RESEARCH IN
HUMAN SOCIAL CONFLICT

Volume 1 • 1995

RACIAL AND ETHNIC CONFLICT:
PERSPECTIVES FROM THE SOCIAL DISCIPLINES

To Marvin and his grandmother Toby Gittler:
"The heart of love that was in her, is in him too."

RESEARCH IN
HUMAN SOCIAL CONFLICT

RACIAL AND ETHNIC CONFLICT:
PERSPECTIVES FROM THE SOCIAL DISCIPLINES

Editor: JOSEPH B. GITTLER
Department of Sociology
Duke University

VOLUME 1 • 1995

 JAI PRESS INC.

Greenwich, Connecticut   *London, England*

CONTENTS

LIST OF CONTRIBUTORS vii

PREFACE xi

ACKNOWLEDGMENTS xiii

DEMOGRAPHY AND ETHNIC CONFLICT
Gray Swicegood, Gillian Stevens, and Allan Parnell 1

RACIAL AND ETHNIC CONFLICT:
PERSPECTIVES FROM HISTORY
David L. Salvaterra 25

PSYCHOLOGICAL PERSPECTIVES ON INTERRACIAL
AND INTERETHNIC GROUP CONFLICT AND THE
AMELIORATION OF INTERGROUP TENSIONS
Martin Lakin 55

ATTITUDES RELATED TO RACIAL
AND ETHNIC CONFLICT
A. Paul Hare 79

RACIAL AND ETHNIC CONFLICT:
PERSPECTIVES FROM ECONOMICS
Robert L. Carter 95

RACIAL AND ETHNIC CONFLICT:
THE VIEW FROM POLITICAL SCIENCE
Herbert Hirsch and Manley Elliott Banks 115

RACIAL AND ETHNIC CONFLICT:
PERSPECTIVES FROM CRIMINAL JUSTICE
Joseph F. Sheley and Victoria E. Brewer 143

RACIAL AND ETHNIC CONFLICT: PERSPECTIVES
FROM SOCIAL AND CULTURAL ANTHROPOLOGY
June Macklin 163

LANGUAGE, CONFLICT, AND
ETHNOLINGUISTIC IDENTITY THEORY
   Aaron Cargile, Howard Giles, and Richard Clément   189

RACIAL AND ETHNIC CONFLICT:
BASIC SOCIOLOGICAL PERSPECTIVES
   Fred D. Hall   209

RACIAL AND ETHNIC CONFLICT:
PERSPECTIVES FROM COMMUNITY INTERVENTION
   George J. McCall   219

INTER-MINORITY GROUP CONFLICTS
   William A. Welch, Sr.   239

ISSUES FROM WOMEN OF RACIAL
AND ETHNIC GROUPS
   Barbara A. Zsembik   257

RACIAL AND ETHNIC CONFLICT:
HUMAN GEOGRAPHIC PERSPECTIVES
   Richard L. Morrill, Harold M. Rose,
   and Judith T. Kenny   275

RACIAL AND ETHNIC CONFLICT: PERSPECTIVES
FROM SOCIAL PHILOSOPHY AND ETHICS
   Michael Levin   301

RACIAL AND ETHNIC CONFLICT: PERSPECTIVES
FROM AMERICAN RELIGIONS
   Leonard J. Pinto   321

A COGNITIVE-EDUCATIONAL APPROACH TO THE
RESOLUTION OF RACIAL AND ETHNIC CONFLICT
   Joseph B. Gittler   343

RACIAL AND ETHNIC CONFLICT STUDIES:
METHODOLOGICAL DILEMMAS
   John H. Stanfield, II   365

LIST OF CONTRIBUTORS

Manley Elliott Banks

Department of Political Science
Virginia Commonwealth University

Victoria E. Brewer

Criminal Justice Center
Sam Houston University

Aaron Cargile

Department of Communication
University of California,
    Santa Barbara

Robert L. Carter

Department of Sociology
Hunter College,
City University of New York

Richard Clément

School of Psychology
University of Ottawa

Howard Giles

Department of Communication
University of California,
    Santa Barbara

Joseph B. Gittler

Department of Sociology
Duke University

Fred D. Hall

Department of Sociology
University of North Carolina,
    Chapel Hill

A. Paul Hare

Department of Behavioral Sciences
Ben-Gurion University of the Negev

Herbert Hirsch

Department of Political Science
Virginia Commonwealth University

Judith T. Kenny   Department of Geography
                                     University of Wisconsin, Milwaukee

Martin Lakin   Department of Psychology
                                     Duke University

Michael Levin   Department of Psychology
                                     City College, City University
                                        of New York

George J. McCall   Department of Sociology
                                     University of Missouri, St. Louis

June Macklin   Department of Anthropology
                                     Connecticut College

Richard L. Morrill   Department of Geography
                                     University of Washington

Allan Parnell   Department of Sociology
                                     Duke University

Leonard J. Pinto   Department of Sociology
                                     University of Colorado,
                                        Boulder

Harold M. Rose   Department of Geography
                                     University of Wisconsin, Milwaukee

David L. Salvaterra   Department of History
                                     Loras College

Joseph F. Sheley   Department of Sociology
                                     Tulane University

John H. Stanfield, II   Department of Sociology
                                     University of California,
                                        Davis

Gillian Stevens   Department of Sociology
                                     University of Illinois

Gray Swicegood

Department of Sociology
University of Illinois

William A. Welch, Sr.

Human Relations Commission
Prince George's County, Maryland

Barbara A. Zsembik

Department of Sociology
University of Florida

PREFACE

Interest in the nature, ubiquity, and effects of social conflict has a long and protracted history. In recent decades, many significant scholarly studies on this subject have been published. Although there are numerous publications, few have approached the problems of conflict from a multidiscipline perspective. We decided, therefore, to address the problem of racial and ethnic conflict through the relevant social disciplines.

This volume is the first of a series dealing with the varied aspects of conflict knowledge and conflict resolution. It is anticipated that the accumulated volumes will lead ultimately to an integrated knowledge concerning the generic aspects of conflict. Integrated generic theory and cognition, of necessity, await empirical verification of the formulated propositions. Only then is it feasible to attempt the formulation of compendent sets of concepts and propositions related to the generic aspects of conflict. Alfred North Whitehead's admonition is here appropriate: "Seek simplicity, but distrust it."

In the last paragraph of the last page of *A History of Western Philosophy*, Bertrand Russell observes that: "In the welter of conflicting fanaticisms, one of the few unifying forces is scientific truthfulness, by which I mean the habit of basing our beliefs upon observation and inferences as impersonal, and as much divested of local and temperamental bias as is possible."

We believe that this statement reflects our motivation and ethos in preparing this volume and those to follow.

We wish to invite critical, scholarly exchange on the contents of the chapters and we shall request that the authors respond to all comments and observations through direct correspondence with the reader.

Joseph B. Gittler
Editor

ACKNOWLEDGMENTS

I wish to thank all those individuals and colleagues who unconstrainedly encouraged me to undertake the editorship of this volume and the contributing authors for their scholarly products.

My special appreciation goes to Susan Gittler for her devotion, patience, endurance, and help in the final editing of the manuscripts.

I am grateful to Charleen Boyd and Richard Collier for their assistance in preparing the manuscripts for publication.

DEMOGRAPHY AND ETHNIC CONFLICT

Gray Swicegood, Gillian Stevens, and Allan Parnell

The core substantive concerns of demography are the population processes of fertility, mortality and migration, the structures generated by these processes, and the spatial distribution of populations. Such concerns may appear to be far removed from the subject of ethnic conflict. But historically demographers have collected much of the data on racial and ethnic populations including the social, economic, demographic, and ecological characteristics of racial and ethnic groups. Issues involving racial and ethnic groups such as ethnic identity and its measurement, the population dynamics of subpopulations, and residential segregation have also been long-standing concerns of the discipline.

Horowitz (1985) suggests that ethnic conflict, especially in its more virulent forms, is episodic in nature. Demographic analysis is not sufficient to understand such episodic events, nor is it likely to provide a complete explanation of more enduring manifestations of racial and ethnic conflict. However, the long-term processes affecting the size and composition of two or more ethnic groups that are spatially proximate and in competition for social or economic resources are fundamentally demographic, and these processes and the conditions generated by them are intrinsically related to ethnic group vitality and boundary maintenance.

Research in Human Social Conflict, Volume 1, pages 1-23.
ISBN: 1-55938-923-0

Demographic research has investigated a wide range of factors that may be implicated in the likelihood and severity of racial and ethnic conflict through more or less direct paths. Patterns of marriage within and between groups affect the boundaries and the long-term identity of ethnic groups. In the long term, the relative sizes of ethnic groups are affected by differential rates of fertility and mortality. Migration within and between countries also affects the sizes of groups in proximity, and, if the groups are in the same labor market, places group members in direct competition. Spatial segregation is often accompanied by differential access to resources such as education, housing, and jobs and clearly plays a role in the social stratification of ethnic groups in many societies.

In this chapter, we review research on the demography of racial and ethnic groups in terms of its relevance for intergroup conflict. Our illustrative examples are largely from North America, where immigration and racial polarization are producing new tensions and raising old concerns, but our observations are pertinent to other contexts as well. We have devoted most of the discussion to conditions such as group size and population structures, differential fertility, immigration, intermarriage, and spatial patterns of residence, all of which may underpin conflict between ethnic groups. We have also briefly considered two perhaps equally salient topics: the measurement of racial and ethnic identity and the symbolic and political implications of demographic data on racial and ethnic groups.

THE MEASUREMENT OF ETHNICITY

The potential for ethnic conflict exists when groups differentiated by race or ethnicity share a geographic region. A common presumption is that regions contain a stable array of mutually exclusive and exhaustive ethnically defined subpopulations. The first step is to define ethnicity. Researchers have drawn upon cultural differences (especially language and religion), nativity, social-psychological identification, and the organization of social relationships to define and differentiate between ethnic groups. The two most common principles governing people's ethnic designations remain, however, parentage and choice, or in anthropological terms, etic and emic identification strategies (Harris, 1990). The first principle assumes that ethnic groups consist of people sharing ancestral origins, or at very least, a subjective belief in common descent whether there exists an objective blood relationship or not. The second assumes that ethnic groups consist of people who identify themselves as members.

In practice, societies have relied on varying combinations of questions on ancestry and self-identification to identify ethnic populations. Australian, Canadian, and British censuses have all asked their populations to identify their ethnic ancestry. The most recent Canadian and the two most recent U.S. censuses have relied on ethnic self-identification questions. The varying types of questions about ethnicity need not, however, produce comparable information. In 1980, for example, over six million Americans identified themselves as "American Indian" in response to the question on their ancestry group yet only one and a half million Americans considered themselves as "American Indian" in response to the question on race (Snipp, 1991).

Furthermore, the inclusion of additional questions, vagaries of question wording, and the inclusion of specific examples in the text accompanying questions, can all change the answers and, hence, the apparent ethnic composition of the country dramatically. A 1979 Current Population Survey pretest of the U.S. census question on ancestry yielded an estimate of 40 million Americans of "English" ancestry. Five months later, the census counts showed almost 50 million Americans of "English" ancestry. The additional 10 million were probably produced by having respondents note that English was their home language just before answering the ancestry question (McKenney and Cresce, 1993).

The contrast between Americans' ethnic affiliations in the two most recent censuses and the affiliations generated by objective measures of ethnic ancestry in earlier censuses exemplify the limitations of official definitions of ethnicity or race. Official ethnic or racial categories clearly can be unreliable and at odds with social reality. Survey and census data in Brazil show that the use of different, but presumably equivalent, terms yields strikingly different frequencies for race-color groupings. Furthermore, neither of the proffered race-color schemes yielded results similar to those generated when respondents were allowed to freely identify their race-color (Harris, Consorte, Lang, and Byrne, 1993).

The official statistics generated by censuses or surveys do, however, matter. Formal recognition of a group's existence in official statistics can encourage group solidarity by constructing a collective identity for the individual members (Neilsen, 1985). Official statistics can be used to depict putative economic and social inequities between ethnic subpopulations and so become a source of grievance. They are also sometimes used to disburse funds and to regulate access to other resources. For example, statistics on ethnic populations in the United States are used to monitor employment and promotion practices, enforce the requirements of the Voting Rights Act, monitor and enforce the Fair Housing Act, and to award federal contracts (OMB, 1994). In Canada, data on ethnic subpopulations are used to support the 1986 Employment Equity Act and the 1988 Multiculturalism Act. These uses of official statistics have motivated ethnic groups to lobby for more data or more "accurate" data to solidify or augment their claims to group-based entitlements (Choldin, 1986).

INTERMARRIAGE AND ETHNIC GROUP MEMBERSHIP

Intermarriage (and other forms of interethnic liaisons) obscures the distinctions between ethnic groups in at least two ways. Individuals involved in such relationships have or may develop sympathies and kinship ties with two ethnic groups. Interethnic marriages are therefore sometimes deliberately arranged or encouraged to symbolically defuse ethnic tensions. European alliances have been forged through such arranged marriages. The dominant ethnic group in Swaziland, the Dlamini (or "Swazi"), emerged through generations of arranged matrimonial alliances between the polygynous Kings, their numerous offspring, and people of other ethnic groups or clans (Van den Berghe, 1987).

The most important threat posed by ethnic intermarriage is, however, the ambiguous ethnic identities of the offspring. The intimate kinship ties to two ethnic groups, the possible muting of any distinct physical markers of membership in one or the other groups, and the imperfect (or dual) socialization in the cultures of two groups make the ethnic identities of offspring of interethnic marriages problematic.

In this section we discuss the effects of relative sizes of groups, the ethnic composition of societies, and sex ratios on the prevalence of ethnic intermarriage. We then discuss some of the responses to ethnic intermarriage: "rules of descent," the formation of the new groups, and finally, reliance on the second principle of ethnic group membership: choice.

The Demographics of Ethnic Intermarriage.

The relative frequency of ethnic endogamy (marriage within an ethnic group) versus ethnic intermarriage in an ethnically complex society is affected by a large number of social considerations. Social distances between groups, the distributions of political and economic resources across the groups, the degree of common participation in important social institutions such as schools, and the rigidity and enforcement of antimiscegenation laws all influence the relative frequency of ethnic intermarriage. If these social and cultural sanctions forbidding intermarriage prevail, then all couples are married endogamously and demographic considerations are irrelevant.

But if the social and cultural considerations do not entirely determine marriage patterns (and they almost never do), demographic considerations come into play. One of the most important demographic predictors of the relative frequency of intermarriage is the relative size of an ethnic group (Besanceny, 1965). The first panel of Table 1 shows the effects of group size for members of a relatively small group, (group A) and a relatively large group, (group B).

The percentages of endogamously married couples are easiest to evaluate if compared against the expectation that social and cultural considerations rule

Table 1. The Relative Frequency of Ethnic Endogamy and Intermarriage in Two Societies Assuming No Social or Cultural Constraints on Ethnic Intermarriage

			Women's Ethnicity		
		Group	A	B	Total
Society I					
	Men's	A	1	9	10
	Ethnicity	B	9	81	90
		Total	10	90	100
Society II					
	Men's	A	25	25	50
	Ethnicity	B	25	25	50
		Total	50	50	100

marriage choices and so 100 percent of couples in both groups marry endogamously. When demographic rather than social considerations prevail, the percentages of men and women in group A who are married endogamously drops by a factor of 10, from 100 percent to 10 percent. Meanwhile, the percentages of men and women in the larger group who are married endogamously drops only from 100 percent to 90 percent (81/90). The effects of relative group size are thus much stronger for smaller groups than for larger groups. In Britain, where whites make up 95 percent of the population, over 99 percent of men and women are in a white/white relationship. Yet almost a quarter of West Indian men and a tenth of West Indian women in Britain have white partners (Diamond and Clark, 1989).

Comparing across Society I and Society II in Table 1 also demonstrates a second effect of the demographic context on rates of ethnic intermarriage. In Society I, only 18 percent of all couples are intermarried. (Of these, 9% consist of B men and A women and 9% consist of the opposite combination). Yet in Society II, which has two groups of equal size, 50 percent are intermarried. Overall, the more equal the sizes of ethnic groups, the higher the overall frequency of ethnic intermarriage (Blau, 1977).

Allied with the effects of the distribution of group sizes on the prevalence of ethnic intermarriage are the effects of sex ratios. The sex ratio at birth is about 105 males to 100 females for almost all ethnic and racial groups. Mortality rates during infancy and childhood usually slightly favor females and so the sex ratio is usually about 100:100 for young adults in most ethnic groups. In unique circumstances, however, sex ratios during the typical marrying ages can vary drastically because of sex-specific patterns of mortality or migration among young adults. There are two major demographic responses to this circumstance: higher rates of non-marriage among the more common sex, or higher rates of intermarriage among the more common sex.[1]

For a variety of social, cultural, and economic reasons, migration streams, which are largely composed of young adults, often favor one or the other sex. Until the 1930s, for example, immigration to the United States was heavily male. Between the 1930s and 1978, migrants to the United States were more likely to be female (Houstoun, Kramer, and Barrett, 1984). More importantly, the migration streams from particular countries are likely to be dominated by one sex (Donato, 1990). For example, the Chinese recruited to build the U.S. railroads in the mid-1800s were almost exclusively men, and the Irish brought in as domestic servants during the late 1800s were primarily women. The more extreme the sex ratio among migrants, the more likely the migrants are to contract ethnic intermarriages (Pagnini and Morgan, 1990).

The participation of men in military operations outside of their own country is also often attended by a high frequency of intermarriage among soldiers. The 1946 War Brides Act, for example, was enacted to allow American soldiers to bring home their Japanese brides. The U.S.'s military bases in Korea, Japan, the Philippines, and Germany have resulted in numerous women migrating to the United States as wives of American servicemen (Jasso and Rosenzweig, 1990).

The overall prevalence of ethnic intermarriage in a society is, however, determined by the degree of contact between members of ethnic groups within the society. The degree of geographic segregation between ethnic or racial groups, whether measured at the state, city, or neighborhood levels, is strongly and negatively related to levels of ethnic intermarriage (Stevens and Swicegood, 1987). Social segregation, the structured unequal participation of members of ethnic groups in major social institutions such as schools, churches, and the labor force, further lowers the probability that members of different ethnic groups meet and marry (Bozon and Héran, 1987; Schoen and Kluegel, 1988).

Responses to Interethnic Relationships

The ambiguities posed by ethnic intermarriage always test the principle that ancestry determines ethnic group identity. In societies characterized by two or more relatively large groups participating in overlapping geographic and social spheres, the demographic structure exerts upward pressure on overall rates of intermarriage. Even in the former Yugoslavia, for example, around 12 percent of marriages contracted between the 1960s and 1989 were exogamous (Botev, 1994). If ethnic groups continue to presume that parentage determines ethnic group membership, they must respond to the threats posed by the offspring of intermarriage.

One response is to ban intermarriage through antimiscegenation laws. Until the 1940s, a majority of states in the United States prohibited marriage between people of various ethnic and racial groups. The North Carolina Act of 1715 specified, for example, that a white person could not marry "an Indian, Negro,

Mustee, or Mulatto or any person of Mixed Blood to the Third Generation" (Forbes, 1993). Other U.S. states outlawed marriages between Caucasians and Mongolians, Whites and Malays, Negroes and Indians, or Malays and Negroes (Spickard, 1989). In South Africa, the 1949 Prohibition of Mixed Marriages Act banned marriages between whites and nonwhites and nullified mixed marriages contracted abroad by South Africans (Riley, 1991).

But forbidding intermarriage is seldom entirely effective. In fact, the details of antimiscegenation laws, which often outline in excruciating detail who cannot marry whom, confirm that interethnic relationships, and their concomitant, children of mixed ancestry, are prevalent. For example, the North Carolina Act of 1715, by banning marriage between a white person and "any person of Mixed Blood to the Third Generation" forthrightly acknowledged that "miscegenation" had been occurring for generations. Although Rwanda has a long history of bloody conflict between its two major ethnic groups, Tuzi (Tutsi) men have regularly had Hutu concubines (Van den Berghe, 1987, p. 73) and so a growing proportion of the Rwandan population have both Hutu and Tuzi ancestry.

A second response to the problem of mixed ancestry is to codify "rules of descent" to dissipate the ambiguities surrounding children with complex ethnic ancestries. In Russia, for example, socially determined rules of descent ordain that children inherit the ethnic parentage of the mother. In Canada, children inherit the father's ethnic identification. The infamous "one-drop" rule throughout much of the United States considered a child with either a black mother or a black father to be black (Davis, 1991).

A third, usually geographically based, response to intermarriage is ethnogenesis, the formation of new ethnic groups. The Melungeons of Tennessee, for example, combine varying elements of American Indian, Black, and Irish (or other white) descent. The Métis of Canada, who eventually settled in the Red River Valley, are the descendants of Canadian Indian women and French, Scots, or English men (Burley, Horsfall, and Brandon, 1992).

A fourth response is to de-emphasize ancestry in favor of choice. Early U.S. censuses relied on "objective" measures of Americans' ethnic ancestry (birthplace if foreign-born, birthplaces of foreign-born mothers and fathers, mother tongue). But the 1980 and 1990 censuses asked Americans the ancestry or ethnic group with which they identified. Because of generations of high rates of ethnic intermarriage, the result was a welter of complex and unreliable ethnic responses (Farley, 1991). Children's ethnic identities were inconsistent with their parents' (Lieberson and Waters, 1993) vividly demonstrating that ancestry is not a reliable measure of white Americans' ethnic affiliations. The willingness of Americans to opt for one (or more) of the ethnicities represented in their background also meant that some groups drastically increased in apparent size. Millions more Americans identified themselves as of German or Irish ancestry in the 1980 census than were expected by demographers (Hout and Goldstein, 1994).

DEMOGRAPHIC PROCESSES AFFECTING GROUP SIZE

In spite of the difficulties involved in determining ethnic group membership, one of the clearest demographic factors affecting racial and ethnic conflict is the relative size of groups. Relative size is central to some theoretical formulations of ethnic relations (e.g., Blalock, 1967), and the stability of relative sizes of groups in a spatially defined area (assuming stability of group membership) are entirely a product of demographic processes. Relative size is theoretically linked to racial and ethnic discrimination, racial and ethnic inequality (e.g., Frisbie and Niedert, 1977; Wilcox and Roof, 1978), and to majority group attitudes toward minorities (e.g., Fossett and Kiecolt, 1989).

In the following two sections, we review the two primary demographic processes affecting the relative sizes of racial and ethnic groups in a society: migration and fertility. Passel and Edmonston's (1994) projections of the racial and ethnic composition of the United States underscore the importance of immigration to the growth of ethnic groups. They project that nearly 70 percent of the growth of the Asian-American population, and 50 percent of the growth of the Hispanic population, will be attributable to net immigration between 1990 and 1995. In a parallel fashion, Swicegood and Morgan's (1994) projections highlight the importance of differential fertility. Their projections imply a 2050 population of Hispanics that is 34 percent larger (about 20 million more people) than it would be if Hispanics had the same fertility rate as non-Hispanic whites. The African-American, Native-American, and Asian-American populations would be 30 percent, 48 percent, and 14 percent larger than they would be in absence of differential fertility. Together, the projections of migration trends and fertility differentials among ethnic groups imply an increasingly ethnically diverse society.

Immigration

Immigration is the primary way new racial and ethnic groups enter a society. The potential for conflict is immediate. Immigrants compete with prior residents for land, housing, employment, and marriage partners. Whether the competition flares into conflict depends on the perceived clarity of the ethnic distinctions between the newcomers and established residents, the perceived degree of competition for and the relative scarcity of resources, and the perceived alternatives for dealing with the situation.

One of the founding ideologies of the United States is the welcoming of immigrants to its shores. The articulation of this ideology has, however, waxed and waned throughout U.S. history (cf. Daniels, 1991). The first major expression of ethnic antagonism arose in response to the heavy immigration of Irish Catholics, many of them desperately poor, during the 1820s and 1830s. Nativism during this era was excused through the purported threat of

Catholicism to the new republic, but the immigrants' poverty and the port cities' need to aid the impoverished immigrants were significant factors. By the 1840s and 1850s, the American or "Know-Nothing" party was denouncing immigration and calling for a requirement of twenty-one years of residence for immigrants to become naturalized.

After the Civil War, Congress did change the naturalization act, but not in the way that the "Know-Nothings" had imagined. Instead, the focus of the country's xenophobia shifted to Asians. The Fourteenth Amendment, ratified in 1868, granted citizenship to all persons born in the United States and established uniform requirements for citizenship. In 1870, new legislation pointedly excluded the thousands of Chinese who had migrated to the country to build the nation's railroads. The 1882 Chinese Exclusion Act, extended in 1892 and made permanent in 1902, confirmed the racist bent of Congress. This legislation was designed to protect the economic interests of white working men in California and other western states and territories while not unduly interfering with American trade with China.

In the late nineteenth century, the origin of the major immigration streams to the United States shifted from Northern and Western Europe to Southern and Eastern Europe. Coinciding with the closing of the American frontier and the economic depression of the 1890s, these newcomers were viewed with alarm as "down-trodden, atavistic and stagnant" (Solomon, 1956). The initial response was to limit immigration through literacy tests, culminating in the 1917 legislation barring immigration from Asia, and the National Quota Acts of 1921 and 1924 in which the numbers of migrants from Southern and Eastern Europe, Africa, and Asia were drastically capped.

The prosperous decades after World War II saw low levels of migration into the United States, and possibly in consequence, a weakening of nativistic sentiments. A new immigration policy passed in 1965 turned to principles of family reunification for admission. Overall levels of legal immigration increased. A return of anti-immigration sentiment among the general American public as a weakening economy accompanied the rise in levels of legal immigration. The public's anti-immigration sentiment focused, however, on undocumented Mexican migrants working in the United States. "Controlling the borders" became a watchcry. The 1986 Immigration Reform and Control Act was intended to deter illegal migration by removing the economic incentives drawing illegal migrants to the States.

The Immigration Act of 1990 was the most major revision of U.S. immigration laws in 25 years. It included provisions for family reunification, labor shortages, and entrepreneurial immigrants. It also provided "diversity" visas for immigrants from underrepresented countries with 40 percent of those visas between 1992 to 1994 reserved for Irish applicants (Passel and Edmonston, 1994).

The waves of nativism that periodically surface in the United States are rooted in the presumed "unassimilatable" characteristics of the immigrants and the perception of "unfair" economic competition and consumption of social resources. Immigrants have been accused at numerous times during the country's history of undercutting American labor by their willingness to work for low wages. Some Americans believe that immigrants, particularly illegal immigrants, are more likely to receive welfare benefits or to impose a fiscal burden on their municipality. As immigration levels rise, the perception of competition increases, and the probability of ethnic hostility and outbreaks of ethnic conflict increases. The perception of competition also appears to intensify when levels of immigration fluctuate from year to year because of the difficulties accompanying the incorporation of a suddenly large number of immigrants into stable labor and housing markets (Olzak, 1987).

The extent to which immigrants compete with native-born Americans in most labor markets is, however, fairly low. Despite the escalating numbers of immigrants to the United States in the postwar period, scholars have reached a wide-ranging consensus that immigration does not negatively affect the economy as a whole, although the declining levels of skills among recent immigrants may have increased levels of economic inequality during the 1980s. Studies considering the effect of immigration on particular ethnic groups, especially African Americans, have drawn substantially similar conclusions (e.g., Reischauer, 1989). However, Bean, Fossett, and Park (1994) note that these conclusions are based on national-level data from the 1970s and 1980s. Their analysis demonstrates that the effect of immigration on African-American unemployment varies according to local labor market conditions. These results indicate the crucial importance of considering the salience of racial and ethnic competition for jobs in terms of the local context.

There is a wealth of historical evidence confirming the linguistic, social, economic, and cultural integration of the millions of immigrants from Southern and Eastern European countries and their descendants who were previously thought to be "unassimilatable." However, two main conditions of ethnic conflict, a large flow of immigrants and the perception of economic competition, are firmly in place. Massey (1994) points out that the United States had the luxury of about half a century (1930 to 1980) to integrate the last major flow of immigrants and enjoyed an expanding economy during several of those decades. The ethnic distinctions between many of the contemporary immigrants and most resident Americans are seemingly clear and buttressed by linguistic, phenotypic, and cultural differences. The numerous proposed "English-Only" amendments are obviously aimed at immigrants and their children. The increasing restrictions in immigration law, the growing public unrest about the reliance of immigrants on public aid, and the distrust of immigrants among the lesser educated Americans may just be isolated phenomena in an increasingly ethnically complex society. They may also be harbingers of further ethnic antagonism and conflict.

Racial and Ethnic Differentials in Fertility

Like immigration, differential patterns of childbearing for racial and ethnic groups affect the demographic conditions salient to ethnic conflict. Net of other demographic factors, groups with higher levels of fertility will grow faster than those with lower levels, and so the relative sizes of ethnic groups will shift over time. Such changes may be perceived as a threat by the groups in decline while creating political and economic opportunities for the growing populations.

Despite a relatively low overall fertility rate, there is considerable diversity among U.S. ethnic groups in their reproductive regimes. In Table 2 we show the total fertility rates[2] (TFR) for several racial and ethnic groups in 1990. The overall total fertility rate for the country in 1990 was 2.08. The rate for non-Hispanic white women was 1.85; for black women, the rate was 2.55. Historically, the fertility differentials between blacks and whites have commonly been this large. With the exception of Cuban Americans, Hispanic groups tend to have even higher levels of childbearing relative to non-Hispanic whites. Mexican Americans, for example, had a TFR of 3.21 in 1990, nearly 75 percent higher than their non-Hispanic counterparts. Within the broad Asian/Pacific Islander category there is also considerable variation. Chinese and Japanese American women have TFRs well below replacement levels, while the residual API category, consisting of Korean, South Asian, and Southeast Asians, have a current fertility level about 45 percent higher than non-Hispanic whites. If these differentials persist, they will substantially affect the relative sizes of these groups.

Large ethnic fertility differentials are also found in other societies and, in some cases, carry great political consequences for ethnic relations. In Israel, in 1990, the TFRs for European-origin and Asian-origin Jews were 2.31 and 3.09 respectively. In contrast, the TFR for the Arab-Israeli population is 4.7 (Goldscheider, 1992). While half of the total growth of the Jewish population between 1948 and 1990 was attributable to immigration, 98 percent of the growth of the Arab population resulted from the excess of births over deaths (Goldscheider, 1992). In Thailand the general fertility rate of ethnic Malays (the main component of the Muslim population) is about 75 percent higher than Buddhist Thais (Knodel, Chamratrithirong, and Debavala, 1987).

While differences in levels of childbearing can clearly affect the relative size of subpopulations, other aspects of fertility behavior also generate differences across groups that may be salient to ethnic conflict. Two key examples are differences in timing of childbearing within the life course and the marital status of the mother at the birth of her children. We can get a sense of the former by examining differences in the fertility rates for teenage women (aged 15-19). There are striking racial/ethnic differences in the fertility of teenage women. The fertility rate for teenage African-American women is 2.7 times higher than

Table 2.   Childbearing and Age Structure for
Selected Racial and Ethnic Groups, United States, 1990

Racial and Ethnic Classification	Total Fertility Rate (TFR)	ASFR per 1,000 Women Ages 15 to 19	% Non-Marital Births	Median Age of Group	Dependency Ratio
Non-Hispanic					
White	1.85	42.5	16.9	34.9	1.65
Black	2.55	116.2	66.7	28.2	1.48
Hispanic					
Mexican American	3.21	108.0	33.3	23.8	1.39
Puerto Rican	2.30	101.6	55.9	25.7	1.49
Cuban American	1.46	30.3	18.2	38.9	1.94
Other	2.88	86.0	41.2	27.2	1.80
Asian/Pacific Islander (API)					
Chinese American	1.36	4.7	5.0	32.1	2.16
Japanese American	1.11	10.4	9.6	36.3	2.22
Hawaiian	3.22	120.9	45.0	26.3	1.54
Filipino American	1.88	27.0	15.9	31.1	1.87
Other API	2.68	33.4	12.6	29.0	1.94
American Indian	2.18	81.1	53.6	26.7	1.41

Sources: Centers for Disease Control (1993) and U.S. Bureau of the Census (1991).

that of non-Hispanic whites. Hispanic groups (except for Cuban Americans) all have intermediate levels of teenage childbearing. In contrast, the Asian and Pacific Islander groups, including those with relatively high fertility levels, all have lower levels of teenage childbearing than non-Hispanic whites.

Differences in the timing of fertility imply differences in the typical life course experienced by members of various ethnic groups. Young mothers are more likely to be unmarried mothers. Childbearing among unmarried mothers, in turn, is related to a variety of negative educational and economic outcomes for the mother. Because patterns of early nonmarital childbearing tend to be transmitted across generations (e.g., McLanahan, 1988), variation in ethnic reproductive regimes are involved in the regeneration of ethnic stratification. To the extent that contact between members of different ethnic and racial groups is structured by age and social roles, differences in the timing of parenthood can restrict such interactions and create a sense "of otherness" with regard to outgroup members. Differences in timing of childbearing may also affect schooling and work patterns, two potential areas of competition and conflict between groups.

Age Structure

Variation in the quantity and timing of childbearing also differentiates racial and ethnic groups by influencing the age structure of the subpopulations. Fertility and mortality levels both contribute to the age structure of a population, but under current mortality conditions, fertility plays the dominant role. The median age of the entire U.S. population in 1990 was 32.9. But the median age for non-Hispanic whites was 34.9 while the median age for the African-American population was 28.2. Within the Hispanic population, there are even greater differences. The median age of Mexican Americans was 23.8 versus 38.9 for the Cuban-origin population. Age selectivities associated with recent immigration can also significantly shape the age structures of groups. For example, the Hmong, a high-fertility group that recently arrived in the United States, has a median age of only 12.5.

Age structure determines the relative proportion of a group that is potentially economically active. Demographers traditionally measure this concept via dependency ratios. Here we define the dependency ratio as the number of people aged 18-64 divided by the number of children aged less than age 18 plus the number of older people aged 65 or older. For the non-Hispanic whites this ratio was 1.65 in 1990 and for blacks, 1.48. The figures are fairly similar because the higher proportion of children for blacks is offset by their lower proportion of elderly. By contrast the ratio for Japanese Americans was 2.2, and only 1.39 for Mexican Americans.

Differing age structures can influence a variety of conditions underlying ethnic tensions and conflict. Groups with higher dependency ratios must, all else equal, divide available resources across a greater number of people, thus lowering the average standard of living. Higher dependency ratios may constrain group members' social, economic, and residential mobility by reducing the capital available for savings and investments. A large young population concentrated by residential segregation may also put downward pressure on local wage rates (Azar and Farah, 1984) and upward pressure on unemployment rates. The combination of higher unemployment and the strong age-grading of criminal (Cohen and Land, 1987) and deviant behavior means that groups with relative young age structures are likely to experience greater levels of social disorganization, especially in the presence of ethnic discrimination. These conditions in turn may increase the severity of ethnic conflict (Choucri, 1984).

Age structure also influences the political agenda and allocation of resources in age-stratified societies. Preston (1984) argues that the aging of the American population has been accompanied by increases in the relative well-being of the elderly coupled with declines in the relative well-being of children. Because of differences in age structure across ethnic and racial groups (as discussed earlier), racial and ethnic groups with older populations have benefited most from these trends and those with younger populations the least. Indeed, Preston suggests that ethnic considerations may be woven into age-conscious politics, and that middle-aged and elderly voters, who are largely white, are reluctant to devote public resources to a school-age population that is increasingly Hispanic or non-white. (In 1990 Hispanics and non-whites accounted for about 31% of the school age population but only 13% of the population over age 65.) Furthermore, because the elderly are now more likely to vote than any other age group in the United States, their priorities get disproportionate attention even in absence of race/ethnic conscious voting.

SPATIAL SEGREGATION

Demographers have long been concerned with the processes that lead to the spatial segregation of racial and ethnic groups. In this section, we discuss the processes that result in racial and ethnic segregation as well as some of the consequences of segregation pertinent to ethnic conflict.

Dimensions of Segregation

Ethnic segregation is defined generally as the extent to which two or more ethnic groups live separately from one another. Segregation has, however, numerous dimensions. Massey and Denton (1988) outline five: evenness, exposure or isolation, clustering, concentration, and centralization. Of these five dimensions of segregation, the first is the one most commonly discussed and measured. It is usually measured through the index of dissimilarity (D) which compares the distribution of an ethnic group across blocks, tracts, neighborhoods, or some other geographical unit with the distribution of another group (or the entire population).

Exposure or isolation is the dimension of segregation referring to the extent to which members of an ethnic group live with (or without) contact with members of other ethnic groups. A group occupying a relatively small area is said to be concentrated. Centralization is the degree to which members of an ethnic group are found near the central areas of cities rather than on or near the periphery. Clustering is the extent to which ethnic group members live in geographic units that are contiguous to one another. An area with a high degree of segregation on four of the five measures of segregation is referred to as "hypersegregated" (Massey and Denton, 1993).

Racial and Ethnic Segregation in the United States

Immigration history in the United States accounts for the overall geographic distribution of most European ethnic groups in the late twentieth century. The earliest immigrant groups entering the country settled on the East Coast. As the American frontier moved westward, later arriving groups tended to settle in the midwest, southern regions, and finally in the west (Lieberson and Waters, 1988). Over time, however, high rates of residential mobility have distributed descendants of these immigrants fairly evenly across the country. The timing of each group's major immigration stream is thus reflected in only a modicum of concentration in various clusters of states.

Members of some ethnic groups, however, tend to live in ethnic enclaves. Ethnic enclaves are the result of social networks, or what is sometimes referred to as chain migration (Castles and Miller, 1994). Chain migration is set in motion by initial migrants finding an opportunity and then encouraging family and friends to migrate to the same area. These social links between origin and destination, which result in the concentration of migrants in specific locations, lower the economic and psychic costs of migration to migrants (see Tilly and Brown, 1974; MacDonald and MacDonald, 1974; Massey, Alarcon, Durand, and Gonzales, 1987).

Trends and patterns of segregation for the black population differ in degree and kind, however, from those for other U.S. ethnic groups. In 1980, the African-American population was hypersegregated in 16 of the 30 metropolitan areas with the largest black population (Massey and Denton, 1993). The segregation of the black population had increased during and after World War I as blacks moved northward in search of jobs. Competition for housing between blacks and whites occurred and resulted in open conflict with instances of firebombings and riots. The open conflict shaded into more subtle means of restricting blacks' residential choices, notably the spread of covenants specifying that homes could not be occupied by blacks or other minorities. Restrictive lending practices facilitated by the Federal Housing Administration also designated white neighborhoods as credit-worthy while "redlining" racially-mixed transition neighborhoods as areas where home values were slated to decline (Farley and Frey, 1994).

Segregated suburbs emerged after World War II (Hirsch, 1983; Bickford and Massey, 1991). The whites who fled the central cities created a series of obstacles to prevent blacks from following. Institutionalized and federally supported real estate discrimination, through redlining and the refusal of agents to show suburban houses to blacks, was the major factor, but instances of violence and physical intimidation also occurred (Hirsch, 1983).

The segregation of blacks decreased slightly during the 1970s and 1980s although levels of institutionalized segregation remain high in the older, industrial metropolitan areas of the north and in some older southern cities (Farley and Frey, 1994). The lowest levels of segregation are currently found in the newer metropolitan areas of the south and the west where there has been considerable residential construction.

Discrimination against blacks in the real estate market still, however, continues. The evidence of discrimination against blacks that results in residential segregation is persistent and strong (Yinger, 1991). Studies of mortgage rejections have found, for example, that black and, to a lesser degree Hispanic, applicants are more likely to have mortgage applications rejected than are whites when matched on other characteristics other than race (White, 1994).

Massey and Denton (1993) argue that segregation is one of the most important factors associated with the social pathologies commonly reported in central cities and is the most important item remaining on the nation's civil rights agenda. Attempts by the federal government to end residential segregation have largely failed. If residential segregation continues, they maintain, social institutions in the urban black communities will collapse, poverty and crime will expand, and racial prejudice and hostility toward blacks will continue.

SYMBOLIC ASPECTS OF DEMOGRAPHIC DATA

Most of our chapter has been concerned with the ways in which demographic processes may establish the conditions relevant to racial and ethnic relations and conflict. There is another link between demography and ethnic conflict that we have alluded to but not explicitly discussed. Frequently, demographic phenomena become essential elements in the symbolic and political arenas where racial and ethnic relations are played out. Demographic data are used to provide evidence of discrimination and racism, and racial/ethnic demographic differentials often figure into stereotypes and stigmas that carry through public and private discourse.

Determining the size of racial and ethnic groups has been a politically charged issue in the United States since its inception. The details of the U.S. census definitions of "black" have changed markedly over time in response to political and public pressures (Lee, 1993). There are, however, more subtle ways in which the measurement and presentation of official demographic statistics can exacerbate nativistic or racist fears. Until 1970, for example, the U.S. Census Bureau separated the population into the foreign-born or first generation, the second generation, and later generations. The first two generations were considered to be "foreign stock" a term that subsumed an entire generation of American citizens born in the United States under the label "foreign." In the first few decades of this century, the high population growth among the "foreign stock" in the urban centers of the country was a major impetus for Congress to ignore the constitutional mandate to re-allocate congressional seats on the basis of the changing geographic distribution of the population (Anderson, 1988).

Recently, immigration and ethnic diversity have become a polarizing issue in many European countries as well. Often public perceptions of immigration issues are at variance with available data. In France, for example, where LePen's anti-immigrant party become an important political force, about 75 percent of the public disagrees with the conclusion drawn from official statistics that the number of immigrants in the country is about the same as it was a decade ago. Lévy (1992) traces this discrepancy to a widely circulated news article that unfortunately included all second generation French citizens in the count of the immigrant population.

Mortality rates, particularly infant mortality rates, are another example of politically sensitive data. In the United States, the mortality rate of black infants, about 18 deaths per 1,000 births, is twice that of white infants (Zopf, 1992). In South Africa in the early 1980s, the mortality rate for black infants varied from 34 in various urban districts to 280 in rural districts. The overall rate for "colored" infants was about 50 while the overall rate for white infants was 13. The life expectancy of blacks in Harlem has been compared to the life expectancies observed in Bangladesh—a comparison that shocked the American public by overlaying images of the third world conditions onto the American context (*New York Times*, 1990). Because racial and ethnic differentials in mortality rates almost always show the politically less powerful groups with higher rates, the differentials are often considered to be direct and reliable measures of ethnic and racial repression and exploitation (Kent, 1991).

Racial differences in fertility provide another example. Higher levels of childbearing, especially among young unmarried black women, play an important role in academic debates about the underclass (Wilson, 1987) but they also figure prominently in whites' perceptions of blacks. Hacker's (1992) *Two Nations*, a popular account of recent racial schisms in the United States, tightly links racial differences in reproductive regimes with languishing public support for social welfare programs.

Even when official statistics are apparently accurately reported, the measurement strategies adopted by governmental agencies can exaggerate differences between ethnic groups. For example, until 1989 the U.S. National Center of Health Statistics assigned most children born to a white parent and a nonwhite parent to the race of the nonwhite parent (National Center for Health Statistics, 1991). This rule had the effect of spuriously boosting the fertility rate of the black population by about five percent, and may have contributed to the perception among some whites of high and irresponsible childbearing among blacks.

Immigration and fertility issues were intertwined in American politics of the late-nineteenth and early-twentieth centuries. "Race suicide," a commonly used term of the time, referred to the consequences of the large family size among the "foreign stock" (immigrants and second generation Americans) as compared with the presumably lower and declining fertility levels of older generations of Northern European ancestry. King and Ruggles (1990) show that in fact, the combined fertility of immigrants and their children was actually lower than that of native-born women of native-born parentage, but they also suggest that the demographic reality was overlooked because the ideology of race suicide dovetailed so closely with prevailing genetically based theories of the hierarchy of the races.

The measurement and dissemination of demographic data codifies demographic and social differences between groups. Faced with mounting dissatisfaction with official classification schemes for race and ethnicity, and debates and legal action over census undercounts, the U.S. Office of Management and Budget called for proposals to modify their current methodology (OMB, 1994). A notice of public meetings on this issue, which appeared in a recent issue of the Federal Registry, contained a list of possible changes in the classification of racial and ethnic groups. One of the proposed changes was to eliminate racial and ethnic classifications altogether in data collected by federal agencies because these "categories merely serve to perpetuate an overemphasis on race in America and contribute to the fragmentation of our society." Although eliminating racial and ethnic data seems unlikely in the United States in the near future, the proposal clearly seeks to sidestep the potent symbolic and political uses of demographic data in ethnic and racial relations.

CONCLUSIONS

In this chapter we argue that demographic analysis is essential to the understanding of racial and ethnic conflict and offer considerable historical and contemporary evidence in support of this contention. From a theoretical standpoint, we have taken a cautious approach, arguing that demographic processes and structures establish underlying conditions that influence intergroup relations through more proximate factors. Immigration, for example, establishes the possibility for conflict by bringing different racial and ethnic groups into contact, but it does not inevitably result in conflict. In particular instances these demographic factors may be pivotal. Ladner and his colleagues (1981) assign a central role to the recent arrival of large numbers of middle-class Cuban immigrants in their explanation of the Miami riots of 1980.

However, the more general theoretical position of demographic factors in models of racial and ethnic conflict requires greater systematic development. Olzak's (1992) work on ethnic conflict in the United States between 1877 and 1914 successfully draws on human ecology, a perspective that is intertwined with the development of American social demography. Blau's (1977) structural theory of intergroup relations is anchored in the distributional properties of population characteristics, including ethnicity. Both approaches invest considerable explanatory power to demographic processes and structures, but further development depends on clarifying theoretical linkages between these demographic factors and the intervening mechanisms that produce variations in ethnic relations. Olzak, for example, emphasized the role of job competition between groups in shaping conflict, but what are the linkages between residential segregation and job competition?

Further clarification also depends on clearer specification of alternative hypotheses accompanied by rigorous empirical testing. Does the relative size of groups have threshold effects before it becomes a salient factor? Careful attention to measurement issues will be crucial for that empirical work. We have noted that even the basic size of ethnic groups varies dramatically according to the measurement scheme that is used. This issue goes beyond reliability concerns because for some problems self-identification provides a more theoretically relevant measure of ethnicity, while for others an objective measure, such as country of origin, may be preferable.

The resulting explanations of racial and ethnic conflict will incorporate a number of contingencies. Here we have taken a broad view of conflict rather than focus on a specific form, but we expect models linking racial attitudes and demographic conditions to be specified quite differently from models focusing on the occurrence of riots. Levels of analysis are likely to be one important contingency. Local labor markets are especially salient in the operation of economic mechanisms, but symbolic uses of demographic data profiling group differences operate on a broader national scope. Historical context is equally important. The effects of occupational segregation on conflict identified by Olzak pertain to an era when an industrializing economy was based on manual labor. Links between demographic forces and ethnic competition are likely to differ in today's economy.

These considerations argue against simple demographic determinism. Our review of racial and ethnic demography in the United States refers to substantial group differences on many dimensions, and continuing high levels of segregation, especially between African Americans and whites of European ancestry. These conditions may augur continued or even escalating intergroup conflict, but there are countervailing trends as well, such as increasing levels of intermarriage. Both positive and negative demographic forces are largely outside the realm of direct manipulation that might reduce the likelihood of conflict. However, researchers can act to minimize the negative symbolic and political uses of their work by responding in the public arena to divisive interpretations of their research.

NOTES

1. A third possibility is polygamous marriages, either polyandrous (multiple husbands and one wife) or polygynous (one husband and multiple wives). Polygamous marriages are, however, usually the result of cultural traditions rather than demographic shortages.

2. The total fertility rate is the average number of children a cohort of women would have if they experienced prevailing age-specific fertility rates throughout their childbearing years (usually ages 15 to 49). This measure eliminates the effects of age composition and assumes no mortality during the childbearing years. In low mortality populations, a TFR of about 2.1 is necessary to replace the population.

REFERENCES

Anderson, M. 1988. *The American Census: A Social History.* New Haven, CT: Yale University Press.

Azar, E.E., and N.E. Farah. 1984. "Political Dimensions of Conflict." Pp. 157-78 in *Multidisciplinary Perspectives on Population and Conflict,* edited by N. Choucri. New York: Syracuse University Press.

Bean, F.D., M.A. Fossett, and K.T. Park. 1994. "Labor Market Dynamics and the Effects of Immigration on African Americans." In *Blacks, Immigration and Race Relations,* edited by G. Jaynes. New Haven, CT: Yale University Press.

Besanceny, P.H. 1965. "On Reporting Rates of Intermarriage." *American Journal of Sociology* 70: 717-721.

Bickford, A., and D.S. Massey. 1991. "Segregation in the Second Ghetto." *Social Forces* 69: 1011-36.

Blalock, H.M., Jr. 1967. *Towards a Theory of Minority Group Relations.* New York: Wiley.

Blau, P.M. 1977. *Inequality and Heterogeneity: A Primitive Theory of Social Structure.* New York: Free Press.

Botev, N. 1994. "Where East Meets West: Ethnic Intermarriage in the Former Yugoslavia, 1962 to 1989." *American Sociological Review* 59: 461-480.

Bozon, M.. and F. Héran. 1987. "Finding a Spouse. Part 1: Changes and Morphology of the Place of First Encounters." *Population* 42: 943-985.

Burley, D.V., G.A. Horsfall, and J.D. Brandon. 1992. *Structural Considerations of Mtis Ethnicity.* Vermillion, SD: The University of South Dakota Press.

Castles, S., and M.J. Miller. 1994. *The Age of Migration: International Population Movements in the Modern World.* New York: The Guilford Press.

Centers for Disease Control. 1993. "Childbearing Patterns Among Selected Racial/Ethnic Minority Groups—United States, 1990." *Morbidity and Mortality Weekly Report* 42: 398-403.

Choldin, H.M. 1986. "Statistics and Politics: The 'Hispanic Issue' in the 1980 Census." *Demography* 23: 403-418.

Choucri, N. (ed.). 1984. *Multidisciplinary Perspectives on Population and Conflict.* New York: Syracuse University Press.

Cohen, L.E., and K.C. Land. 1987. "Age Structure and Crime: Symmetry versus Asymmetry and the Projection of Crime Rates Through the 1990s." *American Sociological Review* 52: 170-83.

Daniels, R. 1991. *Coming to America. A History of Immigration and Ethnicity in American Life.* New York: Harper Collins.

Davis, J.J. 1991. *Who is Black? One Nation's Definition.* University Park, PA: The Pennsylvania State University Press.

Diamond, I., and S. Clarke. 1989. "Demographic Patterns among Britain's Ethnic Groups." Pp. 177-199 in *The Changing Population of Britain,* edited by H. Joshi. New York: Basil Blackwell.

Donato, K.M. 1990. "Recent Trends in U.S. Immigration: Why Some Countries Send Women and Others Send Men." Paper presented at the Annual Meetings of the Population Association of America, Toronto, Canada.

Farley, R., and W.H. Frey. 1994. "Changes in The Segregation of Whites from Blacks." *American Sociological Review* 59: 23-45.

Farley, R. 1991. "The New Census Question about Ancestry: What Did It Tell Us?" *Demography* 28: 411-30.

Forbes, J.D. 1993. *Africans and Native Americans. The Language of Race and the Evolution of Red-Black Peoples.* Urbana, IL: University of Illinois Press.

Fossett, M.A., and K.J. Kiecolt. 1989. "The Relative Size of Minority Populations and White Racial Attitudes." *Social Science Quarterly* 70: 820-35.

Frisbie, W.P., and L.J. Neidert. 1977. "Inequality and the Relative Size of Minority Populations: A Comparative Analysis." *American Journal of Sociology* 82: 1007-30.

Goldscheider, C. 1992. "Demographic Transformations in Israel: Emerging Themes in Comparative Context." Pp. 1-38 in *Population and Social Change in Israel*, edited by C. Goldscheider. Boulder, CO: Westview Press.

Hacker, A. 1992. *Two Nations.* New York: Charles Scribner's Sons.

Harris, M., J.G. Consorte, J. Lang, and Bryan Byrne. 1993. "Who are the Whites? Imposed Census Categories and the Racial Demography of Brazil." *Social Forces* 72: 451-62.

Harris, M. 1990. "Emics and Etics Revisited." Pp. 48-61 in *Emics and Etics: The Insider/Outsider Debate*, edited by T. Headland, K. Pike, and M. Harris. Beverly Hills, CA: Sage.

Hirsch, A. R. 1983. *Making the Second Ghetto: Race and Housing in Chicago: 1940-1960.* Chicago: University of Chicago Press.

Horowitz, D.L. 1985. *Ethnic Groups in Conflict.* Berkeley: University of California Press.

Houstoun, M.F., R.G. Kramer, and J.M. Barrett. 1984. "Female Predominance of Immigration to the United States Since 1930: A First Look." *International Migration Review* 18: 908-63.

Hout, M., and J.R. Goldstein. 1994. "How 4.5 Million Irish Immigrants Became 40 Million Irish Americans: Demographic and Subjective Aspects of Ethnic Identity." *American Sociological Review* 59: 64-82.

Jasso, G., and M.R. Rosenzweig. 1990. *The New Chosen People: Immigrants to the United States.* New York: Russell Sage.

Kent, G. 1991. *The Politics of Children's Survival.* New York: Praeger.

King, M., and S. Ruggles. 1990. "American Immigration, Fertility and Race Suicide at the Turn of the Century." *Journal of Interdisciplinary History* 20: 347-69.

Knodel, J., A. Chamratrithirong, and N. Debavala. 1987. *Thailand's Reproductive Revolution.* Madison: University of Wisconsin Press.

Ladner, R.A., B.J. Schwarts, S.J. Roker, and L. Titterud. 1981. "The Miami Riots of 1980." *Research in Social Movements* 4: 171-214.

Lee, S.M. 1993. "Racial Classifications in the US Census: 1890-1990." *Ethnic and Racial Studies* 16: 75-94.

Lévy, M. 1992. "Immigration in France: Popular Perceptions Versus Reality." Pp. 6-7 in *Population Today* (volume 20, No. 5). Washington, DC: Population Reference Bureau.

Lieberson, S., and M.C. Waters. 1988. *From Many Strands: Ethnic and Racial Groups in Contemporary America.* New York: Russell Sage.

Lieberson, S., and M.C. Waters. 1993. "The Ethnic Responses of Whites: What Causes Their Instability, Simplification, and Inconsistency." *Social Forces* 72: 421-450.

MacDonald, J.S., and L.D. MacDonald. 1974. "Chain Migration, Ethnic Neighborhood Formation, and Social Networks." Pp. 226-36 in *An Urban World*, edited by C. Tilly. Boston: Little, Brown and Compay.

Massey, D.S., R. Alarcon, J. Durand, and H. Gonzales. 1987. *Return to Atzlan: The Social Process of International Migration from Western Mexico.* Berkeley: University of California Press.

Massey, D.S. 1994. "The New Immigration and the Meaning of Ethnicity in the United States." Paper presented at The 13th Albany Conference, American Diversity: A Demographic Challenge for the Twenty-First Century. SUNY-Albany.

Massey, D.S., and N.A. Denton. 1988. "The Dimensions of Residential Segregation." *Social Forces* 67: 281-315.

Massey, D.S. and N.A. Denton. 1993. *American Apartheid. Segregation and the Making of the Underclass.* Cambridge: Harvard University Press.

McKenney, N.R., and A.R. Cresce. 1993. "Measurement of Ethnicity in the United States." In *Challenges of Measuring an Ethnic World. Proceedings of the Joint Canada-United States Conference on the Measurement of Ethnicity.* Washington, DC: U.S. Government Printing Office.

McLanahan, S.S. 1988. "Family Structure and Dependency: Early Transitions to Female Household Headship." *Demography* 25: 1-16.

National Center for Health Statistics. 1991. "Advance Report of Final Natality Statistics 1989." *Monthly Vital Statistics Report* 40 (8), suppl. Hyattsville, MD: Public Health Service.

Neilsen, F. 1985. "Ethnic Solidarity in Modern Societies." *American Sociological Review* 45: 76-94.

The New York Times. 1990. "Still Invisible, and Dying in Harlem." February 24.

Office of Management and Budget, Executive Office of the President (OMB). 1994. "Standards for the Classification of Federal Data on Race and Ethnicity." Washington, DC.

Olzak, S. 1987. "Causes of Ethnic Conflict and Protest in Urban America, 1877-1889." *American Sociological Review* 16: 185-210.

Olzak, S. 1992. *The Dynamics of Ethnic Competition and Conflict.* Stanford: Standford University Press.

Pagnini, D.L., and S.P. Morgan. 1990. "Intermarriage and Social Distance among U.S. Immigrants at the Turn of the Century." *American Journal of Sociology* 96: 405-32.

Passel, J.S., and B. Edmonston. 1994. "Immigration and Race: Recent Trends in Immigration to the United States." Pp. 31-72 in *Immigration and Ethnicity: The Integration of America s Newest Arrivals,* edited by B. Edmonston and J.S. Passel. Washington, DC: Urban Institute Press.

Preston, S. 1984. "Children and the Elderly in the U.S." *Scientific American* 251:44-9.

Reischauer, R. 1989. "Immigration and the Underclass." *The Annals* 501: 120-31.

Riley, E. 1991. "Major Political Events in South Africa, 1948-1990." New York: Facts on File, INC.

Schoen, R., and J.R. Kluegel. 1988. "The Widening Gap in Black and White Marriage Rates: the Impact of Population Composition and Differential Marriage Propensities." *American Sociological Review* 53: 895-907.

Snipp, C.M. 1991. *American Indians: The First of This Land.* New York: Russell Sage.

Solomon, B.M. 1956. *Ancestors and Immigrants.* Cambridge: Cambridge University Press.

Spickard, P.R. 1989. *Mixed Blood.* Madison: University of Wisconsin Press.

Stevens, G., and G. Swicegood. 1987. "The Linguistic Context of Ethnic Endogamy." *American Sociological Review* 52: 73-82.

Swicegood, G., and S.P. Morgan. 1994. "Racial and Ethnic Fertility Differentials in the United States." Paper presented at the 13th Albany Conference, American Diversity: A Demographic Challenge for the Twenty-First Century. SUNY-Albany.

Tilly, C., and C.H. Brown. 1974. "On Uprooting, Kinship, and the Auspices of Migration." Pp. 108-33 in *An Urban World,* edited by C. Tilly. Boston: Little, Brown and Company.

U.S. Bureau of the Census. 1991. *General Population Characteristics, 1990: U.S. Summary.* Washington, DC: U.S. Government Printing Office.

Van den Berghe, P.L. 1987. *The Ethnic Phenomenon.* New York: Praeger.

White, M.J. 1994. "Housing Segregation: Policy for an Increasingly Diverse Society." Paper presented at The 13th Albany Conference, American Diversity: A Demographic Challenge for the Twenty-First Century. SUNY-Albany.

White, P. 1993. "Ethnic Minority Communities in Europe." Pp. 206-25 in *The Changing Population of Europe*, edited by D. Noin and R. Woods. Oxford: Blackwell Publishers.

Wilcox, J., and W.C. Roof. 1978. "Percent Black and Black-White Status Inequality: Southern versus Non-Southern Patterns." *Social Science Quarterly* 59: 421-34.

Wilson, W.J. 1987. *The Truly Disadvantaged*. Chicago: University of Chicago Press.

Yinger, J. 1991. "Housing Discrimination Study: Incidence and Variation in Discriminatory Behavior." *Office of Policy Development and Research, Department of Housing and Urban Development.*

Zopf, P.E. 1992. *Mortality Patterns and Trends in the United States*. Westport, CT: Greenwood Press.

RACIAL AND ETHNIC CONFLICT:
PERSPECTIVES FROM HISTORY

David L. Salvaterra

U.S. HISTORIOGRAPHY

Expansion and Differentiation

Perhaps the most important development in the field that bears on our concerns has been its expansion and differentiation. Expansion was, first of all, the product of increasing numbers of historians at work in the field. It also resulted from research specialization that has kept pace with the greater number of practitioners writing in the last three decades. A third and related factor that must be considered is the expansion-related phenomenon of vastly greater inclusion. No longer is U.S. history the story of elite, literate, white males. So much has the picture changed that critics charge it has been diluted and denatured and has become "politically correct." They further charge that newer versions of our nation's past are destructive of our shared cultural values because they so often are accompanied by devaluation of the very individuals and groups whose lives and accomplishments used to dominate historical accounts. U.S. historians, themselves, fear that the field has come to be

Research in Human Social Conflict, Volume 1, pages 25-54.

overspecialized and fragmented to the point where synthesis has become nearly impossible (American Historical Association, 1984; Himmelfarb, 1984, 1989; Link, 1985; Bender, 1986; Monkkonen, 1986; Thelen, 1986; Hamerow, 1987; Toews, 1989; Megill, 1989; Anderson and Cayton, 1993; Hollinger, 1993; Levine, 1993).

As both practitioners and research specializations increased a corresponding expansion of research output occurred. Specialized historical organizations and publication outlets proliferated and historians returned to the local, the particular, the unique, and the private. Moreover, historians have recently been striving to be inclusive geographically and chronologically as well as by means of many other characteristics that differentiate Americans (Foner, 1990; Burke, 1991, 1992; Limerick, 1992; Richter, 1993).

Internationalization

U.S. history, once studied in geographical and intellectual isolation, has recently become internationalized on an unprecedented scale. Recognizing that capable practitioners are located on all continents and that research now is an enterprise that goes beyond all national boundaries the profession has responded by moving decisively in this direction. The comparative dimension and recognition that one cannot study world-historical forces such as capitalism, slavery, or migration in specific national contexts only has also contributed to this reorientation (Iriye, 1989; Kaye, 1991; McGerr, 1991; Tyrell, 1991; Thelen, 1992).

Methodological Maturation

Mental and Physical Worlds

If the field has grown and developed in terms of both size and scope of activities, a corresponding transformation in intellectual assumptions and methodological presuppositions has altered the study of U.S. history tremendously of late. Important methodological cross-fertilization from the social sciences, particularly psychology, sociology, and anthropology, has altered historical method and reinforced the emphasis on the local and private mentioned earlier. Moreover, influences from Europe, chiefly England and France, have combined with these influences to bring about the current preoccupation with demography, with family, with quantifiable entities and phenomena, with inner mental worlds and structures of past historical actors, with decoding deeply embedded cultural meanings as past figures lived and moved through their worlds and with reconstruction of their specific historically experienced worlds through previously neglected or heretofore unusable sources (Hamerow, 1987; Himmelfarb, 1989; Krieger, 1989; Levine, 1989, 1993; Foner, 1990).

Self-Consciousness

Historians have recently become extremely interested in both the process and the product of historical reconstruction. What gives historical research validity? Is the product of research in any sense objectively valid? If so, what might the sense be? As the academy becomes more and more insecure about its intellectual moorings, history has shared in the misgivings of postmodernist, deconstructed "reality." All historical evidence can now be seen as "text" and historians must ask whether any timeless meaning can be attached to its explication or whether it is all inescapably culture-bound in a double sense. That is, it was the product of a unique historical culture in which it was generated and therefore, can it ever be adequately rendered by any subsequent, different one? It is also recognized that all such redaction is subject to the vagaries of memory and of interference stemming inescapably from the interpreter's culture and presuppositions (Toews, 1987, 1989; Harlan, 1989a, 1989b; Hollinger, 1989; Megill, 1989; Novick, 1989; Scott, 1989; Kloppenberg, 1989; Harlan, 1990; Haskell, 1990; Matthews, 1990; American Historical Association, 1991; Brown, 1991; Jacoby, 1992; La Capra, 1992).

Three Special Cases

All of these developments have contributed both to greater possibilities as well as greater confusion. Three other special categories of analysis which have figured prominently in the recent historiography have impacted the field in a similar manner but deserve special mention both because of their overall importance for the field and for their bearing on the matters relevant to our concerns. Gender, race and ethnicity, and class considerations have all become extremely important analytical categories in the study of the U.S. past.

Gender

The rise of feminist consciousness, the emergence of sizeable numbers of female historians, and the appearance of specialized research outlets have contributed to the recognition that gender must continue to be taken into account throughout the American past and that it will continue to yield fresh perspectives on many old matters (Scott, 1986; Baron, 1991; Frankel and Dye, 1991; Gordon, 1991; Appleby, 1992; Faue, 1993). Ethnic and racial concerns tend to often get connected together in the current historical literature with race, in this sense, being regarded as a subset of the more generically inclusive ethnic phenomena. This, too was partly due to the expanding number and identity of historians as many blacks entered the field as well as many second, third, and later generation ethnics. Writing from different perspectives and coming from very different backgrounds than earlier historians, they also changed the picture. We shall have more to say on this point later (Hine, 1986; Meier and Rudwick, 1986; Quarles, 1988). Finally, class as a category of analysis, either by itself or in combination with gender and ethnic/racial considerations, has yielded abundant results. It is harder to account for this phenomenon since historians have tended to be from very different socioeconomic backgrounds than the working class, the subjects whose class position interests them most. It might be accurate to say that much of this concern has been motivated by sympathy for the dispossessed of the past and by a diligent search for evidence of class consciousness among Americans of the past (Bloom, 1987; Arnesen, 1991; Frankel and Dye, 1991; Baer and Jones, 1992).

RACE AND ETHNICITY IN RECENT HISTORIOGRAPHY

Native Americans/Mexican Americans and the West

Native Americans have been transformed from being viewed as obstacles to the advancenent of Euro-American progress to historical actors in their own right. It is now possible to tell their story without resorting to victimization models and it is even possible to accord Native Americans volitional, cultural, and other positive attributes. And they are not primarily confined, in accounts, to the period of most active European-American westward movement. The west itself, the arena in which European-Americans encountered them, has undergone significant reinterpretation under the impact or recent environmental history and ethnography (Hirsch, 1988; Worster, 1988; Malone and Etulain, 1989; Limerick, Milner, and Rankin, 1991; Malone, 1991; White, 1991a, 1991b; Cronon, Miles, and Gitlin, 1992; Dowd, 1992; Hoxie, 1992; Limerick, 1992; Nostrand, 1992; Worster, 1992; Farragher, 1993; Richter, 1993). As the west has been reinterpreted so has treatment of Mexican Americans (San Miguel, 1987; Garcia, 1989; Daniel, 1991; Garcia, 1991; Nostrand, 1992; Escobar, 1993; Sanchez, 1993; Skerry, 1993).

The Asian-American Experience

In traditional historical accounts, blacks were confined to certain periods and topics and Asian Americans either did not appear at all or at most got passing mention. Regarded as something other than "immigrants, " even by historians, Asians could therefore be ignored. In recent literature they are beginning to be restored to their rightful place and we now recognize that it is important to tell the story of the peopling of America from both Atlantic and Pacific Ocean perspectives (Patterson, 1985; Tsai, 1986; Daniels, 1988;

Hellweg, 1990; Daniels, Taylor and Kitano, 1991; Fugita and O'Brien, 1991; Appleby, 1992; Espiritu, 1992; Reed, 1992; Rutledge, 1992).

Globalization of Migration

The study of American migration has been globalized in other ways, also. The comparative dimension has yielded great insights. Tracing migrants back to the donor countries has also changed perspectives as have recognition of the significance for several groups of return migration and international patterns of migration, and greater understanding of destinations, the processes of migration and premigration changes in the individuals involved and of the mobile communities to which they belonged (Bailyn, 1986; Gabbacia, 1988; Jasso and Rosenzweig, 1990; Yans-Mc Loughlin, 1990; Altman and Horn, 1991; Vecoli and Sinke, 1991; Morgan, 1993; Nugent, 1992; Wyman, 1993; Reed, 1994; Olson, 1994).

Ethnic Identity

Finally, the complexities of ethnic identity have introduced new perspectives on ethnic community and on the mechanisms and means used by migrants to adjust and cope after their migration. Here again the focus accords immigrants greater scope and greater volition. And the immigrant-ethnic story has been enriched by detailed examination of autobiography and of specific communities over time (Miller, 1985; Morawska, 1985; Stolarik, 1985; Swierenga, 1985; Meagher, 1986; Tsai, 1986; Alexander, 1987; Bukowczyk, 1987; Gerber, 1989; Nadel, 1990; Clark, 1991; Pacyga, 1991; Perlman, 1991; Ramirez.1991; Anderson and Blanck, 1992; Shapiro and Sarna, 1992; Sanchez, 1993; Skerry, 1993; Mormino, 1986; Mormino and Pozzetta, 1987).

AFRICAN AMERICANS IN U.S. HISTORY

The Traditional Account

Traditionally, historical attention to African Americans has focused on the periods of enslavement and emancipation in the early United States. Then in the twentieth century the story revolved around the making of urban black ghettoes along with the consequences thereof. Throughout, blacks were seen as victims of white greed, of the labor requirements of large-scale plantation agriculture and later of industrial capitalism, and of virulent and nearly universal white racism. We now understand this to be an unfairly truncated and distorted picture. It decontextualizes black life by eliminating African connections and fails to accord blacks any status other than that of victim.

After the changes of the 1960s, such a picture would be intolerable. The historical profession, itself, is no longer content to understand blacks as merely passive objects of white whim, as shadowy figures who lived and moved through largely white worlds as unobtrusively as possible and who passively accepted that role (Hine, 1986; Harris, 1987; Meier and Rudwick, 1986; Quarles, 1988; Walker, 1991).

Slavery Reinterpreted

Slavery itself has been returned to its Atlantic context. That is, it was an international phenomenon that originated in the slave trading practices of the early modern world which was essentially a circum-Atlantic Ocean operation. It operated over the four centuries of its existence in accordance with the imperatives of capitalism's labor demands, but this is now read as a capitalism which was international in scope and operation and was significantly shaped by African influences and by Afro-Caribbean and African American as well as European ones (Smith, 1985a; Okihiro, 1986; Kolchin, 1987; Turner and Turner, 1988; Berlin and Morgan, 1991; Solow, 1991; Thornton, 1991, 1992; Mullin, 1992).

Enslavement and the conditions of slavery have also been given an international context by means of the comparative dimension. Slaves are known now to have contributed significant skills and knowlege to the agricultural operations on which they worked, much of which they brought with them from Africa. And many cultural survivals can now be traced back to their African origins, many times through Caribbean connections (Jones-Jackson, 1987; Creel, 1988; Harris, 1991; Ferguson, 1992; Hall, 1992; Hirsch and Logsdon, 1992; Kasinitz, 1992; Holloway and Vass, 1993).

Republicanism and Race in the Era of the American Revolution

Undoubtedly the most fertile and important explanatory concept in early U.S. history over the last three decades has been that of "republicanism." Its exponents have done much to document its origins in earlier centuries of European history and to work it into the very marrow of interpretations of the era of the American Revolution. What is more, they have not stopped there: the concept has been extended in time from the revolutionary era through the Civil War era. Although the concept and its overuse have lately come in for some substantive criticism, its defenders have staunchly risen in its support.

For our purposes it becomes relevant to discussions of revolutionary and later ideology and of their implications for equality. It raises some intriguing questions historians have explored and it makes possible the reading of race relations in the years between the 1770s and 1820s as both a period of relatively harmonious relations and of lost opportunity. Generally, the market economy and changes associated with it are blamed for undermining this period of relative black-white racial concord and relative economic and political opportunity.

The years of the American Revolution themselves were the era of the first wave of slavery elimination and the role of republican ideology in northern state emancipation has been well documented. What later research has revealed is much about free slaves in the years of the greatest expansion of slavery, from about 1780 until adoption of the Thirteenth Amendment to the constitution. The free black population was diverse, sometimes surprisingly well off, especially in some locales, often constituted a black or mixed race elite. Despite legal and social disabilities imposed by the white legal system and by white attitudes, free blacks seem to have often successfully carved out niches of relative security and even relative prosperity in the antebellum north and south. And this pre-Civil War free black community often played a key leadership role in emancipation and in the adjustment to the postemancipation world (Cody, 1987; Nash, 1988; Piersen, 1988; Berthoff, 1989; Farr, 1989; Bolster, 1990; Schweninger, 1990a, 1990b; Alexander, 1991; Nash, 1991; Nash and Soderlund, 1991; ; Mc Curry, 1992; Rodgers, 1992; Buchalter, 1993; Pole, 1993; Walker, 1993).

Black-White Relations in the Slavery Context

It is in the area of black-white relations that probably the greatest change has occurred and it is the area most relevant to our purposes. Although a long-standing historical concern, the study of black reactions to whites and to slavery has taken a significantly new turn. Perhaps the keynote of recent studies of blacks in the slavery context has been black humanization. While overt slave rebellion was relatively rare, black resistance to the attempted dehumanization inherent in slavery was surprisingly universal and spirited. While acknowledging that blacks lacked access to formal power they are now seen as having contested their status and treatment with whites in an amazing variety of ways. Escaping from enslavement is now seen not as the risky action of the desperate but as the purposeful attempt of the bold to strike a direct blow against the institution. Moreover, blacks evolved a host of coping mechanisms that allowed them to endure slavery far more on their own terms than was ever realized. In the main, such mechanisms were completely nonviolent. They malingered, not as their masters claimed, because they were lazy or inadequate workers, but to subvert work discipline and to purposely impact agricultural output. They deliberately damaged, lost, and misused farm equipment for the same reasons. And masters' complaints about slow and shoddy work, when looked at from a slave perspective, can often be seen to be coping mechanisms (Jones, 1987; Fox-Genovese, 1988; Wyatt-Brown, 1988; Jones, 1990; Campbell and Ryce, 1991; Berlin and Morgan, 1991; LaCapra, 1991; Forbes, 1992; Mullin, 1992; Parker, 1993).

The Slave Quarter Community

Finally, insights drawn from cultural anthropology, from folklore studies, from literary analysis, and other areas of scholarship have made it possible to view blacks, even in a slavery context, as having maintained a reasonably autonomous and surprisingly viable community life. The black experience in slavery was a quite diverse one with significant national, regional, occupational, and other variations. But regardless of time or place, when studied from a slave perspective, the institution takes on new meaning. Primarily, we now understand their life experiences far more on their terms than ever before and we now know that they were active shapers of their lives in significant ways. In particular they used language, folklore and oral traditions, music and dance, and other folk customs to shape their worlds. Within the confines of their own living spaces, moreover, they devised and maintained their own sets of values and mores. In spite of the ever-present possibility of disruption of their communities by interventions of whites they produced their own forms of family and even turned religion itself, often imposed by masters for purposes of social control, to their own ends. The world of the slave quarters was, to the fullest extent that they could make it so, a world of their own construction and a world in which they could live and move apart from the slaveowners' scrutiny or even knowledge (Lawson and Merrill, 1984; Patterson, 1985; Singleton, 1985; White, 1985; Mohr, 1986; Okihiro, 1986; Boles, 1988; Blyden, 1989; Burrison, 1989; Watson, 1989; Campbell and Ryce, 1991; Aptheker, 1992; Malone, 1992; Mullin, 1992).

Antislavery and Emancipation

Antislavery has also been subject to reinterpretation. We now know a great deal more than ever about black abolitionism and about black participation in aiding fellow slaves to escape. We have a much greater appreciation of black participation in the Civil War and about the importance of that military service in helping to move the United States toward emancipation. The global context of antislavery and situating abolitionism within an international capitalist context are currently also the subject of lively discussion among historians (Haskell, 1985a, 1985b; Sernett, 1986; Ashworth, 1987; Davis, 1987; Aptheker, 1989; Swift, 1989; Dillon, 1990; Hahn, 1990; Thornton, 1991; White, 1991; Yee, 1992; Eltes, 1993).

The consequences of emancipation have been actively researched by historians, too. Reconstruction is now seen as a process that commenced during the military conflict in certain localities and spread throughout the south by the war's end. At all stages of the process, blacks participated actively and purposively. They made conscious, rational, and self-serving decisions about whether to participate in public life and about the nature and duration of such participation. They took control of, and responsibility for, their own and their family members' lives in numerous ways; they chose where to live, with whom to live, and how to make a living. Moreover, they made such choices and decisions either without reference to white preferences or quite in opposition to them and often despite white threats and reprisals. They made and saved money in surprising amounts, sought out and secured educational advantages for their children whenever possible, and did whatever they felt was necessary to make themselves as independent of whites as possible (Colburn, 1985; Blacket, 1986; Duncan, 1986; Bess, 1987; Foner, 1987, 1988; Mc Caul, 1987; Wallenstein, 1987; Ingalls, 1988; Orser, 1988; Winch, 1988; Fitzgerald, 1989a, 1989b; Gatewood, 1990; Graves, 1990; Hahn, 1990; Cohen, 1991; Kremer, 1991; Ayers, 1992; Mc Glynn and Drescher, 1992; Lowe, 1993; Scott, 1994).

Emancipation and Migration

In cases where white hostility was too great or the opportunities too scarce, blacks defused potentially destructive situations by means of migration. Black population movement, we now realize, was as complex a phenomenon as black-white relations during slavery and emancipation. It was prompted by a wide range of motivations other than moving away from white threats and violence. It involved, especially after the turn of the twentieth century, surprising numbers of people and some surprising destinations. Finally, black volition and agency are apparent here, also. Black kinship networks provided information, lodging, job connections, and cultural sustenance during the critical period of uprooting and reestablishment consequent to large scale population transfer. And once black migrants had arrived at their destinations, black institutional and organizational life helped the black community establish and maintain its identity (Kaczorowski, 1987; Litwack and Meier, 1988; Shapiro, 1988; Mc Millen, 1989; Hamilton, 1991; Kremer, 1991; Ayers, 1992; Mandle, 1992; Frehill-Rowe, 1993).

The Great Migration

Black movement to northern urban centers in the 1920s and 1930s has received considerable recent historical attention and reinterpretation. The comparative dimension has yielded valuable insights as have studies of particular localities and of the black connections that made movement possible and determined its direction and character. Here again, black community structure, black institutional activities, black volition, and black culture are essential elements of the story. We have learned a great deal about who the migrants were, their motives for moving, their methods, destinations, and their lives after migration (Andrews, 1986; Gottlieb, 1987; Grossman, 1989; Marks, 1989; Lemann, 1991; Trotter, 1991).

Blacks in the American City

Building on insights gained from urban history, immigration history, and labor history along with sociological and anthropological methodologies, historians now have a much more complete picture of black life in an urban context. Although predominantly an urban phenomenon it should not be associated solely with major metropolises as many blacks migrated to secondary and smaller cities that, along with the major urban centers, are now being studied (Colburn, 1985; Bigham, 1987; Gottlieb, 1987; Grossman, 1989; Arnesen, 1991; Hamilton, 1991; Lewis, 1990; Hirsch and Logsdon, 1992).

The mid-nineteenth century, the period of most intense urbanization of all U.S. history, has received a good deal of the attention and blacks are an important part of the story. By the Civil War, a number of U.S. cities already had substantial black populations that were concentrated in certain parts of the urban landscape and urban black institutional structures had already begun to make their appearance. Black churches, in particular, were focal points of these communities and helped determine residential patterns. Black social, benevolent and charitable organizations also served their communities (Lane, 1979, 1986, 1991; Andrews, 1986; Wheeler, 1986; Gilje, 1987; Nash, 1988; Winch, 1988; Cooper, 1989; Bernstein, 1990; Cornelius, 1991; Angell, 1992).

Beyond the "Ghetto Model"

Twentieth-century black urban centers, originally studied as ghettoes, have undergone substantial recent reinterpretation also. First of all, they are now studied on their own terms as loci of black life rather than as blighted portions of otherwise respectable cities. Secondly, economic interpretation has risen to great prominence. Black participation in urban economic life is now, according to several recent historians, best understood as involving a "proletarianization" process. This proletarianization, of course, was shared with non-black urban industrial laborers and studying their comparative responses to their laboring and residential conditions was a natural outgrowth of the newer perspective (Greenberg, 1991; Thomas, 1992; Watts, 1992; Green, 1993).

Finally, as with other areas of African-American life, the hallmarks of twentieth-century black urban studies are black autonomy, black volition, and black achievement. Many studies have documented a vibrant black cultural life, significant black religious and organizational life, and an ongoing struggle for black rights and equality led by gifted indigenous black middle-class and leadership elements. Impediments to black advancement and social stigmatization, though formidable obstacles, are currently seen as continuously being confronted and opposed. Blacks, of course, experienced varying degrees of success in their confrontational and oppositional activites but that is now seen as far less important than that they consistently and constantly conducted the opposition. Equally significant, despite major economic obstacles, by the end of World War II urban metropolitan blacks were experiencing substantial social and occupational change. Much of it was undoubtedly due to war-related necessities and came with great difficulty but the fact that it did occur was to prove decisive for the future of the black community (Trotter, 1985, 1991; Cooper, 1987; Hull, 1987; Lornel, 1988; Turner and Turner, 1988; de Jongh, 1990; Harris, 1991; Kubitschek, 1991; Luker, 1991; Thomas, 1992; Lasch-Quinn, 1992).

Post-World War II Black American Life

Like so much of earlier areas of black life in the United States, the post-World War II period is the story of gains and losses, opportunities and obstacles, and above all, of black participation and volition and of black achievement. Diversity and continuity, here again, play a big role also as the postwar story shows long-standing connections with prewar trends and developments and as we learn more about the recent black community the more internally diverse we can know it to have been (Colburn, 1985; Dickerson, 1986; Hall, Korstad, and Lecoudis, 1986; Norrell, 1986; Bauman, 1987; Litwack, 1987; Bullard, 1989; Modell, Goulden, and Magnusson, 1989; Formisano, 1991; Capeci and Wilkerson, 1991; Baer and Jones, 1992; Draper, 1992; Hacker, 1992; Jones, 1992; Mandle, 1992; Kelly, 1993; Nelson, 1993).

Civil Rights

No area has received more recent attention, but the traditional historical picture has been corrected in several ways. The civil rights movment of the 1950s and 1960s did not originate in Supreme Court decisions or the decisions of any other courts. Nor was it the product of only one or, at best, a handful of black leaders. Nor was it severed in any meaningful sense from past black activities and leaders. Nor was it the product of an ideologically homogeneous black community.

Connections with earlier black oppositional activities have become well established. Continuities with past black leadership and with its goals have also been amply demonstrated as have the diversity of the 1950s and 1960s leadership and of its ideological and methodological approaches. And the critical role of black religion and black religious leadership have been confirmed (Anderson and Pickering, 1986; Garrow, 1986; Marable, 1986; Thomas, 1986;

Bloom, 1987; Foner, 1987; Harding, 1987; Organization of American Historians, 1987; Schwieder, Hraba, and Schwieder, 1987; Stuckey, 1987; Tushnet, 1987a, 1987b; Branch, 1988; Haines, 1988; Hall, 1988; Lipsitz, 1988; Cooper, 1989; Darity, 1989; Hine, 1989; Neverdon-Morton, 1989; Weiss, 1989; Chestnut, 1990; Cobb, 1990; Howard-Pitney, 1990; Margo, 1990; Pfeffer, 1990; Cashman, 1991; Cone, 1991; Lawson, 1991; Lewis, 1991; Luker, 1991; Martin, 1991; Robinson and Sullivan, 1991; Staniland, 1991; Aptheker, 1992; Baer and Singer, 1992; Carson, Luker, Russell, and Harlan, 1992; Crawford, Rouse, and Woods, 1992; Irvin, 1992; King, 1992; McCartney, 1992; Miller, 1992; Pratt, 1992; Stewart, 1992; Bayor, 1993; Carson, 1993; Higginbotham, 1993; Kelly, 1993; Sandage, 1993; Wells, 1993).

IMMIGRANTS/ETHNICS IN U.S. HISTORY

The Traditional Picture

Traditional accounts of the immigrant/ethnic dimension of U.S. history have been U.S. focused and focused on the period of mass immigration when record numbers of new arrivals came here chiefly from Europe. Most of the scholarly attention given to these matters by historians was done from the perspective of the new arrivals' postmigration adjustment to life in the United States and, by and large, the groups who received the bulk of the attention were European migrants from the countries that formerly made up the Austro-Hungarian empire, from Russia and from southern and central European nations such as Italy and Poland.

Prior to the late nineteenth century the United States was not considered to have had any particular ethnic dimension in its history as the U.S. population was seen to have been largely homogeneously English in background and "Englishness" was the dominant cultural situation. And until the onset of mass immigration there was nearly universal confidence in the absorptive power of our largely Anglo-American "melting pot" to melt away foreigners' differences. And there was a cultural consensus that this was both appropriate and good as it contributed to the building up of American national unity.

The University of Chicago sociology department gave explanatory power and academic respectability to this cultural consensus. Studies done there were based on Austrian conflict school sociology and on Robert Park's refinement of it into what became known as his "interaction cycle." As late as the 1960s such a view had been elaborated into a multistage process by Milton Gordon, but what is important here is that in any case the immigrant was the largely passive instrument of fate who, responding to mysterious forces much larger than he or she could comprehend, moved rather purposelessly from some European location to one in the United States. Once here, he or she was expected to more or less quickly shed all foreignness and eventually become part of the dominant Anglo-American culture by embracing American culture, dress, food, customs, and beliefs. Of course such a transformation would require the immigrant to pay a certain price, pyschically and otherwise, for the privilege but that was essentially seen as a small price to pay for the inestimable advantages of relocating to America.

Recent Immigration Historiography

Virtually none of the traditional views would be tenable among scholars of ethnicity/immigration today in the historical profession. The globalization of the profession has altered the picture in significant ways as have developments in social and labor history. Also, efforts to be inclusive have made it possible to broaden the focus beyond Europe and to examine the ethnic dimension in U.S. history in a way that includes all groups in all time periods. We now recognize that the Anglo-American identity, itself, is an ethnic one and that the United States was far more ethnically pluralistic from its earliest years than we formerly recognized (Bailyn, 1986; Bodnar, 1985; Tsai, 1986; San Miguel, 1987; Yans-Mc Loughlin, 1990; Altman and Horn, 1991; Vecoli and Sinke, 1991; Appleby, 1992; Morgan, 1993; Nostrand, 1992; Nugent, 1992; Rutledge, 1992; Sanchez, 1993; Olson, 1994; Reed, 1994).

Even more importantly, we now understand how the traditional picture distorted the realities of immigrant life experiences by denying the participants themselves any meaningful involvement in the process. As scholars focused on specific immigrant communities and individuals our understanding of their role in shaping their own reality broadened correspondingly. As was the case with African Americans we began to realize they had always exerted a great deal of control over their own lives, making countless crucial decisions, which from their perspective made a great deal of sense. When we moved beyond studying them as social problems, or at least challenges, and studied them rather as human beings it would have been very difficult to deny their humanity, the validity of their choices, and to fail to appreciate the strategies adopted and accomodations they made to cope with often very difficult situations (Bodnar, 1985; Yans-MCloughlin, 1990; Vecoli and Sinke, 1991; Olson, 1994; Reed, 1994).

Who Was an Immigrant?

This question would have been unaskable earlier. Now with the trend toward universal inclusiveness in the field we tend to answer it as broadly as possible. Current practice has moved well beyond a European focus and recognizes that important population components of the United States have come from Asia and from Latin America as well. Asians, formerly having been largely excluded from discussions of the mass immigration of the late nineteenth century, are now recognized to have constituted an important part of it and of recent immigration. And Latin Americans, especially from the 1920s on, also contributed importantly. We can now recognize that both of these population streams contained significant internal diversity (Tsai, 1986; Daniels, 1988; Patterson, 1988; Garcia, 1989; Hellweg, 1990; Jasso and Rosenzweig, 1990; Daniels and Kitano, 1991; Fugita and O'Brien, 1991; Garcia, 1991; Appleby, 1992; Hollinger, 1993; Skerry, 1993; Foner and Rosenberg, 1993; Olson, 1994; Reed, 1994).

Sources/Destinations/Motivations

Globalization requires that immigrants be studied in an international context that takes into account donor country conditions and cultures in shaping migrants' experiences and choices. It was not simply the abundance of industrial employment opportunities in the U.S. economy in the late nineteenth and early twentieth centuries which uprooted masses of individuals. Global capitalism was causing significant changes in donor countries and massive regional and interregional population movement within donor countries often preceded movement to the United States or to several other destinations in the western hemisphere and elsewhere. The migrant is no longer seen or studied as an isolated individual. We now understand the family and community connections that played an important part in motivation, destination, and survival after arrival. And we have a much better appreciation than ever before of the regional, national, and other variations within immigrant groups. Comparative studies have demonstrated that many of the "new immigrants" of the period from 1880 to World War I were, in intent, temporary migrants and indeed, within certain immigrant groups, return migration was a significant phenomenon (Briggs, 1986; Gabbacia, 1988; Nugent, 1992; Cinel, 1991; Ramirez, 1991; Stolarik, 1992; Wyman, 1993).

The Immigrant Community and Identity

If the immigrants relocated as part of a larger network of human connections, they lived their lives after arrival as parts of larger communities. Community connections impacted destinations, job opportunities, residential patterns, and participation in public life. And it impacted immigrant identity in ways we are just now beginning to understand. As was the case with black Americans, immigrants had vibrant cultural lives, strong and meaningful religious affiliations, and flourishing organizational structures, all of which played crucial roles in mediating individual and group identity (Diner, 1983, 1992; Miller, 1985; Morawska, 1985; Stolarik, 1985; Swierenga, 1985; Meagher, 1986; Mormino, 1986; Alexander, 1987; Green, 1987; Mormino and Pozzetta,

1987; Gabbacia, 1988; Gerber, 1989; Glenn, 1990; Nadel, 1990; Clark, 1991; Pacyga, 1991; Perlman, 1991; Anderson and Blanck, 1992; Stolarik, 1992).

Conflict and the Construction of Identity

Following the lead of social scientists, historians now tend to look at this matter as one less of genetic immutability and more one of cultural construction. Imaginative studies have demonstrated how ethnic festivals and celebrations, both religious and secular, reveal a multifaceted ethnicity that can evolve over time and be related to ancestors in surprisingly indirect and diffuse ways. They reveal further that the individuals and communities involved, themselves shaped their own understanding of who they were and who they were becoming in important ways (Bodnar, 1986; Tsai, 1986; Perlman, 1988; Garcia, 1989; Gerber, 1989; Pula and Dziedzic, 1990; Fugita and O'Brien, 1991; Garcia 1991; Pacyga, 1991; Perlman, 1991; Schulz, 1991; Reed, 1992; Escobar, 1993; Foner and Rosenberg, 1993; Sanchez, 1993).

Detailed studies of various localities, additionally, have revealed that there has been a significant degree of disunity within immigrant groups. Associational life, religious practices, cultural values, regional and village loyalties, and other forces have probably just as often divided immigrants internally as they have united them. And the conflict that resulted from these divisions were often bitter and long-running (Miller, 1985; Mormino, 1986; Bukowczyk, 1987; Green, 1987; Mormino and Pozzetta, 1987; Shapiro and Sarna, 1992).

Pluralism and Postpluralism

In the 1960s and 1970s white ethnics, especially the descendants of the groups involved in the massive late nineteenth-century migration, asserted themselves in what became known as the "ethnic revival." In this first decisive challenge to the Anglo-conformity or assimilationist model, they insisted upon the ability to retain their differentness in some ways and celebrated their differentness as reflective of a healthy diversity. Assimilationist beliefs were harshly criticized as unrealistic and coercive, as destructive of the legitimate diversity which had long characterized American society. And they insisted they could be hyphenate Americans and good Americans at the same time. American tolerance, equality, democracy, and freedom seemed to demand that all groups and individuals be able to preserve and exercise their ethnicity.

The most famous explanation of this phenomenon was rediscovered and applied after the fact. Marcus Hansen's so-called "Hansen's Law" predicted a third generation return to ethnicity after a second generation distancing. In some respects it does seem to have been a generationally based phenomenon but what is important here is that it helped prepare the way for regarding ethnicity as an important force and for viewing it as a cultural and social construction. Scholars of ethnicity, often third and later generation ethnics themselves, helped bring this view into focus.

At about the same time, social scientists were rethinking ethnicity. Anthropologists and sociologists, in particular, noticed that ethnicity was surprisingly long-lived and that it was related to immigrant ancestors in ways that were hard to connect to primordialist or genetic explanations. In a famous reformulation an anthropologist insisted that what was important was not what was enclosed in the boundary, the focus of nearly all attention up to that point. What was important, instead, was the construction, location, and functional meaning of the boundary which essentially became seen as a social and cultural construction. Boundary acceptance and observance, essentially human and utterly subjective, yet real, seemed to indicate that ethnic self-definition and definition by another must be a good deal more complex than recognized in the past.

All of this made possible what might be called a postpluralist view of ethnicity or of ethnic identity. It is now seen as a social/cultural construct in which the individuals and groups involved actively participate and contribute to their own identity. In combination with the dominant culture, then, groups formulate their own self-identity in ways that involve social bartering and mutual exchange in complicated ways (Sollors, 1986; Gleason, 1992; Salvaterra, 1994).

Ethnicity and Class

Perhaps more has been done by historians on this than on any other recent topic. It has long been known that immigrants typically provided unskilled, industrial labor but what about those who migrated prior to U.S. industrialization or just as industrialization was taking hold? And for those who came during the mass industrialization of the United States in the same era as that of mass migration, what was the nature and character of their life experiences?

Historians used to try to answer how industrialization shaped their lives and in a sense still do. Those concerns are now supplemented, however, by an additional and complementary concern about how immigrants participated actively in the industrial economy. As with blacks, once again, the focus is no longer on passive acceptance of inescapable forces but on immigrant volition, ingenuity, and resilience in accomodating such forces to their own purposes. Two European scholars have been especially influential in shaping U.S. historians' approaches to these questions. E.P. Thompson and Antonio Gramsci moved historians' attention to the working-class world and to the culture and ideology which underpinned it (Bodnar, 1985; Montgomery, 1987; Yans-McLoughlin, 1990; Barrett, 1992).

Thompson's insights have been most fruitfully applied in the preindustrial and emergent industrial United States of the mid-nineteenth century where his concept of "artisanal republicanism" has enjoyed great prominence. A concept closely related to the republicanism of the American Revolution era, in fact they are seen as sharing the same roots, artisanal republicanism is now widely understood as the working-class response to the transition from skilled hand labor to market and machine dictated production. Whether this led to class conscious opposition to capitalism itself, usually seen as happening later in the fully industrial age of the late nineteenth century, is a matter of active debate. Gramsci's concept of "cultural hegemony" is used by some to argue just for such class antagonistic ideology, just slightly less conflictual than its Marxist alternative (Diggins, 1985; Lears, 1985; Hall, Korstad, and Lecoudis, 1986; Oestreicher, 1986, 1988; Stansell, 1986; Fink, 1987, 1991; Gorn, 1987; Montgomery, 1987; Organization of American Historians, 1988; Pula and Dziedzic, 1990; Arnesen, 1991; Czitrom, 1991; Franklin, 1991; Fitzpatrick, 1991; Barrett, 1992; Kelley, 1992; Levine, 1992; Eltis, 1993; Way, 1993).

Ethnocultural Political Analysis

If immigrant economic behavior has been the chief concern of recent historical analysis, only slightly less attention has been given to ethnic political behavior. Heavily quantitative, ethnocultural political analysis has been extremely influential in accounting for long-term persistence and change in American electoral and partisan activities. Here again, working-class culture and ideology play a decisive role, but in great contrast to Thompsonian and Gramscian explanations, real significant divisions over crucial cultural and ethnic controversies get expressed in voting behavior, in party affiliations, and political realignments rather than in working-class consciousness (Mink, 1986; Oestreicher, 1988; Argersinger, 1989; Arnesen, 1991; Barrett, 1992).

THE HISTORIAN AND ETHNIC AND RACIAL CONFLICT

Ex-Victims as Heroes

As can be seen, historians address these issues head-on only relatively rarely. When they do it tends to be from a perspective of overt conflict rather indirectly. Current accounts of black American life written by historians have decisively de-victimized blacks to the point where conflict, absent situations of sheer physical violence, seems almost irrelevant to the African-American past. Virtually all the emphasis is currently on continuities in black volition, leadership, contributions to American life, and to their incessant and nobly waged struggle against the constraints placed upon them throughout U.S. history.

In much the same way, ethnic conflict has been turned to the former victims' historiographical advantage. As with blacks, conflict for ethnics has become an element in identity construction or an important element in ideological and political makeup of past ethnics. In the case of both groups we are, perhaps, at the point where de-victimization has come so far that the former victims have been converted into the central characters or almost heroes of our accounts.

Complexities of the Past

Perhaps the chief contribution to this discussion that could be offered from a perspective of U.S. history is that past conflict has been more complex than has been heretofor generally acknowledged. It can no longer be seen in simple victims-victimizers terms. Over the course of the last two decades historical scholarship has repeatedly documented the ability of past humans to resist subjugation and attempted dehumanization, to adjust to conflictual situations with remarkable resilience and tenacity, and to demonstrate surprising resourcefulness.

REFERENCES

Alexander, J. 1987. *The Immigrant Church and Community: Pittsburgh's Slovak Catholics and Lutherans, 1800-1915*. Pittsburgh: Pittsburgh.

Alexander, A. 1991. *Ambiguous Lives: Free Women of Color in Rural Georgia, 1789-1879*. Fayetteville, AR.

Altman, I., and J. Horn. (eds.). 1991. *"To Make America": European Emigration in the Early Modern Period*. Berkeley, CA.

American Historical Association. 1984. "The American Historical Association: The First Hundred Years,.1884-1984." *American Historical Review* 89: 909-1036.

American Historical Association. 1991. "American Historical Review Forum: Peter Novick's That Noble Dream: The Objectivity Question and the Future of the Historical Profession." *American Historical Review* 96: 675-708.

Anderson, A., and G. Pickering. 1986. *Confronting the Color Line: The Broken Promises of the Civil Rights Movmement in Chicago*. Athens, GA: University of Georgia.

Anderson, F., and A. Cayton. 1993. "The Problem of Fragmentation and the Prospects for Synthesis in Early American Social History." *William and Mary Quarterly* 50: 299-310.

Anderson, P., and D. Blanck. 1992. *Swedish-American Life in Chicago: Cultural and Urban Aspects of an Immigrant People*. Urbana, IL: University of Illinois.

Andrews, W. (ed.). 1986. *Sisters of the Spirit: Three Black Women's Autobiographers of the Nineteenth Century*. Bloomington, IN: Indiana University.

Angell, S. 1992. *Bishop Henry Mc Neal Turner and African-American Religion in the South*. Knoxville, TN: University of Tennessee.

Appleby, J. 1992. "Recovering America's Historic Diversity: Beyond Exceptionalism." *Journal of American History* 79: 419-31.

Aptheker, H. 1989. *Abolitionism: A Revolutionary Movement*. Boston: Twayne.

Aptheker, H. 1992. *Anti-Racism in U.S. History: the First Two Hundred Years*. New York: Greenwood.

Argersinger, P. 1989. "The Value of the Vote: Political Representation in the Gilded Age." *Journal of American History* 76: 59-90.

Arnesen, E. 1991. *Waterfront Workers of New Orleans: Race, Class and Politics, 1863-1923.* New York: Oxford.

Ashworth, J. 1987. "The Relationship Between Capitalism and Humanitarianism." *American Historical Review* 92: 813-28.

Ayers, E. 1992. *The Promise of the New South: Life After Reconstruction.* New York: Oxford.

Baer, H., and Y. Jones. (eds.). 1992. *African Americans in the South: Issues of Race, Class and Gender.* Athens, GA: University of Georgia.

Baer, H., and M. Singer. 1992. *African-American Religion in the Twentieth Century: Varieties of Protest and Accomodation.* Knoxville, TN: University of Tennessee.

Bailyn, B. 1986. *Voyagers to the West: A Passage in the Peopling of America on the Eve of the Revolution.* New York: Knopf.

Baron, A. (ed.). 1991. *Work Engendered: Toward a New History of American Labor.* Ithaca, NY: Cornell University Press.

Barrett, J. 1992. "Americanization from the Botton Up: Immigration and the Remaking of the Working Class in the United States, 1880-1930." *Journal of American History* 79: 996-1020.

Bauman, J. 1987. *Public Housing, Race and Renewal: Urban Planning in Philadelphia, 1920-74.* Philadelphia: Temple.

Bayor, R. 1993. "The Civil Rights Movement as Urban Reform: Atlanta's Black Neighborhoods and New 'Progressivism.'" *Georgia Historical Quarterly* 77: 286-309.

Bender, T. 1986. "Wholes and Parts: The Need for Synthesis in American History." *Journal of American History* 73: 120-36.

Berlin, I., and P. Morgan (eds.). 1991. *The Slaves' Economy: Independent Production by Slaves in the Americas.* London: Cass.

Bernstein, I. 1990. *The New York City Draft Riots: Their Significance for American Society and Politics in the Age of the Civil War.* New York: Oxford.

Berthoff, R. 1989. "Conventional Mentality: Free Blacks, Women and Business Corporations as Unequal Persons, 1820-70." *Journal of American History* 76: 753-84.

Bess, B. 1987. *A Revolution Gone Backward: The Black Response to National Politics, 1876-96.* Westport, CT: Greenwood Press.

Bigham, D. 1987. *We Ask Only a Fair Trial: A History of the Black Community of Evansville, Indiana.* Bloomington, IN: Indiana University.

Blacket, R. 1986. *Beating Against the Barriers: Biographical Essays in Nineteenth Century Afro-American History.* Baton Rouge: Louisiana State University.

Bloom, J. 1987. *Class, Race and the Civil Rights Movement.* Bloomington, IN: Indiana University.

Blyden, J. 1989. *A History of Afro-American Literature Vol.1: The Long Beginning, 1746-1895.* Baton Rouge: Louisiana State.

Bodnar, J. 1985. *The Transplanted: A History of Immigrants in Urban America.* Bloomington, IN: Indiana University.

Bodnar, J. 1986. "Symbols and Servants: Immigrant America and the Limits of Public History." *Journal of American History* 73: 137-151.

Boles, J. (ed.). 1988. *Masters and Slaves in the House of the Lord: Race and Religion in the American South, 1740-1870.* Lexington, KY: University of Kentucky.

Bolster, W. 1990. "'To Feel Like a Man': Black Seamen in the Northern States, 1800-1860." *Journal of American History* 76: 1173-99.

Branch, T. 1988. *Parting the Waters: America in the King Years.* New York: Simon and Schuster.

Briggs, J. 1986. "Fertility and Cultural Change Among Families in Italy and America." *American Historical Review* 91: 1129-45.

Brown, R. 1987. "Positivism, Relativism and Narrative in the Logic of the Historical Sciences." *American Historical Review* 92: 908-20.

Brown, R. 1991. *No Duty to Retreat: Violence and Values in American History and Society*. New York: Oxford.

Buchalter, C. 1993. *Afro-Americans in Antebellum Boston: An Analysis of Probate Records*. New York: Garland.

Bukowczyk, M. 1987. *And My Children Did Not Know Me: A History of the Polish-Americans*. Bloomington, IN: Indiana University.

Burke, P. 1991. *New Perspectives on Historical Writing*. University Park: Pennsylvania State.

Burke, P. 1992. *History and Social Theory*. Ithaca: Cornell.

Bullard, R. (ed.). 1989. *In Search of the New South: The Black Urban Experience in the 1970s and 1980s*. Tuscaloosa, AL: University of Alabama.

Burrison, J. (ed.). 1989. *Storytellers: Folktales and Legends from the South*. Athens, GA: University of Georgia.

Campbell, E., and K. Ryce (eds.). 1991. *Before Freedom Came: African American Life in the Antebellum South*. Charlottesville, VA: University of Virginia.

Capeci, D., and M. Wilkerson. 1991. *Layered Violence: The Detroit Rioters of 1943*. Jackson, MS: University Press of Mississippi.

Carson, C. 1993. *The Movement: 1964-1970*. Westport, CT: Greenwood.

Carson, C., R. Luker, P. Russell, and L. Harlan (eds.). 1992. *The Papers of Martin Luther King, Jr. Vol. I: Called to Serve: January, 1929-June, 1951*. Berkeley, CA: University of California.

Cashman, S. 1991. *African-Americans and the Quest for Civil Rights, 1900-1990*. New York: New York University.

Chestnut, J. 1990. *Black in Selma: The Uncommon Life of J.L. Chestnut, Jr*. New York: Farrar, Straus and Giroux.

Cinel, D. 1991. *The National Integration of Italian Return Migration, 1870-1929*. Cambridge, MA: Cambridge University.

Clark, D. 1991. *Erin's Heirs: Irish Bonds of Community*. Lexington, KY: University of Kentucky.

Cobb, J. 1990. "'Somebody Done Nailed Us on the Cross': Federal Farm and Welfare Policy and the Civil Rights Movement in the Mississippi Delta." *Journal of American History* 77: 912-36.

Cody, C. 1987. "There Was No 'Absalom' on the Ball Plantations: Slave-Naming Practices in the South Carolina Low Country, 1720-1865." *American Historical Review* 92: 563-96.

Cohen, W. 1991. *At Freedom's Edge: Black Mobility and the Southern White Quest for Racial Control, 1861-1915*. Baton Rouge: Louisiana State.

Colburn, D. 1985. *Racial Change and Commuity Crisis: St. Augustine, Florida, 1877-1980*. New York: Columbia.

Cone, J. 1991. *Martin and Malcolm and America: A Dream or a Nightmare*. Maryknoll: Orbis.

Cooper, A. 1989. *Between Struggle and Hope: Four Black Educators in the South, 1894-1915*. Ames: Iowa State.

Cooper, W. 1987. *Claude McKay: Rebel Sojourner in the Harlem Renaissance: A Biography*. Baton Rouge: Louisiana State.

Cornelius, J. 1991. *"When I Can Read My Title Clear": Literacy, Slavery and Religion in the Antebellum South*. Columbia, SC: University of South Carolina.

Crawford, V., J. Rouse, and B. Woods. 1992. *Women in the Civil Rights Movement Trailblazers and Torchbearers*. Bloomington, IN: Indiana University.

Creel, M. 1988. *"A Peculiar People": Slave Religious and Community-Culture Among the Gullah*. New York.

Cronon, W., G. Miles, and J. Gitlin (eds.). 1992. *Under an Open Sky: Rethinking America's Western Past*. New York: Norton.

Czitrom, D. 1991. "Underworlds and Underdogs: Big Tim Sullivan and Metropolitan Politics in New York, 1889-1913." *Journal of American History* 78: 536-58.

Daniel, C. 1991. *Chicano Workers and the Politics of Fairness: The FEPC in the Southwest, 1941-5*. Austin, TX: University of Texas.

Daniels, R. 1988. *Asian America: Chinese and Japanese in the United States since 1850*. Seattle, WA.

Daniels, R., S. Taylor, and H. Kitano. 1991. *Japanese Americans: From Relocation to Redress*. Seattle, WA: University of Washington.

Darity, W. (ed.). 1989. *Abram L. Harris Race, Radicalism and Reform: Selected Papers*. New Brunswick: Transaction.

Davis, D. 1987. "Reflections on Abolitionism and Ideological Hegemony." *American Historical Review* 92: 797-812.

Dickerson, D. 1986. *Out of the Crucible: Black Steelworkers in Western Pennsylvania, 1875-1980*. Albany, NY: State University of New York.

Diggins, J. 1985. "Comrades and Citizens: New Mythologies in American Historiography." *American Historical Review* 90: 614-38.

Dillon, M. 1990. *Slavery Attacked: Southern Slaves and Their Allies, 1619-1865*. Baton Rouge: Louisiana State.

Diner, H. 1983. *Erin's Daughters in America: Irish Immigrant Women in the Nineteenth Century*. Baltimore: Johns Hopkins.

Diner, H. 1992. *A Time for Gathering: The Second Migration, 1820-80*. Baltimore: Johns Hopkins.

Dowd, G. 1992. *A Spirited Resistance: The North American Indian Struggle for Unity, 1745-1815*. Baltimore: Johns Hopkins.

Draper, A. 1992. "Do the Right Thing: the Desegregation of Union Conventions in the South." *Labor History* 33: 343-56.

Duncan, R. 1986. *Freedom's Shore: Tunis Campbell and the Georgia Freedmen*. Athens: Georgia.

Eltis, D. 1993. "Europeans and the rise and Fall of African Slavery in the Americas: An Interpretation." *American Historical Review* 98: 1399-1423.

Escobar, E. 1993. "The Dialectics of Repression: The Los Angeles Police Department and the Chicano Movement, 1968-71." *Journal of American History* 79: 1483-1514.

Espiritu, Y. 1992. *Asian American Panethnicity: Bridging Institutions and Identities*. Philadelphia: Temple.

Farr, J. 1989. *Black Odyssey: The Seafaring Tradition of Afro-Americans*. New York: Lang.

Farragher, J. 1993. "The Frontier Trail: Rethinking Turner and Reimagining the American West." *American Historical Review* 98: 106-17.

Faue, E. 1993. "Gender and the Reconstruction of Labor History: An Introduction." *Labor History* 34: 1-10.

Ferguson, L. 1992. *Uncommon Ground, Archaeology and Early African-America , 1650-1800*. Washington, DC: Smithsonian.

Fink, L. 1987. "Labor, Liberty and the Law: Trade Unionism and the Problem of the American Constitutional Order." *Journal of American History* 74: 904-25.

Fink, L. 1991. "'Intellectuals' versus 'Workers': Academic Requirements and the Creation of Labor History." *American Historical Review* 96: 395-421.

Fitzgerald, M. 1989a. "'To Give Our Votes to the Party': Black Political Agitation and Agricultural Change in Alabama, 1865-70." *Journal of American History* 76: 489-505.

Fitzgerald, M. 1989b. *The Union League Movement in the Deep South: Politics and Agricultural Change During Reconstruction*. Baton Rouge: Louisiana State.

Fitzpatrick, E. 1991. "Rethinking the Intellectual Origins of American Labor History." *American Historical Review* 96: 422-8.

Foner, E. 1987. "Rights and the Constitution in Black Life During the Civil War and Reconstruction." *Journal of American History* 74: 863-83.

Foner, E. 1988. *Reconstruction: America's Unfinished Revolution, 1863-1877*. New York: Harper and Row.

Foner, E. (ed.). 1990. *The New American History*. Philadelphia: Temple.

Foner, P., and D. Rosenberg (eds.). 1993. *Racism, Dissent, and Asian Americans from 1850 to the Present*. Westport, CT: Greenwood.

Forbes, E. 1992. "African Resistance to Enslavement: the Nature and the Evidentiary Record." *Journal of Black Studies* 23: 39-59.

Formisano, R. 1991. *Boston Against Busing: Race, Class and Ethnicity in the 1960s and 1970s*. Chapel Hill, NC: University of North Carolina.

Fox-Genovese, E. 1988. *Within the Plantation Household: Black and White Women of the Old South*. Chapel Hill, NC.

Frankel, N., and N. Dye. 1991. *Gender, Class, Race and Reform in the Progressive Era*. Lexington, KY: University of Kentucky.

Franklin, R. 1991. *Shadows of Race and Class*. Minneapolis, MN.

Frehill-Rowe, L. 1993. "Postbellum Race Relations and Rural Land Tenure: Migration of Blacks and Whites to Kansas and Nebraska, 1870-90." *Social Forces* 72: 77-91.

Fugita, S., and D. O'Brien. 1991. *Japanese American Ethnicity: The Persistence of Community*. Seattle, WA: University of Washington.

Gabbacia, D. 1988. *Militants and Migrants: Rural Sicilians Become American Workers*. New Brunswick: Rutgers.

Garcia, M. 1989. *Mexican Americans: Leadership, Ideology and Identity, 1930-60*. New Haven, CT: Yale.

Garcia, R. 1991. *Rise of the Mexican American Middle Class: San Antonio, 1929-41*. College Station: Texas A&M.

Garrow, D. 1986. *Bearing the Cross: Martin Luther King, Jr. and the Southern Christian Leadership Conference*. New York: Morrow.

Gatewood, W. 1990. *Aristocrats of Color: The Black Elite, 1880-1920*. Bloomington, IN: Indiana University.

Gerber, D. 1989. *The Making of an American Pluralism: Buffalo, New York, 1825-60*. Urbana, IL: University of Illinois.

Gilje, P. 1987. *The Road to Mobocracy: Popular Disorder in New York City, 1763-1834*. Chapel Hill, NC: University of North Carolina.

Gleason, P. 1992. *Speaking of Diversity: Language and Ethnicity in Twentieth Century America*. Baltimore: Johns Hopkins.

Glenn, S. 1990. *Daughters of the Shtetl: Life and Labor in the Immigrant Generation*. Ithaca: Cornell.

Gordon, L. 1991. "Black and White Visions of Welfare: Women's Welfare Activism." *Journal of American History* 78: 559-90.

Gorn, E. 1987. ' "Good-Bye Boys, I Die a True American': Homicide, Nativism and Working-Class Culture in Antebellum New York City. *Journal of American History* 74: 388-410.

Gottlieb, P. 1987. *Making Their Own Way: Southern Blacks' Migration to Pittsburgh, 1916-30*. Urbana, IL: University of Illinois.

Graves, J. 1990. *Town and Country: Race Relations in an Urban-Rural Context, Arkansas, 1865-1905*. Fayetteville, AR: University of Arkansas.

Green, L. 1993. "Harlem, the Depression Years: Leadership and Social Conditions." *Afro-Americans in New York Life and History* 17: 33-50.

Green, V. 1987. *American Immigrant Leaders, 1800-1910*. Baltimore: Johns Hopkins.

Greenberg, C. 1991. *"Or Does it Explode?": Black Harlem in the Great Depression*. New York: Oxford.

Grossman, J. 1989. *Land of Hope: Chicago's Black Southerners and the Great Migration*. Chicago: Chicago University Press.

Hacker, A. 1992. *Two Nations: Black and White, Separate, Hostile, Unequal*. New York: Scribner's.

Hahn, S. 1990. "Class and State in Postemancipation Societies: Southern Planters in Comparative Perspective." *American Historical Review* 95: 75-98.

Haines, H. 1988. *Black Radicals and the Civil Rights Mainstream, 1954-70.* Knoxville, TN.

Hall, G. 1992. *Africans in Colonial Louisiana: The Development of Afro-Creole Culture in the Eighteenth Century.* Baton Rouge: Louisiana State.

Hall, J., R. Korstad, and J. Lecoudis. 1986. "Cotton Mill People: Work, Community and Protest in the Textile South, 1880-1940." *American Historical Review* 91: 245-86.

Hall, W. 1988. *The Rest of the Dream: The Black Odyssey of Lyman Johnson.* Lexington, KY.

Hamilton, K. 1991. *Black Towns and Profit: Promotion and Development in the Trans-Appalachian West, 1877-1915.* Urbana, IL: University of Illinois.

Hamerow, T. 1987. *Reflections on History and Historians.* Madison, WI: University of Wisconsin.

Harding, V. 1987. "Wrestling Toward the Dawn: The Afro-American Freedom Movement and the Changing Constitution." *Journal of American History* 74: 718-39.

Harlan, D. 1989a. "Intellectual History and the Return of Literature." *American Historical Review* 94: 581-609.

Harlan, D. 1989b. "Reply to David Hollinger." *American Historical Review* 94: 622-6.

Harlan, L. 1990. "The Future of the American Historical Association." *American Historical Review* 95: 1-8.

Harris, M. 1991. *The Rise of Gospel Blues: The Music of Thomas Andrew Dorsey in the Urban Church.* New York: Oxford.

Harris, R. 1987. "The Flowering of Afro-American History." *American Historical Review* 92: 1150-61.

Haskell, T. 1985a. "Capitalism and the Origins of the Humanitarian Sensibility, Part I." *American Historical Review* 90: 339-61.

Haskell, T. 1985b. "Capitalism and the Origins of the Humanitarian Sensibility, Part II." *American Historical Review* 90: 547-66.

Haskell, T. 1990. "Objectivity is Not Neutrality: Rhetoric vs. Practice in Peter Novick's That Noble Dream." *History and Theory* 29.

Hellweg, A. 1990. *An Immigrant Success Story: East Indians in America.* Philadelphia, PA: University of Pennsylvania.

Higginbotham, E. 1993. *Righteous Discontent: The Women's Movement in the Black Baptist Church 1880-1920.* Cambridge: Harvard University Press.

Himmelfarb, G. 1984. *The New History and the Old.* Cambridge: Harvard.

Himmelfarb, G. 1989. "Some Reflections on the New History." *American Historical Review* 94: 661-70.

Hine, D. Ed.. 1986. *The State of Afro-American History: Past, Present and Future.* Baton Rouge: Louisiana State.

Hine, D. 1989. *Black Women in White: Racial Conflict and Cooperation in the Nursing Profession, 1890-1950.* Bloomington, IN: Indiana University.

Hirsch, A. 1988. "The Collision of Military Cultures in Seventeenth Century New England." *Journal of American History* 74: 1187-1212.

Hirsch, A., and J. Logsdon (eds.). 1992. *Creole New Orleans: Race and Americanization.* Baton Rouge: Louisiana State.

Hollinger, D. 1989. "The Return of the Prodigal: The Persistence of Historical Knowing." *American Historical Review* 94: 610-21.

Hollinger, D. 1993. "How Wide the Circle of the 'We?' American Intellectuals and the Problem of the Ethnos Since World War II." *American Historical Review* 98: 317-37.

Holloway, J., and W. Vass. 1993. *The African Heritage of American English.* Bloomington, IN.

Howard-Pitney, D. 1990. *The Afro-American Jeremiad: Appeals for Justice to America.* Philadelphia: Temple.

Hoxie, F. 1992. "Exploring a Cultural Borderland: Native American Journeys of Discovery in the Early Twentieth Century." *Journal of American History* 79: 969-95.

Hull, G. 1987. *Color, Sex and Poetry: Three Women Writers of the Harlem Renaissance.* Bloomington, IN: Indiana University.

Ingalls, R. 1988. *Urban Vigilantes in the New South: Tampa, 1882-1936.* Knoxville, TN.

Iriye, A. 1989. "The Internationalization of History." *American Historical Review* 94: 1-10.

Irvin, D. 1992. *The Unsung Heart of Black America: A Middle Class Church at Midcentury.* Columbia, MO: University of Missouri.

Jacoby, R. 1992. "A New Intellectual History?" *American Historical Review* 97: 405-24.

Jasso, G., and M. Rosenzweig. 1990. *The New Chosen People: Immigrants in the United States.* New York: Sage.

Jaynes, G. *Branches Without Roots: Genesis of the Black Working Class in the American South, 1862-82.* New York: Oxford.

Jones, H. 1987. *Mutiny on the Amistad: The Saga of a Slave Revolt and Its Impact on American Abolition, Law and Diplomacy.* New York: Oxford.

Jones, J. 1992. *The Dispossessed: America's Underclasses from the Civil War to the Present.* New York: Basic.

Jones, N. 1990. *Born a Child of Freedom, Yet a Slave: Mechanisms of Control and Resistance in Antebellum South Carolina.* Hanover: Wesleyan/New England.

Jones-Jackson, P. 1987. *When Roots Die: Endangered Traditions on the Sea Islands.* New York: Oxford Press.

de Jongh, J. 1990. *Vicious Modernism: Black Harlem and the Literary Imagination.* New York: Cambridge.

Kaczorowski, R. 1987. "To Begin Anew: Congress, Citizenship and Civil Rights After the Civil War." *American Historical Review* 92: 45-68.

Kasinitz, P. 1992. *Caribbean New York: Black Immigrants and the Politics of Race.* Ithaca, NY: Cornell.

Kaye, H. 1991. *The Powers of the Past: Reflections on the Crisis and the Promise of History.* Minneapolis, MN: University of Minnesota.

Kelley, R. 1992. "Notes on Deconstructing 'The Folk.' " *American Historical Review* 97: 1400-8.

Kelly, R. 1993. ' "We Are Not What We Seem': Rethinking Black Working-Class Opposition in the Jim Crow South." *Journal of American History* 80: 75-112.

King, R. 1992. *Civil Rights and the Idea of Freedom.* New York: Oxford.

Kloppenberg, J. 1989. "Objectivity and Historicism: A Century of American Historical Writing." *American Historical Review* 94: 1011-30.

Kolchin, P. 1987. *Unfree Labor: American Slavery and Russian Serfdom.* Cambridge: Harvard.

Krieger, L. 1989. *Time's Reasons: Philosophies of History Old and New.* Chicago: Chicago University Press.

Kremer, G. 1991. *James Milton Turner and the Promise of America: The Public Life of a Post-Civil War Black Leader.* Columbia, MO: University of Missouri.

Kubitschek, M. 1991. *Claiming the Heritage: African-American Women Novelists and History.* Jackson, MS.

LaCapra, D. (ed.). 1991. *The Bounds of Race: Perspectives on Hegemony and Resistance.* Ithaca: Cornell.

LaCapra, D. 1992. "Intellectual History and Its Ways." *American Historical Review* 97: 425-39.

Lane, R. 1979. *Violent Death in the City Suicide, Accident and Murder in Nineteenth Century Philadelphia.* Cambridge: Harvard.

Lane, R. 1986. *Roots of Violence in Black Philadelphia, 1860-1900.* Cambridge: Harvard.

Lane, R. 1991. *William Dorsey's Philadelphia and Ours: On the Past and Future of the Black City in America.* New York: Oxford.

Lasch-Quinn, E. 1992. *Black Neighbors Race and the Limits of Reform in the American Settlement House Movememt. 1890-1945.* Chapel Hill, NC: University of North Carolina.

Lawson, E., and M. Merrill. 1984. *The Three Sarahs: Documents of Antebellum Black College Women.* New York: Edwin Mellen.

Lawson, S. 1991. "Freedom Then, Freedom Now: The Historiography of the Civil Rights Movement." *American Historical Review* 96: 456-71.

Lears, T. 1985. "The Concept of Cultural Hegemony: Problems and Possibilities." *American Historical Review* 90: 567-93.

Lemann, N. 1991. *The Promised Land: The Great Black Migration and How It Changed America.* New York: Knopf.

de Leon, A. *Ethnicity in the Sunbelt: A History of Mexican Americans in Houston.* Houston: Houston.

Levine, B. 1992. *The Spirit of 1848: German Immigrants, Labor Conflict, and the Coming of the Civil War.* Urbana, IL: University of Illinois.

Levine, L. 1989. "The Unpredictable Past: Reflections on Recent American Historiography." *American Historical Review* 94: 671-9.

Levine, L. 1992. "The Folklore of Industrial Society: Popular Culture and Its Audiences." *American Historical Review* 97: 1369-99.

Levine, L. 1993. "Clio, Canons, and Culture." *Journal of American History* 80: 849-67.

Lewis, E. 1991. *In Their Own Interests: Race, Class and Power in Twentieth-Centrury Norfolk, Virginia.* Berkeley, CA: University of California.

Limerick, P., C. Milner, and C. Rankin (eds.). 1991. *Trails: Toward a New Western History.* Lawrence, KS: University of Kansas.

Limerick, P. 1992. "Disorientation and Reorientation: The American Landscape Discovered from the West." *Journal of American History* 79: 1021-49.

Link, A. 1985. "The American Historical Association, 1884-1984: Retrospect and Prospect." *American Historical Review* 90: 1-17.

Lipsitz, G. 1988. *A Life in Struggle: Ivory Perry and the Culture of Opposition.* Phildelphia: Temple.

Litwack, L. 1987. "Trouble In Mind: The Bicentennial and the Afro-American Experience." *Journal of American History* 74: 315-337.

Litwack, L., and A. Meier. 1988. *Black Leaders of the Nineteenth Century.* Urbana, IL: University of Illinois.

Lornel, K. 1988. *Happy in the Service of the Lord": Afro-American Gospel Quartets in Memphis.* Urbana, IL: University of Illinois.

Lowe, R. 1993. "The Freedman's Bureau and Local Black Leadership." *Journal of American History* 80: 989-98.

Luker, R. 1991. *The Social Gospel in Black and White: American Racial Reform, 1885-1912.* Chapel Hill, NC: University of North Carolina.

Malone, A. 1992. *Sweet Chariot: Slave Family and Household Structure in Nineteenth Century Louisiana.* Chapel Hill, NC: University of North Carolina.

Malone, M. and Etulain, R. 1989. *The American West: A Twentieth Century History.* Lincoln, NE: University of Nebraska.

Malone, P. 1993. *The Skulking Way of War: Technology and Tactics Among the New England Indians.* Baltimore: Johns Hopkins University

Margo, R. 1990. *Race and Schooling in the South, 1880-1950 An Economic History.* Chicago: Chicago University Press.

Marks, C. 1989. *Farewell-We're Good and Gone: The Great Black Migration.* Bloomington, IN: Indiana University.

Mandle, J. 1992. *Not Slave, Not Free: The African American Economic Experience Since the Civil War.* Durham: Duke.

Marable, M. 1986. *W.E.B. Du Bois: Black Radical Democrat.* Boston: Twayne.

Martin, M. 1991. *Social Protest in an Urban Barrio: A Study of the Chicano Movement, 1966-1974.* Lanham: University Press of America.

Martin, R. 1991. *Howard Kester and the Struggle for Social Justice in the South, 1904-77.* Charlottesville: University of Virginia.

Matthews, F. 1990. "The Attack on "Historicism": Allan Bloom's Indictment of Contemporary American Historical Scholarship." *American Historical Review* 95: 429-47.

Mc Cartney, J. 1992. *Black Power Ideologies: An Essay in African-American Political Thought.* Philadelphia: Temple.

Mc Caul, R. 1987. *The Black Struggle for Public Schooling in Nineteenth Century Illinois.* Carbondale: Southern Illinois University.

Mc Curry, S. 1992. "The Two Faces of Republicanism: Gender and Proslavery Politics in Antebellum South Carolina." *Journal of American History* 78: 1245-64.

Mc Gerr, M. 1991. "The Price of the "New Transnational History." *American Historical Review* 96: 1056-67.

Mc Glynn, F., and S. Drescher (eds.). 1992. *The Meaning of Freedom: Economics, Politics and Culture After Slavery.* Pittsburgh: University of Pittsburgh.

Mc Millen, N. 1989. *Dark Journey: Black Mississippians in the Age of Jim Crow.* Urbana, IL: University of Illinois.

Meagher, T. 1986. *From Paddy to Studs: Irish-American Communities in the Turn of the Century Era, 1880-1920.* Westport, CT: Greenwood.

Megill, A. 1989. "Recounting the Past: Description, Explanation and Narrative in Historiography." *American Historical Review* 94: 627-53.

Meier, A., and E. Rudwick. 1986. *Black History and the Historical Profession, 1915-80.* Urbana, IL: University of Illinois.

Miller, K. 1985. *Emigrants and Exiles: Ireland and the Irish Exodus to the North America.* New York: Oxford.

Miller, K.1992. *Voice of Deliverance: The Language of Marting Luther King, Jr. and Its Sources.* New York: Free Press.

Mink, G. 1986. *Old Labor and New Immigrants in American Political Development: Union, Party and State, 1875-1920.* Ithaca: Cornell.

Modell, J., M. Goulden, and S. Magnusson. 1989. "World War II in the Lives of Black Americans: Some Findings and an Interpretation." *Journal of American History* 76: 838-48.

Mohr, C. 1986. *On the Threshold of Freedom: Masters and Slaves in Civil War Georgia.* Athens, GA: University of Georgia.

Monkkonen, E. 1986. "The Dangers of Synthesis." *American Historical Review* 91: 1146-57.

Montgomery, D. 1987. *The Fall of the House of Labor: The Workplace, the State and American Labor Activism, 1865-1925.* Cambridge, MA: Cambridge University.

Morawska, E. 1985. *For Bread with Butter: The Life-Worlds of East Central Eurpeans in Johnstown, Pennsylvania, 1890-1940.* New York: Cambridge.

Morgan, P. Ed.. 1993. *Diversity and Unity in Early America.* New York: Routledge.

Mormino, G. 198?. *Immigrants on the Hill: Italian-Americans in St. Louis, 1882-1982.* Urbana, IL: University of Illinois.

Mormino, G., and G. Pozzetta. *The Immigrant World of Ybor City: Italians and Their Latin Neighbors in Tampa, 1885-1985.* Urbana, IL: University of Illinois.

Mullin, M. 1992. *Africa in America: Slave Acculturation and Resistance in the American South and the British Caribbean, 1736-1831.* Urbana, IL: University of Illinois.

Nadel, S. 1990. *Little Germany: Ethnicity, Religion and Class in New York City.* Urbana, IL: University of Illinois.

Nash, G. 1988. *Forging Freedom: The Formation of Philadelphia's Black Community, 1720-1840.* Cambridge: Harvard.

Nash, G. 1991. *Race and Revolution.* Madison: Madison House.

Nash, G., and J. Soderlund. 1991. *Freedom By Degrees: Emancipation in Pennsylvania and Its Aftermath.* New York: Oxford.

Nelson, B. 1993. "Organized Labor and the Struggle for Black Equality in Mobile during World War II." *Journal of American History* 80: 952-88.

Neverdon-Morton, C. 1989. *Afro-American Women of the South and the Advancement of the Race, 1895-1925.* Knoxville, TN: University of Tennessee.

Norrell, R. 1986. "Caste In Steel: Jim Crow Careers in Birmingham, Alabama." *Journal of American History* 73: 669-94.

Nostrand, R. 1992. *The Hispano Homeland.* Norman, OK: University of Oklahoma.

Novick, P. 1989. *That Noble Dream: The "Objectivity Question" and the American Historical Profession.* New York: Cambridge.

Nunnelley, W. 1991. *Bull Connor.* Tuscaloosa, AL: University of Alabama.

Okihiro, G. (ed.). 1986. *In Resistance: Studies in African, Caribbean and Afro-American History.* Amherst: University of Massachusetts.

Olson, J. 1994. *The Ethnic Dimension in American History.* New York: St. Martin's.

Organization of American Historians. 1987. "A Round Table: Martin Luther King, Jr." *Journal of American History* 74: 436-81.

Organization of American Historians. 1988. "A Round Table: Labor, Historical Pessimism, and Hegemony." *Journal of American History* 75: 115-61.

Orser, C. 1988. *The Material Basis of the Postbellum Tenant Plantation: Historical Archaeology in the South Carolina Piedmont.* Athens, GA: University of Georgia.

Oestreicher, R. 1986. *Solidarity and Fragmentation: Working People and Class Consciousness in Detroit, 1875-1900.* Urbana, IL: University of Illinois.

Oestreicher, R. 1988. "Urban Working Class Political Behavior and Theories of American Electoral Politics." *Journal of American History* 74: 1257-1286.

Pacyga, D. 1991. *Polish Immigrants and Industrial Chicago: Workers on the South Side, 1880-1992.* Columbus: Ohio State.

Parker, F. *Running for Freedom: Slave Runaways in North Carolina, 1775-1840.* New York: Garland.

Patterson, R. 1985. *The Seed of Sally Good'n: A Black Family of Arkansas, 1833-1953.* Lexington, KY: University of Kentucky.

Patterson, W. 1988. *The Korean Frontier in America: Immigration to Hawaii, 1896-1910.* Honolulu, HA: University of Hawaii.

Perlman, J. 1988. *Ethnic Differences: Schooling, and Social Structure Among the Irish, Italians, Jews and Blacks in an American City, 1880-1935.* New York: Cambridge.

Perlman, R. 1991. *Bridging Three Worlds: Hungarian-Jewish Americans, 1848-1914.* Amherst, MA: University of Massachusetts.

Pfeffer, P. 1990. *A. Philip Randolph, Pioneer of the Civil Rights Movement.* Baton Rouge: Louisiana State.

Piersen, W. 1988. *Black Yankees: The Development of an Afro-American Subculture in Eighteenth Century New England.* Amherst: University of Massachusetts.

Pincus, S. 1990. *The Virginia Supreme Court, Blacks and the Law, 1870-1902.* New York: Garland.

Pole, J. 1993. *The Pursuit of Equality in American History.* Berkeley, CA: University of California.

Pratt, R. 1992. *The Color of Their Skin: Education and Race in Richmond, Virginia, 1954-1989.* Charlottesville: University of Virginia.

Pula, J., and E. Dziedzic. 1990. *United We Stand: The Role of Polish Workers in the New York Mills Textile Strikes, 1912 and 1916.* Boulder, CO: East European Monographs.

Quarles, B. 1988. *Black Mosaic: Essays in Afro-American History and Historiography.* Amherst: University of Massachusetts.

Ralph, J. 1992. *Northern Protest Martin Luther King, Jr., Chicago and the Civil Rights Movement.* Cambridge: Harvard.

Ramirez, B. 1991. *On the Move: French-Canadian and Italian Migrants in the North Atlantic Economy, 1860-1914.* Toronto: Mc Clelland & Stewart.

Redkey, E. 1992. *A Grand Army of Black Men: Letters from African-American Soldiers in the Union Army, 1861-5.* New York: Cambridge.

Reed, U. 1992. "The Paradox of Irish and Japanese Assimilation: the Persistence of Ethnic Community and Culture." *Reviews in American History* 20: 372-7.

Reed, U. 1994. *Postwar Immigrant America A Social History.* Boston: St. Martin's.

Richter, D. 1993. "Whose Indian History?" *William and Mary Quarterly* 50: 379-93.

Robinson, A., and P. Sullivan (eds.). 1991. *New Directions in Civil Rights Studies.* Charlottesville: University of Virginia.

Rodgers, D. 1992. "Republicanism: The Career of a Concept." *Journal of American History* 79: 11-38.

Rutledge, P. 1992. *The Vietnamese Experience in America.* Bloomington, IN: Indiana University.

San Miguel, G. 1987. *"Let Them All Take Heed": Mexican Americans and the Campaign for Educational Equality in Texas, 1910-81.* Austin: University of Texas.

Sanchez, G. 1993. *Becoming Mexican American Ethnicity, Culture and Identity in Chicano Los Angeles, 1900-45.* New York: Oxford.

Sandage, S. 1993. "A Marble House Divided: The Lincoln Memorial, the Civil Rights Movememt, and the Politics of Memory, 1939-63." *Journal of American History* 80: 135-67.

Schweninger, L. 1990a. "Prosperous Blacks in the South, 1790-1800." *American Historical Review* 95: 31-56.

Schweninger, L. 1990b. *Black Property Owners in the South, 1790-1915.* Urbana, IL: University of Illinois.

Schulz, A. 1991. "'The Pride of the Race Has Been Touched': The 1925 Norse-American Immigration Centennial and Ethnic Identity." *Journal of American History* 77: 1265-95.

Schwieder, D., J. Hraba, and E. Schwieder. 1987. *Buxton: Work and Racial Equality in a Coal Mining Town.* Ames: Iowa State.

Scott, J. 1986. "Gender: A Useful Category of Historical Analysis." *American Historical Review* 91: 859-81.

Scott, J. 1989. "History in Crisis? The Others' Side of the Story." *American Historical Review* 94: 680-92.

Scott, R. 1994. "Defining the Boundaries of Freedom in the World of Cane: Cuba, Brazil and Louisiana After Emancipation." *American Historical Review* 99.

Sernett, M. 1986. *Abolition's Axe: Beriah Green, Oneida Institute and the Black Freedom Struggle.* Syracuse: Syracuse University Press.

Shapiro, H. 1988. *White Violence and Black Response: From Reconstruction to Montgomery.* Amherst: University of Massachusetts.

Shapiro, H., and J. Sarna. 1992. *Ethnic Diversity and Civic Identity: Patterns of Conflict and Cohesion in Cincinnatti since 1820.* Urbana, IL: University of Illinois.

Singleton, T. (ed.). 1985. *The Archaeology of Slavery and Plantation Life.* Orlando, FL: Academic.

Skerry, P. 1993. *Mexican Americans The Ambivalent Minority.* New York: Free Press.

Slotkin, R. 1992. *Gunfighter Nation: The Myth of the Frontier in Twentieth-Century America.* New York: Atheneum.

Smith, J. 1985a. *Slavery and Rice Culture in Low Country Georgia, 1750-1860.* Knoxville, TN: University of Tennessee.

Smith, J. 1985b. *An Old Creed for the New South, Proslavery Ideology and Historiography, 1865-1918.* Westport, CT: Greenwood.

Solow, B. (ed.). 1991. *Slavery and the Rise of the Atlantic System.* Cambridge.

Staniland, M. 1991. *American Intellectuals and African Nationalists, 1955-70*. New Haven: Yale.

Stansell, C. 1986. *City of Women: Sex and Class in New York, 1789-1960*. New York: Knopf.

Stewart, J. (ed.). 1992. *Race Contacts and Interracial Relations: Lectures on the Theory and Practice of Race by Alain Leroy Locke*. Washington, DC: Howard.

Stolarik, M. 1985. *Growing Up on the South Side: Three Generations of Slovaks in Bethlehem, Pennsylvania, 1880-1976*. Lewisburg: Bucknell.

Stolarik, M. 1992. *Slovaks in Canada and the United States, 1870-1990: Similarities and Differences*. Ottawa: Ottawa University Press.

Stuckey, S. 1987. *Slave Culture: Nationalist Theory and the Foundations of Black America*. New York: Oxford.

Swierenga, R. (ed.). 1985. *The Dutch In America: Immigration, Settlement and Cultural Change*. New Brunswick: Rutgers.

Swift, D. 1989. *Black Prophets of Justice: Activist Clergy Before the Civil War*. Baton Rouge: Louisiana State.

Thelen, D. 1986. "The Profession and the Journal of American History." *Journal of American History* 73: 9-14.

Thelen, D. 1992. "Of Audiences, Borderlands and Comparisons: Toward the Internationalization of American History." *Journal of American History* 79: 432-462.

Thomas, L. 1986. *Rise to Be a People: A Biography of Paul Cuffe*. Urbana, IL: University of Illinois.

Thomas, R. 1992. *Life for Us is What We Make It: Building Black Community in Detroit, 1915-45*. Bloomington, IN: Indiana University.

Thronton, J. 1991. "African Dimensions of the Stono Rebellion." *American Historical Review* 96: 1101-13.

Thornton, J. 1992. *Africa and Africans in the Making of the Atlantic World, 1400-1680*. New York: Cambridge.

Toews, J. 1987. "Intellectual History After the Linguistic Turn: The Autonomy of Meaning and the Irreducibility of Experience. *American Historical Review* 92: 879-907.

Toews, J. 1989. "Perspectives on the Old History and the New: A Comment." *American Historical Review* 94: 693-8.

Trotter, J. 1985. *Black Milwaukee: The Making of an Industrial Proletariat, 1915-45*. Urbana, IL: University of Illinois.

Trotter, J. (ed.). 1991. *The Great Migration in Historical Perspective: New Dimensions of Race, Class, and Gender*. Bloomington, IN: Indiana University.

Tsai, Shih-shan H. 1986. *The Chinese Experience in America*. Bloomington, IN: Indiana University.

Turner, W., and J. Turner (eds.). 1988. *Richard B. Moore, Caribbean Militant in Harlem: Collected Writings, 1920-72*. Bloomington, IN.

Tushnet, M. 1987a. "The Politics of Equality in Constitutional Law: The Equal Protection Clause, Dr. DuBois and Charles Hamilton Houston." *Journal of American History* 74: 884-903.

Tushnet, M. 1987b. *The NAACP's Legal Strategy Against Segregated Education, 1925-50*. Chapel Hill: University of North Carolina.

Tyrell, I. 1991. "American Exceptionalism in an Age of International History." *American Historical Review* 96: 1031-55.

Vecoli, R., and S. Sinke (eds.). 1991. *A Century of European Migrations, 1830-1930*. Urbana: University of Illinois.

Walker, C. 1991. *Deromanticizing Black History: Critical Essays and Reappraisals*. Knoxville, TN: University of Tennessee.

Walker, G. 1993. *The Afro-American in New York City*. New York: Garland.

Wallenstein, P. 1987. *From Slave South to New South: Public Policy in Nineteenth Century Georgia*. Chapel Hill: Univeristy of North Carolina.

Watson, A. 1989. *Slave Law in the Americas*. Athens: University of Georgia.

Watts, J. 1992. *God, Harlem U.S.A.: The Father Divine Story*. Berkeley, CA: University of California.

Way, P. 1993. "Evil Humors and Ardent Spirits: The Rough Culture of Canal Construction Laborers." *Journal of American History* 79: 1397-1428.

Weiss, N. 1989. *Whitney M. Young, Jr. and the Struggle for Civil Rights*. Princeton, NJ: Princeton University Press.

Wells, D. 1993. *We have a Dream: African-American Visions of Freedom*. New York: Carroll and Graf.

Wheeler, E. 1986. *Uplifting the Race: The Black Minister in the New South, 1865-1902*. Lanham: Michigan University Press.

White, D. 1985. *Arn't I a Woman? Female Slaves in the Plantation South*. New York: Norton.

White, R. 1991a. *"It's Your Misfortune and None of My Own": A History of the American West*. Norman, OK: University of Oklahoma.

White, R. 1991b. *The Middle Ground: Indians, Empires, and Republics in the Great Lakes Region, 1650-1815*. Cambridge.

White, S. 1991. *Somewhat More Independent: The End of Slavery in New York City, 1770-1810*. Athens: University of Georgia.

Winch, J. 1988. *Philadelphia's Black Elite: Activism, Accomodation and the Struggle for Autonomy*. Philadelphia: Temple.

Worster, D. (ed.). 1988. *The Ends of the Earth: Perspectives on Modern Environmental History*. New York: Cambridge.

Worster, D. 1992. *Under Western Skies: Nature and History in the American West*. New York: Oxford.

Wyatt-Brown, B. 1988. "The Mask of Obedience: Male Slave Psychology in the Old South." *American Historical Review* 93: 1228-??.

Wyman, M. 1993. *Round-Trip to America The Immigrants Return to Europe, 1880-1930*. Ithaca: Cornell.

Yans-Mc Laughlin, V. 1990. *Immigration Reconsidered: History, Sociology and Politics*. New York: Oxford.

Yee, S. 1992. *Women Abolitionists: A Study in Activism, 1828-60*. Knoxville, TN: University of Tennessee.

Zieger, R. (ed.). 1991. *Organized Labor in the Twentieth Century South*. Knoxville, TN: University of Tennessee.

PSYCHOLOGICAL PERSPECTIVES ON INTERRACIAL AND INTERETHNIC GROUP CONFLICT AND THE AMELIORATION OF INTERGROUP TENSIONS

Martin Lakin

Wherever one turns in today's world one is confronted by reports of group against group. An ironic commentary about the Cold War's end is that we have moved from "controlled violence" dominated by superpowers to a "democracy of violence" where every tribe can wage war against its neighbors, limited only by the amount of weaponry it can afford. This chapter examines psychological perspectives on conflicts between domestic racial groups and ethnic groups and those occurring in other lands, and psychologically informed efforts to ameliorate them. These include educational efforts to change prejudiced attitudes and "experiential" intergroup workshops designed to bring about better mutual understanding between participants from antagonist groups. The latter have mainly been undertaken and conducted on the basis of conceptions derived from psychological and sociological observations and experimentation as well as on the basis of certain assumptions about the nature

Research in Human Social Conflict, Volume 1, pages 55-78.
Copyright © 1995 by JAI Press Inc.
All rights of reproduction in any form reserved.
ISBN: 1-55938-923-0

of psychotherapies applied in multiperson treatment contexts. Despite the fact that they have been sporadically used over the past three or four decades, they have never been surveyed in terms of overarching theory, shared procedures, or results. In view of the dangers of the multiple intergroup quarrels to world peace and personal security, it is important to examine the various aspects of a psychological perspective on intergroup conflict afresh, to gauge their usefulness and to assess their shortcomings.

From a psychological perspective, understanding of intergroup relationships, at a minimum, should take into account the following:

1. The relationships between group identity and personal identity;
2. Relationships between individual aggressiveness and group aggressiveness;
3. The state of knowledge about intragroup and intergroup dynamics (including the role of perceptual distortions, e.g., mutual projection in intergroup perception);
4. Pros and cons of social contact in ameliorating intergroup conflict.

The concern that guides the ensuing discussion is whether on the basis of understanding of such factors, it is reasonable to think that skilled psychological intervention might contribute to conflict amelioration of intergroup conflicts.

INTERGROUP CONFLICT: DOMESTIC UNITED STATES

There is ample evidence of conflict between racial and ethnic groups in the United States. Demographic changes as well as frustrated rising expectations sharpen competitive intergroup attitudes in this country. Where problems have recently been perceived mainly in terms of black-white relations, the growing frustrations of Asians and Hispanics add yet another volatile element. Varying degrees of hostility between racial, ethnic, national, and religious groups may have always characterized inter- and intrasocietal relations, but the carnage of two world wars in the modern era moved some academics, psychologists among them, to try to use their knowledge and skills for influencing the course of intergroup conflict. Some were motivated by concerns about mutual destruction caused by wars; others abhorred Nazi racism and wanted to try to eliminate racist attitudes in their own societies. Still others were genuinely hopeful that their knowledge and skills as psychologists or behavioral scientists could somehow be applied to ameliorate the lethal nature of quarrels between groups.

In 1947 Robin Williams, acting for the Social Science Research Council, published one of the earliest resumes of research on intergroup conflict in general. The topics covered involved all of the aforementioned types of domestic group conflicts. Among the implications of his survey were the following:

1. Although intergroup hostility is a universal phenomenon, it varies greatly in intensity.
2. Competitiveness and hostility are more intense where physical distinctions (color, physiognomy, or dress) are a primary basis of difference.
3. In multicultural societies overt intergroup competition is more likely because juxtaposition of diverse groups predisposes to mutual perception of differences and to invidious social comparison.
4. Intergroup conflict is made more probable by rapid and extensive social and/or economic changes. When stable expectations of intergroup conduct (and contingent interpersonal behavior) are disrupted lessened predictability results in heightened interpersonal anxiety.
5. Anxiety and aggressive feelings are readily focused on racial, ethnic, or religious outgroups inside or outside the society.
6. Intergroup conflict may be used by leadership elites to focus attention away from intragroup problems and from criticism of their leadership.
7. If membership of the group to which one feels primary allegiance is relatively stable, competition from outside groups will generate at least initially heightened group "patriotism" since hatred of the common enemy is a very effective short-term mechanism for mobilizing in-group cohesiveness (incidentally, providing unscrupulous leaders with a mechanism for enhancing their own positions).

Intensity of animosity and associated militancy is extremely variable. Militancy is not necessarily characteristic of groups that are most deprived, but rather of those which have acquired rights sufficient such that they may hope to attain more; more specifically, militant attitudes are more likely when a group's position is rapidly improving or when that group's position seems to be rapidly deteriorating—particularly if the deterioration follows a period of rapid positive change. (For an illustration of the phenomenon one may look at many aspects of current relations between African Americans and whites in our own society.) Since the heyday of achievements of voting rights and school integration, resistance to certain aspects of civil rights legislation (affirmative action and busing) has stiffened among many whites. In response, many African Americans conclude that doctrinal allusions to fairness, social justice, and equality are hollow. Claims that affirmative action is "reverse racism" are dismissed as evasive nonsense. Their argument is that only blacks were brought to this country in chains and therefore deserve the compensation that affirmative actions represent. In any event, the predictable increases in militancy and in resistance are both evident.

One finds expressions of mutually antagonistic attitudes not only in the cities; universities, too, are playing a psychodramatically significant role as "cockpits" where intergroup hostilities are acted out (mostly talked out, but there are also implicit threats of violence). While confrontation with attitudes different from one's own can lead one to better understand the other and reflect upon his or her own biases, intergroup confrontations may also be used as a means of reinforcing in-group identification and out-group stereotypes. Thus, some people complain that current programs of "diversity training" on college campuses that could be explorations of difference are in fact used for dramatizing minority group complaints and demands. It is unclear whether such programs are contributing to mutual understanding among groups in this country or exacerbating the tensions between them.

PSYCHOLOGY AND GROUP PROCESSES

For the most part, academic psychology has paid relatively little attention to group interactions, leaving them to the political scientist and the sociologist. Most theoreticians and researchers in psychology didn't consider group behavior a legitimate object for psychological study. Individualism and a focus on self derived mainly from philosophy seems to have shaped psychology's preoccupation with individual experience. Overvaluing individual experience resulted in underestimating tribe, clan, or people as formative influences on self-identity. A similar preoccupation with individualism has been apparent in studying etiological and curative aspects of psychological dysfunction. Thus, it was sociologists, not psychologists, who first recorded the demoralizing effects of alienation from group ties. Only the rare psychologist attributed any feature of psychopathology to a presumed "lack of rootedness" with the consequence of severe and dysfunctional personal insecurity. Burrow (1927) and Fromm (1941) were among those who, like Durkheim (1951) perceived in the loss of primary group ties a social pathology that required therapeutic remediation. Somewhat later, David Bakan proposed an essential tension between individualism (he termed it "agency") and a ubiquitous vital experience of rootedness in one's own group ("communitarian" feelings); the former concerned with independence and individual achievement, and the latter with belongingness, cooperation, and collective achievement. However, when we refer to the major figures of dynamic psychotherapy, Freud and Jung, we find that both were markedly antipathetic to group influences, believing them to be inimical to personal and healthy personal development. Jung especially disliked the repressive pulls of group affiliation. He wrote in response to Illing's inquiry "... in view of the notorious inclination of people to lean on... "isms" rather than on inner security and independence, there is the danger that the individual will equate the group with father and mother, and will, thereby remain as dependent, insecure, and infantile as ever" (Illing, 1963, p. 184)

Despite the caveats of Freud and Jung, few contemporary psychotherapists would quarrel with Bakan's (1966) or Erikson's (1954) counter assertions that group rootedness is an important component of healthy personality. However, Erikson, in particular, recognized that groups are also sources of profound emotional influence for ill as well as for good. Thus, the group loyalties that produce the "good citizen" might also cultivate a group chauvinism so extreme that it defines outsiders as vermin destined to be destroyed. It is a tragic fact that the idealism that encourages self sacrifice can also give rise to demonization of others as the perceived source of misfortune and evil. As Jung wrote (Illing, 1963) "...(the person) will not be disturbed by the greatest infamy as long as his fellows believe in the morality of their cause..." Nazi Germany, of course, provides the salient example of the century.

AGGRESSION AND GROUP BEHAVIOR

Some years ago, Feshback and Singer (1957), then Berkowitz (1968), summarized evidence for innateness of aggression in humans (observed even among deaf and blind children who can make aggressive gestures and threats despite never having seen or heard them). Pugnacity, rivalrousness, and the desire for undisturbed possession over things and persons appear to be innate characteristics of humans and are ubiquitous in our world. Fighting over turf appears to be a major disrupting factor in and between a number of societies. A later confirmation of this conclusion is a major thesis of the review of the subject by Somit (1990).

What is unique to humans is that while they may be quite cruel, even more ruthless than other species when they do aggress against one another, is that they seem to establish complex "justifications" for their aggressions, even constructing comprehensive ideological rationalizations to justify intentions and actions to destroy their rivals. The most general psychological principle seems to be that vast powers and sinister motives are invariably attributed to the group that is feared or envied. Needless to say, emphasizing the "malign" character and hostile attitude of opponents justifies the actions taken against them. By the same token, one's core group may mobilize and release individual frustrations in aggressions against another group. But this does not imply that aggressiveness of group members is necessarily the motivating element in any intergroup conflict.

As the Second World War loomed, Albert Einstein wrote to Sigmund Freud (1933) inquiring about his views of human nature and aggression. Why is it,

Einstein asked, that hatreds are so easily aroused? Could Freud's insights into the "dark places of human will and feelings" shed some light on the question. Freud's response was to reassert his pessimistic view of the determining operation of the "death instinct" at the root of human aggressiveness. It could only be controlled, not eliminated, by imposing mutual obligations and duties of citizenship which would have to be forcibly maintained against the constant danger of its eruption.

Before, during and after World War II some psychological theorists and practitioners began to conceptualize aspects of intergroup conflict in terms of shared psychopathology. Some went so far as to suggest that prejudiced attitudes based on racial and ethnic difference were developed as props for faltering self-esteem and functioned as defenses against repressed impulses of one's own, particularly aggressive and sexual impulses. Thus, H.S. Sullivan and Erik Erikson argued that those who derogate others are in fact attempting to compensate themselves for their own felt inadequacies. Sullivan, in particular, interpreted race hatred and discrimination against negroes in America as arising from failures to cope with experiences of shame, humiliation, and anxiety in one's personal development. The pathological, that if, dysfunctional, consequences of racism were apparent in both the prejudiced and the victims of prejudice (Sullivan, 1948).

Troubled by the onset of war and worried about the future of intergroup relations in this country and abroad, but inspired by Dollard, Doob, Miller, Mowrer, and Sears' (1939) integration of psychoanalytic theory with their notions of behaviorism, and especially their theory of the relationship between frustration and aggression, E.C. Tolman, a personality theorist, advanced the idea of an inverse relationship between satisfaction of needs and propensities to aggress (1942). Simply put, his thesis was an elaboration of the notion that a satisfied people is less aggressive than a frustrated one. Tolman argued that ideological and political "myths"—the Marxian, the Capitalist, the Millenarian Religious myths, and Totalitarian ideologies—had all misled the human quest for life satisfaction and had thereby greatly increased human frustration. To replace these failed myths, Tolman proposed a psychological agenda for meeting human needs that was weighted toward what might be called good mental health practices, especially for the young. Revisiting the skeptical views of Jung and Freud about the effects of group experience, Tolman, who was favorably impressed by the concepts of Kurt Lewin, argued that group influence need not be totalitarian; democratic participation as well as emotional rootedness could find its expression in groups.

GROUP IDENTITIES AND PERSONALITY

In endeavoring to understand the seeming intransigence of group rivalries, we must turn to broad historical perspectives of other behavioral scientists.

One of the most salient is Sumner's characterization of ethnocentrism (1911). He emphasized the concentric influence that characterizes group loyalties, causing group members to exaggerate and intensify every distinction between themselves and others. He exemplifies the lethal extremes of group partisanship by the case of the ancient, Strabo, who is reputed to have said of the Scythians that they were just and kind to one another but savage to all outsiders...so that they regarded shedding the stranger's blood as among the "brightest virtues," but "conjugal union with the stranger" was punishable as a most heinous crime. Fights against hated groups are decked with the mantle of crusades for justice and virtue. Moreover, as Hebb and Thompson (1964) wrote, fear and dislike of the stranger is apparently easily developed. Group differences, particularly those marked by skin color and different facial features, are rapidly registered in consciousness. (One may contrast this conception with the wishful idealization of the musical, "South Pacific," where the sailor in love with a "native girl" bemoans the anticipated rejection by his prejudiced neighbors back in the United States. His musical lament..."You've got to be taught"...contrasts with the fact that little instruction is evidently needed to generate invidious attitudes toward outgroup members.)

The propensity to make invidious distinctions seems to characterize intergroup relations. Even casual categorization as belonging to this or that group has been shown to generate "Us versus Them" value comparisons. Rothbart's (1993) is only the most recent report of how easily one can stimulate intergroup competition through simply assigning to different groups. Sherif, Harvey, White, Hood, and Sherif (1961) had pioneered, in demonstrating how intergroup hostility could be induced, setting up two equal sized groups in a boys' summer camp. Their assignments of the 24 11-year olds to either of two groups led in a remarkably short time to the kinds of name calling and threats associated with characteristic intergroup rivalry, verging on real hostility. Sherif and his colleagues were able to ameliorate the conflict through involving the boys in a "superordinate" task of working together for common benefit. (One version of the story is that the two groups had to work together in order to get an essential supplies truck out of a ditch; apparently, it may have only involved being able to travel to see a movie. In any event, the experience of cooperating is said to have halted the spiraling pattern of hostility.) This field experiment demonstrated processes of developing intergroup conflict where no adversarial history existed. It showed how arbitrary categorizations—as in choose-up games—facilitates group identifications sufficient to potentiate competitive intergroup attitudes. A subsequent series of laboratory studies by Tajfel (1984) and his associates similarly demonstrated that individuals assigned to different groups under a variety of conditions (even patently irrelevant groups such as "under- or overestimators of dots," or preferrers of Klee or Kandinsky's paintings) come to favor unknown fellow assignees for selection as "resource persons" over persons from the "other group."

As Tajfel and Turner (1986) argued, membership in dichotomous categories is itself sufficient to induce preferences for the persons in one's assigned category. Moreover, relative status and choice is quickly tied to group affiliation so that comembers and outgroup members are scaled and evaluated accordingly, that is, "More than, better than, more capable than, smarter than..." One is reminded of Freud's assertion that humans are vulnerable to "the narcissism of small differences." In this section we have been focusing on experiments in "casual" group assignments, but it follows from our discussion that membership in real racial, ethnic, national, or religious core groups can have much more profound significance for one's sense of self.

Given that a sense of group identity becomes important in the course of personal development, what psychological factors foster malign rather than benign sentiments between members of different groups? Partly in response to the rise of Nazism, a group of behavioral scientists, including social and clinical psychologists, attempted to examine personality attributes presumed to be associated with Germany's racist and authoritarian ideology, but reflected in proto-fascist sentiments among some Americans. Specifically, they isolated a cluster of attitudes involving rigidly held moralistic ideas, extreme nationalistic sentiments, and convictions of racial superiority-inferiority according to which they exalted their own group and denigrated others. These were the "Authoritarian Personality" studies launched by Adorno, Frenkel-Brunswik, Levinson, and Sanford (1950). Levinson's (1951) interpretation of the modal "authoritarian" personality is illustrative: "The ardent Nazi/Fascist shows primitiveness...[an excess of] stereotyping tendencies, fears of moral contamination, exaggerated fears of weakness, and compulsive longings to submit to a powerful leader."

One of the pioneers in the study of group processes and intergroup conflict was the aforementioned Kurt Lewin. Almost four decades after his death, he still symbolizes one of the primary aspirations of applied group dynamics research; reducing intergroup conflict and discriminatory prejudice. Himself, a refugee from Nazi Germany, Lewin was a major influence on experimental social psychology and applied psychology. His teachings inspired a generation of dedicated researchers who endeavored to apply his group dynamics concepts in the volatile areas of conflict over interracial housing, school integration, and interfaith relationships.

In retrospect, it might be concluded that Lewin was overly optimistic about prospects for resolving intergroup conflicts. Group experiences are not necessarily democratic; attitude and behavior change induction in them can be authoritarian (as has been demonstrated by examples of "political re-education" (brainwashing) in totalitarian societies. The "regressive" potential in group affiliation so disdained by Freud and Jung is constantly incipient in emotionally powerful group experiences. Finally, is has proven exceedingly difficult to apply Lewin's "field theory" (1951) in a precise manner, even though it remains an excellent heuristic for picturing influences and pressures in the group—the "field of forces"—operating at a given time. Most significantly, in terms of our concern with conflict management and resolution, it has proven extraordinarily difficult to establish clear connections between the dynamics of field and laboratory experiments and "real world" conflicts. Nevertheless, Lewin's basic conceptions (1947, 1948) continue to play an important part in understanding the microcosmic interactional dynamics of intragroup and intergroup processes.

We are faced with the continuing problem of what, from a psychological perspective, might be done to reduce intergroup tensions. For a start, let us refer once again to remediative proposals by Williams (1947) and consider some of his propositions for ameliorating intergroup conflicts: (1) Where reduction of intergroup conflict is intended, the frustrations and insecurities and the attendant anxieties of each group have to be minimized to the extent possible. (2) Efforts at guided change between groups have to try to avoid threatening either group's security. As Allport (1954) pointed out, it is axiomatic that people who feel that they are under attack will not learn positive things about their perceived attackers. Criticism of any group will only mobilize defensiveness among its members in response to the "unwarranted" attacks of outsiders. (3) Moralistic sloganeering or appeals to conscience (guilt induction) is also likely to intensify rather than diminish hostility. On the other hand, expressions of shared values may increase levels of trust, first on interpersonal, then possible on group levels. (4) Socializing between members of antagonist groups is most likely to be successful when participants are of similar, socioeconomic statue and share tastes and interests. (5) The main goal of a psychological intergroup intervention should be to identify possibilities for collaboration where members of the conflicted groups can work together on a task that all believe is in the common interest. Given the period in which Williams formulated these proposals, it should not be surprising that he was mainly concerned (as we still are) with worsening relations between the races in this country. His recommended "reverse role taking, (exchanging white and black persons' roles in acting out job interviews) foreshadowed some of the subsequent changes in discriminatory employment practices.

As has been suggested, psychology's historic focus on individual personality virtually ignored the interrelatedness of personal and group identity. Aspects of both are inextricably involved even though particular group affiliations— racial, ethnic, religious, national, and so forth—may not be salient in every circumstance. What is particularly relevant for intergroup relations and individual behavior is that people are invariably sensitive to condescending or demeaning attitudes toward their own groups from others, even if they, themselves, experience marked ambivalence with respect to their own membership. It is something like the commonly remembered childhood scenarios in which one might feel free to express the most scurrilous attitudes about one's own family members, but rises to attack the outsider who dares to say negative things about them. Differences between groups are inevitably salient in the minds of group members, and, according to the veteran researcher of prejudice, Pettigrew (1986), attempts to reduce intergroup conflict cannot wish them away. On the contrary, conflict resolution attempts must take into account the degree to which personal identity is established around the group's distinctiveness attractive or repugnant. The consequence is that even well-intentioned efforts to deny the differences between groups (to try to resolve conflicts in a "color-blind" manner) are at odds with the realities of the intergroup experience. To ameliorate conflict between groups does not mean, in his view, to deny differences but rather to acknowledge legitimate grievances, but then to work toward their remediation.

Factors such as group-linked reputations for crime, drug abuse, teenage pregnancy, and so forth, are currently seized upon as evidencing an inherently underclass status for Afrrican Americans. But, depending on majority-minority status, and the histories of association, denigrative conceptions of other groups have frequently obtained in the history of this country's intergroup experience. In the United States this has also been characteristic of Asian-black, Asian-white, Hispanic-white, and Hispanic-black as well as Christian-Jewish comparisons ever since the founding of the Republic. That invidious intergroup comparisons will inevitably be made seems a sad fact of human existence. That they are too often associated with lethal intergroup hostilities seems to be another tragic fact of human experience. As Arthur Miller (1987) the playwright, wrote, "the ultimate human mystery...may be the claim on us of clan and race...which may yet have the power, because they defy the rational mind, to kill the world" (p. 54).

The ties of race, language, and culture are like congruities of blood, religion, and social custom in that they have an overpowering coerciveness in and of themselves, such that discontent rooted along these lines is extremely difficult to defuse, wrote Clifford Geertz in 1973. Obviously, conflict among groups that embody such vital elements of personal identity are far more difficult to defuse than that which is induced in experimentally contrived groups. It is nevertheless instructive to see how some of the same processes can be demonstrated in the latter. For example, it is striking that there can be developed a feeling of collectivity even in temporary groups (such as therapy groups) strong enough to displace accustomed exclusivity in relationships. This reaches intensities where no one "dares to be different" (Moscovici, 1985). Even in contrived group experiences aggressiveness that might have been experienced toward fellow members is directed "outward" toward members of other groups.

It appears that the juxtaposition of races, ethnicities, and nationalities makes competition between them almost inevitable (Horowitz, 1985). Horowitz states that one consequence of the passage of white dominance in formerly colonial Africa and Asia has been substitutions of conflict between other racial and ethnic divisions and ultimately ramifications into intra-ethnic "subconflicts." That specific conflicts are not necessarily fixed in character for all time is amply evidenced even on the streets of urban America, where Asian shopkeepers have come to be regarded by their African-American customers with the same kinds of envy and resentment as were Jewish shopkeepers in those same neighborhoods two generations ago.

The interchangeability of rivals, historic alternations in patterns of who are the oppressors and who are the oppressed, shifts in who is seen as powerful and who as powerless, and the associated patterns of envy and resentment do not, in themselves, justify the conclusion that intergroup conflicts are "only psychological" or that current conflicts will diminish with the passage of time and the generations. As Levine and Campbell (1972) asserted, real histories of conflicting claims and real histories of oppression characterize many intergroup conflicts, and their memories will not disappear. On the other hand, the ubiquity of psychological factors in intergroup conflicts is so evident that psychologists must feel impelled to consider how they operate and how to cope with them precisely because of the alarming state of intergroup relations. What has come to be known as the "Tajfel" paradigm is certainly discouraging evidence of the intransigence of intergroup rivalrousness, seemingly so easy to stimulate and yet so difficult to control. Hinkle and Schopler (1986), in particular, worried that in accepting its implications at face value, without further critical analysis, psychologists would be dissuaded from making serious attempts to ameliorate intergroup antagonisms.

In fact ingroup identities seem to be formidably robust to those who see them as obstacles to intergroup harmony. As Peterson wrote (1982) the most powerful and ubiquitous social contrast invariably comes down to: Us versus Them; the implicit norm seems unfortunately to be competition and/or conflict. Personal ambivalence about one's group (the phenomenon of self-hatred) is commonly observed among members of persecuted or oppressed minority groups, but disdain for one's own group may paradoxically transform into sentiments more like ingroup chauvinism, especially among frustrated, but also talented, individuals. Thus, feelings of victimization, particularly in the absence of legitimated alternate identities, not only strengthens ingroup solidarity, but may also strengthen the determination to redeem damaged self-esteem through rising to do battle with the perceived oppressor group. It has been observed that some racial, ethnic, and religious leaders had, early in their careers, recorded their disgust with their own group's "negative traits," a reaction that apparently precipitated the determination to redeem it. Malcolm X's apotheosis may be representative of such a psychological journey as an African-American leader, as was Theodore Herzl's as the founder of Political Zionism. A related phenomenon—also precipitated by envy of the other group and contempt for one's own is a process that Lewin (1948) called "reverse categorization," a process in which one unequivocally takes on the majority's prejudices toward one's own group.

Given the traditions of research in psychology, it is understandable that "peace researching" psychologists would try to examine conflict through the prism of perceptual processes. Bronfenbrenner (1961) and White (1965) were among those whose names are associated with the "mirror image" studies in which each side is supposed to project onto the other its own fears and aggressive impulses. Prejudiced attitudes would be reflected in pejorative views of the other but the defensive process of "projection" would add an additional distortive element to exacerbate intergroup mistrust. Mirror imaging could also lead to the likelihood of dangerous miscalculation of the "enemy's" intent because projective perception involves the most feared motives and behaviors one might be culpable of and attributing them to the rival group. Since the "undercover" attitudes are necessarily destructive, the intentions of the opponent group will be interpreted accordingly. The potentially disastrous consequences are implicit in mutually erroneous perceptions based on such distortive processes.

A related effort that has continued to influence peace research is Janis' speculative analysis of the "conformist, stereotypic, and essentially uncreative" responses among cabinet-level officials in response to foreign policy crises that he characterized as "Groupthink" (1982). It suggested that under certain conditions, people in a group fail to challenge each other's misperceptions and misinterpretations, fearing to interfere with the group's wish for consensus. As Janis interpreted processes in the policy meetings called to deal with Cuba and eventuating in the Bay of Pigs fiasco, the consensus-seeking dynamic may have had a major role in the faulty policy decisions that eventuated. It is important that such perceptual processes should be examined in laboratory situations as well as in real life because they may constitute important components of the cognitive processes underlying the expression of hostility in intergroup conflicts.

THINKING ABOUT CONFLICT RESOLUTION

We have seen that problems of intergroup communication are exacerbated by tendencies to misperceive and misinterpret the other. Does familiarity and knowledge of the other diminish hostility. Do groups that are intimately acquainted understand one another better than stranger groups? The "contact hypothesis" predicts that people will have no wish to harm outgroup individuals they have come to know. The sentiment "getting to know you..." is the theme of multiple experiments in international work projects and youth enclaves; international rescue and relief efforts are also energized by such shared sentiments. Unfortunately, as Back (1992) has written,... "We must be aware that some of the greatest amount of intercultural awareness and (mutual) understanding occurs between hereditary enemies." One is reminded of the saying, "I thought I didn't like him. But now that I really know him, I *know* that I don't like him!"

Despite such obvious reservations, conventional wisdom would have it that people who know one another are less inclined to assault one another; that is, acquaintance and socializing together usually reduce mutual suspicion and replace fear and hostility with friendly curiosity. Amir (1969) reviewed studies where contact had been employed as the major strategy for trying to resolve intergroup conflict. He came to the following conclusions: (1) Changes in relationships between interacting members of conflicted groups can and do occur. "Favorable" conditions influence a change toward more favorable judgments of outgroup members, but "unfavorable" conditions are likely to increase, not decrease, intergroup tensions. (2) Even when there are favorable changes, they may be limited to the specific individuals who participate in the intergroup interactions. Positive attitude change does not generalize to members of the disliked group. (True, participants of higher status from either group may be more receptive to one another; however, again, there is no necessary carryover to lower level persons.) On the other hand, however, if participants in an intergroup experience are too disparate in status and cultural level, intergroup antagonism will likely be increased rather than diminished.

Undeniably, the perception of group differences invites social comparison and invidious categorization. Recognizing its fatefulness, Brewer and Miller (1984) tried to bypass it by developing experimental situations in which participants would relate to one another as individuals, not as group representatives. Apparently they were sufficiently successful that participants acted and spoke as if their group identities were diminished in favor of effective interpersonal relating. How genuinely this was felt could not be assessed. However, what is really important is the unanswerable question of the practical utility of such experimentation in relation to real, not contrived groups. It is of course significant that group members, even of contrived groups, and even transiently, could attenuate group ties in order to relate as fellow humans. One is impelled to recall anecdotal accounts among even hereditary enemies. In literature Romeo and Juliet's was only one, if the most famous, of many such cross-group relationships through history, some carried on in the midst of battle and others in almost completely racially segregated circumstances. Were it possible to really reduce categorical distinctions, it would undoubtedly help heal intergroup quarrels. But we are also reminded by Pettigrew (1986) that obscuring differences between groups will not help in the long run—especially in those cases, where one group has been, or is seen as, the traditional object of oppression and the other is seen as its perpetrator. Even the relative success of intergroup meetings among "higher status" individuals is only temporary, in this view, because those same people later fall back on the outgroup stereotypes endorsed by their groups. After all, Pettigrew argues, prejudiced perception and interpretation of the actions of the other is "functional"; people grow tired of trying to understand the other in all of his or her complexity. Hence, the self-serving perceptions that "keep it simple" and that preserve the psychological status quo about one's own group and about the other group are so enduring and resilient.

The familiar condescension in the phrase "some of my best friends are..." is immediately recognized for its patronizing quality. "Color-blind" approaches to intergroup conflict resolution also appear to be discouragingly at odds with experienced realities of race relations here and elsewhere. Even Brewer and Miller acknowledged that group categorization is inevitably an enduring point of personal reference, particularly for people who are conscious of the disadvantages of their group's position. Even if one succeeds in experimentally diminishing group differences in laboratory groups (as did Brewer and Miller), one must ask whether the results could be applied to the real world. Triandis (1976), an acknowledged expert in the area of intergroup relations, is as skeptical about this possibility as is Pettigrew. They both insist that perceived realities need to be taken into account prior to "let's get to know one another" exercises. On the other hand, it is impossible to dismiss the importance of face-to-face contact in establishing initial trust on which to build more far-reaching mutual accommodation.

PEACE RESEARCHERS

We have mentioned the activities of psychologists who might be called "peace researchers." Some elaborated the theories and built on the research conceptions of the aforementioned Kurt Lewin as they continued to explore the processes of prejudice and methods of coping with it. Efforts to study and to resolve group conflicts which had been centered in the northeast moved from MIT to the University of Michigan where the *Journal of Conflict Resolution* was founded. Harty and Mocell (1991) surveyed the articles of that journal since its beginnings, and found that imaginative interdisciplinary conceptions were soon swamped by the kinds of articles on "game theory" and "decision making" that were too rarely applicable to real world circumstances. Along with such publications as *The Journal of Social Issues, The International Journal of Group Tensions,* and *The Journal of Peace Research, The Journal of Conflict Resolution* continues to publish relevant articles about domestic as well as foreign intergroup conflicts. However, the focus is increasingly restricted to conflicts in this society. As for the goal of training credentialed intervenors, some "dispute resolution practitioners" and "mediation specialists" are being trained at various centers to intervene into intergroup conflicts, but the dream of systematic preparation of credentialed practitioners for interventions into intergroup conflicts remains unfulfilled. To be sure, there are a number of agencies that have sprung up in the wake of a developing market for "diversity training" on college campuses and in industry. But, as noted earlier, their purpose may be indoctrination rather than mediation.

What progress has there been in conceptualizing the psychological factors in intergroup conflict in recent years? It seems fair to conclude that there is greater sophistication about causes and processes of intra- and intergroup conflict than forty years ago, but still relatively limited experience in trying to manage, ameliorate, or resolve it. It is important to take note of what is no longer characteristic of psychologists' perspectives. For one thing, characterizing whole populations and cultures in psychopathological terms is no longer done by responsible psychologists. For another, it is mostly in the pages of the popular press that intergroup conflict is attributed solely to the inner personality of particular leaders (characterized in psychopathological terms) even though particular political leaders may, of course, be so unstable that they precipitate or exacerbate conflicts. (As recently as 1971 the president of the American Psychological Association seriously proposed administering ataractic therapy to national leaders so as to make them less warlike! See Clark, 1971.) While leaders play decisive roles in national affairs and intergroup conflicts, attitudes of groups exist independently of leaders' political and military ambitions, and it is often the case that leaders manipulate those attributes and associated sentiments, often with their group's wholehearted endorsement.

In characterizing intergroup conflict in terms of its accessibility to psychological techniques of intervention, it is important to point out that there has been a significant shift toward cognitive-behavioral treatment strategies and away from traditional psychodynamic (expressive) therapies—especially when trying to treat the interrelated problems of a number of people at the same time (see Burton, 1969). There are a number of reasons for this which have relatively little to do with the intrinsic values of the treatment orientations, but rather with the relative effectiveness of their techniques. As an example, historical analyses are neither fully possible nor useful in relatively brief intergroup contact. For another thing, evocation of emotional reactions must be carefully "titrated" in intergroup contacts. Thus, mutual catharsis is of particularly limited value in multiperson therapies for families, groups, and organizations. While from the perspective of the psychologist, one must take into account the intensity of feelings as well as their sources, in group situations one must also see that they are sufficiently constrained to make effective communication possible. This is, in some ways parallel to the situation in intergroup contacts. Let us examine several "quasi-therapeutic" and somewhat experimental approaches to intergroup conflict that have been attempted over the past three decades.

A surprisingly fertile arena for thinking about and experimenting with intergroup conflict has been labor disputes between workers and management in American industry. Blake and Mouton (1962) pioneered in developing paradigms for intergroup intervention what they hoped would serve to prevent costly and possible violent work stoppages. They offered their "win-win" strategy according to which the conflicting sides would be encouraged to try to understand the positions of their opponents. This means that each would be encouraged to be open to different interpretations of the goals of their opponents. The reasoning was that if mutual understanding could be achieved about this limited aspect of the conflict, the groups could proceed to collaborative problem-solving in order to try to meet as many of the goals of each as possible. Accordingly, they set out their strategy in a series of steps:

1. Participants are chosen not only for their representativeness, but also because they have status in their own groups as "influentials."
2. Each group meets separately to consider its position. Members analyze their own group's position prior to considering the positions of the opposed group.
3. Participants analyze their own group's goals and aims in terms of criteria of fairness as well as relative advantage or disadvantage.
4. The conductors or "facilitators" of the intergroup sessions act as neutral "third parties," dedicated only to finding fair solutions to the problems of both groups.
5. The facilitator's interventions must take into account emotional as well as intellectual interactions among participants from the opposing groups.
6. Although the setting could be almost anywhere, it is advantageous to hold sessions away from where "immediate consequences might be experienced."
7. Since the goal of the intergroup session is mitigation of the conflict, special efforts are directed toward positive progress to mutual agreements on progressively more complex issues.

Basically, the assumption that guides these types of intervention is the conviction that both sides stand to gain from the avoidance of further conflict, a conception that has been found to apply in a straightforward way to most intergroup problems. Obviously, this assumption, applied to intergroup antagonism that is historically racial/ethnic/national, or religious represents a huge leap from a comparatively straightforward conflict over salaries or wages and working conditions.

A similar emphasis on developing conjoint projects on the basis of greater mutual understanding through cognitive analysis of shared problems may be seen in the proposals put forward by Burton (1972). He argued that the realities of existence in a transnational "global" society pose cognitive and emotional challenges that are essentially comprehensible by everyone. The assumptions of previous generations should not prevent us developing an essential sense of such "transnational" or global loyalties alongside our primary group identities. Burton's thesis involved the following points:

1. Conflicts have multiple psychological as well as substantive components and it is necessary to attempt to understand them through conflict analysis.
2. The parties to an intergroup conflict do not respond altogether irrationally—at least no less rationally than industrial firms calculating costs and seeking relative advantage.
3. The opportunity for conflict amelioration and resolution comes with the realization that win-lose conceptions may be self-destructive, not just harmful to the other group. With that realization comes a window of opportunity for introducing possible "win-win" strategies.
4. The intergroup conflict needs to be transformed form confrontation to joint problem-solving. What is needed is to engage in face to face exploration of mutual perceptions and acknowledging the real goals of each group.
5. The mediator should be a trustworthy nonpartisan, who is skilled in managing group dynamics and who defines the task in terms of issues clarification.
6. Intergroup conflicts can be resolved only through progressive mutual understanding and acceptance, moving from transient compromises to more durable settlements. (For industrial examples, see Blake and Mouton, 1978.)

Viewed from such perspectives, it would appear that theories and techniques of psychotherapy do have a significant, if limited, relevance for understanding intergroup conflict. In particular, the lessons of group therapies help in understanding the group dynamics that foster collective and individual change as well as those that are mobilized to enhance group cohesiveness in the face of perceived attack. Of course goals of therapy and of intergroup conflict resolution are markedly different. Nevertheless, there is an overarching shared psycho-technology by means of which change processes are set in motion. Needless to add, it is essential that such processes are channeled to reduce rather than exacerbate conflicts.

We turn now to attempts to ameliorate real world intergroup conflicts that do involve race, ethnicity, and tribal loyalties. Basing their effort on Human

Relations Training's quasi-therapeutic techniques, Doob (1970) and Doob and
Foltz (1973) conducted conflict resolution workshops involving group self-
study, transactional analysis, and interpersonal and intergroup feedback with
rival ethnic/national groups in the Horn of Africa. Their second effort involved
representatives of the antagonistic Catholic and Protestant communities of
Northern Ireland. They also used similar intervention techniques with other
groups, including Turkish and Greek Cypriots.

At about the same time Lakin, Lomranz, and Liebermnan (1969) conducted
conflict resolution workshops in Israel. Since that time, under various auspices,
subsequent Arab-Israeli workshops have involved political figures at many
levels, educators, psychologists, and students in school programs aimed at
better intergroup relations (see Bargal and Bar, 1990). While variable as to
sponsorship, participants, leadership, and procedures, they have been similar
in emphasizing open-ended discussions of differences in a "therapeutic
atmosphere" free from distractions of daily affairs and with assurances of
confidentiality. Facilitators were typically psychologically trained individuals
who were committed to nonpartisan interventions aimed at clarification of
issues and facilitating communication among the participants. While degrees
of expertise in managing a group's dynamics necessarily varied among them,
most facilitators adopted a "therapeutic" strategy of "reflective listening" and
tried to refrain from excessive interpretation. In a number of cases, especially
where educators or political figures were involved, the hope was that there
would be carryover that extended beyond the several days to week-long
workshops to influence attitudes in the communities from which participants
came.

An implicit goal of all these efforts was to "de-demonize" and to "de-toxify"
mutually hostile perceptions as an essential preliminary to progressing toward
collaboration on projects of common interest. In most cases results of this kind
of workshop were described as moderately positive, but even such
comparatively modest results were achieved amid formidable mutual mistrust.
(Incidentally, fears of being ostracized or informed on by members of one's
own group were not unfounded.) It is significant that some of the Northern
Irish Catholics and Protestants continued to doubt the usefulness of
"psychology" for dealing with their community problems. It is certainly easy
to understand their disbelief that their conflicts could be ameliorated through
training in human relations. (As mentioned earlier, their concerns about
retributive consequences were not trivial. "Consorting with the enemy" can be
a dangerous "crime" among groups in conflict.) Their reservations about the
utility of workshops must be taken seriously.

The idea of the workshops in those early applications was clearly social-
psychotherapeutic. That is, they utilized a "protected environment" (a neutral
zone away from daily activity and routine involvements); they emphasized
problems in interpersonal communication, and the facilitators acted as quasi-

therapists. However, those of more recent vintage have been characterized by a somewhat different strategic conception, a more cognitive/analytic and less emotionally oriented point of departure. One could say that they are more in line with Burton's and Blake and Mouton's cognitive focus on controlled analysis and conjoint problem-solving. Even if aspects of intergroup hostility involve psyphopathology, the emotionally toned emphasis of a dynamic psychotherapy approach might be harmful as contrasted with a "cognitive behavioral" controlled communication paradigm.

Using his own adaptation of the model of "controlled communication," Kelman (1991) and Kelman and Cohen (1986) conducted a number of conflict resolution workshops involving Arabs and Israelis and others. Kelman describes them as "experimental journeys from We-They to We-We through examining each other's perceptions and concerns." Informally disclosive interactions facilitate the initial development of interpersonal trust, on the basis of which it becomes progressively possible to examine one another's outlooks and to articulate one's own point of view. His explicitly stated goal is to get each side to recognize and to accept the validity of at least one claim of its opponent. There is, of course, a subtext, which is to expose and to eliminate the mutual stereotyping that limits thinking about the other in constructive ways.

Needless to say, in these as in all such workshops the honesty and trustworthiness of the workshop's organizer/facilitator is a crucial factor. He or she must persuade all of the participants of basic fairness and objectivity in making interventions; especially with regard to the points that are selectively emphasized, the questions that are put to the groups, and the suggestions that are made for how the process can be improved. As I have already noted, suspiciousness is inevitable and typically persists throughout the duration of the workshop.

I have acknowledged that such conflict resolution efforts cannot be judged only on the basis of endorsements by participants or on the basis of the convictions of those who organize and conduct them. As I will suggest, systematic inquiry is needed. However, for illustrative purposes, I will cite the reactions of one participant whose words, it seems to me, reflect sentiments of participants from a variety of similar experiences with different groups. "Despite the initial ease of relating, disagreement in bitter terms escalated almost immediately. It was punctuated by repeated accounts of experienced indignities and humiliations. Sloganeering and implied or explicit threats were characteristic of some of the meetings.... Each side complained that the other side misread its own goals, but that it had correctly assessed the wicked intentions and behaviors of the other. While the facilitator's interventions were sometimes helpful and clarifying, they were often ignored or rejected. Nevertheless, the post-sessions evaluations by each of us were positive endorsements of the meetings, emphasizing their importance and the very profound emotional impact they were having on each one of us....It is very hard to know what the long range effects of my participating here will be. Virtually everyone feels the same way, that solutions to our conflict won't be found in single workshops, but that many such experiences may eventually bring about solutions and real cooperation between us."

It is frequently the case that participants recognize the need to develop "superordinate" cooperative projects to strengthen the fragile bonds resultant from such short-term efforts in trying to understand the "other." This is consistent with the conclusion that "learnings" from guided intergroup interactions must be put into practice or else they dissipate. More specifically, a kind of "rubber-band" effect occurs; participants simply resume majoritarian behaviors and attitudes on their return home. Organizers of conflict resolution workshops must also anticipate the inevitable sharpening of disagreements and the spates of misperceptions and miscommunications that this participant reports.

It seems easy to see why conflict resolution workshop participants have mostly been intellectuals—that is, journalists, educators, health specialists, writers, business people, and even parliamentarians. It may be that, as in analytical forms of psychotherapy, intellectuals are the ones most likely to value psychological "binocular vision," as Kelman terms it. Even though vitally concerned with their own group's welfare, they are also sensitive to issues of moral treatment of others. While intellectual and social challenges are as great as is the emotional one in trying to understand the "other," conflict resolution is also being tried in public schools where there is of course great variance in intellectual levels. In responsibly conducted workshops conflict analysis must be undertaken from as neutral a stance as possible and in the light of psychological knowledge. From this perspective the most general aspects of intergroup conflicts are the following: (1) Acknowledgement that we all live in groups—racial, ethnic, tribal, religious, societal, and so on—and that our identities are at least partially determined by them. (2) As in the case of psychological dysfunction in individuals, a group's psychological trauma (real or imagined) is enlarged in experience and repeatedly reinforced as well as enlivened by perceived opportunities to make up for grievances. Needless to say, such perceptions and experiences often exacerbate the conflicts with the rival or antagonist group. (3) Psychologically ameliorative techniques for intergroup conflicts are based partly on developing greater mutual empathy and partly on increasing mutual understanding among members of the groups about sources of their conflict and possible scenarios for its containment, amelioration, or resolution.

In recent years yet another workshop variant ("track-two diplomacy") has been reported by Azar, Davies, Pickering, and Sahbaze (1990). It involves unofficial, "off the record" meetings between representatives of adversarial groups. While participants bear no official responsibility for their group's policy, as "influentials" they work with each other to develop ways of organizing ameliorative activities that would be mutually acceptable to their own groups. They also work out strategies for influencing their back home policies. One can imagine the delicacy of conducting "track-two" sessions with participants close to decision makers. It is encouraging that their organizers believe they have succeeded in establishing "subjective mutual understanding" in a number of cases and in achieving significant modifications in claims and counterclaims. Their procedures are similar to those we have reported:

1. The facilitator (leader) works with both groups toward identifying the needs underlying the intentions of each group.
2. Achieving mutual understanding of the enduring roots of the conflict between the groups itself reduces tension between the participants and constitutes the first steps in peace building.
3. The facilitator tries to get participants to enlarge perspectives of each group about what might be common or shared concerns rather than group specific interests.
4. Recognitions of each group's "subjective interest," that is, recognition of their human rights, guarantees of security against violent aggression; recognition of the legitimacy of their identity and community are priority goals.

According to Azar and colleagues (1990), who have worked with track-two methods, skilled focus on these sorts of questions seems to facilitate the development of positive "win-win" rather than "zero-sum" outcomes. That is, both groups may plan how to achieve satisfaction of basic (psychological) needs without losses to each other. Once the psychological needs of each group begin to be accommodated, conditions for cooperative negotiations about substantive concerns and conflicts of interest have a better chance of success.

It is hardly necessary to state that none of these types of programs is known to have influenced a particular intergroup conflict. However, collectively, they represent efforts to apply psychological "know-how" to issues of intergroup conflict. At this stage, systematic efforts should be made to evaluate them in terms of the validity of their conceptions, procedures, and effectiveness in real intergroup contexts. Many people who study conflict believe that the kinds of intergroup conflicts we have been discussing are so intransigent that they are inaccessible to psychological mediation. Freud's view, referred to earlier, seems to be in accord with this relatively pessimistic outlook. A somewhat more hopeful view is one that views intergroup conflicts as on a continuum with those of families, clans, and tribes; that is, potentially lethal, but also potentially controllable. It is not that aggression may be eliminated, but that it may be contained. Is it altogether unrealistic to think that intergroup conflict may be ameliorated through using modifications of techniques that are know to us from trying to cope with smaller scale conflicted human relationships?

One might be tempted to dismiss the conception of psychological interventions in intergroup conflict as did Rosenau, the political scientist. "...A pervasive confusion of fact and value, and an unabashed rehashing of long standing concepts that have yet to be proved useful..." (Rosenau, 1965, p. 511). Osgood, the experimental psychologist turned peace researcher, offered a somewhat more hopeful suggestion: "...What is needed is...the dedicated generation of data, and not so much an unyielding commitment to peace as (achieving) comprehension of how to work toward it" (1964). I think that intergroup conflict resolution intervention should be viewed as an area of applied research. The utility (and the defects) of workshops should be examined so that they produce beneficial, not harmful effects. A reasonable start would be to develop greater awareness of what is being done by way of intergroup conflict interventions and how it is being done. Account has also to be taken of the diverse cultural contexts in which conflict resolution workshops are carried out. It will be necessary to evaluate effects on individuals as well as groups, and on representative institutions.

This has been a selective view of psychologists' attempts to understand and to ameliorate intergroup quarrels that escalate into destructive conflict. In the final analysis, it is reasonable to have reservations about the utility of psychological interventions into enduring intergroup conflicts. Perhaps those who protest that psychological intervention strategies are useful only to the "elites" from whom participants are drawn are right. But this, in itself, may be important. A more general—and more ominous—view is that intergroup problems will prove to be refractory to any methods we humans can devise. It seems to me that the only reasonable response to such a gloomy outlook is an empirical one.

REFERENCES

Adorno, T.W., E. Frenkel-Brunswick, D. Levinson, and R.N. Sanford. 1950. *The Authoritarian Personality*. New York: Harper.
Allport, G.W. 1954. *The Nature of Prejudice*. Reading, MA: Addison-Wesley.
Amir, Y. 1969. "The Contact Hypothesis in Ethnic Relations." *Psychological Bulletin* 71: 319-342.
Azar, E.E., J.L. Davies, A.G. Pickering, and H.A. Sahbaze. 1990. In *Annual Review of Conflict Knowledge and Conflict Resolution*, edited by J.J. Gitler. New York: Garland Press.
Back, K.W. 1992. "The Legitimacy of Group Methods." *Duke University Faculty Newsletter*.
Bakan, D. 1966. *The Duality of Human Existence*. Chicago: Rand Mcnally.
Berkowitz, L. 1968. "Aggression: Psychological Aspects." *International Encyclopedia of the Social Sciences* 1: 168-174.
Bargal, D., and M.A. Bar. 1990. "Field Theory and Intergroup Workshops for Arab-Palestinian and Jewish Youth." Presentation, New Brunswick, NJ in honor of Kurt Lewin.

Blake, R.R., and J.S. Mouton. 1962. "Intergroup Therapy." *International Journal of Social Psychiatry* 8: 196-198.

Blake, R.R., and J.S. Mouton. 1978. *The Managerial Grid.* Houston, TX: Gulf Publishing.

Brewer, M.B., and N. Miller. 1984 "Beyond the Contact Hypothesis." In *Groups in Contact: the Psychology of Desegregation,* edited by N. Miller and M.B. Brewer. New York: Academic Press.

Bronfenbrenner, U. 1961. "The Mirror Image in Soviet-American Relations: A Social Psychologist's Report." *Journal of Social Issues* 17: 45-56.

Burrow, T. 1927. "The Group Method of Analysis." *Psychoanalytic Review* 14: 268-280.

Burton, J.C. 1969. *Conflict and Communication: The Use of Controlled Communication in International Relations.* London: Macmillan.

Burton, J.C. 1972. *World Society.* London: Cambridge University Press.

Clark, K.B. 1971. "Pathos of Power." *American Psychologist* 2 (26): 1047-1057.

Dollard, J., L. Doob, N.E. Miller, O.H. Mowrer, and R.R. Sears. 1939. *Frustration and Aggression.* New Haven: Yale University Press.

Doob, L.W. (ed.). 1970. *Resolving Conflict in Africa: The Fermada Workshop.* New Haven: Yale University Press.

Doob, L.W., and W. Foltz. 1973. "The Belfast Workshop: An Application of Group Techniques to Destructive Conflict." *Journal of Conflict Resolution* 17: 489-512.

Durkheim, E. 1953. *Suicide.* Glencoe, IL: Free Press.

Erikson, E. 1954. "Wholeness and Totality: A Psychiatric Contribution." In *Totalitarianism,* edited by D.J. Friedrich. Cambridge: Harvard University Press.

Feshback, S., and R. Singer. 1957. "The Effects of Personality and Shared Trends upon Social Prejudice." *Journal of Abnormal and Social Psychology* 54: 411-416.

Freud, S. 1933. "Unpublished Correspondence Between Messrs. Albert Einstein and Sigmund Freud." Reprinted from S. Freud *Collected Papers vol. 5.* New York: Basic Books.

Fromm, E. 1941. *Escape from Freedom.* New York: Farrar and Rinehart.

Geertz, C. 1973. *Interpretation of Cultures.* New York: Basic Books.

Harty, M., and J. Mocell. 1991. "The First Conflict Resolution Movement: An Attempt to Institutionalize Applied Interdisciplinary Science." *Journal of Conflict Resolution.*

Hebb, D.O., and W.R. Thompson. 1964. "Emotion and Society." In *War,* edited by L. Bramson and G.W. Goethals. New York: Basic Books.

Hewstone, M., and R. Brown (eds.). 1986. *Contact and Conflict in Intergroup Encounters.* Oxford: Basil Blackwell.

Hinkle, S., and J. Schopler. 1986. "Ethnocentrism in the Evaluation of Group Products." In *The Social Psychology of Intergroup Relations,* edited by W.G. Austin and S. Worchel. Monterey, CA: Brooks/Cole.

Horowitz, D.L. 1985. *Ethnic Groups in Conflict.* Berkeley: University of California Press.

Illing, H.A. 1963. "C.G. Jung on the Present Trends in Group Psychotherapy." In *Group Psychotherapy and Group Function,* edited by M. Rosenbaum and M. Berger. New York: Basic Books.

Janis, H.C. 1982. *Groupthink* (2nd ed.). Boston: Houghton-Mifflin.

Kelman, H.C., and S. Cohen. 1986. "Resolution of International Conflict: An Interactional Approach." Pp. 323-342 in *Psychology of Intergroup Relations,* edited by S. Worchel and W.G. Austin. Chicago: Nelson-Hall.

Kelman, H.C. 1991. "Interactive Problem Solving." Pp. 146-160, edited by V.D. Volkan, J.V. Montville, and D.A. Julius. Lexington, MA: Lexington Books.

Lakin, M., J. Lomranz, and M.A. Lieberman. 1969. *Arab and Jew in Israel: Case Study in a Human Relations Approach to Conflict.* Washington, DC: NTL Institute for Applied Behavioral Science.

Levine, R.A., and D.T. Campbell. 1972. *Ethnocentrism: Theories of Conflict, Ethnic Attitudes and Group Behavior."* New York: Wiley.

Levinson, D.J. 1951." Authoritarian Personality and Foreign Policy." Paper presented to American Psychological Association in Convention.

Lewin, K. 1947. *Resolving Social Conflict.* New York: Harper and Row.

Lewin, K. 1948. "Frontiers in Group Dynamics." *Human Relations* 1: 143-145.

Lewin, K. 1951. *Field Theory in Social Science.* New York: Harper and Row.

Miller, A. 1987. *Timebends: A Life.* New York: Grove Press.

Miller, N., and M. Brewer (eds.). 1984. *Groups in Contact: The Psychology of Desegregation.* New York: Academic Press.

Moscovici, S. 1985. *The Age of the Crowd.* Cambridge: Cambridge University Press.

Osgood, C.E. 1964. "The Psychologist in International Affairs." *American Psychologist* 19: 111-118.

Peterson, A. 1982. *Ethnic Identity: Strategies of Diversity.* Bloomington, IN: Indiana University Press.

Pettigrew, T.F. 1986. "The Intergroup Contact Hypothesis Reconsidered." In *Contact and Conflict in Intergroup Encounters,* edited by M. Hewstone and R. Brown. Oxford: Basil Blackwell.

Rosenau, J.N. 1965. "Behavioral Science, Behavioral Scientists, and the Study of International Phenomenon." *Journal of Conflict Resolution* 7: 509-520.

Rothbart, M. 1993. "Intergroup Perception and Social Conflict." In *Conflict Between People and Groups: Causes, Processes, and Resolutions,* edited by S. Worshel and J.A. Simpson. Chicago: Nelson-Hall.

Sherif, M., O.J. Harvey, B.J. White, W.R. Hood, and C. Sherif. 1961. *Intergroup Conflict and Cooperation: The Robbers Cave Experiment.* Norman, OK: University of Oklahoma Press.

Somit, A. 1990. "Humans, Chimps and Baboons: The Biological Basis of Aggression, War, and Peacemaking." *Journal of Conflict Resolution* 34: 531-582.

Sullivan, H.S. 1948. "Toward a Psychology of Peoples." In *The Interpersonal Theory of Psychiatry,* edited by H.S. Sullivan. New York: W.W. Norton.

Sumner, W.G. 1911. *War and Other Essays."* New Haven: Yale University Press.

Tajfel, H. 1984. *The Social Dimension: European Developments in Social Psychology.* Cambridge: Cambridge University Press.

Tajfel, H., and J.C. Turner. 1986. "The Social Identity Theory of Intergroup Behavior." Pp. 7-24 in *Psychology of Intergroup Relations,* edited by S. Worchel and W.G. Austin. Chicago: Nelson-Hall.

Tolman, E.C. 1942. *Drives Toward War.* New York: Appleton-Century- Crofts.

Triandis, H.C. 1976. "The Future of Pluralism." *Journal of Social Issues* 32: 179-191.

White, R.K. 1965. "Images in the Context of International Conflict." In *International Behavior: A Social Psychological Analysis,* edited by H.C. Kelman. New York: Holt, Rinehart, and Winston.

Williams, R.M. 1947. *Reduction of Intergroup Tensions.* New York: Social Science Research Council.

ATTITUDES RELATED TO RACE AND ETHNIC CONFLICT

A. Paul Hare

Attitudes are thoughts and feelings about and tendencies to act toward other persons, concepts, or objects in various situations. Personality is represented by the average of these tendencies over all situations. If an attitude is enacted over a period of time it may become an informal role. If a group or organization finds the role valuable, the role may become formalized. To understand attitudes toward others one must understand the personalities of the actors, the roles that they are playing, the task, and the situation in which the interaction occurs.

The relationship between the attitudes about and between racial and ethnic groups that involves conflict represents one application of a more general theory (cf. Hare 1978 for an earlier version of this perspective). As evidence, first I will describe a set of social-psychological dimensions that underlie the descriptions of self, others, and the situation. Next I will show that only a few studies of attitudes have so far recognized these dimensions explicitly. Finally I will present two applications of this perspective to race and ethnic relations involving conflict. One application draws on data from South Africa, showing that attitudes include conceptions of self as well as conceptions of the other.

Research in Human Social Conflict, Volume 1, pages 79-94.
Copyright © 1995 by JAI Press Inc.
All rights of reproduction in any form reserved.
ISBN: 1-55938-923-0

The second application describes the process of "working through" understandings and feelings about the Holocaust in Hitler's Germany with groups of German and Israeli students. The literature on attitude change and conflict resolution is essentially the same. Thus conflict resolution requires an understanding of self and others in relation to a task in a given situation.

A common definition of attitudes is that given by McGuire. An *attitude* is a response locating an object of thought on dimensions of judgment. Three components of an attitude are cognitive, affective, and conative (1985, p. 242). The cognitive component refers to the set of interpersonal dimensions that are used as a basis for social perception. The affective component includes the associated feelings. In early research evaluation in terms of good or bad, like or dislike, is often the only feeling that is measured. However evaluation is actually a separate dimension. The conative component involves the person's tendency to act in a certain way, often measured by some indication of a tendency to maintain social distance. A *stereotype* is an attitude about the characteristics of members of a social group (DeLamater, 1992, p. 117).

Attitudes about "objects of thought," which may be people or animate or inanimate objects, are associated with attitudes about the self (Hare, Koenigs, and Hare, 1993). The position of other objects in a social field always implies a conception of the position of the self, although the conception of the self may not be explicitly stated. Members of one group cannot see members of another group as dominating without seeing their own group as being forced to submit. Just as there are no leaders without followers, there are no roles without opposing or supporting roles, and there are no attitudes about objects without some opposing or supporting concepts of the self.

Sets of attitudes are joined in support of values. *Values* indicate preferences for certain types of outcomes and for certain types of conduct that will lead to these outcomes (Ball-Rokeach and Loges, 1992, p. 2228). The evaluative component of an attitude, whether one considers an object or type of action as good or bad, is in relation to a preference for a type of outcome represented by one's values. The second example of intergroup attitudes to be given in this paper, involving German and Israeli students "working through" their ideas and feelings about the Holocaust, will demonstrate the connection between one's value position and the possibilities for attitude change.

DIMENSIONS OF ATTITUDES, BEHAVIOR, AND VALUES

In recent years many psychologists have come to agree that a limited number of dimensions can account for most of the variance in descriptions of personality, the "Big Five" (McCrae and John, 1992). Several of these dimensions, or rotations of them, had been identified previously in studies of attitudes, verbal and nonverbal behavior, emotions, and semantic connotations of concepts (Bales, 1985). Current research on the "sociology of emotions" indicated how the cognitive and affective dimensions may be related (cf. Kemper, 1990). The "Big Five" personality dimensions include three dimensions of interpersonal behavior, one of variability, and one of intelligence or problem-solving behavior. Peabody and Goldberg (1989) add two more dimensions to the basic list, an additional dimension of interpersonal behavior, and a measure of evaluation (Good versus Bad).

In many studies of attitudes and of interpersonal behavior the interpersonal dimension of being friendly or unfriendly (warm or cold) was masked by the evaluative component of good-bad. However, as Peabody has demonstrated, members of racial groups can agree on the dimensions of the perceptions of themselves and others while disagreeing on the evaluation. For example, in a study in the Philippines Peabody found that both native Filipinos and persons of Chinese extraction living in the Philippines agree that the Chinese preferred to save their money and the Filipinos preferred to spend it. However the Chinese said that they were "saving" and the Filipinos were "spendthrifts" while the Filipinos said that the Chinese were "stingy" and they were "generous" (Peabody, 1968).

Since at least seven different kinds of intelligence have now been identified (Gardner, 1983) future research will probably include more than one factor or dimension of intellectual activity. Also future theory will probably also include a conceptualization of a complex multidimensional space in which social interaction takes place. However, at present almost all of the studies that identify a number of factors treat them as variables to be measured rather than the dimensions of a social psychological space. Bales is an exception (1970; Bales and Cohen, 1979). He uses a variation of the three interpersonal dimensions that are included in the "Big Five" to define a social psychological field in which persons act, perceive, and relate to others and to objects. The three dimensions are similar to the three dimensions of physical space as they usually appear in a school classroom. The first dimension is dominance versus submission (activity versus inactivity, or "upward" versus "downward" in Bales's terminology). The second dimension is friendly versus unfriendly (positive versus negative, where positive behavior is visualized as being on the right-hand side of the space, facing the front of the room, and negative behavior on the left). The third dimension, which Bales designates as forward versus backward combines task-oriented behavior that conforms to the norms of established authority as forward, as opposed to expressive behavior that is opposed to established authority as backward.

Much of the early research on attitudes with regard to race used a single dimension, such as a measure of "close or distant" (Bogardus, 1925). However, in some early research and some contemporary research questions are asked that would allow the identification of several factors, but the answers to the questions are combined into one single variable such as "prejudice." For example, Pettigrew and Meertens (1993) studied subtle and blatant prejudice using samples of respondents from seven nations in Western Europe. Although the content of some of the ten items on each scale would appear to measure the three dimensions used by Bales, the answers to the items in each set are combined to give a single prejudice score. Examples of research that does identify dimensions of attitudes are Feldman and Hilterman (1975) and Corenblum, Fisher, and Anderson (1976).

IMAGES OF VICTIMS AND VICTIMIZERS IN RACIAL DOMINATION AND GENOCIDE

A theory that explained all of the factors involved in racial domination and genocide would necessarily be complex, as complex as any theory used to analyze the relationships between groups in a society (cf. Charny, 1982). Whether or not one group will dominate another or in the extreme case subject them to genocide will depend on the relative power of the two groups and the willingness of the more powerful group to see those of the less powerful group as a threat (Stryker, 1959).

The focus here is on one aspect of such a theory, namely attitudes about the victims and victimizers in cases of racial domination and genocide, as defined by the United Nations (Brownlie, 1971, pp. 116-120). The cognitive, affective, conative, and evaluative components of attitudes (or values) may be discovered by giving subjects questionnaires, but attitudes can also be inferred from the images that appear in discourse or written material (Bales and Cohen, 1979). However the cognitive component of an attitude is the aspect most frequently reported in studies of domination and genocide. As a further limitation the examples are drawn from two types of victims in the economic area: the middlemen minorities and the labor force (slave) minorities.

In discussing attitudes, the literature on group judgments and national stereotypes represented by the work of Peabody (1985) will be combined with the dimensional analysis of images in interpersonal behavior represented by the work of Bales (1970) and Bales and Cohen (1979). These perspectives can in turn be amplified by the functional analysis of Parsons and Effrat (Effrat, 1968; Loubser, Baum, Effrat, and Lidz, 1976). Taken together these perspectives provide a picture of the way in which the "image" of a victim in racial domination or genocide is related to the position of the victim in the social system and the reciprocal relationship between the image of the victim and the victimizer.

Importance of Social System Variables

Stryker's (1959) analysis of social structure and prejudice documents the importance of social system variables. He compares the experience of three middlemen minorities in the eighteenth and twentieth centuries: Jews in Germany, Armenians in Turkey, and Parsis in India. He is interested in why Jews and Armenians were the subject of prejudice, even genocide, while he found no evidence of anti-Parsism among the Hindus who were the dominant group in the province of Gujarat, India (1959, p. 351). He concludes that "the underlying view is that such systematic prejudice as anti-Semitism results from the conjoining of specific kinds of structural conditions.... a marginal trading people without a strong separatist component would not be subject to prejudice of this order even when set in an expanding nationalist state" (1959, p. 353).

Stryker seems to place the emphasis on whether or not the middlemen minority is separatist or expansionist. He cites the case of India where the Parsis (separatist) do not appear to have been the subject of prejudice from the Hindus while there was antagonism between Hindus and Muslims and Hindus and Christians. Muslims and Christians were described as "expansionist." Since Stryker earlier describes both Jews in eighteenth- and nineteenth-century Germany and the Armenian Christians in nineteenth-century Turkey as "separatist" (1959, pp. 345-346), he has not explained the Jewish and Armenian cases. The difference between these groups and the Parsis seem to be in whether or not the dominant group is expansionist (Germans and Turks), or has a more separatist ideology of castes, each following its own Dharma or duty (Hindus). If the minority group has goods or trade relationships which the majority covet, then prejudice and possibly genocide will follow regardless of whether the minority is separatist or expansionist.

This is of course too simple an explanation to cover all cases of prejudice against middlemen minorities, other variables need to be added. Blalock (1987, p. 84), for example, draws attention to cases where middlemen minorities serve as a scapegoat to inhibit direct attacks against the elite. However the purpose of the present paper is not to provide an overview of theories of domination and genocide, but rather to provide an analysis of the images which form a central component of the attitudes about victims and victimizers.

Social-psychological Analysis of Images

W.I. Thomas is credited with noting the importance of the "definition of the situation" in determining human behavior (Volkart, 1951, p. 7). Once a situation is defined for the individual, the appropriate behavior will follow. It is not necessary that the definition be true. People will act "as if" the situation were true with the same consequences. This point of view has been maintained by functional theorists, following Talcott Parsons, who observe "a well formed definition of the situation is relatively unambiguous in providing the normative grounds for the rationalization of action" (Loubser et al., 1976, p. 144).

Bales takes the idea of defining the situation a step further by emphasizing that people tend to present definitions of situations or aspects of situations or other persons in terms of "images." An image is defined as "a picture of an emotionally loaded focus of attention" (Bales and Cohen, 1979, p. 167). The behavior of an individual tends to follow from the images in his or her mind. Bales's definition of image thus contains both the cognitive and affective components of "attitude" and assumes that the conative component will follow. Bales has developed a scheme for classifying images in terms of three interpersonal dimensions, as described earlier, plus evaluation. But before considering Bales's or other theories in detail, let us examine an example of a set of traits used to form an image of a "middleman minority" group.

Here is a description of a group of people who were the object of genocide in fairly recent history:

> Ironically it is their hard work and their success that have contributed to make the...so unpopular in.... Other characteristics are adduced to explain the antipathy they manage to generate; they are pushful, uppity and aggressive say the detractors ambitious and energetic say the defenders. They are money-loving and mercenary says one school; canny and thrifty says the other. Clannish and unscrupulous in grabbing advantages, say some; united and quick to realize the advantages of education, say others.

This description is similar to that given for Jews in Germany, Chinese in Indonesia, or Indians in Uganda. Actually, it is a description of the Ibo in Nigeria at the time of the genocide before and during the struggle for independence in Biafra (Forsyth, 1969, p. 106). This description is also representative of the type of trait list usually used to stereotype persons who are the subject of prejudice. For example, Allport in his classic book, *The Nature of Prejudice* cites a study done in the United States in 1932 which reports the following list of traits ascribed to Jews (Allport 1954, p. 192): shrewd, mercenary, industrious, grasping, intelligent, ambitious, and sly. The Ibo example also illustrates the common fact that members of the minority group and their detractors may agree on the descriptive elements in the traits but disagree on the evaluative aspect. That is, what one side sees as good, the other side sees as bad (Merton, 1968, p. 482).

Following Allport's general line of research, a set of studies has been conducted to determine the number of independent aspects of dimensions represented in lists of traits like those given here. Although more dimensions can be added in the future using the seven dimensions identified earlier, a beginning has been made using three dimensions similar to those of Bales plus evaluation.

Bales provides an extensive discussion and illustration of the way in which salient images may polarize or unify a group (Bales and Cohen, 1979, pp. 31-57). Group members may be unified by conforming to a positive image or by moving away from a negative image. One device of an authoritarian leader is to divert negative reactions from himself or herself by focusing the group's attention on a scapegoat who is depicted as being even more negative. Bales observes that "many or most individuals try energetically to get rid of anything about themselves that does not fit with their desired self-picture and social image. Perhaps the commonest defense of the self-picture is to 'project' the undesired aspects of the self or the social image on to other persons involved in the interaction, to some outside group, to the society, or to some situational or fantasy object" (Bales and Cohen, 1979, pp. 197-198). Another version is to create an image of another person or group that complements and enhances one's own self-image.

Although Bales' theory and method provides for a complex, multilevel analysis of group behavior, using three interpersonal dimensions plus evaluation, a four-dimensional scheme appears to give a better fit with the analysis of Peabody and Goldberg and with functional analysis (Hare, 1982, pp. 100-105).

Examples of Images in the Economic Area With and Without Genocide

Middlemen minorities and black minorities, when they have slave or near slave status in societies dominated by whites, both fall in the economic area. Images of these groups emphasize the forward-backward dimension. The middlemen, for example Jews, are seen as serious, tight, and high on achievement motivation. In contrast blacks are seen as expressive, loose, and low in achievement motivation. The images also include traits associated with the other two dimensions: Jews are seen as dominant and negative; blacks are seen as submissive and positive.

The traits included in the stereotypic images of Jews and blacks tend to appear across cultures. The list of traits associated with Jews in the United States as reported by Allport (1954, p. 192) has already been noted. From the same study Allport provides a list of traits associated with the stereotype of blacks: superstitious, lazy, happy-go-lucky, ignorant, and musical. Allport goes on to elaborate, in a manner similar to Bales's later analysis, the way in which the psychological mechanism of projection may have been operating for the average white American during the period. The black reflects the impulses of the "Id" while the Jew reflects the violations of the "Superego." According to this psychoanalytic interpretation, ethnic hostility is a projection of unacceptable inner striving onto a minority group (Allport, 1954, p. 199). Although it appears that societal factors play a more important part in prejudice than psychological factors, this psychological mechanism of projection can add fuel to the fire of prejudice to bring the emotional heat to the kindling point.

LeVine and Campbell have noted this causal chain. The hostility to the out-group comes first and then, in the service of this hostility, all possible differences between the out-group and the in-group are opportunistically interpreted as despicable. The most plausibly despicable traits are given the most attention (LeVine and Campbell, 1972, p. 170). As Allport pointed out rather early (1954, p. 233) and J. Levin (1975, p. 127) and Wellman (1977, p. 62) more recently, the hostility arises because the minority group represents some threat to the privileges of the majority. Prejudice is a "mask for privilege."

In the case of South Africa, Adam (1971, p. 10) observed, referring to an earlier period in the history of the country: "it is, therefore, not the right of the White tribe to live in South Africa that is questionable, but its privileged political and economic status compared with the majority of the country's population, and a policy that aims at ensuring its continuation." Adam goes on to say: "Ethnic identification should be seen as the result of efforts by under-privileged groups to improve their lot through collective mobilization, or conversely, the efforts of a super-ordinate group to preserve the privileges they enjoy by exploiting subjected groups" (1971, p. 22). This domination was carried on within the law rather than outside it (Sachs, 1975; Kane-Berman, 1978).

The image projected of Jews by propaganda in Hitler's Germany has been well documented. At worst they were seen as the diabolical enemy, unalterably foreign, and conspiratorial (N. Levin, 1973, p. 14). In Bales's scheme they were projected as being upward-negative-backward. That is, they were classified with revolutionaries who were plotting the destruction of Germany and German life. At best Jews were described as criminals who practiced ritual murder (Hilberg, 1973, p. 656). Again in Bales's terms negative-backward. In contrast, German leaders projected an image of themselves as good, natural leaders, whose only concern was for the group (Bales: upward-positive-forward). For example, Himmler is quoted as saying: "We had a moral right vis-à-vis our people to annihilate this people who wanted to annihilate us" (Hilberg, 1973, p. 656). This image given to the victim is designed to justify and enhance the image projected of the victimizer, especially to justify any negative or dominating behavior on his or her part.

Images of Whites and Blacks in South Africa

Data concerning the images of whites and blacks in South Africa are drawn from research conducted by du Preez during time that apartheid was in force and published in a book, *The Politics of Identity* (1980). Du Preez undertook a content analysis of the Debates of the House of Assembly of the Republic of South Africa on the subject of local African affairs during three one-year periods: 1948, the year the National Party came into power, 1958, and 1968. He compiled a dictionary of the main "constructs" used in the debates. The main concerns during this time were white identity and survival, African identity and survival, the threat of conflict, economic interest, African welfare, and moral and ethical arguments. Although it is evident that problems of identity and survival were not the only issues of concern, du Preez shows them to be the most frequent concern in his sample of arguments.

Du Preez focused on the structure of the identities ascribed to whites and blacks. He based his analysis primarily on "clear cases," for example, the statement made in the House of Assembly that "We should assist the Native to develop according to his own nature and capabilities, and his own traditions, and we should assist him to develop through our guardianship" (1980, p. 86). The following pairs of constructs (dimensions) occurred most frequently (du Preez, 1980, p. 90):

1. Adult-child: whites are construed as adults relative to childish blacks, or more benevolently as guardians of blacks.
2. Traditional-modern: A reflection of the commonplace notion of differences between traditional and modern ways.
3. Estranged-natural: This refers to estrangement from one's own people and attempts to imitate those of a different group (imitation whites, agitators, kaffir-boeties).

In his discussion of the reciprocal nature of identities of white and black, du Preez adds a fourth dimension of evaluation. That is, some combinations of these dimensions are seen as good and others as bad. Again we find a similarity between these four dimensions of constructs and the dimensions of group judgments and interpersonal behavior.

In his book du Preez draws two figures based on the data for the National Party to show the relationships between the system of constructs and the evaluations attached to them and to show the complementary identities they represent. For the constructs, white is superior to black and this superiority is highly valued. For both white and black, traditionalism is positively valued and estrangement is negatively valued. The Trekker was the good Afrikaner of yesteryear who helped the simple tribesman as an adult would a child. The counterpart of the modern Afrikaner of the 1960s was the African Nationalist who developed his homeland into an independent state while still making it possible for his tribesmen to provide migrant labor for South Africa and allowed the South African government and individual entrepreneurs to assist in modernizing his country. Both white and black agitators were viewed with alarm as disturbing the nature of things. Thus for the ideal type of modern Afrikaner, in this earlier period of South Africa's history, the ideal modern black had no "human rights" within South Africa since they were all supposed to be supplied by the homeland. What the white did need was a willing worker (without his family) (Kane-Berman, 1978, pp. 230-252). The whites were seen as good, paternal, natural leaders with the hope that the blacks would play their part as willing workers. If blacks took on rebellious agitator roles severe punishment was administered (Sachs, 1975, p. 229; Kane-Berman, 1978, pp.

37-48). But whites did not propose genocide since blacks provided a necessary part of the labor force.

WORKING THROUGH THE CONSEQUENCES OF THE HOLOCAUST IN ISRAELI AND GERMAN STUDENT SEMINARS

Just as an understanding of the interpersonal dimensions that lie behind attitudes helps to place the images people hold about racial and ethnic groups in a larger social psychological field, so the dimensions can also be used to locate value positions that are in conflict and determine the likelihood that individuals with different value positions will be able to derive more complex solutions to the conflict rather than simplistic solutions.

An example of this type of dimensional analysis is the following summary of research on the extent of change in the process of "working through" the consequences of the Holocaust as observed in two seminars of university students, one in Israel and the other in Germany (Bar-On, Hare, and Chaitin, 1993). The students' value positions with regard to the main value dilemma evident in the group discussions, as indicated on Bales' (SYMLOG) value questionnaires, were compared with the amount of change in working through. Based on Tetlock's (1986) analysis of the relationship between individuals' abilities to reach complex solutions, depending on their value position in relation to the value dilemma they face, the value positions of students in both seminars were ranked according to the expected amount of change that would be apparent in the working through process. In both student groups a high rank based on the SYMLOG questionnaire was associated with more change in the process of working through.

Research involving 2,200 Israelis and Germans on attitudes of youth toward the Holocaust had suggested the existence of a "vicious circle" linking their political and social current attitudes and their attitudes toward the Holocaust that impaired their ability to "work through" the past (Bar-On, 1990; Bar-On, Beiner, and Brusten, 1991; Bar-On, Hare, Brusten, and Beiner, in press; Novey, 1962). Whereas the Israelis tended to overgeneralize the relevance of the Holocaust, the Germans tended to underestimate its relevance. This research was followed by year-long seminars with university students in both Israel and Germany in an attempt to enhance personal working through to arrive at a more differentiated "partial relevance" understanding.

A description of the interaction within and between the groups of Israeli and German university students who participated in the year-long seminars has been reported elsewhere (Bar-On, 1992). In addition to the semi-structured group discussions, members of each seminar held personal interviews with persons of the first and second generation after the Holocaust, took part in reciprocal visits in the two countries which included trips to Holocaust memorials and discussions on the topic, and carried out individual research projects. Each group was facilitated by a faculty member with experience in group dynamics.

The principle hypothesis for this study is based on the work of Tetlock (1986) who observed that the extent to which individuals find more complex solutions to a conflict of value positions is related to their own ranking of the importance of the two sides of the value conflict. He used the Rokeach Value Survey to have individuals rank order the value positions according to their preference. Then he asked them to consider a problem involving values, for example, whether one is willing to pay higher taxes to assist the poor, thus activating a conflict between a concern for personal property and a concern for social equality. He gave subjects five minutes to write down their thoughts on the question and to take a yes or no stand on the policy question. He then judged the responses on their integrative complexity. He found that subjects who place a high rank on the position represented by only one side of the conflict will tend to suggest simpler solutions in line with their value preference. Those subjects who give equal rank to both sides of the conflict are more likely to provide more integrated and complex solutions.

Applying Tetlock's ideas to the value ratings of students in the Israeli and German seminars, it was hypothesized that students whose values supported group teamwork were able to "work through" the issues regarding the Holocaust more effectively assuming that their position was a position midway in the main value conflict represented by the authoritarian versus the humanitarian position. Milgram (1963) had also noted that this was the main value conflict in his experiments.

In terms of Bales' field theory (Bales and Cohen, 1979; Hare, 1989) the continuum from authoritarian values to humanitarian values represents a diagonal in a square space (see Figure 1a) where the horizontal axis goes from unfriendly (negative) values on the left to friendly (positive) values on the right. The vertical axis goes from values accepting authority (forward) at the top to values opposing authority (backwards) at the bottom. The third value dimension from dominant (upward) to submissive (downward) is represented by the size of the circle surrounding the point representing a subject's position with regard to the positive-negative and forward-backward dimensions. The larger the circle, the more dominant is the subject.

In this value space the authoritarian-humanitarian continuum lies along the diagonal from NF, at the upper left corner, to PB, at the lower right corner. Thus the field theory value positions of PF (friendly-accepting authority, favoring group teamwork) and NB (unfriendly-nonacceptance of authority) would both appear in the center of the authoritarian-humanitarian continuum if only the authoritarian scale were used. However, in terms of field theory, only persons on the positive side of the space and midway between the positions

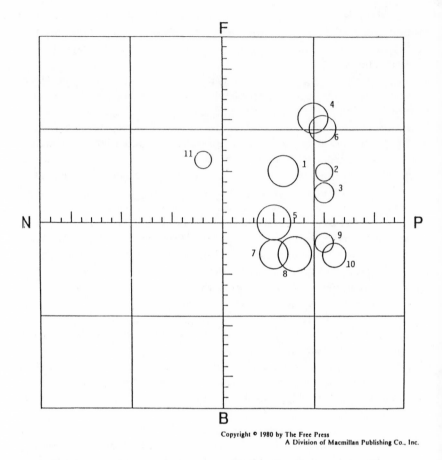

Figure 1a. German Group: Vale positions on SYMLOG field diagram

in conflict (PF in this case) would be able to find integrated and complex solutions. Persons whose values are on the negative side of the space (NB in this case) would be in radical opposition to the PF persons and might even become scapegoats in a value laden discussion if the authoritarian and humanitarian persons sought a scapegoat as a way of bringing some unity into the group.

When group members are placed in rank order according to the likelihood that they would develop integrated and complex solutions as a result of working through the main value dilemma in the discussions of the Holocaust, the persons with PF values would rank highest, next those with PB values, then NF values, and lowest NB values. An additional reason why one might expect persons with PF values to be able to work through the problem is that they are task oriented enough (forward) to be interested in working through, and

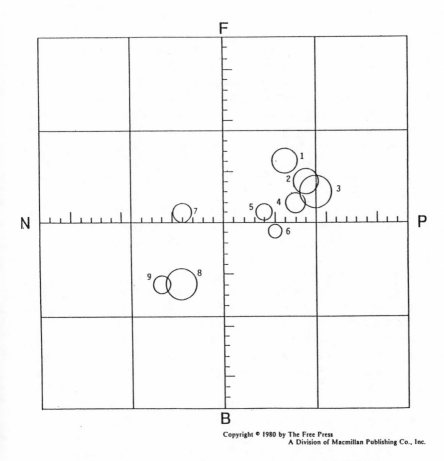

Figure 1b. Israeli Group: Value positions on SYMLOG field diagram

friendly enough (positive) to have a set of group members giving social support to their attempts to work through.

The participants in the study were two groups of university students. One group was comprised of eleven German undergraduates at a German university and the other of nine Israeli undergraduates in a university in Israel.

Several times during the life of each group the facilitators and members made ratings of all group members using German and Hebrew translations of the Bales' value questionnaire (Bales and Cohen, 1979; Hare, 1989). Ratings were made of the values of each group member, as well as the values that the rater would tend to wish for or reject, and how the rater expected to be rated. At the end of the year the principal facilitator of each seminar group ranked each of the members on the extent to which they had been able to work through their attitudes toward the Holocaust.

The median of the ratings made by the group facilitators and two or three group members who had similar ideas concerning the ideal values that should be exhibited in this type of "group dynamics" seminar (namely being supportive of members regardless of their task orientation, or PB, positive-backward) was used as an indication of the values of each group member. The median scores for the German students are represented in Figure 1a. The circles representing the value positions of the students appear mainly in two clusters. One cluster, of five persons, is in the PF quadrant and the other, of four persons, in the PB quadrant. One student is only P (neither F nor B) and one student is in the NF quadrant.

The median scores for the Israeli students are represented in Figure 1b. Their value positions are more dispersed than those of the German students. Five students are in the PF quadrant, one in the PB quadrant, one in the NF quadrant, and two in the NB quadrant.

Three dimensional value scores for members of each group were placed in a rank order with those closest to the center of the positive-forward quadrant given the highest ranks. A score that was dominant (upward) was given a higher rank that one that was submissive (downward). Second highest ranks were persons in the positive-backward quadrant, next the negative-forward quadrant, and finally those in the negative-backward quadrant. The rank order of a student's value position is given by a number next to the circle in each of the field diagrams.

For both the German and Israeli group the amount of "working through" as judged by the group's facilitator was positively associated with the rank order of the student's value position. This supports Tetlock's hypothesis that an individual with a value position midway between the poles of a value dilemma is more likely to be able to work through the dilemma to reach a more complex solution.

As yet, the literature on attitudes, attitude change, and social perception has not been brought together in one framework. When that happens we will expect to find that all of these phenomena can be understood in the context of a field theory in which individuals and groups interacting in a n-dimensional space seek agreement on a definition of the situation that will allow them to reach preferred goals either together or apart.

REFERENCES

Adam, H. 1971. *Modernizing Racial Domination*. Berkeley: University of California Press.
Allport, G.W. 1954. *The Nature of Prejudice*. Reading, MA: Addison-Wesley.
Bales, R.F. 1970. *Personality and Interpersonal Behavior*. New York: Holt Rinehart & Winston.

Bales, R.F. 1985. "The New Field Theory in Social Psychology." *International Journal of Small Group Research* 1(1): 1-18.

Bales, R.F., and S.P. Cohen. 1979. *SYMLOG: A System for the Multiple Level Observation of Groups.* New York: Free Press.

Ball-Rokeach, S.J., and W.E. Loges. 1992. "Value Theory and Research." Pp. 2222-2228 in *Encyclopedia of Sociology* (volume 4), edited by E.F. Borgatta and M.L. Borgatta. New York: Macmillan and Maxwell.

Bar-on, D. 1990. "Children of Perpetrators of the Holocaust: Working through One's Own Moral Self." *Psychiatry* 53: 229-245.

Bar-On, D. 1992. "Israeli and German Students Encounter the Holocaust." *Group Tensions* 22 (2): 81-118.

Bar-On, D., F. Beiner, and M. Brusten. 1991. "The Holocaust and its Relevance to Current Social Issues in the Federal Republic of Germany and Israel." Pp. 214-220 in *Der Holocaust-Familiale und Gesellschactliche Folgen-Aufarbeiung in Wissenschaft und Erziehung?*, edited by D. Bar-On, F. Beiner, and M. Brusten. Wuppertal: University of Wuppertal.

Bar-On, D., A.P. Hare, M. Brusten, and F. Beiner. in press. "'Working through' the Holocaust? Comparing the Questionnaire Results of German and Israeli Students."

Bar-On, D., A.P. Hare, and J. Chaitin. 1993. "Working through the Consequences of the Holocaust in Israeli and German Student Seminars." Report to German-Israeli Foundation.

Blalock, H.M., Jr. 1967. *Toward a Theory of Minority-group Relations.* New York: Wiley.

Bogardus, E.S. 1925. "Measuring Social Distance." *Journal of Applied Sociology* 9: 299-308.

Brownlie, I. 1971. *Basic Documents in Human Rights.* London: Oxford.

Charny, I.W. with C. Rappaport. 1982. *How can we Commit the Unthinkable? Genocide: The Human Cancer.* Boulder, CO: Westview Press.

Corenblum, B., D.G. Fisher, and K. Anderson. 1976. "Occupational Differences and Attributions of Trait Adjectives to Ethnic Groups." *Psychological Reports* 39 (2): 535-542.

DeLamater, J.D. 1992. "Attitudes." Pp. 117-124 in *Encyclopedia of Sociology* (volume 1), edited by E.F. Borgatta and M.L. Borgatta. New York: Macmillan and Maxwell.

du Preez, P. 1980. *The Politics of Identity.* Oxford: Basil Blackwell.

Effrat, A. 1968. "Editor's Introduction: Applications of Parsonian Theory." *Sociological Inquiry* 38(3): 97-103.

Feldman, J.M., and R.J. Hilterman. 1975. "Stereotype Attribution Revisited: The Role of Stimulus Characteristics, Racial Attitude, and Cognitive Differentiation." *Journal of Personality and Social Psychology* 31(6): 1177-1188.

Forsyth, F. 1969. *The Biafra Story.* Harmondsworth, UK: Penguin.

Gardner, H. 1983. *Frames of Mind: The Theory of Multiple Intelligence.* New York: Basic Books.

Hare, A.P. 1978. "Images of Victims and Victimizers in Racial Domination." Paper presented as Second International Conference on Psychological Stress and Adjustment in Time of War and Peace, Jerusalem, Israel.

Hare, A.P. 1982. *Creativity in Small Groups.* Beverly Hills: Sage.

Hare, A.P. 1989. "New Field Theory: SYMLOG Research, 1960-1988." Pp. 229-267 in *Advances in Group Processes* (volume 6), edited by E. Lawlor. Greenwich, CT: JAI Press.

Hare, A.P., R.J. Koenigs, and S.E. Hare. 1993. "Implicit Personality Theory and Social Desirability: In the Context of New Field Theory SYMLOG." Paper presented at meeting for the Society for Experimental Social Psychology, Santa Barbara, CA.

Hilberg, R. 1973. *The Destruction of European Jews.* New York: New Viewpoints.

Kane-Berman, J. 1978. *SOWETO: Black Revolt, White Reaction.* Johannesburg: Raven.

Kemper, T.D. 1990. "Social Relations and Emotions: A Structural Approach." Pp. 207-237 in *Research Agendas in the Sociology of Emotions*, edited by T.D. Kemper. Albany: State University of New York Press.

Levin, J. 1975. *The Functions of Prejudice.* New York: Harper and Row.

Levin, N. 1973. *The Holocaust*. New York: Schoken.

LeVine, R.A., and D.T. Campbell. 1972. *Ethnocentrism: Theories of Conflict, Ethnic Attitudes and Group Behavior*. New York: Wiley.

Loubser, J.J., R.C. Baum, A. Effrat, and V. Lidz. 1976. *Explorations in General Theory in Social Science: Essays in Honor of Talcott Parsons*. New York: Free Press.

McCrae, R.R., and O.P. John. 1992. "An Introduction to the Five Factor Model and its Implications." *Journal of Personality* 60 (2): 175-215.

Merton, R.K. 1968. *Social Theory and Social Structure*. New York: Free Press.

McGuire, W.J. 1985. "Attitudes and Attitude Change." Pp. 233-346 in *Handbook of Social Psychology*, edited by G. Lindzey and E. Aronson. New York: Random House.

Milgram, S. 1963. "Behavioral Study of Obedience." *Journal of Abnormal and Social Psychology* 67(4): 371-378.

Novey, S. 1962. "The Principle of 'working through' in Psychoanalysis." *Journal of the American Psychoanalytic Association* 10: 658-676.

Peabody, D. 1968. "Group Judgements in the Philippines: Evaluative and Descriptive Aspects." *Journal of Personality and Social Psychology* 10: 290-300.

Peabody, D. 1985. *National Characteristics*. Cambridge: Cambridge University Press.

Peabody, D., and L.R. Goldberg. 1989. "Some Determinants of Factor Structures from Personality-trait Descriptors." *Journal of Personality and Social Psychology* 57: 552-567.

Pettigrew, T.F., and R.W. Meertens. 1993. "Subtle and Blatant Prejudice." Paper presented at meetings of Society for Experimental Social Psychology, Santa Barbara, CA.

Sachs, A. 1975. "Instruments of Domination in South Africa." Pp. 223-249 in *Change in Contemporary South Africa*, edited by L. Thompson and J. Butler. Berkeley: University of California Press.

Stryker, S. 1959. "Social Structure and Prejudice." *Social Problems* 6(4): 340-354.

Tetlock, P.E. 1986. "A Value Pluralism Model of Ideological Reasoning." *Journal of Personality and Social Psychology* 50(4): 819-827.

Volkart, E.H. 1951. *Social Behavior and Personality: Contributions of W. I. Thomas to Theory and Social Research*. New York: Social Science Research Council.

Wellman, D. T. 1977. *Portraits of White Racism*. Cambridge: Cambridge University Press.

RACIAL AND ETHNIC CONFLICT:
PERSPECTIVES FROM ECONOMICS

Robert L. Carter

INTRODUCTION

One could arbitrarily select almost any area of human social activity for an analysis of the cognitive and resolutive aspects of conflict. This is so because not only is conflict endemic to social life, and ubiquitous to boot, but, it seems ours is an age in which conflict is celebrated. We speak of "taking it to them," or "in your face" as if these are newly discovered principles of social interaction.

Thus while we may have become more accepting of conflict, we, as social scientists, should never take it for granted. We must continue to interrogate its nature cognitive dimensions, and try to understand the conditions necessary for its development and control. From acts of domestic violence to organized war, it is clear that certain aspects of conflict must be controlled or we as a species will not flourish.

All this I believe to be true in the most general way. But I seek to focus on a more limited terrain of social conflict, namely racial and ethnic conflict in an era of putative declining economic growth, increasing societal, structuation, and the proliferation of group identity as a driving force in social

Research in Human Social Conflict, Volume 1, pages 95-113.
ISBN: 1-55938-923-0

organization. We must not only understand the social bases of continuing racial and ethnic conflict, we must understand its cognitive base; that is, we must understand how those caught up in various kinds of social conflict situate themselves, understand, and experience the conflict.

In this paper I will present empirical data, rational argument, and speculation from historical and contemporary economic perspectives relative to what has been happening over the last three decades, in the conflict dimensions of intergroup relations in the United States. What is presently going on, and what is developing, or is likely to develop in the immediate years ahead.

These relationships have multiple dimensions and I will focus deeply on the economic aspects of ongoing racial conflict, realizing quite well that other aspects are important. Economic perspectives are the foundations for understanding modern race relations. As Joe Feagin (1986) argues, "modern race relations begins in the late 1400's with Pope Alexander VI's bill of demarcation and the treaty of Tordesillas between Spain and Portugal." These two diplomatic instruments, according to Feagin, "put all the heathen peoples and their resources" at the disposal of European nations, beginning first with Spain and Portugal. Thereafter, it was as if all exploits of others, non-European nations, were minimally fair, and even sanctioned by God. Thus, began, arguably the social, political, and economic quagmire from which European nations, with their generally capitalist means of production, would spend the next five hundred years trying to extricate themselves.

The story of American race relations from an economic perspective is one crucial part of this much larger, world-scale, economic story.

RACE AND ECONOMICS

Practically speaking, the economics of race relations in this country began with the Trans-Atlantic slave trade. True, it must be noted that Native Americans (so-called Indians) were here before any of the rest of us, and that they were, from all I can tell, doing just fine, economically and otherwise. They never could be made into mere economic artifices for European consumption and purposes, and thus not only had, in the European imagination, to be subdued but destroyed. Aided by various pernicious myths, genocide nearly completely happened (Fitzpatrick, 1992).

Blacks, on the other hand, were a different story. The heavy labor needs of colonial America were met by the then increasing enslavement of African workers (Feagin, 1986). While this story is generally well known, authors differ in their assignment of the pivotal explanatory roles of slavery as a system of labor (Genovese, 1966) or as a functionally more dialectical system of relations between the dominators and the dominated (Patterson, 1982).

Three things, however, are clear about the place of slavery in American history and economic development:

1. that, formally, slavery was predominantly an institution of the agrarian American South (Cox, 1948);
2. that the system of African exploitation in the Americas, which is what slavery was, provided much of the economic basis for subsequent industrial development of the entire United States (Perelman, 1977; Allen, 1974);
3. that the legacy of slavery is directly implicated in the current status of contemporary African Americans in the social structure of American society, and is productive of continuous racial conflict.

AN ECONOMIC CASTE

Since the end of slavery after the Civil War, blacks have been relegated to the lowest, dirtiest, most menial occupations in American society. Nieman (1991) points out that with most nonagricultural jobs closed to blacks after the Civil War and on into the twentieth century, "Blacks were segregated into the least desirable, lowest paying, most vulnerable positions...." Clearly much of this changed in the early part of the twentieth century, but it left blacks as a virtual caste within the occupational structure of American society, a caste so nearly rigid that white immigrants generally became more successful, materially, than native or immigrant blacks (Butcher, 1994; Chiswick, 1978). Moreover, throughout the 1940s and 1950s the relative economic positions of blacks to whites remained flat, and perhaps, even deteriorated (Smith, 1984). It would be the mid-1960s before a contrary pattern—one in which comparable years of education begin to close the white/black income gap—was discovered to be developing. This led to even greater emphasis on the *Human Capital* argument (Smith, 1984), that is, the role of education and on-the-job training as the basic preconditions for blacks moving ever closer to bridging the income gap.

However pertinent and truthful the *Human Capital* argument may prove to be in explaining the existence and/or elimination of a racial income gap after the mid-1960s, the radical changes brought about in the political status of blacks by political changes since *Brown*, the 1964 Civil Rights Act, and the 1965 Voting Rights Act, had in no sense been matched by changes in the economic status of blacks. In fact, as a corollary to a "dual labor market" there had nearly developed a dual society, "One black One white" (The Kerner Commission Report, 1968) by 1965. Though there clearly was improvement of blacks' absolute economic status since World War II, white economic improvement was also substantial (Feagin, 1986). Thus, for example, Feagin puts it, "in hard times and good times black unemployment rate has stayed about twice that of whites, leaving the overall economic picture somewhat murky.

RACE, LABOR MARKETS, AND PUBLIC POLICY

Surely there was improvement in both the absolute occupational and economic status of blacks, as well as the income gap relative to whites in post-1960s America (Heckman and Payner, 1989). Something real and economically significant did happen. In the next few pages I try to define what did happen and with what results for blacks in American Society.

To accomplish this I review research seeking to explain what has happened to the black population, to some extent *before* Myrdal (1944), and certainly *since* his monumental work. This research can be explained by four competing theories, according to King (1993). She notes these as (1) an improvement in black men's human capital, (2) economic growth and tight labor markets, (3) government intervention in the labor market, and (4) the pressure of sociopolitical movements both directly on business and indirectly via the government.

The Human Capital Story

Representative of this approach is the work of Smith and Welch (1989). They present data showing that the economic gains of the black U.S. population between 1940 and 1980 were sufficient, not only to begin to significantly bridge the black/white income gap, but to produce a sizeable black middle class. Moreover, Smith and Welch believe that "slowly evolving historical forces—education and migration—were the primary, determinant of Black economic improvement" (p. 55).

These authors produce data showing significant growth in wage ratios by education level. "Black male wages rose relative to whites between 1940 and 1980 at every schooling level," in fact, according to these researchers, even surpassing white men (p. 527). While Smith and Welch recognize that there has always been controversy surrounding the question of the role of education in shaping the economic history and present plight of blacks, they, nevertheless, conclude that: (1) the historical record strongly challenges the view that education is not a route to economic improvement for blacks; (2) the next two most powerful explanatory variables in accounting for black economic progress between 1940 and 1980 are concentration of the black population in the South and increasing urbanization; subsequent migration out of the South and a shift from rural to urban within the South were critical to narrowing the income gap; (3) A new black leadership group—apparently more market orientated—gives reason for optimism as to continued black economic progress, while at the same time, (4) a still large black "underclass" may persist well into the future.

Economic Growth and Tight Labor Markets

In the context of a discussion of black economic progress the concept of "tight labor market" is crucial to understand, and functionally necessary for, black employment because very often in American history blacks found employment only when and where there were no others available and/or willing to take the jobs. In this sense, black economic prospects were a function of the ups and downs of white male employment. If times were especially good for whites, certain menial jobs not taken by them became available to blacks and sustain marginal subsistence.

Heckman and Payner (1989) argue, cogently, I think, that the concept of the "tightness" of labor markets is "the only viable alternative to the story of government as the agent of change in the [South Carolina] textile industry" (p. 173). They find the human capital thesis less compelling as an account of black economic progress, since large groups of blacks possessing the essentially low skills necessary for the textile industry were still heavily unemployed between 1960 and 1970.

Indeed, it makes intuitive sense that a booming economy of the mid-1960s would have absorbed any excess white farm labor, creating the incentive to "draw on new sources of low wage labor...." In a further, important speculation, these authors assert that "what cannot be dismissed and indeed seems quite plausible is that in 1965 entrepreneurs seized on the new federal legislation and decrees to do what they wanted to do anyway" (p. 174). Thus driven by market necessity, these owners could claim either to be "doing the right thing," with government prodding of course, or, alternatively and depending on audience, that they are being forced by government to violate the generally historic and accepted pattern of Jim Crow. Either way the confluence of law, morality and necessity could be good for the pockets of the entrepreneurs.

Government Intervention: The Continuing Controversy

Of all the efforts to improve the negatively constructed economic position of blacks in American society, government intervention in markets, especially labor markets, has been most controversial. Even while citizens have enjoyed the benefits of government programs of assorted types, they have also criticized government's "meddling" in, presumably, our business. This, of course has far more to do with technical economic factors. But again, the fundamental questions of economic livelihood and survival interpenetrate all others.

Specifically, the government intervention and legislation under consideration are the various efforts called affirmative action. Benjamin Ringer (1993) has said that "few issues have aroused more hostility and controversy in academic circles than has that of Affirmative Action" (p. 325). Arguably nothing has more distorted and inflamed the actual nature and workplace application of affirmative action than has academic discourse that has been more ideological than scholarly or incisive. Leonard (1990) has stated that "Affirmative Action is one of the most controversial government intervention into the labor market since the abolition of slavery" (p. 47). And though Smith and Welch (1989) are deeply imbedded into the explanatory power of the human capital story as productive of black economic progress, they allow (p. 557), that there is an indirect effect of affirmative action on the wages of black men via its effect on education.

Two important researchers (Freeman, 1973; Leonard, 1990) find significant impact of affirmative action in the past on "promoting the integration of blacks into the workplace" (Leonard, 1990, p. 62). Further, as Leonard points out, affirmative action is criticized both on the basis that it does not work, as well as for the claim that it does not work. A number of empirical studies argue that AA is effective, others say that it is not. There remains, after twenty odd years of research, no definitive, no dispositive answers to the question. There is some agreement that it works in certain industries and to certain extents.

While as a program intending to have economic impact on targeted groups, AA is rightly evaluated through econometrics, however, much of the conflict surrounding AA is a conflict of ideology, of world views and presuppositions. In this respect, Hawkesworth (1988) has written a very useful analysis of AA showing how "fundamental differences in the understanding of the nature of individual identity and freedom not only shapes the interpretation of contemporary social life, but structures the very capacity to perceive the existence of discrimination in the contemporary United States" (p. 119). It became impossible to see the status quo of taken-for-granted privileges as discriminatory, as other than entitlements.

To the extent that many citizens do not even perceive continuing discrimination as problematic, coupled with a sluggishly performing economy in the early to mid-1970s, there is, for me, little wonder that affirmative action is viewed as an unnecessary, derisive program of preferential treatment for blacks, and should be the object of a scorn so deep as to endanger the mental and physical health of proponents and opponents of Affirmative Action. Add to this collective mentality the demagoguery of some politicians and you get the volatile mix that gives social expression to what might have remained latent conflict. In large measure racial conflict, latent or expressed, is driven by varying perceptions of whether the society is fair and just or not.

African Americans generally believe that there is still too much racial discrimination in the United States. Fully three quarters believe both that there exist too much discrimination and that the push for equal rights is moving "too slow" (The National Urban League, 1990). And this finding is reported to be up from forty-seven percent on the same question in 1970 (Feagin, 1986). Thus, from virtually any way in which the issue of affirmative action is viewed, it merely signals deeper perceptions and experience of social division as between blacks and whites in contemporary America. Affirmative Action does not cause these divisions, nor will its demise eliminate them. For this gulf between black and white is part of the much larger identity of what it means to be American and has been present since the founding of the country. In these United States we continue to struggle to form a different sense of who we are; one shaped by the promise of the ideals contained in the American Declaration of Independence and the Preamble to its Constitution. This promise suggested *citizen* as the highest status within the body politic. But everywhere it denied, often, even the title, almost always the substance, of citizenship to blacks. And this was systematically done through processes and forms of law. "Citizenship" for blacks guaranteed nothing in the way of protection from the arbitrary use of authority, nor from the exploits of private power.

The struggle to craft this new American identity has been shaped by a number of recent court cases that are worth brief note. And these cases are employment/workplace related cases.

LAW, RACE, AND CLASS

The court signaled its early approval of affirmative action in its 1971 landmark ruling in *Griggs v. Duke Power*. Duke Power had historically tracked blacks into its labor department where they received the lowest wages relative to whites. In fact, the highest wage in this department was lower than the lowest wage paid to employees in other departments (Nieman, 1991). In deciding in 1965 to end its departmental apartheid, Duke Power put in place a set of criteria that required all applicants from other departments, or to Duke Power from outside, to have high school diplomas or to pass an aptitude test. Facially, the policy was fair since it applied equally to all. No one should have been at all surprised to discover that blacks failed the test at a much higher rate than whites, ninety-four to forty-two percent (Nieman, 1991, p. 203). Thus, while the policy sought to treat a historically disadvantaged group formally equal, the impact of this "color-blindness" would perpetuate the continued substantively unfair dominance of the workplace and high wages by incumbents whose defining and sustaining characteristic is that they are the inheritors of social and educational privilege relative to their black counterparts who had education once denied their parents altogether and themselves to a large extent.

Because a large number of blacks were denied transfers to the better paying jobs, they brought a lawsuit against the company charging violation of Title VII of the 1964 Civil Rights Act since the tests were unrelated to the performance of the jobs they sought. Thus, the policy amounted to discrimination against them. The Court agreed.

In a unanimous decision written by Chief Justice Burger the Court declared the company's policy illegal, arguing that the objective of the U.S. Congress was precisely to "remove barriers that had operated in the past to favor an identifiable group of white employees over other employees" (Nieman, 1991, p. 204). Burger went on to say that criteria that had an adverse impact on blacks could be justified only if employers could prove that they were job related. In Berger's own words: "The touchstone is business necessity... if an employment practice which operates to exclude Negroes cannot be shown to be related to job performance, the practice is prohibited" (Nieman, 1991, p. 204).

In fact it was often the case that so-called objective tests did not measure anything remotely related to job performance, if to anything else, other than as a measure in proxy, of the hidden legacy of the institution slavery and the era of Jim Crow. *Griggs* held out the promise that this would no longer be constitutionally protected.

Another important case raising questions of both law and livelihood as part of the affirmative action strategy of intervention into the employment is *Fullilove v. Klutznick*. Fullilove upheld Congressional legislation mandating that at least ten percent of federal funds granted for local public works projects must be used to obtain services or supplies from businesses owned by minority groups. The claim by H. Earl Fullilove and several associations of contractors and subcontractors that they had sustained injury under the "set-aside" provisions of the law which, on its face, violated the Equal Protection Clause of the Fourteenth Amendment and the equal protection aspects of the Due Process Clause of the Fifth Amendment, was rejected by the Court. These two cases *Griggs* and *Fullilove* went a long way toward improving the economics competitive basis of many black individuals and businesses. These, however, were basically pre-Reagan era labor market interventions. After Reagan came to power in 1980 there is evidence of some significant reversal in affirmative action practice and in the collective economic improvement of blacks.

More and more interracial conflict over employment practices would surface during the Reagan years. The roots of these conflicts, as I earlier have said, lay deep in the American distant and recent past. But it would be the social climate of the Reagan era that would give the most pervasive expression to some of the most pernicious views American populace held about one another. Racism in the raw resurfaced with a political agenda. Acts of violence, covert and overt, against Asians, blacks, Hispanics, Jews, women, gays, and an assortment of groups defined as "others," constituting a perked threat to the continued dominance by white males of power and income, became pervasive. Ugly racial incidents on college campuses and in the workplaces of America were daily news items.

Ethnicity

Triggered in large measure by the facts of the decline of the United States in the international economy, due to a growing trade imbalance, shift from an essentially producer nation to a consumer nation, coupled with a low rate of personal savings, the search for social scapegoats began in earnest.

Asian Americans were succinctly posited as the "model minority" whose behavior should be emulated by the rest of us as this very behavior confirmed the contradictory perceptions of both the persistence and viability of the American Dream of material success no matter what, and that the Asian hordes are taking away our jobs.

The empirical reality that Asians in the United States are generally located in the labor market's secondary sector, generally absent from the higher levels of corporate administration, and generally earn less than white males in personal income (Takaki, 1995), seemingly has not altered the persistent and varied, now multicultural version of "the white man's burden."

Hispanics, an appellation that is neither agreed upon by, nor satisfying to, the assortment of peoples who share Latin-American or Spanish ancestry, are a rapidly growing part of the racial-ethnic mix of American society and mainly urban landscape. They currently represent about 8.1 percent of the American population and are growing. Selective empirical features help to locate them within the United States economic order. Puerto Ricans, for example, have a median income less than half that of non-Hispanic whites. Half of all Hispanic adults lack a high school diploma. The unemployment rate of Hispanics is more than fifty percent above that of non-Hispanic whites, and the poverty rate of Hispanics is two and one half times the rate of non-Hispanic whites (Farley, 1990).

The story with respect to Native Americans is worse yet:

> Indians remain the least urbanized of any major American racial or ethnic group, with just over half living in urban areas. Most rural Indians live on or near reservations. As of 1980, more than one American Indian out of four lived below the federal poverty level— about three times the white poverty rate of that year. On reservations, where Indian poverty is most intense, about half of the population lives below the poverty level. The 1980 unemployment rate for Indians was 13.2 percent, and on reservations it was higher yet (Farley, 1990, p. 319).

Thus it would seem through this cursory look at "ethnicity" that there is an on-going struggle of a number of groups in American society to close the socioeconomic gap between dominant group males and everybody else.

SOCIOPOLITICAL MOVEMENTS,
GOVERNMENT, AND ECONOMY

We cannot close this part of the discussion without mentioning the Civil Rights Movement. Granted that talking about the Civil Rights Act, voting rights, and affirmative action is to recognize these legal constructions as products of the movement itself. But not all the impacts were on government; the culture of racism and bigotry was itself set in turbulence and produced levels of racial violence unheralded since the throes of violence against blacks in the period between the Civil War and the 1920s.

Arguably, the search for calm and stability after protest demonstrations, sit-ins, bombing and burning, American business, no less its government, merely desired peace, or as it was then put, "law and order" to be able to get on with the nation's business which is, fundamentally, business.

Though I do not have the data to measure any one-to-one correspondence between specific acts of violence or their threat and specific employment or economic opportunities opened up to blacks as a result of such action, I am convinced that there was in a limited, rather than lasting, way some real connection and some real benefit of this turbulent era. Not only did it engender ever greater awareness that 1950s style quiescence was based on the myth of unending economic growth, producing sufficient commodities for all to become integrated into the social logic of wasteful consumption, but also the periods of turbulence forced the realization that some people wanted more out of American democracy than the magnitude of often surperflous commodities; they wanted equal political rights, democracy, citizenship, respect, and dignity. Moreover, blacks had announced, in thunderous tones, that they were no longer willing to only fight other nations and peoples under the flag of the United States, but would challenge the government itself in behalf of "these rights we have." Politics mattered. And much, not all, of the violence of the period was politics, in the search for new and effective ideas and tactics to confront a perceived unjust system.

Surely nonviolence was significant in conveying power and economic pressure. Nonviolence represented a confrontation of what Berger (1966, p. 92-104) and Luckman call "symbolic universes," in that these realities were outside the scope of the everyday experience of white persons' way of viewing Negroes, but were meaningful in integrating a worldview for blacks that allowed them to live in the social world of that time but to have a way of transcending its stigma, its taint, its perceived wholesale injustice. It was as if those who put their lives on the line in that era were following a different, higher voice. Hardfought concessions were won from city fathers across the country and these very often were translated into marginal economic benefits such as open housing agreements.

Couple these small gains with the emphasis on political rights and dignity and we begin to understand how a tenacious nonviolence lent fervor, built organizations, and challenged and transformed the sociopolitical order of the United States of the late 1950s and early 1960s. Economically speaking, however, blacks had not overcome, in this period or since. They had made a major impact on government and on society, but their economic plight was still serious.

CURRENT STATUS OF BLACK AMERICA

Based on the March 1992 Current Population Statistics, we know the following about the economic characteristics of black Americans.

Highlights

Blacks, like whites, are older in 1992 than in 1980. The black population had a median age of 28.2 years in 1992, compared with 24.8 years in 1980. The corresponding median ages for whites were 34.3 and 30.8 years.

In 1980, 8 percent of adults (25 years old and over) had a bachelor's degree or more. By 1992, this proportion had increased to 12 percent.

The annual average labor force participation rate for black men is down slightly in 1992 as compared to 1980. Black women's labor force participation rates were up slightly as were those of white women.

Black family, real median income of $21,550 in 1991 is essentially the same as in 1980. The ratio of black-to-white median income for all family types in 1979 and 1991 did not statistically differ.

- In 1991, the median earnings of year-round, full-time black workers 25 years old and over who were high school graduates was $18,620; 55 percent of them had earnings below $20,000. In contrast, the median earnings of comparable black workers with a bachelor's degree or more was $30,910, or 66 percent higher than black high school graduates. Only 16 percent of black workers with at least a bachelor's degree earned less than $20,000.
- In occupations with statistically significant earnings differentials between black and white males who worked year-round, full-time, the median earnings ratio of black men to white men ranged from an apparent low of $64 per $100 for men employed in farming, fishing, and forestry, to an apparent high of $87 for men employed in service occupations.
- Black men with high school education employed as executives, administrators, and managers earned about $60 for every $100 earned by comparable white men. Three percent of black and 9 percent of white

male high school graduates were employed in these jobs.

- Among college educated males who worked year-round, full-time, a higher proportion of whites than of blacks were employed in executive, administrative, and managerial jobs. The median earnings of black college educated males in these jobs was 77 percent of comparable white males earnings.
- Thirty-three percent of all black persons were poor in 1991, similar to their 1979 poverty rate of 31 percent. Among white person, 11 percent were poor in 1991 and 9 percent in 1979.[1]

With respect to per capita income, in 1991 the per capita income of the black population ($9,170) was about 60 percent of the white population's ($15,510). The ratio (0.59) of black-to-white per capita income was similar in both 1979 and 1989. Unemployment, as well as occupational, educational, work experience, and earnings differentials, all contribute to these ratios.

Families

The income levels of families are related to a number of factors such as family composition (including the increase in the proportion of families maintained by women), the number of earners in the family and their educational attainment levels, as well as the economic conditions of the nation.

Black median family income was $21,550 in 1991, 57 percent of that of white families ($37,780). After adjusting for inflation, neither the ratio (0.57) nor the median family income for black and white families in 1991 differed from their 1979 levels.

Clearly education makes a difference in the earning capacity, particularly when blacks are compared to other blacks. But black male executives, administrators, and managers earned about $60 for every $100 earned by comparable white men. Generally, for every $60 earned by members of the black population whites earn $100. Thus, for all the evidence of specific cohort analyses of blacks and whites, the economic benefit for comparably expended resources (years of experience, education, occupational titles) still differs according to race.

How then can Wilson (1978) claim the "declining significance of race?" He returns to aspects of that issue later, and in more thorough going manner in his important book *The Truly Disadvantaged*, (1987). This work adds to the significant body of research (Gephart and Pearson, 1988). On the urban underclass, a concept that is as specious as it is controversial.

Wilson marshals an impressive array of facts to argue that what has in large measure happened to black, inner city neighborhoods is a normative shift of major and catastrophic proportions. What has changed is "ghetto behavior, norms, and aspirations" (Wilson, 1987, p. 7), resulting in a loss of "a sense of community, positive neighborhood identification, and explicit norms and sanctions against aberrant behavior."

On the contrary, I think that what has been lost here, or perhaps never found, or maybe found once and lost again, is a sense of critical perspective. I agree with Fishman and Gomes (1989, p. 78) that the serious problem is less about the "facts" used to "support their underclass theory... rather, our difference is more in the philosophical and theoretical understanding of society and history that provides the "scientific" explanation of these data—permanent unemployment and poverty, etc."

The chagrin of these authors, and mine, is that none of the "underclass" discussion takes seriously the macrostructural, economic processes of the accumulation of capital and its resultant production of unemployment and poverty. These "underclass" theorists, the "culture of poverty" revisited under another name, perhaps, do not agree with the notion of a logic of capital accumulation; but worst, do not offer evidence of or critique its tenets, and may, indeed, not even take it seriously, as is the case for most American social scientists (Ritzer, 1992). Marx is not vintage "underclass" theory, but deserves to be taken seriously.

Though Wilson is, in my view, related to the "culture of poverty" theory in some ways, he clearly and significantly differs in other important ways. His perspective has emphasized "demand side, claiming that the substantial restructuring of the economy in the last 15 years [now 21 years] eliminated jobs that were disproportionately held by inner-city blacks" (Smith and Welch, 1989, p. 550), as compared to the "supply-side" arguments that the labor market in "underclass" black men is tight to nonexistent because these men are involved in various government support programs—so-called "safety net" type programs. This is one reason why some business leaders and their intellectual supporters like Charles Murray (1984) are eager to dismantle most of these programs (Smith and Welch, 1989).

These basic disputes over "models" are not definitively disposed of in the economic and policy literature, even less so in the literature of sociological theory which is increasingly taking policy issues and "politics" more seriously than heretofore.

There is little doubt that the facts of debilitating poverty have trapped and broken the lines of large and growing numbers of African Americans during the period since roughly 1965. The question of what works to alleviate this situation is utmost for those who think about it and for those living it. But it is also a question, as stated, that is not sufficiently conflict ladened with element of a conflict theory of the racial status quo or the aspirations of blacks as a driving force in the disruption of the "normal" processes of the reproduction of group subordination and diminished economic prospect. Race, in this country, is real, has been from its founding moment and, if Derrick Bell (1992) is right, is likely to remain so.

CONFLICT THEORY

I have focused heavily on occupational changes and income because these are crucial measures of socioeconomic status and contribute easily observable static and dynamic aspects of the working of the economy of the maketplace. In this sense they reproduce social patterns indicative of either institution transformation or the latent power of the status quo. These data coupled with recent research by Kinder and Mendelberg (1995) suggest a somewhat ominous prospect for racial harmony and economic viability of the largest number of blacks as a group in American society. Kinder and Mendelberg (p. 1) warrent quoting at length:

> For all the substantial accomplishments of the Civil Rights Movement, the United States remains today in many respects a profoundly segregated society. Jim Crow is gone, swept aside by federal legislation, Supreme Court decisions, and waves of protest and demonstrations. But in communities across the country, blacks and whites are separated more completly now than they were at the turn of the century.

At the very end of this century it seems that we are grappling ever more with ideas, problems, and conflicts whose orgins are located squarley within the "unelightened" nineteenth century. "Scientific Racism" is a formidably resilient social form which seeks to hide its harsh and discriminitory face behind, not a "veil of ignorance," but an array of numbers that parade as complex operationalizations, but signify simple racism.

Were I to be wrong in this analysis, what matters is that so many African Americans hold such a view of what is going on with the assortment—small though it is—of "scientists" who are "discovering" that blacks, perhaps, simply do not have the cognitive acumen to "cut it" in the labor market of this country.

Assimilation was this country's race realtions objective soon after it was recognized that Native Amerians would not die and that African Americans were human beings, with or without entitlement. Neither group would long be contained. With the apparent intractibility of poverty both on the reservation and in the ghetto, many Americans lost faith in the American Dream of assimilation and equality. Some thinkers now begin to imagine a condition in which this country will and can only have a permanant group that is economically denied and socially downtrodden. What this means is that simultaneously we are witnessing an expansion of formal legal rights while a real diminution of viable economic existence is occuring. Formal legal rights in a legal culture subsumed under a logic of capitalist accumulation are important expressions of the society's highest ideals. Devoid of the economic means to assert these rights—as in purchasing housing, not having employment hiring committees stacked against you numerically and/or culturally, being able to have a meaningful vote, or to hire a taxi anywhere in New York City—

their very existence constitutes a cruel joke on the citizenry and a farce within the constructed ideology of equality. Patricia Williams (1991, p. 28) has commented on the nexus of law and economics in the following way:

> The discussion of economic rights and civil liberties usually assumes at leasy two things— that equal protection guarantees equality of opportunity 'blindly' for the benefit of those market actors who have exercised rational choices in wealth-maximizing ways; and that those who make irrational non-profit-motivated choices have chosen, and therefore deserves to be poor.

These "free market" relations are presumed to exist and to account, from behind a "veil of ignorance," for the relative disparity in the economic status of persons as individuals endowed with the capacity for intelligent choice, as well as for the ensuing group structuation (or placement) in society realative to one another.

Nowhere is this argued to be more true than in the area of race (Allport, 1958; Billig, 1978; Gossett, 1965; Jensen, 1969; Jordon, 1977). But if Held (1975, p. 33 and quoted in Hawkesworth, 1988, p. 115) is correct dominant group males should not so confidently proclaim either that other racial and ethnic groups are lacking in mental capicity, or that a strategy of rational choice and it's necessarily related cognitive understandings are sufficent explanation of their rate of incumbency to the "best" positions available in a socially stratified society for: "they are members of a group of persons who have been privileged in hiring and promotion in accordance with normal practices of long-standing, persons who have been offered better educational preparation than others of the same basic talents, persons whose egos have been stenghened more than members of other groups." This is a thin theoritical basis for articulating an anti-group-preference position and it has even less a basis as a philosophical anthropology. For in the structuation of dominant males witin the status quo of privleges and benefits, we learn nothing about the human attributes they possess that are invariant and species specific, or that are particularistic and local, namely with respect to only themselves. Rather, we note that status for these white males is an accumulated history of strong social preferences established and maintained by their historic control of the most extensive set of resources ever created by human collective efforts. These resources include power, violence, wealth, and a host of symbolic and ideological forms that enlist the support of others who may themselves not stand to benefit from the organized present. If this account is correct, then it is indeed strange, that in a country proclaiming and regularly celebrating the general abstract principle of "the rule of law," we find sacrosanct the social results of arbitrariness.

The American Constitution pemits such a stutus quo, and arguably, may even require it. Katznelson and Prewitt (1979, p. 33 and quoted in Campbell and Skocpol, 1995, p. 101) puts it thusly: "The Constitution does not establish...[an administratively centralized] state that in turn manages the affairs of society toward some clear conception of the public welfare; rather, it established a political economy in which public welfare is the aggregate of private preferences....The United States is a government of legislation and litigation...Politics becomes the struggle to translate social and economic interest into law.... *The political culture defines political power as getting a law passed.*"

Dissatisfaction most frequently takes the form of trying to force a new and more favorable interpretation of the Constitution. Never in this endless shuffling does the Constitution itself become the target. Rather, constitutional principles, legitimate claims for a fair share of "the American way of life," and constitutional interpretations and reinterpretations are the means for forcing reallocations.

What this suggests for the present analysis is that since there is no constitutionally mandated economic "floor" under citizens, the operation of private social power is legally protected and compels toward patterns of interest articulation. People choose with whom they wish to associate; they choose the neighborhoods in which to live; and they choose the professionals to whom they wish to go.

And yet, this "aggregate of private preferences" is not unencumbered. Sometimes individuals are able to enhance their ability to make these choices through their interrelationships (connections?) with others similarly situated. Other times they are able to thwart the exercise of these same choices by others. There emerges from this interaction patterns of power and influence on virtually everything; these patterns reproduce the racial status quo and give it the appearance of naturalness and normalcy.

Racial groups seeking to effect change in the racial status quo are, then, faced with not only challenging it on its face for what it is—seriously constituted forms of social power—but must carry on a struggle against its deep legitimacy in law. Blacks must not only struggle against dominant group members in social spheres but also against government as it, in large part, protects the racial status quo and is constituted by its members. This to is an ominous prospect; for if black struggles cannot crack the austere, external face of racism thruough changing the law, then few legitimate options are left available to a black activist, movement organization, and movement group.

Thus the law constrains in serious and effective ways the shape of ensuing racial conflict now and into the future.

SUMMARY

If Jerome Mc Cristal Culp (1993) is right, we can expect near future racial conflict to continue in large measure to be defined by struggles over economic and political resources through the application of a combination of remedies that invoke both policy argument and moral ones, and generally confuse the two. Culp's emphasis on solving racial problems with racial remedies invites a thorough critique of color-blindness as a constitutional principle sufficient to transform the racial status quo. Such a policy parading as moral principle consigns blacks in a permanent position of racial and socioeconomic subordination.

As I write, affirmination action is, it seems, everywhere under attack. It is attacked for all sorts of reasons and is said to cause and account for all sorts of things, some contadictory of each other. For example, affirmation action is critized because it effectively enhances blacks getting more and better economic positions, that is, it works; it is critized because it has not significantly changed the plight of, among others, blacks in American society, that is, it does not work; it is overenclusive; it is underenclusive; it merely "creams" the best blacks; it produces mediocraty. Critics of affirmative action seem to want to have it both ways. They claim that affirmative action's objective can be met in other and better ways, but in recent history have never proposed any of these alternatives. This leads me to strongly suspect that the attack on affirmative action is an orchestrated attack against virtually all the government interventions in various economic markets ever the last fifty years; and, it is also part of the campaign to limit and control the racial and ethnic diversifying of the workplace and of American society. It is not that conservative forces are totally set against any conception of "racial intergration," but, rather, would like to force its expression in ways consonant with continued white supremacy and capital accumulation.

If race and capitalism are as interconnected as I believe, then, clearly, racial conflict will continue to have a deep economic component to it; capitalism will continue to reproduce a deep racism, and neither can be reduced to the other. Both race and class will, for a very long time, continue as related but relatively autonomous logics for the continued subordination of blacks in America society. This is so, I believe, not because of any invariant laws or inevitability, rather, I believe, this is so because the society is objectively segregated and interracial, precluding any geniune basis for a cross-racial "community of persons" (Adams, 1976, p. 113). As I write, affirmative action is still the law of the land. It is not the same law that it had been, however; it has been seriously modified through judicial actions over the last seven to ten years. Nieman (1991) argues that with the courts—notably the Supreme Court and Federal Appeals Courts—chipping away at important pieces of the edifice of equal opportunity law, we can expect that just as at the inception of the American Constitution in 1776, race and racial conflict will "remain a major fault line of controversey and debate during the nation's third century under the constitution" (Nieman, 1991, p. 227).

Inconcluding, I invoke and paraphase Martin Luther King Jr. He said that the Civil Rights Movement was not an undertaking merely to integrate

American society, or to win this or that concession. We are in this struggle in order to "change the soul of America." I submit, America is a soul not yet transformed.

NOTE

1. All of the information is from "The Black Population in the United States: March, 1992, with respect to per capita income, in 1991 the per capita income of the black population ($9,170) was about 60 percent of the white population's ($15,510). The ratio (0.59) of black-to-white per capita income was similar in both 1979 and 1989. Unemployment, as well as occupational, educational, work experience, and earnings differentials, all contribute to these ratios.

REFERENCES

Adams, J.L. 1976. One Being Human Religiously. Boston, MA: Unitarian University Assn.
Allen, R. 1974. Reluctant Reformers. Washington, DC: Howard University Press.
Allport, G. 1958. The Nature of Prejudice. Garden City, NY: Doubleday
Bell, D 1992. Faces at the Bottom of the Well: The Permanence of Racism in America. New York: Basic Books.
Berger, P., and T. Luckman 1966. The Social Construction of Reality. Garden City, NY: Doubleday.
Billig, M. 1978. "Patterns of Racism: Interviews With National Front Members." Race and Class 20(2): 161-79.
Butcher, K. 1994. "Black Immigrants in the U.S.: A Comparison With Native Black and Other Immigrants." Industrial and Labor Relations Review 47(2): 265-282.
Campbell, J.L., and T. Skocpol. 1995. American Society and Politics: Institutional, Historical and Theoretical Perspectives. New York: McGraw Hill.
Chiswick, B. 1978. Human Resources and Income Distribution: Issues and Policies. New York: Norton.
Cox, O.C. 1948. Caste, Class and Race. Garden City, NY: Doubleday.
Culp, J.M. 1993. "The Intersectionality of Oppression and its Negation of Color Blind Remedies: Affirmative Action, Race, Class, and Gender." New York Law Review 69(16): 162-83.
Farley, J. 1990. Sociology. Englewood Cliffs, NJ: Prentice-Hall.
Feagin, J. 1986. Social Problems: A Critical Power Conflict Perspective. Englewood Cliffs, NJ: Prentice-Hall.
Fishman, W.K., and R.C. Gomes 1989. "A Critique of The Truly Disadvantaged: A Historical Materialist (Marxist) Perspective." Journal of Sociology and Social Welfare XVI(4): 77-98.
Fitzpatrick, P. 1992. Sociology of Law and Crime: The Mythology of Modern Law. London, England: Routledge.
Freeman, R. 1973. "Changes in the Labor Market for Black Americans, 1948-1972." Brookings Paper on Economic Activity 1,: 67-120.
Genovese, E. 1966. The Political Economy of Slavery. London, England: MacGibbon and Kee.
Gephart, M.A., and R.W. Pearson 1988. "Contemporary Research on the Underclass." Social Science Research Council 42: 1-10.
Gossett, F. 1965. Race: The History of An Idea in America. New York: Schocken Books.
Hawskeworth, M.E. 1988. Theoretical Issues in Policy Analysis. Albany, NY: State University of New York Press.

Heckman, J.J., and B.S. Payner 1989. "Determining the Impact of Federal Antidiscrimination Policy on the Economic Status of Black: A Study of South Carolina." *The American Economic Review* 79: 138-177.

Held, V. 1975. "Reasonable Progress and Self-Respect." *Ethnics and Public Policy,* Edited by T.L. Beauchamp. Englewood Cliffs, NJ: Rowman and Littlefield.

Jensen, A. 1969. "How Much Can We Boost I.Q. and Scholastic Achievement?" *Harvard Education Review* 39: 1-123.

Jordon, W. 1977. *White Over Black: American Attitude Toward the Negro, 1520-1812.* New York: Norton.

Katznelson, I., and K. Prewitt. 1979. "Limits of Choice." In *Capitalism and State* edited by R. Fagen. Standford, CA: Standford University Press.

Kinder, D.R., and T. Mendleberg. 1995. "Cracks in American Apartheid: The Political Impact of Prejudice Among Desegregated Whites." *The Journal of Politics* 57(2): 402-24.

King, M.C. 1993. "Black Women's Breakthrough into Clerical Work: An Occupational Tipping Model." *The Journal of Economic Issues* 27: 1097-1125.

King, M.L. Jr. et al. 1968. "Beyond Vietnam." Reprint by Clergy and Laymen Concerned About Vietnam, pp. 10-17.

Leonard, J.S. 1990. "The Impact of Affirmative Action Regulation and Equal Employment Law on Black Employment." *Journal of Economic Perspectives* 4(4): 47-63.

Murray, C.A. 1984. *Losing Ground: American Social Policy.* New York: Basic Books.

Myrdal, G. 1944. *An American Dilemma.* New York: Harper and Brothers.

Nieman, D.G. 1991. *Promises to Keep: African-Americans and the Constitutional Order, 1776 to the present.* New York: Oxford University Press.

Patterson, O. 1982. *Slavery and Social Death.* Cambridge, MA: Harvard University Press.

Perelman, M. 1977. *Farming for Profits in A Hungry World.* New York: Universe Books.

Ringer, B. 1993. "From Nondiscrimination to Affirmative Action: Retrogression or Profession?" *Journal of Social Distress and the Homeless* 2(4): 325-341.

Ritzer, G 1992. *Classical Sociological Theory.* New York: McGraw Hill.

Smith, J.P. 1984. "Race and Human Capital." *The American Economic Review* 74(4): 685-698.

Smith, J.P., and F.R. Welch. 1989. "Black Economic Progress After Myrdal." *Journal of Economic Literature* 27: 519-564.

Takaki, R. 1995. "The Myth of the 'Model Minority'." In *Sociology: Exploring the Architecture of Everyday Life,* edited by D. Newman. Thousand Oaks, CA: Pine Forge Press.

U.S. National Advisory Commission on Civil Disorders. 1968. *Report of the National Advisory Commission on Civil Disorders.* New York: Bantam Books.

Wilson, J. 1978. *The Declining Significance of Race: Blacks and Changing American Institutions.* Chicago: University of Chicago Press.

Wilson, J. 1987. *The Truly Disadvantaged.* Chicago: The University of Chicago Press.

Williams, P. 1991. *The Alchemy of Race And Rights: Diary of a Law Professor.* Cambridge, MA: Harvard University Press.

RACIAL AND ETHNIC CONFLICT:

THE VIEW FROM POLITICAL SCIENCE

Herbert Hirsch and Manley Elliott Banks

INTRODUCTION

Political science is a schizophrenic discipline. On the one hand, political scientists study votes of all kinds, votes in elections, in legislatures, in courts, and so on. This analysis is one aspect of the study of political conflict. On the other hand, there is another group of scholars, smaller in number to be sure, who focus their attention on the more lethal forms of conflict such as violence, war, and genocide. This chapter will attempt to provide a taste of both forms of analysis. We want to start with the most violent and move to what is a more traditional form of analysis. We will, consequently, first examine the conditions under which violent conflict occurs. Our basic argument is that in order for conflict to occur, groups or individuals develop a sense of identity of themselves as separate from and superior to others. This identity is formed within a political context, and within that context, myths and stereotypes develop and are socialized and passed on from generation to generation. Under these conditions language is used to motivate individual human beings to engage in violent acts. Following this, we will amply demonstrate the schizophrenic nature of our discipline as we turn our attention to a more traditional case study of political conflict in the city of Atlanta.

Research in Human Social Conflict, Volume 1, pages 115-142.
Copyright © 1995 by JAI Press Inc.
All rights of reproduction in any form reserved.
ISBN: 1-55938-923-0

POLITICAL PSYCHOLOGY AND POLITICAL CONFLICT

There is little doubt that we live at the end of the most consistently violent century in human existence. Recent estimates of the toll taken in the twentieth century are astounding; war alone has claimed 87 million lives. Brzezinski (1993, p. 17) estimates that "167,000,000 to 175,000,000 lives have been deliberately extinguished through politically motivated carnage." This is, according to his calculations, "the approximate equivalent of the total population of France, Italy, and Great Britain; or over two-thirds of the total current population of the United States. This is more than the total killed in *all* previous wars, civil conflicts, and religious persecutions throughout human history" (Brzezinski, 1993, p. 17).

Clearly, as one allows one's mind to wander through the events of the twentieth century it is difficult to avoid the pessimistic perception that we have failed to control or resolve the seemingly endless spiral of racial and ethnic conflict that seems to be racing through our era. While national and international political systems have undergone remarkable and swift transformations since the end of the Second World War, individual perceptions appear to remain mired in the morass of race and ethnicity. Groups as well as nation-states, construct myths that involve the glorification and romanticization of themselves and the denigration of others. Whether in war or peace your particular group is "correct," or your interests are justified, and "God" and righteousness, in whatever form you choose, are always on your side. Race, along with religion and ethnicity, are often the basis for myths used to motivate violent action and, during or after the violence, to justify the death of individuals killed both serving the myth and opposing it, as worthy and necessary sacrifices. These myths eventually become self-perpetuating and function as mechanisms used by persons to organize their views of the world. In order to understand how they develop into the root causes of racial and ethnic conflict we need to understand how identity develops and, following that, we need to understand how people are motivated to commit violence.

FORMING RACIAL AND ETHNIC IDENTITY

Identity does not develop in a vacuum. While this simple notion seems obvious, scholars interested in the development of identity often neglect important contextual environments within which the person develops their racial and ethnic identity, but also which have important effects on that development throughout the person's life. Attempts to measure and analyze the development of identity have, as one observer notes, "run aground in a conceptual fog" (Adam, 1978, p. 68) because they ignore the context of politics. What does it mean to talk about racial or ethnic or any form of identity, if the conditions are not specified? All social phenomenon are, after all, embedded in social and political structures and any research that hopes to be remotely connected to reality must consider these an integral part of the conceptual framework. In fact, identity is manifestly political since it reflects and is influenced by the social, economic, and political circumstances within which a particular individual or group of individuals finds him- or herself.

Ethnic and racial identity become sociopolitical creations when they are related to power and to the dominant or subordinate position in which an individual or group is placed (Adam, 1978, p. 10). Thus, access to, or denial of, opportunities in a society are generally related to the characteristics that have been declared by that society to be valued, to be positive or negative. It might be the value placed on the color of a person's skin, religion, or gender. These "subjective" judgments are transformed into "objective" categories as they are used by those occupying positions in society that allow them to bestow or withhold the rewards of the system. In short, seemingly objective criteria are actually the result of highly subjective political evaluations that have developed within a society over time. Once these criteria are established, groups will engage in political battle to maintain or change them and to pass them on to succeeding generations. The status of the criteria for status and success become embedded in the memory and become an accepted part of the conventional wisdom and dominant ideology of a culture or state. Hence, they also become political means and ends and are tied to the maintenance of the status quo or to change. The battles over these definitions may become heated and occasionally violent and they, in turn, have an impact on the identity which is developing within that context. In other words, racial and ethnic identity cannot be divorced from a serious consideration of politics, and we must, consequently, examine identity as it operates within boundaries formed by the political environment.

THE POLITICAL ENVIRONMENT OF IDENTITY

Even though it has been historically foolhardy to attempt to define precisely what the term "political" means, it is still necessary to venture into that territory if one is to have any notion of the context within which identity is formed.

Political thinkers have grappled with this problem for thousands of years. From Aristotle to Marx they have struggled to define "politics," and there are a multiplicity of older and modern definitions. Most contemporary definitions involve the concept of "power"—which itself is very difficult to define. Other definitions use terms such as "influence," and attempt to distinguish between influence and power. These efforts at definitional clarity ultimately, in modern political science, give way to attempts to frame the concepts in mathematical symbols and thus to make them "scientific." While "scientific" definitions are useful for empirically based studies, especially if they are grounded in theory and based on historical understanding, very often the method becomes an end in itself and results in trivialization in the name of science. Since I believe that the human being must be the primary focus of inquiry (Hirsch, 1989), the definition I wish to use is that of a humanist.

Terrence Des Pres (1988, p. 73) approached politics by writing about poetry. He once defined politics as the manipulation of regular people by agents of power, generally of the modern nation-state. His view of the "political" means that identity formation takes place in an environment in which people are unable to escape the penetration of politics into their everyday lives because politics is, as Des Pres (1988, p.74) notes "insistent," "penetrating," and "widespread." Even if the individual does not personally experience incidents such as terrorism or violence or political chaos and uncertainty, he or she cannot escape "knowing" such facts and the mere "knowing" "changes the way you feel about being in the world" (1988, p. 74). Politics now intrudes on all aspects of life and there are no more bystanders. The personal has been transformed into the political and the disintegration of the boundary between them has left the modern individual face to face with the power of the modern state. The reality formed by this erosion of boundaries means that the human person is no longer isolated and that his or her identity is formed within a crucible of political turmoil and unpredictability. The realities of contemporary political life intrude upon the formation of identity and these political realities may be destructive or constructive—may destroy or preserve life. If we adopt Des Pres' definition and focus on the acts of power addressed toward generally powerless people, then the realities are often not pretty.

Reflect for a moment on some of the more somber realities. Within the United States individuals face poverty, homelessness, environmental destruction and disintegration, increasing gaps between rich and poor, unemployment, recession, drugs, violence, disintegrating cities and a disintegrating infrastructure, and increases in the incidents of racism, sexism, and anti-Semitism. Internationally, individuals are confronted with and exposed to war, nationalism and ethnic hostility rising and giving birth to violence, the widening gap between rich and poor nations, increasing interethnic conflict, starvation and famine, the destruction of the rain forest, and genocide against indigenous populations. The list is almost beyond comprehension and almost immediately depressing.

These political episodes become an integral part of our daily diet of overwhelming information and become part of the structure within which identity is formed and conflict carried out. Politics, thus, intrudes into the process of identity formation, and must have important repercussions for the developing identity. If this is the case, it is important to explain how identity is being formed in the political cauldron of contemporary civilization and what conditions give rise to racial and ethnic conflict.

CONDITIONS FOR CONFLICT

Modern political science demonstrated little interest in racial and ethnic conflict. Of course, there have been a few conspicuous exceptions that have been interested in exploring why people are willing to engage in violent conflict. Three works, mainly psychologically based analyses, are of particular importance. Milgram's (1974) pioneering work on obedience, of which more later, Staub's (1989), *The Roots of Evil*, and Kelman and Hamilton's (1989), *Crimes of Obedience*. These latter works recognize Milgram's contribution, although not always acknowledging it, and they start with the realization that many of the greatest examples of conflict are committed in the name of obedience. As a result, much of the focus has been on explaining the roots and results of unquestioning obedience to authority.

Take Kelman and Hamilton as an example. They attempt to account for the apparent repetition throughout history of what they call crimes of obedience by focusing on what they refer to as "the consequences that often ensue when authority gives orders exceeding the bounds of morality or law..." (p. xi). According to their definition, an act of obedience becomes a crime of obedience "if the actor knows that the order is illegal, or if any reasonable person— particularly someone in the actor's position—'should know' that the order is illegal" (p. 47). An act of obedience is a crime if the orders issued by superiors *cause* or *justify* the act of violence. The issues confronted thrust us into the uncharted and precarious terrain of individual and collective responsibility.

As one of their prime examples, Kelman and Hamilton begin with the village of My Lai where on March 16, 1968 a company of American soldiers commanded by Lieutenant William C. Calley committed a crime of obedience. After describing the massacre, the military code of justice and the trial of Calley, Kelman and Hamilton attempt to account for this particular crime of obedience which they refer to as "sanctioned massacre." I want to discuss their analysis by placing it more directly in the context of an already existing literature which they refer to from time to time, but often leave out when it seems most relevant. In so doing I do not intend to make light of their contribution, but to connect their book and this one with the larger narrative and explanatory tradition of work in this area. According to Kelman and Hamilton, "sanctioned massacres" are "violent acts":

...of indiscriminate, ruthless, and often systematic mass violence, carried out by military or paramilitary personnel which engaged in officially sanctioned campaigns, the victims of which are defenseless and unresisting civilians, including old men, women, and children (p. 12).

Sanctioned massacres, they argue, have occurred throughout history and examples include: the actions of American troops in the Philippine war, the massacres of the American Indians, the Nazi extermination of the European Jews, the extermination of the Armenians by the Turks in the period 1915 to 1917, the liquidation of the Russian kulaks, the massacres that have taken place in Indonesia, Bangladesh, Biafra, Burundi, South Africa, Cambodia, and others—clearly there is no paucity of examples. Violent conflict has, according to Kelman and Hamilton, certain common features. They focus on two: context and target.

All sanctioned massacres, they argue, occur "in the context of an overall policy that is explicitly or implicitly genocidal: designed to destroy all or part of a category of people defined in ethnic, national, racial, religious, or other terms" (p. 13). The massacres themselves may not be explicitly planned but the overall policy sanctions the violent acts as a strategic necessity.

The second feature they identify is that the targets or victims are "often defenseless civilians and the primary question they ask is why so many people are willing to formulate, participate in, and condone policies that call for the mass killings of defenseless civilians" (p. 15). To answer this difficult and most important question, Kelman and Hamilton identify three social processes that tend to create conditions under which sanctioned massacre occurs: authorization, routinization, and dehumanization.

Sanctioned massacres are authorized with an authority situation within which "a different kind of morality, linked to duty to obey orders, tends to take over" (p. 16). As far as I am aware, this condition was first identified by Stanley Milgram (1974, p. 8) when he noted that a person acting under orders does not lose their moral sense, but that the moral sense "acquires a radically different focus...." Moral concern now shifts to a consideration of how well a person is living up to the expectations that the authority has of her or him. "In wartime," as Milgram notes, "a soldier does not ask whether it is good or bad to bomb a hamlet; he does not experience shame or guilt in the destruction of a village: rather he feels pride or shame depending on how well he has performed the mission assigned to him." In short, as Kelman and Hamilton, and Milgram argue, individuals see themselves as agents, as having no choice but to accept the legitimacy of orders they are given. This, in turn, allows them to be relatively free of guilt when their actions cause harm to others because they are required and permitted to do so by the authorities from whom the orders came. Acts of violence are thus legitimated and the perpetrators are rendered free of guilt because they are acting out the orders of higher authority.

The second condition, routinization, "transforms the action into routine, mechanical, highly programmed operations" (p. 18). Routinization operates at both the individual and organizational level as the performance of a job is broken down into steps and divided among different offices. Responsibility is consequently diffused. This is very close to Weber's (1946, p. 54) classic arguments about the nature of bureaucracy. Weber identified several characteristics of bureaucracy noting that it was characterized by hierarchy and levels of graded authority where the responsibility for jobs was divided and where there was a firmly ordered system of super- and subordination. Routinization normalizes atrocity and masks the atrocity with language rendering it seemingly harmless.

The third condition is dehumanization. Dehumanization is necessary, according to Kelman and Hamilton, because the usual moral inhibitions against killing can be overcome once the victims are "deprived in the perpetrator's eyes of the two qualities essential to being perceived as fully human and included in the moral compact that governs human relationships: *identity—standing as independent, distinctive individuals...and community—* fellow membership in an interconnected network of individuals who care for each other and respect each other's individuality and rights" (p. 19). When people are removed from these, the moral restraints against killing them are weakened. Once again, however, these notions have been developed elsewhere, and Kelman and Hamilton's work should be tied to this earlier work.

The idea of the "universe of moral obligation" was first developed by Helen Fein (1979) in a very important work *Accounting for Genocide*. Fein was the first to point out that excluding fellow humans from the universe of moral obligation loosened the restraints and defined them as likely victims of sanctioned massacre.

In short, Kelman and Hamilton identify three conditions under which the type of violent conflict they call sanctioned massacres are likely to take place. Ultimately, if we view conflict, at least in part, as a response to these conditions, we are left with the profoundly disturbing conclusion that acts of large-scale destruction of human life might be committed by any individual or nation under the "right" cultural, psychological, or political circumstances. But, in order for violence and conflict to occur, individuals must be motivated to participate. Very often the motivator is language.

LANGUAGE AND CONFLICT

It is through language that the primal impulses, the likes and dislikes, the hatreds and enmities, the stereotypes and degrading and dehumanizing portraits of those who are not desirable or are rivals for political or economic power or status, are transmitted. Language is a powerful political tool.

The seemingly mysterious connection between words and actions, between language and behavior, has been a puzzle of enduring interest and fascination for scholars of many disciplines. In the contemporary era this fascination continues as scholars explore what Thomas Mann referred to as the connection between language and human responsibility (Steiner, 1977, p. 102). Unfortunately, most of the philosophical investigations of language are written at a level of abstraction which renders their utility as interpretative tools questionable. Those of us interested in how language works in the "real world," in particular in the world of politics, power, and human conflict, have relatively few sources to which to turn.

C. Wright Mills (1984, p. 13) pointed the way when he noted that "... we must approach linguistic behavior, not by referring it to private states in individuals, but by observing its social function of coordinating diverse actions." The matter, however, is not quite as simple as it sounds for at least two reasons. First, language "does not have the fixity or stability of meaning implied by the dictionary definitions of the words that comprise it. The crucial feature of language is that meaning is not fixed—it is emergent—tied to specific situations and constantly changing. The meaning of language is really no more stable than the particular situations it may be used to describe" (Weinstein, 1980, p. 17).

Second, language is a dialectical phenomenon that both shapes and reflects experience (Bolinger, 1980, p. ix). It not only describes events but is itself "a part of events, shaping their meaning and helping to shape the political roles officials and the general public play. In this sense, language, events, and self-conceptions are a part of the same transaction, mutually determining one another's meanings" (Edelman, 1977, p. 4). Events, then, are defined by the language used to describe them and this language, in turn, functions to "create shared meanings, perceptions, and reassurances among mass publics" (Edelman, 1971, p. 65). Perceptions of reality are linguistically created and meaning derives from the cultural, social, and political context.

In this sense, language may be a potent cultural and political weapon for it carries the cultural imperatives and transmits the dominant themes of a culture into the minds and hearts of the people. Language is the carrier and formative agent of the ideologies and mythologies prevalent in a culture or nation-state (Poliakov, 1971; Mosse, 1978; Becker, 1975).

LANGUAGE AND MYTH

All states, all cultures, and every society construct political myths which are usually based on claims that explain the origin of its people or of the nation-state. Generally, these are phrased metaphorically and "suppress the recognition of reality" (Edelman, 1971, p. 74). They eventually become self-perpetuating and serve as mechanisms used by the public to organize their views of the world. Usually, the metaphors become myths (Edelman, 1977, p. 17). The creation myths very often hold that the members of the group or the state descend from divine origins, or are protected by divine intervention. In the case of groups of people, the group may be said to descend from God or gods or from some mythic hero or animal. When the nation-state is involved, there is usually a founding myth which is often based on presumptions of divine intervention resulting in divine protection.

In addition, of course, the founders, generally male, were the wisest, most beneficent individuals who were representative of the best the culture had to offer. The "Founding Fathers" in the United States are, for example, revered as the "best and the brightest" who created a heavenly mansion on the hill which would be protected by God and which would always be on the side of right and justice. They were, in short, not human individuals and were, consequently not motivated by normal human passions. In fact, when I discuss some of the more mundane motivations for some of the founders in my introductory government class, students often get defensive and accuse me of "ridiculing" the great men. But it is not ridicule to examine the motivation of human individuals—whether to build a government or destroy a group of people. In both cases, and in the example of any founding myth, we are witnessing a very rudimentary type of historical thinking which operates to differentiate the group or the state from other groups or states, and to invest the actions of the state or group with a legitimacy beyond that normally accorded the actions of mere human beings. After all, if you are descended from, or inspired by gods, your actions are not questionable since they are not merely normal human acts. Such myths of divine origin are sometimes extended to define other peoples as outside the "universe of obligation" (Fein, 1979, pp. 4-5). Once defined as a member of the "out-group," as no longer protected, as not one of the privileged members of the society, the creation myth becomes a tool of destruction. These tools are not allowed to rest peacefully in one generation. On the contrary, they become part of the folklore and the "history" of a people or a nation and are passed from generation to generation. Passed along with the myths are the accompanying stereotypes and hatreds and desires for revenge or redemption—all of which may ultimately lead to extermination. These myths, and the propaganda that accompanies them, may function to dehumanize those outside the mythical boundaries—the potential victims—and eventually justify their extermination. As Edelman points out, the basic themes often revolve around a threatening out-group conspiracy against the in-group from which the benevolent political leaders will save the people. Victory, according to the leaders, may be achieved if the group works hard, sacrifices, and, most importantly, obeys its leaders (Edelman, 1971, p. 77). These types of myths, which often form the base of the language of extermination, perform at least four functions. First, they define the out-group—in this case the Jews. Second, they call for certain actions on the part of the in-group which are justified by the myth. Third, they require unquestioning obedience to the leaders who will function, if they are obeyed, as the saviors of the people. Fourth, they disguise reality and justify the acts of destruction.

DEFINING THE OUT-GROUP

When political leaders want to target a population for abuse they will produce negative characterizations that are usually linguistically found in deprecating nouns such as: *Kike, Wop, Spik, Bohunk, Jap, Chink, Dago* (Bollinger, 1980, p. 79).

Once these are accepted, the stereotyped group is now defined as being outside the "universe of obligation" (Fein, 1979, pp. 4-5). This means that they are not protected by the state because they are not considered official citizens and do not have the protection of the law—similar to African Americans in the Southern United States until 1964. Legal victimization of African Americans, was justified—was not considered against the law. Consequently, as it was "legal" to kill a black person in the south—even during the civil rights years there were killings for which no person was convicted. Several examples come to mind: on August 28, 1955 Emmett Till, a young African-American male from Chicago who was visiting his relatives in Mississippi was killed for talking to a white woman; Medgar Evers was killed June 12, 1963; and James Chaney, Andrew Goodman, and Michael Schwerner were killed on June 21, 1964—"justice" was never meted out in any of these cases.

It is obvious that there are connections that are not only theoretical between different forms of prejudice and the expressions that these take. Ideologies of hate and racism function to dehumanize the people at whom they are directed and to prepare the way for oppression or even extermination. Dehumanizing ideologies are justifications to the perpetrators. All racist terminology may conceivably function in this fashion. It is language that might be used to motivate or justify extermination.

Color symbolism, which forms a powerful set of negative stereotypes and images, functions in this fashion. James Baldwin recognized this and pointed out that as a black writer in an English speaking country he was forced "to realize that the assumptions on which the language operates are his enemy.... I was forced to reconsider similes: as black as sin, as black as night, blackhearted" (quoted in Bollinger, 1980, p. 89). Black is synonymous with negative images with evil, while white is symbolically positive and beautiful. Why this is the case has been explored by Moffic (1988, pp. 3-4) who notes that one might discover the source of the negative connotation of black by examining synonyms in the English language. In a paragraph meriting a long quotation he notes that:

> Even before the 16th-century discovery of darker people in Africa, the Oxford English Dictionary indicated negative associations to the term black. The meaning of black back then included 'deeply stained with dirt, soiled, foul...having dark or deadly purposes...deadly ...iniquitous, atrocious, horrible, wicked.'

Recent studies support the continuation of these associations. The great majority of Roget's Thesaurus synonyms for 'white' embrace positive qualities, while most (at least 60%) synonyms for 'black' have negative connotations. Examples of 'white' synonyms include pure, moral, fair, and honorable. For 'black,' in contrast, we have such synonyms as disastrous, repulsive, sinister, and wicked. In Webster's Dictionary, concepts or words hyphenated with the term black are mainly negative, including blackball, blacklist, black magic, blackmail, and black market.... For children learning the English language, negative associations to black are quickly reinforced.

This type of racist stereotyping takes additional forms and is not limited to color. For example, "People executed as witches in the seventeenth century and those persecuted in witch hunts in the twentieth century suffered from the definitions applied to them regardless of the correctness of either form of belief in witches" (Edelman, 1977, p. 9). Moreover, during the Vietnam War, negative symbolism was used to characterize Vietnamese people as "gooks," "dinks," "slant eyes," and so on (Lifton, 1973; Caputo, 1977; Baker, 1981, Downs, 1987). In an earlier period of American history Native American people were negatively labeled as the groundwork was prepared for their eventual destruction. They were saddled with terms such as "indians," "savages," "infidels," "heathen," and "barbarians" (Berkhofer, 1979). As understood at the time, a "barbarian" was to be contrasted with a person who was "civilized" which, as Berkhofer (1978, p. 16) notes, was also interchangeable with Christian. A prime example of this type of language may be found in a description sent back to England by one Alexander Whitaker, a minister in Henrico, Virginia, who wrote in 1613:

...let the miserable condition of these naked slaves of the divell move you to compassion....Wherefore they serve the divell for fear, after a most base manner, sacrificing sometimes (as I have heard) their own children to him....Their priests...are no other but such as our English witches are. They live naked in bodie, as if their shame of their sins deserved no covering: Their names are as naked as their bodie: they esteem it a virtue to lie, deceive and steal as their master the divell teacheth to them (Berkhofer, 1978, p. 12).

This use of language would, of course, be of little consequence if it were not accompanied by calls for action, for behavior. As noted earlier, the call to the in-group to act is a second function of myths created by the language of extermination.

CALL TO ACTION

There is a relationship between negative symbols and mass murder. The symbols are a legitimating mechanisms and a call for action. Once it has been established that the state or group is threatened by vermin or some other mythic creation, however defined, the protection, cleansing, extermination must be put into motion. Leaders prepare a population for participation in mass murder by issuing the calls for action. When leaders talk of violent action as necessary in defense of the state or in defense of a "way of life," they are legitimating extermination. There is always a ready supply of people willing to act out the hostile impulses if they are reinforced by those in positions of influence. Political authority perpetuates an image of order and stability against a background of potential chaos. In this context familiar language may be used to "represent traditional standards," or to "change the language because the familiar has failed or appears to be failing" (Weinstein, 1980, p. 18). Political leaders are, therefore, like dramatists in that they "can manipulate the common capacity for a willing suspension of disbelief. But whereas people follow the dramatist in his work because nothing is lost if they do, they must follow political leaders because everything may be lost if they do not" (Weinstein, 1980, p. 18). The words of the leader were used to induce action and to insure obedience to the commands of authority.

LANGUAGE AND OBEDIENCE

Language is used to obscure the reality of mass murder and to numb the participants (Fleming, 1982). That this is a commonplace use of language is a depressing and all too often denied reality. Leaders prepare a population for violence by positing a connection between the well being of a particular country or group and obedience to the leaders. This results in citizens perceiving leaders as "correct," simply because they are leaders. Authority is to be obeyed, the exterminations are to be carried out as ordered.

Obedience is rewarded, encouraged by "the glory words like duty, honor and valor" (Baker, 1981, p. 168). It is also reinforced by indoctrination and the destruction of identity and self-worth. Rituals of induction often function to transmit into the psyches of individuals the words of the leaders. Military training is a prime example. Philip Caputo (1977, pp. 9-10) sums up military indoctrination as mental and physical abuse the objective of which was to eliminate the weak who were collectively known as "unsats," for unsatisfactory. The reasoning was that anyone who could not take being shouted at and kicked in the ass once in awhile could never withstand the rigors of combat. But such abuse was also designed to destroy each man's sense of self- worth, to make him feel worthless until he proved himself equal to the Corp's exacting standards.

Once the self-worth is destroyed what message replaces it? Again Caputo is a perceptive observer who notes that "The psychology of the mob, of the Bund rally, takes command of his will.... In time, he begins to believe that he really does love the Marine Corps, that it is invincible, and that there is nothing improper in praying for war..." (p. 12). The result, of course, is obedience. One is not supposed to consider the consequences of acts one is ordered to undertake. Once the orders are executed the behavior, especially if destructive, must be justified. One mechanism of justification is to manipulate and disguise reality.

LANGUAGE AND JUSTIFICATION

In some cases, acts of human destructiveness are disguised by euphemisms. Jargon is an example of euphemism and it functions "to mask what one does not wish to face....If Pentagon pronouncements speak of structures in Vietnamese villages, people feel better than they would if they read that huts or houses were being destroyed" (Edelman, 1971, p. 74). In fact, categorizations were developed to label human beings so that when U.S. troops entered a village they were able to place the villagers in categories according to their supposed involvement with the National Liberation Front (Schell, 1987, p. 241). The categories were: "confirmed VC," "VC suspect," "VC supporter," "detainee," "refugee," and "defector." Schell goes on to describe what happened when the troops actually entered a village and rounded up the villagers. Those who were to be evacuated were categorized as "VC supporters" or "VC suspects," but when the same villagers were removed to a camp the Army categorized them as "refugees." By the same token, a Vietnamese who had been shot by our troops was almost invariably categorized as a "confirmed VC." (The soldiers had a joke that ran, "Anything that's dead and isn't white is a VC.") (p. 241).

The language of violence and conflict is not a historical aberration, it is all to common. Used to create myths which function to simplify a complex world, to call people to action against specified targets, to motivate obedience, and justify destruction, the language of extermination is designed to touch what Steiner (1971, p. 31) refers to as the "dark places" which are "at the center" of all human beings. These dark places are probably not part of the consciousness of most people. Afterall, no person intends to commit evil. "No eighteen-year-old kid went to Vietnam thinking, 'Oh boy, now I'm going to be evil.' But most of them met their darker sides face to face in that war" (Baker, 1981, p. 168). Until we confront and begin to understand how language functions to touch that "darker side," we will remain potential victims and executioners. Evil is encouraged and rewarded with symbols that may come in many forms, sometimes medals or honors of assorted types, but most often words. These words are transmitted from generation to generation through the process of socialization and they perpetuate the myths and negative stereotypes and hatreds which keep the cycle of violence going. Very often these words and myths involve, as we have seen, race and class. The remainder of this chapter, therefore, provides a brief illustrative case study of conflict in the city of Atlanta, Georgia under the administration of Mayor Andrew Young, where it appears to have been tied to questions of race and class.

RACIAL AND ETHNIC CONFLICT IN ATLANTA

Conflict in Atlanta appears to be tied to questions of race and class. Since the early 1970s, an increasing number of cities in the United States have become "black regimes." Black or African-American regimes are "black-led and black-dominated administrations backed by solid council majorities" (Reed, 1988, p. 1). Thirteen cities with populations over 100,000 are governed by African-American regimes. These cities include: Detroit, Washington, DC, New Orleans, Atlanta, Oakland, Birmingham, and Richmond (Reed, 1988, p. 174). They share the following common socioeconomic characteristics: majority-African-American populations, large numbers of poor residents, intense fiscal stress, and high central city-suburban economic disparities. Interestingly, there are an even larger number of black regimes in cities under 100,000.

In these cities, downward redistributive policies are favored by many residents, because a large number of them are working class. As a result, their mayors make populist and racial appeals to remain in office. However, at the same time, upward redistributive policies are sought by the business-dominated governing coalition which exists in these and most medium and large cities (Fainstein and Fainstein, 1982; Friedland, 1983; Reed, 1988; Stone, 1989). Consequently, there is a high potential for conflict between the governing and electoral constituencies of many mayors, but especially those in African-American regimes.

Furthermore, this conflict heightens the latent tensions between middle- and upper-strata African Americans vis-à-vis those of the lower strata. The possible conflict stems from the greater governmental benefits that middle- and upper-stratum African Americans (combined and referred to hereafter as upper-strata) receive as compared to their lower-strata counterparts. Several scholars contend that upper-strata African Americans are the prime beneficiaries of such affirmative action policies as municipal government employment and contracts to minority businesses (Piliawasky, 1985, pp. 18-19; Nelson, 1987, pp. 172-173; Reed, 1988, pp. 156-157; Stone, 1989, pp. 183-199).

This high potential for rancorous conflict underscores the importance of conflict management for these regimes. "Managing conflict in matters of political importance," claims Banfield and Wilson, is a key function of municipal government (Banfield and Wilson, 1963, p. 18). This means, according to Friedland and colleagues, that city government seeks "political integration of the urban population" (Friedland, Piven, and Alford, 1984, p. 274).

POLITICAL INTEGRATION AND SYSTEM SUPPORT

How well this has been accomplished may be indicated by examining the level of political or "system support" among its citizens (Bowman, Ippolito, and Levin, 1972). Political support, referred to as political trust in some studies, contains two components: diffuse and specific support. Diffuse support is defined as the "reservoir of favorable attitudes or goodwill that helps members to accept or tolerate outputs to which they are opposed or the effects of which they see as damaging to their wants" (Easton, 1975, p. 444). Specific support is characterized as "the satisfaction that members of a system feel they obtain from the perceived outputs and performance of the political authorities" (Easton, 1975, p. 435).

In contrast, diffuse support is "independent of outputs and performance in the short run" and more enduring than specific support (Easton, 1975, pp. 444-445). A decline in diffuse support means the "loss of a generalized capacity of authorities to commit resources to attain collective goals" (Gamson, 1968, p. 43).

The few studies examining the political trust attitudes of citizens in cities with African-American mayors have found African Americans more politically trusting than whites (Abney and Hutcheson, 1981; Foster, 1978; Fowler, 1974). There are, however, limitations. One study (Foster, 1978) investigated the political trust attitudes of preadults and most of the remaining studies did not explore intra-racial or interclass attitudinal differences (Bowman et al., 1972; Abney and Hutcheson, 1981; Fowler, 1974). This lack of attention to possible intra-racial attitudinal differences may have been partly due to a failure to consider certain alternative explanations and partially due to not studying African-American regimes. Given the previously discussed possibility of political conflict in these cities, it is important to consider intra-racial and interclass attitudinal differences.

This is achieved by examining three alternative explanations: the unitary city interest, race, and class. According to the unitary city interest explanation, a relatively high level of diffuse support is expected among citizens regardless of their race or class backgrounds (Peterson, 1981). Where race is used as the explanation, significant attitudinal differences are predicted to occur along racial lines (Eisinger, 1984; Judd, 1988; Jones, 1978, 1990; Levine, 1974). Class explanations claim that, instead of race divisions, significant class differences will be evident among support attitudes; they predict contrasting diffuse support attitudes will exist between upper- and lower-strata residents (Katznelson, 1976; Friedland et al., 1984; Fainstein and Fainstein, 1982).

This study attempts to determine which explanation provides the most appropriate description of the diffuse support attitudes of neighborhood organization leaders in Atlanta, Georgia, a city governed by an African-American regime. This, in turn, helps to delineate the implications for the regime's conflict management. The findings of this study support, with some modifications, the race explanation. However, significant class differences were found in the attitudes of African Americans.

This paper proceeds as follows. First, the three alternative explanations on the conflict management effectiveness of African-American mayors are examined. In the second section, the methodology is discussed. Third, the findings and the implications of the findings are elaborated. The concluding section provides an overall summary of these findings and their implications for urban conflict.

THREE ALTERNATIVE EXPLANATIONS DISCUSSED

Paul Peterson, creator of the unitary city interest explanation, argues that a mayor, regardless of whether he or she is an African American or white, is constrained by the city's need to have a prospering economy (Peterson, 1981, 1984). This entails pursuing policies that will attract investment capital to the city. Thus, most mayors give primary emphasis to development policies, which Peterson claims are policies that promote economic growth (Peterson, 1981, p. 41). Such policies include tax abatements for businesses, infrastructure improvements and development, downtown renewal projects, tourism and convention promotions, and actions to promote a good business climate. Moreover, mayors are prompted by the fierce competition that exists among cities to obtain investments and to maintain their own exporting industries.

Popular awareness of these realities fosters widespread consensus, claims Peterson, among a city's governmental leaders, business leaders, and citizens on the need for emphasizing economic development policies. In contrast, redistributive policies, according to Peterson, are not considered "because a wide variety of political groups active in local politics implicitly appreciate the impracticality of locally financed redistribution" (Peterson, 1984, p. 325). Mayors seek to minimize redistributive social policies because the tax burden they place on middle- and upper-class residents encourages these people to leave the city. Moreover, these policies, however desirable from the perspective of the poor and their advocates, undermine the city's competitive advantage vis-à-vis other cities; they reduce revenue that could be used on economic development and increase taxes on businesses (Peterson, 1981, pp. 43-44). Since the mayor and citizens of all races and classes recognize their common interest in fostering economic development, no significant differences in diffuse support are expected among residents. A pro-growth mayor should foster positive diffuse support.

In contrast, scholars emphasizing race as an explanation would predict significant racial differences in diffuse support levels (Eisinger, 1976, 1984; Judd, 1986; Jones, 1978, 1990; Levine, 1974). They contend that an African-

American mayor pursues a dual strategy to maintain the support of his or her two chief constituencies: the African-American community and the white business community. One component of this strategy is emphasizing economic development policies with the expectations that they will provide profits for downtown businesses and jobs for African-American residents. The second part of this strategy is utilizing affirmative action policies to provide municipal jobs for African Americans and government contracts for minority-owned businesses (Eisinger, 1984).

Middle- and working-class whites are not likely to be members of these mayors' electoral constituency for several reasons. They compete with their African-American counterparts for the jobs and benefits created by these policies. Secondly, since these mayors have a majority-African-American electorate, they are not dependent on middle-class white voters. Moreover, a populist political alliance between African Americans and working-class whites is not sought by these mayors, because it would promote the kind of class politics that would make a political alliance with the business community extremely difficult and, possibly, deter business investments (Eisinger, 1984). Lastly, given the intense racial polarization that exists in these cities, it is unlikely that working-class or even middle-class whites would respond positively to such political overtures by African-American mayors without unrealistic reassurances or concessions being made by these officials.

This dual strategy fosters significant racial differences among city residents in their levels of diffuse support. Therefore, white middle- and working-class residents will have significantly lower diffuse support levels than their African-American counterparts. It should be noted that some race explanation scholars would also argue that there is potential conflict between African Americans of the middle and upper stratum and those of the lower strata (Stone, 1989; Reed, 1988; Nelson and Meranto, 1977; Jones, 1990; Manning, 1980). However, they contend it is effectively managed by these mayors' adroit manipulation of racial appeals to obscure or redefine divisive issues (Manning, 1980; Jackson, 1990; Reed, 1988).

Such intra-racial class differences in diffuse support are predicted by class explanation scholars in both racial communities. Some class explanation scholars as Friedland, Piven, and Alford argue that city government has the dual functions of "meeting the infrastructural and service requirements of capital accumulation," while managing the "popular discontent generated by the social costs of the accumulation process" (Friedland et al., 1984, p. 274). They claim that African-American mayors, as do any other mayors, must respond to the mobility of capital by pursuing a policy of maintaining a highly favorable business environment for capital investments (Katznelson, 1976; Fainstein and Fainstein, 1982; Stone, 1989; Friedland, Piven, and Alford, 1984). In doing so, these mayors promote economic development policies that entail considerable social costs for many working- and middle-class residents.

Friedland asserts that the "policies necessary to growth have high social costs while the policies necessary to social control cut into the revenues necessary to support growth" (Friedland, 1983, p. 221).

As a result, these mayors are often placed in the dilemma of satisfying the demands of the business community for favorable economic development policies vis-à-vis the demands of the African-American community for increased social expenditures. The former seeks pro-business economic development policies, which entail such social costs as destruction of housing for the poor, dislocation of indigent people, traffic congestion, and reduced taxes or postponement of tax collection. Consequently, the latter, who are often the victims of aforementioned policies, demand more social service expenditures to offset the social costs of economic development policies, as well as to improve their impoverished conditions. This dilemma frequently occurs in a situation of declining city revenues. These scholars argue that economic development policies are favored over the social welfare policies, because government is biased toward the interests of the powerful upper class.

As a result of this bias, political alienation and class consciousness increase among minorities, working-class whites, and gays. These groups acquire a "corporate group consciousness" that challenges the dominant "legitimate" belief system (Katznelson, 1976, pp. 222-223). Therefore, significant class differences are expected among citizens in their levels of diffuse support. The upper-strata African Americans and whites are expected to have relatively high levels of diffuse support, whereas their lower-strata counterparts will have very low levels of diffuse support.

METHODOLOGY

Diffuse support is vital to any regime that does not rely completely on its power of coercion to obtain the obedience and support of its citizens. Gamson claims political trust (diffuse support) is "a creator of collective power" (Gamson, 1968, p. 45). The effectiveness of political leadership, argues Gamson, "depends on the ability of authorities to claim the loyal cooperation of members of the system without having to specify in advance what such cooperation will entail" (Gamson, 1968, p. 45). Gamson and Easton contend that a decline in diffuse support entails a decrease in the capability of the political system to achieve its collective goals (Gamson, 1968; Easton, 1975).

Diffuse support, according to Easton and Gamson, involves a sense of attachment beyond the incumbent authorities. This attachment extends, cumulatively, to the incumbent authorities, the regime institutions and rules, and the larger community (Easton, 1965, p. 220; Gamson, 1968, p. 53). Since each level is a generalization of support attitudes from the previous level, dissatisfaction with an outcome at one level, according to Gamson and Easton, may be generalized by a citizen to other levels. Dissatisfaction begins, according to Gamson, when an undesirable outcome is regarded by a citizen as "a member of a class of decision with similar results" (Gamson, 1968, p. 51). As dissatisfaction grows, system effectiveness declines because diffuse support is now becoming political alienation.

To determine the levels of diffuse support of Atlanta's citizens, ninety African-American and white Atlanta neighborhood organization leaders of Atlanta were interviewed by telephone in spring of 1986. They were asked a series of close-ended questions. Jukam's diffuse support questionnaire was used, because of its high inter-item correlations and scale reliabilities (Jukam, 1979, pp. 14, 21, 22). The specific support questions were derived largely from Jukam's specific support questionnaire along with some political evaluation questions from Abney and Hutcheson's government evaluation questionnaires (Jukam, 1979; Abney and Hutchinson, 1981, pp. 98-99). The external political efficacy question was derived from Iyengar's political efficacy instrument (Iyengar, 1980, p. 40). After gathering the diffuse support data on the neighborhood organization leaders, their attitudes were categorized using Gamson's typology of group support.

According to the unitary city interest explanation, we should expect neighborhood organization leaders of all class and racial groups to constitute a confident group. In contrast, the race explanation scholars predict that African-American and white neighborhood leaders will comprise separate groups with that of the African Americans being a confident group and that of the whites being a neutral group. The class explanation suggests that upper-strata African-American and white leaders will constitute a confident group; whereas their lower-strata counterparts will compose an alienated group.

Atlanta was chosen as the case study site for four reasons. First, Professor Banks has considerable familiarity with the city's history and politics. Second, its politics have been the subject of several noteworthy political studies (Hunter, 1953, 1980; Jennings, 1964; Stone, 1989; Orfield and Ashkinaze, 1991). In addition, its citizens' political attitudes have been examined in several attitudinal studies (Bowman et al., 1972; Fowler, 1974; Abney and Hutcheson, 1981). These earlier studies allow us to make longitudinal comparisons, which are important because Atlanta has had an African-American regime since 1977.

Furthermore, Atlanta is similar to most African-American regimes. This is evident in the 1980 statistical comparisons between Atlanta and the seven other cities with African-American regimes, and populations over 200,000: Baltimore, Birmingham, Detroit, New Orleans, Newark, Richmond, and Washington, DC. The African-American population of Atlanta was 66.6 percent; the average for the seven others was 58.3. One highly revealing statistic involves the percentage of people below the poverty line. In Atlanta the percentage was 27.5, while for the other regimes it was 27.4 percent. Median family income in Atlanta was $13,591 compared to $15,870 average for the seven regimes. The population of Atlanta decreased by -14.8 percent from 1970 to 1986, whereas its metropolitan area experienced a 19.8 percent increase in population from 1980 to 1986. During the years from 1970 to 1986, the seven regimes averaged a -15.6 decrease in central city population, while their metropolitan area grew by 3.7 percent from 1980 to 1986 (U.S. Census Bureau, 1990).

Lastly, in the 1980s, Atlanta's African-American mayor, Andrew Young, as typical of most African-American regime mayors, was a noted pro-growth advocate. Mayor Young strongly supported policies favored by business and commercial interests. For example, he led the Atlanta Chamber of Commerce's lobbying efforts to get the adoption of a sales tax that would be used to reduce property taxes. Despite the shortage of housing for lower-income people, Mayor Young aggressively pursued the construction of middle- and upper-income housing nearby the downtown business district. However, in keeping with the dual strategy pursued by many African-American mayors, he vigorously sought 35 percent minority participation in major public-funded construction projects (Jones, 1990, pp. 140-141).

Neighborhood organization leaders were interviewed instead of citizens for the following reasons. These leaders are participants in the city's citizen participation program, Atlanta Neighborhood Planning Unit program. This program is a direct effort by the Atlanta city government to bolster political trust in city government among its residents (Prejean, 1986). Thus, the leaders' diffuse support attitudes provide one clear means of assessing the city's efforts to promote political integration.

The leaders' participation in this program enhances their knowledge of the processes and plans of Atlanta city government. As a result, they should be better able to evaluate the performance of city government than most citizens. But, more importantly, their knowledge of public affairs, their access to government information, and their leadership positions are apt to make them highly influential opinion leaders in their respective neighborhoods.

They are also likely to exercise some political influence on government elites. These leaders, unlike many citizens, are active in city politics. Virtually all of them indicated in their questionnaire responses that they are extremely active in most forms of political participation. Since they are well-educated, community leaders with some grass-roots support, there is a strong likelihood that the incumbents will consider them likely political challengers. For example, in the 1973 city elections, five neighborhood organization activists were elected to the city council. The political behavior and attitudes of such community leaders, claims Eisinger, are far more important than those of most citizens in "determining the structure of the context of elite interaction" (Eisinger, 1976, p. 18).

The neighborhood organization leaders interviewed were chosen on the basis of the socioeconomic characteristics of their neighborhoods, which was provided in a study of Atlanta neighborhood organizations (Urban Life Associates, 1975). The objective was to achieve a representative cross section of neighborhoods on the basis of race and class background. The leaders interviewed constituted 41 percent of the leadership of the 219 formally organized city neighborhood organizations.

Their socioeconomic characteristics are as follows. There are 49 African Americans (56%) and 38 whites (44%). Approximately 14 percent had only some high school or high school diploma and 20 percent had only some college training. Sixty-six percent of the leaders had college degrees and 50 percent had post-college training. In 1985 dollars, one-fourth of the leaders had family incomes of less than $19,000. Whereas, 56 percent had family incomes between $20,000 and $59,000 and 20 percent had incomes of $60,000 and up. The majority of the leaders held professional or managerial occupations (57%) and 16 percent were self-employed and 3 percent were semiskilled (Banks, 1987).

FINDINGS

The diffuse support attitudes of the leaders reveals two significant groups based on race. As shown in Table 1, both upper- and lower-strata African Americans have higher diffuse support scores compared to all stratum of white leaders.

There is, however, a considerable difference between upper- and lower-strata African-American leaders in diffuse support scores (23 to 30.43). Upper-strata African Americans scored considerably higher than their lower-strata brethren. The mean score of the lower-strata African-American leaders is closer to the score of upper-strata whites than that of upper-strata African Americans. Whereas, the margin of difference is small between upper-strata and lower-strata whites.

Table 1. Mean Diffuse Support Scores of Upper and Lower SES Groups

	Blacks		Whites	
	Upper SES	*Lower SES*	*Upper SES*	*Lower SES*
Mean	23.00	30.43	36.05	37.61
Minimum (positive)	13	10	23	18
Maximum (Negative)	30	68	57	54
Range	17	58	34	36
N =	10	38	20	18

These findings suggest that the race explanation is the most accurate of the three explanations. As predicted by race explanation scholars, significant racial differences in diffuse support were found. However, it is clear that there are important class differences in diffuse support scores within the African-American community. Thus, the race interpretation needs to be qualified to account for the significant internal class divisions of the African-American community.

Similar findings were found regarding specific support. Specific support differences among leaders of both racial groups were considerable. Approximately 55 percent of the African-American leaders of both strata gave city government high evaluations in its performance across several important policy areas, such as attracting industry, treating all citizens fairly, providing strong capable political leadership, guaranteeing protection and security for individuals, promoting economic growth, and improving employment opportunities of citizens. In contrast, only 22 percent of the white leaders gave similar assessments, while almost three-fourths of the white leaders evaluated city government as only average in its performance.

Among the class groupings within the African-American community, the vast majority of the upper-strata leaders evaluated the performance of city government as high; whereas, only two-fifths of the lower-class African Americans gave a high rating. Approximately, two-thirds of the upper- and lower-strata white leaders gave moderate ratings and slightly less than a third evaluated it high.

Class differences were greater than race differences on the leader's assessment of whether his or her neighborhood received "better or about the same or worse services than most other neighborhoods," regarding such services as garbage collection, parks, police, and fire protection. Approximately, 35 percent of all upper-class leaders perceived their neighborhood receiving better services than most other neighborhoods and six percent saw it as worse. Whereas, 35 percent of the lower-class leaders saw their neighborhoods as receiving worse services than the others. The evaluation of city services among African-American and white leaders were similar to the 1981 findings of Abney and Hutcheson. For example, they found 76 percent of white Atlanta as rating their city services as "about same" and 15 percent as "better than" those provided in other neighborhoods of the city (Abney and Hutcheson, 1981, pp. 98-99). Similarly, in this study 69 percent of the white leaders chose the "about same" response and 18 percent selected the "better than" response.

Even in external political efficacy (perception of governmental responsiveness), the more significant attitudinal difference was between the racial groups instead of biracial class groupings. Over half of the African-American leaders (58%) claimed people like themselves had a lot of power in city politics, whereas, over half of the white leaders (55%) believed that people like themselves had little power in city politics. Among upper-income African-

American leaders the percentages of those seeing people like themselves as having a lot of power in city politics was 79 percent. Whereas, only 41 percent of their lower-income brethren reported similar perceptions. Only one-third of the upper-income whites saw people like themselves as having a lot of power.

Interestingly, there was considerable agreement in their perceptions of distribution of power between African American and whites in city politics. Forty percent of the African-American and white leaders claimed that African Americans had about "equal power" to whites. However, 55 percent of the white leaders claimed that "blacks had too little or somewhat less power than whites" in politics, while only 33 percent of the African-American leaders answered similarly.

POLITICAL CONFLICT IN ATLANTA

The findings of this study endorse, with some modifications, the race model as providing the most appropriate explanation of the diffuse support attitudes of Atlanta's neighborhood organization leaders. Since significant differences were found in the levels of diffuse support between African-American and white leaders, these findings basically confirm the race explanation. However, there were important class differences found among African Americans in their diffuse support, which are not accounted for in the race explanation. In interpreting the implications of these findings, it should be underscored that the results are the diffuse support levels of neighborhood organization leaders. Their diffuse support levels are apt to be higher than those of most citizens because they have more political trust and confidence in their local governmental officials than nonparticipants (Cole, 1974, p. 111). As discussed earlier, these leaders are participants in a citizen participation program that seeks to bolster their trust (support) in city government; that is, to further their political integration (Prejean, 1986). Friedland and colleagues argue that the political integration function of city government is generally placed in agencies that have relatively little power but high visibility such as a citizens participation program (Friedland et al., 1984, p. 285). This is the case in Atlanta (Banks, 1987).

Furthermore, the more educated and politically efficacious persons tend to have higher levels of political trust (Abramson, 1983; Erickson, Luttbeg, and Tedin, 1991, p. 126; Wildavsky, 1964, p. 264). Participants in Atlanta's citizen participation program are more educated and more politically efficacious than ordinary citizens.

However, the failure at politically integrating upper-strata whites lessens the likelihood of maintaining, as well as luring middle- and upper-class white residents. As a result, there will be fewer middle-class white residents to rely on to bolster the community's tax base and to offset the negative investment effects of being a virtually all African-American city. For studies have shown that businesses are adverse to investing in communities with large concentrations of African Americans (Bradbury, Downs, and Small, 1982). Further, there is the belief that if a city exceeds 70 percent African American, as an Atlanta newspaper editor argues, "investors, for whatever reasons, begin to shy away from an area" (Stone, 1989, p. 174). These results could have serious consequences for these financially stressed cities.

The resultant declining economic conditions of these cities may exacerbate the ability of their mayors to manage political conflicts between their governing and electoral constituencies and within the African-American community itself. As mentioned earlier, failure to politically integrate middle-class whites may lead to negative investment consequences by external and internal white businesses. This occurrence may result in the business community placing greater demands on these regimes, so as to protect their local investments. Moreover, the business community in this situation is apt to gain increased leverage against city government, because government leaders will be even more dependent on them for maintaining the city's business climate, if not its economic vitality.

Declining economic conditions coupled with increasing business community demands will more than likely lessen the regime's ability to provide benefits to lower-strata, as well as the upper-strata African Americans. The declining ability to maintain political integration within the African-American community is apt to have some major consequences in the future.

This lack of community political cohesiveness may lead to heightened skepticism and scrutiny in some segments of the African-American community toward the regime's policies. This study's findings suggest that cynicism may be underway. The economic plight of Atlanta's lower-strata African Americans is a likely contributing factor. The proportion of city households below the poverty line practically doubled from 1970 to 1982 (Orfield and Ashkinaze, 1991, p. 52). This cynicism is apt to weaken the capability of these mayors to manipulate racial symbols or redefine issues or policies, especially pro-growth development policies, in generic racial interest terms. As discussed earlier, this capability is seen by several scholars as one of the most effective noncoercive means that these mayors have for managing conflict between their governing and electoral constituencies and within the African-American community.

Moreover, the increasing political cynicism among lower-strata African Americans may lead to some significant changes in the recruitment patterns of candidates and in the candidates' electoral campaign strategies. Jennings contends that such changes are likely to occur (Judd, 1986, p. 166):

> As the conditions for blacks continue to worsen, we will see more clearly the two faces of urban politics. While one kind of black politician will seek accommodation with

corporate America, other black politicians will become more vociferous and sophisticated in their challenges to the powerful. It is the latter face of black and urban politics that will be able to mobilize the masses of blacks and the poor in the electoral arena.

However, these and other conventional political changes, such as mass-based populist organizations, are not likely to be fully realized unless significant numbers of middle-class African Americans become increasingly cynical enough to promote such changes. This appears to have been the case in Chicago with the 1983 election of the populist African-American mayor, Harold Washington. However, the opposition was a white-controlled party machine. Anyhow, there exist few, if any, independent, grass-roots political organizations in most of these cities to check African-American mayors, much less function as an independent power base (Nelson, 1987, p. 175).

The possible growing political cynicism of lower-strata African Americans may lead, however, to such nihilistic political behaviors as riots and civil disorders (Judd, 1988, pp. 418-420). This phenomenon would present these regimes with a highly serious political conflict problem and a reduced capability to manage it.

CONCLUSION

Racial and ethnic conflict may, therefore, be studied from disparate perspectives that conceivably provide interesting insights into its possible roots and future occurrence. Traditional political science, as we have just seen in the case study of Atlanta, examines variables such as race, class, and different measures of support, in an attempt to ascertain whether conflict is likely between certain specified groups. On the other hand, explanations based in political psychology focus on more abstract issues such as the role of identity and language in causing and motivating conflict. Both are important and, we argue, that the insights from both must be merged empirically and theoretically if political science is to make further advances in the study of ethnic and racial conflict.

ACKNOWLEDGMENT

The section of this chapter entitled "Racial Confict in Atlanta" is drawn from a larger study entitled "Political Support Attitudes Toward an African American Regime: A Case Study of the Andrew Young Administration in Atlanta," *National Political Science Review* 6: (1996).

REFERENCES

Abney, F.G., and Hutcheson, Jr. J.D. 1981. "Race Representation, and Trust: Changes in Attitudes After the Election of a Black Mayor." Public Opinion Quarterly 45: 91-101.

Abramson, P. 1983. *Political Attitudes in America*. San Francisco: Freeman.

Adam, B.D. 1978. *The Survival of Domination*. New York: Elsevier.

Baker, M. 1981. *NAM*. New York: Berkley Books.

Banfield, E.C., and Wilson, J.Q. 1963. *City Politics*. Cambridge: Harvard University Press.

Banks, M.E. 1987. "Consociational Democracy: The Outcome of Racial Political Polarization in Atlanta, Georgia, 1973-1986." Unpublished dissertation, University of Texas at Austin.

Becker, E. 1975. *Escape from Evil*. New York: The Free Press

Berkhofer, R.F., Jr. 1978. *The White Man's Indian*. New York: Random House.

Bollinger, D. 1980. *Language-The Loaded Weapon*. Chicago: Longman.

Bowman, L., D. Ippolito, and M. Levin. 1972. "Self Interest and Referendum Support: The Case of A Rapid Transit Vote in Atlanta." In *People and Politics in Urban Society, edited by H. Hahn. Beverly, CA: Sage*.

Bradbury, K., A. Downs, and K. Small. 1982. Urban Decline and the Future of American Cities. Washington, DC: Brookings.

Brzezinski, Z. 1993. *Out of Control*. New York: Charles Scribner's Sons.

Caputo, P. 1977. *A Rumor of War*. New York: Ballantine.

Cole, R.L. 1974. *Citizen Participation and the Urban Policy Process*. Lexington, MA: Lexington Books.

Des Pres, T. 1988. *Praises and Dispraises: Poetry and Politics in the 20th Century*. New York: Viking.

Downs, F. 1978. *The Killing Zone*. New York: W.W. Norton.

Easton, D. 1975. "A Re-Assessment of the Concept of Political Support." *British Journal of Political Science* 5 (October): 435-457.

Easton, D. 1965. *A System Analysis of Political Life*. New York: John Wiley.

Edelman, M. 1971. *Politics As Symbolic Actions*. San Diego: Academic Press.

Edelman, M. 1977. *Political Language: Words that Succeed and Policies That Fail*. San Diego: Academic Press.

Edelman, M. 1988. *Constructing the Political Spectacle*. Chicago: The University of Chicago Press.

Eisinger, P.K. 1976. *The Patterns of Interracial Politics: Conflict and Cooperation in the City*. New York: Academic.

Eisinger, P.K. 1980. *The Politics of Displacement: Racial and Ethnic Transitions in Three American Cities*. New York: Academic.

Eisinger, P.K. 1984. "Black Mayors and Racial Economic Advancement." Pp. 249-260. In *Readings in Urban Politics*. Edited by H. Hahn and C. Levine. New York: Longman.

Erikson, R. TS., N.R. Luttbeg, and K.L. Tedin. 1991. *American Public Opinion: Its Origins, Content, and Impact*. (4th ed.). New York: Macmillan.

Fainstein, N., and S. Fainstein. 1982. "Restructuring the American City: A Comparative Perspective." In *Urban Policy Under Capitalism*, edited by N. Fainstein and S. Fainstein. Beverly Hills, CA: Sage.

Fein, H. 1979. *Counting for Genocide*. New York The Free Press.

Fein, H. 1992. *Genocide Watch*. New Haven: Yale University Press.

Felming, G. 1982. *Hitler and the Final Solution*. Berkeley: University of California Press.

Foster, L.S. 1978. "Black Perception of the Mayor." *Urban Affairs Quarterly* 14: 245-252.

Fowler, F. 1974. *Citizen Attitudes Toward Local Government, Services, and Taxes*. Cambridge, MA: Ballinger.

Friedland R., F.F. Piven, and R. Alford. 1984. "Political Conflict, Urban Structure, and The Fiscal Crisis." Pp. 273-297 in *Marxism and the Metropolis: New Perspectives in Urban Political Economy,* edited by W.K. Tabb and L. Sawers. New York: Oxford University Press.

Friedland, R. 1983. *Power and Crisis in the City.* New York: Schocken.

Gamson, W.A. 1968. *Power and Discontent.* Homewood, IL: Dorsey.

Hirsch, H. 1989. "Trivializing Human Experience: Social Studies Methods and Genocide Scholarship." *Armenian Review* 42(4): 71-81.

Iyengar, S. 1980. "Trust, Eefficacy and Political Reality: A Longitudinal Study of Indian High School Students." *Comparative Politics* 13 (October): 90-117.

Jackson, B. 1990. "Black Political Power in the City of Angels: An Analysis of Mayor Tom Bradley's Electoral Success." *National Political Science Review* 2: 169-175.

Jennings. M.K., 1964. *Community Influentials.* New York: Free Press.

Jones, M. 1978. "Black Political Empowerment in Atlanta: Myth and Reality." *The Annals of the American Academy of Political and Social Sciences* 439 (September): 90-117.

Jones, M. 1990. "Black Mayoralty Leadership in Atlanta." *National Political Science Review* 2: 138-144.

Judd, D.R. 1986. "Electoral Coalitions, Minority Mayors and the Contradictions in the Municipal Policy Agenda." In *Cities in Stress: A New Look at the Urban Crisis,* edited by M. Gottdiener. Beverly Hills:: Sage Publications.

Judd, D.R. 1988. *The Politics of American Cities: Private Power and Public Policy.* Boston: Scott, Foresman.

Jukam, T.O. 1979. "Political Support in the United States." Paper delivered at the Latin American Studies Association Meeting, Pittsburg, Pennsylvania, April 5-7.

Katznelson, I. 1976. "The Crisis of the Capitalistic City: Urban Politics and Social Control." In *Theoretical Perspectives on Urban Politics,* edited by W. Hawley, M. Lipsky, S. Greenberg, J.D. Greenstone, et al. Englewood Cliffs, NJ: Prentice-Hall.

Kelman, H.C., and V.L. Hamilton. 1989. *Crimes of Obedience: Toward a Social Psychology of Authority and Responsibility.* New Haven: Yale University Press.

Levine, C.H. 1974. *Racial Context and the American Mayor.* Lexington, MA: Lexington.

Lifton, R.J. 1973. *Home from the War.* New York: Simon and Schuster.

Lifton, R.J. 1979. *The Broken Connection.* New York: Simon and Schuster.

Lifton, R.J. 1986. *The Nazi Doctors.* New York: Basic Books.

Lifton, R.J. 1987. *The Future of Immortality and Other Essays for a Nuclear Age.* New York: Basic Books.

Lifton, R.J., and E. Markusen. 1990. *The Genocidal Mentality: Nazi Holocaust and Nuclear Threat.* New York: Basic Books.

Manning, M. 1980. *From the Grassroots: Social and Political Essay Toward Afro-American Liberation.* Boston: South End.

Milgram, S. 1977. *The Individual in a Social World.* Boston: Addison-Wesley.

Milgram, S. 1974. *Obedience to Authority.* New York: Harper & Row.

Mills, C.W. 1984. "Situated Actions and Vocabularies of Motive." Pp. 13-24. In *Language and Politics,* edited by M. Shapiro. New York: New York University Press.

Moffic, H.S. 1988. *What's In A Name? Labelling and Group Tensions in the United States.* Paper prepared for delivery at the Conference of the International Organization for the Study of Group Tensions, Princeton University.

Moffic, H.S. 1989. "Labelling and Group Tensions in the United States." *International Journal of Group Tensions* 19(2): 152-164.

Mosse, G.L. 1975. *The Nationalization of the Masses.* New York: Meridian.

Mosse, G.L. 1978. *Toward the Final Solution.* New York: Harper & Row.

Mosse, G.L. 1990. *Fallen Soldiers.* New York: Oxford University Press.

Muller, E, and T. Jukam. 1977. "On the Meaning of Political Support." *American Political Science Review* 71 (December): 1561-1595.

Nelson, W.E., and P.J. Meranto. 1977. *Electing Black Mayors.* Columbus: Ohio University Press.

Nelson, W.E. 1987. "Cleveland: The Evolution of Black Political Power." In *The New Black Politics: The Search for Political Power,* edited by M.B. Preston, L. Henderson, and P. Puryear. New York: Longman.

Orfield, G., and C. Ashkinaze. 1991. *The Closing Door: Conservative Policy and Black Opportunity.* Chicago: University of Chicago Press.

Peterson, P.E. 1981. *City Limited.* Chicago: University of Chicago, Press.

Peterson, P.E. 1984. "A Unitary Model of Local Taxation and Expenditure Policies." In *Readings in Urban Politics: Past, Present and Future,* edited by H. Hahn and C.H. Levine. News York: Longman.

Poliakov, L. 1971. *The Aryan Myth.* New York: New American Library.

Prejean, M. 1986. Administrative Assistant to President of Atlanta City Council. Interviewed by author, 19 July, Atlanta Georgia.

Piliawsky, M. 1985. "The Impact of Black Mayors on the Black Community: The Case of New Orleans' Ernest Morial." *The Review of Black Political Economy* (Spring): 5-23.

Reed, A. 1988. "The Black Urban Regime: Structural Origins and Constraints." In *Power Community and the City: Comparative Urban and Community Research,* edited by M. Peter Smith. New Brunswick, NJ: Transaction.

Schell, J. 1987. *The Real War.* New York: Pantheon Books.

Staub, E. 1989. *The Roots of Evil.* New York: Cambridge University Press.

Steiner, G. 1971. *The Bluebeard's Castle.* New Haven: Yale University Press.

Steiner, G. 1977. *Language and Silence.* Atheneum.

Stone, C. 1989. *Regime Politics: Governing Atlanta, 1946-1988.* Lawrence: University of Kansas Press.

United States Department of Commerce, Bureau of Census. 1990. *Summary of Social, Economic and Housing Characteristics.* Washington, DC: Bureau of Census.

Urban Life Associates, Georgia State University. 1975. *Organized for Action: A Narrative Survey of Atlanta's Neighborhood Organizations.* Atlanta: Urban Life Associates, Georgia State University.

Weber, M. 1946. "Bureaucracy." Pp. 27-55 in *From Max Weber: Essays in Sociology,* edited by H.H. Gerth and C. Wright Mills. New York: Oxford University Press.

Weinstein, F. 1980. *The Dynamics of Nazism.* San Diego:

Wildavsky, A. 1964. *Leadership in a Small Town.* Towata, NJ: Bedminister.

RACIAL AND ETHNIC CONFLICT:
PERSPECTIVES FROM CRIMINAL JUSTICE

Joseph F. Sheley and Victoria E. Brewer

In the fall of 1992, police in a New York college town questioned every African-American and Hispanic male registered at the college following an assault by a black man on an elderly white woman (Schemo, 1992). The following spring, police in a Florida town randomly stopped young black males for questioning in connection with the slaying of a tourist by otherwise unidentified black male juveniles (Beck, 1993).

Such events are not rare, and the theme underlying them likely is not lost even on the most casual observer. Race is implicated in the practice of criminal justice in the United States. Through the eyes of some, this is to be expected given the allegedly disproportionate involvement of African Americans and members of certain other minority groups in criminal activity. Through other eyes, however, the criminal justice system is a stage, one of many, upon which is enacted a smoldering and varyingly explosive larger conflict between racial and ethnic groups in this country.

In this chapter, we examine historical criminal justice involvement in this conflict, remedial efforts by the courts to introduce "color blindness" to our system of justice, and the implications for color-blind justice in the larger

Research in Human Social Conflict, Volume 1, pages 143-161.
Copyright © 1995 by JAI Press Inc.
All rights of reproduction in any form reserved.
ISBN: 1-55938-923-0

struggle for equality. Prior to pursuing this agenda, however, two issues must be addressed. The first involves assessment of the extent to which purported criminal justice discrimination is but a manifestation of disproportionate minority involvement in crime. The second concerns discretion, the feature of the criminal justice system that most lends itself to racial and ethnic strife. Importantly, the focus of the present paper is primarily upon African Americans and European Americans. This is not intended to suggest that other racial or ethnic minorities are without problems regarding crime and the administration of justice. The problems of others tend to be more localized than do those of African and European Americans.

DIFFERENTIAL CRIMINAL INVOLVEMENT

Are African Americans overly represented in the criminal population in this country? The answer depends, certainly, on the crimes to which we refer. If we focus upon "silk-collar" (corporate) offenses, underrepresentation of African Americans is apparent and understandable. Yet, it is street crime—homicide, robbery, rape, assault, burglary—that the public fears. Here, most measures point to a higher-than-statistically-expected level of involvement of the black population. Annual FBI *Uniform Crime Reports* concerning race of arrestees consistently show African Americans, comprising approximately 12 percent of our population, to be disproportionately involved in most predatory crime. Rate-adjusted ratios of blacks to whites arrested are approximately 8.3 to 1 for homicide, 5.2 to 1 for rape, 10.8 to 1 for armed robbery, 2.9 to 1 for burglary (Harris, 1991).

At the close of 1991, African Americans constituted roughly half of the U.S. prison population (Bureau of Justice Statistics, 1992). While one of every sixteen white males between twenty and twenty-nine years of age is somehow being supervised by the criminal justice system, the comparable figure for their black counterparts is one of every four (Mauer, 1990).

These statistics leave open the possibility that apparent race differences in criminal involvement are artifacts of discriminatory arrest practices. However, these findings hold as we move from arrests to offense behaviors. Self-report data (wherein individuals respond, usually anonymously, to survey items about illegal activity) indicate overrepresentation among African Americans in serious, predatory delinquencies and in serious crimes by adults (Elliott and Ageton, 1980; Petersilia, 1985). Analyses of victimization data (wherein individuals respond to survey items about episodes in which they were crime victims, including questions about the perceived race of the perpetrator) similarly point up disparities in involvement across races in "personal" crimes (predominantly rape, robbery, assault, and certain types of theft). Computing race- and age-specific involvement rates for these offenses, Hindelang (1981) reported exceptional differences by race—35,000 robberies per 100,000 black males eighteen to twenty years old versus 2,245 per 100,000 for comparable white males.

The traditional response to such discrepancies is to note that, net of socioeconomic class differences, they would not exist. That is, since African Americans are overly represented among lower economic status groups, the only meaningful comparison is between white and black members occupying the same rung of the class ladder. However, self-report research results indicate that, for more serious predatory offenses (robbery and burglary, for instance) by juveniles, both class and race matter, and race matters more strongly. Even for African-American youth from more affluent families, the rate for serious offenses exceeds that of European American youth from less affluent families (Harris, 1991; Elliott and Ageton, 1980). Viewed from the perspective that the cultural and economic histories of whites and blacks of all classes in America differ so greatly, the finding that class effects do not wholly mediate race effects probably should not surprise (Sheley, 1985).

Given this, it is difficult to ascribe race differences in criminal involvement *solely* to criminal justice bias. This hardly suggests that such bias is only imagined, however. Nor, were it substantially imagined, would we dismiss that which exists as nonproblematic. As we shall see later, criminal justice discrimination in any amount is embedded in the socioeconomic fabric of this society; the more pervasive and systematic the discrimination, the larger are the socioeconomic divisions and related conflicts.

CRIMINAL JUSTICE SYSTEM DISCRETION

Understanding racial and ethnic discrimination by criminal justice organizations in larger societies is best accomplished through an appreciation of the *discretion* inherent in criminal justice activity. Discretion influences decisions at the levels of both organization and individual operative. It translates to relative freedom to act without direct supervision. For example, police officers have discretionary powers in arrest situations, district attorneys in negotiating pleas, and judges in sentencing offenders.

Two determinants of criminal justice production are, of course, the size and industry of the subpopulation committing crimes. Criminal behavior (and some types of criminal behavior more than others) clearly raises one's chances of being the target of criminal justice attention. Yet we know that criminal behavior, even when detected, does not guarantee the application of the official label "criminal" by the system. And we are aware of the possibility that persons who have committed no crimes may be officially labeled "criminal." In fact, the criminal justice system can alter the size and composition of its product (labeled criminals) regardless of changes in the population of those committing offenses (Sheley and Hanlon, 1978).

If the freedom to choose among policy and behavioral options is also the freedom to discriminate against segments of the population in the conduct of criminal justice activity, the task at hand is to describe the extent to which race and ethnicity represent or have represented the variable around which discrimination is clustered. We begin this endeavor with a brief historical examination of the intertwining of race and criminal law.

HISTORICAL OVERVIEW

For all intents and purposes, race relations in the United States have never *not* been fused with criminal justice. The subjugation of people in a legalistic society necessarily required the formulation of legal codes by which to define rights of ownership among slaveowners and the related acceptable boundaries of behavior of the enslaved. Finkelman (1993) reports that South Carolina's 1712 slave code provided such possible punishments for runaway slaves as whipping, castration, branding, and hamstringing. Most antebellum southern states not only forbade blacks to learn to read but forbade whites to teach them (Higginbotham, 1978). Colonial Virginia law, by way of similar example, took pains to define conversion from heathen ways as insufficient grounds by which to win freedom from slavery though those same heathen ways served philosophically to justify the enslavement of a people in the first place (Davis, 1966, 1984). Though clearly economic at heart, laws aimed at control of blacks had the additional effect of stereotyping blacks as criminal in nature, that is, as by disposition demanding separate and harsher statutes. Finkelman (1993) details colonial Massachusetts' laws by which members of the "criminal classes" (including Indians and blacks) could not sell goods that "appeared" to be stolen, could not be found on the streets after nine o'clock, and could not be served in taverns. He notes that free adult blacks could be bound into servitude for loitering or misusing time.

The use of criminal (and civil) law to control blacks in the South after the War Between the States is well known (Adamson, 1983; Rafter, 1990). Recent research ties lynching and incarceration of blacks in Georgia at the turn of the century to changes in the supply and location of black male labor (Myers, 1990; Soule, 1992). Rates of lynching varied with level of competition between blacks and whites in both agriculture and manufacturing. The incarceration rate of blacks was influenced by demands for convict labor, especially in the agrarian sector (Myers and Massey, 1991).

Well into the middle segment of this century, some criminal law still had its roots directly in racial distinctions. African Americans who refused to conduct their behavior in accord with segregationist practices could be jailed.

In both 1964 and 1967, the Supreme Court overturned laws based solely on racial status. In the former instance (*McLaughlin v. Florida*, 379 U.S. 184), a racially mixed couple had been sentenced to jail terms and fines for interracial cohabitation. In the latter (*Loving v. Virginia*, 388 U.S. 1), a couple was convicted of a felony for interracially marrying (Sickels, 1972; Finkelman, 1993). Such examples, of course, speak not at all to the criminal justice system's failure during the era in question to pursue culprits when African Americans were the victims of crime or of lynchings.

The point of this historical sketch is that, to the extent that racial and ethnic discrimination occurs in the criminal justice arena today, it does so following nearly three centuries of cultural conditioning. If we understand the law as an evolving institution influenced by its own past, then even apart from the influences of the larger society's prejudices, the criminal justice system is unlikely to have purged itself of bents abruptly denied it only thirty years ago when race and the administration of justice were uncoupled *officially*.

While allegations of criminal justice discrimination were plentiful in the 1970s, the era was quiet relative to the succeeding one. The late 1980s and early 1990s have been characterized by increasing racial conflict. Much of this has been fueled by economic difficulties. In the face of competition for jobs and growing resistance to taxation, government policies aimed at improving the lot of minorities (school busing, open housing laws, anti-job-discrimination laws, and affirmative action programs) have generated considerable animosity among whites (Bobo and Kluegel, 1993; Schuman, Steeh, and Bobo, 1988). More pertinent to the present discussion, the 1980s generally saw a leveling out of the trend toward increasing crime rates that characterized the prior two decades. But it was clear also that crime and, especially, violent crime rates exceeded those of any period in this century (Gurr, 1989). The focus of the 1960s on the social (primarily opportunity-related) forces underlying crime found less interest and still less sympathy in the late 1970s and through the 1980s.

Encouraged by conservative criminologists (Wilson, 1975; van den Haag, 1982), the criminal justice system set its sights on deterrence and custody. That is, efforts were made to raise the costs of engaging in criminal activities and, whether or not this served to deter potential criminals, to lock away serious, convicted offenders for the majority of their otherwise criminally active years. However, as the 1980s came to a close, it became apparent that, at least as a strategy to reduce crime, the custody-deterrence approach had accomplished little. In essence, it had directed more attention to the flow of water than to the faucet that was its source. Court dockets swelled, longer sentences were imposed, and prison and jail populations reached new highs (Shover, 1991). But crime rates failed to decline substantially as new offenders replaced those taken off the streets. Research and commentary in professional journals and, to a lesser extent, popular media, increasingly have returned to social-causation issues as problems no longer able to be ignored (Krisberg, 1991). The general public has yet to reach the same conclusion.

Against this backdrop, we now appreciate that the interrelated issues of race and criminal justice were on their way to public debate well before the Los Angeles riots of 1992. Government's failure to decrease crime levels, the perception that African Americans' representation among those processed by the criminal justice system exceeded their representation in the general population, and the 1988 Republican presidential nominee's attention to race and crime invited outrage concerning the "black problem" in many sectors of the white community and the criminal justice system (Burrell, 1990) and, in turn, counterclaims of racism, especially in the administration of justice, from African Americans. Within the context of this conflict, cases that likely would have drawn less attention now capture the nation's interest. In the wake of the Rodney King case in Los Angeles, for example, front-page coverage has been given to a homicide charge brought against police officers in Detroit for the beating death of Malice Green, an African-American man stopped for a "possible drug violation" (*The New York Times*, 1992). Once again, we have been forced to confront the issue of the possibility of a color-blind justice system.

THE QUEST FOR COLOR-BLIND JUSTICE

The attempt to remove discrimination from the legal system took the obvious direction of the deletion of statutes pertaining to particular racial and ethnic groups. This, however, could not insure color-blind application of the newly cleansed laws, especially regarding decisions to investigate, arrest, prosecute, and sentence suspected or alleged offenders. Several avenues were considered appropriate to this quest. The less traveled ones involved raising levels of awareness of discrimination through public education, the recruitment of minority officers onto police departments, and the attempted transformation of the police from occupational to professional status. Professional status was considered exceptionally important because professions generally possess codes of ethics thought to require commitment on the part of the practitioner as opposed to externally imposed regulations thought to motivate only to the extent they deterred.

The more traveled avenue was process oriented, the structuring of formulas by which cases must be handled uniformly at all stages of criminal justice activity. We have come to represent this path through reference to the Warren Court decisions of the 1960s. In fact, however, the modern emphasis on procedural law traces to the late 1940s when post-realist legal scholars opined an important distinction between issues of substance—politically determined notions about what is to be punished—and those of process (Peller, 1988).

Determinations of substantive law were said to be subjective at all junctures and belonged in the legislative rather than the judicial realm. Procedural matters, in contrast, could be treated as objective at all junctures.

Procedural issues, Peller argues, ultimately were stated as issues of institutional competence. While substantive decisions were subjective and thus political in nature, legal action was considered apolitical by virtue of the application of objective standards to substantive matters. Thus, Peller (1993; see also Ely, 1980) points out, the Warren Court was less progressive and liberal than often is the charge, since that Court maintained a very sharp distinction between process and substance. Rather than holding vagrancy and loitering statutes unconstitutional because they caused no harm, for example, the Warren Court ruled that the actions were not clearly defined statutorily. The Court therefore carved out as its province regarding criminal law the reigning in of discretion in criminal justice activity.

The process consciousness of the 1960s corresponded with the race consciousness of the same era and, some scholars argue, procedural reform of the period must be interpreted within the context of conflict between the races (Peller, 1993). For it was directed at what, until that era, was the major instrument of control of African Americans by the more powerful European Americans—the police. Context notwithstanding, the Court argued its procedural position in color-blind terms. Random field interrogations of blacks were ruled unconstitutional in terms of the vagueness of the common standards by which these interrogations were conducted rather than in terms of racial bias they reflected. Thus procedures could be made neutral by shrinking discretionary latitude to the point that racial bias would be so obvious in practice that it could not occur with the impunity attendant to ambiguity. Race, no longer a focal point of criminal justice activity, could then become less significant in the conduct of social interaction generally.

RACE AND THE POLICE

The charge of racial discrimination is directed at the police more often than at any other segment of the criminal justice system (Dannefer and Schutt, 1982). The most controversial discrimination-related issues are those involving encounters between the police and African Americans. These include complaints ranging from incivility to differential use of interrogation and arrest and include the discriminatory application of deadly force (Chevigny, 1969).

It is quickly acknowledged that much criminal justice discrimination is the work of individual "bad apples" who were not screened out during their training. Some police officers, regardless of race, are brutal and abusive. Some are better able to handle the pressure of encounters with citizens. We must also note that police spend the better part of their occupational lives dealing with dangerous persons and frightening acts. As rates of serious crime have risen, police work has become more dangerous (Geller, 1982), and serious street offenders increasingly have become concentrated in underclass, thus often largely black, populations. In short, the everyday pressures of police work are intense.

However, the ascription of some police misconduct to individual officers should not obscure the possibility of more system-wide discrimination. Brown (1993) has chronicled a sufficient number of deadly-force cases over the past two decades in New York City alone to provide grounds at least for the *perception* that police, in the aggregate, apply such force discriminatorily. Among the many recent cases she presents is that in which an African-American youth arrested in 1984 for drawing graffiti in the subway was choked to death; police were acquitted of all charges though the family of the youth prevailed in civil court. In 1985, a Stanford University-bound black prep-school graduate was shot to death by a police officer who claimed that the youth had attempted armed robbery. In 1988, four officers were convicted of using stun guns to extract confessions from black arrestees. In 1989, a black retarded man was choked to death by members of a specially trained police unit; two years earlier a white officer in the same unit had been acquitted in the shotgun death of a sixty-three-year-old black woman who allegedly threatened the police with a kitchen knife.

More systematic research concerning racial discrimination in the conduct of police work offers ambiguous findings both in the sense of the methodological adequacy of the studies in question and of the contradictory nature of the studies' results. Regarding method generally, Mastrofski and Parks (1990) point out that despite advances in quantitative studies of police behavior, research remains restricted. Much of what police do and how they do it remains unexplored. The quantitative behavioral literature relates only a small portion of what police say and how and why they say it. The more visible and dramatic dispositions of encounters remain the focus of attention, yet we lack extensive knowledge of the processes by which events come to the ends they do.

Much research on police misconduct is hampered by the low visibility of incidents and, as expected, we consistently meet with conflicting accounts of the episodes producing the injuries. Survey research fills the void, though only partially. Powell (1990), for example, analyzed self-reported use of discretion in nonfelony situations by police officers in both large and small southern cities. He found a significant difference in the overall reported use of discretion by offense, in relation to the race of the offender. The greatest disparity involved decisions made in public intoxication and domestic encounters and, except for speeding offenses, more punitive action was taken toward black offenders than toward white offenders. In such studies, we confront issues of validity regarding measurement of conduct. As well, we encounter problems of generalizability.

Note, for example, that Powell found large regional (city-by-city) differences in the use of discretionary power for similar types of offenses.

The real difficulty in interpreting data on race and police conduct lies in the problem of controlling for the effects of other pertinent variables. At the aggregate level, for example, we know that the majority of civilians struck by police bullets in major United States cities are African American. However, the racial distribution of police shootings also closely matches the racial distribution of participation in serious crime (Geller and Darales, 1981; Geller, 1982).

At the individual level, oft-cited but now likely dated research on police assaults of citizens in the field and at police headquarters found that class, rather than race, was the influential variable: lower-class citizens ran a higher risk of such treatment, while within the same class whites and blacks were treated roughly equally (Reiss, 1971). In his investigation of police misconduct (including the use of excessive force by black versus white police officers) in three cities in the mid-1960s, Reiss (1971, 1980) found that both black and white officers were more likely to use excessive force against members of their own race. Reiss also found that white citizens were more likely than black citizens to be victims of excessive force (5.9 to 2.8 per 1,000 citizens) and that white offenders were more likely than black offenders to be the victims of excessive force by the police (41.9 to 22.6 per 1,000 offenders). Clearly, here we encounter measurement problems regarding type of excessive force as well as the effects of the general policy of police departments to assign black officers to African-American communities.

The federal government's role in protecting the civil rights of citizens against police misconduct historically appears largely one of neglect. Since 1985, for example, the Department of Justice has brought an average of 42 lawsuits per year against police officers, although they investigated more than 15,000 cases (Committee on the Judiciary, 1992). This is especially puzzling in the face of the distribution of complaints of police brutality; approximately half of the complaints were filed against members of just 187 agencies. Yet, it is also clear that convictions of offending police are difficult. Proof that individual officers intended to violate the law is problematic. And jurors are reluctant to brand as criminals the very people on whom they rely for their safety.

Not the least of the complaints of African Americans is that the police view their role as control rather than protection of black neighborhoods. In this vein, research findings indicate that law enforcement personnel are more numerous in metropolitan areas in which economic inequality is most pronounced (Jacobs, 1979). Additionally, following civil disorders in the south in the 1950s, 1960s, and early 1970s, whites in cities with large nonwhite populations and less residential segregation perceived chances of crime victimization as greater regardless of whether actual crime rates changed; they demanded and received more police protection (Liska, Laurence, and Benson,

1981). Conversely, the most frequent charges of African-American citizens against the police involve inadequate protection and service in their neighborhoods (Radelet, 1986). As blacks move up the socioeconomic ladder, complaints of this type decrease, suggesting again the confounding of the racial discrimination issue with the issue of class (Murty, Roebuck, and Smith, 1990).

Just as it shapes the average white citizen's notion of the dangerous offender, the stereotype of the young black male as offender structures much of law enforcement. African-American males consistently charge that police field interrogations and arrests are based on no more than skin color (Greene, 1993). *The New York Times* carried a story in 1991, for example, concerning a black professor of literature held as a robbery suspect in a suburban mall jewelry store because he did not look as if he belonged there.

The conflict inherent in pursuit of this stereotype is precisely the stuff of legal challenges by African Americans against the criminal justice system. *Florida v. Bostick* (111 S. Ct. 2382, 1991) has come to embody that conflict. In their ongoing fight against drugs, police in Florida set up surveillance at public transportation sites such as bus stations and airports. Officers approached individuals either randomly (i.e., without regard to sociodemographic characteristics) or because of suspicions of criminal activity, asked questions and, often, asked permission to search the individuals and their luggage. By law, officers could not convey a message that individuals were required to acquiesce to such searches.

In the *Bostick* case, police boarded a bus at an intermediate stop and chose to interrogate two men at the back of the vehicle. Standing in the aisle before Bostick, a black man, the officers—one with a hand on his gun—asked for his identification and ticket. They then requested to look inside a bag Bostick was using as a headrest; he consented. Finding nothing, the police then searched a second bag and discovered cocaine. Bostick disputed that he had consented to the search of the bag, arguing as well that no reasonable person possessing drugs in a bag would consent to such a search unless coerced. The Court disagreed.

Two important issues proceed from *Bostick*, one addressed by the Court, the other left unsaid. The first involves the constitutional issue of Fourth Amendment seizure without reasonable suspicion. For the Court minority, Justice Marshall argued that Bostick was not advised of his various rights regarding the search and easily could have perceived the situation as coercive. However, the Court majority concluded that, as long as no obligation to comply was conveyed by the police and the *overall* situation was not coercive, the search was legal. The second issue, that of Bostick's skin color, was not addressed by the Court. Clearly, the Court perceived the specification of process as sufficient to produce color-blind police conduct. Yet, it can as easily be argued that traditional police treatment of young black males has left a legacy by which any interrogation by the police of such males can be perceived by them as coercive and threatening. Further, police routinely consider a suspect's race in detention decisions (Cloud, 1985; Johnson, 1983). In *State v. Dean* (543 P.2d 425,427, Ariz. 1975), for example, the Supreme Court of Arizona ruled that the presence of a Mexican male in a dented car parked on a street containing white middle-class homes can be employed *in concert* with other factors as reasonable cause for investigation and detention. The courts have upheld the stopping of a black man alone in a white Cadillac based on the report of a bank robbery by three black men driving a brown car of the same make (Johnson, 1983; Roberts 1993). As well, the courts have made it clear that it is permissible to stop and frisk individuals if they fit the profile, developed through police experience, of drug couriers; the profile can include skin color, gender, and age (*Florida v. Bostick*, 111 S. Ct. 2382, 2390 n.1, 1991; see also Powell and Hershenov, 1991). In effect, the attempt to construct color-blind process has opened the door to criminal justice targeting on the basis of race and, in laying the burden upon defendants to prove discrimination in their particular cases, has made it exceptionally difficult to constrain the high potential for racist police conduct inherent in the discretion characterizing their work.

RACE AND THE COURTS

Charges of racial bias also surface regarding court processing of defendants. A recent New York State Judicial Commission, for example, characterized the courts of that state as two systems of justice—one for whites and a second for poor persons and minorities (New York State Judicial Commission on Minorities, 1991). Race may influence decisions to prosecute, including decisions to negotiate a plea (Gibson, 1978; Myers, 1991). It may extend into trial proceedings in pretrial publicity, voir dire and opening statements at trials, testimony, closing arguments, jury instructions, and jury deliberations (Johnson, 1985, 1993; Lipton, 1983). It may affect the sentencing process (Peterson and Hagan, 1984).

As with the research findings involving police misconduct, those involving the judicial process are ambiguous. Investigations indicate that prosecutors pursue cases more aggressively if the victim of a crime is white (Paternoster, 1983; Hawkins, 1987). Rape charges are more likely to be processed if the suspect is African American and the victim European American (LaFree, 1989). Race appears to enter the picture as well in the plea bargaining process, but the outcome varies by jurisdiction; sometimes whites benefit, sometimes blacks (Myers, 1991). African Americans are significantly less likely than are European Americans to gain pretrial release and to secure the services of a private attorney, thus ultimately negatively influencing their case outcomes (Spohn, Gruhl, and Welch, 1981-82). However disturbing, these findings must be viewed cautiously. What is lacking across many of the studies that produced them are uniform controls for legally relevant variables such as seriousness of the injury to the victim.

Studies only recently have been able to offer sophisticated research findings regarding racial disparities in sentencing. Where once discrimination was quite likely, the general conclusion now is that it remains an important factor only in selected contexts (Myers, 1991). African Americans are more likely than are European Americans to be imprisoned in states in which the black population is a small percentage of the total population and is predominately urban (Bridges and Crutchfield, 1988). Race effects are significant for cases involving some violent crimes: black men convicted of rape receive longer sentences than do white men, but the opposite is true for those found guilty of homicide (Zatz, 1984). Black drug users have been found to receive lighter sentences than do white users, but the sentences of black drug traffickers exceed those given to white traffickers (Peterson and Hagan, 1984). Racial disparities do not appear in sentences given to offenders who victimized someone they knew, but African Americans are more likely than European Americans to be incarcerated if the victim was a stranger. Harsher treatment yet is given to African Americans who victimize European American strangers (Myers, 1991).

The one aspect of discrimination about which there is currently little question is its appearance in the assignment of the death penalty to convicted killers. The focus of *Furman v. Georgia* (408 U.S. 238) in 1972 was upon capriciousness and arbitrariness inherent in some states' death-sentence laws. Because race of offender, de facto, could easily enter capital cases, the Supreme Court ruled extant death penalty statutes unconstitutional. In 1976, in *Gregg v. Georgia* (428 U.S. 153), a majority of the justices determined that revisions of state laws had eliminated arbitrariness sufficiently to permit reinstatement of the death penalty. Executions resumed in 1977. A number of studies followed in an effort to determine whether or not race remained a factor in capital punishment. They found consistently that, while race of offender plays little role in death-penalty sentences, race of victim clearly does. Persons killing European Americans are four times more likely to be assessed a death sentence than are persons killing African Americans, even after taking into account a host of legal and extralegal circumstances that might influence this pattern (Baldus, Pulaski, and Woodworth, 1983; Baldus, Woodworth, and Pulaski, 1985). Sources of the bias seem as likely located in prosecutorial decisions to seek the death penalty as in jurors' decisions to apply it (Smith, 1991).

Notwithstanding these findings, court cases involving race bias appear regularly on appeals court dockets. Overall, the courts have been unreceptive to such cases. In cases charging prosecutorial bias, for instance, the court routinely demands from the person alleging discrimination proof that a real and immediate injury has been suffered, that such injury is traceable to allegedly unlawful conduct by the prosecutor, and that the injury can be redressed by the relief being sought. In short, it does not suffice to present aggregate findings of past discrimination in prosecutorial decisions. To prove a case of selective prosecution, for example, a defendant "must show both that the government singled him out for prosecution while others similarly situated were not prosecuted for similar conduct and that the government's action [against the specific defendant] was based on an impermissible motive such as race...." (*United States v. Holmes*, 794 F.2nd 345, 347 8th Cir., 1986).

This same theme appears in Supreme Court decisions regarding the death penalty. In *McCleskey v. Kemp* (481 U.S. 279, 1987), for example, the Court acknowledged the validity of research findings concerning aggregate racial bias in the assignment of capital punishment. As noted earlier, the findings demonstrated that, net of the effects of other important variables, the race of the homicide victim was influential in death penalty cases. Yet, by a vote of five to four, the Court determined that the defendant, McClesky, could not prove that the aggregate findings applied to his particular circumstance.

Currently, the major issues involving criminal justice-related racial bias in the courts involve choice of venue and the racial composition of juries. Interestingly, the more celebrated cases pertaining to venue—that involving the trial of the Los Angeles police officers accused of beating Rodney King and that involving the trial of a Miami police officer for the shooting death of a motorcyclist and the death of his passenger in the ensuing crash—pertain to white and Hispanic defendants, respectively, accused of victimizing African Americans. The interest in these cases focuses on balancing the right to a fair trial in highly publicized cases with the need to provide assurances that African Americans are not excluded from juries by virtue of the relocation of trials to overwhelmingly white jurisdictions. In the wake of the Los Angeles riots of 1992, the judge in the state-court trial of those accused of beating King seems to have failed to be sensitive to the alienation of the African-American community from the judicial system; the case was moved from Los Angeles to a predominantly white small town and a white jury. The Miami case ultimately was heard in Tallahassee, overwhelmingly white, and before a jury of three whites, two Hispanics, and one African American. Each trial ended in acquittals.

Addressing the charge that prosecutors systematically exclude blacks from juries serving in cases with black defendants through use of peremptory challenges on the basis of race, the Supreme Court, in *Batson v. Kentucky* (476 U.S. 79, 1986) framed the issue in terms of provision of a representative jury rather than a jury of the defendant's peers. The Court ruled that if the defendant makes a prima facie case that a prosecutor has utilized a peremptory challenge to exclude a potential juror on the basis of that juror's race, the prosecutor must respond with a race-neutral explanation; the challenge is disallowed if the prosecutor cannot do this. Thus, it remains possible, given the prosecutor's potential for race-neutral explanation, to construct an all-white jury in the trial of a black defendant in a predominantly black jurisdiction. In short, the Court has continued its pursuit of the color-blind process under the assumption that any racial "bias" remaining beyond the corrected process is a matter of substance to be addressed by legislatures.

SUMMARY AND IMPLICATIONS

By way of summary, we have argued that, above and beyond any case that can be made that African Americans contribute disproportionately to the nation's crime rate, a strong case can be made that racial bias lurks systematically in the administration of criminal justice. That case is certainly made through a review of a historical record that demonstrates nearly three centuries of cultural conditioning that race and crime are inseparable. The major vehicle by which discrimination enters into the conduct and policies of criminal justice organizations and their agents is the behavioral discretion that characterizes the enforcement and judicial branches of the law. Police departments may deploy their patrols in a racist manner, for example. Individual officers may exercise discretion discriminatorily in the field. Racial factors may shape prosecutorial decisions. Jurors may be unable to separate race from fact in the testimony they hear. Judges may vary the harshness of their sentences based on the racial characteristics of those found guilty.

Recognizing these possibilities, the courts since the 1960s have directed their efforts toward reining in the discretionary elements of the criminal justice system. The philosophy underlying this agenda is the belief that justice can be made color-blind if the procedures governing criminal justice activity are broader in number and narrower and more specific in scope. Peller (1993, p. 2248) notes that:

> [T]he intervention that the Court pursued [has been] wide reaching and dramatic. Expansion of the right to counsel; protection against abusive interrogation procedures and unreliable identification evidence; stricter supervision of the power to search, stop, and arrest; and the various improvements in trial requirements were all important progressive reforms of the criminal justice system in general, and its relation to people of color in particular. In fact, the progress...has been so dramatic that, for nearly the last two decades, it has been difficult to imagine any other way to approach the issue of race and the criminal law.

To what extent have these efforts succeeded? The research literature offers ambiguous findings. Apart from the clear demonstration of race bias (based on the race status of homicide victims) in the application of the death penalty, we encounter uneven methodological rigor, problems of generalizability, the failure often to sort race from class effects, and the contradictory findings flowing from such problems.

Given the cases that now appear in the courts, however, it is obvious that the intertwining of race and criminal justice in America is far from past us. This problem has several roots. Foremost, it reflects a relatively new effort, now just three decades old and one that cannot be expected fully to have produced the results that are its goal. Second, as with the promise of equality in all aspects of the race movement in the United States, the promise of equality in the administration of criminal justice was made in better economic times. As African Americans were prepared to enter the basic structure of opportunity, the industrial economy underpinning that structure eroded. Production jobs which fueled the assimilation of immigrant groups earlier in the century were replaced by generally lower-paying and relatively stagnant service sector jobs. Expectations increased as possibilities decreased. The ensuing decades and, especially, the 1980s witnessed serious expansion of the gap between haves and have nots; the poor have gotten poorer—so much so that we now distinguish between the working poor and an impoverished underclass. Crime and its skewed distribution across class and race lines have increased to the point of tolerance by some segments of the majority of some level of racial discrimination as an evil necessary to the control of crime.

Third, the distinction drawn by the courts between substance and process likely is erroneous, and the color-blind justice thought to flow from strengthening process probably is unattainable—at least beyond the present point. The Supreme Court now seems not to understand the social context of the administration of even the most specified of procedures. Thus, the majority of the justices could not fathom that, unlike the average white male, a black male like Bostick could not have perceived of himself as having "choices" when confronted by police officers in the back of a bus. As Greene (1993, p. 2039) argues, "Black men must be concerned about the type of car they drive; the wrong car, like ... the BMW today, causes the police to assume that the car must be stolen or that [driver] must be a drug dealer." Color-blind procedures have not produced the color-blind social world that was hoped for. Rules followed perfectly nonetheless can produce discrimination if, for example, the attention of the functionary selectively attaches to a particular subpopulation.

That the courts themselves are becoming aware of this is obvious in *McCleskey* wherein the justices admit that racism exists but deem a process-based solution impossible. In effect, they have punted the ball back to the legislature, recognizing that, ultimately, substantive bias cannot be overcome by applying neutral procedures to its manifestation in conduct and policy. Whether the legislature is willing or ready directly to pursue racism in the criminal justice system remains to be seen. To this point, for example, no legislation has been passed to remedy the problem raised by *McCleskey* (Herman, 1993).

Finally, and related, the overall failure of the process-based attempt to reduce racial conflict may lie in its commitment to discourage rather than to encourage conflict. To strive for color-blind criminal law as we have done is to seek to assimilate African Americans into the opportunity structure of this society, all else status quo. It can be argued in a more radical vein that simply opening the opportunity structure to members of a predominantly lower socioeconomic group does little more in the short- to mid-run than bleach the majority conscience. At one time, black separatists argued that the assimilation of African Americans into the mainstream could only occur when blacks were on the same economic footing as whites (Peller 1993). Unable to embrace separatism, we now debate the merits of race-targeted "preferential treatment" over "compensatory" policies (Bobo and Kluegel, 1993). Some view this acrimonious debate as counterproductive. Others label such conflict as necessary to meaningful social change and far more productive than pronouncements regarding an open opportunity structure. In the area of criminal law, the courts have for thirty years resided in the former camp. In so doing, they have slowly moved from viewing process-based criminal law as a potential vehicle for change to viewing it as having little relation to change.

REFERENCES

Adamson, C.R. 1983. "Punishment After Slavery: Southern State Penal Systems, 1865-1890." *Social Problems* 30: 555-69.

Baldus, D.C., C. Pulaski, Jr., and G. Woodworth. 1983. "Comparative Review of Death Sentences: An Empirical Study of the Georgia Experience." *Journal of Criminal Law and Criminology* 74: 661-753.

Baldus, D.C., G. Woodworth, and C.A. Pulaski, Jr. 1985. "Monitoring and Evaluating Contemporary Death Sentencing Systems: Lessons from Georgia." *U.C. Davis Law Review* 18: 1375-1407.

Beck, M. 1993. "In a State of Terror." *Newsweek*, September 27: 40-1.

Bobo, L., and J.R. Kluegel. 1993. "Opposition to Race-Targeting: Self-interest, Stratification Ideology, or Racial Attitudes?" *American Sociological Review* 58: 443-64.

Bridges, G., and R. Crutchfield. 1988. "Law, Social Standing and Racial Disparities in Imprisonment." *Social Forces* 66: 699-724.

Brown, W.R. 1993. "Book Review of 'For the Color of His Skin: the Murder of Yusuf Hawkins and the Trial of Bensonhurst.' By John DeSantis, New York: Pharos Books, 1991." *Tulane Law Review* 67: 2371-86.

Bureau of Justice Statistics. 1992. *Sourcebook of Criminal Justice Statistics-1991.* Washington DC: U.S. Department of Justice. USGPO.

Burrell, S. 1990. "Gang Evidence: Issues for Criminal Defense." *Santa Clara Law Review* 30: 739-42.

Chevigny, P. 1969. *Police Power.* New York: Vintage Books.

Cloud, M. 1985. "Search and Seizure by the Numbers: The Drug Courier Profile and Judicial Review of Investigative Formulas." *Boston U. Law Review* 65: 843-921.

Committee on the Judiciary, U.S. House of Representatives. 1992. *Hearing Before the Subcommittee on Civil and Constitutional Rights.* Washington, DC: USGPO, May 5.

Dannefer, D., and R.K. Schutt. 1982. "Race and Juvenile Justice Processing in Court and Police Agencies." *American Journal of Sociology* 87: 1113-29.

Davis, D.B. 1966. *The Problem of Slavery in Western Culture.* Ithaca, NY: Cornell University Press.

Davis, D.B. 1984. *Slavery and Human Progress.* Ithaca, NY: Cornell University Press.

Elliott, D., and S. Ageton. 1980. "Reconciling Race and Class Differences in Self-Reported and Official Estimates of Delinquency." *American Sociological Review* 45: 95-106.

Ely, J.H. 1980. *Democracy and Distrust: A Theory of Judicial Review.* Cambridge, MA: Harvard University Press.

Finkelman, P. 1993. "The Crime of Color." *Tulane Law Review* 67: 2063-2112.

Geller, W. 1982. "Deadly Force: What We Know." *Journal of Police Science and Administration* 10: 151-77.

Geller, W., and K. Darales. 1981. "Shootings of and by Chicago Police." *Journal of Criminal Law and Criminology* 72: 1813-66.

Gibson, J.L. 1978. "Race as a Determinant of Criminal Sentences: A Methodological Critique and a Case Study." *Law and Society Review* 12: 455-478.

Greene, D.L. 1993. "Justice Scalia and Tonto, Judicial Pluralistic Ignorance, and the Myth of Colorless Individualism in 'Bostick v. Florida.'" *Tulane Law Review* 67: 1979-2062.

Gurr, T.R. 1989. "Historical Trends in Violent Crime: Europe and the United States." In *Violence in America* (volume 1), edited by T.R. Gurr. Newbury Park, CA: Sage.

Harris, A.R. 1991. "Race, Class, and Crime." Pp. 95-119 in *Criminology: A Contemporary Handbook,* edited by J.F. Sheley. Belmont, CA: Wadsworth Publishing Co.

Hawkins, D.F. 1987. "Beyond Anomalies: Rethinking the Conflict Perspective on Race and Criminal Punishment." *Social Forces* 65: 719-745.

Herman, S.N. 1993. "Why the Court Loves 'Batson': Representation-Reinforcement, Colorblindness, and the Jury." *Tulane Law Review* 67: 1807-54.

Higgenbotham, A.L., Jr. 1978. *In the Matter of Color: Race and the American Legal Process in the Colonial Period.* New York: Oxford University Press.

Hindelang, M. 1981. "Variations in Sex-Race-Age-Specific Incidence Rates of Offending." *American Sociological Review* 46: 461-74.

Jacobs, D. 1979. "Inequality and Police Strength: Conflict Theory and Coercive Control in Metropolitan Areas." *American Sociological Review* 44, 913-25.

Johnson, S.L. 1983. "Race and the Decision to Detain a Suspect." *Yale Law Journal* 93, 214-58.

Johnson, S.L. 1985. "Black Innocence and the White Jury." *Michigan Law Review* 83: 1611-76.

Johnson, S.L. 1993. "Racial Imagery in Criminal Cases." *Tulane Law Review* 67: 1739-1806.

Krisberg, B. 1991. "Are You Now or Have You Ever Been a Sociologist?" *Journal of Criminal Law and Criminology* 82: 141-155.

LaFree, G. 1989. *Rape and Criminal Justice: The Social Construction of Sexual Assault.* Belmont, CA: Wadsworth Publishing Co.

Lipton, J.P. 1983. "Racism in the Jury Box: The Hispanic Defendant." *Hispanic Journal of Behavioral Science* 5: 275-93.

Liska, A., J. Laurence, and M. Benson. 1981. "Perspectives on the Legal Order: The Capacity for Social Control." *American Journal of Sociology* 87: 413-26.

Mastrofski, S., and R.B. Parks. 1990. "Improving Observational Studies of Police." *Criminology* 28 (3): 475-96.

Mauer, M. 1990. *Young Black Men and the Criminal Justice System: A Growing National Problem.* Washington, DC: The Sentencing Project.

Murty, K.S., J.B. Roebuck, and J.D. Smith. 1990. "The Image of the Police in Black Atlanta Communities." *Journal of Police Science and Administration* 17 (4) 250-57.

Myers, M.A. 1990. "Black Threat and Incarceration in Postbellum Georgia." *Social Forces* 69: 373-93.

Myers, M.A. 1991. "The Courts: Prosecution and Sentencing." Pp. 359-77 in *Criminology: A Contemporary Handbook*, edited by J.F. Sheley. Belmont, CA: Wadsworth Publishing Co.

Myers, M.A., and J.L. Massey. 1991. "Race, Labor and Punishment in Postbellum Georgia." *Social Problems* 38: 267-86.

New York State Judicial Commission on Minorities. 1991. *Report of the New York State Judicial Commission on Minorities, Executive Summary, 1.* Albany, NY: Govt. Printing Office.

The New York Times. 1991. "Action by Missouri Police Raises Question of Racism." Nov. 24: 1, 24.

The New York Times. 1992. "4 Detroit Officers Charged in Death." Nov. 17: A1.

Paternoster, R. 1983. "Race of Victim and Location of Crime: The Decision to Seek the Death Penalty in South Carolina." *Journal of Criminal Law and Criminology* 74: 754-85.

Peller, G. 1988. "Neutral Principles in the 1950s." *University of Michigan Journal of Legal Reform* 21: 561-622.

Peller, G. 1993. "Criminal Law, Race, and the Ideology of Bias: Transcending the Critical Tools of the Sixties." *Tulane Law Review* 67, 2231-51.

Petersilia, J. 1985. "Racial Disparities in the Criminal Justice System: A Summary." *Crime and Delinquency* 31: 15-34.

Peterson, R.D., and J. Hagan. 1984. "Changing conceptions of Race: Towards an Account of Anomalous Findings of Sentencing Research." *American Sociological Review* 49: 56-70.

Powell, D.D. 1990. "A Study of Police Discretion in Six Southern Cities." *Journal of Police Science and Administration* 17 (1): 1-7.

Powell, J.A., and E.B. Hershenov. 1991. "Hostage to the Drug War: The National Purse, the Constitution and the Black Community." *U.C. Davis Law Review* 24: 557-616.

Radelet, L.A. 1986. *The Police and the Community* (4th ed.). New York: Macmillan Publishing Co.

Rafter, N.H. 1990. *Partial Justice: Women, Prisons, and Social Control* (2nd ed.). New Brunswick, NJ: Transaction Publishers.

Reiss, A.J., Jr. 1971. *The Police and the Public.* New Haven, CT: Yale University Press.

Reiss, A.J., Jr. 1980. "Police Brutality." Pp. 274-96 in *Police Behavior: A Sociological Perspective*, edited by R.J. Lundman. New York: Oxford University Press.

Roberts, D.E. 1993. "Crime, Race, and Reproduction." *Tulane Law Review* 67: 1945-78.

Schemo, D.J. 1992. "College Town in Uproar Over 'Black List' Search." *New York Times*, Sept. 27: 33.

Schuman, H., C. Steeh, and L. Bobo. 1988. *Racial Attitudes in America: Trends and Interpretations.* Cambridge, MA: Harvard University Press.

Sheley, J.F. 1985. *America's "Crime Problem."* Belmont, CA: Wadsworth Publishing Co.

Sheley, J.F., and J.J. Hanlon. 1978. "Unintended Effects of Police Decisions to Actively Enforce Laws: Implications for Analysis of Crime Trends." *Contemporary Crisis* 2 (65): 265-75.

Shover, N. 1991. "Institutional Correction: Jails and Prisons." Pp. 279-397 in *Criminology: A Contemporary Handbook*, edited by J.F. Sheley. Belmont, CA: Wadsworth Publishing Co.

Sickels, R.J. 1972. *Race, Marriage, and the Law.* Albuquerque, NM: University of New Mexico Press.

Smith, M.D. 1991. "Capital Punishment." Pp. 479-94 in *Criminology: A Contemporary Handbook*, edited by J.F. Sheley. Belmont, CA: Wadsworth Publishing Co.

Soule, S.A. 1992. "Populism and Black Lynching in Georgia, 1890-1900." *Social Forces* 71: 431-49.

Spohn, C., J. Gruhl, and S. Welch. 1981-82. "The Effect of Race on Sentencing: A Reexamination of an Unsettled Question." *Law and Society Review* 16: 71-88.
van den Haag, E. 1982. "Could Successful Rehabilitation Reduce the Crime Rate?" *Journal of Criminal Law and Criminology* 73: 1022-35.
Wilson, J.Q. 1968. *Varieties of Police Behavior.* Cambridge, MA: Harvard University Press.
Wilson, J.Q. 1975. *Thinking About Crime.* New York: Basic Books.
Zatz, M.S. 1984. "Race, Ethnicity, and Determinate Sentencing." *Criminology* 22: 147-71.

RACIAL AND ETHNIC CONFLICT:
PERSPECTIVES FROM SOCIAL AND CULTURAL ANTHROPOLOGY

June Macklin

INTRODUCTION

A recent volume on peace and war claims that "[a]nthropology is the behavioral science that has delved most deeply into the question of how diverse societies solve their social problems" (Foster and Rubinstein 1986, p. xi). At once eloquent and parsimonious, Peter Worsley pursues the point: We must "examine the relevance and usefulness of anthropology, not in order to improve our understanding of warfare among Them but to find ways to peace for Us. To change the world we need to understand it" (1986, p. 293).

That racial and ethnic conflicts are increasingly frequent and increasingly intense seems to be a perception shared by layman and social scientist alike. Anthropologist Richard Thompson's masterful *Theories of Ethnicity* cites violent expressions of racial and ethnic hostility from the late 1980s, drawing on headlines that called our attention to deadly "sectarian fighting" in Lebanon; to a study that "finds Black economic growth not enough; and reported that

Research in Human Social Conflict, Volume 1, pages 163-187.
Copyright © 1995 by JAI Press Inc.
All rights of reproduction in any form reserved.
ISBN: 1-55938-923-0

"Irish guerrillas vow revenge" (1989, p. 1). From a single week's headlines in February, 1995, one can conclude only that there has been no diminution of global racial and ethnic violence: Mexico's government has started a new offensive against the Highland Maya; an attack on Austrian Gypsies deepens fear of neo-Nazis; the World Tribunal charges Serbs with genocide of Bosnian Muslims; Islamic violence accelerates fear of a showdown in Algeria; and the Irish Protestants and Irish Catholics still are not at peace. To remark on the need to understand and resolve human conflict and suffering based on racial and ethnic differences is superfluous: these examples provide their own stark comment.

It is only recently, however, that anthropologists have devoted much professional time or energy to the concept of ethnicity, let alone how that knowledge might be applied to resolving conflicts. Such neglect is somewhat surprising, given the intellectual legacy bequeathed us by Franz Boas. *Engage* throughout his professional life, Boas' "liberal ideology was aroused by his concern for the inhumanity surrounding racism" (Hyatt, 1990, p. 85). Hyatt tells us that Boas deplored the inaccurate application of scientific data (e.g., the use of the cephalic index), and adds: "Few Americans were more concerned with the immigration problem than Franz Boas.... The same forces were at work in Boas's defense of immigration as in his attack on theories of black inferiority" (1990, p. 105). Further, as early as 1885, the Women's Anthropology Society of Washington urged the study of their own society (Beals, 1968, p. 407). Clark Wissler, writing in 1920 (pp. 1-12), thought that anthropologists were "itching to lay their hands on Europeans and their culture," and suggested the "foreign colonies" in America presented an ideal starting point. However, surveying the situation in 1955, in a special issue of the *American Anthropologist* devoted to the study of American society, Melford Spiro (1955, p. 1240) found that fewer than thirty publications had been devoted to the cultures of ethnic groups in the intervening 35 years. In the same issue, Ruth Landes lamented that anthropological method had not contributed new insights to the "already rich literature of American Negro life" (1955, p. 1253).

It is the purpose of this chapter (1) to review briefly the distinctive characteristics of the field which have retarded anthropological research on ethnicity, and consequently, on racial and ethnic conflict and conflict resolution; (2) to examine the historical shifts that effected changes in the discipline's conceptual, methodological, and theoretical viewpoints; and finally, (3) to inventory the major propositions that deal with conflict and conflict resolution, gleaned from anthropological research. I submit that anthropologists do know a great deal about these issues, as Foster and Rubinstein claim, but this knowledge emerges from the field data in case studies rather than from recent attempts to synthesize the bewildering (and too often jargon-ridden) array of publications. The concepts and theories informing the best of these studies are, perforce, interdisciplinary.

Anthropologists have been notoriously oblivious to their discipline's history (cf. Wolf, 1982, p. 394; Nash, 1981, p. 396), and such neglect encourages enthusiastic claims of newly-discovered paradigms for understanding racial and ethnic relations. Clarion calls are issued regularly, urging greater appreciation of the complexities involved. But many of the new models are based on "old" insights, which have been well understood and applied for nearly half a century. Unfortunately, not many "new" questions are raised in these syntheses. If we are to "reinvent" or "recapture" anthropology, our discoveries in these areas must become more cumulative than they have been to date.

DISABLING CONCEPTS AND METHODS

The Unit of Study and Its Context

In the middle 1970s, I surveyed anthropological approaches to ethnic minorities in the United States. It is dismaying to realize that many of those points and the propositions I inferred from the literature then are being emphasized anew in the middle 1990s. I noted then that American anthropologists had been slow to study such groups, in part because the unit of study with which they worked and how they defined it precluded focusing on ethnicity. The units anthropolgists defined as bands, tribes, and villages were conceived of as small scale, primitive isolates: "our" people were considered to be living in self-sufficient, closed, homogeneous systems which we could approach holistically (Macklin, 1977). We collected data that ignored the macrocosmic contexts in which the units were embedded. But early on, Gutkind remarked sourly that "...we have *always* studied complex societies, many of them with pluralistic characteristics and any anthropologist who insists otherwise is either blind or a fool" (1968, p. 20). A decade earlier, Peter Worsley (1957) had perceived clearly that "for the most part, anthropologists had studied not backward and primitive peoples, but rather *colonial* peoples" (1957, p. 350, emphasis in the original) who were parts of more complex societies, often with state institutions.

Functionalist interpretations were dominant during these years, as Eric Wolf (1982) points out, and attempted to "derive explanations from the study of the microcosm alone, treating it as a hypothetical isolate...Thus, a methodological unit of inquiry was turned into a theoretical construct by assertion, a priori. The outcome was series of analyses of wholly separate cases" (p. 14). Within the equilibrium model preferred by functionalism, conflict and change were perceived as dysfunctional traits to be explained away. Functionalism notwithstanding, British anthropologists working in what is now Zambia realized they were investigating complex societies, and were concerned specifically "with social change and with the meaning and significance of 'tribalism' in the industrial towns of the Copperbelt" (Despres, 1984, p. 9; cf. Worsley, 1957, p. 352). Although they were not trying to develop a new theory of ethnicity, they concluded that "the term 'tribe' carried different meanings in rural and in urban areas," thereby anticipating the subjective approach to ethnicity usually credited to Fredrik Barth (Despres, 1984, p. 9). Certainly, anthropologists can no longer expect to understand racial or ethnic microcosms without taking into account the macrocosms in which they are embedded.

Changing Emphases in the Concept of Culture

The prevailing· view of culture that served to organize the collection and analysis of data was also disabling. Although it was and remains the key concept with which anthropologists work, and is the unique perspective the discipline has to offer, anthropologists increasingly realized that the "holistic, humanistic view of culture synthesized by Kroeber and Kluckhohn includes too much and is too diffuse for analytical purposes" (Keesing, 1974, p. 74).

Not only do anthropologists tend to ignore the discipline's history; they also have been reluctant to "take a critical look at [their] basic assumptions" (Wolf, 1982, p. 393). Much earlier, Anthony F.C. Wallace (1952, p. 747) had questioned the adequacy of the notion "that culture is a unitary, external, 'superorganic,' environmental force which mechanically...molds individual behavior." He urged then, and later (1970), that attention be given to diversity as well as uniformity in cultural behavior. Pertti and Gretel Pelto (1975, p. 12) argued that assuming intra-cultural *heterogeneity* would greatly strenghten the theoretical significance of the concept itself.

Barth's watershed volume came out in 1969, which shifted anthropological interest in ethnic groups as cultural units to the now-prevailing view of "ethnicity as social organization...a much needed corrective..." (Thompson, 1989, p. 8). These points also were made in Roger Keesing's (1974) discussion of the concept of culture. Scholars tend to analyze ethnicity either as objectively defined behavioral patterns, a structural category; or they emphasize the cultural, phenomenological point of view, and describe ethnicity as *systems of knowledge*. The more adequate approaches consider *both* structural, contemporary socioeconomic constraints and subjective, historically transmitted culture to be important determinants of ethnic behavior. Therefore, part of the not-so-new paradigm for studying ethnicity considers culture at times to be an independent variable, the *explicans*; and in other situations culture is a dependent variable, the *explicandum*, that which must be explained.

Finally, anthropologists' own enculturation also accounts for their failure to focus on conflict. I shall return to this point later to show that the propositions on race and ethnicity generated by American anthropologists in particular, reflect the cultural discourse within the United States more than the reality of their empirical data (Ortner, 1991, p. 169).

THE CHECKERED HISTORY OF A CONCEPT

The Dawning of an Era

By the early 1970s—Radcliffe-Brown had seen it as early as 1940 and A.I. Hallowell saw interaction between American Indians and Europeans as important in the 1950s (1957)—it had become clear to nearly all anthropologists that "our" "people were becoming parts of newly emerging nation-states. Although they were migrating into rapidly growing, urbanizing, modernizing areas, and becoming parts of larger social systems" (Macklin, 1977, p. 100), the terms "ethnic groups" and "ethnicity" were slow to enter the literature. "Ethnic groups" appears three times in the first *Biennial Review of Anthropology* (1959) and then only in connection with studies done in the United States, and three times in its 1961 successor (cf. Pi-Sunyer, 1971). Important in popularizing these concepts was the inclusion of an emic point of view. As Ronald Cohen observed in 1978:

Once the new states of the Third World emerged, once American Indian groups, Inuit... and others saw themselves as parts of larger wholes, and used this as a major feature of their own group identities, then multiethnic contexts became essential to the anthropological understanding of these groups.

But the grip of the paradigm with which anthropologists had been working, and which still was being transmitted to apprentice anthropologists, is reflected in a telling survey of the indexes of 13 major anthropological textbooks published between 1916 and 1970: no references to either "ethnic" or "ethnic groups" were found (DesPres, 1975). It seems clear that we continued to believe the appropriate unit of study to be something exotic—"strange and other-worldly" (Mead, 1973, p. 13). By 1971, however, the text by Ralph Beals and Harry Hoijer, along with that of Marvin Harris appeared, using the terms "ethnic," "ethnic populations," and "minorities." By the 1990s, all introductory texts—and they are legion—include specific sections devoted to the definitions and dynamics of ethnicity. Those publishers who failed to predict where the discipline's winds listed, hastened into print with corrected, more marketable, versions.

Two Decades of Definitions

In 1977, I observed "more often than not, ethnicity is left undefined in the social science literature." Isajiw (1974) surveyed 65 sociological and anthropological studies, and showed that only 13 included some definition. Although current definitions vary according to the proposition with which the investigator is working, most include, explicitly or implicitly, the notion that an ethnic group is a collectivity of people who share patterns of normative behavior, a common history (objectively and/or subjectively defined), and a "primordial" notion (Shils, 1957; Geertz, 1963) of "peoplehood," of consciousness of kind. Ubiquitous—found in both developing and developed countries, past and present (Cohen, 1974)—ethnicity is seen as a matter of a double boundary, one a subjective, emic, view "maintained by the socialization process; the other, an [objective, etic] boundary from without, established by the process of intergroup relations" (Isajiw, 1974, p. 122). Ronald Cohen, addressing ethnicity as "problem and focus in anthropology" for the 1978 *Annual Review of Anthropology* covered much of the same ground earlier surveys had summarized, concluding that "'ethnicity' signals a change that should be understood from several angles—historical, theoretical and ideological," as indeed Glazer and Moynihan had stated clearly in 1975. They, too, believed this was not a simple shift in labels, but reflected a new phenomenon. Cohen focused much of his synthesis on the complexity of defining key terms, and rightly concludes that "much less attention has been given to understanding what conditions tend to evoke ethnic identities of particular scale and intensity than to describing what ethnicity is as a pheonomenon" (1978, p. 389). During the 1970s and early 1980s, those determining conditions became the focus of anthropological research.

As noted earlier, anthropology has had a "worldwide scope" since its origin; but as June Nash emphasizes, "[w]hat distinguishes the present interest in the world scope of anthropology is the paradigm of integration of all people and cultures within a world capitalist *system*" (1981, p. 393). She traces clearly the history of this model, showing that Worsley (1964; cf. Wolf, 1982) had "stated the dimensions of the system a decade before the publication" of the volume by Wallerstein (1974) on the operations of a world system. The latter has made a major impact subsequent anthropological theorizing about racial and ethnic realities. Another "new" insight reclaimed.

After Two Decades, the Impasse

"Different and contentious conceptions of ethnicity are currently amplified in the literature," Leo Despres (1984) informs us, "and it has become almost a matter of standard procedure for anthropologists to interrogate the relative utility of these conceptions to the significance of one's empirical research" (p. 8). But Despres's perspicuous comment has not deterred 16 more years of intrepid synthesizers, each evidently hoping to transcend the impasse and develop a more perfect general theory of ethnic phenomena. The *Annual Reviews* published by various disciplines purportedly represent the latest and clearest statements of major issues. Slogging through an overwhelming slough of studies, and losing battle after battle with the English language, the most recent essays extending and explaining "new" paradigms seem to have brought little illumination, and less clarity to the subject. For example, in 1989 "A Class Act: Anthropology and the Race to Nation Across Ethnic Terrain," (Williams, 1989, pp. 401-445), touches all bases in its title alone. The author concludes that:

> They [the members of an ethnic category] cannot eradicate the category—either by processes of individual material assimilation to different class strata or by their shedding of inappropriate cultural enactments across generations, or by a socialization process that directs individuals to apish acculturation of [sic] a national mainstream to which their contributions ultimately are calculated by those who metonymize the nation [sic] (1989, p. 439).

The same prestigious series offered, in 1994, a discussion of "state formation, nationalism, and ethnicity." Here we learn that:

> [t]he widely held notion of the state as the representative of the public will, a neutral arbiter above the conflicts and interests of society, is an effect of a topography of hierarchized binaries whose terms are constructed as autonomous spaces [sic] (Alonso, 1994, p. 381).

Lloyd Fallers wisely opined, in his clear, but little-noticed 1971 Henry Lewis Morgan lecture, *The Social Anthropology of the Nation-State*, that "such general ideas as we possess are most useful...when they are applied to particular cases" (1974, p. 27). I shall move to some of the propositions gleaned from anthropology's "particular cases."

PROPOSITIONS

Even as we owe the British the early recognition that anthropologists were working with complex societies, we also owe to "social anthropology the insight that the arrangements of a society become most visible when they are challenged by conflict" (Wolf, 1990, p. 593; cf. Gonzalez, 1989; also Ross, 1993, pp. 39, 190) What seems to be needed, then, is not a new theory of ethnicity but rather a look at how current theories are linked to practice on both micro- and macrolevels (Despres, 1984, p. 8; Gonzalez, 1986; Thompson, 1989, p. 4). I have relied heavily on Richard Thompson's pellucid presentation and critical appraisal of current theories as they can be applied to particular case studies.

All of the subdisciplines of anthropology have contributed to the understanding of racial and ethnic conflict. However, although biological anthropology produced many studies of the biology of race, few were done on the impact of differing socially constructed perceptions of race. Post-seventies archaeology particularly has made contributions to understanding the significance of ethnic conflicts that can be inferred from their data, especially in the formation of archaic and preindustrial states; lately linguists have been paying attention to violent conflicts produced (or at least mobilized) by "primordial" attachments to a group's language. Sociolinguists has collected data on conflictful misunderstandings that can be evoked by differences in speech styles, as well. However, this chapter attempts to summarize those propositions suggested primarily by the work of social and cultural anthropologists.

Propositions have been generated from the two major theoretical positions mentioned earlier. The first, and earlier, focuses on a "primordial" sense of "peoplehood" (Shils, 1957; Geertz, 1963), and how historically transmitted, observable, "objective," patterns of culture—language, religion, dress, dietary preferences, music—have persisted, been modified, or disappeared. Occasionally referred to pejoratively as the "laundry list" approach, post-Barth (1969), studies have turned attention from "ethnic groups as cultural units" to ethnic groups as social organization. These authors believe the interaction among groups and "boundary-maintaining" behavior are as important as cultural content. Barth's views are congruent with the second, currently more fashionable approach, that which interprets racial and ethnic conflicts to be the result of competition for locallly-valued resources within the nation-state, and within the world capitalist system (Cohen, 1978; Despres, 1975, 1984; Gonzalez, 1989, 1986; Graves and Graves, 1974; Nash, 1981; Wallerstein, 1974; Wolf, 1969, 1982, 1990; Worsley, 1964;). The nation-state becomes an important link between local groups and the world system, because it involves:

> not only the economic centralization of the market; not only the concentration of political power in the hands of a dominant class and the creation of a centralized bureaucracy; but also cultural standardization—the subordination of 'subaltern' ethnic communities. That is, the nation-state is opposed to the 'tribe' (Worsley, 1984, p 187; cf. Avruch, 1991, pp. 11-14).

Although the latter position detracts from "culture as a source of causality sui generis" (Roosens, 1989, p. 11), "... one cannot understand let alone explain ethnic behavior without reference to both content and boundary, symbols and behavior" (Royce, 1982, p. 7).

I shall return first to the "disabling" enculturation of American anthropologists, which purportedly has limited their theorizing about racial and ethnic conflicts. I shall then summarize propositions from selected analyses of conflicts resulting from interactions among groups linked on local, national, and international levels of sociocultural integration; finally, I shall reprise the concept of culture, which remains critically important to an understanding of how the global and local histories intersect. (Nash, 1981; Ortner, 1991; Wolf, 1968; Worsley, 1957, 1964, 1984, 1986).

Of Postmodernism, Anthropology, Race, Ethnicity, and Class

Of late, some critics have embraced enthusiastically postmodernist critiques of anthropology, claiming that the practitioners of all academic disciplines are experiencing a crisis of representation. Accordingly, a brief summary of propositions *about* the creators of propositions does not come amiss. This exercise in reflexivty offers several deconstructed metanarratives anthropologists are said to have imposed on racial and ethnic data. For example, having done comparative work on Chinese, Chinese American, and American societies early on, Francis Hsu concluded that American anthropologists "avoid delving deeply... into how human beings relate to each other" because they have "been reared in an individual-centered culture in which men do not form lasting and close ties with each other" (Hsu, 1973, pp. 9-10). Therefore, they rely on deterministic theories to explain human behavior, including the study of American ethnic groups and their antagonistic, competitive relations with each other.

Sherry Ortner recently began the study of "American culture as a capitalist system, and the study of American capitalism as a cultural system." She makes two important points to assist our reading of these "texts." First is her cogent claim that "although class is central to American social life, it is not a native cultural category" in American discourse, and is rarely spoken of in its own right. The United States "has presented itself as more open to individual achievement than it really is" (Ortner, 1991, p. 164). Nancie Gonzalez made the same point, arguing that it is the "American 'way'" to obfuscate the issue of poverty "by emphasizing ethnicity in order to divert attention from socioeconomic class distinctions. People are not so much 'poor' as they are 'ethnic'" (1989, p. 129). Therefore, anthropological literature that "ignores class in favor of any other set of social idioms is... merely reflecting this fact" (Ortner, 1991, p. 169). Second, Ortner repeats the now-familiar criticism that anthropological studies of complex societies have had "a chronic tendency to 'ethnicize' the groups under study, to treat them as so many isolated and exotic tribes" (Cohen, 1978; Gutkind, 1965; Macklin, 1977; Worsley, 1957). This leads investigators to ignore macrocosmic analyses which might address the "conditions of inequality under which we are all produced" (Ortner, 1991, pp. 166-167).

As early as 1970, Nancy Lurie surmised that the "new ethnicity" may be in part a function of white intellectual attention (Macklin, 1977), an observation for which Richard Thompson provided an interesting historical context twenty years later. Not only does the new ethnicity say more about OBSERVERS than about the observed; Thompson proposes further that newer theories of ethnicity—sociobiology, primordialism, and the "new" ethnicity—stem from disillusioned assimilationists seeking to explain what their theories could not: the persistence of unassimilated black Americans. He presents convincing data that the "rediscovery" of ethnicity has been made by mostly Americans. His point corroborates that of Ortner, but with an interesting fillip: having defended and legitimated the black protest movements of the 1960s as an *ethnic* but not primarily as a *class* movement, policymakers provided solutions that did not have to acknowledge or address the conditions of inequality (Thompson, 1989, p. 102) which Ortner later highlighted. Thompson agrees with Ortner (1991) and Gonzalez that once in a pluralistic society, ethnicity is "often a euphemism for lower class" (Gonzalez, 1989, p. 129). Therefore, he concludes, compellingly, even the new American theme of racial equality "has become a sophisticated ideology for continued racial domination by whites," who monopolize the means of production (Thompson, 1989, pp. 170-171).

Social science theories generated in the West, remarks Laura Nader, "reflect the belief that conflict is bad and in need of explanation, while its opposite [i.e., harmony] is valued behavior, and needs no explanation" (1991, p. 41). There is general agreement with Nader's position, although a small but respectable set of propositions concerning conflict and conflict resolution has emerged from the subdiscipline known as the anthropology of war.

Conflict, Harmony, and the Anthropology of War

Peace and War: Cross-Cultural Perspectives: The title of Foster and Rubinstein's recent volume emphasizes the importance of explaining harmony as well as conflict: peace also is caused. But they add that "anthropologists have said little on [either] subject..." (1986, p. xii). Although a spate of books and articles has been published since 1965 on the anthropology of war, (Ferguson, 1984; Ferguson and Whitehead, 1992; Haas, 1990; Ross, 1993), they pay scant attention to the conditions of peace. Evidently the latter are not seen as relevant to understanding the conditions of conflict. Although these investigations have focused primarily on indigenous warfare, or the impact of expanding European colonialism in indigenous areas, there is much to be learned from the study of war and peacemaking among acephalous polities: the world system is an "acephalous political field" also, as Worsley points out (1986, p. 294).

Ronald Cohen takes on issues of "war and war proneness in pre- and postindustrial states," and several of his propositions are directly relevant to understanding other group conflicts. Cross-cultural data do *not* support the theory that some societies have more "bellicose cultures than do others." Therefore, war proneness cannot be predicted from a knowledge of "cultural ideology" only (Cohen, 1986, p. 265). Ferguson and Whitehead survey the field, also, and firmly dismiss any "idea that an innate sense of tribalism inclines people toward collective violence," calling it sheer fantasy to believe otherwise.

Nor does difference in and of itself generate collective violence (1992, p. 28; cf. Gonzalez, 1989, pp. 5-6).

James Silverberg sees politics as the "interplay" of the processes of integration and conflict. His conclusions are useful to understanding racial and ethnic interactions. Conflict "reflects contradictory or competitive adaptive needs," while "integration is most likely to occur where *shared* adaptive problems are most critical" (1986, p. 288). Jill Furst suggests the root of conflict often is identification with and ownership of land. When such claims (which may be symbolic and mythic) are based on divine sanctions, conflict may become endemic. Although her analysis is based on data from the pre-Hispanic Mixteca, she compares their conflicts with those of the present-day Middle East. She concludes that before any solution to a conflict can be found, "there is a need to separate quite firmly the practical reasons of a war from its rhetoric" (1986, p. 103).

Worsley's thinking, as always, is chockablock with illuminating and original propositions: "...relations between societies at war never take place in an anomic social vacuum," and never take place without "rules which define what may and may not be done." In a trenchant aside, he notes that if an opponent is defined as "virtually nonhuman," then the "normal considerations of enmity do not apply" (1986, p. 296). This insight makes more intelligible the intensity of much apparently senseless intergroup violence.

Although anthropological interest in war and peace has produced high quality, synthetic thinking on this new subject, it has not produced yet the development of a general theory. However, there is strong evidence to support the conclusion that what had been assumed to be "pristine" indigenous warfare seems more likely to be a "reflection" of an European presence (Ferguson and Whitehead, 1992, pp. 26-27). Therefore, inferences about universal causes of conflict or harmony among human groups must be drawn with caution. As Worsley sums up, if there is competition for scarce resources, "war becomes a mode of appropriation"; but if resources are perceived as unlimited, armed conflict may develop "norms in which heroism becomes a value in itself" (1986, p. 296). After carefully comparing "the superpowers and the tribes," Worsley's caveat is to avoid simplistic reductionism:

> The ends of war...are not universal: human propensities to aggression or structural imperatives for conflict, drives to expansion or the acquisition of materials goods. *They are cultural* (1986, p. 297, emphasis added).

Microcosm and Macrocosm Linked in Racial and Ethnic Conflict and Resolution

Once anthropologists began to take macrolevel issues into account, a more general theoretical framework was needed. Peter Worsley's early prescient discussion of the post-colonial world economy lays out clearly the points comprised by later world system, dependency theories. Third world states are seen as part of a single international division of labor, the result of the emergence of a capitalist world economy. These "proletariat nations," then, are accomplices of imperialism, passively or actively (1966, p. 229). From this viewpoint, the European or North American worker also is a capitalist, even though he, too, is "oppressed" and "alienated": he and *all of the rest of the 'overdeveloped' world*, benefit from the exploitation of Afroasia and Latin America (1966, p. 228). The concatenation of ideas Worsley connected to explain the "development of underdevelopment" anticipated sociologist Immanuel Wallerstein's modern world-system theory by a decade. Wallerstein asserted that the life of a world system (which, of course, transcends the political boundaries of the world's states):

> is made up of conflicting forces which hold it together by tension, and tear it apart as each group seeks eternally to remold it to its advantage (1974, pp. 347-348; cf. Nash, 1981, pp. 395-396).

There is, then, but a single world in which the characteristics observed at the industrialized "core" are connected to and often causative of the characteristics found in those preindustrial, premodern "peripheries" of the world in which anthropologists traditionlly have worked. Wallerstein's influence is so pervasive that many anthropologists use concepts derived from his theory without specific acknowledgment or perhaps awareness of their debt. Because he applied his paradigm specifically to racial and ethnic conflicts, it is particularly relevant in modified form to the present discussion (cf. Nash, 1981; Wolf, 1982; Despres, 1984; Gonzalez, 1989; Thompson, 1989).

Although a capitalist mode of production is central to her model, Gonzalez's perspicuous analysis points out that "ethnic" distinctions—*whether or not they are so labeled*—do not disappear under socialism or communism" (Gonzalez, 1989, p. 122). The following propositions are among those emanating from, or illuminated by, a world-system framework.

Ethnicity as an Adaptative Strategy

Roosens demonstrates that both the techniques of production and the products of the West have an "intrinsic" attraction to all peoples; this ultimately involves them in a global system from which they cannot escape (1989, p. 11). In addition, sharing these new values with people everywhere has created a perpetual demand for low-paid factory and service workers in virtually all 'developed' countries today (Gonzalez, 1989, p. 7). Ethnicity, then, is potentially more, not less, salient in modern nation-states because there "simply are more goods, services, and social statuses—offices, scholarships, development projects, cabinet posts, patronage, licenses, jobs, etc.—in the sociopolitical environment that are considered important ends" (Cohen, 1978, p. 397). Opportunities for ethnic mobilization and conflict are therefore greater. Roosens strengthens this analysis by presenting the negative case. He describes the Aymara of Bolivia, who always had shared a high degree of cultural continuity, and therefore, presumably experienced "ethnic salience." Nonetheless, as recently as 1975-1980, they were completely oriented to urbanization, "progress" and "economic-development," and had come to believe in their own inferiority as a group: their "objective" cultural distinctiveness did *not* promote ethnic salience.

Important, and distinct, is Roosens's conclusion that before a group can see and use its own culture as a right, it members must have achieved a degree of cultural reflexivity. Specifically, he claims, at least "some leaders must have gone to the West via an acculturation...or...assimilation process before an ethnic struggle could occur in terms of *the right to one's own culture*" (1989, p. 151, emphasis in original). That is, ethnicity "has no existence apart from interethnic relations [but]...depends upon a proclaimed difference between groups" (Cohen, 1978, p. 389; cf. Roosens, 1989, p. 13).

As was mentioned earlier, ethnic solidarity often is seen as an adaptive strategy in the competition for scarce resources. Ethnicity is only one of several possible identities by means of which people may organize themselves (Cohen, 1974; Despres, 1975; Glazer and Moynihan, 1975; Graves and Graves, 1974; Hannerz, 1969; Macklin and Teniente, 1979). Therefore, it follows that the more cleavages—socially, politically, economically—among groups within one boundary, the greater the probability of conflict among them. Conversely, the "greater the number of crosscutting cleavages, the greater the degree of integration and the lower the probability of intergroup conflict" within a society (Cohen, 1978, p. 395, summarizing one of Max Gluckman's early insights: "We marry our enemies." cf. Ross, 1993, p. 39). Although direct relationships across ethnic and racial lines may not prevent intergroup conflicts, they do mean that many people will have personal reasons for wanting to see the conflicts end as soon as possible; these latter are "ready-made intermediaries" (Worsley, 1986, p. 300). They, like other cultural brokers, "mediate between community-oriented groups...and nation-oriented groups which operate through national institutions" (Wolf, 1956, p. 1075), and tend to reduce conflict between ethnic groups by providing assistance in coping with larger society.

Further, if a group constitutes a segmented society (e.g., the Rom Gypsies; also, Amish, Hutterites), held together by kinship, and whose parts replicate each other in form, function, and potential for equal rank, it can survive "severation." Each segment is a "minaturized" whole (Gropper, 1975).

Similar to Roosens's discussion of the Aymara, Cohen proposes that a threshold of "issue salience" must be present in "a cognitive and evaluative sense" before leaders can use significant ethnic diacritical markers to mobilize an ethnic group. A particular level of the we/they dichotomy must be created vis-à-vis those others who are defined as competitiors for scarce resources and rewards. Related is Thompson's proposal that in developed states, ethnic groups vye for greater equality; in new states, where state power is still weak, the ethnic movements are more likely to take the form of nationalist movements (1989, p. 94). The mobilized group's "own recognized, and now salient, ethnic status is seen as a real factor in the denial or achievement of desirable goals" (Cohen, 1978, p. 389). Not all cleavages are equally salient, but must be understood by the groups concerned as involving important issues.

In sum, it has been well established empirically that the persistence and organization of ethnic groups are "significantly related to the competition for material resources...[which] occurs in the political domain and is essentially political in form" (Despres, 1984, p. 18; cf. Guidieri, Pellizzi, and Tambiah, 1988; Keefe, 1989; Keefe, Reck, and Reck, 1989; Keefe and Padilla, 1987; Worsley, 1984, p. 187). However, to assume there was no conflict before the development of the state is a "pastoral myth" (Worsley, 1986, p. 299).

On the other side of the ledger, intergroup competition increases awareness of intragroup identity, tightens group boundaries, reduces conflict within the group, increases punishment and rejection of defectors, and increases ethnocentrism (Levine and Campbell, 1972, pp. 32-33; cf. Gonzalez, 1989, p. 88). Ethnicity then provides an idiom which promotes solidarity as a moral duty in the struggle for common resources (Hannerz, 1974, p. 38). Where scarcity of resources is combined with ethnic consciouness, continuous *ethnic* rivalry may result in the "pyramidal-segmentary integration" of the ethnic group, and class conflict will be reduced. Conversely, where there are *cross-cutting* rather than pyramidal loyalty structures, then there will be more intraethnic group conflict (Levine and Campbell, 1972, pp. 43-45; Hannerz, 1974). Further, when a group experiences deterioration in its economic position, its members are likely to vent anxieties and fears on the group or groups perceived as benefiting at their expense. For example, during the 1970s, Thompson points out, ethnic whites blamed their economic plight on government programs aimed at improving the situation of blacks. White workers saw the degree to which black organizations influenced state action "and the readiness of the state to deal with ethnic rather than class claims," and for their own organizations to press their claims on the state. Thompson adds wryly: ...the "Ethnic Heritages Act (1973), which, while hardly alleviating the conditions of white workers, has paid lip service to the 'rights' of white ethnics... by providing grants for... ethnic festivals, ethnic history projects, and the recognition of ethnic associations..." The definition of both self and group in ethnic terms is enhanced if not actually generated by conflict (Thompson, 1989, p. 78). One can conclude that ethnicity *works* precisely because it combines interests of group, power, and economics with affective ties.

The "New" Ethnicity, Ethnogenesis, and Ethnoregensis

"The new ethnicity" Thompson claims, is new only to baffled American assimilationist theorists. To suggest that these movements are contemporary inventions "is to admit to a rather wide-ranging historical blind spot." Frequent and intense ethnic conflicts can be traced historically to the process of state formation, at least 6,000 years ago (1989, p. 92). He goes on to say that blacks, Asian-American, Hispanic, and other minority movements in America have been defined in terms of interest, and are *not* primarily focused on their recognition of distinct ethnicities; they are rooted in inequality, as it has historically affected racial and ethnic groups. He agrees with Cohen (1978), Despres (1975, 1984), Gonzalez (1989), Ortner (1991), and others, as shown earlier: "The new ethnicity is...an expression of latent class sentiments that, in the absence of effective class organization in the contemporary United States, has taken on an ethnic form or appearance" (Thompson, 1989, p. 94).

By way of contrast, in new states, where power has not yet been consolidated, and is "'still up for grabs,'...ethnic movements tend to take the form of nationalist movements wherein the calls for autonomy and self-determination are often calls for separate statehood and independence" (Thompson, 1989, p. 94). He alleges further that even as the new ethnicity is not a mass-participation, grass-roots movement, it might best be viewed as "an ideological position that has been offered by upper- and upper-middle-class ethnic elites," who have a stake in "maintaining economic and political influence over their claimed ethnic constituencies" (1989, p. 79). Roosens realized that this creates a paradox for leadership in his observation that organizers must transcend their indigenous origins, and move toward a Western orientation. Such ethnic claims and slogans are mainly formulated by people who seem to have moved markedly away from their own culture of origin, which they want to "keep." However, he says, seeing one's culture "from the outside" does not imply that one can no longer be "authentic" or "truthful" when claiming the right to keep one's own tradition (1989, p. 15).

Local elite leadership has played just the opposite role in some attempts to improve conditions of ethnic groups in the third world:

> As a more democratic philosophy permeates development discussions and projects, [Gonzalez reports], there is the danger that the more privileged and dominant local groups, fearing for their vested interests will tighten their grip, not permitting fiscal and other reforms necessary for overall improvement of standards of living.

She points out that the Kanjobal Maya of Guatemala were on the "brink of development until their ideas were labeled communist and radical and they were driven out of their homelands altogether" (Gonzalez, 1989, p. 7). They now live in Indiantown, Florida, where their cheap agricultural labor supplies inexpensive fruits and vegetables to American dining tables.

Hawkins (1984, pp. 3-14, 377-38) offers the original suggestion that the ethnic differences between "colonized masses" of Indians in the New World and their colonial Ladino overlords have little to do with their culturally and historically derived pasts. Rather, the ethnicity of the Guatemalan Indians he studied results from their having accepted and become "inverse images" of the positive evaluations the overlords give to their own society and culture. This, he claims, is their way of rebelling against and rejecting the hated figures in power.

Ethnic group formation, then, is a dynamic, continuing and often innovative cultural process of boundary maintenance, reconstruction, and occasionally construction from whole cloth. Mary O'Conner's (1989) account of the creation of Chumash (Santa Barbara, California) Indian ethnicity where there had been none before is instructive, and demonstrates clearly the power of outside local and state economic resources. To wit: Two extended family groups (both of whom had "learned" to be Chumash from anthropologists, and only one of which could prove any Chumash descent), were competing for the right to rebury presumed ancestral bones. Why? First, to enjoy economic advantages (being hired as monitors on present and future excavation and development projects); and second, to exercise political power in future county decision-making procedures affecting the management of environmental resources. Ironically, the group that had no demonstrable Chumash connections won the right to handle the reburial; the media hyperbole surrounding the conflict further validated their right to their new ethnic identity (p. 11). So, as Roosens says, "humans may manipulate and even re-create or invent the old in order to attain the new in an attempt to bypass competitive achievement" (1989, p. 161), with the state holding the trump card.

Conflict often seems to trigger ethnogenesis or ethnoregenesis. Martin Diskin discusses how the impact of international and national influences reshaped the ethnicity of the Nicaraguan Miskitu Indians on the microlevel. The "reshaping" factors, Diskin tells us, included not only the development of a worldwide network of indigenous and indigenist advocacy groups, but also the decision by the United States to use Indian aspirations for self-determination as part of its effort to overthrow the Sandinistas. Finally, he shows that the ethnoregenesis was given additional impetus, in part as a response to the leveling of social classes, imposed by the authoritarian Sandinista government, ideologically bent on redressing economic injustices.

This provides an interesting contrast with the denial of class in American discourse, where we "ethnicize" class problems; here one might argue the Sandinistas attempted to "classicize" an ethnic problem (Diskin, 1989). State apparatuses, when faced with internal conflict caused by ethnic expressions, may try to coopt the dissidents by playing down ethnic differences and at the same time promote loyalty to the larger whole, even as did the Sandanistas with their ethnic groups in conflict.

The World Community and Ethnic Conflict

The moral and ethical climate of the world community is an important variable in understanding the creation of ethnic groups, claims Eugene Roosens. Having compared the dynamics of ethnicity among the Huron Indians in Canada, the Aymara of Bolivia, the Luba of Zaire, and multiethnic Belgium, he finds recurrent ethnic reactions and patterns among peoples from widely disparate areas and sociohistorical conditions. He concludes that a condition for the "ethnic struggle" is the concept of cultural relativism, most prominently developed in social and cultural anthropology in the 1930s. This concept now "has fully penetrated the conceptual world of a broader mass of politicians, journalists, authors, academicians, and many layers of the working population only after World War II" (1989, p. 152), particularly during and after the 1960s. "*At least officially*, (emphasis added) cultural relativism has become a basis for the development of relations with the post-colonial West," says Roosens. But a second variable also must be present, viz., "a significant degree of prosperity in the global society. The 'minority' must be able to act against the administration of the welfare state," as an internal group or as an external proletariat, "as a Third World country versus a former colonizer or a great power." The dominant opponent is always a country or the administration of a country with a Western culture, a West which has what others wish to have, "social security, comfort, all kinds of products, prestige, luxury, intellectual insights, and technological mastery in many domains—in spite of all the ideologies that contend otherwise" (1989, p. 153).

Obviously, ethnogenesis or ethnoregenesis becomes a much more effective adaptive strategy if the group in question can project an attractive image of themselves and their cause. For example, North American Indians have succeeded in becoming popular in many parts of the world, which has increased considerably their power within the United States. Associated in the popular mind with many current if vaguely expressed social and ecological anxieties— respect for Mother Earth, harmonious, democratic community life, eco-feminism, animal rights—along with a nostalgia for a pristine and simpler life, many Native Americans have received the federal recognition necessary to attract foreign investments, and regenerate their pasts, often hiring anthropological and archaeological assistance to do so. The Mashantucket-Pequot of New England are a case in point. At this writing (1995), they are enjoying the fruits of *the* single most profitable casino/gambling establishment in the world. Nestled in the woods of rural Connecticut, in less than a decade, they have built a multimillion dollar entertainment center, which is to include a ten-million-dollar museum to recreate and represent their past to visitors; reputedly they are attempting to locate a linguist from whom they can learn their long-lost language.

There is no evidence of comparable sympathy for foreign workers in Europe—they have a negative profile and are merely a problem...The culture of most immigrants is an unappealing 'workers' culture. A 'tribe' of Indians is believed to have an entirely original culture, common to all the Indians of that particular group without any class distinction. This gives them a noble cachet (Roosens, 1989, p. 161).

Roosens concludes optimistically, however, that in spite of the increasing uniformity our consumption patterns produce, the mass media—television, film, radio, music—as a "gigantic production sector in themselves...permit the creation of new ways of expressive invention and cultural differentiation" (1989, p. 160).

The World Capitalist System, Migration, and Ethnicity

Nancie Gonzalez makes the point that "conflict both produces and is a product of migration, and that ethnic phenomena are interwoven with both" (1989, p. 1). She makes it clear that the process of commercial and industrial development, is not a "panacea for the world's ills," and indeed may encourage emigration, in part because "the benefits of development are unequally distributed." She argues further that the development process "in the contemporary world is likely to exacerbate or create conflict at the local level" (1989, p. 7).

Certain classes of people are relegated to more or less permanent dependency on wage labor—wherever they can get it, in whatever country. Therefore, local conflict in a third world country may benefit its more developed neighbors by directing a flow of migrant labor their way (Gonzalez, 1989, p. 7).

International institutions have evolved that help create and maintain a continual migration or circulation of peoples from the less industrialized to the more highly industrialized areas—from rural to urban in the third world, and from less developed to more highly developed countries (Gonzalez, 1989, p. 7). By way of example, a recent study of a multinational corporation, the United Fruit Company, illustrates vividly the unequal relations between this powerful "core" company and two peripheral governments. One of its plantations straddles the Costa Rican-Panamanian border, where UFCO profits not only by bribing government officials, but also by shifting (or threatening to shift) operations from one side of the border to the other, thereby improving its tax-bargaining position with the two governments. The United Fruit Company also creates competitive strife among its workers, importing Indians from Costa Rica, and manipulating local Indians as well as imported blacks and Nicaraguans, thereby keeping wages low (Bourgois, 1989).

Gonzalez continues, proposing if the flow of people is larger than the number of jobs, then wages will be depressed, but employers will benefit. Massive unemployment will result, which in turn fuels unrest and increases both latent and violent conflict. Thus both the United States and Germany face potential internal unrest as a result of their immigration policies. Gonzalez adds that most modern states have not developed effective ways of resolving or managing fundamental disputes engendered by territorial or economic competition, oppression, or by disagreement over fundamental rights and values by which to live. Such political failures may promote protracted conflict—both latent and violent—among groups, as well as outmigration of those who find themselves helpless to improve their situation (Gonzalez, 1986, p. 7).

Local conflict spawns refugeeism, and creates new interethnic tensions. The refugees come to be seen as unwelcome intruders. Gonzalez, writing as recently as 1989, says that in the United States it is not "fashionable" to admit resentment of the use of national funds to pay for health and educational needs of newcomers, but by 1995, such resentment has become the focus of openly and stridently voiced conflict in several states, which have passed legislation denying precisely these basic human rights to their new immigrant laborers and neighbors.

Further, newly acquired literacy and access to knowledge about the larger society through the mass media tend to increase the sense of relative deprivation suffered by many of groups in the developing world, which in turn becomes an additional "push" factor (Gonzalez, 1989, p. 3).

Many global institutions have evolved that help create and maintain a continual migation or circulation of peoples from the less industrialized to the more highly industrialized areas, from rural to urban areas in the third world, and from less developed to more highly developed countries.

For example, migration also has effected a change in the dynamics of the "delicate" ethnic and racial balance in Belize. McCommon, calling this country a "cauldron of ethnic tensions," offers several interesting general proposals. Independence from British rule in 1982 eliminated the common enemy which had created an uneasy unity between the two major black groups, the English-speaking Creoles and Garifuna, who share a Caribbean cultural orientation. Coinciding with the end of the colonial period was the steady exodus of the African-descent Creoles and Garifunas to the United States, and the increasing immigration into Belize of often-illegal Central Americans, who arrive without knowledge of the dominant language, are poverty stricken, in need of emergency assistance, and make demands for social services. These demographic shifts brought fear of hispanizacion and loss of power among the blacks, along with competition for limited resources. McCommon concludes that the core of the immigration debate is the shift in ethnic balance, and with this, the defintion of national identity" (1989, p. 99).

The importance of external pressures can be seen in the case of the Arab immigrants in Honduras. Primarily Christian Palestinians, they found themselves in a conflictful and ambivalent position in the host society, caused in part by developments in their country of origin. Some had been "hovering on the brink of assimilation," their acceptance aided by their being co-religionists with other Christian Hondurans (although some of their envious hosts perceived the Arabs economic success as having come about because of pacts with the devil). Then conflict in Palestine heightened national consciousness both abroad and in Honduras. Arab assimilation now seemed an act of disloyalty to their country of origin; newly displaced emigrants from Palestine joined them in Honduras, reminding them not only of their ethnic distinctiveness, but adding pressure to the guilt they already experienced about their near-assimilation. Gonzalez reports that some even began practicing some "Arab" characteristics they had learned from books. Finally, the presence of the new immigrants also reminded their hosts of their foreignness—which was beginning to diminish (Gonzalez, 1989).

Durham, summarizing papers on migration and ethnic conflict, concluded that "ethnicity blossoms as part of a continuing attempt to negotiate improved position within a social system" (1989, p. 144).

ON SELF-DETERMINATION: A PARADOX

A paradoxical concern arises among those advocates of self-determination of peoples around the world. As Cohen observes, in a multiethnic society in which a plurality of groups vie for scarce rewards, stressing individual rights, as does Western democratic theory, leads ultimately to unequal treatment. Today, in an effort to "counter invidious access by some and impossible or rare access by others, democratic theory and ideology have shifted to include both individual and group rights. In this sense, ethnicity has been legitimized in political theory" (Cohen, 1978, p. 402). But Maybury-Lewis expresses concern that organizations such as the United Nations focus on the rights of individuals and "in practice is most solicitous of the rights of states while at the same time taking little interest in the rights of ethnic groups which do not... coincide" with the nation-state. The latter, he avers, is the vehicle of a single nationality, and a theoretical hangover from the French Revolution. Contrary to Worsley's position ("The nation-state is opposed to the 'tribe', 1984, p. 187), Maybury-Lewis argues that inequality is a problem to many states, but that American Indian ethnicity is no threat. If I read him rightly, he seems to return wistfully to the Shils/Geertz argument of basic "primordial" attachements of humans: "...the very persistence of ethnic associations and their constant resuscitation in the face of [state] hostility suggest that they *fulfill important human needs* which cannot otherwise be satisfied," and argues on both anthropological and libertarian "humanitarian grounds that ethnic associations be accommodated" (1984, p. 228, emphasis added). It is precisely this kind of theorizing against which Thompson (1989, p. 91) rails: it "not only makes it difficult to understand ethnic processes, but it also positively obscures them. It asserts that the cause of alienation, anomie, interethnic hostility, and conflict is due to some mysterious loss of a basic, necessary, and affectively fulfilling identity that is rooted in a primordial ancestral tie" (1989, p. 58). He then presents the obverse side of this coin, quoting Orlando Patterson, who argues that the "pluralist creed, despite the good intentions of its liberal promulgators, consists of 'intellectual malevolence...which...becomes an apologia for continued separation and inequality...[and has] reactionary consequences...which works against a respect for individuality.'" Clearly these theoretical and political differences are not yet resolved.

ON THE IMPORTANCE OF CULTURE AND STRUCTURE

Although most anthropologists working in the field of ethnic groups and ethnicity realize the importance of studying the relationship between micro and macro levels of society, most also re-emphasize the traditional mission of anthropology, namely, to "represent coherent and valuable systems of meaning and order for those who live within them" (Ortner, 1991, p. 186). A.P. Royce remarks that one has a more distinct, more individual identity as a member of an ethnic group than as a member of a social class, and adds that the satisfaction of participating in an ethnic festival is missing from events connected with one's social class (1982, p. 232). Many contemporary, carefully detailed ethnographic studies of ethnic identity return to the persistent theme of the ways in which people use their existing cultural patterns to mold and reshape outside influences and make them their own (Gonzalez, 1992; Klor, 1992; Nagata, 1984; Ossio, 1992; Taussig, 1992). Lynn Stephen's analysis of identity construction in a Oaxacan (Mexico) village is particularly instructive. She demonstrates that the identity the villagers have constructed for outside consumption emphasizes community solidarity and homogeneity, while the internal version of their ethnic identity emphasizes heterogenity, allowing the contradiction of "class differentiation, age, and gender to slip through in subtle ways." Important is Stephen's conclusion. These two dimensions are *part of one cultural construction*. Stephen demonstrates how a traditional anthropological community study, detailed on the micro level, can show the dynamic relationship the village has with regional, national, and international levels of sociocultural integration.

SUMMARY AND CONCLUSIONS

Most anthropologists reject the opposition of American "cultural" and British "social" anthropology. But anthropology's unique contribution to the understanding of racial and ethnic conflict and conflict resolution is the concept of culture. Ortner summarizes well:

As we study the ways in which the cultures of dominant and subordinate groups shape one another, or the ways in which a particular culture is reshaped through colonial encounters, capitalist penetration, or class domination, we must at the same time work against *the denial of cultural authenticity* that this may imply and the related implication that the ethnography of meaningful cultural worlds is no longer a significant enterprise (Ortner, 1991).

But Peter Worsley shall have the final word. He first makes a cultural point, following Max Weber: "Power is the capacity to carry out one's will despite resistence, but is always, immanently, about ideas, not simply about force" (cited in Worsley, 1986, p. 293). Weber showed clearly that force is never a "force-in-itself, that it is always used to achieve social ends and to express cultural values" (1986, p. 293). Worsley adds that "What formal sociology does not capture is the vastly different social content of the respective protagonists..." and concludes acknowledging structure also, but warning that:

The danger of the notable Real-Politik theorists who see politics in narrow "porkbarrel" terms as simply as a matter of who get what, when and how is that it underestimates the power of ideas...

REFERENCES

Alonso, A.M. 1994. "The Politics of Space, Time and Substance: State Formation, Nationalism, and Ethnicity." *Annual Review of Anthropology* 23: 379-405.

Avruch, K., P.W. Black, and J.A. Schimecca (eds.). 1991. *Conflict Resolution: Cross-Cultural Perspectives.* Westport, CT: Greenwood Press.

Avruch, K. 1991. "Introduction: Culture and Conflict Resolution." Pp. 1-17 in *Conflict Resolution: Cross Cultural Perspectives,* edited by K. Avruch, P.W. Black, and J.A. Schimecca. Westport, CT: Greenwood Press.

Barth, F. 1969. "Introduction." Pp. 9-38 in *Ethnic Groups and Boundaries: The Social Organization of Cultural Difference,* edited by F. Barth. Boston: Little, Brown and Co.

Beals, R. 1968. "Comments on Social Responsibilities Symposium." *Current Anthropology* 9: 407-408.

Bourgois, P.I. 1989. *Ethnicty at Work: Divided Labor on a Central American Banana Plantation.* Baltimore: Johns Hopkins University Press.

Cohen, A. 1974. "The Lesson of Ethnicity." Pp. ix-xxiii in *Urban Ethnicity,* edited by A. Cohen. London: Tavistock.

Cohen, R. 1978. "Ethnicity: Problem and Focus in Anthropology." *Annual Review of Anthropology:* 379-403.

Cohen, R. 1986. "War and War Proneness in Pre- and Postindustrial States." Pp. 253-268 in *War and Peace,* edited by M.L. Foster and R.A. Rubinstein. New Brunswick: Transaction Books.

Despres, L. 1984. "Ethnicity: What Data and Theory Portend for Plural Societies." Pp. 7-29 in *The Prospects for Plural Societies,* edited by D. Maybury-Lewis. Washington, DC: American Ethnological Society.

Despres, L. 1968. "Anthropological Theory, Cultural Pluralism, and the Study of Complex Societies." *Current Anthropology* 9: 3-16.

Despres, L.A. (ed.). 1975. *Ethnicity and Resource Competition in Plural Societies.* The Hague: Mouton.

Diskin, M. 1989. "Revolution and Ethnic Identity: The Nicaraguan Case." Pp. 11-27 in *Conflict, Migration, and the Expression of Identity,* edited by N.L. Gonzalez and C.S. McCommon. Boulder: Westview Press.

Durham, W.H. 1989. "Conflict, Migration, and Ethnicity: A Summary." Pp. 138-145 in *Conflict, Migration and the Expression of Ethnicity,* edited by N.L. Gonzalez and C.S. McCommon. Boulder, CO: Westview Press.

Fallers, L. 1974. *The Social Anthropology of the Nation-State.* Chicago: Aldine Publishing Co.

Ferguson, R.B. (ed.). 1984. *Warfare, Culture, and Environment.* New York: Academic Press of America.

Ferguson, R.B, and N.L. Whitehead (eds.). 1992. *War in the Tribal Zone: Expanding States and Indigenous Warfare.* Santa Fe, NM: School of American Research Press.

Foster, M.L., and R. Rubenstein. 1986. *Pease and War: Cross-cultural Perspectives.* New Brunswick, NJ: Transaction Books.

Foster, M.L., and R. Rubinstein (eds.). 1988. *The Social Dynamics of Peace and Conflict: Culture in International Security.* Boulder, CO: Westview Press.

Furst, J.L. 1986. "Land Disputes and the Gods in the Prehispanic Mixteca." Pp. 93-104 in *Peace and War,* edited by M.L. Foster and R.A. Rubinstein. New Brunswick: Transaction Books.

Geertz, C. 1963. "The Integrative Revolution: Primordial Sentiments and Civil Politics in the New States." Pp. 105-157 in *Old Societies and New States: The Quest for Modernity in Asia and Africa,* edited by C. Geertz. New York: The Free Press.

Glazer, N., and D.P. Moynihan. 1975. "Introduction." Pp. 1-28 in *Ethnicity: Theory and Experience,* edited by N. Glazer and D.P. Moynihan. Cambridge, MA: Harvard University Press.

Gonzalez, N.L. 1992. "Identidad etnica y artificio en los encuentros interetnicos del Caribe." Pp. 403-428 in *De Palabra y Obra en el Nuevo Mundo,* edited by M.G. Estevez et al. Mexico: Siglo Veintiuno Editores. Gonzalez, N.L. 1989. *Conflict, Migration, and the Expression of Ethnicity.* Boulder, CO: Westview Press.

Graves, N.B., and T.D. Graves. 1974. "Adaptive Strategies in Urban Migration." *Annual Review of Anthropology:* 117-151.

Gropper, R.C. 1975. *Gypsies in the City.* Princeton, NJ: The Darwin Press.

Guidieri, R., F. Pellizzi, and S.J. Tambiah (eds.). 1988. *Ethnicities and Nations: Processes of Interethnic Relations in Latin America, Southeast Asia, and the Pacific.* Houston: The Rothko Chapel.

Gutkind, P.C.W. 1968. Comments on L.A. Despres, Anthropological Theory, and the Student of complex Societies. *Current Anthropology* 9:20.

Haas, J. (ed.). 1990. *The Anthropology of War.* New York: Cambridge University Press.

Hallowell, A.I. 1957. "The Impact of the American Indian on American Culture." *American Anthropologist* 59: 201-217.

Hannerz, U. 1969. *Soulside: Inquiries into Ghetto Culture and Community.* New York: Columbia University Press.

Hannerz, U. 1974. "Ethnicity and Opportunity in Urban America." In *Urban Ethnicity,* edited by Abner Cohen. London: Tavistock Publications.

Hawkins, J.P. 1984. *Inverse Images: The Meaning of Culture, Ethnicity, and Family in Post Colonial Guatemalan Society.* Albuquerque: University of New Mexico Press.

Hsu, F.L.K. 1973. "Prejudice and Its Intellectual Effect in American Anthropology: An Ethnographic Report." *American Anthropologist* 75: 1-19.

Hyatt, M. 1990. *Franz Boas, Social Activist: The Dynamics of Ethnicity.* Westport, CT: Greenwood Press.

Isajiw, W. W. 1974. "Definitions of Ethnicity." *Ethnicity* 1: 111-124.

Keefe, S.E. (ed.). 1989. *Negotiating Ethnicity: The Impact of Anthropological Theory and Practice.* *NAPA Bulletin, #8.* Washington, DC: American Anthropological Association.

Keefe, S.E., G.G. Reck, and U.M.L. Reck. 1989. "Measuring Ethnicity and Its Political Consequences in a Southern Appalachian High School." Pp. 27-28 in *Negotiating Ethnicity,* edited by S.E. Keefe. Washington, DC: The American Anthropological Association.

Keefe, S.E., and A.M. Padilla. 1987. *Chicano Ethnicity.* Albuquerque: University of New Mexico Press.

Keesing, R. 1974. "Theories of Culture." *Annual Review of Anthropology:* 73-97.

Klor de Alva, J.J. 1992. "La invencion de los origenes etnicos y la negociacion de la identidad latina, 1969-1981." Pp. 457-488 in *De palabra y obra en el nuevo mundo,* edited by M.G. Estevez et al. Mexico: Siglo Veintiuno Editores.

Landes, R. 1955. "Biracialism in American Society: A Comparative View." *American Anthropologist* 57: 1253-1263.

LeVine, R., and D. Campbell. 1972. *Ethnocentrism: Theories of Conflict, Ethnic Attitudes and Group Behavior.* New York: John Wiley & Sons, Inc.

Macklin, J. 1977. "Ethnic Minorities in the United States: Perspectives from Cultural Anthropology." *International Journal of Group Tensions* 7(3/4): 89-119.

Macklin, J., and A.T. de Costilla. 1979. "La Virgen de Guadalupe and the American Dream: The Melting Pot Bubbles on in Toledo, Ohio." Pp. 111-143 in *The Chicano Experience,* edited by S.A. West and J. Macklin. Boulder, CO: Westview Press.

McCommon, C.S. 1989. "Refugees in Belize: A Cauldron of Ethnic Tensions." Pp. 91-102 in *Conflict, Migration, and the Expression of Ethnicity,* edited by N.L. Gonzalez and C.S. McCommon. Boulder, CO: Westview Press.

Maybury-Lewis, D., and S. Plattner (eds.). 1984. *The Prospects for Plural Societies.* Washington, DC: The American Ethnological Society.

Maybury-Lewis, D. 1984. "Conclusion: Living in Leviathan: Ethnic Groups and the State." In *The Prospects for Plural Societies,* edited by D. Maybury-Lewis. Washington, DC: The American Ethnological Society.

Mead, M. 1973. "Changing Styles of Anthropological Work." *Annual Review of Anthropology:* 1-26.

Nader, L. 1991. "Harmony Models and the Construction of Law." Pp. 41-59 in *Conflict Resolution: Cross-Cultural Perspectives,* edited by K. Avruch et al. Westport, CT: Greenwood Press.

Nagata, J. 1984. "Particularism and Universalism in Religious and Ethnic Identities: Malay Islam and Other Cases." Pp. 121-135 in *The Prospects for Plural Societies,* edited by D. Maybury-Lewis. Washington, DC: The American Ethnological Society.

Nash, J. 1981. "Ethnographic Apects of the World Capitalist System." *Annual Review of Anthropology* 10: 393-423.

O'Connor, M.I. 1989. "Environmental Impact Review and the Construction of Contemporary Chumash Ethnicity." In *Negotiating Ethnicity: The Impact of Anthropological Theory and Practice,* edited by S.E. Keefe. Washington, DC: American Anthropological Association.

Ortner, S. 1991. "Reading America: Preliminary Notes on Class and Culture." Pp. 163-189 in *Recapturing Anthropology,* edited by R.G. Fox. Santa Fe: School of American Resarch Press.

Ossio, J.M. 1992. "El otro en la cosmologia andina." Pp. 349-378 in *De palabra y obra en el nuevo mundo,* edited by M.G. Estevez et al. Mexico: Siglo Veintiuno Editores.

Pelto, P., and G.H. Pelto. 1975. "Intra-cultural Diversity: Some Theoretical Issues." *American Ethnologist* 77 (2): 1-18.

Pi-Sunyer, O. (ed.). 1971. *The Limits of Integration: Ethnicity and Nationalism in Modern Europe.* Amherst, MA: Research Reports Number 9, Department of Anthropology.

Roosens, E.E. 1989. *Creating Ethnicity: The Process of Ethnogenesis.* Newbury Park, CA: Sage Publications.

Ross, M.H. 1993. *The Culture of Conflict*. New Haven: Yale University Press.

Royce, A.P. 1982. *Ethnic Identity: Strategies of Diversity*. Bloomington, IN: Indiana University Press.

Silverberg, J. 1986. "The Anthropology of Global Integration: Some Grounds for Optimism about World Peace." Pp. 281-292 in *Peace and War*, edited by M.L. Foster and R.A. Rubinstein. New Brunswick: Transaction Books.

Spiro, M. 1955. "The Acculturation of American Ethnic Groups." *American Anthropologist* 57: 1240-1252.

Stephen, L. 1991. *Zapotec Women*. Austin: University of Texas Press.

Tambiah, S.J. 1988. "Foreword." Pp. 1-6 in *Ethnicities and Nations*, edited by R. Guidieri, F. Pellizzi, and S.J. Tambiah. Houston: The Rothko Chapel.

Taussig, M. 1992. "La magia del estado: Maria Lionza y Simon Bolivar en la Venezuela contemporanea." Pp. 489-518 in *De palabra y obra en el nuevo mundo*, edited by M.G. Estevez et al. Siglo Veintiuno Editores.

Thompson, R.H. 1989. *Theories of Ethnicity: A Critical Appraisal*. Westport, CT: Greenwood Press.

Wallace, A.F.C. 1952. "Individual Differences and Cultural Uniformities." *American Sociologial Review* 17: 747-750.

Wallace, A.F.C. 1970. *Culture and Personality* (2nd ed.). New York: Random House.

Wallerstein, I. 1974. *The Modern World-System: Capitalist Agriculture and the Origins of the European World-Economy in the Sixteenth Century*. New York: Academic Press.

Williams, B.F. 1989. "A Class Act: Anthropology and the Race to Nation Across Ethnic Terrain." *Annual Review of Anthropology* 18: 401-444.

Wissler, C. 1920. "Opportunities for Coordination in Anthropological and Psychological Research." *American Anthropologist* 22: 1-12.

Wolf, E. 1969. "American Anthropologists and American Society." Pp. 251-263 in *Reinventing Anthropology*, edited by D. Hymes. New York: Panteon Books.

Wolf, E. 1982. *Europe and the People Without History*. Berkeley: University of California Press.

Wolf, E. 1990. "Facing Power: Old Insights, New Questions." *American Anthropologist* 92: 586-596.

Worsley, P. 1957. *The Trumpet Shall Sound: A Study of 'Cargo' Cults in Melanesia*. London: Macgibbon and Kee.

Worsley, P. 1964 *The Third World*. Chicago: University of Chicago Press.

Worsley, P. 1984. "The Three Modes of Nationalism." Pp. 187-206 in *The Prospects for Plural Societies*, edited by D. Maybury-Lewis. Washington, DC: The American Ethnological Society.

Worsley, P. 1986. "The Superpowers and the Tribes." Pp. 293-306 in *Peace and War* edited by M.L. Foster and R.A. Rubinstein. New Brunswick: Transaction Books.

LANGUAGE, CONFLICT, AND ETHNOLINGUISTIC IDENTITY THEORY

Aaron Cargile, Howard Giles, and Richard Clément

Ethnic relations and identities have been, and continue to be, closely intertwined with language (Kachru and Nelson, 1992). Language issues have often been implicated in cultural conflicts and there are countless instances where efforts at linguistic and political change have coincided worldwide. For example, after an independent government was established in Vanuatu, Bislama became the lingua franca rather than English and French that predominated during colonial times (Hassall, 1992). More recently, the Soviet empire crumbled along nationalistic fissures marked by language and, in many instances, language alone became reason enough to kill. As the central Soviet press reported, a young Russian was murdered in Kizil after failing to reply in Tuvinian to the question, "Do you have a smoke?" (Dobbs, 1990). The bitter and protracted conflict in former Yugoslavia also centers around language. When four Slovenians were sentenced to prison in a military trial conducted not in their native language, but in Serbo-Croatian, the ethnic republics were drawn down a path to war (Tollefson, 1993).

Research in Human Social Conflict, Volume 1, pages 189-208.
Copyright © 1995 by JAI Press Inc.
All rights of reproduction in any form reserved.
ISBN: 1-55938-923-0

Hence, language is clearly an important feature of interethnic, and other intergroup, relations (see Giles and Coupland, 1992). In this chapter, we outline three roles that language plays in these, often conflictive, relations. First, language articulates existing conditions and, as such, can serve to define situations as conflictive. Individual leaders and institutions can mobilize groups through timely and skillful rhetoric. Second, it serves as a marker of group boundaries and people can use it to establish and refute claims of ethnic group membership. Third, language is a means of negotiating group identities as it not only assists in ethnic categorization, but helps establish and display the meaning of those social categories. In order to understand how these identities are negotiated in interaction and to appreciate better the conflict that can result, we explore the sociopsychological territory of ethnolinguistic identity theory and a family of phenomena known as communication accommodation (viz., convergence and divergence). Finally, we argue that this theoretical framework would profit from embracing more situated and constructivist accounts of identity.

LANGUAGE ARTICULATES CONFLICT

Pruitt and Rubin (1986, p. 4) define conflict as a "perceived divergence of interest." This definition reflects the view of conflict held by many conflict researchers, namely that perceptions matter. Because conflict is not a tangible object, it should not be defined objectively. Certainly there are very "real" indicators of conflict, such as demonstrations and war, but the essence of conflict is a situation or relationship viewed as such. In Fisher's (1984) terms, conflict can be said to exist when the stories being told are perceived as incompatible. This view not only reflects the importance of perceptions, but also the role of language and communication as both a vehicle for, and an influence on, such perceptions.

If conflict resulted from the mere divergence of interests, and not from the perceptions thereof, language would fail to be an important consideration in realizing or avoiding conflict. However, interests are oftentimes ambiguous and their divergence is debatable. For example, is affirmative action an interest of African Americans? At one time most would agree, yet today there is much debate (Steele, 1990). Even when a group's interests are agreed upon, people may not realize the extent to which they are incompatible with the interests of others. In California, Mexican farm laborers were satisfied to be working and did not recognize fully their exploitation until Cesar Chavez appeared, showed them their problems, and suggested solutions (Taylor, 1975). Because the identification of interests arises out of social interaction and perceptions of interest compatibility can be manipulated, language and rhetoric is thereby essential to creating, maintaining, and ending conflict.

But why should it be the case that we sometimes allow others to define our own reality? Perhaps because these definitions offer understandings. If individuals or institutions can provide an explanation of events for which we had none previously, or which better fits our experiences, we may accept it for the order it provides. Thus conflict can be created where none was before if it is a consequence of the accepted articulation. This was, arguably, the case in Germany following World War I. After this defeat, the German people were struggling when Hitler rose to power partly on the appeal of his expressed explanation for what was happening and why. The racial doctrine of his political party read that "Jews are an inferior race and that their influence on the economic, political, and cultural life of Germany, past and present, is responsible for *all* that was and is evil" (Abel, 1938, p. 155, emphasis added). Unfortunately, Hitler was successful at defining this "reality" for those willing to have their negative experiences understood.

Articulation alone though cannot transform any relationship into conflict as other societal forces must also work in concert. Some basis for group grievances, dissatisfaction with the distribution of wealth or power, or some level of anxiety vis-à-vis other groups is necessary if definitions of the situation engendering conflict are to be accepted by a large number of people. Hence, the appearance of another Hitler is unlikely given the circumstances surrounding his reign in Germany will never be repeated.

Even though the success of articulation at creating (and ending) conflict is constrained greatly, it is nonetheless an important element in ethnic group conflict. Today, the media often serve as influential agents of articulation and Price (1989) has developed a three-step theoretical model that helps us understand how they fill this role. First, a media message about group conflict initiates the process of social categorization: "recipients of the message are cued to think of themselves and others in relation to the issue primarily as members of those groups rather than isolate persons" (p. 203). As an example, the British press in the 1960s focused attention on the "problem" of immigration. Even though blacks represented but one third of immigrants, the press reported that Britain had a black immigration problem; the words "immigrant" and "colored" were used synonymously (Husband, 1977). In Price's model, this represents the social categorization process whereby (white) readers learned to view all blacks in terms of the immigration issue. Second, the salience of this categorization leads to stereotypical information processing of people's opinions: "perceived disagreements between social groups are accentuated, and opinion differences within groups are discounted" (p. 203). Whites believed that all other whites felt immigration was a problem, and that blacks did not. Third, the model posits that the increased salience of group membership also enhances behavioral conformity to perceived group norms. Hence, encouraged by what they perceived to be a white anti-immigration sentiments (via the model's second step), the British parliament passed a series of (discriminatory)

Immigration Acts. Other whites also conformed to salient norms by engaging in extensive popular discrimination on the shop floor, in management, in housing, and in education (Smith, 1976). As Husband summarizes his analysis of these events, "the mass media had played a significant part in generating and sustaining [a] separation between Black and White in Britain" (p. 232). Price's theoretical model then appears to be a useful tool in understanding exactly how the media, as an agent of articulation, can succeed in shaping the genesis of conflict. In Price's words, "It is thus in contextualizing public issues— in representing the way people and groups within the public are responding to issues—that the mass media may exert much of their influence" (p. 198).

Language is important to ethnic relations because it is a vehicle through which many agents can compete to define social realities. However language is important not only for the views it expresses, but also for its forms, as we shall now explain.

LANGUAGE MARKS GROUP BOUNDARIES

Quite unintentionally, our language may "give off" information that others employ in developing their views of us (see Cargile, Giles, Ryan, and Bradac, 1994). For example, an American may think a stranger to be "cultured" or "refined" simply because of her British accent. Yet, we may consciously fashion our language to deliberately convey tacit yet clear messages. Such is the case of a shopkeeper speaking Welsh to a man asking for directions in (Oxford-accented) English (Hogg and Abrams, 1988). Despite the former's English proficiency, he chooses to emphasize communicative distance through his choice of language. Language varieties and speech styles contain social markers (Scherer and Giles, 1979) that (ostensibly) contain information about speakers' personality, social status, and social group membership, and so forth. Because language contains such markers that can be changed (on occasion) with ease, it is a widely-used means of conveying group affiliation in particular situations.

For orientation in a complex environment, individuals need to organize their world, including social categorization of its inhabitants. Language is central here because it has the flexibility and overt physical presence to reference a range of social categories. Language characteristics are, in fact, often essential for distinguishing group memberships—for example, Canadians from Americans, New Zealanders from Australians, Catholics from Protestants in Northern Ireland, and so on (see linguistic shibboleths, Hopper, 1986). Many aspects of language performance (e.g., accent) can be acquired and modified developmentally and situationally. Therefore, language is sometimes a stronger cue to an individual's sense of ethnic belongingness than inherited characteristics (such as skin color). A newspaper account of the life of a Mexican mafia godfather reported that although the man was Anglo, he identified strongly with the Latino culture and spoke fluent Spanish. As an acquaintance recounted, "as far as we were concerned, he was Mexican" (Katz 1993, p. B4). As this illustrates, others especially rely on language as an indicator of the extent of our group identifications since acquired characteristics may be attributed "internally" (as conscious decisions about how to self-project) rather than "externally" (as historical accident).

It is not the case, however, that language always shapes perceptions of every group boundary. For instance, Smolicz (1984) argued that language was not a core value (i.e., elements that epitomize the intimate essence of a group) of Dutch people in Australia, whereas it did far more for Poles and Greeks there. Even so, Conversi (1990) reports that "the most universal core value in the contemporary world... is language" (p. 52; see also, Fishman, 1972). Indeed, a series of multidimensional scaling studies has shown that some French Canadians felt closer to an English Canadian who spoke French than to a French Canadian who did not (Taylor, Bassili, and Aboud, 1973). Not surprisingly then, ethnic group members in some communities who do not endorse their ethnic affiliation linguistically may be labeled cultural traitors (Hogg, D'Agata, and Abrams, 1989) and their language regarded as improper, insulting, and disloyal. The multidisciplinary literature reflects a debate regarding whether language is such a universal and central element in ethnic identity, and elsewhere we have attempted to mediate that controversy (Giles and Johnson, 1981). Here, we wish to advocate the position that communication variables rather than language ones per se may be integral to ethnic identity; admittedly, a distinctive language, dialect, or nonverbal style may be a crucial symbolic facet of this. Othertimes, they may not be and identity can be sustained by the overt communication of ethnic values, habits, dance, artefacts, and so forth.

Notwithstanding, language is often a most important means of exercising one's ethnicity. The use of a distinct language or an ethnic speech style (e.g., slang) is a reminder of a shared past, of a shared solidarity in the presence of a shared destiny in the future (Ryan, 1979). Additionally, it is also a way of excluding out-group members from within-group participation (Drake, 1980).

At the same time that language helps draw prosocial group boundaries, it can also erect barriers. Language is a malleable dividing line that can be called upon as threatened parties see fit. Discussing so-called ethnoterritorial politics, Luhman (1993, p. 35) argues that "language is not an 'automatic issue'... but a flexible strategy to be placed in play in varying gambits according to the competitive circumstances of peripheral elites." If too many people are gaining access to resources, those in control can use language to separate out particular groups. Myers-Scotton (1993) calls this language strategy "elite closure" and it is accomplished when powerful groups manage language policies and their own patterns of communication to exclude others from political office and economic improvement. Tollefson (1991) also reports instances of linguistic discrimination and concludes that it marginalizes subordinate power groups. Watson (1992) observes that highly linguistically-heterogeneous countries are often underdeveloped and that developed nations always exhibit considerable linguistic uniformity. His explanation is that linguistic heterogeneity is responsible, in part, for internal division and a consequent lack of development. Thus language can serve as powerful boundaries between groups worldwide and the divisions it creates can have important consequences. The importance of language to ethnic relations does not end there though. In addition to marking group boundaries, language is also a way of negotiating the meaning of group memberships and is sometimes aimed at avoiding conflict, while othertimes facing it squarely.

LANGUAGE NEGOTIATES GROUP IDENTITIES

Consider the fact that sometimes accents seem quite strong yet, at other times, are almost imperceptible. Sometimes people try to sound like those with whom they are interacting, and sometimes try to sound different. These processes of convergence and divergence are at the heart of our third function of language, that of negotiating identities. When people speak in a manner that unambiguously ties them to a particular ethnic group, it is usually done, as stated, to express pride in their group. Members of other social groups can respond to this implicit statement in one of three ways. They can ignore it by not shifting their own style of speech. They can endorse it by converging toward the style of speech they perceive. Or they can challenge it by diverging and emphasizing their own speech style. Whatever the outcome, this accommodative dance can be a way in which interlocuters negotiate the meaning of various social groups (see also, Eastman and Stein, 1993). Ethnolinguistic identity theory (ELIT: Giles and Johnson, 1987) was developed in order to understand better certain features of this process. Accordingly, we now turn to explicating and extending this framework which was derived, in part, from social identity theory (Tajfel and Turner, 1986).

Following this, knowledge of category memberships, together with the values attached to them, is defined as one's social identity. It has meaning only in social comparison with other relevant groups. Social identity forms an important part of the self-concept, and it is assumed that we try to achieve— by various comparatively differentiating means (see Brewer and Weber, 1994)—a positive sense of social identity so as to make our in-group favorably distinct from other collectivities on valued dimensions (see also, Luhtanen and Crocker, 1992). This process enables individuals to achieve a satisfactory social identity, and thereby enhances their own positive *self*-esteem. It could well be that this process has even more currency in collectivistic than in individualistic cultures (see Burns and Brady, 1992; Hinkel and Brown, 1990); pursuing group-oriented goals is more socially-relevant in the former, whereas attaining personal uniqueness and accomplishments are valued more in the latter. In any case, when ethnic group identity becomes important for individuals, they may attempt to make themselves favorably distinct on valued dimensions such as language. The accentuation of a whole panoply of ethnic speech and nonverbal markers (such as vocabulary, slang, gesture, discourse styles, and accent) can therefore realize a process termed, "psycholinguistic distinctiveness" (Giles, Bourhis, and Taylor, 1977), and in line with the previous section, we would now wish to extend this notion to that of *"communicative distinctiveness."* But first, it must be recognized that strategies of distinctiveness are only one of two generic sets of strategies adopted when in-group members attempt to change a negative ethnic identity that has resulted from unfavorable social comparisons. Before making themselves more distinct, in-group members may first try to "pass" into other, better-evaluated groups as a means of achieving a more positive self-concept. Whether one or both of these types of strategies are chosen, ELIT illustrates that changes sought in group identity are often accomplished communicatively.

Individual Mobility and Group Assimilation

This general strategy is one where individuals wish to pass out of a group in which they experience comparative discomfort into a more positively valued one (usually the dominant ethnic collectivity). They will attempt to acquire, or at least aspire toward, the characteristics (physical, linguistic, and/or psychological) of this other group. This is enacted when objections raised by either in-group or out-group to the shift are not considered strong. An important tactic for individual upward mobility in such a situation is convergence toward the linguistic characteristics believed prototypical of the ethnic out-group, and attenuating the in-group's distinctive speech and non-linguistic markers. Banks (1987) argues that ethnolinguistic minorities in some organizations, such as Hispanics in Anglo-American settings, must cross the boundary from "marked" usage (that is, interactionally salient, non-normative speech) to "unmarked" usage if they are going to bridge the great divide between low and high managerial positions.

Ultimately, this strategy of upward mobility is not always successful in attaining a more satisfactory social identity. It may instead lead to anomie, intragroup conflict, and a loss of cultural distinctiveness for those individuals who still, in some respects, value their ethnic group membership. Acquiring another ethnic group's speech style can sometimes lead to "subtractive bilingualism" (second language learning leading to subsequent losses in one's first language and culture) for a group with an inferior sense of social identity (Lambert, 1977). Indeed, the intergroup model of second language acquisition

(Giles and Byrne, 1982)—which developed as an emergent satellite of ELIT—claims that such sociopsychological processes are at the heart of understanding how and why certain minority group individuals and/or immigrants lack native-like proficiency in the dominant/host language (see Kelly, Sachdev, Kottsieper, and Ingram, 1993). Further, and despite the rewards for increased social stability and control, the dominant group frequently may not fully accept the subordinate group even after it has attempted to assimilate, as this, in turn, diminishes its own psycholinguistic distinctiveness, creating another form of conflict. First the dominant group could refuse to acknowledge linguistically-assimilated individuals as sounding fully "correct." In other words, however much the individual objectively has acquired competence in the dominant group's variety or code, the latter may still *perceive* the former to "sound ethnic" (or dialectal) if they can predicate this from other cues, such as name or skin color (Williams, 1976). Second, if linguistic assimilation by ethnic minorities occurs with such levels of proficiency, and in such numbers, as to dilute the dominant group's cultural distinctiveness, powerful members of the latter may respond by "upwardly" diverging away, and thereby create a new standard for comparison (such as emergent forms of pronunciation, lexicon, nonverbals, etc.). Predictably, subordinate groups may find the high-prestige language or dialect of the dominant group an ever-shifting target to pursue. At the level of the (minority) group itself, large-scale defection can blur group boundaries, decrease in-group cohesiveness, reduce the potential for collective awareness, and be deemed unworkable for attaining parity. Then the minority may seek other forms of collective action aimed at redefining the group on its own terms rather than on the pre-existing terms of the dominant group. This, of course, can be accomplished by linguistic means and the advocation of language rights, laws, and policy (Bourhis, 1984; Nelde, Labrie, and Williams, 1992).

Communicative Differentiation

Following on from Tajfel and Turner (1986), we would expect to find at least two strategies of linguistic or communicative differentiation available to subordinate ethnic group members—social creativity and competition. In contrast to the above, which implied a linguistic abandonment of the group, the following strategies are aimed at protecting the group's identity and restoring its positive distinctiveness.

Social creativity strategies are those which attempt a redefinition of different elements of the comparison between subordinate and dominant ethnic groups. One way this is accomplished is through an avoidance of "painful" comparisons with the out-group deemed responsible for the negative in-group image. However, it is unlikely that groups can be successfully insulated from interethnic comparisons in the long term, especially in situations of close proximity, so the strategy seems precarious, and other creativity strategies will often need to be undertaken. A more compelling tactic is to change the values attributed to in-group characteristics in a more positive direction, so that negative in-group comparisons are much mollified. The example par excellence is the "black is beautiful" slogan. Again, language assumes significance in that the often-termed "inferior" or "substandard" language or dialect of ethnic in-groups are no longer stigmatized but heralded proudly as symbols of group pride. If the value shift succeeds, we would find strategies of language retention and dialect maintenance within the minority group (see Giles, Leets, and Coupland, 1990). Another creative strategy compares the in-group with the out-group on some new dimensions. Ukranian nationalists replaced letters of the Russian alphabet with new (Ukranian) ones to emphasize the distinctiveness of their language, and Bones (1986) refers to lexical and semantic aspects of Rastafarian language, called Afro-Lingua, as an instance of linguistic creativity. However, having these new forms recognized and legitimized by the dominant out-group is often difficult and itself conflictual.

Social competition refers to the strategy adopted by individuals who wish to reverse the perceived status of in-group and out-group on valued dimensions. Direct competition is viewed as taking place when (a) group members identify strongly with their group, and (b) intergroup comparisons are still active (perhaps despite previous attempts at social creativity) and/or become insecure. Among the determinants considered crucial in fostering "insecure social comparisons" is the awareness of cognitive alternatives to a group's status, conceived in terms of two dimensions: perceived legitimacy-illegitimacy, and stability-instability. Thus, when subordinate group members come to (1) attribute their inferiority externally to historically oppressive and discriminatory measures of the out-group (and do not now attribute it internally to group inadequacies), and (2) see their subordination as illegitimate and potentially changeable or even reversible, between-group comparisons will become more active than quiescent. In Gurin, Miller, and Gurin's (1980) terms, the group will become more politically conscious and collectively mobilized into redressing the power imbalance and their social discontent.

Examples of linguistic competition abound cross-nationally (for instance, in Spain, France, India, Sri Lanka) where individuals take part in civil disobedience on behalf of their beleaguered language and in The Welsh Language Society's tenacious fight for their language to be represented in the media and in education (Roberts, 1987). Not only do group members wish to revitalize their traditional languages, but they move to have these recognized in formal public contexts. In this sense, people will wish to accentuate their in-group language markers and actively diverge away from what they perceive as focally out-group styles. Testing ethnolinguistic identity propositions, Giles and Johnson (1987) found that Welsh people who valued their cultural identity strongly and who believed the intergroup hierarchy was illegitimately biased against them, claimed that they would use more divergent strategies in interacting with English people (e.g., use more Welsh phrases and accent) than those who identified less with their Welshness and saw prevailing intergroup relations as more legitimate (see Giles and Viladot, in press for a Catalonian test of ELIT). We would argue now that divergence is not merely a dependent variable of strong in-group identification, but may also, in its communication, act as an independent variable evoking heightened feelings of in-group belongingness and solidarity among its self-monitoring perpetrators as well as, correspondingly, out-group recipients of it.

Here we have the seeds of potential ethnic conflict since dominant groups are unlikely to ignore actions which not only increase the status of the subordinate group but also, by implication, threaten their own social and communicative distinctiveness. Indeed, it would appear that dominant group members being aware of cognitive alternatives (recognizing, for example, that their superiority is illegitimate and unstable) make them prime candidates for adopting reciprocal strategies of social creativity and competition in order to restore their positive ethnic identity. Brown (1978) suggested an extension to the notion of illegitimacy to include cases where the dominant group saw its superiority—through comparisons with other dominant groups (e.g., colonial powers) as illegitimately small. Then, we would witness derogatory language, abrasive verbal humor, oppressive language policies, and patriotic rhetoric elevating the dominant group's language to the only one with official status and currency. As Stephens (1989, p. 141) reports in his work on ethnicity in Brazil, "pejoration or dysphemism marks the majority of acts of out-group identity and demonstrates the power of the dominant group."

Accommodative Variations

This discussion maps out identity as the product of intergroup relations and more precisely, as a result of converging and diverging linguistic strategies. As argued by Giles, Coupland, and Coupland (1991), divergence and convergence can take many forms.[1] Two broad distinctions are particularly important. The first distinction relates to the subjective/objective nature of accommodation. Much research points to the fact that our perception of speech styles is dependent on various social and cognitive biases (Street and Hopper, 1982). Minority interlocutors may, for example, sound more nonstandard (Williams, 1976). Objective accommodation refers to the speaker's shift in speech independently measured as moving toward (convergence) or away from (divergence) others. Subjective accommodation, on the other hand, concerns the speakers beliefs regarding whether they are converging or diverging. Subjective and objective strategies may be in tune. Nonetheless, it is possible for speakers to converge to where they *believe* the others to be or to where the others expect them to be. Thus, the definition of the target speech style, on which the distinction between convergence and divergence rests may not be shared by all interlocutors. Intriguingly, situational and societal factors may bias the perceptions of interlocutors. Indeed, a challenge for ELIT is now to specify the contextual conditions under which linguistic differentiations are managed not merely in a cognitively-distancing manner but, rather, are enacted as variably aggressive acts, and/or interpreted by its recipients as conflict-sustaining or conflict-creating. Clearly, the undoubtedly disparate motives underlying various forms of ethnolinguistic differentiation need also to be specified and will play an important role in contributing to this dynamic.

A related distinction concerns the contrast between linguistic and psychological accommodation. So far, our discussion has centered upon the former. It is, however, entirely possible that the psychological intention to converge dictates divergent speech, such as in role-discrepant situations where discrepancies are not only acceptable but even expected. For instance, a sensitive interviewee is hardly likely to be evaluated favorably if he or she assumes communicatively the directive, interrogative language and nonverbal controlling stances of the interviewer; complementarity on certain levels is expected by both parties.

The mirror-image of this exists when psychological divergence is allied to linguistic convergence. In Montreal in the 1970s, many English Canadian students reported effortful instances of accommodating to French Canadians in what to them was nonfluent French. This was replied to, and often interrupted by, fast, fluent English by French Canadians in what was interpreted by recipients as in a prosodically-denigrating manner. Woolard (1989) has reported a similar pattern in Catalonia, where the linguistic etiquette of an "accommodation norm" is that "Catalan should be spoken only by Catalan"; Castillian Spanish speakers attempting Catalan would be replied to in Castillian. Much of the interpretation of these phenomena, such as what may be termed, "divergent convergence" rests on the relationship between the interlocutors, the situation and, more importantly the language norms which dictate appropriate linguistic behavior for a particular interaction. Much seems to rest on the intent of the sender and the fact that the recipient recognizes the obverse signification of convergent accommodation.

Taken together, variations observed in the accommodation process compel us to re-evaluate some basic assumptions underling the original ELIT framework. Language variations, then, should not be understood *merely* as responsive to the semi-permanent existence of well-defined intergroup boundaries but also would appear to fluctuate with situational norms and with them, the points of reference which define converging and diverging strategies (Coté and Clément, 1994). This perspective leads us next to considering theories of identity construction as richer foundations for understanding more of the complexities of ethnolinguistic and accommodative phenomena and processes than more static, positivistic accounts of group belongingness.

IDENTITY DYNAMICS AND ELIT

Gergen (1991) encapsulated a broad historical perspective and described three major conceptualizations of self identity: romanticism, modernism, and postmodernism in which we could also locate the ethnicity traditions discussed previously. The so-called *romanticist* view of identity arose during the nineteenth century and its tenets were influenced by Christianity. For the romanticist, each individual was believed to possess a soul at the core of their being which bridged the gap to God and the natural world. The soul was considered an enigma. It lied beyond observation and was more a matter of spirit; individuals were forever a mystery and their characteristics seen as innate, natural instincts. With the arrival of Freudian psychology during the early part of the twentieth century, however, the core of an individual being was believed to be on the level of unconsciousness, it was no longer a mysterious unattainable entity and the *modernist* perspective emerged. Psychology, not Christianity, furnished the vocabulary to discuss identity and self. Individuals were felt to be predictable and open to observation. A person's identity resided in beliefs, opinions, and behavior. Most recently, the *postmodernism* view posits there is not a true and knowable self, eradicating the two previous views. One's identity is relative, constantly being negotiated through relationships and situational contexts. No identity is taken for granted. Instead of a core self or identity, there is a plurality of selves, fighting for expression. Given the appropriate situation, one of any numerous selves may spring to life. This view claims that in the modern world there is no longer one true identity to which an individual remains committed.

As for ethnicity, the definition of ethnic identity has therefore changed toward a conceptualization of the phenomenon as more variable and more subject to the active construction of the individual. Two theoretical traditions encapsulate this perspective: *symbolic interactionism* and *constructionism*. Many scholars have contributed to the ideas behind the former, in particular the work of Mead, Blumer and pragmatism, Darwin and behaviorism. The individual is not thought to be a product of society so much as an actively involved actor in its development (Charon, 1989). With regards to identity, symbolic interactionists explicitly link it to situated social relationships. An individual does not have one identity but multiple identities which are negotiated through interaction with others. In essence, the symbolic interactionist attends to changes in identity across situations, acknowledging that individuals actively engage in different identity stages according to the social context. They would therefore represent ethnic identity as emerging when the social context underscores those aspects that are particularly related to categorization of individuals along ethnic lines. Social constructionism (e.g., Gergen, 1985), like the previous and other perspectives (e.g., humanistic psychology, ethnomethodology, poststructuralism), is an approach that embraces the notion of a subjective and historically constructed identity, challenging the objective basis of conventional knowledge (i.e., objective, individualistic, ahistoric knowledge). While the notion of "identity construction" may be linked to Berger and Luckmann's (1966) seminal work, Gergen (1991) has been a major exponent of this position. He explains that to the constructionist, identity is not comprised of a psychological state, but is created by people in a relationship. Instead of looking for one true identity, the constructionist examines the process of articulating identity (the starting point of this chapter).

Thus, in addition to embracing the varied situational salience of ethnic identity, as symbolic interactionists would, constructionists would argue in favor of its *emergent* qualities. Ethnic identity is not only the result of situational interactions, it is enacted and value-expressive. It involves the active participation of the individual using it as a badge and as a relational canvas. Hecht and associates (e.g., Hecht, Larkey, and Johnson, 1992) show how ethnic labels are related to conversational issues such that characteristics of a verbal exchange are not evaluated identically whether one identifies as an Afro-American or black American, for example. Case studies by Luborsky and Rubinstein (e.g., 1987) show that among elderly widowed men, "returning to one's ethnic roots" acts as a catalyst for public expression of feelings and a reconstruction of life meaning in periods of bereavement. Finally, Deaux (1993) illustrates the dynamics of identity by showing how ethnic affiliation associated with family matters as freshmen enter college becomes linked to campus activities at the end of the first year. All of these examples, we would suggest, are instances of the active, structuring role of ethnic identity. They also illustrate its dependence on context, and its variable salience and valence. Ethnic identity is neither pervasively important, nor necessarily positively-valued.

Accommodating Variations

This does not detract markedly from the intent reflected in social identity theory. For Tajfel and Turner (1986), the social self implicated in intergroup comparisons represents only a fraction of the self-concept. Thus, while ELIT pertains to situations where group characteristics (and mainly from the point of view of the minority) are salient, the introduction of situational variations would not be dissonant to its conceptual underpinnings. Indeed, it is entirely possible that situational factors may override the effects of societal factors (Giles and Johnson, 1987) and promote, if only momentarily, membership in groups defined along dimensions other than language. Several researchers (e.g., Argyle, Furnham, and Graham, 1981) have emphasized the importance of situational analysis in psychological investigation. Research to this end has included the development of taxonomies, the examination of scripts, and the elaboration of cognitive representations of interaction episodes. Within the realm of studies of ethnicity and ethnic identity, Okamura (1981) has stressed the relevance of a situational analysis. Ethnolinguistic identity may thus best be conceived as situationally-bound, such that individuals slip in and out of particular group memberships as required by immediate contextual demands (Collier and Thomas, 1988).

The role played by contextual demands is central to situated identity theory (Alexander and Beggs, 1986) which shares with ethnolinguistic identity theory the assumption that individuals seek to view themselves positively and that a positive image is determined socially. It posits further that when confronted with alternative courses of action, individuals will choose the one that will enhance his or her self-presentation, given the context. This goal is achieved to the extent that social acts are accepted by interactants and referent others as being appropriate. When this is the case, the individual feels no pressure to alter his or her actions and situated identity is validated.

This theorizing has three consequences for ELIT. First, the proposition that situated identity is maintained because of social approval for an act implies the existence of well-defined and shared situational norms regarding appropriate accommodation behaviors (Gallois and Callan, 1991) and shared beliefs about expressing and managing one's identity. A sudden lack, or break-up, of such social consensi would mean that the norms are becoming volatile within the group and therefore individual members are negotiating identity in different ways. It would further follow that this kind of norm erosion would be symptomatic of large-scale language shift and concomitant cultural assimilation (Clément, Gauthier, and Noels, 1993). Second, it would seem that ethnolinguistic identity and communication accommodation should be viewed and assessed so as to reveal situational variations (cf. Forgas, 1982). Edwards (1985), for one, has suggested that ethnic markers such as language may have both symbolic and communicative functions which reflect private and public facets of ethnicity, respectively. Public facets may include the use of language in interaction with others in the community. Private facets may encompass language use in religious or family rituals. Communication accommodation could occur in any situation. Its meaning and relationship to identity could, however, vary along the private-public continuum.

Third, it would be expected that situational variations would interact with the structural characteristics of the membership groups of the interlocutors. For example, Waddell and Cairns (1986) found that the Catholic Irish rated themselves as Irish more consistently across situations than did Protestant Irish, attributing this finding to the former's status as a minority. In the same vein, Edwards (1985) has suggested that visible and public markers of ethnicity, such as language in its communicative sense, will tend to become assimilated faster and more completely than those, such as language in its symbolic sense, that are intangible or restricted to private domains. Thus, the more private an ethnic marker is, the more likely it is to be exempt from acculturative pressures. One might therefore expect that, in public situations, minority group members would show greater identification to the majority group than vice-versa.

The situation might, however, be more complex. Clément and Noels (1992) asked Canadian Anglophone and Francophone university students to evaluate separately their degree of identification to the French and English groups in a series of everyday situations. Indeed, studies show, in ways not theoretically acknowledged by ELIT to date, that individuals can identify highly with both ethnic in- and out-groups (Berry, Kim, Power, Young, and Bujaki, 1989); doubtless, the nature of this, arguably, dialectical relationship can also be context-dependent. The two groups were further subdivided into minority and majority groups based on their geographical origin. Separate factor analyses of identification scores to one's own group and to the other group revealed that Anglophones' (the majority group) identified to their own group along two dimensions corresponding to Edward's private/public distinction. The Francophones identification to their own group, however, spanned four factors distinguishing two types of private aspects and two types of public aspects. Ethnolinguistic status therefore appears to have an influence on degree of identity diversification as much as it might have on language variations. Furthermore, contrary to hypotheses, minority Francophones identified more with Anglophones in private situations. The explanation was that since private situations are less normatively controlled, usage of English might be taken as a matter of personal choice and, therefore, interpreted as directly reflecting identity. If correct, that would link linguistic norms and linguistic accommodation via an attributional mechanism similar to that proposed by Nisbett and Valins (1972). Such a position is not entirely foreign to ELIT (e.g., Ball, Giles, Byrne, and Berechree, 1984). Its illustration and further empirical exploitation, however, requires, in our view, a recourse to a more versatile conceptualization of identity of the type offered earlier.

CONCLUSION

By investigating the ways in which people use language, both as an explicit vehicle for ideas and as an implicit expression of membership and identity, we have seen that language clearly plays a number of important roles in episodes of human conflict. Because conflict is a status assigned to situations based on people's subjective perceptions, language is a critical forum of debate and influence that dominates such perceptions. Racial and ethnic conflict also depends on language to help establish who belong to which groups. In order to focus attacks in any form, people must be able to identify members of the other (out-) group and language is a marker often used for this purpose. Lastly, language is a means of changing negative group identities and this process of negotiation frequently results in conflict. As ethnolinguistic identity has previously outlined, when group members try to pass linguistically into the dominant group or try to redefine and revitalize the status of their language, these moves will often be met with resistance. Conflict then takes the form of dominant group members failing to acknowledge the speech of others, upward divergence, or even pejoration. However, we have seen that this outline provided by ELIT is incomplete. Conflict does not always and unconditionally take these forms. Instead, the linguistic manifestation of conflict is now recognized to be dependent on variations in the situation. The further development of this notion, in concert with more macro-societal frameworks and forces in the context of *both* individualistic and collectivistic cultures, should lead to both a more robust theory of ethnolinguistic identity and to a better understanding of the significant and complex relationship between language and human conflict.

ACKNOWLEDGMENT

We wish to gratefully acknowledge the input of Hiroshi Ota on issues relating to cultural variation.

NOTE

1. Herein we have characterized both convergence and divergence as arising out of intergroup-oriented motives, albethey contrastive of course. Although the distinction has never been made explicit previously, it is useful to conceptualize convergence and divergence in a 2 x 2 format of intergroup versus inter-individual motives. With regard to the latter, convergence would arise when speaker's wished another group member's respect and adopted their communicative modes, while divergence would arise in response to disdain for, say, an obtuse other who espouses different codes of conduct.

REFERENCES

Abel, T. 1938. *Why Hitler Came into Power.* New York: Prentice Hall.
Alexander, C.N., and J.J. Beggs. 1986. "Disguising Personal Inventories: A Situated Identity Strategy." *Social Psychology Quarterly* 49: 192-200.
Argyle, M., A. Furnham, and J.A. Graham (eds.). 1981. *Social Situations.* Cambridge: Cambridge University Press.
Ball, P., H. Giles, J. Byrne, and P. Berechree. 1984. "Situational Constraints on the Evaluative Significance of Speech Accomodation: Some Australian Data." *International Journal of the Sociology of Language* 46: 115-129.
Banks, S.P. 1987. "Achieving 'Unmarkedness' in Organizational Discourse: A Praxis Perspective on Ethnolinguistic Identity." *Journal of Language and Social Psychology* 6: 171-90.
Berger, P.L., and T. Luckmann. 1966. *The Social Construction of Reality.* Garden City, NY: Doubleday.

Berry, J.W., U. Kim, S. Power, M. Young, and M. Bukai. 1989. "Acculturation Attitudes in Plaural Societies." *Applied Psychology: An International Review* 38: 185-206.

Bones, J. 1986. "Language and Rastafari." In *The Language of Black Experience*, edited by D. Sutcliffe and A. Wong. Oxford: Blackwell.

Bourhis, R.Y. (ed.). 1984. *Conflict and Language Planning in Quebec*. Clevedon: Multilingual Matters Ltd.

Brewer, M.B., and J.G. Weber. 1994. "Self-evaluation Effects of Interpersonal versus Intergroup Social Comparison." *Journal of Personality and Social Psychology* 66: 268-275.

Brown, R.J. 1978. "Divided we Fall: An Analysis of Relations between Sections of a Factory Workforce." Pp. 395-430 in *Differentiation Between Social Groups*, edited by H. Tajfel. London: Academic Press.

Burns, D., and J. Brady. 1992. "A Cross-cultural Comparison of the Need for Uniqueness in Malaysia and the United States." *Journal of Social Psychology* 132: 487-495.

Cargile, A., H. Giles, E.B. Ryan, and J.J. Bradac. 1994. "Language Attitudes as a Social Process: A Review and Heuristic Model." *Language and Communication* 14: 211-236.

Charon, J.M. 1989. *Symbolic Interactionism*. Princeton, NJ: Prentice Hall.

Clément, R., R. Gauthier, and K. Noels. 1993. "Choix Langagiers en Milieu Minotaire: Attitudes et Identite Concomitante" ("Language Choices in a Minority Setting: Concomitant Attitudes and Identity"). *Canadian Journal of Behavioral Science* 25: 149-164.

Clément, R., and K. Noels. 1992. "Towards a Situated Approach to Ethnolinguistic Identity: The Effects of Status on Individuals and Groups." *Journal of Language and Social Psychology* 11: 203-232.

Collier, and Thomas. 1988. "Cultural Identity: An Interpretive Perspective." Pp. 79-122 in *Theories of Intercultural Communication*, edited by Y.Y. Kim and W.B. Gudykunst. Newbury Park, CA: Sage.

Conversi, D. 1990. "Language or Race?: The Choice of Core Values in the Development of Catalan and Basque Nationalisms." *Ethnic and Racial Studies* 13: 50-70.

Coté, P., and R. Clément. 1994. "Language Attitudes: An Interactive Situated Approach." *Language and Communication* 14: 237-252.

Deaux, K. 1993. "Reconstructing Social Identity." *Personality and Social Psychology Bulletin* 19: 4-12.

Dobbs, M. 1990. "The Empire of Ethnic Russians Retrenches: Return to Soviet Heartland Reverses Six Centuries of Expansion." *The Washington Post*, October 7, A1, 34-35.

Drake, G.F. 1980. "The Social Role of Slang." Pp. 63-70 in *Language: Social psychological perspectives*, edited by H. Giles, W.P. Robinson, and P.M. Smith. Oxford: Pergamon.

Eastman, C.M., and R.F. Stein. 1993. "Language Display: Authenticating Claims to Social Identity." *Journal of Multilingual and Multicultural Development* 14: 187-202.

Edwards, J.R. 1985. *Language, Society, and Identity*. Oxford: Blackwell.

Fisher, W.R. 1984. "Narration as a Human Communication Paradigm: The Case of Public Moral Argument." *Communication Monographs* 51: 1-22.

Fishman, J.A. 1972. *Language and Nationalism*. Rowley: Newbury House.

Forgas, J.P. 1982. "Episode Cognition: Internal Representations of Interaction Routines." Pp. 15, 19-101 in *Advances in Experimental Psychology*, edited by L. Berkowitz. New York: Academic Press.

Gallois, C., and V.J. Callan. 1991. "Interethnic Accommodation: The Role of Norms." Pp. 245-269 in *The Contexts of Accommodation*, edited by H. Giles, J. Coupland, and N. Coupland. Cambridge: Cambridge University Press.

Gergen, K.J. 1985. "The Social Constructionist Movement in Modern Psychology." *American Psychologist* 40: 266-275.

Gergen, K.J. 1991 *The Saturated Self: Dilemmas of Identity in Contemporary Life*. America: Basic Books.

Giles, H., and J.L. Byrne. 1982. "The Intergroup Model of Second Language Acquisition." *Journal of Multilingual and Multicultural Development* 3: 17-40.

Giles, H., and N. Coupland. 1992. *Language: Contexts and Consequences.* Pacific Grove, CA: Brooks/Cole.

Giles, H., and P. Johnson. 1981. "The Role of Language in Ethnic Group Relations." Pp. 199-243 in *Intergroup Behavior*, edited by J. Turner and H. Giles. Oxford: Basil Blackwell.

Giles, H., and P. Johnson. 1987. "Ethnolinguistic Identity Theory: A Social Psychological Approach to Language Maintenance." *International Journal of the Sociology of Language* 68: 69-99.

Giles, H., and A. Viladot. in press. *Ethnolinguistic Differentiation in Catalonia.* Multilingua.

Giles, H., R.Y. Bourhis, and D.M. Taylor. 1977. "Towards a Theory of Language in Ethnic Group Relations." Pp. 307-348 in *Language, ethnicity, and intergroup relations*, edited by H. Giles. London, Academic Press.

Giles, H., N. Coupland, and J. Coupland. 1991. "Accommodation Theory: Communication, Context, and Consequence." Pp. 1-68 in *Contexts of accommodation*, edited by H. Giles, J. Coupland, and N. Coupland. New York: Cambridge University Press.

Giles, H., L. Leets, and N. Coupland. 1990. "Minority Language Group Status: A Theoretical Conspexus." *Journal of Multilingual and Multicultural Development* 11: 1-19.

Gurin, P., H. Miller, and G. Gurin. 1980. "Stratum Identification and Consciousness." *Social Psychology Quarterly* 43: 30-47.

Hassall, G. 1992. "Nationalism and Ethnic Conflict in the Pacific Islands." *Conflict Studies* 255: 1-34.

Hecht, M., L. Larkey, and J. Johnson. 1992. "African American and European American Perceptions of Problematic Issues in Interethnic Communication Effectiveness." *Human Communication Research* 19: 209-236.

Hinkel, S., and R.J. Brown. 1990. "Intergroup Comparisons and Social Identity: Some Lins and Lacunae." Pp. 48-70 in *Social Identity Theory: Constructive and Critical Advances*, edited by D. Abrams and M.A. Hogg. New York: SpringerVerlag.

Hogg, M.A., and D. Abrams. 1988. *Social Identifications.* London: Routledge.

Hogg, M.A., P. D'Agata, and D. Abrams. 1989. "Ethnolinguistic Betrayal and Speaker Evaluations Among Italian Australians." *Genetic, Social and General Psychology Monographs* 115: 153-181.

Hopper, R. 1986. "Speech Evaluation of Intergroup Dialect Differences: The Shibboleth Schema." Pp. 126-136 in *Intergroup Communication*, edited by W.B. Gudykunst. London: Edward Arnold.

Husband, C. 1977. "News Media, Language and Race Relations: A Case Study in Identity Maintenance." Pp. 179-196 in *Language, Ethnicity and Intergroup Relations*, edited by H. Giles. London: Academic Press.

Kachru, B.B., and C.L. Nelson (eds.). 1992. "Language and Identity." *Journal of Asian Pacific Communication* 3: 1.

Katz, J. 1993. "Reputed Mexican Mafia Leader Dies in Prison at 64." *The Los Angeles Times*, November 10: B1, 4.

Kelly, C., I. Sachdev, Kottsieper, and M. Ingram. 1993. "The Role of Social Identity in Second-language Proficiency and Use: Testing the Intergroup Model." *Journal of Language and Social Psychology* 12: 288-301.

Lambert, W.E. 1977. "The Effects of Bilingualism on the Individual: Cognitive and Sociocultural Consequences." Pp. 1-27 in *Bilingualism: Psychological, social and educational implications*, edited by P.A. Hornby. New York: Academic Press.

Luborsky, M.R., and R.L. Rubinstein. 1987. "Ethnicity and Lifetimes: Self-concepts and Situational Contexts of Ethnic Identity in Later Life." Pp. 35-50 in *Ethnic dimensions of aging*, edited by G. Gelfano and C. Barresi. New York: SpringerVerlag

Luhman, R. 1993. "The Role of Language Issues in Ethnoterritorial Political Movements." Unpublished Manuscript, Eastern Kentucky University, Richmond, KY.

Luhtanen, R., and J. Crocker. 1992. "A Collective Self-esteem Scale: Self-evaluation of One's Social Identity." *Journal of Personality and Social Psychology* 18: 302-318.

Myers-Scotton, C. 1993. "Elite Closure as a Powerful Language Strategy: The African Case." *International Journal of the Sociology of Language* 103: 149-164.

Nelde, P.H., N. Labrie, and C.H. Williams. 1992. "The Principles of Territoriality and Personality in the Solution of Linguistic Conflicts." *Journal of Multilingual and Multicultural Development* 13: 387-406.

Nisbett, R.E., and S. Valins. 1972. "Perceiving the Causes of One's own Behavior." Pp. 63-86 in *Attribution: Perceiving the Causes of Behavior*, edited by E.E. Jones, D.E. Kanouse, H.H. Kelley, R.E. Nisbett, S. Valins, and B. Weiner. Morristown, NJ: General Learning Press.

Okamura, J. 1981. "Situational Ethnicity." *Ethnic and Racial Studies* 4: 452-465.

Price, V. 1989. "Social Identification and Public Opinion: Effects of Communicating Group Conflict." *Public Opinion Quarterly* 53: 197-224.

Pruitt, D.G., and J.Z. Rubin. 1986. *Social Conflict: Escalation, Stalemate, and Settlement.* New York: Random House.

Roberts, C. 1987. "Political Conflict over Bilingual Initiatives: A Case Study." *Journal of Multilingual and Multicultural Development* 8: 311-322.

Ryan, E.B. 1979. "Why do Low-prestige Language Varieties Persist?" Pp. 145-157 in *Language and Social Psychology*, edited by H. Giles and R.N. St. Clair. Oxford: Blackwell.

Scherer, K.R., and H. Giles (eds.). 1979. *Social Markers in Speech.* Cambridge: Cambridge University Press.

Smith, D.J. 1976. *The Facts of Racial Disadvantages.* London: P.E.P.

Smolicz, J.J. 1984. "Minority Languages and the Core Values of Culture: Changing Policies and Ethnic Response in Australia." *Journal of Multilingual and Multicultural Development* 5: 23-41.

Steele, S. 1990. *The Content of our Character: A New Vision of Race in America.* New York: St. Martin's Press.

Stephens, T.M. 1989. "The Language of Ethnicity and Self-identity in American Spanish and Brazilian Portuguese." *Ethnic and Racial Studies* 12: 138-145.

Street, R.L., Jr., and R. Hopper. 1982. "A Model of Speech Style Evaluation." Pp. 175-188 in *Attitudes Towards Language Variation*, edited by E.B. Ryan and H. Giles. London: Arnold.

Tajfel, H., and J.C. Turner. 1986. "An Integrative Theory of Intergroup Conflict." Pp. 7-24 in *The Social Psychology of Intergroup Relations*, edited by W.C. Austin and S. Worchel. Monterey, CA: Brooks/Cole.

Taylor, D.M., J.N. Bassili, and F. Aboud. 1973. "Dimensions of Ethnic Identity: An Example from Quebec." *Journal of Social Psychology* 89: 185-92.

Taylor, R.B. 1975. *Chavez and the Farm Workers.* Boston: Beacon Press.

Tollefson, J. W. 1991. *Planning Language, Planning Inequality.* London: Longman.

Tollefson, J.W. 1993. "Language Policy and Power: Yugoslavia, the Philippines, and Southeast Asian Refugees in the United States." *International Journal of the Sociology of Language* 103: 73-96.

Waddell, N., and E. Cairns. 1986. "Situational Perspectives of Social Identity in Northern Ireland." *British Journal of Social Psychology* 25: 25-31.

Watson, K. 1992. "Language, Education and Politcal Power: Some Reflections on North-South Relationships." *Language and Education* 6: 99-122.

Williams, F. 1976. *Explorations of the Linguistic Attitudes of Teachers.* Rowley, MA: Newbury Park.

Woolard, K.A. 1989. *Double Talk: Bilingualism and the Politics of Ethnicity in Catalonia.* Stanford: Stanford University Press.

RACIAL AND ETHNIC CONFLICT:
BASIC SOCIOLOGICAL PERSPECTIVES

Fred D. Hall

What is sociology, and what light does it shed on the now ubiquitous phenomena of racial and ethnic conflict in human societies? This is the fundamental question that will be addressed in the body of this chapter. One of my most enlightening experiences as an undergraduate student years ago was the discovery in the introductory text used in my very first sociology course, Robert Bierstedt's (1974) *The Social Order*, that virtually all fields and disciplines in modern university settings had their origins in ancient Greek philosophy. Natural philosophy evolved into what Mannheim (1936) designated the natural sciences (Naturwissenschaften), while social philosophy evolved into the social sciences (Geisteswissenschaften). I became so enamored with sociology that I chose it as my major field of concentration. But it is gratifying to be able to contribute to this particular volume whose aim is not to promote the further fragmentation and differentiation of fields of study, but rather their reconciliation and unification, by focusing on their varying approaches to examining racial and ethnic conflict.

Research in Human Social Conflict, Volume 1, pages 209-218.
Copyright © 1995 by JAI Press Inc.
All rights of reproduction in any form reserved.
ISBN: 1-55938-923-0

SOCIOLOGY'S BACKGROUND

Sociology is the scientific study of systematic patterns of relations among persons and groups. The present discipline of sociology is considered to have germinated in the matrix of transformative intellectual currents swirling around the period of European Enlightenment in the seventeenth and eighteenth centuries, coupled with counter-current elements of what has been labeled a "Romantic-Conservative Reaction" (Zeitlin, 1990). The eponymous "Father" of sociology is widely regarded among sociologists as Auguste Comte (1957). It must however be indicated here in a spirit of honesty and forthrightness that since he so freely borrowed many of his ideas from his proto-socialist forbear, Henri de Saint-Simon, Comte could rightly be labeled an unmitigated plagiarist. The corpus of Comte's writings reveal that from today's vantage point, he would also be considered elitist, sexist, racist, and ethnocentric. The very term "sociology" can itself be regarded as an etymological bastardization, a hybrid made up of both Greek and Latin elements. And regrettably, a little-known fact to which Frazier (1972) has drawn attention is that, quite possibly, the very first use of the term "sociology" in published discourse in the United States was by aristocratic antebellum U.S. Southerner George Fitzhugh (1854), who attempted to use the newly-emerging science of sociology to justify and legitimate the institution of slavery.

Classical and Contemporary Sociology

These rather ignoble origins aside, it was largely as a result of the tremendous contribution of his making more transparent the linkages between theory and praxis, issues of value and issues of fact, the realm of the material and nonmaterial by Karl Marx (1970) that the real promise of sociology as a potential contributor to amelioration of certain problematic aspects of *la condition humaine* began to truly emerge. After Marx, the ongoing transformation in human social relations wrought by the onset of industrialization, the accompanying rise of science, and the process of rationalization of organizations and institutions was brilliantly adumbrated by Max Weber (1968). Finally, After both Marx and Weber, the continued secularization of society and aspects of the consequent need to maintain its cohesion by normative inculcation of civic virtues was explored by Emile Durkheim (1933).

With the work of these three—Marx, Weber, and Durkheim—the basic ideological, ontological, and epistemological terrain of sociology became explicitly delineated. Sociology's central insight, and a point of agreement among these three classical as well as contemporary sociologists, can be summed up in the following proposition: *an individual's position in the social structure of his or her society tends to shape the sum total of "life chances" she or he is likely to experience.* Although social class, gender, age, educational attainment, and other characteristics of individuals may also serve as proxies for their "position in the social structure," for present purposes, race and ethnicity become most relevant. Indeed in America today, one's ethnicity may matter at times, but one's race remains what it has been since the the nation's founding and through the days of slavery and Jim Crow: a "master status-determining" characteristic (Bennett, 1993; Janowitz, 1978).

DEFINING RACE AND ETHNICITY

Due primarily to the Greek philosophical antecedents of scientific disciplines discussed earlier, the classificatory empiricism characteristic of Western science can be seen as resting at its base on solidly Aristotelian foundations. When it comes to defining ethnic, and to a degree sub rosa racial groups, use of Aristotelian-based logic has led to the conclusion that crucial components can be seen to include (1) a group's overt behavior, (2) its covert identification, and (3) the existence of its societal designation (Gittler, 1988). In this regard, over the years the most useful definitions I have found to help my students understand precisely what one means by the terms "race" and "ethnicity," incorporating the three criteria noted earlier, are provided by van den Berghe (1967). He indicates "...we consistently use the term race...to refer to a group that is socially defined but on the basis of physical criteria," while "Ethnic groups...are socially defined but on the basis of cultural criteria." (van den Berghe 1967, pp. 9-10, emphases in original).

In the United States, the physical characteristics of groups that have been most salient in their designation have been primarily skin color and, secondarily, physiognomic features, while the cultural characteristics that have loomed most largely in differentiating among ethnic groups have been those of language, religion, and national origin. Thus "white" people have been racially distinguished from "nonwhite" people such as blacks, Native Americans, and Chinese, while Hispanics, Jews, and Australians have been considered ethnic groups on the basis of their shared religion, language, and national origin respectively. Note that racial groupings may cut across ethnic ones, and ethnic groupings may intersect with racial ones. Thus, one may be racially "black" and at the same time ethnically "Jewish," and it would therefore be erroneous to designate Jews collectively as a "race," as some have done (see Patai and Patai, 1989). But precisely because of the existence of the "peculiar institution" of chattel slavery, the aftermath of Jim Crow, and the enduring legacy of both, observers as removed from one another in time as Alexis de Toqueville (1966) and Gunnar Myrdal (1944) indicate that race has been, and to this very day remains, the quintessential American obsession. This has resulted in the existence of what one political scientist describes as "two nations/black and white, separate, hostile, unequal" (Hacker, 1995).

Racism and Ethnocentrism

Linked to the phenomenon of race is that of racism, and linked to ethnicity is ethnocentrism. Like race and ethnicity, racism and ethnocentrism are often confounded with one another, but there are crucial important differences. Following van den Berghe and Wilson (1973), racism can be defined as a philosophy or ideology which justifies racial exploitation on the basis of presumed differences in innate endowment, accounting for Group A's superiority over Group B. Ethnocentrism can be defined as a principle of invidious group distinction in which vicissitudes of history account at any given moment for Group A's (possibly temporary) superiority over Group B. The crucial point here is that racism, as we know it today, came into existence only in particular societies like the United States and South Africa at particular historical junctures, while ethnocentrism has been historically and geographically universal (Lenski, 1984). Racism is a characteristic of only some racial groups in some societies, while ethnocentrism is characteristic of virtually all ethnic groups in all societies.

THEORETICAL PERSPECTIVES

Theory is both the starting and ending point of sociology. Theory indicates what one looks for in examining human social interrelationships, and it also represents the cumulation and summation of systematic knowledge generated regarding such interrelationships (Wallace, 1969). There are basically three different vantage points from which sociologists view social phenomena. These are *conflict, interaction,* and *consensus.* Conflict theorists attempt to account for patterns of domination, exploitation, and oppression in society. Marx is the classical archetype of a conflict-oriented theorist. Interactionists claim to be "value-neutral," and as dispassionate observers simply map out and categorize patterns of relationships existing among persons and groups. This approach was classically modeled by Weber. Consensus theorists attempt to show how societies cohere as relatively unified and stable entities, and have Durkheim as their classical theoretical progenitor.

In this century, a theoretical perspective tracing its roots to Marx has been Hawley's (1950) human ecology (which a colleague of mine once described as "Marxism without the ideological axe to grind"); one tracing its roots to Weber has been Herbert Blumer's (1969) symbolic interactionism; and one tracing its roots to Durkheim was Parsons' (1951) structural-functionalism. Echoes of these different approaches can be seen even today in studies of race and ethnicity. For example, Stanfield (1985) discusses race-relations cycle, structural-functionalist, and radical-critical approaches in examining the phenomenon of "race-making"; these can be seen as representing Weber's, Durkheim's, and Marx's orientations respectively. Use of variants of these different theoretical emphases can also be seen explicitly in Leggon (1979) and Hirschmann (1980), and implicitly in virtually all sociological examinations of race and ethnicity.

To date, no single theoretical orientation has been able to claim absolute hegemony, although because of how race and ethnicity have played themselves out in history and contemporaneously, if there is a near-dominant one, in my view, it would have to be said to be that of conflict. The ways in which patterns of domination and exploitation exist and shift over time in societies, while maintaining intact the underlying structure of asymmetrical relationships is ably described by van den Berghe. He observes that with the onset of industrialization, race relations tend to transform themselves from what are designated *paternalistic* to *competitive* ones. Paternalistic relations were characteristic of the antebellum U.S. South, while competitive ones were characteristic first of the industrial North, and since the civil rights era, of the U.S. North and South. Under paternalistic race relations, the pervasive social ethos is one of "benevolent despotism," while under competitive race relations it evolves into "survival of the fittest"—but the underlying reality remains unchanged. Whites are superordinate, and nonwhites are subordinate.

As van den Berghe, Wilson, and Blalock (1982) note, an additional crucial element that shapes the eventual outcome of how racial as well as ethnic groups relate to one another is that of resources these groups can mobilize in given social contexts. Based on how such "competitive resources" like economic clout and "pressure resources" such as voting are obtained and used, possible outcomes of relations between racial and ethnic groups range all the way from the extremes of integration/assimilation to segregation/extermination. What particular eventual arrangements actually come into being are historically shaped and depend greatly on the degree to which oppressive structures prove to be obdurate, and subordinate group members are individually and collectively able to maximize the efficacy of their own agency. Indissolubly linked to and often conditioned by matters of theoretical orientation are those of methods of analysis, which will now be discussed.

EMPIRICAL DIMENSIONS

Units and Levels of Analysis

In sociological research, one must decide if one wishes to focus on individuals or aggregates as analytical units. Properties of aggregates are not necessarily reducible to those of individuals, although as Mills (1959) observes, they may be intimately connected. An *individual* may be black or Hispanic, but the *percentage* of persons in a city who are black or Hispanic is a phenomenon of a different order of magnitude. It is analogous to how water, which is a combination of hydrogen and oxygen, has properties that differ from those of hydrogen and oxygen existing singly as elements. In like manner, how an individual white person behaves toward an individual black person is a little different from how whites in the aggregate respond to blacks in the aggregate, as the visible reality of "white flight" and continued pervasive residential segregation in America amply demonstrate (Massey, 1993). Such segregation paradoxically persists in the face of a documented decline, since World War II, in prejudiced attitudes of individual whites toward individual blacks and blacks in general (Pettigrew, 1980; Pinkney, 1986).

To focus in the first instance on interpersonal relationships and small group dynamics is to conduct a *micro*-level analysis, while to focus in the second on larger groups, institutions, and whole societies is to conduct a *macro*-level analysis. These designations may, in a particular context, be arbitrary and relative; the entire United States with respect to its individual inhabitants is macro-level, but with respect to the community of nations it is micro-level. Given today's powerful computers as tools of analysis, researchers are increasingly able to explore the complex relationships between micro and macro levels by means of multilevel modeling (Goldstein, 1987). This portends a potential "sea change" in the exploration of conflictive dynamics among racial and ethnic groups, and should be expected to become more prominently addressed in scholarship produced and consumed by those of us interested in these matters.

Methods of Analysis

Researchers must also decide whether to make use of qualitative or quantitative methodologies. Qualitative ones may be ethnographies such as Zaniecki and Thomas' (1927) *The Polish Peasant*, Liebow's (1967) *Tally's Corner*, and more recently Anderson's (1990) *Streetwise*. But overwhelmingly, sociologists (in emulation of the natural sciences) make use of sophisticated quantitative techniques such as multiple regression and log-linear analysis, usually with survey data—a staple of sociologists. A methodological approach increasingly making its appearance is network analysis, the promise of which for race and ethnic studies has already been discussed by Anderson and Christie (1982). Most research articles published in contemporary sociology journals make use of these quantitative empirical approaches.

Interestingly, multidimensional scaling analysis of sociology articles published since the Second World War in scholarly journals reveals that studies of race and ethnic relations have remained a central component of the sociological enterprise (Hall and Simpson, 1990). Furthermore, my own search of articles published between 1974 and 1994 as compiled and publically available on CD-ROM in SOCIOFILE shows that 11,264 of them touch on "race," and 9,102 of them on "ethnicity." More precisely, 6,619 deal with the topic of "race relations," and 6,064 with "ethnic relations." This corroborates the existence of the greater concern in America with the former than the latter, even among social scientists.

CONTEMPORARY ISSUES AND CONCLUSIONS

The field of race and ethnic studies, like sociology itself, is tremendously diverse, and it is exceedingly difficult to summarily characterize it, though admirable attempts have been made to do so (Williams, 1975; See and Wilson, 1988). Nevertheless, three particular issues related to race and ethnicity are of tremendous concern in both society and sociology today, and will, in closing, be touched on here. They are: (1) race versus class, (2) social policy and affirmative action, and (3) pluralism and multiculturalism. For at least the remainder of this century and in all likelihood into the next one, some of us will be as sociologists and all of us will be as citizens, coming to terms with developments in all three of these areas.

Race versus Class

At least since Wilson's (1978) publication of *The Declining Significance of Race*, a debate has been raging in sociology over whether one's race or one's class (sic, not one's ethnicity) is the more crucial determinant and more powerful predictor of "life chances." Evidence in support of both sides of this question is readily forthcoming (see for example Wilson, 1987 for an argument favoring the prevalence of class over race, and Massey for one of race over class). The catalyst for this discussion is the putative emergence in advanced industrial American society of a disproportionately black, largely urban "underclass," the intractability of whose amelioration has bedevilled policymakers on both the ideological right and left (Hall, 1989). Some like Gans (1989) argue in favor of the continued need for governmental assistance to help this group get itself "out of the poverty trap," while others as emphatically assert the need to terminate all federal income support for members of this group, irrespective of race, and wish to see a cessation of race-based targeted programs like affirmative action (Murray, 1984). Indeed, affirmative action looms as the second pressing issue that revolves around race in modern America. At this writing, the continued need for affirmative action is shaping up as *the* issue of the 1996 Presidential election.

Affirmative Action

Throughout American history, this nation has viewed itself as one of immigrants who, if they came with strong backs and willingness to work, could experience upward mobility. This is seen as no less true for America's newest immigrants from both Asian Rim nations and south of the U.S. border. But there was, at one time, recognition that real life situations of black Americans would not easily improve without an emphasis on attempts to move from an emphasis on putative equality of individual opportunity to increasing equality of group condition (Ezorsky, 1991). Thus, such a race-specific policy as affirmative action became progressively enacted in American society, although ironically, its chief beneficiaries have been shown to be white women (Hacker, 1995). What the eventual outcome of this controversy will be remains to be seen, and may in fact hinge on blacks' and other minorities' ability to wield the "competitive" and "pressure" resources alluded to earlier.

Pluralism and Multiculturalism

The view of America as a "melting pot" where we all blend together like cheese fondue is becoming subsumed under its being viewed as a "salad bowl" or "stew," where the elements remain distinct and identifiable, yet all make unique contributions to flavoring the whole. This is the position known as racial/ethnic pluralism, and is ensconced in contemporary debates in American public education over multiculturalism (D'Souza, 1991). The essence of race and ethnicity as meaningful categories lies in the ability to differentiate among categories. The trick we have not yet mastered is how to have horizontal differentiation without vertical ranking. It is also not clear how we will be able to get beyond the "Anglo-Saxon core" of a multiethnic America (Aguirre and Turner, 1995), which may render us as a nation decreasingly competitive in the evolving world economy, where less heterogeneous nations like Japan and China may, in the next century, surge ahead of an America which proved itself incapable of growing past the stage of adolescent bickering.

And there are other trouble spots: recent intensification of black-Jewish tensions following decades of cooperative relationships; a recrudescence of racial intolerance epitomized by five Greenwich, Connecticut white males' coded yearbook message to "Kill All Niggers"; not-so-subtle attempts to resurrect the ghost of racial and ethnic eugenics by Herrnstein and Murray (1994), and America's sustained failure to give adequate justice to its forgotten race and its forgotten ethnicities—its aboriginal population (Nabokov, 1991).

With the exception of America's first inhabitants, it has been said "we may have come over here on different ships, but we're all now in the same boat." It has also been said that "no one of us alone is as smart or knows as much as all of us together." Fellow contributors to this volume, in psychology, political science, and philosophy for example, may shed additional light on how we may collectively evolve toward transmuting outworn shibboleths of this racial group's or that ethnic group's supposed superiority or inferiority into a concrete and pragmatic emphasis on making real the common ties that bind us all together. We are here as scholars making a crucial first step; let us individually and collectively muster the strength and will to continue the journey we have begun.

REFERENCES

Aguirre, A., Jr, and J.H. Turner. 1995. *American Ethnicity: The Dynamics and Consequences of Discrimination.* New York: McGraw-Hill.

Anderson, E. 1990. *Streetwise: Race, Class, and Change in an Urban Community.* Chicago: University of Chicago Press.

Anderson, G.M., and T.L. Christie. 1982. "Networks: The Impetus for New Research Initiatives." Pp. 207-225 in *Research in Race and Ethnic Relations* (volume 3), edited by C.B. Marrett and C.B. Leggon. Greenwich, CT: JAI Press.

Bennett, L., Jr. 1993. *Before the Mayflower.* New York: Penguin.

Bierstedt, R. 1974. *The Social Order.* New York: McGraw-Hill.

Blalock, H. 1982. *Race and Ethnic Relations.* Englewood Cliffs, NJ: Prentice-Hall.

Blumer, H. 1969. *Symbolic Interactionism.* Berkeley: University of California Press.

Comte, A. 1957. *La Sociologie.* Paris: Presses Universitaires de France.

D'Souza, D. 1991. *Illiberal Education: The Politics of Race and Sex on Campus.* New York: Free Press.

Durkheim, E. 1933. *The Division of Labor in Society.* New York: Free Press.

Ezorsky, G. 1991. *Racism and Justice: The Case for Affirmative Action.* Ithaca: Cornell University Press.

Fitzhugh, G. 1854. *Sociology for the South, or the Failure of Free Society.* New York: Burt Franklin.

Frazier, E.F. 1972. "Sociological Theory and Race Relations." Pp. 15-25 in *Intergroup Relations: Sociological Perspectives,* edited by P. van den Berghe. New York: Basic Books.

Gans, H. 1989. "Sociology in America: The Discipline and the Public." *American Sociological Review* 54: 1-16.

Gittler, J.B. 1988. "Social Ontology and Aristotelian Criteria as an Approach in Defining an Ethnic Group." *International Journal of Group Tensions* 18: 3-19.

Goldstein, H. 1987. *Multilevel Modelling in Educational and Social Research.* London: Charles Griffin and Company.

Hacker, A. 1995. *Two Nations.* New York: Ballantine Books.

Hall, F. 1989. "Race, Sex, and Entrapment in the Web of Urban Change." *Humanity and Society* 13: 29-42.

Hall, F., and R. Simpson. 1990. "The Division of Sociological Labor in Postwar America." Unpublished manuscript, University of North Carolina at Chapel Hill.

Hawley, A. 1950. *Human Ecology: A Theory of Community Structure.* New York: George Ronald Press.

Herrnstein, R.J., and C.A. Murray. 1994. *The Bell Curve: Intelligence and Class Structure in American Life.* New York: Free Press.

Hirschman, C. 1980. "Theories and Models of Ethnic Inequality." Pp. 1-20 in *Research in Race and Ethnic Relations* (volume 2), edited by C.B. Marrett and C.B. Leggon. Greenwich, CT: JAI Press.

Janowitz, M. 1978. *The Last Half-century*. Chicago: University of Chicago Press.

Leggon, C.B. 1979. "Theoretical Perspectives on Race and Ethnic Relations: A Socio-historical Approach." Pp. 1-16 in *Research in Race and Ethnic Relations* (volume 1), edited by C.B. Marrett and C.B. Leggon. Greenwich, CT: JAI Press.

Lenski, G.E. 1984. *Power and Privilege: A Theory of Social Stratification*. Chapel Hill: University of North Carolina Press.

Liebow, E. 1967. *Tally's Corner: A Study of Negro Streetcorner Men*. Boston: Little, Brown, and Company.

Mannheim, K. 1936. *Ideology and Utopia*. New York: Harcourt, Brace, and World.

Marx, K. 1970. *A Contribution to the Critique of Political Economy.*. New York: International Publishers.

Massey, D.S. 1993. *American Apartheid: Segregation and the Making of the Underclass*. Cambridge, MA: Harvard University Press.

Mills, C.W. 1959. *The Sociological Imagination*. New York: Grove Press.

Murray, C. 1984. *Losing Ground: American Social Policy, 1950-1980*. New York: Basic Books.

Myrdal, G. 1944. *An American Dilemma: The Negro Problem and Modern Democracy*. New York: Harper.

Nabokov, P. (ed.). 1991. *Native American Testimony*. New York: Penguin.

Parsons, T. 1951. *The Social System*. New York: Free Press.

Patai, R. and J. Patai. 1989. *The Myth of the Jewish Race*. Detroit: Wayne State University Press.

Pettigrew, T. 1980. "Racial Change and the Intrametropolitan Distribution of Black Americans." Pp. 52-79 in *The Prospective City*, edited by A.P. Solomon. Cambridge, MA: MIT Press.

Pinkney, A. 1986. *The Myth of Black Progress*. Cambridge: Cambridge University Press.

See, K.O., and W.J. Wilson. 1988. "Race and Ethnicity." Pp. 223-242 in *Handbook of Sociology*, edited by N. Smelser. Newbury Park: Sage.

Stanfield, J.H. 1985. "Theoretical and Ideological Barriers to the Study of Race-making." Pp. 161-181 in *Research in Race and Ethnic Relations* (volume 4), edited by C.B. Marrett and C.B. Leggon. Greenwich, CT: JAI Press.

Tocqueville, A. 1966. *Democracy in America.*. New York: Harper and Row.

van den Berghe, P.L. 1967. *Race and Racism: A Comparative Perspective*. New York: Wiley and Sons.

Wallace, W.L. 1969. *Sociological Theory: An Introduction*. New York: Aldine.

Weber, M. 1968. *Economy and Society*. New York: Bedminster Press.

Williams, R.L. 1975. "Race and Ethnic Relations." Pp. 125-164 in *Annual review of sociology* (volume 1), edited by A. Inkeles, J. Coleman, and N. Smelser. Palo Alto: Annual Reviews, Inc.

Wilson, W.J. 1973. *Power, Racism, and Privilege: Race Relations in Theoretical and Sociohistorical Perspectives*. New York: Macmillan.

Wilson, W.J. 1978. *The Declining Significance of Race: Blacks and Changing American Institutions*. Chicago: University of Chicago Press.

Wilson, W.J. 1987. *The Truly Disadvantaged: The Inner City, the Underclass, and Public Policy*. Chicago: University of Chicago Press.

Zeitlin, I.M. 1990. *Ideology and the Development of Sociological Theory*. Englewood Cliffs, NJ: Prentice-Hall.

Znaniecki, F., and Thomas, W.I. 1927. *The Polish Peasant in Europe and America* (2d ed.). New York: Knopf.

RACIAL AND ETHNIC CONFLICT:
PERSPECTIVES FROM COMMUNITY INTERVENTION

George J. McCall

THE FIELD OF COMMUNITY CONFLICT INTERVENTION

As a distinct field of knowledge and practice, community conflict intervention (Laue, 1981b, 1982, 1987; Nicholau and Cormick, 1972) emerged only in the course of the turbulent American civil rights movement of the 1960s. Establishment of a federal agency for community conflict intervention—the Community Relations Service (CRS)—provided initial impetus for the professionalization of what had been an ancient human undertaking (Pompa, 1981, 1987). For its principles of practice, early training and formalization efforts borrowed extensively from those of community organizers (Alinsky, 1946, 1971; Schaller, 1966; Zald, 1967) and from applied sociological practice roles in industrial relations (Kerr, 1954) and intergroup tension reduction (Dean and Rosen, 1955; Rose, 1947; Williams, 1947). For conceptual and empirical underpinnings, those early efforts relied heavily on the still-new field of conflict resolution (Lewin, 1948) and the developing sociology of conflict (Angell, 1965; Bernard, 1950, 1957; Coser, 1956, 1957, 1961, 1967; Mack and Snyder, 1957; Simmel, 1955). Especially important from the latter specialty

Research in Human Social Conflict, Volume 1, pages 219-237.
Copyright © 1995 by JAI Press Inc.
All rights of reproduction in any form reserved.
ISBN: 1-55938-923-0

were early sociological studies of race riots (Chicago Commission on Race Relations, 1922; Clark, 1944; Lee and Humphrey, 1943) and of rancorous community conflicts more generally (Coleman, 1957; Crain, Katz, and Rosenthal, 1969; Gamson, 1966).

Ford Foundation funding of counterpart private agencies—for example, the Institute for Mediation and Conflict Resolution (Nicholau, 1981)—keyed a wider and more reflective phase of this professionalization process. A distinct scholarly literature first emerged in 1970, including a short-lived journal, *Crisis and Change*. Although community conflict intervention never attained the status of a separate discipline that the late James H. Laue had sought for it (Laue, 1982, 1993), it has maintained itself as one (comparatively slender) thread within the broader field of conflict resolution, figuring regularly in the programs of the National Conference on Peacemaking and Conflict Resolution (NCPCR), the Society of Professionals in Dispute Resolution (SPIDR), and the National Institute for Dispute Resolution (NIDR).

Beyond the United States, the self-conscious development of community conflict intervention has taken hold primarily in South Africa, where a changing political climate has fostered a recent flowering of old seeds. Scholarly literature from that country is just now really coming on stream (Anstey, 1993; Pretorius, 1993; van der Merwe, 1993).

What most distinguishes community conflict intervention from (or within) the broader field of conflict resolution are (1) its consideration of a wider spectrum of conflict roles and outcomes, and (2) the centrality of a "social change and social justice" orientation.

> Intervention in community disputes refers to deliberate attempts by outside or other organizations, persons, or forces to influence the course of events in a conflict or crisis situation. Generally, the intervenors perceive their role as helping the disputing parties resolve their differences in what the *intervenors* see as a positive or socially desirable manner (Laue and Cormick, 1978, p. 208, emphasis added).

Intervention is ubiquitous and itself a key dynamic in social conflict. Moreover, intervention in social conflict is plural, involving several types of intervenor role and, often, multiple occupants of each such role. In any one conflict, it is typical that some intervenors are advocating for a particular *party*, other intervenors are advocating for a particular *outcome*, and yet other intervenors are advocating for a particular *process* to be employed in conducting the conflict (Laue, 1978, 1981a). Emphasizing that negotiation plays a particularly vital part in all social conflicts, and that a just and proper negotiation process requires adequate representation of all parties, community conflict intervention does in practice focus on the key role of negotiation-process advocates, or *mediators*. Here, mediation is viewed not as a means of social control, of settlement, but rather as a means of social change

(Scimecca, 1987)—by empowering all parties within the negotiation process, the power structure of the community may be altered (Laue, 1971, 1978).

Not surprisingly, therefore, mediators tend to be viewed as meddlesome and unwanted (Bash, 1981; Doob, 1993; Touval, 1993; Zartman, 1990, 1991). Any potential mediator therefore has to build leverage, through preparatory positioning and prenegotiation. In positioning, a potential mediator strives to maintain contacts with all parties, to promote legitimate discussion of the problem, at whatever level it may exist, and stay attuned to the tactics of pluralism within either side. In prenegotiations, a potential mediator tries to foster discussions among the sides, to build up and legitimize moderate groups and leaders on both sides, and to help them develop a common sense of the problem and of its solution (Zartman, 1990).

Therefore, even in negotiation-process advocacy, community conflict intervention consists less in direct mediation than in leverage building, through various tactics of positioning and prenegotiation on the part of potential mediators. These tactics are, further, complicated by the fact that virtually every social conflict "tends to involve many would-be mediators.... Multiple efforts are a desirable feature of mediation, but so is coordination. Uncoordinated, many mediators present the parties with continual occasions to try to improve the latest offer, by turning to another mediator, and thus they destroy the mediator's basis for leverage" (Zartman, 1991, p. 313).

Overall, the scholarly literature of community conflict intervention is relatively scant, even in the form of case studies (Assefa and Wahrhaftig, 1988; Salem, 1984; Shellow and Roemer, 1966), for a number of reasons. First of all, the activities of positioning and prenegotiation are usually humdrum and quite indeterminate in outcome. Second, the mediator's needs to assure the confidentiality of the process, to avoid the glare of publicity, and to allow the parties to take all credit for success, constrain the detailed documentation even of major cases of direct mediation. Third, as in most practicing professions, scholarly writing is distinctly a secondary activity. Most community mediators prefer practice to writing, and tend to become involved in new cases before they get around to writing up the last ones.

Even so, the field of community conflict intervention does provide a distinctive and important perspective on racial and ethnic conflicts. It cannot be overlooked that:

- most episodes of ethnic collective violence actually occur within community conflicts (Grimshaw, 1969) and, conversely,
- most community conflicts do in some way involve matters of race or ethnicity (Laue and Cormick, 1978).

What is it about community conflict that serves to explain these two major facts?

COMMUNITY AND SOCIETY

Communities can be understood only against the backdrop of societal dynamics.

The political economy perspective in sociology, for example, emphasizes the co-evolution of national economy and the state. A key point that follows from that perspective (linking the state, the labor market, and the money market) is that the expansionist dynamic of a capitalist economy necessarily entails *uneven development.* "Within an economy, not all industries or regions develop at the same rate or along the same path...; newer areas emerge because economic activities face limits to expansion in existing sites" (Bartelt, Elesh, Goldstein, Leon, and Yancey, 1987, p. 182). Populations flow from one industry or location to another, in response to these changing patterns of industrial investment.

"[C]ities are settlements that emerged largely because of production and distribution requirements of geographically extensive economic and political orders.... Cities emerge, grow, shrink, and even disappear in response to shifts in the emphasis and growth of the entire economy" (Bartelt et al, 1987, pp. 180-181).

The settlements of any national economy are thus functionally specialized components. Settlements function as manufacturing cities, wholesale centers, retail centers, transportation or communication centers, mining towns, college towns, medical centers, capital cities, military towns, finance-insurance-real estate centers, resort or retirement towns, fishing or lumbering towns (e.g., Nelson, 1955). This functional specialization of a settlement determines most of its community characteristics: its size, internal spatial structure, occupational distribution, and demographic composition (Duncan and Reiss, 1956) as well as its relationships with other communities and the larger society (Warren, 1978). As a specialized "subcultural lump" within the mass society, a community provides its members a more congenial social setting for daily life-rounds and the suspension or relaxation of certain demands, pressures, and status anxieties imposed by the larger society (McCall and Simmons, 1982). In fact, outsiders may find that such communities can be hard lumps to crack.

The extent of impingement of outsiders is largely determined by that community's rank in the urban hierarchy of central places, defining the extent of the hinterland served by that community as a source of various goods and services (Berry, 1967).

All this is important here because the functional specialization of a settlement—together with the spatial and social characteristics which that specialization produces—largely determine the contours of community conflict (Canan, 1992). For example, resort towns experience resort riots, manufacturing or mining towns have wildcat strikes, college towns have student riots, and capital cities experience protest marches and sit-ins. Because of their skewed age distributions, retirement centers are less likely to experience riots of any sort; lower-order retailing centers in the Southwest are more likely than other communities to experience significant conflict between whites and Indians.

A community's functional specialization and its rank in the urban hierarchy also influence its organizational links with the outside world (Canan, 1992)— a key factor in its either suffering (unwanted) or obtaining (desired) conflict intervention from beyond the community. For example, certain industries are more heavily unionized; communities specializing in those particular industries will exhibit a greater number and variety of vertical linkages to higher-ranking cities and to national society than will otherwise similar communities.

COMMUNITY CONFLICTS

Sources of Community Conflicts

The expansionist dynamic and resultant uneven development of the larger economic order destines continual change in the character of any local settlement.

First of all, expansion into different industries and different regions will inevitably affect the functional specialization of any community. The decline of an entire industry, such as rail transportation or coal mining, threatens the economic base of all communities that have specialized in that industry. Opening a bigger and newer factory in another region often entails closing of the company's local plant. Shifts in the technology of an industry affect the labor market, pulling in workers with a different set of social characteristics. All these sorts of effects on communities frequently trigger community conflict.

Second, the internal spatial structure of a settlement is continually reshaped as a result of the expansionist dynamic and uneven development. The land-use map of any city reflects a "mosaic of financial interests" (Molotch, 1976). Investment decisions about the siting of new local developments differentially affect particular neighborhoods, conferring positive externalities on some while imposing negative externalities on others (Harvey, 1973). "Because changes to the urban fabric introduce new sources of positive and negative externalities, they are potential generators of local conflicts" (Johnston, 1984, p. 171).

Third, because neighborhoods thus "have different stakes in the future of a city" (Bartelt et al, 1987), public and private provision of service amenities is necessarily unevenly developed across neighborhoods (Pinch, 1985), and is frequently another potent generator of community conflicts.

Fourth, the established social character of a community or a neighborhood —its integrity as a "subcultural lump"—is continually threatened by the operation of cultural diffusion processes (Brown, 1971). Uncharacteristic beliefs or practices—creation science, crack cocaine use, gang colors, fluoridation—first gain tentative foothold in a community through either "relocation diffusion" (brought along by immigrants) or "expansion diffusion" (spreading throughout the larger territory, covering an ever-greater portion). (Hierarchical expansion diffusion is the leapfrogging of an innovation from urban center to urban center, temporarily bypassing the less developed territory between them.) Like Professor Harold Hill warning River City about the arrival of a pool table, moral entrepreneurs (Becker, 1963) often make a community issue of cultural innovations. Such issues, especially if injected into the arenas of school, library, or publicly financed facilities, may engender serious community controversy (Coleman, 1957).

Fifth, national-level social movements may, through strategic or tactical decision, induce or impose community conflict at a particular locality. Induced local conflict may occur when a national-level social movement organization pressures its local chapter or affiliate to demonstrate its strength and its loyalty. Imposed local conflict most often results from the national-level organization targeting and converging on a particular locality as the site for its rally or other collective action. A well-studied example is the Southern Christian Leadership Council's targeting of Selma, Alabama, for a very strategic mass confrontation (Garrow, 1978).

Dynamics of Community Conflict

By whichever of these modes a community conflict is initiated, the developmental process of its unfolding is essentially similiar in outline:

> The most important changes in *issues* are: (a) from specific disagreements to more general ones, (b) elaboration into new and different disagreements; and (c) a final shift from disagreement to direct antagonism. The changes in the *social organization* of the community are as follows: the polarization of social relations as the controversy intensifies, as the participants cut off relations with those who are not on their side, and elaborate relations with those who are; the formation of partisan organizations and the emergence of new, often extremist partisan leaders to wage the war more efficiently; and the mobilization of existing community organizations on one side or the other. Finally, as the pace quickens and the issues become personal, word-of-mouth communication replaces the more formal media (Coleman, 1957, p. 13).

How far these changes proceed depends on *characteristics of the community* and on *the nature and timing of intervention efforts* by activists, advocates, monitors, enforcers, and mediators.

Community Characteristics

In community conflict, the community tends to break apart "along the line of least attachment" (Coleman, 1957, p. 12). Sometimes that line is the enduring heritage of earlier community conflicts (Kreps and Wenger, 1973). But even the most peaceful and homogeneous of communities has its lines of latent cleavage, whether these be lines of kinship, class, length of residence, party, religion, age, race, ethnicity, and/or neighborhood. Such lines of cleavage define potentially opposing "sides" in any community conflict that might arise. In communities where several of these lines of cleavage essentially coincide, marking off similar sets of individuals, the course of community conflict is likely to escalate farther and faster than in communities where the lines of cleavage are cross-cutting (Coleman, 1957; Coser, 1956; Simmel, 1955).

According to Coleman (1957), the extent of such cross-pressures on residents is a function of the "horizontal patterning" of the community (Warren, 1978)— that is, the network structure obtaining among its local voluntary associations and other community organizations. The greater the organizational density and the interlocking character of that network, the greater the potential for cross-pressures. The higher the percentage of residents who participate in that network and/or who identify themselves with the community as a whole, the stronger are the restraining effects of that horizontal patterning.

The vertical pattern of community (Warren, 1978)—the nature and types of organizational linkages with other levels of society—may also influence the scope of community conflict. In many communities far down the urban hierarchy, some segments have few vertical linkages; in remote and isolated mining or farming communities, for example, laborers have few influential ties to higher-level organizations, so that their violent struggles are unlikely to attract external intervention.

The more pluralistic the power structure of a community (Aiken and Mott, 1970; Canan, 1992), the more constrained are political actors in community conflict (Clark, 1968; Kreps and Wenger, 1973). Communities where power is very strongly centered—for instance, company towns owned and operated by a remote corporation—are notorious for bitter and violent conflict.

The role of local government is a very important influence (Crain, Katz, and Rosenthal, 1969). In locational disputes and the grievances of particular neighborhoods, local government authorities almost always serve as the key decision makers. Where those authorities are seen as biased decision makers, local government effectively yields its third-party role and assumes the role of second party (i.e., adversary). The conflict thereby departs the arena of polite politics and enters that of protest politics or even the politics of violence (Lofland, 1985).

Intervention Efforts

The development of a community conflict depends greatly on the nature and the timing of intervention efforts by activists, advocates, monitors, enforcers, and mediators (Laue, 1981a).

Grass-roots neighborhood and community activists (Cox and McCarthy, 1982; Woliver, 1993) are the key principals, of course, although outside agitators (Marx, 1974) and community organizers often prove influential. A more generalizing sort of support is contributed by advocates, who speak (and perhaps negotiate) for the principals within more formal or more privileged arenas. Advocates, local but especially external (Suskind and Cruikshank, 1987), frequently serve to redefine or even hijack the grass-roots agenda.

Enforcers—usually the local police and judiciary—are supposed to ensure a level playing field for all these participants in the community conflict. If and when they appear to fail in that effort—by suppressing the conflict or seeming to favor one side—the conflict is very likely to escalate from polite politics to the politics of protest or even violence (Feagin and Hahn, 1973; Gamson, Fireman, and Rytina, 1982). The pressure then mounts for local government authorities or, more likely, the national state itself to intervene to restore the semblance of procedural justice.

Mediators, in all their variety and multiplicity, seek centrally to slow, halt, ameliorate, and eventually reverse the reciprocal effects of social and psychological polarization:

> As participants in a dispute become psychologically "consistent," shedding doubts and hesitancies, they shun friends who are uncommitted, and elaborate their associations with those who feel the way they do. In effect, the psychological polarization leads to social polarization. The latter, in turn, leads to mutual reinforcement of opinions, that is, to further psychological polarization.... Increasingly, his opponents' position seems preposterous— and in fact, it is preposterous, as is his own; neither position feeds on anything but reinforcing opinions.
>
> The outcome, of course, is the division of the community into socially and attitudinally separate camps, each convinced it is absolutely right (Coleman, 1957, p. 13).

Mediators strive to create doubts in the minds of these absolutistic camps (Colosi, 1987), to provide some alternatives to the stereotyping and hostile interpretations that result from the prevailing rumor process (Knopf, 1975; Rosnow and Fine, 1976; Shibutani, 1966), and to augment the slender lines of communication between camps by acting as a go-between. Through such positioning and prenegotiations, a mediator may eventually encounter a realistic opportunity to assist the parties in negotiating a settlement.

Although their early intervention may avert or slow the escalation of community conflict, mediators seek not to prevent or suppress the conflict but rather to regulate it (Wehr, 1979). Mediators advocate for a constructive and productive process of community conflict—that is, conflict that (1) leads to a more articulated and more inclusive organizational network, with revised structures of interorganizational exchange, communication, and power, which (2) enhances community adaptation to the shifting emphases within the larger economic and political order.

ETHNIC CONFLICTS

Ethnic conflict must be understood at both community and societal levels.

Societal Level

Every economy and state is multi-ethnic. As these economic and political orders develop their hegemony over geographically extensive territories, they capture, conquer, incorporate, and/or recruit people of various racial and ethnic categories. As development emphasis shifts from industry to industry over time, these industries—with the cooperation of the state authorities—recruit new waves of immigrants, internally or internationally (Hughes and Hughes, 1952). In the nineteenth-century U.S. economy, for example, the cotton industry recruited African fieldworkers, the railroad industry recruited Chinese laborers, and the mining industry recruited Welsh miners. Within each economy, a customary ethnic division of labor emerges (Jiobu, 1988).

Ethnic stratification—the social ranking of these ethnic groups (Shibutani and Kwan, 1965)—results not so much from this division of labor as from mode of inclusion, seniority of inclusion, extent of physical and cultural differences from the charter group, and rate of social mobility.

From such social comparison of groups flows the passionate, symbolic, and apprehensive process of ethnic conflict (Hogg and Abrams, 1988; Horowitz, 1985). "Ethnic conflict arises from the common evaluative significance accorded by the groups to acknowledged group differences and then played out in public rituals of affirmation and contradiction" (Horowitz, 1985, p. 227). That is to say, ethnic conflict (subsuming racial conflict as a special case) is fundamentally the struggle of ethnic groups to socially establish their comparative worth and legitimacy—a struggle for honor that is conducted primarily in the political arena, in a politics of group entitlement. In the modern western states, however,

Virtually never is one whole, organized cultural entity pitted against another in the clear-cut fashion of the classic paradigms of ethnic conflict. Instead, claims are made by some political actors in the name of groups. Nor have ethnic differences led to extensive and protracted violence, except in the two cases noted....Even massive demands tend to be dealt with through policy responses, bargaining, or negotiated institutional or constitutional adjustments—within frameworks suited to the orderly management of issues and claims in dispute (Heisler, 1990, pp. 27, 28).

All these points require elaboration. First of all,

only partial, structurally fragmented ethnic identity and group organization survived the dual thrust of modernization and the increasingly pervasive, centripetal state...*ethnicity no longer demarcated people but only some aspects of their lives*. Ethnic identity...became intermittent as well as partial... (Heisler, 1990, p. 33).

For individuals in modern—and even in modernizing societies (Maré, 1992)—ethnic identity is only situationally salient (McCall and Simmons, 1978).

Second, the most significant factor that intermittently makes salient one's ethnic identity is ethnic mobilization—the attempt by ethnic entrepreneurs to develop a following as a basis for political or economic power. "Politicized ethnicity...answers the need to mobilize geographically and across classes; it legitimates and explains present conditions in terms of a past history of conquest and incorporation (whether actual or reinterpreted); and it provides a multitude of readily-available cultural symbols for group formation and exclusion of the 'other'" (Maré, 1992).

Third, in ethnic conflicts everywhere, state authorities are almost always the key decision makers:

> Drawing on latent grievances in their communities, ethnic and regional intermediaries make various and contradictory claims on state authorities.... How the state will react to these collective demands is situational and depends largely on the intensity of demands, the structure of power relations, the political culture, the perceptions of elites, and the skill and effectiveness of leaders (Rothchild, 1991, p. 205).

Where state authorities come to be seen as ethnically biased, those authorities assume the role of second party rather than third, and ethnic conflict is transformed into the politics of ethnic protest (nonviolent or violent) or even ethnic rebellion (Gurr, 1993). How the character of state/ethnic interactions then conditions the mixes and back-and-forth sequencing of these three conflict strategies (Gamson, 1990; Gurr, 1993; Zartman, 1990) has been well studied, particularly in the United States (Killian, 1984; Lipsky, 1968; Lofland, 1985; McAdam, 1982, 1983; Morris, 1993). Group interests are nonunitary at every phase and also shift by phases (Gurr, 1993), so that each phase is marked by internal factional struggle and by changes in leadership (Zartman, 1990). These phase-shifts both complicate and afford opportunity for mediation efforts (Horowitz, 1990; Montville, 1990; Touval, 1993; Zartman, 1991).

Whatever the form that societal-level ethnic conflict assumes, mediation efforts encounter formidable social psychological barriers to constructive negotiation between rival ethnic groups (Fisher, 1990; Miller and Brewer, 1984; Oudenhoven and Willemsen, 1989; Turner, Hogg, Oakes, Reicher, and Wetherell, 1987). These social psychological barriers include cross-cultural communication (Avruch and Black, 1993), ethnocentrism (Le Vine and Campbell, 1972; Ross, 1992, 1993a, 1993b), racial and ethnic stereotyping (Grant, 1990; Hamilton, 1981; Jackman and Senter, 1983), prejudice (Bobo, 1992), and intergroup dynamics (Hewstone and Brown, 1986; Hogg and Abrams, 1988; Tajfel, 1982). Many of the positioning and prenegotiation interventions by mediators of societal-level ethnic conflicts (Kelman, 1972; Mitchell, 1993; Rothman, 1992; Taylor and Taylor, 1988) represent small-scale efforts to reduce these social psychological barriers to constructive negotiation, at elite levels of the respective ethnic groups.

Community Level

From the community conflict intervention perspective, the foregoing is important because societal-level ethnic conflicts induce, impose, or at least potentiate local ethnic conflicts.

On the whole, it is local conflict events that bring out most clearly the passionate, symbolic, and apprehensive character of ethnic conflict. Localized gatherings generate distinctive emotional force, through face-to-face interaction, large numbers of people expressing mutual solidarity, and proximity of many others expressing hostility that implies physical danger (Lofland, 1985). In these respects, of course, urban ethnic conflicts (Clarke and Obler, 1976; McCord and McCord, 1977) are particularly dramatic for their scale and destructive potential.

Mobilization by Societal-Level Ethnic Movements

Social movements—including ethnic movements—seek to create local conflict events, in order to harness the power of such gatherings (Miller, 1985).

Induced local ethnic conflicts are those conflict events organized and staffed by an ethnic movement's locally resident members or adherents, at the inspiration, coaxing, cajoling, or bullying of the national movement. This sort of stimulation of activism amounts to mobilization of an ethnic community and is far more challenging than mobilization of checkbooks (Lo, 1992). Even mobilization to nonviolent protest actions, such as peaceful demonstrations and rallies, demands of adherents some social and physical risk-taking; after all, the power of a protest event lies in the veiled potential for violence (Eisinger, 1973). Higher-risk conflict events, such as the raids or "communal riots" of violent protest (McPhail, 1994) or the guerilla actions of rebellion (White, 1989), require far more selectively targeted micromobilization tactics. Although Gamson (1990) refers to the "combat readiness" of protest movements, most violent protest events actually involve comparatively little physical combat and a great deal of symbolic tokenism (Berk, 1972; McPhail, 1994; Nieberg, 1972). Potential participants probably overestimate considerably the degree of physical risk these events entail.

Imposed local ethnic conflicts are those conflict events that are organized extra-locally by higher levels of an ethnic movement, as targets of strategic opportunity, and are staffed significantly by nonresidents—either the national core elite of the movement (Garrow, 1978) or a special flying squad (McAdam, 1986). Local mobilization is mainly reactive, as the exciting presence of these prominent operatives of the movement serves as a high-leverage tool for stimulating local co-participation. The presence of these prominent outsiders also serves to raise the stakes, so that even nonviolent protest actions are somewhat more likely to provoke violent local reaction. Whether the strategy of the American civil rights movement in imposing local conflict events on targeted cities was predicated on provoking violent response from local whites remains a controversial question (McAdam, 1982, 1983; Morris, 1993).

Community variation in susceptibility to induced or imposed local ethnic conflicts has not been studied systematically, but some of the community characteristics favoring escalation of community conflict (cited in a previous section) may prove relevant.

Mobilization through Community Disputes

Some local ethnic conflicts are neither induced nor imposed by ethnic movements, but are merely potentiated by them. Societal-level ethnic conflicts prosecuted by ethnic movements increase the salience of ethnicity in every community by challenging received notions of the ethnic stratification system. Almost everywhere, then, ethnicity provides lines of at least latent community cleavage (Williams, 1977; Williams, Dean, and Suchman, 1964).

As noted earlier, community conflict situations are ubiquitous in the major cities. Because conflict situations in cities lead people to feel threatened, ethnicity is heightened and ethnic category members—especially recent migrants and those of lower-ranking ethnic categories—tend to cluster defensively into discrete, ethnically homogeneous territories (Boal, Murray, and Poole, 1976; Merry, 1981; Suttles, 1968). One's ethnic group is thought of as "a fictive, greatly extended family, a unit that provides blood solidarity and personalistic help in an increasingly impersonal environment—in short, ascription in an ostensibly nonascriptive world" (Horowitz, 1985, p. 74). Clustering together within some neighborhood of the city serves four principal functions: common defense against threats to security; buffering from the hostile attitudes of the larger society; preserving and promoting cultural heritage; and a base for action in economic and political struggles (Boal, Murray, and Poole, 1976).

Because of this territorial segregation (de facto or de jure), locational disputes and the grievances of particular neighborhoods will tend to affect ethnic categories differentially. Consequently, community conflict mobilization in response to these issues is likely to assume an ethnic form or flavor (Cormick, 1992; Merry, 1987; Suttles, 1968). Recent American experience suggests that ethnic mobilization of this sort is most likely within disputes about territorially uneven provision of public and private services (Harvey, 1973)—most especially the quality of police services (Feagin and Hahn, 1973; Hundley, 1968).

Since local government authorities are almost always the key decision makers in these types of urban conflict, where such authorities are seen as being biased against some neighborhood or ethnic group, they are cast in the role of a second party rather than third. Polite politics give way to protest politics, often pitting an ethnic minority against a majority establishment (Eisinger, 1973; Harvey, 1973; Lofland, 1985).

Ethnic protest arising in this fashion tends to engender only a temporary mobilization, whether in nonviolent protest (Cormick, 1992) or violent protest in the form of "commodity riots" (Feagin and Hahn, 1973; Hundley, 1968; McCall, 1970; McPhail, 1994). Local mechanisms of micromobilization for nonviolent protest and for commodity riots are critically examined by Gamson, Fireman, and Rytina (1982), McPhail (1994), and Miller (1985). Community variation in susceptibility to commodity riots has been studied very extensively and critically reviewed by Snyder (1979).

Intervention in Local Ethnic Conflicts

Even in the comparatively brief durations of most local ethnic conflicts, the involvement of mediators largely takes the form of positioning and prenegotiations. Process-promoting and problem-solving workshops, for instance, are not uncommon prenegotiation activities even at this level (Doob and Foltz, 1973; Rothman, 1992). Somewhat more distinctive are efforts at tension monitoring and rumor control (Knopf, 1975; Ponting, 1973; Rosnow and Fine, 1976).

In the United States, the Community Relations Service functions as a highly professionalized flying-squad community intervention service specifically for racial and ethnic conflicts (Pompa, 1981, 1987). Even for this elite corps, positioning and prenegotiations—in the forms of entry, assessment, conciliation, and technical assistance—turn out to be the largest part of the mediator's work (Salem, 1980, 1982). Until a local conflict meets a demanding set of criteria, the CRS mediator is not likely to propose formal mediation, even though:

> There are clear advantages to bringing a community dispute to mediation. First, the signed, publicized agreement is likely to be more binding than one reached during informal conciliation. Second, the formal process legitimizes the protest group, making it easier to open negotiations if there are future disputes. Also, the structured mediation process helps sensitize the parties to each other's positions and tends to increase understanding between divergent groups (Salem, 1982, p. 97).

CONCLUSIONS

The community focus of the perspective sketched out here enlarges our understanding of racial and ethnic conflict by showing the necessity of a bilevel view of those conflicts. Just as community can be understood only against the backdrop of the larger political economy, so local ethnic conflicts can be understood only against the background of societal-level ethnic conflicts. By understanding how and why ethnic movements induce, impose, or at least potentiate local ethnic conflicts, the potential for inappropriate policy responses to local conflicts can be diminished. Certainly, this analysis—challenging the classical "ethnic nominalist" view of conflict, through emphasizing the situational nature of ethnicity and the central role of ethnic mobilization—shows that ethnic conflict at either level (1) involves struggle around genuine issues (McPhail, 1994; Rule, 1988), not merely shared sentiments of fear and loathing or pride and prejudice; (2) can therefore possibly prove to be productive as well as constructive; and (3) is importantly shaped by the nature and timing of every sort of third-party intervention, particularly by government authorities.

REFERENCES

Aiken, M., and P.E. Mott (eds.). 1970. *The Structure of Community Power*. New York: Random House.

Alinsky, S. 1946. *Reveille for Radicals*. Chicago: University of Chicago Press.

Alinsky, S. 1971. *Rules for Radicals: A Pragmatic Primer for Realistic Radicals*. New York: Vintage.

Angell, R.C. 1965. "The Sociology of Human Conflict." Pp. 91-115 in *The Nature of Human Conflict*, edited by E.B. McNeill. Englewood Cliffs, NJ: Prentice-Hall.

Anstey, M. 1993. *Practical Peacemaking: A Mediator's Handbook*. Johannesburg: Juta.

Assefa, H., and P. Wahrhaftig. 1988. *Extremist Groups and Conflict Resolution: The MOVE Crisis in Philadelphia*. New York: Praeger.

Avruch, K., and P.W. Black. 1993. "Conflict Resolution in Intercultural Settings: Problems and Prospects." Pp. 131-145 in *Conflict Resolution Theory and Practice: Integration and Application*, edited by D.J.D. Sandole and H. van der Merwe. Manchester: Manchester University Press.

Bartelt, D., D. Elesh, I. Goldstein, G. Leon, and W. Yancey. 1987. "Islands in the Stream: Neighborhoods and the Political Economy of the City." Pp. 163-189 in *Neighborhood and Community Environments*, edited by I. Altman and A. Wandersman. New York: Plenum.

Bash, H.H. 1981. "Conflict Intervention and Social Change: Sociological and Ideological Contexts of Professional Social Meddling." *Journal of Intergroup Relations* 9 (2): 12-30.

Becker, H.S. 1963. *Outsiders*. New York: Free Press.

Berk, R.A. 1972. "The Emergence of Muted Violence in Crowd Behavior: A Case Study of an Almost Race Riot." Pp. 309-328 in *Collective Violence*, edited by J.F. Short and M.E. Wolfgang. Chicago: Aldine.

Bernard, J. 1950. "Where is the Modern Sociology of Conflict?" *American Journal of Sociology* 56: 11-16.

Bernard, J. 1957. "The Sociological Study of Conflict." Pp. 33-117 in *The Nature of Conflict*, edited by International Sociological Association. Paris: UNESCO.

Berry, B.J.L. 1967. *The Geography of Market Centers and Retail Distribution*. Englewood Cliffs, NJ: Prentice-Hall.

Boal, F.W., R.C. Murray, and M.A. Poole. 1976. "Belfast: The Urban Encapsulation of a National Conflict." Pp. 77-131 in *Urban Ethnic Conflict: A Comparative Perspective*, edited by S.E. Clarke and J.L. Obler. Chapel Hill: University of North Carolina, Institute for Research in Social Science.

Bobo, L. 1992. "Prejudice and Alternative Dispute Resolution." *Studies in Law, Politics, and Society* 12: 147-176.

Brown, L.A. 1971. *Innovation Diffusion: A New Perspective*. New York: Methuen.

Canan, P. 1992. "Environmental Disputes in Changing Urban Political Economies: A Dynamic Research Approach." *Studies in Law, Politics, and Society* 12: 287-308.

Chicago Commission on Race Relations. 1922. *The Negro in Chicago: A Study of Race Relations and a Race Riot*. Chicago: University of Chicago Press.

Clark, K.B. 1944. "Group Violence: A Preliminary Study of the 1943 Harlem Riot." *Journal of Social Psychology* 19: 319-337.

Clark, T. 1968. *Community Structure and Decision-making: Comparative Analysis*. San Francisco: Chandler.

Clarke, S.E., and J.L. Obler (eds.). 1976. *Urban Ethnic Conflict: A Comparative Perspective*. Chapel Hill: University of North Carolina, Institute for Research in Social Science.

Coleman, J.S. 1957. *Community Conflict*. New York: Free Press.

Colosi, T. 1987. "A Model for Negotiation and Mediation." Pp. 86-99 in *Conflict Management and Problem Solving: Interpersonal to International Applications*, edited by D.J.D. Sandole and I. Sandole-Staroste. New York: New York University Press.

Cormick, G.W. 1992. "Environmental Conflict, Community Mobilization, and the 'Public Good': Linkages and Contradictions." *Studies in Law, Politics, and Society* 12: 309-329.

Coser, L.A. 1956. *The Functions of Social Conflict*. New York: Free Press.

Coser, L.A. 1957. "Social Conflict and the Theory of Social Change." *British Journal of Sociology* 8: 197-207.

Coser, L.A. 1961. "The Termination of Conflict." *Journal of Conflict Resolution* 5: 347-353.

Coser, L.A. 1967. *Continuities in the Study of Social Conflict*. New York: Free Press.

Cox, K.R., and J.J. McCarthy. 1982. "Neighborhood Activism as a Politics of Turf: A Critical Analysis." Pp. 196-219 in *Conflict, Politics and the Urban Scene*, edited by K.R. Cox and R.J. Johnston. London: Longman.

Crain, R.L., E. Katz, and D.B. Rosenthal. 1969. *The Politics of Community Conflict: The Fluoridation Decision*. Indianapolis: Bobbs-Merrill.

Dean, J.P., and A.A. Rosen. 1955. *A Manual of Intergroup Relations*. Chicago: University of Chicago Press.

Doob, L.W. 1993. *Intervention: Guides and Perils*. New Haven: Yale University Press.

Doob, L.W., and W.J. Foltz. 1973. "The Belfast Workshop: An Application of Group Techniques to a Destructive Conflict." *Journal of Conflict Resolution* 17: 489-512.

Duncan, O.D., and A.J. Reiss, Jr. 1956. *Social Characteristics of Urban and Rural Communities, 1950*. New York: Wiley.

Eisinger, P.K. 1973. "The Conditions of Protest Behavior in American Cities." *American Political Science Review* 67: 11-28.

Feagin, J.R., and H. Hahn. 1973. *Ghetto Revolts: The Politics of Violence in American Cities*. New York: Macmillan.

Fisher, R.J. 1990. *The Social Psychology of Intergroup and International Conflict Resolution*. New York: Springer-Verlag.

Gamson, W.A. 1966. "Rancorous Conflict in Community Politics." *American Sociological Review* 31: 71-81.

Gamson, W.A. 1990. *The Strategy of Social Protest* (2nd ed.). Belmont, CA: Wadsworth.

Gamson, W.A., B. Fireman, and S. Rytina. 1982. *Encounters with Unjust Authority*. Homewood, IL: Dorsey.

234   GEORGE J. McCALL

Garrow, D.J. 1978. *Protest at Selma: Martin Luther King, Jr., and the Voting Rights Act of 1965.*
New Haven: Yale University Press.

Grant, P.R. 1990. "Cognitive Theories Applied to Intergroup Conflict." Pp. 39-57 in *The Social
Psychology of Intergroup and International Conflict Resolution*, edited by R.J. Fisher.
New York: Springer-Verlag.

Grimshaw, A. (ed.). 1969. *Racial Violence in the United States.* Chicago: Aldine.

Gurr, T.R. 1993. *Minorities at Risk: A Global View of Ethnopolitical Conflicts.* Washington, DC:
United States Institute of Peace Press.

Hamilton, D.L. (ed.). 1981. *Cognitive Processes in Stereotyping and Intergroup Behavior.*
Hillsdale, NJ: Erlbaum.

Harvey, D.W. 1973. *Social Justice and the City.* London: Arnold.

Heisler, M.O. 1990. "Ethnicity and Ethnic Relations in the Modern West." Pp. 21-52 in *Conflict
and Peacemaking in Multiethnic Societies*, edited by J.V. Montville. Lexington, MA:
Lexington Books.

Hewstone, M., and R. Brown. 1986. *Contact and Conflict in Intergroup Encounters.* Oxford:
Blackwell.

Hogg, M.A., and D. Abrams. 1988. *Social Identifications: A Social Psychology of Intergroup
Relations and Group Processes.* London: Routledge.

Horowitz, D.L. 1985. *Ethnic Groups in Conflict.* Berkeley: University of California Press.

Horowitz, D.L. 1990. "Ethnic Conflict Management for Policymakers." Pp. 115-130 in *Conflict
and Peacemaking in Multiethnic Societies*, edited by J. V. Montville. Lexington, MA:
Lexington Books.

Hughes, E.C., and H.M. Hughes. 1952. *Where Peoples Meet: Racial and Ethnic Frontiers.* New
York: Free Press.

Hundley, J.R., Jr. 1968. "The Dynamics of Recent Ghetto Riots." *Detroit Journal of Urban Law*
45: 627-639.

Jackman, M.R., and M.S. Senter. 1983. "Different Therefore Unequal: Beliefs about Trait
Differences Between Groups of Unequal Status." *Research in Social Stratification and
Mobility* 2: 309-335.

Jioubu, R.M. 1988. *Ethnicity and Assimilation.* Albany: State University of New York Press.

Johnston, R.J. 1984. *City and Society* (2nd ed.). London: Hutchinson.

Kelman, H .C. 1972. "The Problem-solving Workshop in Conflict Resolution." Pp. 168-204 in
Communication in International Politics, edited by R.L. Merritt. Urbana: University of
Illinois Press.

Kerr, C. 1954. "Industrial Conflict and its Mediation." *American Journal of Sociology* 60: 230-
245.

Killian, L.M. 1984. "Organization, Rationality and Spontaneity in the Civil Rights Movement."
American Sociological Review 49: 770-783.

Knopf, T.A. 1975. *Rumors, Race and Riots.* New Brunswick, NJ: Transaction Books.

Kreps, G., and D. Wenger. 1973. "Toward a Theory of Community Conflict: Factors Influencing
the Initiation and Scope of Conflict." *Sociological Quarterly* 14: 158-174.

Laue, J.H. 1971. "A Model for Civil Rights Change through Conflict." Pp. 256-262 in *Racial
Conflict*, edited by G.T. Marx. Boston: Little, Brown.

Laue, J.H. 1978. "Advocacy and Sociology." Pp. 167-199 in *Social Scientists as Advocates: Views
from the Applied Disciplines*, edited by G.H. Weber and G.J. McCall. Newbury Park,
CA: Sage.

Laue, J.H. 1981a. "Conflict Intervention." Pp. 67-75 in *Handbook of Applied Sociology*, edited
by M.E. Olsen and M. Micklin. New York: Praeger.

Laue, J. H. 1981b. "The Development of Community Conflict Intervention." *Journal of Intergroup
Relations* 9 (2): 3-11.

Laue, J.H. 1982. "The Future of Community Conflict Intervention." *Journal of Intergroup Relations* 10 (2): 3-11.

Laue, J.H. 1987. "The Emergence and Institutionalization of Third Party Roles in Conflict." Pp. 17-29 in *Conflict Management and Problem Solving: Interpersonal to International Applications*, edited by D.J.D. Sandole and I. Sandole-Staroste. New York: New York University Press.

Laue, J.H. 1993. "The Conflict Resolution Field: An Overview and Some Critical Questions." Pp. 21-32 in *Dialogues on Conflict Resolution: Bridging Theory and Practice*. Washington, DC: U.S. Institute of Peace.

Laue, J.H., and G. Cormick. 1978. "The Ethics of Intervention in Community Disputes." Pp. 205-232 in *The Ethics of Social Intervention*, edited by G. Bermant, H.C. Kelman, and D.P. Warwick. Washington, DC: Halsted Press.

Lee, A.M., and N.D. Humphrey. 1943. *Race Riot*. New York: Dryden Press.

Le Vine, R.A., and D.T. Campbell. 1972. *Ethnocentrism: Theories of Conflict, Ethnic Attitudes, and Group Behavior*. New York: Wiley.

Lewin, K. 1948. *Resolving Social Conflict*. New York: Harper.

Lipsky, M. 1968. "Protest as a Political Resource." *American Political Science Review* 62: 1144-1158.

Lo, C.Y.H. 1992. "Communities of Challengers in Social Movement Theory." Pp. 224-247 in *Frontiers in Social Movement Theory*, edited by A.D. Morris and C.M. Mueller. New Haven: Yale University Press.

Lofland, J. 1985. *Protest: Studies of Collective Behavior and Social Movements*. New Brunswick, NJ: Transaction.

Mack, R.W., and R.C. Snyder. 1957. "The Analysis of Social Conflict: Toward an Overview and Synthesis." *Journal of Conflict Resolution* 1: 212-248.

Maré, G. 1992. *Brothers Born of Warrior Blood: Politics and Ethnicity in South Africa*. Johannesburg: Ravan Press.

Marx, G.T. 1974. "Thoughts on a Neglected Category of Social Movement Participant: The Agent Provocateur and the Informant." *American Journal of Sociology* 80: 402-442.

McAdam, D. 1982. *Political Process and the Development of Black Insurgency, 1930-1970*. Chicago: University of Chicago Press.

McAdam, D. 1983. "Tactical Innovation and the Pace of Insurgency." *American Sociological Review* 48: 735-754.

McAdam, D. 1986. "Recruitment to High-risk Activism: The Case of Freedom Summer." *American Journal of Sociology* 92: 64-90.

McCall, G.J., and J.L. Simmons. 1978. *Identities and Interactions*. (revised ed.) New York: Free Press.

McCall, G.J., and J.L. Simmons. 1982. "The Community Level." Pp. 305-328 in *Social Psychology: A Sociological Approach*, by G.J. McCall and J.L. Simmons. New York: Free Press.

McCall, M.M. 1970. "Some Ecological Aspects of Negro Slum Riots." Pp. 345-362 in *Protest, Reform and Revolt*, edited by J. Gusfield. New York: Wiley.

McCord, A., and W. McCord. 1977. *Urban Social Conflict*. St. Louis: Mosby.

McPhail, C. 1994. "The Dark Side of Purpose: Individual and Collective Violence in Riots." *Sociological Quarterly* 35: 1-32.

Merry, S.E. 1981. *Urban Danger: Life in a Neighborhood of Strangers*. Philadelphia: Temple University Press.

Merry, S.E. 1987. "Crowding, Conflict, and Neighborhood Regulation." Pp. 35-68 in *Neighborhood and Community Environments*, edited by I. Altman and A. Wandersman. New York: Plenum.

Miller, D.L. 1985. *Introduction to Collective Behavior*. Belmont, CA: Wadsworth.

Miller, N., and M.B. Brewer (eds.). 1984. *Groups in Contact: The Psychology of Desegregation.* New York: Academic Press.

Mitchell, C.R. 1993. "Problem-solving Exercises and Theories of Conflict." Pp. 78-94 in *Conflict Resolution Theory and Practice: Integration and Application,* edited by D.J.D. Sandole and H. van der Merwe. Manchester: Manchester University Press.

Molotch, H. 1976. "The City as a Growth Machine: Toward a Political Economy of Place." *American Journal of Sociology* 82: 309-332.

Montville, J.V. (ed.). 1990. *Conflict and Peacemaking in Multiethnic Societies.* Lexington, MA: Lexington Books.

Morris, A.D. 1993. "Birmingham Confrontation Reconsidered: An Analysis of the Dynamics and Tactics of Mobilization." *American Sociological Review* 58: 621-636.

Nelson, H.J. 1955. "A Service Classification of American Cities." *Economic Geography* 31: 189-210.

Nicholau, G. 1981. "The Institute for Mediation and Conflict Resolution: A Private Sector Approach to Community Disputes." *Journal of Intergroup Relations* 9 (2): 54-61.

Nicholau, G., and G.W. Cormick. 1972. "Community Disputes and the Resolution of Conflict: Another View." *The Arbitration Journal* 27 (June) : 98-112.

Nieburg, H.L. 1972. "Agonistics—Rituals of Conflict." Pp. 82-99 in *Collective Violence,* edited by J.F. Short and M.E. Wolfgang. Chicago: Aldine.

Oudenhoven, J.P., and T.M. Willemsen (eds.). 1989. *Ethnic Minorities: Social Psychological Perspectives.* Amsterdam: Swets and Zeitlinger.

Pinch, S.P. 1985. *Cities and Services: The Geography of Collective Consumption.* London: Routledge and Kegan Paul.

Pompa, G.G. 1981. "The Community Relations Service: Public Sector Mediation and Conciliation of Racial Disputes." *Journal of Intergroup Relations* 9 (2): 46-53.

Pompa, G.G. 1987. "The Community Relations Service." Pp. 130-142 in *Conflict Management and Problem Solving: Interpersonal to International Applications,* edited by D.J.D. Sandole and I. Sandole-Staroste. New York: New York University Press.

Ponting, J.R. 1973. "Rumor Control Centers: Their Emergence and Operations." *American Behavioral Scientist* 16: 391-401.

Pretorius, P. (ed.). 1993. *Dispute Resolution.* Johannesburg: Juta.

Rose, A. 1947. *Studies in Reduction of Prejudice.* Chicago: American Council on Race Relations.

Rosnow, R.L., and G.A. Fine. 1976. *Rumor and Gossip: The Social Psychology of Hearsay.* New York: Elsevier.

Ross, M.H. 1992. "Ethnic Conflict and Dispute Management: Addressing Interests and Identities." *Studies in Law, Politics, and Society* 12: 107-146.

Ross, M.H. 1993a. *The Culture of Conflict: Interpretations and Interests in Comparative Perspective.* New Haven: Yale University Press.

Ross, M.H. 1993b. *The Management of Conflict: Interpretations and Interests in Comparative Perspective.* New Haven: Yale University Press.

Rothchild, D. 1991. "An Interactive Model for State-Ethnic Relations." Pp. 190-215 in *Conflict Resolution in Africa,* edited by F.M. Deng and I.W. Zartman. Washington, DC: Brookings Institution.

Rothman, J. 1992. *From Confrontation to Cooperation: Resolving Ethnic and Regional Conflict.* Newbury Park, CA: Sage Publications.

Rule, J.B. 1988. *Theories of Civil Violence.* Berkeley: University of California Press.

Salem, R.A. 1980. "The Use of Mediation and Conciliation to Resolve Racial Disputes in the USA." Pp. 183-194 in *Race and Ethnicity: South African and International Perspectives,* edited by H.W. van der Merwe and R.A. Schrire. Cape Town: David Philip.

Salem, R.A. 1982. "Community Dispute Resolution through Outside Intervention." *Peace and Change* 8 (2/3): 92-104.

Salem, R.A. 1984. "Mediating Political and Social Conflicts: The Skokie-Nazi Conflict." *Mediation Quarterly* 5: 65-75.

Schaller, L.S. 1966. *Community Organization: Conflict and Reconciliation.* Nashville: Abingdon.

Scimecca, J.A. 1987. "Conflict Resolution: The Basis for Social Control or Social Change?" Pp. 30-33 in *Conflict Management and Problem Solving: Interpersonal to International Applications,* edited by D.J.D. Sandole and I. Sandole-Staroste. New York: New York University Press.

Shellow, R., and D.V. Roemer. 1966. "The Riot that Didn't Happen." *Social Problems* 14: 221-233.

Shibutani, T. 1966. *Improvised News: A Sociological Study of Rumor.* Indianapolis: Bobbs-Merrill.

Shibutani, T., and K.M. Kwan. 1965. *Ethnic Stratification: A Comparative Approach.* New York: Macmillan.

Simmel, G. 1955. *Conflict and the Web of Group Affiliations.* New York: Free Press.

Snyder, D. 1979. "Collective Violence Processes: Implications for Disaggregated Theory and Research." *Research in Social Movements, Conflicts and Change* 2: 35-61.

Suskind, L., and J. Cruikshank. 1987. *Breaking the Impasse: Consensual Approaches to Resolving Public Disputes.* New York: Basic Books.

Suttles, G.D. 1968. *The Social Order of the Slum.* Chicago: University of Chicago Press.

Tajfel, H. (ed.). 1982. *Social Identity and Intergroup Relations.* Cambridge: Cambridge University Press.

Taylor, P.A., and D.A. Taylor (eds.). 1988. *Eliminating Racism: Profiles in Controversy.* New York: Plenum.

Touval, S. 1993. "Gaining Entry to Mediation in Communal Strife." Pp. 255-273 in *The Internationalization of Communal Strife,* edited by M.I. Midlarsky. London: Routledge.

Turner, J.C., M.A. Hogg, P.J. Oakes, S.D. Reicher, and M.S. Wetherell. 1987. *Rediscovering the Social Group: A Self-categorization Theory.* Oxford: Blackwell.

van der Merwe, H. 1993. "Relating Theory to the Practice of Conflict Resolution in South Africa." Pp. 263-275 in *Conflict Resolution Theory and Practice: Integration and Application,* edited by D.J.D. Sandole and H. van der Merwe. Manchester: Manchester University Press.

Warren, R.L. 1978. *The Community in America* (3rd ed.). Chicago: Rand McNally.

Wehr, P. 1979. *Conflict Regulation.* Boulder: Westview.

White, R.W. 1989. "From Peaceful Protest to Guerilla War: Micromobilization of the Provisional Irish Republican Army." *American Journal of Sociology* 94: 1277-1302.

Williams, R.M., Jr. 1947. "The Reduction of Intergroup Tensions." *Social Science Research Council Bulletin* 57: 1-153.

Williams, R.M., Jr. 1977. *Mutual Accommodation: Ethnic Conflict and Cooperation.* Minneapolis: University of Minnesota Press.

Williams, R.M., Jr., J.P. Dean, and E.A. Suchman. 1964. *Strangers Next Door: Ethnic Relations in American Communities.* Englewood Cliffs, NJ: Prentice-Hall.

Woliver, L.R. 1993. *From Outrage to Action: The Politics of Grass-roots Dissent.* Urbana: University of Illinois Press.

Zald, M.A. (ed.). 1967. *Organizing for Community Welfare.* Chicago: Quadrangle.

Zartman, I.W. 1990. "Negotiations and Prenegotiations in Ethnic Conflict: The Beginning, the Middle, and the Ends." Pp. 511-533 in *Conflict and Peacemaking in Multiethnic Societies,* edited by J.V. Montville. Lexington, MA: Lexington Books.

Zartman, I.W. 1991. "Conflict Reduction: Prevention, Management, and Resolution." Pp. 299-319 in *Conflict Resolution in Africa,* edited by F.M. Deng and I.W. Zartman. Washington, DC: Brookings Institution.

INTER-MINORITY GROUP CONFLICTS

William A. Welch, Sr.

INTRODUCTION

The predominate mass of extant data available today, irrespective of what ever it may be titled, is primarily the result of studies concerning dominant minority conflict and its resolution. Perhaps this rightly suggests that the areas of inter-minority and dominant minority conflict are inseparable as issues. It would appear, from the writers limited review, that absent the dominant groups behavior affecting minority groups, much of the present tension experienced between minorities would not exist. Having said this, considering what we know about "liberated" groups and nations, minority groups, in the absence of dominant group influence, may well discover other tensions just as debilitating, just as conflictual, as those imposed by the presence of a dominant group (Bok, 1989). The evidence that each group differentially values the other minority groups would lead us to that conclusion. There is much to be learned from the existing data and there are significant opportunities to contribute to the developing discourse on inter-minority conflict and resolution.

Some statement or definition of what is meant by dominant and minority groups is in order at the outset. Marden and Meyer (1978) defined a dominant group as one existing in a country "...whose distinctive culture and/or

Research in Human Social Conflict, Volume 1, pages 239-256.
Copyright © 1995 by JAI Press Inc.
All rights of reproduction in any form reserved.
ISBN: 1-55938-923-0

physiognomy is established as superior in the society, and which treats differentially or unequally other groups in the society with other cultures or physiognomies in order to maximize its own group interest" (p. 22). Anthropologists Wagley and Harris (1958) have defined minority groups as:

> (1) Minorities are subordinate segments of complex state societies; (2) minorities have special physical or cultural traits which are held in low esteem by the dominant segments of the society; (3) minorities are self conscious units bound together by the special traits which their members share and by the special disabilities which these bring; (4) membership in a minority is transmitted by a rule of descent which is capable of affiliating succeeding generations even in the absence of readily apparent physical or cultural traits; (5) minority peoples, by choice or necessity, tend to marry within the group (p. 10).

While both of these definitions have been with us for some time, they are sufficient for our purposes.

Discussion in this chapter, has been primarily limited to inter-minority conflict and resolution efforts in the United States. These efforts will be examined in the light of selected relevant data, and suggestions made for increased effectiveness in approaching resolution. A brief examination of some of the underlying factors that fuel conflict between minorities, and between them and their dominant group counterparts is explored, particularly as they ramify into the resolutive aspects of conflict between them.

Conflict has been defined "...as an incompatibility of behaviors, cognitions (including goals), and/or affect among individuals or groups that may or may not lead to an aggressive expression of this social incompatibility" (Boardman and Horowitz, 1994, p. 4). Whether or not the aggression is expressed, "...any conflict management strategy motivated by the intent to harm the other [is considered] as being aggressive and...ultimately destructive" (Boardman and Horowitz, 1994, p. 4). Our focus then, in inter-minority conflict resolution, is to assist parties in not only restraining the expression of such motives, but in managing toward the elimination of the causal factors that give rise to them. In order to achieve this condition, considerable effort will have to be expended on those factors generated by the dominant group. It is the intent of the writer, to review what has been done, and provoke some thought on possible directions that might be taken toward the development of more effective models for inter-minority conflict resolution.

EARLY AND ENDURING CONTRIBUTIONS TO INTERGROUP CONFLICT

The seeds of enduring intergroup conflict were sown long before the explorers ever reached these western shores. Racial, ethnic, and religious animosity, without question, pre-existed the establishment of colonies in what was to become the United States of America. As far as we are able to determine, gender bias has a history as long as humankind itself. It is of little wonder then, that the principal settlers in the new world would continue the practice.

It has been said that the study of America is the study of immigration. A brief review of the immigration policies of the United States in its early days, reveals a steady stream of efforts to manage immigration in a manner that would reduce the possibility of multicultural and multiracial numbers becoming significant among the population (Cose, 1992). Additionally, it must be stated that the limitations were not uniformly applied among the various minority groups.

There were also considerable efforts directed at maintaining the religious status quo. Although history assures us that a multitude came to these shores to escape religious intolerance, this did not deter many of those who found their way here from exhibiting such attitudes and behaviors toward others. At the time of the American Revolution "... America had become not so much a haven for the worlds theologically oppressed as a refuge for dissenting Protestants" (Cose, 1992, p. 17). It is useful to note that Protestants at that time represented an estimated 98 percent of the population. "... Many of the Protestants so feared the pollution from competing sects that they refused to sanction religious freedom for others" (Cose, 1992, p. 17). In our early history, non-Protestants were barred from full membership in the communities in Virginia and South Carolina. In Massachusetts, the vote was limited to Catholics. There are many other examples of these practices by the various faiths. The early advantage was to the Protestants however.

Whites also began to be disaggragated in the eyes of the dominant group. In the mid-eighteenth century many of the non-German settlers insisted that the German newcomers were of inferior quality (Stephenson, 1926). Their disdain for the Germans was based not on religion as it was with the Irish, but on their ethnicity, their foreignness, the possible effects on the English language (Cose, 1992). In the 1800s we witnessed the differentiation of certain other Europeans as being undesirable for immigration (Slavic, Mediterranean) and of course, nonwhites. The categorizations and ascriptions imposed upon these groups created the basis for additional intergroup conflicts.

The *San Francisco Chronicle*, in 1905, informed its readers that irrespective of how dreary a failure an individual Croat, Slav, or Pole may have been, his children, like as clay in the hands of the potter, in one generation would wipe away the squalor and freedom would banish even the inherited memories of repression. As for Asians, the *Chronicle* was not so encouraging. "The Asiatic can never be other than Asiatic, however much he may imitate the dress of the white man, learn his language and spend his wages for him" (Feb. 11, 1905). So that while there was in fact a pecking order among Europeans, there was no mistaking the preference for all Europeans over non-Europeans. These attitudes have persisted over time. A 1990 Gallop Poll found that 54 percent of respondents believed too many immigrants came from Latin America and 49 percent felt too many came from Asia.

Slavery as a legal institution ended in 1865, its descendants however, existed in legalized apartheid for over one hundred years thereafter. Perhaps of all of the groups who have found disfavor, the African American has faced and continues to face the most enduring animus. Thomas Jefferson offered that the differences between blacks and whites were so great that conflict between the two groups "will probably never end but in the extermination of one or the other race" (Jefferson, 1904, p. 49). The question of IQ was used as a basis for ascriptions of inferiority and made the news again in 1994 with the publication of *The Bell Curve* (Herrnstein and Murray, 1994), irrespective of whatever intent the authors may have had in its writing. When our nation celebrates the heroes, of its earlier years in particular, the founding fathers included, it is reasonable to assume that a significant portion of our population will find themselves in a state of some ambivalence to say the least.

Various groups have suffered continuing practices of various forms of discrimination. These discriminatory practices have been based on a myriad of factors, from immutable characteristics such as race, sex, and sometimes physical disabilities, to such choices as religion, association, and political orientation. These and other societal factors have continued to serve to maintain old issues, create others, and serve to generate among the various groups, mutually incompatible goals. These same factors also affected the strategies of the various groups as they sought to meet their needs which in some cases gave rise to intragroup goal incompatibilities. For example, the goals of the Talented Tenth African Americans, assimilation, was certainly not compatible with the majority of their African-American counterparts any more than the goals of the small band of powerful and politically privileged Jews who sought the same ends were compatible with the majority of the Jews in the country at that time. Just as the more affluent Jews were unhappy, to say the least, with many of the less affluent and less educated immigrants, so were northern African Americans unhappy with their less educated counterparts who had migrated from the south (Lewis, 1992). "The members of the Talented Tenth... believed themselves (despite episodic race riots) well along toward full citizenship through circumspect politics and ostentatious patriotism, by good manners, education, and industry, and by quiet cultivation of influential WASP" (Lewis, 1992, p. 21). It is easy to discern the myriad if conflictual possibilities that could arise from this background. It is easy to see how these and other factors further exacerbated existing intra- and intergroup tensions and how these factors may subsequently ramify into future intergroup interactions, in unproductive ways; an expected outcome where goals are mutually incompatible.

Azar (1970), insists that "...Mutually incompatible goals among parties amidst a lack of coordinating or mediating mechanisms give birth to conflict"

(p. 5). The interaction of different cultures who have significantly different goals is problematic (Doob, 1970) and as a part of a multicommunal society, is deeply affected by access to the superstructure of society for relief (Azar, 1990). Access to the governing body, its social institutions, is generally differentially available in relationship to the value the group is assigned within the community. The in-group will have the greatest access. It is through access that satisfaction of wants and needs are fulfilled. It is through first, the denial of access and then, of the satisfaction of group needs that intergroup conflict is created and/or exacerbated.

Minorities in the United States have continued to have differential access to the means of relief based on the externally ascribed value that has been imposed upon them, and their lack of resources to resist the imposed categories of ascription. "Multicommunal societies... are characterized by disarticulation between the state and society as a whole, with the state usually dominated by a single communal group or a coalition of...groups that are unresponsive to the needs of other[s].." (Azar, 1990, p. 7). This appears to be the condition in which we find ourselves as a society today. It is from this position that we must examine ways through which conflicts may be managed toward a more enduring resolution. It is also in this area that a great deal of additional research is needed.

Gert Hofstede (1984) insists that the survival of humankind will depend, to a large extent, on the ability of people who think differently to act together for the collective good of all. This would appear to be the dilemma facing our nation today as our population becomes more diverse in character, and larger in general. Given the protracted nature of the existing social conflicts (Azar, 1986, 1984, 1979), what knowledge and skills are needed by the population in general and by those who are or will be charged with the responsibility of bringing about this condition of intergroup comity? What role must be played by governments, local, state and federal? Are present models adequate? If not how should they be altered? Are new ones suggested? These questions were the foci of the writers brief review of the present condition in the area of intergroup conflict and resolution, particularly where social conflict was a factor.

THE INDIVIDUAL AND INTER-MINORITY CONFLICT

The single individual is a vital link in the improvement of the general population's ability to resolve conflict in constructive ways and to establish a climate that encourages the use of positive conflict resolution strategies. Deutsch (1994) points out that "... it is important to recognize that institutional and cultural changes are often necessary for an individual to feel free to express his constructive potential" (p. 28). This would suggest that through comprehensive training in constructive conflict resolution we may achieve not only individual change but a change in the society as well. The individual then, must know something about the behaviors that are most likely to cause conflict to become constructive or destructive, and develop the skills to apply them.

"Most conflicts are mixed motive conflicts in which the parties involved have both cooperative and competitive interest"(Deutsch, 1994). These two interests result in two processes that have been termed by Walton and McKersie (1965) as integrative bargaining and distributive bargaining. Deutsch (1973) termed them cooperative and competitive processes. Deutsch (1994) asserts that conflict can be constructive or destructive. The direction the conflict will take (constructive or destructive) will be affected by the level of interest of the parties regarding cooperativeness and competitiveness, and how these interests may vary during the conflict.

The dual interests under discussion here arise from a dual concern model, concern for self and concern for the other (Blake and Mouton, 1984; Cosier and Ruble, 1981; Pruitt and Rubin, 1986, Thomas, 1976). Deutsch (1973) distinguished three basic types of motivational orientations to conflict: cooperative, individualistic, and competitive. Under the cooperative orientation the party has an interest in both his or her welfare and the welfare of the other. Under the individualistic orientation the party is concerned about his or her interest and unconcerned about the interest of the other. Under the competitive orientation the party is concerned about doing the best he or she can for themselves and better than the other.

As may be surmisable, the concern for self and other are independent of each other and therefore various combinations are possible. More importantly however, is the affects of the various combinations on whether or not the conflict will take a constructive or destructive course. "... Research (Deutsch, 1973; Kelley and Stahelski, 1970) as well as theory (Deutsch, 1982) suggest that only the reciprocal combinations are stable and that nonreciprocal combinations tend to move... toward... mutual competition if either party has a competitive orientation" (Deutsch, 1994, p. 15). Succinctly stated, a party to a conflict needs to know the specific behaviors that are likely to result in keeping the conflict moving toward a constructive course. A party must also know when he or she is actually displaying them. The same party needs also to know what behaviors lead to a destructive course and be able to determine when he or she is displaying them. Knowing is not enough, parties in conflict must have the skills to actually use the behaviors. This further requires parties to have the ability to detect and accept feedback on their interactive skills. This seems obvious enough but is seldom the case. "In conflict, people often do not question whether they have communicated well or not; they assume they have done so without checking with the other or examining their internal feelings" (Deutsch, p. 25). The foregoing exploration of the interactions in this model, as presented by the writer, implies an assumption of interpersonal authenticity, and / or the skill of detecting when others are being deceitful. There is a need for this skill as well as the skill of soliciting and detecting feedback.

The individual, as aforestated, is a vital link in developing interpersonal competence in the general community, and in the development of a community climate that permits and encourages the practice of conflict resolution skills. However, it is well settled that individuals do not interact in a vacuum. They are not robots, inanimate objects, they are social beings. Therefore even within groups there will be friction as they seek settlement of their differences. There are social and emotional factors to be considered. Irrespective of these factors, individuals offer us some advantages in dealing with some of them. For example there is a greater degree of discontinuity between groups than between individuals (Insko, Schopler, Graetz, Drigotas, Currey, Smith, Brazil, and Bornstein, 1994). That is to say, that individuals, when competing with one another, will be less competitive than will competing groups. That is not to say that individuals will not be affected by the groups to which they are accountable. Barley (1991) points out that the values and beliefs of the group to which an individual belongs shape their beliefs and cognition. Whether or not the individual identifies with the other party or the degree to which he or she identifies, and the degree to which the individual feels accountable, will further influence whether or not the individual will use a self-interested or an other-interested decision (Kramer, Sommerenke, and Newton, 1993). "...The identity in any given situation can range from highly individuating personal identities to shared collective or group identities" (Kramer et al., 1993, p. 637). The sense of accountability the individual feels has been found to increase competitive or contentious bargaining tactics, reduce concessions, and decrease the likelihood of agreement (Ben-Yoau and Pruitt, 1984; Carnevale, Pruitt, and Britton, 1979). It has also been suggested that resolution of individual parties may well be situation specific. For example, a person may well resolve concerns with another who represents another ethnic or racial group in a work setting without resolving those differences with the group as a whole (Jackson, 1993, p. 46). There are equally strong suggestions that if a sufficient number of individuals are affected, a critical mass could thus be created through which change could occur on a larger scale. One of the proponents of social change through the training of individuals is Carl Rodgers. Gurnah (1984) has a different view. He sees racism as a power relationship between groups within the society as opposed to between individuals. He does see individual training in racism awareness as important but not sufficient unto itself. Jackson (1993) states "viewing an outgroup member individually, rather than categorically, may facilitate favorable attitudes toward that individual, but not toward his or her group" (p. 46). Positive views, developed for a particular out-group individual in the group, will not generalize to out-group members (Hewstone and Brown, 1986). From another view we find evidence that having a number of out-group friends will have more impact than having one intimate one

(Jackman and Crane, 1986). Allport (1954) insists that "...it is only individuals who can feel antagonism and practice discrimination" (p. xvi). Perhaps it is not either/or, rather a combination of both acting in concert, particularly since there is no them without an us from which we may develop our group supported biases.

GROUP PROCESS METHODS IN INTER-MINORITY CONFLICT

"...Groups can often create short-term changes, but many of them are not conducted in a manner which ...[insure]...the continuance of those changes" (Smith, 1987, p. 166). The purpose for intergroup and in this case inter-minority conflict intervention, is to bring about continuing change. There have been a number of studies on how best to resolve intergroup animosities and resulting behaviors (Allport, 1954; Sherif, 1966; Stephan, 1985; Worchel and Austin, 1986). While most of the studies dealt with dominant minority conflict, the writer takes the position that they are directly relevant to the dynamics that occur between minority groups. If we revisit our definition of a dominant group, and consider the general attitudes of the various minorities in American society toward the "others," we come easily to the conclusion that these attitudes are remarkably similar to those of the dominant culture. This is particularly true as they relate to those they consider occupying a position in the societal hierarchy, lower than that they perceive their group as occupying. Power is perceived by many such groups in direct relationship to their social proximity to the dominant group.

Based on the findings of Cook (1984, 1985), Johnson and Johnson (1989), and Sherif (1966), the deepest and most lasting changes will occur when members of a group cooperatively successfully achieve superordinate goals. The key ingredient here and in the process is "cooperatively." Each member must do his or her share. It implies a crucial role for group leaders particularly in assisting the members to select goals that are meaningful and challenging and most importantly "doable." This becomes vital when we consider that one of the critical elements in this approach is that the outcomes of the group's needs must be positive and that the contacts between members must be extended over time. One of the reasons advanced for the quick fade out of group interventions has been the fact that the groups have been temporary, convened for one specific purpose and no relationship existed beyond that for which the group was aggregated (Smith, 1987). The selection of the groups would appear to be an enormously important task. The groups should have some continuing purpose. There is an additional caveat, that the contacts between the groups occur in diverse situations. This may well assist members is generalizing the outcomes to a larger context.

One of the most important factors was reported to be the status of the group members. The literature insist that the members be of equal status. At first glance this would not appear to present any particular difficulty. However, Avruch (1991) raises some concern with his assertion that "... blacks and whites in negotiation are not co-equal... white society dominates black... " (p. 5). How much of this in the perception of the interactants, how this affects the negotiation process between groups, and the nature and longevity of the outcomes, are questions that sorely need to be answered, both for purposes of inter-minority and dominant minority interventions.

Similar values, beliefs, and levels of competence are important factors. Members needing help may well be perceived of as being less competent; respect and liking for that member, is likely to decrease (Cook, 1984). Thus, member selection is again highlighted as a critical element in increasing the probability of a successful intergroup intervention.

There is a need to recognize the support for the position that, needs long denied, tend to increase cohesion within the denied group and increase the hostility toward those who are perceived as denying those needs (Azar, 1990). There is also the belief that the longer the needs are denied the more intractable positions become. The need on the part of some minority groups to distance themselves from those groups having less favor with the dominant culture is also a factor to be considered if we are to improve inter-minority relations. What ever model or combination of models are to be used in efforts to bring about more positive inter-minority group interactions must take these factors into account.

CULTURE AND INTER-MINORITY CONFLICT

There is wide agreement that culture is involved in intergroup interaction. The disagreement is centered around the degree to which it affects the interactive process. A person's perception of reality, their organization of their negotiating behavior which is fashioned as a response to their perception of the behavior of the other party or parties, is based on culture (Faure and Sjostedt, 1993).

Culture has been defined by Harris and Moran (1979) as "... knowledge for human coping within a particular environment that is passed on for the benefit of subsequent generations" (p. 32). The definition can be divided into three elements. If we consider the first two together, it becomes easily apparent that if two groups do not occupy the same environment they will in fact develop different cultures. It is important to also note that the authors, when speaking of environment were not speaking primarily of geographic proximity, rather of social proximity. The mere spatial proximity of bodies does not provide access to either of the others social environment. The third element speaks to the enduring quality of culture. Members of particular groups have maintained values, beliefs, and behaviors over generations which are still closely held and with slight, if any, awareness of from whence they came.

Vontress (1981), and Harris and Moran (1991), support the view that culture is conscious and unconscious, it is visible and it is invisible. It is the invisible part that causes the greatest difficulty as members of various groups seek to settle their differences. It is easy to see how inadvertent offenses could occur so very easily while the offended party may well feel the offender is simply socially incompetent or worse. The visible portion of our culture is but the tip of the iceberg and yet that is the part that becomes the target of so much attention in some cultural awareness sessions. Relying on this definition and the accompanying discussion, the genesis for disparate cultural development, given the power differential and social separation between dominant and inter-minority populations, can easily be seen. The longer the separation, the more rigid the differences are likely to be.

Stewart and Bennett (1991) highlight two aspects of culture, subjective and objective. Subjective culture is defined as "...the psychological features of culture, including assumptions, values, and patterns of thinking" (p. 2). Objective culture is defined as "...the institutions and artifacts of a culture, political structures and processes, arts, crafts, and literature" (p. 2). Again, it is that which we cannot see that becomes necessary for our focus if we are to successfully improve inter-minority group salience.

Faure and Sjostedt (1993) define culture as "...a set of shared and enduring meanings, values, and beliefs that characterize national, ethnic, or other groups and orient their behavior" (p. 3). There are many other definitions. Kroeber and Kluckhohn (1963) gathered over 160. From those we have examined here, it appears that they are mutually supportive.

As stated in the beginning of this section, the concern is centered around the degree that culture may affect the interactive process. Selected for purposes of illustration is one of the models in considerable use for conflict resolution in the United States, negotiation. The particular theory of negotiation is derived from the dominant culture although used by minorities as well. In this approach parties are asked to leave emotions out of the process, to remain calm, to think logically, and to calculate rationally. Kochman (1981) argues that this model is not by any means universally valid, that black and white Americans have a different view:

> In general, whites take a view of the negotiation procedure that is markedly different from the view taken by blacks. Though blacks view whites as devious in insisting that emotions be left in front of the meeting-room door, whites think that blacks are being devious by insisting on bringing those emotions into the room. [Whites believe that] If the meeting is to be successful, the black's anger and hostility will be allayed by the results of the meeting.... Blacks simply do not see things that way. To leave their emotions aside is not their responsibility; it is the white's responsibility to provide first with a reason to do so (p. 40).

Having raised the issue of emotionality, of heightened animation among some African Americans, how does this affect their ability to negotiate with, for example, Koreans and vice versa. The Prince George's County Human Relations Commission was asked to intervene in a conflict with some members of an African-American community and several Korean and Vietnamese managers of several convenience stores. The request came on behalf of the managers. The two groups had sought to work out their difficulties through a meeting and had been unsuccessful. The African Americans were characterized as hostile, angry, and even dangerous. The Koreans and Vietnamese felt that they had been treated with disrespect, while they had been most respectful in their treatment toward their African-American clientele. The African Americans felt that they had been treated with disrespect, contempt even. They felt that their patronage was not appreciated. As is often the case, both groups were right. In their own eyes, from their own cultural perspective they had been treated with disrespect.

An example may be in order. One of the African Americans complained that he had gone into the store to purchase an item. When he asked for it the young Korean male stated that they did not have any. When he turned to leave he saw several on a shelf. When the managers were subsequently confronted with this allegation by the facilitator it was determined that the incident did in fact happen. The young man in the store was not proficient in English and did not understand what the customer had wanted. It was considered improper to tell the customer he could not understand him and thus his response. His intent was to be polite, the effect was the opposite.

The Commissions intervention, which lasted over an extended period, was successful as evidenced by the end of overt acts against the merchants and by their reports of satisfaction. The point to be made, however, is that the barrier to their understanding, in fact the genesis of their misunderstanding and resulting conflict, was the differences in their respective cultures. If we return to the individual competencies briefly treated in the earlier portion of this chapter, we can see that these competencies may well have helped, however, without some understanding of their cultural differences probably not much. This is particularly true if we are seeking an improvement in the level of acceptance between the groups.

Inter-minority interaction appears to be far less frequent than dominant minority interactions, both socially and work related. Given the definitions of culture and the discussion of cultural differentiation, inter-minority isolation portends grave consequences as the various groups compete within the same community for scarce resources. "...It appears that the issue of allocation of resources is a more important source of conflict when parties to the conflict occupy the same territory" (Landis and Boucher, 1987, p. 21). The literature is replete with positions on both sides of the contact argument. It would appear however, that there is sufficient support for the appropriate structuring of such contacts, and that they be frequent and favorable (Pettigrew, 1986; Linville, 1982).

GOVERNMENTAL INVOLVEMENT IN INTER-MINORITY CONFLICT

One of the major implications of this discussion of the present condition of inter-minority conflict, is that something must be done to improve the level of inter-minority group acceptance. The larger question that remains is, who is to do this? Does the various levels of government have a role to play? A review of Azar's (1990) definition and description of protracted social conflict, would easily lead us to respond, that governments not only have a role, but an obligation, to positively involve themselves. It is after all the governments that have played and still play a major role in maintaining some of the conditions that give rise to intergroup conflict, among those, unmet needs; needs only the government can satisfy, such as distributive justice, access to housing, and other basic needs. For the example, imposing area restrictions or requirements on housing that leads to economic discrimination, a safe haven around racial, ethnic, religious, and national origin discrimination but often motivated by same. One of the obvious effects of these practices is to increase intergroup isolation. The inclusion of members from all segments of the community, where ever possible, would not only provide much needed cross-cultural input, but establish the basis for continuing groups, which under appropriate conditions, could very well lead to increased intergroup salience. There are those who would term this a type of social engineering and that such should be outside the governments purview. The writer would suggest the following offered by Azar (1990):

> The level of satisfaction or deprivation of basic needs is generally influenced by the intervening or mediating role of the state. Indeed an ideal state characterized by a fair and just mode of governance should be able to satisfy human needs regardless of communal or identity cleavages, and promote communal harmony and social stability (p. 10).

A healthy democracy with a culturally pluralistic population requires, as Hofstede (1984) suggests, an electorate that while thinking differently, is able to act together for the collective good of all. Thus it is reasonable to conclude that the government's duty is no less than the assurance that the inter-minority community is able to function in substantial numbers within each group to that end. Governments at each level must reframe from unnecessary acts that exacerbate intergroup tensions and support those actions that reduce it. Governments, in the view of the writer, have a responsibility to create a climate of acceptance among and between its citizens.

ETHNOCENTRISM AND INTER-MINORITY CONFLICT

Ethnocentrism has been defined by Stewart and Bennett (1991) as "...centrality of culture" (p. 161), and by Random House Dictionary as:

> Belief in the inherent superiority of ones own group and culture; it may be accompanied by feelings of contempt for those others who do not belong; it tends to look down upon those considered as foreign; it views and measures alien cultures and groups in terms of ones own culture.

"Ethnocentrism is conducive to the occurrence of conflict but not conducive to its constructive conclusion" (Deutsch, 1994, p. 20).

There is a need for dominant culture Americans to finally and squarely face their ethnocentrism and resulting racism. It is this ethnocentrism that fuels much of the conflict that affects American minorities. It is probable that white Americans haven't a clue as to the extent or the effects of their ethnocentrism or their racism. "...Racism may be viewed as a historically specific facet of the general social phenomenon of ethnicity" (Jenkins, 1986, p. 174). The level to which the ethnocentrism of the dominant culture ramifies throughout our society cannot be recounted here. An example however, can be seen in the former reference to the basic negotiation model. The standards of "good" negotiation is determined by the dominant group irrespective of the needs, culture, and standards of the minority groups. The standards for this model require a calm demeanor, logical thinking, and to calculate rationally. These very requirements are culturally based. This model represents "a" way to negotiate. It is the dominant cultures insistence that it is "the" way to negotiate that ethnocentrism comes into play.

The effects of dominant culture ethnocentrism at the very least, is that minorities must consistently accommodate to ways that are not necessarily in their best interest. It also means that only the dominants may define "good" and only they may determine when it is demonstrated. Value then, issues from the dominants and their ability to confer value also reaches to deciding how groups will be valued.

As mentioned earlier, in 1905 the *San Francisco Chronicle* commented that the Asian would never be other than an Asiatic (as if that was or is something awful to be), in contrast to, the then considered undesirable, Croat or Slav who could assimilate. This rejection of the Asian was based on physiognomy and race. To this group must be added African Americans and other persons of color. These groups are not equally valued, however, on one point they are totally equal, they are considered as objectionable as equal human beings from the standpoint of the dominant group as a whole. Each of the minority groups also, in some ways, find the other objectionable as equals, thus the insidiousness of intergroup enmity is not limited to dominant minority relations.

It must be said quickly, that nothing in this chapter is intended to deny the fact that individual variation does occur and that there is no intent to say that all members of any group act in lockstep with traits we identify as cultural attributes. The purpose of this discourse is to make the point that there are influences within a community or a nation that differentially inhibit the efforts of portions of the populations from interacting as productively as desirable and that, that limitation has consequences for the society as a whole.

Ethnocentrism does violence to the concept of an America of one people. It encourages, and in some cases, forces us to be a nation of separate groups, with their own very special interest, which more often than not, is incompatible with other groups. "The multiethnic dogma abandons historic purposes, replacing assimilation by fragmentation, integration by separation. It belittles *unum* and glorifies *pluribus*" (Schlesinger, 1992, p. 16). This would appear to infer that this zealous tendency toward ethnocentristically motivated group identification, coupled with the disdain for others, threatens the very kind of society and ethos we espouse. A society of free men and women, who believe in the inherent dignity of all human beings, and the right of every human being to have equal opportunity to the pursuits "guaranteed" by the constitution.

If ethnocentrism is so pervasive and destructive, why is it so difficult for both dominant and minority groups to come to grips with it? Aside from the fact that in some cases there are significant payoffs for its retention, one of the great difficulties lies in the fact that many persons do not understand the extent to which they and their group as a whole, are carriers. Three true experiences come to mind that may help us see through the eyes of the "other." In 1959, Howard Griffin, a white journalist, disguised himself as an African American, traveled in the rural South, and wrote a book about his experiences. In the 1970s, Grace Halsell, a white woman, told of her experiences as she lived as an African-American, Hispanic, and Native-American woman. In 1994, Joshua Solomon decided to replicate the experience. This excerpt from the *Washington Post*, relate his feelings in the beginning, at the end, and on the subway in Atlanta as he began his return home to Silver Spring, Maryland:

> I'd sympathized with my friends, and I wanted to support them, but secretly, inside, I'd always felt that many black people used racism as a crutch, an excuse. Couldn't they just shrug off the rantings of ignorant people?...I began to cry as I recounted the events of the last two days, the drip-drop of indifference and fear from the white people I had encountered. Their lack of patience, their downright contempt...A young black woman leaned against the seat next to me. She dozed off occasionally. In her arms she cradled a sack of books. Around her neck hung a stethoscope. Why hadn't she given up? I could return home to my comfortable world. I could wait for my skin to turn white again. She would have to endure (October 30, 1994).

It is no doubt an interesting, revealing, and sometimes frightening experience to see ourselves as others see us. We can only conjecture what the results would be if we could all take such a walk in the shoes of the other for a while.

We are a diverse people. The fact that groups are different in and of itself does not mean conflict until something triggers it, until anxiety increases and a rationale is developed for its escalation (Landis and Boucher, 1987; Rommell, 1976). We are the envy of much, if not most, of the world. We have much to preserve and even more to experience if we are able to maintain a constructive course in the intergroup conflicts we are experiencing and will experience in the future. As we consider the alternative, a stern warning is sounded by Azar (1990):

> The process of protracted conflict deforms and retards the effective operation of political institutions. It reinforces and strengthens pessimism throughout the society, demoralizes leaders and immobilizes the search for peaceful solutions...a siege mentality develops which inhibits constructive negotiation for any resolution of the conflict (p. 16).

There needs also to be a change in the perception of how conflict in general is viewed. Conflict in and of itself is not to be abhorred. It can be used as a catalyst for learning about and from, one another. "...Social conflict is not an aberration to be seen as part of the abnormal psychology, but a problem in the construction of the social world" (Landis and Boucher, 1987, p. 26). The focus then, must be brought to bear on how this flawed construction occurs and how to remedy it to the extent that it does not do violence to the ability of diverse humans to live in comity.

Somewhere along the way, it will be necessary to identify the payoffs, the benefits that accrue from the various conflicts, that fuel their continuance, and to whom they accrue. Many persons in the inter-minority community gain their power, prestige, and in some cases their livelihood, from continuing destructive conflict. These payoffs, once identified, must be removed.

It has not been the intent of the writer to present a blow-by-blow description of conflicts within the inter-minority community, rather to highlight some underlying factors that will continue to fuel conflicts if thoughtful and constructive interventions are not made. Underlying factors that we all know perhaps, but all too frequently seem to forget or relegate to the no longer revelant category. It is the writer's contention, that it is this historical perspective that infects inter-minority discussions and makes resolution so difficult today. So that when African Americans and Jews discuss, for example, particular members of the Nation of Islam, the explicit subject may be what is kept on the table but the interaction goes far beyond the ostensible. They are in reality, discussing their history with each other, and in relation to the dominant culture. It is important to note, that their respective views of that history are not congruent.

Members of the Jewish community often remind African Americans of the support they gave for the cause of African Americans in the early history of the country, as evidence of their good will toward them. African Americans respond that the motivation for that help was the need for certain rights that the Jews themselves had but did not find in their best interest to fight for directly, an interest influenced by the dominant culture. Does this retort mean that African Americans did not appreciate their support irrespective of the perceived motivation? Probably not. The point sought to be made here is that inter-minority conflict is, as aforestated, rooted in history, is imbedded deeply within the culture, and into the very psyche of the group members. If we can recall the third element of Harris and Moran's (1979) definition of culture, that it is passed on, transmitted to future generations, we understand that we do not have to have been there to house the vestiges of its meaning.

In the final analysis, if we are to improve the condition in which we find the cognitive and resolutive aspects of inter-minority conflict, it will be necessary to narrow the gap between theory and praxis. It is not surprising that practice is out front of theory, as there is wide sentiment for the view that practice drives theory (Avruch, 1991). There are a plethora of opportunities for significant research on which solid practice may be based. There are a number of entities throughout the country that could serve as useful partners in this endeavor and have some investment. There are hundreds of human relations commissions throughout America, specifically charged with improving relations between people and have great need of help. There are community mediation boards and a multitude of other organizations, public and private, religious and secular, that may be engaged. The possible outcomes from a coalescence for such a purpose as discussed here are exciting to imagine.

Finally, the words of Fisher (1994) seem a fitting close:

> The bottom line in the constructive management of intergroup conflict is this: We can learn to understand, respect, collaborate, and share with our neighbors, or we and future generations can suffer in varying degrees of debilitation and destruction with them (p. 63).

REFERENCES

Allport, G. 1954. *The Nture of Prejudice*. Cambridge: Addison Wesley.

Avruch, K. 1991. "Introduction: Culture and Conflict." In *Conflict Resolution: Cross Cultural Perspectives*, edited by K. Avruch, W. Black, and J. Scimecca. Westport, CT: Greenwood Press.

Azar, E. 1976. "Peace Amidst Development." *International Interactions* 6 (2): 203-40.

Azar, E. 1984. "The Theory of Protracted Social Conflict and the Challenge of Transforming Conflict Situations." In *Conflict Processes and the Breakdown of International Systems*, edited by D.A. Zinnes. Denver: Graduate School of International Systems, University of Denver.

Azar, E. 1986. *Management of Protracted Social Conflict in the Third World: Ethnic Studies Report* 4: 2.

Azar, E. 1990. *The Management of Protracted Social Conflict: Theory and Cases.* VT: Gower.

Barley, S. 1991. "Contextualizing Conflict: Notes on the Anthropology of Disputes and Negotiations." Pp. 165-202 in *Research on Negotiation in Organizations,* edited by M. Bazerman, R. Lewicki, and B. Sheppard. Greenwich, CT: JAI.

Ben-Yoau, O., and D. Pruitt. 1984. "Accountability to Constituents: A Two Edged Sword." *Organizational Behavior and Human Performance* 34: 282-295.

Blake, D., and J. Mouton. 1984. *Solving Costly Organizational Conflicts.* San Francisco: Jossey-Bass.

Boardman, S., and S. Horowitz. 1994. "Constructive Conflict Management and Social Problems." *Journal of Social Issues* 50: 1 1-12.

Bok, S. 1989. *A Strategy for Peace.* New York: Pantheon.

Carnevale, P., D. Pruitt, and S. Britton. 1979. "Looking Tough: The Negotiator Under Constituent Surveillance." *Personality and Social Psychology Bulletin* 5: 118-121.

Cook, S. 1984. "Cooperative Interaction in Multiethnic Context." Pp.155-185 in *Groups in Contact: The Psychology of Desegregation,* edited by N. Miller and M. Brewer. New York: Academic Press.

Cook, S. 1985. "Experimenting on Social Issues: The Case of School Desegregation." *American Psychologist* 40: 452-460.

Cose, E. 1992. *A Nation of Strangers: Prejudice, Politics, and the Populating of America.* New York: Morrow.

Cosier, R., and T. Ruble. 1981. "Research on Conflict Handling Behavior: An Experimental Approach." *Academy of Management Journal* 24: 816-831.

Deutsch, M. 1973. *The Resolution of Conflict.* New Haven: Yale.

Deutsch, M. 1982. "Independence and Psychological Orientation." Pp. 16-43 in *Cooperation and Helping Behaviors: Theories and Research,* edited by V. Delaga, and J. Grzelak. New York: Academic Press.

Deutsch, M. 1994. "Constructive Conflict Resolution: Principles, Training, and Research." *Journal of Social Issues* 50 (1): 13-32.

Doob, L. (ed.). 1970. *Resolving Conflict in Africa: The Fermeda Workshop.* New Haven, CT: Yale University Press.

Faure, G., and G. Sjostedt. 1993. "Culture and Negotiation." In *Culture and Negotiation: The Resolution of Water Disputes,* edited by G. Faure, and J. Rubin. Newbury Park, CA: Sage.

Fisher, R. 1994. "Generic Principles for Resolving Intergroup Conflict." *Journal of Social Studies* 50: 47-66.

Gurnah, A. 1984. "The Politics of Racism Awareness Training." *Critical Social Policy* 10: 16-20.

Harris, P., and R. Moran. 1979. *Managing Cultural Differences.* Houston: Gulf.

Harris, P., and R. Moran. 1991. *Managing Cultural Differences* (3rd ed.). Houston: Gulf.

Herrnstein, R., and C. Murray. 1994. *The Bell Curve.* New York: Crown.

Hewstone, M., and R. Brown. 1986. "Contact is not Enough: An Intergroup Perspective on the 'contact hypothesis'." In *Contact and Conflict in Intergroup Encounters,* edited by M. Hewstone and R. Brown. Oxford: Blackwell.

Hofstede, G. 1984. *Cultures Consequences.* Beverly Hills: Sage Publications.

Insko, C., J. Schopler, K. Graetz, S. Drigotas, D. Currey, S. Smith, D. Brazil, and G. Bornstein. 1994. "Interindividual-intergroup Discontinuity in the Prisoner's Dilemma Game." *Journal of Conflict Resolution* 38 (1): 87-116.

Jackson, J. 1993. "Contact Theory of Intergroup Hostility: A Review and Evaluation of the Theoretical and Empirical Literature." *International Journal of Group Tensions* 23 (1): 43-65.

Jackson, M., and M. Crane. 1986. "'Some of my Best Friends are Black....': International Friendship and Whites Racial Attitudes." *Public Opinion Quarterly* 50: 459-486.

Jefferson, T. 1904. "Notes on the State of Virginia." In *The Works of Thomas Jefferson*, edited by L. Ford. New York: Putnam.

Jenkins, R. 1986. "Social Anthropological Models of Inter-ethnic Relations." In *Theories of Race and Ethnic Relations*, edited by J. Rex and D. Mason. Cambridge: Cambridge University Press.

Johnson, D., and R. Johnson. 1989. *Cooperation and Competition: Theory and Research.* MN: Interaction Book Company.

Kelly, M., and A. Stahelski. 1970. "The Social Interactive Basis of Cooperators' and Competitors' Beliefs about Others." *Journal of Personality and Social Psychology* 16: 66-91.

Kochman, T. 1981. *Black and White Styles in Conflict.* Chicago: University of Chicago Press.

Kramer, R., P. Pommerenke, and E. Newton. 1993. "Social Context in Negotiation." *Journal of Conflict Resolution* 37: 4, 633-654.

Kroeber, A., and C. Kluckhohn. 1963. *Culture: A Critical Review of Concepts and Definitions.* New York: Random House.

Landis, D., and J. Boucher. 1987. *Ethnic Conflict.* CA: Sage.

Lewis, D. 1992. "Parallels and Divergences: Assimilationist Strategies of Afro-America and Jewish Elites from 1910 to Early 1930s." In *Bridges and Boundaries: Africa American and American Jews*, edited by J. Salzman. New York: Braziller.

Linville, P. 1982. "The Complexity-extremity Effect and Age Based Stereotyping." *Journal of Personality and Social Psychology* 42: 193-211.

Marden, C., and G. Meyer. 1978. *Minorities in America Society* (5th ed.). New York: Van Nostrand.

Pettigrew, T. 1986. "The Intergroup Contact Hypotheses Reconsidered." In *Contact and Conflict in Intergroup Encounters*, edited by M. Hewstone and R. Brown. Oxford: Blackwell.

Pruitt, D., and J. Rubin. 1986. *Social Conflict.* New York: Random House.

Rommell, R. 1976. *Understanding Conflict and War.* New York: John Wiley.

Schlesinger, A. 1992. *The Disuniting of America.* New York: Norton.

Sherif, M. 1966. *In Common Predicament: Social Psychology of Intergroup Conflict and Cooperation.* Boston: Houghton Mifflin.

Smith, P. 1987. *Strategies for Improving Race Relations: The Anglo-America Experience.* NH: Manchester.

Solomon, J. 1994. "Skin Deep." *The Washington Post*, October 30: C1,C4.

Stephan, W. 1985. "Intergroup Relations." Pp. 599-658 in *The Handbook of Racial Psychology* (3rd ed.), edited by G. Lindzey, and E. Aronson. New York: Random House.

Stephenson, G. 1926. *History of America Immigration: 1840-1924.* Boston: Ginn and Company.

Stewart, E., and M. Bennett. 1991. *American Cultural Patterns: A Cross Cultural Perspective.* ME: Intercultural Press.

Thomas, K. 1976. "Conflict and Conflict Management." Pp. 889-935 in *Handbook in Industrial and Organizational Psychology*, edited by M. Dunnette. Chicago: Rand-McNally.

Vontress, C. 1981. "Racial and Ethnic Barriers in Counseling." In *Counseling Across Cultures*, edited by P. Pedersen, J. Draguns, W. Lonner, and J. Trimble. Hawaii: University Press.

Wagley, C., and M. Harris. 1958. *Minorities in the New World: Six Case Studies.* New York: Columbia University Press.

Walton, R., and R. McKersie. 1965. *A Behavioral Theory of Labor Negotiations: An Analysis of a Social Interaction System.* New York: Mcgraw Hill.

Worchel, S., and W. Austin. 1986. *Psychology of Intergroup Relations* (2nd ed.). Chicago: Nelson Hall.

ISSUES FOR WOMEN OF RACIAL
AND ETHNIC GROUPS

Barbara A. Zsembik

After considerable neglect, the voices of women of color are being incorporated into our accounts of both women's lives and racial and ethnic experiences. The postwar inclusionary model initially gained foothold in the humanities, followed by the social sciences (Stacey and Thorne 1985). Social science's cross-disciplinary efforts in diversifying scholarship, especially consideration of the amalgam of consequences emanating from interlocking systems of stratification, accumulate more readily in particular research areas. While we know a lot about ethnic families and households, and the contemporary women's civil rights and cultural nationalism movements, we have yet to develop a truly gendered understanding of race and ethnic relations. Attention to the multifaceted nature of women's identity and lives, opportunities and social action with regard to race and ethnicity will contribute to a deeper understanding of the gendered nature of race and ethnic relations, and of race and ethnic relations among women.

The multiplicity of racial and ethnic experiences impedes full consideration, in a single review, of how women's lives are simultaneously racialized and gendered. The recency of the effort to include women's voices, a development

Research in Human Social Conflict, Volume 1, pages 257-273.
Copyright © 1995 by JAI Press Inc.
All rights of reproduction in any form reserved.
ISBN: 1-55938-923-0

occurring unevenly across disciplines and typically reflecting the African-American experience, further complicates this review's analysis and interpretation. An unconscious demographic tyranny overlooks the experience of the relatively small populations of Latinas and Asian-American, and Native-American women, muting their voices, trivializing their experiences, and reducing diversity in scholarship. A number of scholars strive to insert the Asian-American (e.g., Takaki, 1989) and Native-American (e.g., Snipp, 1989) experience into the historical record, though gender, when considered, more often serves as an "independent variable" than as a cross-cutting social experience. Majority-minority relations have justifiably played center stage, witnessed in the volume of writings devoted to the subject, yet such research falsely presumes a shared culture of poverty among various ethnicities (Deloria, 1981). Intra-ethnic diversity and interethnic minority relations are major fault lines in women's and men's racial topography, yet their necessary incorporation into social analysis is deterred by a paucity of data. The dilemma posed by the need to integrate the gendered nature of multiple cultural heritages without complete data is necessarily resolved through analysis of extant data, recognizing the bias toward the better-documented African-American and Chicana experiences.

A cross-cultural thread is spun from the idea of gendered space, women's and men's differential activities in public and private places. Discussions of race and ethnic relations typically focus on struggles in public arenas, consequently omitting much of women's experiences and underestimating the depth of ethnic conflict. Public places—the workplace, the political arena, organizations, and associations—are becoming more hospitable to women, but remain arranged with little regard for women's interests. Women's activities are disproportionately concentrated in private places, household and family settings, informal networks, and semi-private places like the neighborhood or local community. Women's lives are stretched across a gendered space more so than men's lives, calling attention to the multiple levels at which race, ethnicity, and gender coincide. I draw from recent social science literatures, a broad rather than exhaustive review, to show how women's race and ethnic struggle unfold in both public and private arenas, compromising their physical well-being, constraining their access to the extant opportunity structure (social class), and occasionally compelling them into social action. The everyday survival of women of color is a form of collective resistance (Collins, 1990) to the intertwined, deeply embedded nature of racism, sexism, and classism.

HEALTH

Health issues are important issues among women of color as they manifest the long-term and short-term effects of classism, racism, and sexism. In addition, the physical and psychosocial well-being of minority women shed much-needed light on the health and well-being of minority children; evaluating women's health offers a glimpse of another, more silenced minority. Many of the health issues of concern to minority women are most amenable to social change, creating an opportunity for women's social action.

The physical integrity of women of color and their children is at risk due to their residence in unsafe environments, lack of incorporation into the medical system, and lifetime exposure to poverty. Minority women's health is at risk in public places due to the confluence of residential segregation and the political economy of waste storage and waste disposal. Racism and sexism also compromise minority women's and children's health through their absence in medical research and through intentional and unintentional barriers in medical service delivery (Carr and Lee, 1978; Pol and Thomas, 1992). Health risks exist within private places as well as public places. A significant number of women of color reside in substandard housing, experience intentional domestic injuries, and, overall, have the morbidity and mortality profile of residents of an industrializing country.

Environmental Safety

Women of color are exposed to health risks in environments made unsafe by toxic waste disposal and storage in minority neighborhoods, decaying housing stock (Wallace, 1981), and violence inside and outside the home. The recent environmentalism movement has uncovered a number of minority neighborhoods with industries, waste disposal sites, or waste storage sites in close proximity to community residents. Residents of these low-income communities are beginning to organize against what has been called "eco-racism" or "environmental racism." Native Americans are increasingly reluctant to permit industry to store waste on tribal lands, although the revenue is desperately needed. The Environmental Protection Agency's recognition of the prevalence of eco-racism is demonstrated in the 1992 establishment of the Office of Environmental Equity. The disproportional poverty of women of color directly translates into women's and children's exposure to toxins such as asbestos insulation, lead poisoning from wall paint, pest infestation, and to the adverse health effects from housing decay, inadequate ventilation, heating, wiring, and plumbing systems (Jaynes and Williams, 1989; Rodriguez, 1991). Violence, or intentional injury, occurs in both community (semi-public) and domestic (private) settings (Jaynes and Williams, 1989). Minorities are subject more frequently than whites to violent deaths and injuries (O'Carroll and Mercy, 1986). Women are victims of violence in public space such as experiencing violence at the hands of strangers. Women also are victims of violence in private space, assaulted by one's own (Steinmetz and Pellicciaro, 1986).

Morbidity and Mortality

Ethnic variation in profiles of morbidity and mortality discloses the chronic effect of long-term poverty, ignorance, and barriers to service stemming partially from racism and sexism (Jones and Rice, 1987; Lawson and Thompson, 1994). The private space of the body sometimes becomes a proxy battleground for racism and sexism. The morbidity and mortality profiles of African Americans, Puerto Ricans, Chicanos, and Native Americans resemble residents of a newly-industrializing country more than the majority white residents of the United States. For instance, communicable diseases are more prevalent among poorer and thus ethnic populations (Sumaya, 1992).

The public space of morbidity and mortality is defined by access to the knowledge base of medicine, and access to both curative and preventive medical services. Public exclusion from or ghettoization in the medical knowledge base on biological, behavioral, and sociocultural aspects of morbidity and mortality places women of color at greater risk of undetected medical problems. Medical research is built upon the white male subject, presuming that women and minorities present identical medical experiences. Recent comparisons of men's and women's cardiovascular risk and treatment suggest that women have unique cardiovascular risk and have poorer survival rates given a cardiovascular trauma. Relative to white men and women, Native Americans appear to be less tolerant of alcohol (Carr and Lee, 1978), Chicanos and Mexicanos are more likely to suffer from adult-onset diabetes mellitus (Bradshaw and Fonner, 1978), and African Americans are at greater risk of hypertension (Manton, Poss, and Wing, 1979).

Many of the diseases that are prevalent in minority populations have a socioeconomic component, wherein thinner income streams hamper adequate nutrition and health-promoting behaviors such as adequate prenatal care. Prenatal care must start in the first trimester to fully realize its beneficial effect on maternal and infant health, and entails little more than monitoring the pregnancy for signs of fetal or maternal complications. Inadequate prenatal care is associated with an increased risk of premature birth, low birth weight, and infant mortality (Brown, 1988; National Institute of Medicine, 1986). Prenatal care also identifies women and children at risk of poor health that may be supported by another community health program. Moreover, women acquire information during regular prenatal visits that promote healthy behaviors for themselves (e.g., regular gynecological examinations) and for their infants and children (e.g., childhood immunizations). Significantly fewer Latina, Native-American, and African-American women than majority women receive adequate prenatal care. Consequently, African Americans are more likely to bear low birth weight infants (Chavkin, Busner, and McLaughlin, 1987; Cramer, 1987; Kallan, 1993; Powell-Griner, 1988), who bear the detrimental effects of an unhealthy start into adulthood. In contrast, low socioeconomic-status Latinas bear remarkably healthy infants (Cramer, 1987; Forbes and Frisbie, 1991; Powell-Griner, 1988), who acquire their health disadvantage later in childhood.

Community-based health services are touted as an effective way to meet the U.S. Public Health Service's goals of reduction of black low birth weight and infant mortality, and of expansion of early and continuing prenatal care among Latinas, African Americans, and Native Americans (U.S. Public Health Service, 1990). Prevention and management of these health risks are frequently compromised by insufficient government funding, understaffing, and bureaucratic cultural insensitivity. Yet community clinics intending to promote the health of women, infants, and children are economically hindered from significantly ameliorating "the traumas of urban survival" (Cisneros, 1992).

Older Women

The longevity of women over men, and the sensitivity of the quality of life at older ages to social class, makes the health of older, minority women a salient issue among women of color. The lifetime consequences of racism, sexism, and classism on the health of minority women are clearest at the older ages. Minority individual's physical well-being is so thoroughly assaulted by everyday discrimination that it yields the epidemiological oddity of the mortality crossover. The favorable mortality and morbidity conditions earlier in the lives of majority women extends life expectancy. The unfavorable mortality and morbidity conditions earlier in the lives of minority women remove the more frail individuals, effectively culling minority populations' into a selectively healthy subpopulation (Manton, 1980). The consequence of different age-graded mortality and morbidity conditions between majority and minority women shifts the mortality advantage from majority women at younger ages to minority women at older ages. By implication, the disappearance of the minority mortality crossover may be a sign of ethnic social mobility and equality.

The mortality crossover is not evidence of the health of minority women, but a statement of the degree of their adverse-health circumstances. Minority women's poor health stems from a lifetime of economic disadvantage accrued through a racialized and gendered space. Limited economic resources shift health behavior among minority populations to the curative management of acute conditions rather than the healthier and more cost-effective preventive management of acute and chronic conditions. Older minority women are especially plagued by limited economic resources, obliging them to turn to family members for support (National Council of La Raza, 1991). The older economically disadvantaged women band together with the younger economically disadvantaged women to survive. Reliance on family members to provide support drives race and ethnic inequities deep into private places.

Women's and minorities' well-developed and utilized social support networks for older minority individuals, typically women (Lubben and Becerra, 1987; Taylor, 1988), mean that women and minorities disproportionately bear the social and economic costs of long-term care.

OPPORTUNITY STRUCTURE

The material expression of the opportunity structure is "the distribution in space of people, housing, jobs, transportation and other urban elements" (Hershberg, Burstein, Ericksen, Greenberg, and Yancey, 1992). Regional concentration of individual ethnic groups (Bean and Tienda, 1987; Jaynes and Williams, 1989; Snipp, 1989) and the mediation of national economic trends through local economic opportunity structures (Rodriguez, 1991) introduce substantial ethnic variation in women's production, social reproduction, and consumption of goods and services. Labor and source of economic support are a litmus test for Americans preoccupied with individualism and associated explanations of racial and ethnic inequality. Women's labor garners the most cross-disciplinary attention, yielding the definition of activities in the private sphere as labor (Beneria and Sen, 1986), the description of changes in public and private places attendant to women's advent in public places (Ehrenreich, 1983), and the analysis of the articulation of public and private lives of women and men (Blau and Ferber, 1986; Baca Zinn, 1987).

This review focuses on minority women's position in the formal economy and only briefly comments on the nature of the informal economy and its relationship to the formal. The formal economy refers to production and social reproduction of jobs and consumption of goods and services regulated by the state. The features of the formal economy permit description of minority women's employment status, occupational concentration, and earnings and benefits components of the income stream. Economic restructuring and other effects of participation in a global economy change the demand for women's and men's labor, yielding a new international division of labor by gender. Transnational corporations link women and men, majority and minority, to the international division of labor, deliberately exploiting the confluence of race, ethnicity, and gender in the quest for cheap labor (Fuentes and Ehrenreich, 1981).

The informal economy refers to the production, social reproduction, and consumption of goods and services that are not regulated by the state. Embedded within the usually private or semi-private space of the informal economy are hidden costs of racism and sexism because of the gendered nature of informal work. Women typically produce and exchange goods and services that fall under their purview in private spaces. Women of color provide to each other and to white women child care, home-cooked foods, personal services such as hair care. Poverty presumably activates any ethnic value of assistance, and given the more profound effect of poverty on women of color, suggests that informal networks in ethnic groups might be well-developed (Wagner and Shaffer, 1980). Women exchange goods and services (Stack, 1974; Baca Zinn, 1982), readily transferred intergenerationally due to either the culture of poverty or the ethnic culture. Often informal work is not only compatible with family and household demands on women's lives, but extensions of those daily chores.

Support systems appear meager for minority women of higher social standing (Benjamin, 1991). The type of network that professional minority women need becomes more similar to the needs of professional white women. Middle-class professional women, regardless of race and ethnicity, are in need of professional networking and mentoring to achieve economic well-being, in contrast to poorer women's needs for material support. Although all women share the need for quality but affordable child care, elite minority women purchase better services for a lower proportion of their income.

Labor Force Participation

Women's labor force participation in the formal economy partially reflects society's view of the appropriate role for women, with exceptions made for minority women. Minority women's historically disproportionate concentration in physically demanding work, typically lower-class women, was justified through defeminizing them (Davis, 1981; Maddox, 1991). Minority women vary among themselves to the extent that they participate in productive activity in the formal economy, indicating significant variation in traversing public places among minority women. Asian women have the highest labor force participation rates, followed closely by African-American women, whereas Latinas and Native-American women are least likely to be employed (Amott and Matthaei, 1991). Ratios of intra-ethnic men's employment to women's employment show that gender differences in the twentieth century have narrowed within all minority groups, though the gender gap remains widest for Latinas and Native-American women (Amott and Matthaei, 1991).

Occupational Sex Segregation

Women tend to recreate in the formal sphere what they produce in the informal sphere, demonstrating the blurring of public and private space among women. Occupational sex segregation has reduced income and prestige differences among ethnic women, though racism confers different returns to work and education. Asian women have the highest earnings, whereas African-American women and Latinas fall at the bottom of the wage scale (Amott and Matthaei, 1991). Women typically have lower levels of income and prestige than the men of their ethnicity, although gender differences are much narrower among African Americans. There remains a pervasive myth, especially believed of blacks (Benjamin, 1991), that the "double-minority" status of race- ethnicity and gender confers greater advantage in the workplace than among whites or minority men. The truth of the matter is revealed when considering social class.

Classism funnels women into a two-tiered service-based economic system, white-collar professionals (e.g., nurses and teachers) and unskilled service workers (e.g., child care and domestic service). African-American women have moved out of domestic service both in the formal and informal market, drawing unskilled immigrant women, typically Latinas, in to meet the increasing demand for domestic service. Women have different intergenerational mobility patterns than men, though this is not a ringing endorsement of assimilationism. Minority women achieve some mobility, opening up the bottom rung of the opportunity structure for the new migrant women. Feminists have some difficulty in reconciling the fact that a foreign-born woman may regard work as a nanny or cleaning woman to an economically privileged white woman as social mobility.

The level and adequacy of a minority woman's earnings and benefits issue in part from the sexism inherent in occupational sex segregation. Earnings and benefits are also shaped by classism and racism, forcing lower-income, full-time working minority women to supplement their meager earnings. The significantly lower wages of minority women relative to majority women for comparable work presses minority women to supplement an inadequate income stream with social support services. For example, more white women and children receive cash or services from the government than do women and children of color, however, the disproportionate prevalence of transfer payments among women and children of color draws public scrutiny. Growing recognition that a service-sensitive lifestyle may be transmitted intergeneration-ally (McLanahan, 1985) motivates reformers to base transfers on mothers' and children's preparation for, and participation in, the formal workforce, a process called "workfare."

SOCIAL ACTION

The social action of minority women responds to injustices in public and private places. The physical and economic well-being of women and their families compel them to act for survival, a form of social resistance. Social action may be aimed at national or supra-local change (e.g., civil rights movement), at change in one's community (e.g., environmental equity movements), and among intimate relationships (e.g., gender roles in primary relationships).

Macrolevel Action

Collective action takes place in the public arena, ranging from activities surrounding a local issue or a single community to those addressing multiple issues at a supra-local level. Women's multiple identities yield simultaneous urges to participate in multiple struggles. Polarization of the ethnic and feminist movements and finite amounts of disposable time and energy oblige women of color to embrace one struggle over another. The identity dilemma, one's primary identity is either gender or ethnic, translates into the liberation dilemma, one's primary goal is ethnic or gender equality.

Race and Ethnic Movements

Ethnic movements are intended to secure the integration of public places (Brisbane, 1976; Franklin and Moss, 1988) and expressed virtually no concern about integration of private places such as social associations and organizations, friendship networks, and families and households. Consequently, minority women and their issues often sat at the margins in the contemporary civil rights and cultural nationalism movements (Baca Zinn, 1975; Blauner, 1989; Chow, 1987; Davis, 1981; Dill, 1983; Garcia, 1989; hooks, 1984), although women shared in the deepening rediscovery and redefining of ethnic group identity. Minority women rarely filled leadership positions in the civil rights and cultural nationalism movements, and thus were not in a position to argue for items on a gendered agenda. When women did press for women's issues within the ethnic struggle, their ethnic identity was questioned. The fatigue from being stretched across public and private spaces inhibits women's gender struggle within ethnic movements.

When minority women's dual identity as woman and ethnic citizen conflict, some women stress ethnicity over gender. Ethnic liberation is equated with family survival, whereas gender liberation is equated with individual survival. Women's quest for full participation in public places is trivialized within all ethnic groups as more of a woman's preference for activities in public rather than private places and of less of a civil right. Ethnic liberation essentially calls for color-blind access to public places, a struggle implicitly treated as more important than gender-blind access to public places or gender equality in private places.

Contemporary Feminist Movement

The cultural nationalism and civil rights movements of the 1960s and 1970s evoked majority and minority women's interest in the contemporary feminist movement. Women's initial participation in the civil rights movement granted them practical experience in mobilizing for collective action, skills that transferred readily to the feminist movement. Minority women also joined the feminist movement in frustration with the gender-narrow ethnic movements. Different cultural heritages and local opportunity structures blend to produce ethnic variation in levels of gender and feminist consciousness and participation in the contemporary feminist movement.

The multiple identities of women of color, especially their ethnic pride and loyalty, prevented them from focusing exclusively on the struggle against sexism. Minority women's defeminization from racism interferes with formation of their identity as women, thus attenuating their motivation to join the feminist movement (hooks, 1981). The contemporary feminist movement diversified through mixed coalitions of racially and ethnically homogeneous organizations rather than through integration into a single organization (Giddings, 1984).

Integration into the movement and coalition building between white women's organizations and organizations of Chicana, black, Asian, and Native-American feminists were complicated by whites' belief that gender is a woman's primary identity, thus neglecting cultural identity and racial oppression (Cheng, 1984; Chow, 1987; Dill, 1983; Garcia, 1989; hooks, 1981). Moreover, the middle-class agenda of white feminists precluded full incorporation of issues salient to women of color such as an expansion of community services (Chow, 1987; Dill, 1983; Garcia, 1989; King, 1974). Despite a common concern with racism, sexism, and poverty, women of color tended to preserve their autonomous ethnic organizations, preferring to build minority, interethnic coalitions rather than a single minority organization (Chow, 1987; Garcia, 1989). Ethnic diversity within and among feminist groups generates distinct agendas for social change, further taxing coalition-building.

Mesolevel Action

The community provides a natural environment in which women of color flourish as social activists. The conspicuous social problems of ethnic neighborhoods, barrios, and reservations, communities typically abandoned by governing, protective, financial, and employment organizations, reflect women's social space in which public and private lives are most amalgamated. Minority community residents act collectively in response to concern over physical safety and neighborhood socioeconomic opportunity (Blauner, 1989; Pachon, Arguelles, and Gonzalez, 1994; Rodriguez, Elizondo, Mena, Rojas, Vasquez, and Yeverino, 1994; Valadez, 1994).

Women of color are motivated into community action to resolve social issues, such as educational system problems (Santiago-Santiago, 1987), although local groups tend to be ethnically homogeneous. For example, an analysis of the expansion of racial diversity in a local anti-rape movement concludes that women "successfully work together in mixed [race] coalitions when they have powerful common interests, but independent bases" (Matthews, 1989, p. 531). Minority women are the key actors in the effort to eradicate environmental racism, leading local groups in Austin, Texas, Chicago, Illinois, Emelle, Alabama and many other communities across the country. Some local groups' strategy is to secure sponsorship by the national environmental movement, joining macrolevel and mesolevel sites of action.

Microlevel Action

Racism and classism directly and indirectly influence sexual and social interactions. Scholarly oversight of gendered space underestimates the degree to which racism and sexism is prevalent. Yet assaults to physical and economic well-being occur in private places, generating injustices that may evoke social action. At the microlevel action is usually evoked in private places, rousing interest in minority women's experience with marriage, intermarriage, heterosexual gender roles between lovers, and intimate relations among women.

Between Lovers

Marriage and intermarriage reflect intra-ethnic and interethnic variation in gender relations and social class. For example, the higher marriage rates, earlier age at first marriage, and marital stability of Latinos and Asian Americans (Sweet and Bumpass, 1987) are posited to rest in ethnic gender norms that promote men's power over women. White, Latina, Asian-American, and Native-American women spend more time married than African-American women (Sweet and Bumpass, 1987). The unfavorable sex ratio in the African-American population has generated a "marriage squeeze" that leaves women unmarried for considerable lengths of adulthood. One interpretation of the African-American marriage squeeze declares that the very low sex ratio is a result of racism's killing or incarcerating black men. An alternative interpretation faults the classism of middle-class African-American women, who refuse to marry the plentiful, but less-educated black men.

Intermarriage reflects race and ethnic relations at a very intimate level. Intermarriage occurs as the direct effect of a racialized private space. Asian-American and Native-American women are most likely to marry exogamously (Sweet and Bumpass, 1987). In contrast, intermarriage rates are lowest for blacks, though men are more likely to marry exogamously than women (Snipp, 1989). During the 1980s, the intermarriage patterns of blacks and whites shifted. The intermarriage of black husbands and white wives declined as black men increasingly married women of color, whereas the proportion of black wife-white husband marriages increased as women married nonblack men (Spigner, 1990). Despite increasing levels of racial exogamy among black women, they remain frustrated by the preference of educated black men to marry white women (Benjamin, 1991).

Historically, Native-American and African-American gender relations have been more egalitarian than Euro-Americans, Asian Americans or Latinos (Hatchett, 1991; Ortiz and Cooney, 1984; Taylor, 1991). Indeed Native-American culture provides the basis for historical women's movement (Allen, 1986). Yet minority men cannot escape from enculturation into the patriarchal value of male dominance by struggling against racism. They subject minority women to sexism in private and public places. Women perform the majority of social reproductive tasks despite trends indicating men's widening attitudinal acceptance of a more egalitarian household division of labor (Ferree, 1979).

Concomitantly the increasing accommodation of women in public places and declining economic opportunities for minority men changes the nature of gender relations in private places. But these larger economic trends affect race and ethnic groups differently, owing to the larger concentration of minority populations at the lower levels of educational achievement. Occupational sex segregation and economic restructuring in the United States since the 1970s, has reduced employment opportunities for men with moderate or low levels of education, simultaneously creating opportunities for similarly educated women (Kuhn and Bluestone, 1987). Consequently, minority couples are negotiating intimate relationships under conditions in which the conventional gender roles of male breadwinner and female hearthtender are less valid, straining intimate relations (Blauner, 1989; Hanson, 1980; Franklin, 1984; Prieto, 1992; Safa, 1992; Ybarra, 1982; Zsembik and Peek, 1994). It remains unclear whether the increasing economic contributions of women to the household economy is evidence of liberation from microlevel patriarchy or further manifestation of the structural integration of classism, racism, and sexism (Baca Zinn, 1987; Zavalla, 1987; Zsembik and Peek, 1994).

Among Women

Minority-majority relationships among women are complicated by racism in general (Palmer, 1983), and sexual racism in particular. Women of color are at risk of sexual racism by white men, which strains relations among majority and minority women, and among white women and men (Davis, 1981). Women's own racism prevents interethnic friendships. While public places have become integrated, private places remain segregated. Women's shared occupational and family experiences are insufficient to forge intimacies across the racial divide. Women's informal referral networks, offering advice, mentorship, and opportunities, remain racially and ethnically homogenous.

SUMMARY AND CONCLUSIONS

Minority women, and their infants and children, continue to pay a physical price for class, race-ethnic, and gender inequality at the end of the twentieth century. The manifestation of race and ethnic conflict on the private place of the body demonstrates the gendered space of race and ethnic relations. Economic health is intertwined with physical well-being. Minority women disproportionately experience financial stress, largely observed in the interstices of private places. Racial, ethnic, class, and gender inequities in health and economics press women to act for social change for themselves and their children.

Despite the success of the civil rights and cultural nationalism movements, race and ethnic relations grow increasingly strained. For example, Latinos currently identify ethnic issues as the main problem the ethnic group faces, followed by educational issues and social problems (de la Garza, DeSipio, Garcia, Garcia, and Falcon, 1992). College students cite race and ethnic relations as one of the countries most pressing social problems, and enrollment in diversity classes is expanding. The younger generation of women and men, the so-called Generation X, prefers to envision itself as possessing a deeper awareness of racism and sexism than earlier generations. Ferree and Hess (1985) note that the most recent wave of the feminist movement has a broad class and ethnic base.

Yet the younger cohort face a different social climate than their parents and grandparents did. The integration of public places secured with the civil rights and cultural nationalism movements leaves the younger cohorts with the more intractable challenge of integrating the private spaces of friendship, family, and kinship networks. Women of color have been proposed as the bridge which will connect white women and women of color (hooks, 1989; Lourde, 1984). Consequently, the integration of racially-homogeneous women's organizations will permit movement toward improved race and ethnic relations in general. Recognizing and managing race and ethnic relations among women of color may be the natural starting place for building community among women (Anzaldua, 1992).

Following the thread of gendered space effectively demonstrates that women's struggle occurs across multiple situations in everyday life, activating one of several identities and implications for social action. More importantly, envisioning women's ethnic conflict across a gendered space stresses that there are subtle, yet chronic effects of race and ethnic conflict. Their marginal position provides women of color with a remarkable vantage point on gender, race, and ethnic experiences. Clearly there is a gendered nature to the intergenerational reproduction of sexism and racism as women remain child keepers. The arrangement of women's lives across public and private spaces highlights women's management of multiple, noncompartmentalized identities. Greater exposure to discrimination may endow women of color with a larger awareness of social injustice and a sharper motivation to struggle for justice. Perhaps women of color may indeed be the bridge which connects multiple coalitions.

REFERENCES

Anzaldua, G. 1992. "This Bridge Called my Back." In *Race, Class, and Gender in the United States* (2nd ed.), edited by P.S. Rothenberg. New York: St. Martin's Press.

Allen, P.G. 1986. *The Sacred Hoop.* Boston: Beacon Press.

Amott, T.L., and J.A. Matthaei. 1991. *Race, Gender, and Work: A Multicultural Economic History of Women in the United States.* Boston: South End Press.

Baca Zinn, M. 1975. "Political Familism: Toward Sex Role Equality in Chicano Families." *Aztlan* 6: 13-27.

Baca Zinn, M. 1982. "Urban Kinship and Midwest Chicano Families: Evidence in Support of Revision." *De Colores* 6: 85-98.

Baca Zinn, M. 1987. "Structural Transformation and Minority Families." Pp. 155-172 in *Women, Households, and the Economy*, edited by L. Beneria and C.R. Stimpson. New Brunswick, NJ: Rutgers University Press.

Bean, F.D., and M. Tienda. 1987. *The Hispanic Population of the United States.* New York: Russell Sage Foundation.

Beneria, L., and G. Sen. 1986. "Accumulation, Reproduction, and Women's Role in Economic Development: Boserup Revisited." Pp. 141-157 in *Women's Work: Development and the Division of Labor by Gender*, edited by E. Leacock, H.I. Safa, and contributors. New York: Bergin and Garvey.

Benjamin, L. 1991. *The Black Elite: Facing the Color Line in the Twilight of the Twentieth Century.* Chicago: Nelson-Hall Publishers.

Blau, F.D., and M.A. Ferber. 1986. *The Economics of Women, Men, and Work.* Englewood Cliffs, NJ: Greenwood Press.

Blauner, B. 1989. *Black Lives, White Lives: Three Decades of Race Relations in America.* Berkeley, CA: University of California Press.

Bradshaw, B.S., and E. Fonner. 1978. "The Mortality of Spanish-surnamed Persons in Texas: 1969-1971." Pp. 261-282 in *The Demography of Racial and Ethnic Groups*, edited by F.D. Bean and W.P. Frisbie. New York: Academic Press.

Brisbane, R.H. 1976. "Black Protest in America." Pp. 537-579 in *The Black American Reference Book*, edited by M.M. Smythe. Englewood Cliffs, NJ: Prentice-Hall.

Brown, S.S. 1988. *Prenatal Care: Reaching Mothers, Reaching Infants.* New York: Holmes and Meier.

Carr, B.A., and E.S. Lee. 1978. "Navajo Tribal Mortality: A Life Table Analysis of the Leading Causes of Death." *Social Biology* 24: 279-287.

Chavkin, W., C. Busner, and M. McLaughlin. 1987. "Reproductive Health: Caribbean Women in New York City." *International Migration Review* 21: 609-625.

Cheng, L. 1984. "Asian American Women and Feminism." *Sojourner* 10: 11-12.

Chow, E.N. 1987. "The Development of Feminist Consciousness among Asian American Women." *Gender & Society* 1: 284-299.

Cisneros, H.G. 1992. "Cooperative Action for Minority Health Policy." Pp.12-21 in *Health Policy and the Hispanic*, edited by A. Furino. Boulder, CO: Westview Press.

Collins, P.H. 1990. *Black Feminist Thought: Knowledge, Consciousness, and the Politics of Empowerment.* New York: Routledge.

Cramer, J.C. 1987. "Social Factors and Infant Mortality: Identifying High-risk Groups and Proximate Causes." *Demography* 24: 299-322.

Davis, A.Y. 1981. *Women, Race and Class.* New York: Vintage Books.

de la Garza, R.O., L. DeSipio, F.C. Garcia, J. Garcia, and A. Falcon. 1992. *Latino Voices: Mexican, Puerto Rican, and Cuban Perspectives on American Politics.* Boulder, CO: Westview Press.

Deloria, V., Jr. 1981. "Identity and Culture." *Daedalus* 110.

Dill, B.T. 1983. "Race, Class, and Gender: Prospects for an Inclusive Sisterhood." *Feminist Studies* 9: 131-150.

Ehrenreich, B. 1983. *The Hearts of Men: American Dreams and the Flight from Commitment.* Garden City, NY: Anchor Press/Doubleday.

Ferree, M.M. 1979. "Employment without Liberation: Cuban Women in the United States." *Social Science Quarterly* 60: 35-50.

Ferree, M.M., and B.B. Hess. 1985. Controversy and Coalition: *The New Feminist Movement.* Boston: Twayne Publishers.

Forbes, D., and W.P. Frisbie. 1991. "Spanish Surname and Anglo Infant Mortality: Differentials over a Half-century." *Demography* 28: 639-660.

Franklin, C. 1984. *The Changing Definition of Masculinity.* New York: Plenum.

Franklin, J.H., and A.A. Moss, Jr. 1988. *From Slavery to Freedom: A History of a Negro Americans* (6th ed.). New York: McGraw-Hill.

Fuentes, A., and B. Ehrenreich. 1981. *Women in the Global Factory.* Boston: South End Press.

Garcia, A.M. 1989. "The Development of Chicana Feminist Discourse." *Gender & Society* 3: 217-238.

Giddings, P. 1984. *When and Where I Enter: The Impact of Black Women on Race and Sex in America.* New York: Bantam.

Hanson, W. 1980. "The Urban Indian Woman and her Family." *Social Casework: The Journal of Contemporary Social Work* 61: 476-483.

Hatchett, S. 1991. "Women and Men." Pp. 84-104 in *Life in Black America,* edited by J. Jackson. Newbury Park, CA: Sage.

Hershberg, T., A.N. Burstein, E.P. Ericksen, S. Greenberg, and W.L. Yancey. 1991. "A Tale of Three Cities: Blacks, Immigrants, and Opportunity in Philadelphia: 1850-1880, 1930, and 1970." Pp. 185-208 in *Majority and Minority: The Dynamics of Race and Ethnicity in American Life,* edited by N.R. Yetman. Boston: Allyn and Bacon.

hooks, b. 1981. *Ain't I a Woman: Black Women and Feminism.* Boston: South End Press.

hooks, b. 1984. *Feminist Theory: From Margin to Center.* Boston: South End Press.

hooks, b. 1989. *Talking Back: Thinking Feminist, Thinking Black.* Boston: South End Press.

Jaynes, G.D., and R.M. Williams. 1989. *A Common Destiny: Blacks and American Society.* Washington, DC: National Academy Press.

Jones, W.J., and M.F. Rice. 1987. "Black Health Care: An Overview." In *Health care issues in Black America: Policies, Problems and Prospects,* edited by W.J. Jones and M.F. Ricez. Westport, CT: Greenwood Press.

Kallan, J.E. 1993. "Race, Intervening Variables, and Two Components of Low Birth Weight." *Demography* 30: 489-506.

King, M.L. 1974. "Puertorriquenas in the United States: The Impact of Double Discrimination." *Civil Rights Digest* 6: 20-26.

Kuhn, S., and B. Bluestone. 1987. "Economic Restructuring and the Female Labor Market: The Impact of Industrial Change on Women." Pp. 3-32 in *Women, Households, and the Economy,* edited by L. Beneria and C.R. Stimpson. New Brunswick, NJ: Rutgers University Press.

Lawson, E.J., and A. Thompson. 1994. "The Health Status of Black Women: A Historical Perspective and Current Trends." Pp. 278-296 in *The Black Family: Essays and Studies*, edited by R. Staples. Belmont, CA: Wadsworth.

Lourde, A. 1984. *Sister Outsider*. Trumansberg, NY: The Crossing Press.

Lubben, J.E., and R.M. Becerra. 1987. "Social Support Among Black, Mexican, and Chinese Elderly." Pp. 130-144 in *Ethnic Dimensions of Aging*, edited by D.E. Gelfand and C.M. Barresci. New York: Springer.

McLanahan, S. 1985. "Family Structure and the Reproduction of Poverty." *American Journal of Sociology* 90: 873-901.

Maddox, L. 1991. "Bearing the Burden: Perceptions of Native American Women at Work." *Women: A Cultural Review* 2: 228-237.

Manton, K.G. 1980. "Sex and Race Specific Mortality Differentials in Multiple Cause of Death Data." *Gerontologist* 20: 480-493.

Manton, K.G., S.S. Poss, and S. Wing. 1979. "The Black/White Mortality Crossover: Investigation from the Perspective of the Components of Aging." *Gerontologist* 19: 291-300.

Matthews, N.A. 1989. "Surmounting a Legacy: The Expansion of Racial Diversity in a Local Anti-rape Movement." *Gender & Society* 3: 518-532.

National Council of La Raza. 1991. *On the Sidelines: Hispanic Elderly and the Continuum of Care*. New York: National Council of La Raza.

National Institute of Medicine. 1986. *Preventing Low Birthweight*. Washington, DC: National Academy Press.

O'Carroll, P.W., and J.A. Mercy. 1986. "Patterns and Recent Trends in Black Homicide." Pp. 29-42 in *Homicide among Black Americans*, edited by D.F. Hawkins. Lanham, MD: University Press of America.

Ortiz, V., and R.S. Cooney. 1984. "Sex-role Attitudes and Labor Force Participation among Young Hispanic Females and Non-Hispanic White Females." *Social Science Quarterly* 65: 392-400.

Pachon, H., and L. Arguelles, with R. Gonzalez. 1994. "Grass-roots Politics in an East Los Angeles Barrio: A Political Ethnography of the 1990 General Election." In *Barrio Ballots: Latino Politics in the 1990 Elections*, edited by R.O. de la Garza, M. Menchaca, and L. DeSipio. Boulder, CO: Westview Press.

Palmer, P.M. 1983. "White Women/Black Women: The Dualism of Female Identity and Experience." *Feminist Studies* 1: 151-170.

Pol, L.G., and R.K. Thomas. 1992. *The Demography of Health and Health Care*. New York: Plenum.

Powell-Griner, E. 1988. "Differences in Infant Mortality among Texas Anglos, Hispanics, and Blacks." *Social Science Quarterly* 69: 452-467.

Prieto, Y. 1992. "Cuban Women in New Jersey: Gender Relations and Change." Pp. 185-201 in *Seeking Common Ground: Multidisciplinary Studies of Immigrant Women in the United States*, edited by D. Gabaccia. Westport, CT: Greenwood Press.

Rodriguez, C.E. 1991. *Puerto Ricans Born in the U.S.A.* Boulder, CO: Westview Press.

Rodriguez, N.P., N. Elizondo, D. Mena, R. Rojas, A. Vasquez, and F. Yeverino. 1994. "Political Mobilization in Houston's Magnolia." In *Barrio Ballots: Latino Politics in the 1990 Elections*, edited by R.O. de la Garza, M. Menchaca, and L. DeSipio. Boulder, CO: Westview Press.

Safa, H.I. 1992. "Development and Changing Gender Roles in Latin America and the Caribbean." Pp. 63-79 in *Women's Work and Women's Lives: The Continuing Struggle Worldwide*, edited by H. Kahne and J.Z. Giele. Boulder: Westview Press.

Santiago-Santiago, I. 1987. "Aspira v. Board of Education Revisited." *American Journal of Education* 95.

Snipp, C.M. 1989. *American Indians: The First of this Land.* New York: Russell Sage Foundation.

Spigner, C. 1990. "Black/White Interracial Marriages: A Brief Overview of U.S. Census Data, 1980-1987." *The Western Journal of Black Studies* 14: 214-216.

Stacey, J., and B. Thorne. 1985. "The Missing Feminist Revolution in Sociology." *Social Problems* 32: 301-316.

Stack, C. 1974. *All our Kin: Strategies for Survival in a Black Community.* New York: Harper and Row.

Steinmetz, S.K., and J. Pellicciaro. 1986. "Women, Ethnicity, and Family Violence: Implications for Social Policy. Pp. 206-223 in *Ethnicity and Women,* edited by W.A. Van Horne and T.V. Tonnesen. Madison, WI: University of Wisconsin System.

Sumaya, C.V. 1992. "Major Infectious Diseases Causing Excess Morbidity in the Hispanic Population." Pp.76-96 in *Health Policy and the Hispanic,* edited by A. Furino. Boulder, CO: Westview Press.

Sweet, J.A., and L.L. Bumpass. 1987. *American Families and Households.* New York: Russell Sage Foundation.

Takaki, R. 1989. *Strangers from a Different Shore: A History of Asian Americans.* Boston: Little, Brown and Company.

Taylor, R.J. 1988. "Aging and Supportive Relationships among Black Americans." Pp. 259-281 in *The Black American Elderly: Research on Physical and Psychological Health,* edited by J.S. Jackson, P. Newton, A. Ostfield, D. Savage, and E.L. Schneider. New York: Springer.

Taylor, R.L. 1991. "Childrearing in African-American Families." Pp. 119-155 in *Child Welfare: An Africentric Perspective,* edited by J. Everett, S. Chipungu, and B. Leashore. Princeton, NJ: Rutgers University Press.

U.S. Public Health Service. 1990. *Healthy People 2000: National Health Promotion and Disease Prevention Objective.* Washington, DC: Department of Health and Human Services.

Valadez, J. 1994. "Latino politics in Chicago: Pilsen in the 1990 General Election." In *Barrio Ballots: Latino Politics in the 1990 Elections,* edited by R.O. de la Garza, M. Menchaca, and L. DeSipio. Boulder, CO: Westview Press.

Wagner, R., and D. Shaffer. 1980. "Social Networks and Survival Strategies: An Exploratory Study of Mexican-American, Black and Anglo Female Family Heads in San Jose, California." Pp. 173-190 in *Twice a Minority: Mexican American Women in the United States,* edited by M. Melville. St. Louis: CV Mosby.

Wallace, E.C. 1981. "Housing for the Black Elderly: The Need Remains." In *Community Housing Choices for Older Americans,* edited by M. P. Lawton and S.L. Hoover. New York: Springer.

Ybarra, L. 1982. "When Wives Work: The Impact of on the Chicano Family." *Journal of Marriage and the Family* 44: 169-178.

Zavella, P. 1987. *Women's Work and Chicano Families.* Ithaca: Cornell University Press.

Zsembik, B.A., and C.W. Peek. 1994. "The Effect of Economic Restructuring on Puerto Rican Women's Labor Force Participation in the Formal Sector." *Gender & Society* 8: 525-540.

RACIAL AND ETHNIC CONFLICT:
HUMAN GEOGRAPHIC PERSPECTIVES

Richard L. Morrill, Harold M. Rose, and Judith Kenny

INTRODUCTION

The year 1993 was marked by an intense consciousness of racial and ethnic identity. Newspaper headlines often were dominated by racial and ethnic conflict, from the Rodney King beating trial to ethnic cleansing in Bosnia, from a rising backlash against "unwanted" immigrants in the United States, Europe, and other parts of the world, the retreat from mandatory busing, and a question of the efficacy of affirmative racial gerrymandering to black-on-black conflict in South Africa on the eve of their rise to power sharing.

Race and ethnicity are primary human categories that continuously influence individual and collective behavior. Even within those territories where historical racial tensions were observed to have abated, periodic outbursts continue to occur. Primordial bonds are much more difficult to minimize than had been earlier thought. This raises the question—why does race and ethnicity loom so important within and between countries? What makes it so "real?" How is the fact of racial and ethnic identity played out in the geographic landscape? And to what extent have geographers documented the conflict growing out of racial and ethnic tensions?

Research in Human Social Conflict, Volume 1, pages 275-300.
ISBN: 1-55938-923-0

In this paper, we will briefly examine selected aspects of race and ethnicity that have often led to the promotion of conflict and tension in the United States: first, how the categories became institutionalized; second, a review of the dilemma of pluralism and assimilation in the context of the heritage of slavery and of ethnic immigration; and third, the impact of race and ethnicity on the landscape through spatial separation or segregation. There is no space in this brief chapter to treat such important topics as geographic aspects, or tools to address racial and ethnic discrimination and conflict, or the politics of racial and ethnic representation.

It should be noted that few geographers have devoted attention to these issues. As a consequence, these topics are frequently overlooked in introductory human and cultural geography texts and are often only superficially treated in some advanced texts in the field. Yet a small cadre of geographic researchers have been involved in addressing selected issues that are known to promote racial and ethnic tension. While racial and ethnic diversity in general has been observed to produce tension, it is the black-white relationship that is probably the single most important definer of status in America after the individualist social system itself. And it is this relationship that has transcended all others in terms of its potential for conflict.

Gunnar Myrdal long ago recognized this in his classic *An American Dilemma*. Except in remote rural areas of the North, race is an obsession, a pervasive element of our social, economic, political, and cultural life. Along with income, race relations are the major insoluble aspect of inequality in America. The word "insoluble" was used deliberately. The honest social scientist, even the optimistic radical, has to be sobered by the reality and depth of this dilemma. But this does not mean that relations have not improved and cannot be relieved.

THE PHYSICAL AND THE SOCIAL CONSTRUCTION OF RACE AND ETHNICITY

What we call "race" and "ethnicity" are the products of hundreds of thousands of years of human evolution and interaction with the environment. It is true that what is popularly perceived as "race" emphasizes differences in external appearance, essentially skin color. For example, in the United States, broad groupings of "white," "black or African American," "Asian," and "Native American" are employed to describe the notion of racial diversity. The ambiguity of these categories is demonstrated by the millions of people who responded to the census by answering "other." How do Latin Americans who are a mixture of European and Indian respond to the standard census question? Individuals who may be three-quarters "white" genetically are classed as "black" if there is any doubt concerning their racial identity. Even though one's race is self-identified for the census, persons tend to accept a color-coded, socially defined category.

In the biological sciences race has long been dismissed as a meaningful concept, yet it remains in common usage as a metaphor for difference (see Gates, 1986). Racial categories, in popular opinion, are based on genetically transmitted characteristics which imply the presence or absence of certain socially relevant traits. As such, racial identities are imposed by the more powerful group on the less powerful.

These beliefs, or racism, are composed of interrelated ideologies and practices that have profound material consequences. The research of several social geographers has recently focused on significantly different racisms, each of which are historically specific and expressive of the societies in which they appear (Jackson, 1987). Some forms of racism are based in terms of cultural rather than purely physical definitions of difference. A recent survey of research conducted on the institutional and territorial expressions of racism (see Jackson, 1987) includes an examination of relationships of the Irish community in London and the mythical nature of Irish stupidity (Chance, 1987) as well as segregation and beliefs in Asian business success (Cator and Jones, 1987), Puerto Rican docility (Jackson, 1987), and the indolence of Southern blacks (Silk, 1987).

Ethnicity, in contrast, is commonly interpreted as evolving among broad racial, religious, or language groups sharing territory within a single national state. By far, the strongest definers of ethnicity are language and religion, but certainly ethnic status is not confined to these attributes. Ethnic identities are stable or fleeting as a joint function of the group's acceptance by the host society and/or its tendency to cling to those cultural attributes that distinguish it from the other, broader society. Because of this, ethnic assimilation takes place slowly or rapidly as outgrowth of both external pressures and/or internal needs. Ethnicity is often heightened when the broader society is guilty of engaging in oppressive and stigmatizing behavior.

GEOGRAPHY, HISTORY, AND RACE

When it is asked how race and ethnicity arose, the answer is essentially geographic. Environmental differences and sheer physical separation influenced the development of various physical adaptations to conditions such as levels of solar radiation. These adaptive characteristics were then further modified by population migration and interaction. The significant biological adaptations that mark the distinctions between Caucasoid, Mongoloid, and Negroid groups evolved during prehistoric periods.

When it is asked how race has been represented by society, the answer is related to both geography and history. The social construction of race has a complex history and evolving nature. As summarized by Sivandan:

Racism does not stay still; it changes shape, size, contours, purpose, function—with changes
in the economy, the social structure, the system and, above all, the challenges, the resistances
to that system (Sivandan, 1983, p. 132).

As indicated previously, racial categories are representations constructed by
dominant groups. Demonstrating this, assumptions of "white" superiority
appear to date from the last 500 years of European-led technological, economic,
and military change and domination. As one historian has described this
"ascendancy," Europeans viewed "machines as the measure of men" with the
growing strength of Western science and technology (Adas, 1989).

European contact with other peoples theoretically offered the options of
responding to the "Other" in terms of identity or difference. Henri Baudet has
traced the changing image of Europe's "Other" over the centuries,
demonstrating that it has not been uniformly a negative one (Baudet, 1965).
By charting the changes in direction, Baudet's analysis emphasized the
relational aspects of representation.

Said's (1979) analysis of the sciences' nineteenth-century contribution to
racial stereotyping has been embraced by both historical and cultural
geographers (e.g., Livingstone, 1992: Kenny, 1991). Livingstone's summary of
the discipline of geography in the nineteenth-century discipline revealed an
"evolutionary-inspired marriage of society and environment" (Livingstone,
1992, p. 193). Environmental determinism did not create racism but provided
additional, scientific support for interpretations of a human racial history that
already tied race and region. The "indelible mark" of climate, it was taught,
tied physiological characteristics together with psychological and moral
qualities. A representative assessment of "climate's moral economy" which
stated: "...none of these tropical peoples...has a native civilisation, or is fitted
to play any part in history..." (cited in Livingstone, 1992, p. 224). Standard
texts in climatology (Miller, 1931) and human geography (Huntington, 1924)
legitimized this link between racial character and the environment well into
this century.

THE NATURE OF AND THE CREATION OF RACIAL AND ETHNIC CONFLICT

Contact between different racial and ethnic groups occurred as peoples had
to move to better environments, or as they conquered and settled or were
conquered and settled by others. The heritage of U.S. racial and ethnic conflict
stems, perhaps especially, from the rise of European exploration and then trade
and colonization. Europeans, perhaps in part to justify conquest, colonization,
and enslavement, transformed a technical and military advantage into a general

notion of white superiority across all aspects of life, a myth that continues to be supported by an almost universal adherence to values of Western origin.

The settlement and development of what has become the United States was from the very start steeped in racial conflict—wars against the "native savages" control of and dependence on a vast army of slaves brought from Africa. Viewing other races as less than fully human appeared to justify both extermination and enslavement.

The roots of white ethnic conflict were embedded in the long prior history of wars between the states of Europe that revolved around questions of territory, of resources, and religious conflict. A kind of "rank order" of ethnic quality, as prevailed at the turn of the century in the United States, appeared to have a dual basis: first, the degree of "difference" from the English norm, and second, a technical and economic hierarchy—conveniently arraying groups from English, Scots, and Dutch down to Eastern European Jews, Bulgarians, and Gypsies.

More deeply, it may be argued that the basis for viewing others as inferior (and the degree of inferiority) is the very fact of difference, to ward off the slightest possibility that other colors, languages, or religions might be even as good as one's own required that they be labeled inferior. Racial and ethnic tension and conflict became aggravated when the "lesser" group was seen as a threat to the "dominant" group.

GEOGRAPHIC FORMS OF RACIAL AND ETHNIC CONFLICT

Geography deals with how people compete for, and use territory, how they create community or place, and how and why they move. Not surprisingly, over time and at present, by far the main conflict among races and ethnic groups is over land, and especially over a group's autonomy in a place or area. The Bosnian dispute is a representative example. Unequal power leads to attempts by stronger groups to displace weaker groups. Racial and ethnic groups may also have conflicts over geographic access—to resources, services, transportation, jobs, and markets. Dominant groups may try to restrict the mobility of minority groups. They may be able to restrict the economic development and income potential of areas where minority races or looked-down-upon ethnic groups reside. Separation and external hostility may lead to withdrawal, harassment, despair, and acceptance of "second-class citizenship."

A common perception of the more powerful groups is that their power, well-being, and real income will be eroded by the presence of inferior groups, and that "natural segregation" of groups will reduce conflict, by keeping competing or hostile groups apart. On the other hand, some scholars of social history might argue that the separation itself maintains ignorance and breeds distrust and hostility, and that conflict would be more readily resolved if diverse peoples had more contact and interacted within common environments.

It may seem especially advantageous for the dominant group to encourage an acceptance of patterns of spatial separation on grounds of the sanctity of cultural pluralism, as that would lead the subdominant group itself to indirectly help perpetuate the continuation of unequal status—for example, the dilemma associated with the persistence of native American Indian reservations.

THE U.S. HERITAGE OF RACE AND ETHNICITY: SLAVERY AND ASSIMILATION

American history, from the beginning, is a story in which race and ethnicity loom large. The very act of settlement and its spread began the drama of conflict with Native Americans, the "Indians." From 1619 to the present, from the time of initial arrival of blacks in this country, black-white conflict has been a central part of the American experience. Any potential guilt associated with the virtual genocide of American Indians and for enslavement of blacks was warded off by assumptions of the inherent inferiority of the other races.

The new country incorporated numerous groups of European origin, and continued to be fairly tolerant of continuing immigration; after all, most were Northern European and Protestant, and were willing to embrace and enrich a consensus Anglo-Saxon culture. But it was more the pragmatic need for sheer numbers of bodies—to defend the fledgling country, to expand settlement west to ward off additional colonies or countries; and later to supply huge reserves of labor for a burgeoning capitalist economy; plus the sheer abundance of land and resources, that led the country to adopt a liberal immigration policy throughout most of its subsequent history. Labor demands and the pressure for migration from then impoverished and overpopulated European countries were so great that groups came or were recruited from parts of Europe that had not previously provided large numbers of immigrants. The potential for racial/ethnic conflict was enhanced as Eastern and Southern Europeans arrived just ahead of black migrants from the American South. Since the U.S. Constitution guaranteed unfettered movement for free whites, it was inevitable that ethnic groups would try to occupy the same territories, compete for space, and thereby fuel the potential for ethnic conflict.

The American frontier was always the zone of the most overt conflict between whites and native American Indians—not only the series of Indian wars, but also the present day confrontational relations typical throughout most of the country. The proximate cause of most conflict and war has been competition for land (and its resources), although underlying the territorial tension has always been the bald reality of conquest and near extermination, leaving only the semblance of continuing nationhood.

Dominant white policies toward the native American Indians has been explicitly geographic, and subsequently paternalistic. Military actions were used to remove tribes from areas desirable for white settlement, and peoples were either forcibly removed from their accustomed areas in which they had developed and survived, or restricted to a small remnant, or reservation, of the former territory, usually of marginal economic value as well as geographically inaccessible. Then when it proved impossible either to maintain a traditional way of life on an inadequate and inappropriate base, or to assimilate into the white culture and economy, because of inaccessibility and discrimination, the failure was interpreted by the white majority as proof of "wardship," or a dependent relationship. (What a legacy for resentment, distrust and conflict!)

But the experience of the slaves from Africa, now African Americans or blacks, was yet worse. Even though the Indians were defeated, they had been able to fight, retained some land, and a degree of legal autonomy. African slaves were, by definition, without rights, mere property for use and transfer. Especially in the United States, slaves were forcibly stripped of their language and partially stripped of other overt aspects of their former cultures, though not entirely. These populations were also often denied traditional family relationships; nevertheless, the slave family has been shown to have been far less disorganized than earlier historical accounts had pictured it (Gutman, 1976).

The geography of slavery was one of mainly rural dispersion across a commercial agricultural landscape, largely made up of plantations, where the slaves were usually housed in separate quarters, but not far from the place of residence of their white owners (Joyner, 1984). The immense legal gap maintained a "distance" between superior and inferior. The immense gap in the legal rights of owners and their slaves maintained the distance between them. The slaves were effectively immobile, with no rights of movement, although there is evidence that some slaves did escape and/or purchased their freedom, whereas others rebelled against their status as slaves (Blassingame, 1972).

It is important to recall that this legal slavery prevailed for more than 200 years, from 1660 to 1865, compared to only half that time since emancipation; such a heritage of legally defined and enforced inferiority, absence of rights, and arbitrary manipulation of peoples' lives and relationships, remains the underlying basis for continuing racial conflict today. This heritage of suppression makes the changes of the last 25 years seem fairly remarkable and encouraging. Some may thus believe that prejudice is on the way out, but the slow pace in the development of primary relations between the races belies that assumption.

But the Civil War did not pretend to thrust the "Negroes" into the American mainstream. Instead, there were at least another hundred years (1865-1964) of legal and extra-legal forms of discrimination and suppression, much of which was supported by the so-called "Jim Crow" laws. Much of this discrimination was geographic. While, as citizens, blacks could in theory move, their mobility was restricted in many ways. Many blacks were sharecroppers on former southern plantations; if in debt to the owners, as most were, they could not leave the county. Yet many slipped away during "the dead of night" and headed north for the mythical promised land (Henri, 1975; Grossman, 1989; Marks, 1989).

"Jim Crow" or "petty apartheid" laws restricted access to schools, transportation, public services, accommodations, ensuring that the races lived in distinct "spaces," superior and inferior. But the main geographic tool for maintaining the superiority-inferiority relationship and for ensuring adequate distance was through spatial segregation, restricting ownership and where blacks could live, and in the North as well as the South. This will be discussed in detail later, as it remains a dominant arena for interracial conflict.

Blacks did gradually leave the South in anticipation of a better life in the North. Although some fugitive slaves moved north on the "underground railroad" prior to the Civil War, the first large flows were initiated by the "great migration" (1914-1920) in response to opportunities opened up in northern industries by white mobilization and the curtailment of European immigration during World War I. The extreme concentration in a few large and easily reachable northern cities, for example, New York, Chicago, Philadelphia, Pittsburgh, and St. Louis, suggests the severity of prejudice and discrimination faced, so that only the anonymous slums permitted a grudging entry. The next, even larger northward and westward migration reinforcing the metropolitan ghettos took place during World War II, as industrial opportunities again opened, and continued until the mid-1970s (Johnson and Campbell, 1981). Blacks moved, as well, to growing southern towns and cities and later metropolitan areas, as discrimination lessened. Since 1975, the flow of blacks out of the South has slowed and return movement to the region now exceeds outmovement (McHugh, 1987).

The restrictions on access to parks and beaches, schools and hospitals, and constraints on the right to vote, were sources of recurring conflict, and occasionally of major demonstrations and severe riots, for example, the Detroit riots of 1944 were set off by a beach incident. (But they were also the route by which civil rights for racial minorities began to be taken seriously. It was almost always a combination of patient litigation, large scale demonstration, and increasing unrest, culminating in riot and destruction of property that was required to obtain meaningful change—that is, provoking rather than avoiding conflict, because working through the courts was not enough to compel a shift in societal attitudes.) For example, arrests from illegal use of "white" facilities, loss of jobs, or even death by lynching for daring to register to vote, and arrests for picketing discriminatory realtors were all prerequisite to the civil rights advances of the 1960s. The Montgomery bus boycott, 1955, helped initiate an era of change, and more rapid change was triggered by such events as the 1963 March on Washington, the site of the Reverend Martin Luther King's "I Have a Dream" speech.

The experience of Asian racial minorities was distinct from that of blacks and American Indians. Chinese, Korean, Filipino, Japanese, and other groups were imported as contract laborers to the West at selected times of perceived labor shortage between 1850 and 1930 to work on the farms and forests, or mines and railroads. Although not intended to become permanent residents, except in Hawaii, a territory where they could be kept from power, many did gradually gain citizenship. They were subjected to similar, if not so severe, restraints as blacks, including restrictions on land ownership, residential segregation, even occasional riots against them and expulsion from communities. The internment of Japanese Americans to "relocation centers" during World War II was one of the most extreme demonstrations of racial prejudice in U.S. history.

But a critical psychological difference was that they had usually been invited rather than forcibly enslaved, and that some of their countries (e.g., China, Japan) had never been conquered. As a result, their struggles for greater equality began from a higher position of self-esteem.

But for all these racial minorities, the reality of life has been one of "second-classness," or of belonging to distinct strata of society. They were all expected to conform to the dominant Anglo-Saxon cultural norm, yet could not expect to reap the full potential rewards of truly free movement, economic equality, or the right to live where they chose.

The story of white ethnic groups has been fundamentally different, because they had all been assumed not only to adopt Anglo-cultural norms, but then to be able to obtain those rewards by fully assimilating, both economically and geographically, or residentially. The reality was not quite so simple, of course, and white ethnic groups have varied in the degree of assimilation versus retention of cultural distinctiveness and geographic segregation. But such distinctiveness or segregation was somewhat voluntary in the end, and the possibility of full integration existed for most. As suggested at the start, the greater the perceived "difference" in appearance (color shading?) or culture, the greater the barriers to such assimilation. Assimilation was far easier and quicker for Protestant Northern Europeans than for Southern and Eastern European Catholics, than, in turn, for European Jews, and today, for Latin Americans, who may be "not quite" white.

It is true that each ethnic group, as it arrived in significant numbers, was subject to discrimination and was residentially segregated, and often relegated to the worst inner-city slums. Each experienced a period of accommodation and gradual assimilation, preserving nonthreatening attributes, but abandoning or softening modes which hindered success in the American mainstream. But other races could not change the distinctive appearance that was seen as a threat to white well-being.

Ethnic conflict in the United States never approached the level of warfare or even of severe riot or property destruction, as was characteristic of Northern Ireland or Lebanon or Bosnia. Conflict tended to be quite local, and expressed in the form of ephemeral youth gangs, or of unrest at the workplace, especially in times of economic downturn, as new groups were willing to work for less than more established groups.

Discrimination, in the workplace and residentially, was undoubtedly great(est) against Jews, since they (most) overtly differed from the Christian norm. But the resolution of this ethnic discrimination, although again not until the 1950s or 1960s in many cases, came via court litigation or legislative action, without the necessary recourse to civil disobedience and riot.

Among ethnic whites, then, class was a far greater mediator or enabler than for racial groups. Economic and linguistic "success" was the passport to assimilation in the workplace and community, but such success has not yet enabled assimilation of racial minorities, especially blacks.

RACIAL AND ETHNIC SEGREGATION

Racial Segregation

Every major American city and hundreds of smaller ones have distinct racial and/or ethnic communities (Rose, 1971, 1972). These residentially segregated areas house the large majority of the 30 million blacks, and probably half the 22 million Hispanics, and up to half the 7 million Asians. These areas constitute the geographic expression of the combined operation of racially discriminatory forces and personal choice. The weight assigned to the contribution of these forces differs among individual scholars. Among geographers, Darden (see Darden, 1987) would assign the bulk of the weight to the former, while Clark (see Clark, 1986, 1991) currently favors the latter explanation. Regardless of the combination of forces responsible for the spatial evolution of ghettos, they reflect the existence of inequality.

The term "ghetto" originally referred to the distinct, often walled area of medieval European cities set aside for Jews. Black communities in the United States best fit the definition of ghettos in the present context because of the power of outside forces to contain them and of inside forces to sustain them. Ghettos are universally found in large central cities, extending in a sector or wedge (or more than one) from near the downtown outward, and increasingly spilling over into older suburbs in a growing number of metropolitan areas (Rose, 1976). Because of discrimination over time, they are usually initially sited in less desirable sectors, intermingled with industry, railways, and other noxious nonresidential activity.

Ghettos are disproportionately characterized by high levels of poverty and older housing, although like the historic Jewish ghettos, they usually contain all classes within their borders and thus possess a full array of amenity and disamenity attributes. For example, the Chicago southside ghetto extends from destitution in the north to affluence in the south, and the Los Angeles ghetto from abject poverty in the east to a group of prosperous areas in the west. The poverty sector of the ghetto is remarkably deficient in services, jobs, and stores; a growing number of the stores are operated by recently arrived immigrants, that is, Asians, Arabs, and so on, from outside the community. Much housing is also owned by people from outside, and like a colony, workers and income flow outside. Inside there is a dual or second economy, with both bartering and unrecorded transactions, both legitimate and illegitimate, taking place. Crime levels are high in large areas of the ghetto, a condition that some perceive as being officially tolerated.

In the 1980s some ghetto populations became more polarized economically, deepening levels of despair are said to have supported the emergence of zones of so-called underclass residence. The expansion of zones of concentrated urban poverty (> 40% poor) has led some researchers to confine their definition of the ghetto to areas satisfying that criterion (Wilson, 1991; Jargowsky and Bane, 1991). Hughes, a geographer, has indicated his opposition to this simplistic labeling. The scale of these zones of despair varies substantially between metropolitan areas as a function of employment opportunity.

The Chicago "Southside" is often viewed as a classic black ghetto (Figure 1). Comparing its character to that of Cook County as a whole, reveals the degree of disparity and the severity of deprivation. Unemployment rates are four times that of the region (19 versus 4.5), and for males six times. Poverty rates are five times that of whites in the region (33 versus 6.5), and the proportion of female-headed households six times as great (21 versus 3.5). Values of homes are one-half that of Cook County. Levels of college are one-third (10 versus 29), and infant mortality rates triple that of the wider community. Tremendous losses of jobs and of businesses have occurred over time—in part because retail and service outlets fail as local incomes decline, a fact associated with the relocation of industry to the suburbs and/or the increasing automation of jobs, in part because of crime, and in part from discrimination, whether intentional or inadvertent. This results in high unemployment, ignorance of possible opportunities elsewhere, that is, the so-called spatial mismatch, and long or difficult commutes to distant suburban jobs (see Orfield, 1991).

How segregated are American cities? The answer to this question in large measure depends on the scale at which measurement is conducted and the measure of segregation employed to assess levels of segregation. At smaller spatial scales, segregation will usually show higher levels than when evaluating at a larger scale, regardless of measure used.

Percent Black in Chicago and Cook Country—1990

Percent Latino in Chicago and Cook Country—1990

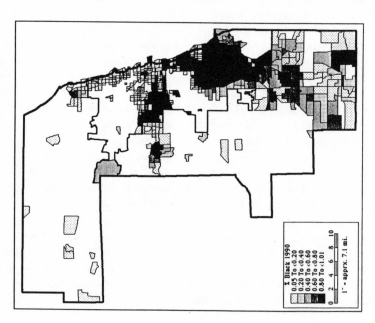

Figure 1.

Segregation is usually defined as the spatial separation of groups on the basis of race, ethnicity, or class. Most measurements are structural—that is, they measure concentration of groups in territories, but a few are spatial and measure the probability of contact between groups. Most measurement is indebted to the scale developed by Duncan and Duncan (1955) in the 1950s, and its subsequent use by the Taeubers in the 1960s (1965), to demonstrate the intensity of black residential segregation in U.S. cities. Duncan's index of dissimilarity (D) continues to dominate among measures employed for this purpose. It measures the degree to which a group is concentrated or overrepresented in particular areas. It is interpreted as the proportion of the minority population that would have to move for all areas to have the same proportion minority.

The more recent work of Massey and Denton (1993), utilizing data from the 1980 and 1990 census, demonstrates the continuing utility of the index of dissimilarity. In the years since the appearance of Duncan's index, a number of additional indexes have emerged that are often used to complement the earlier measure. The more widely used among these newer measures is the index of exposure, an asymmetrical index that measures the degree to which a group dominates or shares particular territories, for example, it is the percent black experienced by the average black person. It does recognize that segregation is different for the minority and for the majority—that is, if there are more whites, they will be more segregated (have less exposure). The proximity or spatial interaction index was developed to measure the probability of contact as a function of spatial separation of groups, and is a measure of the proportion of interaction of blacks, for example, that is within the group.

How segregated are American cities? Comparisons using D, the index of dissimilarity, show for the 1990s, values in the range of 70 to 85 for blacks, which would translate to perhaps 50 to 60 in the spatial interaction index. This degree of segregation means that the majority of blacks will have little contact with whites, and an even higher 80 percent of whites are likely to have little contact with blacks.

The degree to which blacks are segregated is higher than that for Hispanics, with perhaps 30 to 50 as a typical range in the spatial interaction index, or for Asians, with a yet lower range of values, from 20 to 40, and for white ethnic communities, with segregation values of perhaps 10 to 30. As a general rule, the larger the ethnic or racial community, the more highly segregated it will be. Thus because of sheer numbers, the millions of Hispanics in southern California cities are far more segregated than are the thousands in Washington or Oregon cities. Similarly, the more recent the group's arrival in the United States, the greater the cultural differences, and subsequently the more discrimination they are likely to face and the more segregated their communities will be for their own comfort and security.

Segregation also varies regionally. It is the highest in large mid-western cities, especially Detroit, Cleveland, and Chicago, is similarly high in the Northeast and in the South, and is lowest in the West. Over the last thirty years, the South has become more segregated as spatial segregation substitutes for legal separation, while segregation has fallen most in the Northeast and in the West, as middle-class blacks have increasingly migrated to the suburbs.

Mechanisms Leading to and Maintaining Segregation

Considering the power and pervasiveness of historic forces for segregation, it is surprising that racial separation is not even greater. Forces that have contributed to segregation include: legal barriers, discriminatory real estate practices, discriminatory financial practices, and the location of land use barriers. Many of the techniques associated with these external forces are no longer legal, but were until rather recently and thus are responsible for the separate and unequal structure that exists today as a legacy of past institutions.

Deed restrictions or restrictive covenants were the earliest means of placing a legal barrier to open housing. These specified that property could not be sold (or leased/rented) to proscribed groups such as blacks, Asians, and Jews. Supreme Court decisions in 1948 and 1953 determined that enforcement of such restrictions was in violation of equal protection rights as specified in the Fourteenth Amendment and therefore unconstitutional (see Johnson, 1984, pp. 80-83).

In effect, exclusionary zoning has replaced the restrictive covenant (Perin, 1977). When practiced in either cities or suburbs, it has served to control the housing market by dictating patterns of development such as the elimination of multifamily housing or requirements for larger lot sizes. As a consequence, minority groups whose incomes continue to be generally lower than whites' have limited access to these housing markets. Exclusionary zoning has also been challenged in court by appealing to the equal protection argument (Cox, 1973, p. 119), but exposure of discriminatory zoning is made difficult by the continued segregation of housing by value (Adams, 1987).

Official federal and state housing and lending policies, especially those of the FHA (Federal Housing Administration), were particularly influential in maintaining segregation through discriminatory financial and real estate practices. Studies in the 1930s purported to show that where races shared residential space, the sale and rental value of properties fell, as a direct measure of social incompatibility. Since individuals, banks, the courts, and governments all worked to maintain the value of property, it remained official policy to segregate by race, in public as well as private housing, and via loans or the insuring of loans, until 1938. These policies were only rescinded following studies in the 1960s which showed no or little decline in property values with racial integration.

The real estate industry has been a further bulwark against integration. As recently as 1950, the National Association of Real Estate Brokers (NAREB) included an official policy of racial separation in its code of ethics. Agents were cautioned that a "realtor should not be instrumental in introducing into a neighborhood...members of any race or nationality...whose presence will clearly be detrimental to property values in the neighborhood" (Hartshorne, 1992, p. 295). A dual housing market existed, with separate companies, listings, and territories. Unwritten real estate practices included "steering" whereby realtors simply showed homes to persons deemed appropriate for that market.

Even if the real estate agent or a private owner were to show a house, a further mighty barrier existed: the financial sector. It was also official policy of banks and savings and loan institutions not to make loans for purchase or improvements that would lead to racial heterogeneity. In collaboration with the real estate industry, cities were actually zoned in a manner that fostered a differential likelihood of being able to obtain loans.

A further line of defense, but also the main wedge for integration, was the individual seller (or landlord), and this remains true today. In general, even at present, the individual can sell or not sell to whomever he wishes. To the extent he is prejudiced, or simply views a minority buyer as a greater risk, or responds to please his former neighbors, the individual seller remains a force for segregation. On the other hand, some individual sellers are willing to sell to minority buyers who are ready to offer more, and this route has long been critical to the degree of integration that does exist, or to the physical expansion of the minority communities.

Landlords, especially of apartments, have an even greater incentive for discrimination, as they fear the loss of other renters, who can escape much more easily than owners. While rental discrimination on the basis of race is usually illegal, the rental apartment sector in the United States remains very highly segregated.

Organizations have played an important role, both in maintaining and in weakening segregation. Property owners' associations are formed to "hold the color line," certainly to the point of buying the property if necessary. On the other hand, in some communities, liberal churches and other social groups have aided integration and formed interracial groups to reduce discrimination. Within the minority community, both kinds of organizations and sentiments existed: civil rights groups aimed at testing and fighting discrimination and improving opportunities for housing outside, but also groups that stressed identity with the group and appealed to group solidarity, reducing the likelihood of people seeking to "pioneer" by a move into white areas.

At a wider geographic or community scale, there were several other ways to maintain segregation—or more recently, perhaps, to further integration. Physical barriers, for example freeways, have been located to provide a buffer or a no-man's-land between racial groups. Urban renewal, ostensibly to clear blighted slums, was effectively used in the 1950s and 1960s to "upgrade" some areas, replacing lower-class housing and activities with middle-class, usually white ones. Other giant developments were built expressly for minorities, at times in questionable locations.

In the 1970s and 1980s "gentrification" was very effective in "containing" or rolling back minority populations from near the downtowns or more desirable environmental or historic areas, most simply on the basis of economic competitiveness. The location of public housing, especially in the 1950s and 1960s, strongly reinforced racial segregation. In a few large urban centers gentrified housing has expanded into zones previously occupied by low-income blacks. Nowhere is that practice more advanced than in the nation's capital. This has often led to overt conflict between the gentry and lower-income black youth with whom they share public spaces (see Gale, 1987).

Finally, if all those mechanisms failed, and a minority household dared to succeed in moving into a white neighborhood, powerful weapons for separation remained and remain today: the probability of harassment and/or isolation, especially directed against the children. Every year, cross-burning and physical harassment incidents, in all regions of the country, are testament to the power of racial prejudice in our society.

Mechanisms of Racial Transition: How Ghettos Expand

Despite these formidable forces, minority communities do grow in number and must expand territorially. How is such expansion accommodated? Historically, the ghetto usually got its start in a classic way, from pioneer "squatters" on unwanted, undesirable, or abandoned land, possibly on industrial or railroad land, and tolerated by those industries, or in the most rundown and transient areas bordering the CBD.

The expansion of the ghetto, or even the formation of new areas, was very likely decided upon by the real estate industry, the lending institutions, and local governments, by agreeing that selected areas were in the "path of change" and should be "sacrificed." Rapid transitions were achieved, but substantial profits as well, despite the attempts of such neighborhoods to preserve themselves, by such techniques as "redlining" and "blockbusting," abetted by rumors. Redlining meant not making or insuring loans to whites in a transition area, thereby almost impelling a sale to minorities. Blockbusting meant the deliberate sale by a real estate industry "front" to a minority buyer, accompanying this by rumors of doom and letters to other property owners designed to induce panic selling. While blockbusting and direct realty industry selling became illegal by the 1960s, rumor still occurs to hasten transitions. Similarly, while redlining is illegal, that is the designation of whole areas for no loans, bankers remain logically resistant to loans that they deem a credit risk.

Perhaps as important historically, and certainly since the 1970s, is the behavior of individuals and groups. A major force for expansion of the ghetto was the upward mobility and more or less voluntary relocation of bordering groups, that manifests itself in a racial residential turnover process that is primarily responsible for expanding the ghetto along the black-white border. Probably the most important action occurring in many American cities was the rise of middle-class ethnics who, beginning in the late 1940s to 1960s, initiated their move to suburbia, making housing more readily available to blacks via the "trickle down" process. Blacks were more likely to be able to purchase in areas of prior Jewish settlement, in part because Jews, too, were subject to discrimination, and also because entire Jewish communities or congregations tended to make a corporate decision to relocate the synagogue or temple. Thus in New York, Los Angeles, Chicago, and even in smaller cities like Indianapolis and Seattle, the growth of the black ghetto proceeded along corridors of strongly ethnic Jewish settlement, but conspicuously not into areas occupied by white lower-class ethnic groups, which were not economically able to relocate. Thus in Chicago, resistance was and remains almost absolute in the area west of State Street, but the ghetto moved rather rapidly south into both Jewish and later some Catholic areas. But the latter group displayed strong resistance in their effort to stymie the flow (see Berry and Kasarda, 1977).

The process of spread indicates that integrated settlement is unstable and an equilibrium status is difficult to maintain. In general, as the proportion of minorities, especially of blacks, rises to 10 to 20 percent, the demand of whites to property on the market begins to weaken, unless they are economically immobile or are protecting access to major institutions. There is thus a "tipping point" at perhaps 25 to 30 percent at which typically white replacement stops, and a fairly rapid, 5 to 10 years transition to 80 to 90 percent minority level takes place.

Somewhat stable integrated areas do exist—often at about 15 to 35 percent—not at 50 percent which whites view as predominantly "black." These include some very poor, transient areas, where no one has much choice, a few rather rich areas, where class status overrides race, areas of very high educational status, as around universities, and some counter-cultural areas. Beginning in the 1960s and continuing to the present, ghettos in a number of the nation's larger urban centers having reached the city's edge, have now begun to spill over into adjacent suburbs, as to the west and south of Chicago or into Inglewood west of Los Angeles. By 1990 the spillover process had led to larger numbers of blacks residing in the suburbs of Washington, Atlanta, Los Angeles, and St. Louis than in the central city ghetto (Rose, forthcoming). A major theoretical and practical issue is the extent to which "class" can overcome "race"—that is, if a rise to middle- or upper-class status can permit and encourage residential integration. The majority of studies (i.e., Alba and Logan, 1991, Morrill, 1995) support the "stratification" position that segregation by race is far stronger than by class, and that achieving middle-class status is no guarantee or predictor of racial integration.

Point and Counterpoint: The Perceived Advantages and Disadvantages Associated with Minority Spatial Clustering

Segregation is a consequence of racial prejudice and discrimination. Yet the fact that it is so pervasive suggests that it must have social benefits as well as costs to both the dominant and subdominant social groups. What are the advantages to the minority itself?

An emerging force favoring spatial concentration is no longer external discrimination but an internal preference to reside among one's own race or within zones where the minority culture tends to dominate. Blacks often choose to associate with other blacks, even in the most demographically integrated of settings, for example, military bases in recent years. In part this may represent the need for mutual support and assistance in the face of a hostile external world; in part it is a measure of the extent to which separate development over 200 years has resulted in a somewhat distinct culture. While it is easy to exaggerate black-white culture differences in the United States, the extent to which these differences lead to the formation of race-specific communities has not been thoroughly documented. Class differences have been far more frequently invoked to explain these differences than has culture.

Deriving from such group identification is an appeal to group solidarity; from that, two powerful forces come into play which support separation. First is the desire to create a degree of economic independence predicated on the idea that greater numbers might encourage internal ownership and job opportunities, whereupon it is often assumed greater economic independence could take place. Second is the very real possibility of political representation. Since racial block voting can be invoked in the United States to a remarkable degree—often 80 to 90 percent—segregation has been the absolute prerequisite to significant black representation in Congress, in state legislatures, city halls, and school districts. Not only does "black power" through representation offer a sense of achievement and recognition, it permits some access to, and some control over, fiscal resources, and the ability, within jurisdictions under minority control, to remove discriminatory laws and practices. In those cities where black majorities or near majorities are found, blacks have generally gained control of city hall. In a few places these gains have been lost under conditions of emotional and ethnic and racial turmoil, where voter turnouts run high across all groups. The intensification of racial tensions in such locations often lead to very bitter political conflicts that transcend party interest.

The disadvantages associated with spatial clustering are many. First is the fact that separate territory permits the more powerful outside world to ignore and exploit the ghetto as desired. One result is the likelihood of lesser quality goods and services, public or private, for a given level of expenditures; another is the probable lack of jobs; yet another is the ability to exploit the area as a kind of colony, to extract rent and income from external ownership, to pay low wages to a captive labor market. The separateness reduces chances for social and geographic mobility and for information about outside opportunities.

A second disadvantage is that separation may foster ignorance about the other group, and lead to greater prejudice and discrimination. This concern is a principal reason behind the integration of the armed forces and of public schools.

Are there any solutions to this portrait of disaster? The two broad theoretical approaches are to compel integration, on the argument of a higher social need, or to compensate the disadvantaged minority, what has been called the "gilded ghetto" approach. Both are correctly directed to the idea that the only escape from hopelessness is to rise to middle-class status.

Ethnic Discrimination and Segregation

The United States is a nation of immigrants, goes the cliche; certainly the "ethnic" experience is a major part of American social history. By ethnic is meant here basically "white" groups but which are deemed "culturally different" from the dominant culture, at least for a time. Ethnic discrimination today is mainly directed at fairly recent, Spanish-speaking immigrants, some of whom view themselves as "people of color," if not "nonwhite."

There is always a fundamental ambivalence on the part of both the ethnic group and of the wider society between integration and assimilation—the melting pot analogy—and maintenance of ethnic identity—the glorification of cultural diversity and pluralism. Members of the ethnic minority understand the competitive reality of the society, and that they need to conform to the society in order to enjoy its material rewards; yet they insist on maintaining historical cultural traditions. Once here, ethnic communities often split, with the younger, more competitive and successful favoring assimilation, and the older or less secure, preferring cultural preservation and the maintenance of a separate community.

For most of U.S. history, "capital"—that is, the business community, have been advocates of free immigration, in order to maintain a surplus of cheap and willing labor; the poor, and even many earlier immigrants wanted to restrict further immigration as a means of limiting competition for scarce jobs. The debate over our earlier immigration policy, that is, the Immigration Act of 1965, has heated up as the volume of immigration, both legal and illegal, has grown dramatically since 1970. Even scholars who earlier suggested that the new immigration did not negatively affect poor and minority native workers are beginning to alter their previous views (Borjas, Freeman, and Katz, 1992).

Each new group, yes, even Swedes and Norwegians—were initially viewed as contemptible and savage, subject to discrimination in many forms, and segregated to the worst inner-city tenements and ghettos. Why? They were poor and "different"; those already here discriminated in order to slow competition for jobs and housing; they also feared and distrusted different customs and religions—thus the particularly strong discrimination against Jews. The new immigrants themselves clustered together for physical protection, for the security of familiar language and religion, for housing, for loans, and especially for entry into the job market, no matter how lowly. The ethnic ghetto provided a transition space from the old world to the new. But as people moved up the social ladder, they were increasingly faced with competing pressures for integration and solidarity with the mainstream culture. For most groups, especially those numerically small, assimilation usually won out, because of the dominance of the economic motivation to escape poverty and because of the sheer power of the WASP culture in schools and the workplace.

A common economic strategy was first to learn English; then to get jobs that provided entry to the lower middle class; and then to physically leave the community of origin for residence in the outer city of inner suburbs. At the same time, a strategy of bicultural development had evolved that led immigrants to adopt the WASP language and occupational aspirations but to maintain religion, food, and clubs. Some ethnic newcomers insisted on their children attending special weekend ethnic schools.

The process of even white ethnic assimilation was slow; while small groups in big cities, and all immigrants to small places, tended to assimilate within one to two generations, large groups and larger cities still maintain recognized ethnic communities after one hundred years. Often the latter communities simply represent residual communities, but for many they are symbolic of the struggle associated with becoming an American.

The Location of Ethnic Communities

Rural ethnic communities were common in the United States, especially in the mid-west and Great Plains, in response to the opportunities for land under the Homestead Act, and in mining and lumber towns of the West, but the classic ethnic community was located in the large city. In large cities, as a group improved in status and were encroached on by newer, poorer groups, some dispersed, but others shifted outward, usually in the same corridor or sector of the city (see Figures 2, 3, and 4).

As noted earlier, blacks tend to replace some ethnic groups which moved outward, but other, especially poorer white ethnic groups, resisted change. Since World War II, the dominant ethnic population has been Latino—including millions from Mexico, Cuba, Puerto Rico, the Caribbean, and the rest of Latin America. To the degree that society and the groups view

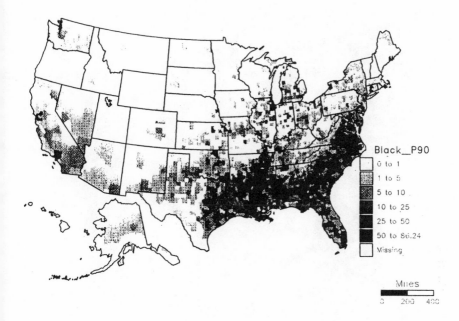

Figure 2. Percent Black, 1990

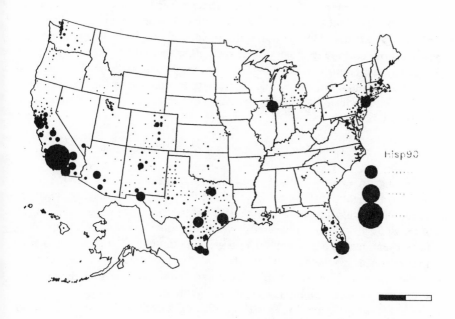

Figure 3. Hispanics 1990

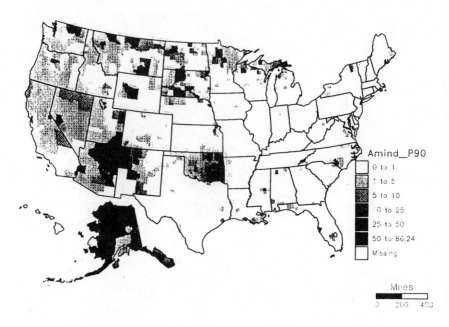

Figure 4.   Percent Native American

themselves as "people of color," their ethnic experience and spatial structure is intermediate between that of earlier white ethnic groups and American blacks. Space does not permit a discussion of this increasingly important population. Nor are we able to treat such other significant geographic aspects of racial and ethnic conflict as the evaluation of tools and policies to address racial discrimination and conflict, for example, mandatory busing for school integration, inclusionary housing policies, or the politics of racial and ethnic representation.

The Underclass Label as a Bone of Contention

During an era of economic restructuring, inequality has become more pervasive. The top income group's share of the pie increased during the period 1970-1990, while the bottom one-fifth of the population saw their share decrease. Those who found themselves at the absolute bottom of the heap, have been identified as members of a growing underclass, a term that is used to describe those persons who fall outside of the normative class system. Among social scientists who have adopted this label, most concur that the group is disproportionately comprised of blacks. William Julius Wilson's book *The Truly Disadvantaged* (1987) focuses exclusively on that segment of the black community in which social isolation and underclass residence is said to predominate. In a few short years, scholars have focused a great deal of attention on the attributes and behaviors of the underclass, but clearly without agreement as to its origins and/or just who may legitimately be described as holding underclass membership.

Wilson argues that the underclass has evolved in response to growing black joblessness, but other scholars reject that assertion. Some are more comfortable with public policy explanations (Murray, 1984); cultural explanations (Magnet, 1993); or explanations based on segregation (Massey and Denton, 1993). Yet others reject the label and suggest that it is simply another stigmatizing effort to demonstrate that a growing segment of blacks are outside of the mainstream culture or that this is part of the continuing effort to legitimate the existence of a caste-like structure within the larger national social structure (Gans, 1993). A few geographers have entered this debate, but none as vigorously as Hughes (1989, 1990). Hughes admits to the seriousness of the problem but rejects the label out of hand, preferring instead the label "impacted ghetto."

The conflict associated with the use of the underclass label operates at two different levels: one represents that described earlier, which largely takes place among members of the research community; the other is associated with media effort and subsequently that of other mainstream organizations to isolate and demean segments of the black community whom they perceive as failing to support mainstream values. In response to this second level of conflict there are growing signs of the emergence of an oppositional culture that is being spearheaded by black youth (Lott, 1992; Massey and Denton, 1993). To what extent this turn of events is likely to have an effect on promoting further alienation and conflict is unknown at this time.

The issue of the underclass has taken on larger proportions than that of simply describing the end process assumed to be associated with the United States making the transition from an industrial to a postindustrial nation. Underclass terminology is presently being used as a part of the normative discourse to describe negative or undesirable behaviors that pervade segments of black and Hispanic communities. The media, both the visual and the print, have no doubt done more to popularize its use and legitimacy than have any other agencies in American society (Lott, 1992). Unfortunately, media treatments most often portray those whom they deem members of the underclass as victims of their own human shortcomings rather than as human beings with specific qualities reacting to forces which originate outside of their control.

Geographers were late in addressing issues associated with the underclass, but there is evidence suggesting that interest in the topic is growing. Given Wilson's emphasis on the social and spatial isolation of those that he identifies as the underclass, geographers would seem to be readily attracted to this topic. Is the concentrated poverty primarily a function of the spatial mobility of the black middle- and upper-working classes or some other form or combination of mobility behavior that flies in the face of Wilson's deduction? On a number of the so-called behavioral attributes generally associated with underclassness, geographers no doubt assume that they more logically fall within the domain of other social sciences. But, as mentioned earlier, the underclass issue may simply be viewed as a surrogate for the race-ethnic-class conflict that pervades the larger society.

On a final note, it should be reported that underclass behavior as a promulgator of racial conflict and tensions seems to have shifted from concerns with passive nonethical behaviors, for example, welfare dependence, out of wedlock births, and weak attachment to the labor force, to more active behaviors which are said to generate fear among white populations. That fear is said to stem from accelerating acts of violence committed by young black males. James Q. Wilson, a noted criminologist, states that "Whites are afraid of young black males and young Latino males. It is not racism that keeps whites from exploring black neighborhoods, it is fear" (1992, p. 90).

Thus the spillover of violence into the larger community seems to be bringing to the fore a concern that had been only weakly expressed in the recent past. The fact is that uncontrolled violence has raged in zones of high poverty during much of the latter half of the decade of the eighties without it becoming a concern of persons who resided outside of harm's way. But with an increase in the incidence of random robbery killings along major traffic corridors and the carjacking and killing of white suburbanites, attention has quickly turned to the more violent expressions of underclass life. So much so that when a number of tourists were recently killed by predatory black youths in Florida it made headlines in newspapers around the world.

Thus violent crime on America's mean streets tends to foster increased racial tension. These tensions are no doubt best played out in the growing conflict between blacks and Jews emanating from New York City's Crown Heights killings. In that instance a car carrying the Hasidic Rebbe struck and killed a black child, but in the melee that ensued a visiting Hasidic scholar was said to have been intentionally killed by a black youth. The police handling of that case was partially responsible for unseating a black mayor, as a growing number of Jews, who have traditionally supported black candidates, provided support for the opposition candidate.

Unfortunately this redirected attention toward the underclass has done little more than increase the cries for increasing sentence lengths, building new prisons, and restoring the death penalty in states where it no longer exists. Although black communities frequently find themselves under siege from increasing random acts of crime and violence they continue to seek solutions that would direct youth in a positive direction long before they adopt codes of conduct that enable the larger society to define them as members of an underclass.

REFERENCES

Adams, J.S. 1987. *Housing America in the 1980s*. New York: Russell Sage Foundation.

Adas, M. 1989. *Machines as the Measure of Men: Science, Technology, and Ideologies of Western Dominance*. Ithaca, NY: Cornell University Press.

Alba, R., and J. Logan. 1991. "Variation on Two Themes: Racial and Ethnic Patterns of Attainment of Suburban Residence." *Demography* 28: 431-454.

Baudet, H. 1965. *Paradise on Earth: Some Thoughts on European Images of Non-European Man*. New Haven, CT: Yale University Press.

Berry, B.J.L., and J. Kasarda. 1977. *Contemporary Urban Ecology*. New York: Macmillan.

Blassingame, J.W. 1972. *The Slave Community, Plantation Life in the Ante-Bellum South*. New York: Oxford University Press.

Borjas, G.J., R.B. Freeman, and L. Katz. 1992. "On the Labor Market Effects of Immigration and Trade." Pp. 213-247 in *Immigration and the Workforce*, edited by G.J. Borjas and R.B. Freeman. Chicago: The University of Chicago Press.

Cater, J., and T. Jones. 1987. "Asian Ethnicity, Homeownership and Social Reproduction." In *Race and Racism: Essays in Social Geography*, edited by P. Jackson. London: Allen & Unwin.

Chance, J. 1987. "The Irish in London: An Exploration of Ethnic Boundary Maintenance." In *Race and Racism: Essays in Social Geography*, edited by P. Jackson. London: Allen & Unwin.

Clark, W.A.V. 1986. "Residential Segregation in American Cities: A Review and Interpretation." *Population Research and Policy Review* 5: 95-127.

Clark, W.A.V. 1991. "Residential Preferences and Neighborhood Racial Segregation." *Demography* (February): 1-19.

Cox, K. 1973. *Conflict, Power and Politics in the City*. New York: McGraw-Hill.

Darden, J.T. 1987. "Choosing Neighbors and Neighborhoods: The Role of Race in Housing Preference." Pp. 15-44 in *Divided Neighborhoods Changing Patterns of Racial Segregation*, edited by G.A. Tobin Newbury Park, CA: Sage Publications.

Duncan, O.D., and B. Duncan. 1955. "A Methodological Analysis of Segregation Indexes." *American Sociological Review* XX (April): 210-217.

Gale, D. 1987. *Washington, D.C., Inner-City Revitalization and Minority Suburbanization*. Philadelphia: Temple University Press.

Gans, H.J. 1993. "From 'Underclass' to 'Undercaste': Some Observations about the Future of the Postindustrial Economy and its Major Victims." *Journal of Urban and Regional Research* 17 (3): 327-335.

Gates, H.L. 1986. *"Race," Writing and Difference*. Chicago: University of Chicago Press.

Grossman, J.R. 1989. *Land of Hope, Chicago, Black Southerners, and The Great Migration*. Chicago: The University of Chicago Press.

Gutman, H.G. 1976. *The Black Family in Slavery & Freedom, 1750-1925*. New York: Pantheon Books.

Hartshorne, T.A. 1992. *Interpreting the City: An Urban Geography* (2nd ed.). New York: John Wiley & Son.

Henri, F. 1975. *Black Migration: Movement North, 1900-1920*. Garden City, NY: Doubleday.

Hughes, M.A. 1989. "Misspeaking Truth to Power: A Geographical Perspective on the Underclass 'Fallacy.'" *Economic Geography* 65 (July): 187-.

Hughes, M.A. 1990. "Formation of the Impacted Ghetto: Evidence from Large Metropolitan Areas, 1970-1980." *Urban Geography*: 265-284.

Huntington, E. 1924. *The Character of Races, as Influenced by the Environment*. New York: Scribners.

Jackson, P. 1987. "The Idea of 'Race' and the Geography of Racism." In *Race and Racism: Essays in Social Geography.* London: Allen & Unwin.

Jackson, P. 1987. "'A Permanent Possession'?: US Attitudes towards Puerto Rico." In *Race and Racism: Essays in Social Geography.* London: Allen & Unwin.

Jargowsky, P.A., and M. Bane. 1991. "Ghetto Poverty in the United States 1970-1980." Pp. 235-273 in *The Urban Underclass,* edited by C. Jencks and P.E. Peterson. Washington, DC: The Brookings Institution.

Johnson, D.M., and R.R. Campbell. 1981. *Black Migration in America: A Social Demographic History.* Durham, NC: Duke University Press.

Johnson, R. 1984. *Residential Segregation, The State and Constitutional Conflict in American Urban Areas.* London: Academic Press.

Joyner, C. 1984. *Down by the Riverside: A South Carolina Slave Community.* Urbana, IL: University of Illinois Press.

Kenny, J. 1991. "'Discovery' of the Hills: British Environmental Perceptions and the Indian Hill Station of Ootacamund." *The National Journal of Indian Geography* (June).

Livingstone, D. 1992. *The Geographical Tradition: Episodes in a Contested Enterprise.* London: Blackwell.

Lott, T. 1992. "Marooned in America: Black Urban Youth Culture and Social Pathology." Pp. 71-85 in *The Underclass Question,* edited by B. Lawson. Philadelphia: Temple University Press.

Magnet, M. 1993. *The Dream and the Nightmare: The Sixties Legacy to the Underclass.* New York: William Morrow and Co.

Marks, C. 1989. *Farewell-We're Good and Gone: The Great Black Migration.* Bloomington, IN: Indiana University Press.

Massey, D.S., and N. Denton. 1993. *American Apartheid, Segregation and the Making of the Underclass.* Cambridge, MA: Harvard University Press.

McHugh, K. 1987. "Black Migration Reversal in the United States." *The Geographical Review* (April): 171-182.

Miller, A.A. 1931. *Climatology.* London: Methuen.

Murray, C. 1984. *Losing Ground: American Social Policy, 1950-1980.* New York: Basic Books.

Orfield, G. 1991. *The Closing Door.* Chicago: University of Chicago Press.

Perin, C. 1977. *Everything in Its Place: Social Order and Land Use in America.* Princeton NJ: Princeton University Press.

Rose, H.M. 1971. *The Black Ghetto: A Spatial Behavioral Perspective.* New York: McGraw-Hill Book Company.

Rose, H.M. 1972. *Perspectives in Geography 2: Geography of the Ghetto.* DeKalb IL: Northern Illinois University Press.

Rose, H.M. 1976. *Black Suburbanization.* Cambridge, MA: Ballinger Publishers.

Rose, H.M. forthcoming. "The State of Ghettoization in Late 20th Century America." In *Cities in the 21st Century* (2nd ed.), edited by G. Gappert. Sage Publications.

Said, E. 1979. *Orientalism.* New York: Vintage Books.

Silk, J. 1987. "Racist and Anti-racist Ideology in Films of the American South." In *Race and Racism: Essays in Social Geography.* London: Allen & Unwin.

Sivandan, A. 1983. "Challenging Racism: Strategies for the '80's." *Race and Class* 25: 1-11.

Taeuber, K., and A. Taeuber. 1965. *Negroes in Cities.* Chicago: Aldine.

Wilson, J.Q. 1992. "Crime, Race, and Values." *Society* 30 (1): 90-93.

Wilson, W.J. 1987. *The Truly Disadvantaged, The Inner City, The Underclass, and Public Policy.* Chicago: The University of Chicago Press.

Wilson, W.J. 1991. "Studying Inner-City Social Dislocations: The Challenge of Public Agenda Research." *American Sociological Review* 56 (February): 1-14.

RACIAL AND ETHNIC CONFLICT:
PERSPECTIVES FROM SOCIAL PHILOSOPHY AND ETHICS

Michael Levin

INTRODUCTION

It is generally agreed that tension between blacks and whites in the United States is high, and shows few signs of abating. What can philosophy say about this issue?

Philosophy is concerned with clarifying concepts and articulating norms. Waiving conceptual difficulties for a moment, there are obviously normative issues raised by race conflict. By what standard should responsibility for it be assigned? How does morality constrain means to its reduction? If racial justice conflicts with social peace, how is a proper balance between these values to be determined?

While it is a commonplace that norms are logically independent of facts, policies and prescriptions cannot be developed in an empirical vacuum. A priori norms are too general to possess directive force. The universally accepted norms of compensatory justice, for instance, that those worse off because of a wrong be "made whole" by those responsible for the wrong, says nothing whatever

Research in Human Social Conflict, Volume 1, pages 301-320.

specific about who owes what to whom. To have any practical use, compensatory justice must be supplemented with empirical data about who did what to whom.

Likewise, an adequate theory of race conflict is needed prior to any discussion of what should be done to reduce it. The conventional theory assumed by most current prescriptions about race seems to me incorrect; I present an alternative theory and in later sections indicate some normative conclusions this theory supports.

DEFECTS OF THE CONVENTIONAL THEORY

The conventional explanation of black/white tension is racism, and attendant black mistrust of whites. Slavery, segregation, and discrimination have stigmatized blacks and excluded them from full participation in society. The damage done by these practices has not abated. Thus, one of their lingering effects is the high rate of violent crime committed by young black males, which of course alarms whites. According to the conventional theory, young black males are more prone to crime than their white counterparts because they see long-range goals as unattainable in a racist society; better to take what one wants when one wants it than to work hard and get nowhere because of racism. Blacks commit proportionately more crime against whites than do whites, on this theory, because of resentment against whites, and disproportionately more crime against blacks because they have internalized white hatred of blacks.

Black attitudes toward work are explained similarly: racism discourages the entrepreneurial optimism needed to run one's own business, and black unemployment is high, with blacks reluctant to take low-end jobs and resistant to the discipline of the workplace, because work remains associated with slavery. Alienation from work causes black men to deny their offspring support, creating a large subpopulation of unmarried black women and their children living on welfare. Black children do poorly and misbehave in school because teachers assume black children are intellectually deficient, do not allow for the less abstract black learning style, and do not permit the freedom to move around black children need (Hacker, 1992, pp. 170-172; the conventional theory thus implicitly recognizes race differences in cognition). Black conduct drives whites from neighborhoods that blacks begin to enter, creating a cycle in which public schools are considered a lost cause, neighborhoods decay, and more whites flee. Black despair is reflected in the intemperateness of black rhetoric—for instance, the conviction of many blacks that AIDS is a genocidal white plot (Taylor, 1992, p. 103-104).

The conventional theory predicts that race tension would abate if whites convinced blacks that they have a stake in American society. This whites can do by continuing to extend affirmative action privileges to blacks, intensifying their efforts to be less racist, teaching all children about African and African-American culture (exaggerating black achievements if necessary), and using federal civil rights laws to achieve residential integration (Massey and Denton, 1993, p. 230ff.).

These prescriptions are starkly asymmetrical. The conventional theory finds the immediate cause of racial tension to be deviant black behavior, yet it places full responsibility on whites for reducing racial tensions and black deviance itself, which, according to the conventional theory, are understandable and perhaps legitimate responses to past wrongs. "In order to survive and retain their sanity in impossibly unjust situations," writes Bernard Boxill, "people may have to resort to patterns of behavior and consequently develop habits or cultural traits which are debilitating and unproductive in a more humane environment" (1984, p. 164). On this view, to criticize blacks is "blaming the victim," although, to white victims of black crime, this phrase may seem more descriptive of the conventional theory itself.

Moral perverseness aside, the conventional theory does not explain the data it sets out to explain, and conflicts with other data. In many cases there is no plausible mechanism to mediate between racism and black behavior. For instance, neighborhood decay subsequent to white flight is standardly attributed to a reduction in municipal services, such as garbage collection, but a reduction in services because of the racial composition of a neighborhood would violate the 1972 Amendments to the Civil Rights Act, and no evidence has been presented that this does in fact occur. (It is highly unlikely that whites sneak into black neighborhoods to blight them.)

Speaking more broadly, it is prima facie implausible that, five generations after slavery ended, its effects should remain as strong as the conventional theory requires. The effects of no more remote historical events on other groups have attenuated into insignificance. The nineteenth-century ancestors of American Jews were subjected to abuses as great as those suffered by blacks, yet Jews are among the most prosperous subgroups in the United States. Asians were treated very badly in the United States in the nineteenth century, but their earning power now exceeds that of European-Americans.

Moving toward the present, the end of de jure segregation in the public schools in 1954 was quickly followed by busing to end de facto segregation. Private discrimination against blacks was outlawed in 1964, and by 1971 "affirmative action" was reserving jobs and academic positions for blacks. White attitudes have also changed; the average white in 1994 has a more flattering estimate of black ability than the average white of 1930. In short, it cannot plausibly be maintained that blacks are more oppressed now than earlier in the century. Yet black crime and illegitimacy increased dramatically in the period 1968-1972, *after* the civil rights revolution had ended in triumph (Herrnstein and Wilson, 1985; Jaynes and Williams, 1989; Murray, 1984), and the academic performance of black children has improved only marginally, if, at all, since integration. Furthermore, while whites have made what are by any objective standards great efforts to undo the perceived consequences of slavery and segregation, black anger at whites seems to be increasing, and receiving ever-freer expressions. The cover of an album by the rap group Public Enemy shows a white policeman in a gunsight. Such gestures menacing nonblacks, unthinkable fifty years ago, are staples of current black culture.

In short, not only has racial tension not abated in the last half-century, the phenomenon most in need of explaining is the failure of blacks to be mollified by the efforts of whites.

AN ALTERNATIVE THEORY

A different approach to black-white relations is psychobiological. It begins from the race differences in phenotypic ability and temperament, conjectures that these differences are significantly genetic in origin, and construes "racial tension" as a consequence of these genetic differences. This approach predicts that the interaction of races with divergent central tendencies must produce some level of animosity and misunderstanding. For reasons to become apparent, I call this the "crossed signals" theory.

Since I and others have discussed race differences at length elsewhere (Rushton, in press; Levin, in preparation), I will merely summarize them here. It is known that the mean intelligence of whites exceeds that of American blacks by about one standard deviation (Garner and Wigdor, 1982). On the conventional scaling of IQ tests, the mean IQ of whites is about 100, and that of blacks about 85. The phenotypic difference detected by these tests corresponds to the intuitive property of intelligence, and the slope and intercept of the regressor of criterion performance on IQ is the same for both races (Garner and Wigdor, 1982). In other words, IQ is an unbiased measure of an observable reality.

In the human population generally, the heritability h^2 of intelligence, the proportion of between-individual variance in intelligence explained by genetic variance, is known to be high. Recent twin studies place h^2 between .7 and .8 (Bouchard et al., 1990; Pedersen et al., 1992), and even critics of "genetic determinism" concede a value of .5 to h^2 (see e.g., Horgan, 1993). While nonzero heritability for individual differences in a trait does not logically implicate genetic factors in group differences, that inference becomes more plausible as between-individual heritability and between-group differences in both increase (see Dolan, 1993; Jensen, 1973; Levin, in preparation, for mathematical details). Given current estimates for h^2 and the size of the race gap in IQ, a genetic contribution to the race gap seems likely.

Further evidence of the involvement of genes is the fact that by late adolescence the IQs of blacks adopted at infancy by highly educated middle-class white families is 89, considerably below the white mean, and more than one standard deviation below the IQs of the birth children and white adoptees of these families (Weinberg, Scarr, and Waldman, 1992). In addition, IQ correlates with head size and presumably brain size both within and between races, and a 4 percent to 5 percent race difference in head size when body size is controlled for has proven to be robust. Several studies (Andraesen et al., 1991; Raz et al., 1993; Willerman, Schultz, and Rutledge, 1992; Wickett and Vernon, 1994) have established correlations in the .35 to .5 range between IQ and *in vivo* brain mass in white samples. Finally, the scores of African blacks fall about two standard deviations below the white mean on the most culture-reduced IQ tests (Lynn, 1991; Owens, 1992). Given that American blacks generally have some white ancestry, it is natural to interpret the IQ level of American blacks, about midway between that of Africans and American whites, as a nonlinear effort of hybrid vigor. The evidence is thus quite strong for a generic race difference in basic cognitive processes.

There are also differences in temperament between the races. Kochman (1983, p. 18) reports that the black communicative style is more "confrontational and personal," and discomforts whites. A number of authors have pointed to what has variously been called greater black impulsivity, lack of self-restraint, rapid decay of reinforcement, high time preference, and inability to defer gratification (Banfield, 1974). In addition, blacks show relatively lower levels of empathy, rule-following, cooperation, altruism and respect for law, a higher sex drive, greater interest in producing as opposed to rearing offspring, and greater aggressiveness (Rushton, in press). Black scores on the Minnesota Multiphasic Personality Index exceed those of whites on the Hypomania, Schizophrenia, Psychopathic Deviance, and Masculinity scales (Dahlstrom, Lachar, and Dahlstrom, 1986). Moreover, contrary to the conventional theory that black work habits and academic performance reflect low self-esteem, black self-esteem is regularly found to exceed that of whites (Shuey, 1966; Tashakkori, 1993).

There is no direct evidence from transracial adoptions implicating genetic factors in the race difference in personality, but recent twin studies indicate that, among humans generally, traits of personality are highly heritable (Bouchard et al., 1990). Once again, it seems reasonable to infer a genetic factor at work in a between-group difference, when, as in the case of blacks and whites, the mean environments of the two groups seem relatively similar. After all, blacks and whites see the same movies and TV shows, attend schools with identical curricula, vote for the same political candidates, and so on. The typical black slum is certainly a different place than the typical white suburb, but, since genotypes tend to make their own environments (see DeFries, Loehlin, and Plomin, 1979) a significant portion of the difference between black slums and white suburbs is probably itself due to genetic factors. While the condition of black slums may reinforce black impulsiveness, the state of the black slums must ultimately be explained in terms of the traits of their individual residents.

Perceived black/white differences in central tendencies are encoded as "stereotypes." Whites think of blacks as less intelligent and reliable than themselves, louder, more prone to crime, and more concerned with sex. Blacks find whites "up tight" and complain with particular bitterness about the coldness of Asians.

RACE TENSIONS

The sheer fact of difference between whites and blacks explains some aspects of "race tensions." By definition, people are loyal to their own norms, hostile to conflicting norms and individuals who follow them. If whites endorse a certain level of sexual restraint as appropriate—that marriage should be a precondition for children, for instance—they will be antipathetic to those who tend to be less restrained. (Whites will certainly resent demands to subsidize illegitimate children, which they see as a consequence of irresponsibility). There may moreover be a biological basis to xenophobia (Rushton, 1987). Genes are more apt to leave partial copies of themselves if their phenotypes selectively aid other phenotypes expressing similar genes. There will therefore be selection for relative antipathy toward observable correlates of genetic dissimilarity, such as skin color is man.

At the same time, sheer aversion to those with dissimilar values appears to explain only a rather superficial part of the dynamic called "race tension." It does not explain the concessiveness of whites toward black demands, the experience called "white guilt," or white willingness to support black illegitimacy with Aid to Families with Dependent Children, food stamps, and other subsidies.[1] Aversion based on dissimilarity seems patently inconsistent with affirmative action, by which whites prefer blacks over better qualified members of their own race. It is usually said that blacks deserve compensation for the harm done them by whites, but a desire to compensate does not explain the shape or scope of affirmative action. Societies do not seek to rectify all injuries, especially those done in previous generations, and rectification itself is usually casewise. Affirmative action will extend a black preference for a job absent evidence that he, in particular, was ever harmed by anyone, or that the particular white he is competing against ever benefited from discrimination. Furthermore, the cost of affirmative action is very great—$350 billion annually in the United States, by the estimate of *Forbes* magazine (Brimelow and Spencer, 1993); no society has ever undertaken compensation on so vast a scale. More curiously, whites do not deduct welfare, the cost of schooling black children,[2] or black crime from the debt they believe blacks are owed. This willingness to make unilateral concessions is rare in human behavior. Whites grumble privately about black crime and seek to avoid blacks, but, despite the fact that the United States is a democracy, white dissatisfaction with blacks receives no political expression. As already noted, blacks for their part rail against whites with increasing stridency. There is more to these patterns than simple xenophobia.

I propose that whites misunderstand black social signals because black and white social signals evolved differently. Whites attribute to signals emitted by blacks the meaning these signals have when emitted by whites; more specifically, the same signal when emitted by a white indicates a greater injury than when emitted by a black, and, when emitted by a black, evokes from whites the strong response appropriate to that greater injury. These signals and evoked responses are largely innate, creating positive feedback between black anger and white concessiveness.

The known race differences suggest indirectly that natural selection differentiated black and white social behavior. Climatic differences between Eurasia and Africa, where blacks evolved in isolation for at least 100,000 years, are more direct evidence. It is natural to conjecture that the colder Eurasian climate selected for greater cooperativeness as well as intelligence. In addition to having to master fire, invent clothing, and store food, Caucasoids and Mongoloids had to hunt large, dangerous animals. The hunt presumably favored cooperation and rule-following, since, if it was to succeed, everyone had to be where he was expected to be, and everyone had to be satisfied with the subsequent division of spoils. The warmer African climate permits acquisition of enough food for oneself and family by solitary gathering and hunting of small game. Rules for distributing stored food are unnecessary, since stored food goes bad. The African climate would thus be expected to select for the lower levels of cooperation, rule-following, and impulse control African Americans are observed to display.

Among the phenotypes enhancing the inclusive fitness of social animals like man are signals by which group members indicate internal states. Some expressions, like smiles and screams, have acquired an innate signaling function. The crossed signals theory rests on the fact that the same expression may acquire different signaling functions in different populations.

I present the theory first in a schematic form. Assume that, among whites, R is the most fitness-enhancing response to someone who has sustained an injury of severity I. R might include offering comfort, feeling sympathy, readiness to attack the cause of the injury, and, if the cause of the injury is perceived to be oneself, guilt. There will be selection among whites for regarding R as intrinsically appropriate for I. Suppose also that, initially, anyone sustaining I might utter two different cries, u or u'. Suppose also that, for some reason, u (say) becomes more apt to be uttered when I is sustained, or more apt to elicit R. There will be selection for uttering u rather than u' on sustaining I and for responding to u with R. We may suppose there is, at the same time, increased selection for uttering u' upon sustaining more serious injury Γ, and for reacting to u' with the more distressed response R'. Eventually, among whites, u will become a natural indicator of I and elicitor of R, and u' a natural indicator of Γ and elicitor of R'.

Had contingencies differed, I noted, u would have become associated with, and a natural signal for, Γ. In fact—this is the heart of the hypothesis—we may suppose that just such an association between u and Γ *was* established among blacks. Perhaps u' is louder than u, and among blacks, who are on average less empathetic, a more strident signal is needed to elicit the response appropriate to I. It is also possible that, among blacks, the most adaptive response to I is not R but R''. The situation is depicted in Figure 1.

Consider what happens when whites and blacks communicate. Whites interpret a black utterance of u' as indicating the more serious injury Γ rather than the less serious injury I, and will react with the stronger response R'. In other words, whites will overestimate the seriousness of a black protest of injury, responding to it as if it indicated the more serious injury that same protest would signify if uttered by another white. The same expression *does* mean more serious harm among whites, and a serious response is the evolved white reaction to signals of serious harm.

White misreading of black expressions of anger triggers a corresponding "inappropriate" reaction from blacks. Within a population, the optimal response to an injury tends to remedy it, thereby suppressing both the utterance which signals the injury and the response itself. This negative feedback is familiar enough: soothing remarks usually calm an agitated man, end the agitation, and permit the soothing remarks to be replaced by normal conversation. But anger may not dampen when signal systems cross. R' may mollify the injury Γ that u' signals *among whites*, but not necessarily the injury I that U' signals *among blacks*. Indeed, R may not mollify blacks either, since R'', not R, is the best response to I among blacks. The same signal means a different injury; the white response, wrongly targeted, may leave blacks angrier. At the third phase of the cycle, the failure to mollify blacks on the part of a response that mollifies other whites will leave whites bewildered and guilty.

I have described a feedback loop in which whites misread black anger, blacks reject white responses, and intensified black anger provokes further

Group	Injury	Signal	Within-Group Elicited Response
W	I	u	R
W	I'	u'	R'
B	I	u'	R''

Figure 1.   Crossed Signals

unsatisfying responses from whites. A final accelerant may enter when black stridency convinces whites to compensate black truculence with sympathy and concrete goods, thereby reinforcing the truculence. This model explains such puzzling phenomena as white concessiveness, the phenomenology of "white guilt," and the failure of blacks either to express gratitude for white efforts or to apologize for black crime.

Two analogies suggest themselves. (1) Human babies have an innate repertoire of cries to indicate various needs, and human adults have a repertoire of innate responses evolved to meet those needs, and incidentally suppress the crying. But evolution has not made the mediating emotions entirely pleasant. Prolonged infantile bawling is irritating, and many a father has attended a baby "just to get some peace." Hence, a baby whose cries bore an atypical relation to his wants would not be appeased by the responses evolved in normal humans to meet his cries. Such a baby's crying would be expected to intensify, and a normal adult forced to deal with him would soon become unstrung. (2) The sexes have evolved signals by which females indicate receptiveness to cue male approaches. But imagine a population of females whose signals were so scrambled that what normally expresses receptiveness expressed ambivalence, and what normally expresses ambivalence expressed revulsion. A man dealing with such women would soon find himself confused and demoralized. It is along these lines, I suggest, that one think of black/white interactions. The difficulties some American businessmen report in dealing with the Japanese, and the stereotype of Asians as "inscrutable,' may also be instances of the problem of reading social signals across races with different evolutionary histories.

FURTHER EXAMPLES OF THIS PATTERN

The pattern I have described fits a number of incidents widely covered in the American media in recent years.

To escape an angry stepfather, a 15-year-old black girl named Tawana Brawley hid for a few days, covered herself with dog feces, wrote "Nigger et [sic] shit" on her torso, and claimed that white policemen had raped her. She immediately became a symbol of the mistreatment of black women by white men, and continued to be such after being exposed as a fraud. The credibility to blacks of her preposterous story was itself cited as evidence of the extent of white abuse. Although warrants were issued for the arrest of members of the Brawley family involved in the hoax, no arrests were made, apparently from fear of riots.

In 1989 eight black teenagers raped and savagely beat a white woman jogging in New York's Central Park. When they described their activity as "wildin'"—which turned out to be the everyday black term for banding together for random acts of violence—many prominent blacks scolded the media for publicizing the word. Sonny Carson, a "community organizer" who had just finished a prison term for extortion, complained on television about the number of black males interrogated by the police for the rapists, and threatened violence against Koreans who did not show black women "respect." The received interpretation of the incident was that the city had provided too few social services to keep black youths from becoming bored. The jogger's employer, the investment firm Salomon Bros,. donated several hundred thousand dollars to build a park where the rapists lived (Walls, 1989).

Edmund Perry was a Harlem teenager recruited on full scholarship to Exeter, an exclusive New England preparatory school, despite having performed academically at a level far below that of the typical Exeter entrant. A few weeks after graduating he was shot to death by a plainclothes detective he was attempting to mug. Angry black demonstrations followed, an Perry's act—by ordinary standards a display of monstrous ingratitude—was explained as a consequence of Exeter's alienating atmosphere. New York magazine observed that Perry's classmates favored the Rolling Stones and took little interest in Aretha Franklin, whom Perry preferred. His death was taken to show how far whites still have to go to make blacks feel comfortable.

A black Milwaukee alderman named Michael McGee announced the formation of a black militia to shoot white people if his district did not receive more money. "Our militia will be about violence," he said, "I'm talking actual fighting, bloodshed and urban guerrilla warfare" (cited in Wilkerson, 1990, p. A12). While McGee drew some muted criticism, a fellow white alderman commented, "He is certainly pricking our conscience about the real world. Where are our priorities when you spend millions for downtown amenities and dribbles for the neighborhood" (1990). The New York Times described McGee's remarks as "a cry of despair."

Blacks at the University of North Carolina, who had already been given a black student center in a campus building, demanded a free-standing separate building of their own. After numerous disruptive demonstrations, and being promised a separate building by the UNC administration, blacks resumed their demonstrations—this time accompanied by rap music—when it was announced that the black building would be across the street from the main campus instead of on it. When asked to explain the point of the agitation, one black student replied, "I start from the fact that my great-grandfather used to be a slave. Then I try to put that out of my mind. For a while that works really well. Then I turn on the television and see there was a Ku Klux Klan march in town. That takes me right back" (Sanoff et al., 1993). A second replied, "I don't think it's the responsibility of black people to step outside of who were are" (1993).

In each case, black behavior which by white standards ranged from obnoxious to criminal to depraved was represented, with the eager agreement of many prominent whites, as victimization. The white population as a whole was thrown on the defensive. Sympathy, concessions, and tangible goods intensified black anger and provoked new demands. The UNC case especially illustrates how getting one's way and the intimidation of whites often become ends in themselves. As one commentator put it, "[The] blacks students define progress in terms of more power, rather than in terms of education or reconciliation" (Leo, 1993a, p. 65). On the present theory, the bafflement of whites stems from their assumption that blacks want what whites would want were whites to behave similarly, and, working from that assumption, whites have responded to injuries that do not exist.

Race differences in signaling are a matter of degree. Bluff, aggressive posturing, and dominance display occur among whites, and, one assumes, went on among paleolithic hunters. Among hunters is a harsh climate, however, the ultimate function of bargaining must have been an upshot acceptable to everyone, that is, "reconciliation." Whites did not evolve to deal with groups form whom bargaining has a different function.

TWO APPROACHES TO BARGAINING

Thomas Kochman, cited earlier on the difference between the black and white communicative styles, has also suggested that whites are more "process-oriented" than blacks (cited in Leo, 1993b, p. A11). Whites emphasize fairness and attention to procedure, in his view, while blacks want results. This leads to a conjecture implicit in the previous paragraph, and a natural extension of the crossed signals theory, namely that the races differ in their conceptions of bargaining. White inability to "read" black bargaining may explain more puzzling features of black/white interaction.

It is helpful to follow game theorists in distinguishing two phases of bargaining (see Nash, 1953; Luce and Raiffa, 1957, Chapter 6; Gauthier, 1984). First, all parties adopt a "status quo" point, from which the bargaining begins. Second, the parties agree on a "joint strategy," which makes all parties better off than they were at the status quo. The best-known problems about bargain arise at the second phase, but the first is not trivial. Nash (1953) suggested that the status quo is fixed by an initial noncooperative game in which each player seeks to put himself in the most advantageous position possible. One move in this initial game is the *threat,* a declaration of intent on the part of one bargainer to act in a way which will worsen the position of his competitor(s) and possibly himself if his competitor adopts a strategy the threat maker does not want him to. The status quo that emerges, the equilibrium fixed by each bargainer's best "threat strategy," is the "threat point."

Many commentators reject Nash's analysis on moral and conceptual grounds. Walking along the beach, you and I each find two beautiful, delicate shells. We put all four in a box, which I carry. I suddenly announce "Let's pretend we have no shells, which is what we'll have if I drop the box, which I'll do unless you give me one of your shells." I point out that by going home with one shell you are better off than you would have been at the no-shell status quo. If you agree, your agreement, made under threat, seems coerced— hence not really an agreement—and biased toward the most reckless gambler. If this bargain is acceptable, I could in theory declare, as we are driving home, that I will wreck the car unless you give me all four shells plus your aqualung. If my threat is credible, you will end up worse off than you were before we interacted. Purely from the point of view of self-interest, negotiating from threat-points defeats the purpose of bargaining, which is to make everyone better off than he was when bargaining began. It defeats this purpose to retreat in imagination to a point at which anyone is worse off than he is at the start of negotiations.

Gauthier's approach to bargaining conceives the status quo as the set of positions the bargainers are actually in when the process begins. No one need retreat to get to the bargaining table. Bargaining of this sort is what economists call "productive": no bargainer is worse off in the status quo than he would have been had he never heard of the other bargainers, nor can bargaining make anyone worse off than he was beforehand, as bargaining from a threat-point can.

I suggest that Nash's theory of bargaining is more descriptive of black negotiations, while white negotiations tend to be more productive. Moreover, because whites evolved to be more apt to view threats as defeating the productive purpose of bargaining, threats tend to be less credible and less common among whites and in institutions developed by whites. An automobile dealer trying to sell an option to a reluctant buyer is unlikely to do or say he will do anything that will make both the buyer and himself worse off. He will not tell a potential customer "If you won't want air conditioning then get the hell out of my showroom," depriving the customer of the car he wants and jeopardizing his sale and possibly his job.[3]

If productive bargaining was more adaptive than Nash bargaining when whites evolved, whites will be unprepared to deal with negotiators who regularly resort to threats. Whites are geared to productive interactions; blacks, being less cooperative, more concerned with dominance—perceived as a desire to "get one's way" for its own sake—and more inclined to discount the long-term aversive consequences of their own behavior, are more comfortable with threats. As a result, whites find it difficult to negotiate with blacks. Viewing threats as a last resort, whites are at a loss when threats are a first resort. Threats can of course be checked by counter-threats, but, on the present analysis, whites are less skilled than blacks at this sort of escalation. That is why whites are constantly making deals which leave them worse off than they were in the first place. Similarly, whites are less willing than blacks to aggravate by threat those conflicts in which there is no natural productive status quo, and do not respond efficiently to what strikes them as reckless raising of stakes. Whites, for instance, have difficulty comprehending the dynamic by which one black will kill another because of a show of "disrespect."

It would be useful to test conjectures about race differences in bargaining behavior, by determining, say, whether the ease of bargaining between people is a function of their genetic similarity. But consider the demonstrations blacks frequently stage, such as the one at UNC, in which blacks threatened a disruption of campus life which could only be harmful to everyone, for an announced goal of no obvious utility. The point of many boycotts, another tactic favored by black "activists," seems to be merely to penalize some group doing better than themselves, such as Korean grocers. The black boycotters do not realize or do not care that "getting the Koreans out of the neighborhood" will harm blacks as well as Koreans, by depriving black residents of convenient places to shop, giving other nonblack merchants pause about moving into black neighborhoods, and causing food outlets that remain to raise their prices.

Threats of boycotts against large firms like Nike footwear or Coca-Cola have a similar downside: potential loss of access to goods which blacks themselves desire. It is remarkable, and seldom observed, that black dealings with such firms never consist in the offer of a good for a good that will benefit both sides. Thus, when the NAACP asked Coca-Cola for more black dealerships, it did not offer to accept those dealerships on terms especially favorable to Coca-Cola, but on terms favorable to themselves. (Other "offers" typically include requests for jobs set aside for blacks and money for black organizations.) In most cases, the firms being made these offers could easily withstand black boycotts or counter with a threat not to sell to blacks, yet they do not bring such counterpressure to bear. In fact, whites in effect have forbidden themselves from bringing such counterpressure, since white threats not to sell to blacks, even in response to a black boycotts, would certainly be regarded as violating current civil rights laws. To put the point abstractly, whites, not having evolved to engage in uneconomic interactions, yield to blacks and bargain from threat-points.

Everyday black/white interaction conforms to this overall pattern. Kochman refers to blacks' more "confrontational" personal style (1983, p. 18). Abuse and attacks from rebuffed black beggars have become common occurrences in large American cities. I suspect that a significant factor in black/white interaction is white awareness of a black readiness to resort to violence, and black awareness of this awareness.

IS THIS DYNAMIC INEVITABLE?

That the dynamic described here was not in evidence in the American South during and immediately after slavery argues against a biological cause.

I cannot speak with the assurance of a historian, but I suspect that the experience of the South involved a rare conjunction of historical contingencies. The black population was small. Since most blacks were slaves or descendants of slaves, whites were taught from infancy that they were superior, and blacks that they were inferior. There was no assumption of equality: whites treated each other by one set of rules and blacks by another. Blacks were aware that whites could be quite brutal to blacks who failed to show what was considered proper deference. At the same time, whites cared for their slaves reasonably well. Finally, and perhaps most important, blacks and whites lived close together from infancy. The South was not integrated, but there was probably more daily contact between blacks and whites than in the American North today. As a result, southern whites may have developed a strong intuitive sense of measures useful in controlling black aggression.

Even given these factors, the experience of the antebellum South may show less than it seems to about race relations. The situation there might have been unstable, two centuries being an eyeblink in evolutionary time.

If there is a genetic element in the feedback between black anger and white amelioration, activated under some environmental circumstances (but not all, as the American South shows), is the loop self-sustaining once begun? It is impossible to say without more empirical research. There is no reason to expect black aggressiveness to abate, and at an individual level whites may always have difficulty in coping with it. However, there are large-scale factors that might disrupt the loop. The cost to whites of subsidizing black behavior may at some point become prohibitive. Whites might also become desensitized; concessive responses to black anger might habituate and weaken as the anger that elicits them continues. Finally, if as seems likely whites have evolved the highly efficient tit-for-tat strategy (Axelrod, 1984)—initiate cooperation, but withhold it next time if it is not reciprocated—they will eventually withdraw their altruistic assistance if blacks fail to reciprocate it. Continuation of the responses whites have evolved to perceived cries of distress may itself depend on evidence of distress reduction.

MORAL ISSUES

The moral issues raised by the feedback between black anger and white concessiveness concern the steps whites are permitted to take if they wish to disrupt it. But there are a number of preliminary issues on which the present analysis promises to shed light.

First, it is idle to lay blame for racial conflict. If it is biologically inevitable, it is no one's fault. No group can control its central tendencies, so it is pointless, if emotionally gratifying to search for the parties in the wrong who are then to be told to stop doing what they are doing. There are no such parties.

In particular, racial tensions are not due to white misdeeds, a conclusion congruent with the fact previously noted that tensions have increased despite the disappearance of anything that can be called "racism."

A deeper issue is raised by the essentially statistical character of black/white interactions, which gives rise to what Humphries (1991) has called "actuarial facts" about the behavior of the races. For example, while it is impossible to say beforehand just which blacks will commit crimes, it is actuarially certain that the crime rate in an area will increase if the black population does. Does such statistical knowledge justify whites in leaving such an area, or taking steps to prevent blacks from moving into their own neighborhoods, by (say) exclusionary covenants?

In ordinary circumstances, when sufficient knowledge is available, it is understood that each person should be treated on the basis of his specific traits. A student should be graded on his test performance, not that of the average member of his age group. So it might seem wrong to limit black entry into a neighborhood just because there will be an overall mismatch between black behavior and white norms. However, common sense does take purely statistical data into account when individual knowledge is unavailable or too costly. All 15 year olds are forbidden to drive, even though some 15 year olds are doubtless mature enough to drive safely. Needing uniform rules, and finding it impractical to give all 15 year olds extensive psychological tests to find the precociously mature few, society must choose between two alternatives: licensing all 15 year olds or licensing none. The latter alternative is found more attractive on balance, and chosen, despite its statistical character. The need for rules is not essentially connected to the public character of roads. If all roads were privatized, as libertarians urge, road owners would still have to screen road uses, and, given the volume of traffic, would have to impose statistical tests. Circumstances sometimes make it impossible to treat people as "individuals."

In this connection it helps to reflect that "treating each person on this basis of his unique traits" is in any case an irrational ideal. Most of the traits that distinguish individuals from each other, such as their exact place and time of birth, are irrelevant to any judgments we might wish to make about them. Quite to the contrary, most of the traits we do use in "judging" people, such as possessing a sense of humor, are widely shared and not individuating at all. It is also thought that people should be "treated as individuals" in that they may only be judged on the basis of traits that they choose to have, whereas race is unchosen. This idea too is at variance with common sense, since people are constantly being judged on the basis of traits of personality which nobody chooses. (Hereditarians believe that personality is shaped by genes, environmentalists that it is shaped by early training; neither one's genes nor one's early training are chosen.) I am permitted to avoid people whose personalities offend me even if they are not responsible for their personalities.

Attitudes toward the use of actuarial facts in racial issues often hinge on one's conception of moral rules. One might think of moral rules as basically utilitarian in form, commanding each person to do what he can to maximize certain goods or minimize certain evils. "Do what you can to lower the level of aggression in society" is a utilitarian rule. Followers of Kant, on the other hand, think of moral rules as commanding individuals to act in certain ways, whatever the overall consequences. "Don't aggress, period" is a Kantian rule. The big difference is that utilitarian rules permit a little evil in the service of a likely net good, while Kantian rules do not. For this reason, utilitarians are more tolerant than Kantians of the use of valid statistics, in racial and other contexts. If an influx of blacks into a white neighborhood is actuarially sure to increase crime, a utilitarian who values personal security will allow the whites to keep blacks out, even if so doing wrongs individual blacks who would conform to the law, so long as the exclusionary methods themselves do not do more harm than good.

Most contemporary philosophers, faced with this choice, would insist that everyday morality is Kantian, not utilitarian. Children are told to be honest, not to maximize honesty. Yet at heart we are all maximizers. A captured terrorist refuses to disclose where he has hidden atomic bomb which, if detonated, will kill millions of people. Would it be permissible to torture his infant son in front of him to make him talk? Kantians say no, maximizers say yes. Over the years I have found that most people I ask, including most of my philosophy students, approve of torturing the baby—in other words, of aggressing against one innocent to prevent aggression against sufficiently many. I suspect that ordinary morality *appears* Kantian because, under ordinary conditions, adherence to Kantian rules is the best way to achieve maximizing ends. Under most circumstances, aggression is minimized when everyone refrains from aggression. In extraordinary cases in which Kantianism and utilitarianism conflict, however, we go utilitarian. Since morality is unlikely to have a dual structure—Kantian when Kantianism and utility coincide, utilitarian when they diverge—morality must always be utilitarian at bottom.

So ordinary morality permits the violation of Kantian rules to prevent large-scale evils. Statistical generalizations involving race often validly predict large-scale evils. So taking "statistical actions," such as prevent all blacks from entering a neighborhood, is consistent with ordinary morality.

ANTICIPATED MOTIVATIONAL STATES

"Treating people as individuals" and the conflict between Kantianism and utilitarianism are staples of moral philosophy. To the extent that racial conflict leads to these issues, it does not enter new moral territory. However, the present theory of racial conflict also raises a normative problem that has only recently come to the attention of philosophers.

In its general form, the problem is created by conflict between the motivational states of persons existing at different times (see Ainslie, 1992; Elster, 1979; Herrnstein, 1990). On Monday I think I should jog on Tuesday, but on Tuesday I will feel lazy and not jog—an omission I will regret on Wednesday. Suppose on Monday I *know* what my Tuesday desire promises to be, and have a fail-safe device I can engage to prevent my Tuesday's desire from arising; I can for instance make a promise to meet a friend for jogging that I will be too embarrassed to break. Common sense seems to hold that it is rational to engage fail-safe device, in effect identifying with my Monday rather than my Tuesday desire. Since I will be glad on Wednesday for having done so, identifying with my Monday desire maximizes my overall satisfaction.

Philosophers have traditionally discussed problems of this sort in the context of temptation, moral weakness, and personal identity, but, on the present theory, it also arises for whites interacting with blacks. For suppose whites are prone to respond to black cues in ways which whites would regard as inappropriate if examined before or after the interaction. Whites presumably do not wish to make unwarranted concessions to blacks or collude in unproductive bargaining. If whites are persuaded that upon interacting with blacks they will want to make concessions that from a more global perspective they find irrational, they will, like the jogger who fears his own laziness, begin to look for fail-safe mechanism to guard against their future motivational states. One might imagine the problem as that facing whites who live on the opposite end of an island from a group of blacks. The groups begin migrating toward each other, the whites aware that when the groups meet they will feel like making concessions they currently hope they will not feel like making. What steps may they take to prevent their future motivational states from arising?

In the jogging case, we saw, common sense urges identification with the motivational state which promises the greatest long-run satisfaction. Odysseus didn't want to want to succumb to the Sirens, and every reader of the *Odyssey* admires his cleverness in tying himself to the mast (and blocking his crew's ears with wax) so that he could frustrate his future preference while indulging his curiosity about the Sirens' song. Since, then, it is rational and morally permissible to seek to short circuit wants one does not want and will regret having, the whites on the desert island can take steps to short-circuit their desire to make concessions to blacks. And by the same token, it is rational and permissible for whites in an on-going multiracial society to seek to forestall what they see as a dispreferred shift in their preferences caused by interaction with blacks. One technique is to avoid stimuli that cue the dispreferred preferences. The whites on the desert island can change course; whites in an on-going multiracial society can seek to minimize their contact with blacks. Second, whites may permissibly make a conscious effort to acquaint themselves with the evidence about race differences, white undercuts the intellectual case for white guilt, and may fortify whites against black anger.

CONCLUDING REMARKS

Speaking somewhat more generally, I would suggest that it is unrealistic to expect a multiracial society to be as harmonious as a racially homogeneous one. Despite great public and private efforts made over the last forty years, blacks and whites in the United States do not mingle. It is not simply that white adults avoid blacks when choosing residences and white children avoid black children when socializing in schools; blacks, while favoring the amenities of white society, seem no more eager to associate with whites. There is nothing surprising or scandalous in this, if in fact our genes program an affinity with those who look genetically related. "Sensitivity" training and "multicultural education" either paper over or misrepresent group differences obvious to everyone. Telling college students that "diversity" must be prized—*and* that stereotyping is wicked!—simply adds another loop to the cycle of black recrimination and white confusion.

Possibly the best way to break the cycle, and "reduce racial tension," is to indulge people's propensity for associating with whom the please. Benign disengagement of whites and blacks might also prove to be in the interest of blacks. Anger is rarely a useful emotion, and it profits blacks only insofar as it elicits rewards from whites. The end of guilt-driven responses by whites would end these rewards for black anger, and perhaps prepare the way for more constructive approaches to race relations.

NOTES

1. Blacks are 12 percent of the U.S. population, and the wage of the average black about 66 percent that of the average white (Jaynes and Williams, 1989). Given the progressive tax code in the United States, blacks may be assumed to pay about 50 percent of the taxes per capita that whites do, or 6 percent of the cost of welfare. At the same time, over 40 percent of families receiving AFDC are black (Hacker, 1992; Rector, 1992). So blacks receive about $7 from whites for every $1 they contribute to welfare.

2. The per capita net worth of blacks is about 21 percent that of whites (Jaynes and Williams, 1989). Public schools are supported primarily by property tax, and in most major cities they are significantly or predominantly black. Blacks thus have access to an educational system whose cost they bear relatively little of, on the cross-cultural evidence, could not create by themselves.

3. Deterrent threats are not Nash in character. In threatening to harm you if you harm me, I promise to do something that won't help me but will hurt you if you first make me worse off. I do not promise to harm you unless you make me better off.

REFERENCES

Ainslie, G. 1992. *Picoeconomics.* New York: Cambridge University Press.

Andraesen, N. et al. 1993. "Intelligence and Brain Structure in Normal Individuals." *American Journal of Psychiatry* 150: 130-134.

Axelrod, R. 1984. *The Evolution of Cooperation.* New York: Basic Books.

Banfield, E. 1974. *The Unheavenly City Revisited.* Boston: Little, Brown.

Bouchard, T. et al. 1990. "Sources of Human Psychological Differences: The Minnesota Study of Twins Reared Apart." *Science* 250: 223-228.

Boxill, B. 1985. "The Morality of Preferential Hiring." Pp. 158-174 in *Today's Moral Problems,* edited by R. Wassertrom. New York: Macmillan.

Brimelow, P., and L. Spencer. 1993. "When Quotas Replace Merit, Everybody Suffers." *Forbes,* Feb. 15: 80-102.

Dahlstrom, W. G., D. Lachar, and L. Dahlstrom. 1986. *MMPI Patterns of American Minorities.* Minneapolis, MN: University of Minnesota Press.

DeFries, J., J. Loehlin, and R. Plomin. 1976. *Genotype-Environment Interaction and Correlation in the Analysis of Human Behavior.*" *Psychological Bulletin* 34: 309-322.

Elster, J. 1979. *Ulysses and the Siren.* New York: Cambridge University Press.

Garner, W., and A. Wigdor. 1982. *Ability Testing I and II.* Washington, DC: National Academy Press.

Gauthier, D. 1984. *Morals by Agreement.* Oxford: Oxford University Press.

Hacker, A. 1992. *Twin Nations.* New York: Scribners.

Herrnstein, R. 1990. "Behavior, Reinforcement and Utility." *Psychological Science* I: 217-223.

Herrnstein, R., and J. Wilson. 1985. *Crime and Human Nature.* New York: Simon and Schuster.

Hogan, J. 1993. "Eugenics Revisited." *Scientific American* 268(6): 122-127.

Humphries, L. 1991. "Limited Vision in the Social Sciences." *American Journal of Psychology* 104: 333-353.

Jaynes, G., and R. Williams. (eds.) 1989. *A Common Destiny: Blacks in American Society.* Washington, DC: National Academy Press.

Jensen, A. 1973. *Educability and Group Differences.* New York: Harper and Row.

Kochman, T. 1983. *Black and White: Styles in Conflict.* Chicago: University of Chicago Press.

Leo, J. 1993a. "Separatism Won't Solve Anything." *US News and World Report,* April 19: 65.

Leo, J. 1993b. "Moving Away from Tribalism." *Santa Barbara News-Press,* Sept. 10: A11.

Levin, M. In preparation. *Why Race Matters.*

Luce, R. D., and H. Raiffa. 1957. *Games and Decisions.* New York: John Wiley and Sons.

Lynn, R. 1991. "Race Differences in Intelligence: A Global Perspective." *Mankind Quarterly* 31: 254-296.

Massy, D., and C. Denton. 1993. *American Apartheid.* Cambridge, MA: Harvard University Press.

Murray, C. 1984. *Losing Ground.* New York: Basic Books.

Nash, J. F. 1953. "Two-person Cooperative Games." *Econometrica* 21: 128-140.

Owen, K. 1992. "The Suitability of Raven's Standard Progressive Matrices for Various Groups in South Africa." *Personality and Individual Differences* 13: 149-159.

Pedersen, N. et al. 1992. "A Quantitative Analysis of Cognitive Abilities During the Second Half of the Life Span." *Psychological Science* 3: 346-353.

Raz, N. et al. 1993. "Neuroanatomical Correlates of Age-Sensitive and Age-Invariant Cognitive Abilities: An *in vivo* MRI Investigation." *Intelligence* 17: 407-421.

Rector, R. 1992. "Requiem for the Welfare State." *Policy Review* 61: 40-46.

Rushton, J. P. 1987. "Genetic Similarity, Human Altruism, and Group Selection." *Behavioral and Brain Science* 12: 503-517.

Rushton, J. P. In press. *Race, Evolution and Behavior: A Life History Perspective.* New Brunswick, NJ: Transaction.

Sanoff, A. P. et al. 1993. "Race on Campus." *US News & World Report,* April 19: 52-64.

Shuey, A. 1966. *The Testing of Negro Intelligence* (2nd ed.). New York: Social Science Press.

Tashakkori, A. 1993. "Race, Gender and pre-Adolescent Self-Structure: A Test of Construct-Specificity Hypothesis." *Personality and Individual Differences* 14: 591-598.

Taylor, J. 1992. *Paved With Good Intentions.* New York: Carroll & Graf.

Walls, J. 1989."Salomon Jogging Park Memories." New York, Aug. 28: 11-12.

Weinberg, R., S. Scarr, and I. Waldman. 1992. "The Minnesota Transracial Adoption Study: A Follow-up of IQ Test Performance at Adolescence." *Intelligence* 16: 117-135.

Wickett, J., P. Vernon, and D. Lee. 1994. "*In Viro* Brain Size, Head Perimeter, and Intelligence in a Sample of Healthy Adult Females." *Personal and Individual Differences* 16: 831-837.

Wilkerson, I. 1990. "Call for Black Militia Stuns Milwaukee." *New York Times,* April 6: A12.

Willerman, L. et al. 1991. "*In vivo* Brain Size and Intelligence." *Intelligence* 15: 223-228.

RACIAL AND ETHNIC CONFLICT:
PERSPECTIVES FROM AMERICAN RELIGIONS

Leonard J. Pinto

INTRODUCTION AND OVERVIEW

The general inattention of historians and social scientists to America's history of violent anti-Catholicism and Catholic response, dramatically demonstrated in the various reports produced for President Johnson's National Commission on the Causes and Prevention of Violence, is a classic instance of the politically conservative effects of "social amnesia." Our inability or unwillingness to recall that history has crippled efforts to understand interracial and interethnic conflict and violence from a religious perspective.

There has been lengthy and sometimes heated sociological disagreement about the relation between religion and social conflict in America, with particular reference to the racial conflict of the 1960s. "Consensus theorists" have argued that in America, mainline religions support the status quo; "dissensus theorists," that religion is a force for social change. The debate has turned into a morass.

The mandate of the Commission may extricate us from this confusion. The Commission was expressly charged, and expressly charged its researchers, with

Research in Human Social Conflict, Volume 1, pages 321-341.
Copyright © 1995 by JAI Press Inc.
All rights of reproduction in any form reserved.
ISBN: 1-55938-923-0

inquiring into the history of violence in America and one Commission researcher, Samuel Klausner (1969, p. 1296), noted that while there was much general theorizing about the integrative functions religion performed for society, "little effort has been made to derive general propositions from the historical material on religion and violence (in America)." This paper is an initial attempt at that.

Although none of the myriad consultants and researchers who provided reports to the Commission did more than mention Protestant-Catholic conflict in passing, Klausner (1969) came closest in his fine, relevant essay for the Commission, "Invocation and Constraint of Religious Zealotry". However, he focused on other matters: he drew on diverse cross-cultural and historical contexts, including some American examples, to study religiously induced violence, and also provided a helpful discussion of religion and race relations in the 1960s. Hence, although Klausner points the way, the Commission failed to discuss the history of Protestant-Catholic pitched battles and mutual distrust, and therefore forfeited the opportunity to explore the sociological implications of that history to better understand racial and ethnic conflict. This paper explores that opportunity.

America's continuing "social amnesia" on this subject has strategic sociological significance since we as a people have forgotten that, over three centuries, from the 1600s to at least the early 1900s American Catholics filled the sociocultural role of "internal enemy." More importantly, from the dawn of the new nation this internal enemy filled a strategic sociopolitical role, in two-party politics as well. Frequently violent, and almost continuously rabid opposition to the sociopolitical integration of Catholics in civil society by even the nonaffiliated but Protestantly-self-identified masses put off and shaped the eventual inclusion of Roman Catholics in the American political community. That bellicose past had a second profound consequence for American life: it successfully maintained the socioeconomic status quo. Elite social and economic power was safe because attention was deflected away from class cleavages and the less powerful were fractionalized along religious and ethnic lines. The more manifest goal of retaining the religious status quo by keeping the United States a Protestant country, even if only an informally established one, was not successful in the long run, but the interreligious conflicts certainly held the Catholics at bay for 150 years after the founding of the nation.

In the case at hand, forgetting about religious conflict blinds us to the dynamics and political consequences of interracial conflict centering around African Americans, who replaced Catholics as America's preeminent "internal enemy" about the mid-twentieth century. The third goal of this paper is to articulate the dynamics of social amnesia, and reflect on the parallel socioeconomic and sociopolitical consequences of both religious and racial conflict, once that amnesia has been cured.

It is beyond the range of this paper to document the persistence of our social amnesia, but, given the charge to the Commission to uncover our violent past, the present paper analyzes various documents produced by and for the Commission to demonstrate the process and suggest some of the consequences of our collective amnesia. Its negative effects on efforts to understand the racial conflict of the 1960s, and the role of race in the politics of the 1980s and 1990s will also be discussed.

RELIGION, VIOLENCE, AND CONFLICT AND RELIGIOUS VIOLENCE AND CONFLICT

The 1960s convinced observers that religion functions either as an integrating institution or as a force for social change, or both; it performs these different functions either at different times or simultaneously. Such a broad, unsystematic statement may inform us on religion and social stability and change, but not much. The limits of consensus theory were clearly articulated by the end of the decade: the confounding of sociological and religious perspectives within it, first noted by Alvin Gouldner (1970), could not but profoundly effect the study of the relationship between religion and social life generally.

The connection between sociology and theology is reflected in the fact that, *To Establish Justice, To Insure Domestic Tranquility*, the final report of President Johnson's National Commission on the Causes and Prevention of Violence, included "Religion and the Problem of Violence," an essay by Terence Cardinal Cooke (1969) that parallels both consensus and, to a lesser extent, dissensus theorizing—except of course, he does, but the sociologists do not, refer to God as ordaining all of this. It is interesting to note, too, that even more than some sociologists, the Cardinal remains totally silent on the past history of religious conflict in America.

At the pivotal point in our history when "race riot" no longer meant "lynch mob," and therefore took on an unfamiliar urgency in white society; when the myth of an American history of idyllic, peaceful social change and development was exploded, unsuccessful official efforts to remember our violent religious past in relation to social resistance to change reinforced our shared ignorance. At the end of the decade, the very part of our past that could shed most light on the racial violence of the sixties remained totally forgotten or at best significantly marginalized.

Roman Catholic Americans were, from colonial times on into the nineteenth century and even into the twentieth century, a strategically placed threat to the religious and political status quo, and therefore, became the preeminent "internal enemy." African Americans became the preeminent internal enemy after a short interval during the McCarthy period when internal Communists were the internal enemy. African Americans at that point were socially situated for the first time to threaten the racial status quo through their own nonviolent and confrontational resistance to racial discrimination. Their candidacy for the role of preeminent internal enemy was enhanced by the increase in the number of race riots in which African Americans were not merely victims of white mobs.

Another way to put this last point is that American social amnesia about the role of violence in the process that finally led to the inclusion of Catholics into American political life has generated in us a trained incapacity to understand the dynamics of modern racial conflict. To frame our history to highlight religious violence and tensions illuminates not only the causes but also the contemporary political uses and consequences of racial conflict. Further, it places in a meaningful context the political confrontations and divisions over equal rights for women and homosexuals, just as it can illuminate other "cultural wars" (Hunter, 1991).

The similarities between interreligious violence and interracial violence suggest which social conditions qualify some, but disqualify other social groups for the role of preeminent internal enemy. For instance, there are significant parallels between early Catholic history and later African-American history. The 1968 "Kerner Report" (The Report of the Commission on Civil Disorders) warned, after close to twenty years of racial conflict and violence, that America might become a nation, divided into two, black and white, separate and unequal. The only other significantly large social group about which that statement could be made accurately was the Irish Catholics from 1830 through the Civil War. When Irish Catholics immigrated to the States in large numbers beginning in the 1830s, their arrival was even more traumatic than the great Negro migrations from the rural South to the northern cities of Chicago and the eastern seaboard around World War I.

Admittedly, the parallels between religious and racial confrontations are limited. Protestant-Catholic conflict persisted in America so long for unique religious reasons: Roman Catholics were seen as un-American and subversive because of their loyalty to an international religious authority and Catholic beliefs were offensive to virtually all Americans.

From the 1830s, however, religious intergroup warfare was intense for another reason. Not only did Irish Catholics begin to arrive in large numbers, but in most of the states they were able to assume that with citizenship would come equal civil rights. However, their very noticeable presence and their exercise of their civil liberties produced stiff opposition, and ultimately, they had to fight for them in the face of concerted, if not politically astute, resistance, first by mob rule, later by the violence occasioned by the emergence of the Know Nothing Party, and finally in the political arena during the heyday of Know Nothing electoral victories.

The unskilled immigrants' alien and untutored ways, their poverty, their willingness to work for low wages, and intransigent Roman Catholicism were sure to offend native Americans, and the confluence of all these social attributes of the immigrants had a profound effect on Protestant-Catholic/Native-Immigrant confrontation. It requires that they all be taken into account when referring to the causes of anti-Catholicism, so that the parallels between it and racist, antiblack, sentiment may be assessed properly. This requirement means taking a different stance from that of Higham's ([1955] 1969) excellent work on religious and ethnic nativism, in which he seeks to distinguish between "religious nativism" directed at Catholics from other forms of Protestant-Catholic hostility.

Anti-Catholicism was linked to the desire to keep the English colonies, and later the United States, Protestant, and free from the threat of Catholic "aliens"—ethnically different, or not—whose loyalty was thought to be in doubt. These sentiments were intense even in the early colonial period when Catholics shared with Protestants the same ethnicity and the number of Catholics was minuscule. Although the sentiments against religious and social change underwent several metamorphoses, especially after a large contingent of ethnic Catholics arrived beginning in the mid-1800s and kept arriving until the early 1900s, the hostile sentiments linked to religion lingered at least until the 1950s.

Religious Conflict: A Sociohistorical View

Anti-Catholicism arrived in America even before the Catholics did in 1632, brought from England by still earlier Puritan and Anglican immigrants. Anti-Catholicism expressed itself through state repression and state condoned violence throughout the colonial period to the eve of the Revolution, when our national dependence on Catholic France and Spain muted popular anti-Catholic sentiment. In the Federalist period, nativism, including anti-Catholic nativism, first took on the hue of partisan two-party politics.

Violence against Catholics peaked in the 1830s, in what has been described as a "Protestant crusade" (Billington, 1938). A convent and schools and churches were burned in several cities, and riots leveled Irish sections of eastern cities as well. Methodical German Catholics dressed in uniforms drilled and marched around their churches. After the burning of the Charlestown convent and the widespread rioting and destruction of church property in the City of Brotherly Love, the Know Nothing mayor of New York appeared to be fanning the flames of violence there. Things quieted down when its Roman Catholic archbishop warned him that if one Catholic church burned, New York would become a second Moscow (a rather graphic threat, given its proximity to the Russians' destruction of their capital before advancing French troops). New York remained quiet.

In the 1840s and 1850s, violent political confrontations were connected with Catholic assertions of their political and civil rights and the rise of the Know

Nothing Party which sought to abrogate those rights. Pitched battles were fought for physical control of polling places, people were killed and maimed. Social cleavages took a less physically violent form with the dawn of the Civil War: during that bloodletting, Irish Catholics, strong northern partisans of the Democratic Party, were attacked in the press as a drunken, depraved, disloyal, subversive alien element that thwarted the noble political efforts of Lincoln, and the military success of the Union.

Never far from the surface, anti-Catholic nativism reemerged in the latter part of the nineteenth century with the activity of the American Protective Association: the effort included attempts to exclude Catholics from jobs and other economic and political activities. It survived at least into the first third of the twentieth century in the rhetoric of the Ku Klux Klan, and its political fallout was still visible in voting patterns of Catholics and Protestants up to the mid-twentieth century.

Even if Protestant-Catholic animosity persisted over a long period of time, and then lessened, can its sociologically significant implications for other forms of group violence be demonstrated? I have suggested that the social change that moved the United States from a generally informal but genuinely Protestant nation to relatively pluralistic, religiously inclusivist civil society, was fraught with religious violence and conflict. A second empirical generalization that can be drawn from the historical record is that the religious conflict that was, on one level, a battle over societal change and resistance thereto, was not limited to mob rule, but involved political institutions early, including the two-party and spoils systems, and eventually has entered into the realm of the courts. Lastly, this very long-lived conflict was the first form of wedge politics—before they had that name—which powerfully protected the interests of the economic elite and therefore assured the economic status quo. Hence this history should furnish insight into modern wedge politics which rely on racial (and other "cultural") conflicts to attain the same ends.

There are many sociological reasons, linked to concrete historical factors, for anti-Catholicism's long tenure as the basis of wedge politics. It is important to note first that anti-Catholic sentiment has been intense as well as persistent. In Frederic Jaher's (1994, p. 93) recent book on American anti-Semitism, he writes that during the colonial period "Israel's cherished contributions to Christianity, combined with the greater fear and threat of Catholics, made Jews the less hated minority in Protestant America.... Slurs against Judaism were rarely as vitriolic" as those against Catholics. It is also the case that Jews were welcome in colonies that excluded Catholics.

Admittedly, even in the colonial period, anti-Catholicism and economic and political interests were intertwined: once Maryland was established as a haven for all English Christians, including Catholics and Puritans who having been persecuted by Anglicans in Virginia were invited there by Catholic Lord Baltimore, the Puritans repressed Catholic religious freedom, and protected their newly gained lands from Catholic subversion. It was claimed, too, that the latter were also worthy of prosecution because of their royal politics. However, sociopolitical and economic factors alone do not explain the religious hatred and fear. Catholics were hated and feared in all the colonies, independent of whether or not they had anything worth stealing, whether or not they ever appeared to show tell-tale signs of disloyalty to Protestant monarchs or subversion in the service of Catholic ones.

Clinton Rossiter ([1953] 1956, pp. 89-90), in order to characterize to a mid-century readership the distrust and fear aroused by a tiny band of English Roman Catholics throughout our colonial period, wrote, "The Catholic occupied much the same position in colonial America that the Communist does today."

Political Uses of Anti-Catholicism

The early political uses of anti-Catholicism are found on the eve of the Revolution. The Loyalists warned of dire consequences (Catholic hegemony, subversion, and tyranny) if the colonies took Spain and France as allies against Protestant England. Conversely, the Patriots, led by Alexander Hamilton, a brash seventeen-year-old student pamphleteer, stirred up religious fear and hatred by publicizing the offensive and dangerous terms of the Quebec Act. This act, which granted religious freedom to French Canadian Catholics, was used as a successful gambit to recruit to the Revolution those nonpolitically engaged citizens who could be mustered by their fear of Rome (Schachner, 1961). Given American dependency on Catholic France and Spain, and the desire to enlist French Canada to the revolution, the American patriots quickly gave up that argument, the Loyalists lost the war, and Catholic Americans felt the breath of freedom even more strongly than did the other revolutionaries. The respite was to be short.

Rossiter opined that because "The Catholic was feared and despised with the same unthinking passion as is the communist today... he was therefore the acid test of the good intentions of the new Republic...." and he found the speed with which Catholic "disqualifications were erased from state laws and constitutions... a stunning triumph of common sense and democracy." He fails to point out, however, that if it were a triumph, it was so because there were opponents to the religious freedom of Papists, and it was not a universal triumph at that.

He ignores the fact that while most of the established state churches did disappear relatively soon after the ratification of the Federal Constitution, with its amendment that dictated separation of church and state on the federal level of government, some states retained their established churches into the nineteenth and even the twentieth century. One remained until 1818 in Connecticut, and until 1824 in Massachusetts. New Hampshire, a state that experienced a large influx of French Canadians, defeated Catholic emancipation in 1850; it remained a Protestant state as late as 1902, when it became a Christian one, only to give up all religious labels in 1912 (Littell, 1962, p. 28). Admittedly these states were "exceptions to the rule."

The rule, however, was an informally established Protestant state-church throughout the nation, and as we have seen, its transition to pluralism—independent of what the federal and state constitutions pledged— was a rocky one for Catholics. Freedom of religion was not won by the stroke of a pen, neither at the signing of the Declaration of Independence, nor at the Constitutional Convention. Given this history, being Catholic in America was, at least until the mid-twentieth century, a "master status."

Since the rule was that the Protestant establishment was for the most part informal, the means to curtail Catholicism at least on the civil and political level could be expected to be surreptitious, at least most of the time: The Know Nothing Party got its name from its members' assertions that they "knew nothing" about a party whose not so secret, but avowed purpose was to curtail Catholic civil rights. The Catholic master status was both the most significant aspect of Catholic life, and the one that on the manifest level was supposed to have no effect on their rights as citizens.

The attempt to limit Catholics' rights without referring to their religion emerged early, in the Federalist period, not too distant from the ratification of the Constitution and its commitment to the separation of church and state. Thus, there is reason to believe that the small number of United Irishmen, Catholics, and some distinguished nonbelievers, who supported Irish revolution against England, and were strong supporters of the French Revolution as well, were particular targets of the Alien and Sedition Acts (Billington, 1938; Elkins and McKitrick, 1993), acts which Smith (1956, p. xviii) compared to McCarthy's anti-Communist crusade: "I discovered more and more modern parallels—arguments over presumptive guilt and protests against anonymous informers are prime examples—but I have resisted any temptation to belabor them."

If for Rossiter, the anti-Catholicism of the colonial period is identical to the anti-Communism of the McCarthy period, and for Smith, the Alien and Sedition Acts are similar to the ploys of the McCarthy period, and Catholics were their main target even though now they were not so named, it is clear that Rossiter's acid test of the "good intentions" of the new republic suggests "common sense and democracy" had something less than a stunning success.

During the Federalist period, not long after either the Declaration of Independence or the Constitution, it would not be surprising if the same "internal enemy" that was targeted earlier for disabilities would no longer formally and explicitly be identified with its "master status": being a Catholic. This was a rather simple task because that master status is a confluence of other attributes that will account for the effectiveness of wedge politics: That a very small number of visible Catholics were ethnically distinct immigrants—poor uneducated aliens—pro-Irish and anti-English revolutionaries, as well as anti-Federalist—an Anglophile party—and Jeffersonian democrats to a man. Those who hated Catholics were likely to get the drift of the new Alien and Sedition Acts; Catholics didn't have to be mentioned in them by name to be targeted by them in fact.

The fact that there were still so few Irish Catholic immigrants during the Federalist period should not be overlooked. In a word, a contemporary social and cultural phenomenon—the apparent revival of European anti-Semitism where there are no Jews—is not an anomaly. Similar dramas with different actors have played in America. The Federalist period produced anti-Catholic legislation with a smattering of visible foreign Catholics (and invisible "native" English Catholics) just as McCarthyism featured anticommunism without internal communists. Apparently, "internal enemies" can animate society as a form of theater—that can play for keeps. It demonstrates that any group can fulfill the role of internal enemy, especially if it is small, or preferably, nonexistent.

The Know Nothings also avoided mentioning Catholics by name: they sought legislation requiring all immigrants to live in the United States for twenty years before being granted the right to vote, and requiring all office holders to take oaths of allegiance that would preclude Catholic assent. In spite of the failure of that political agenda, Catholics remained something less than full citizens, whose loyalty to the United States was doubted because of their religious adherence to the Bishop of Rome. Given this climate of opinion it is not surprising that during the "trustee controversy" in the latter half of the eighteenth century, when some Catholic laymen were pitted against Catholic bishops over control of church property and the right of laymen to call priests to minister to parishes, several state legislatures passed laws that would have imposed Protestant church order on Catholics.

Of all the groups that were internal enemies, why have Roman Catholics held the role longest, and can even be characterized as the "preeminent" internal enemy for most of our history? A major reason for their unique status probably is that they were the first outsiders positioned to pressure the society to become more pluralistic—in this case, religiously pluralistic. Their very presence threatened the informal Protestant establishment, and raised fears because of the general assumption that American freedom rested upon a Protestant citizenry. But they also fought for their ongoing political inclusion, and insisted on retaining their unique religious character.

Including Catholics required the most significant social change involving intergroup relations up to that time: it meant moving from a de facto Protestant commonweal to a civil society in which religion really was separated from the rights of citizenship. They remained in the geographical center rather than on the periphery of the nation, came to be a significant minority of the population, and quickly attained urban political power to further their claims. For these reasons Catholics retained their unique status as "preeminent internal enemy" for three hundred years. None of the other "lesser" internal enemies possessed similar social attributes, nor were they similarly socially situated.

Admittedly, the "real Native Americans," as nineteenth-century Roman Catholic spokesmen liked to call them, were the targets of genocide, those who were not slaughtered were pushed westward and interned in prisoner of war camps. Mormons, who came on the scene as an internal enemy late in our history, sought their own separate society beyond the frontier; when the United States finally caught up with them, it was in the boondocks. After they officially renounced polygamy, the federal government's war on them ended. Groups like the Perfectionists and Masons often were either contained in time or number of adherents, and either died out or were integrated into society without producing traumatic social change. These groups seem to be perceived as Talcott Parsons once wrote of a white, Anglo-Saxon, academic, self-avowed Buddhist was in the 1950s: all were Protestants, albeit strange ones. Hence, the integration of these groups into the larger society has generally not required the extent of social change that integrating Roman Catholics did, and only they were poised even as early as the 1840s to press for sociopolitical inclusion and the radical social change that it would necessitate.

What of African Americans? It would seem that if any group can reasonably be characterized as a likely candidate for the role of early internal enemy it is they. But it is my contention that African Americans become an internal enemy rather late in our history. The very fact of their existence, as opposed to the illusiveness of McCarthy's internal communists, put constraints on African Americans' potential to play that social role.

When were African Americans similarly socially and politically situated as the Catholics were from the 1830s on? When could they assert their right to be fully included in civil society, and by that very act, threaten significant social change and dislocation? It is the thesis of this paper that their objective and absolute social marginality and powerlessness precluded their being an internal enemy for much of our history. Their marginality was social and political, first as slaves and later as victims of Jim Crow laws; it was even geographical until the early 1900s. The fact that the Supreme Court struck down the doctrine of separate but equal educational opportunities only after 1950, and it still caused a public furor, is indicative of their absolute political marginality throughout most of our history. Segregation itself was only attacked in the South after that late date and met significant institutional resistance.

Admittedly, African Americans were feared, especially when slave revolts were so much on white minds, but the futility of such efforts is attested to by their aftermath. Too, at least later, African Americans were hated: they were easy targets of violence—most dramatically that of lynch mobs—and their murderers went unpunished. With rare exceptions, African Americans were not positioned to make claims for their own civil rights and their own civil liberties until late in our history. When they did begin to make such claims frequently and forcefully, only around the middle of the twentieth century, they become eligible for the status of internal enemy, and they immediately attained the dubious distinction of internal enemy par excellence.

The special role that intergroup violence and conflict played in the careers of Catholic Americans and African Americans as preeminent internal enemies will tell much about ethnic and racial conflict from the perspective of religious history. Minimally, it is clear that interracial confrontation and violence and race riots ceased to be lynch mobs and took on a different quality only in the 1940s. The newer forms of racial violence fruitfully can be compared to anti-Catholic violence and Catholic response in the nineteenth century.

The most significant comparison between early anti-Catholic violence and response and later racial violence is that in the first case, the Catholics did not remain the victims for long; they threatened to fight back, and they did fight back rather early on. The fighting Irish got their name and logo from this history: a cleaned up version of an ethnic slur became the little pugnacious man in the green suit and top hat that signified Irish Catholicism to America. It seemed to be the social character of this ethnic group that they refused to assume the role of victim. Because of the way they were socially situated— gaining control of city political machines, the mayor's office, and the urban police departments—they had the power to make their counter identity stick. Indeed, some of their bellicose reactions to violence perpetrated against them convinced many Protestants that their own freedom of speech and assembly would be curtailed by Catholic power. And sometimes it was. Ignorance of this history makes it virtually impossible to meaningfully situate the history of racial violence and confrontation of the 1960s, and understand their implications for social change.

FORGETTING WHAT WAS BARELY REMEMBERED: THE NATIONAL COMMISSION ON THE CAUSES AND PREVENTION OF VIOLENCE

The concept of social amnesia, or social forgetting, is not new, and the potential advantages of remembering the forgotten past have been discussed by Thomas F. O'Dea (1960). The idea was picked up later by Mary Douglas (1986). She concluded, from the work of Robert K. Merton, that to study what is esteemed and valued, it is best to examine what is discarded or unmemorable.

Some Analytical Distinctions

"Soft social amnesia" is essentially a failure to analyze and theorize. An incident or series of incidents is known and reported at least by a small group of educated persons, but the historical events are known merely as discrete phenomena. No successful effort is made to place them in context, or examine their consequences. Events may be recalled but only within classificatory systems that exclude some pertinent cases or ignore significant aspects of their existential reality. "Hard social amnesia" involves forgetting a fact or event *tout court,* and it can include distorting past events or even creating a mythic past opposite to the failed fact. The myth of a peaceful transition to freedom of religion in 1789 is a case in point.

In the research papers scholars submitted to the Commission staff, in the reports written by the staff from these research papers (as well as other sources), and especially in the Commission's final report, both soft and hard social amnesia abound. Interestingly, there appears to be a pattern of moving from soft to hard social amnesia as one progresses from the scholarly papers, to the staff reports, and ultimately to the Commission's final report. The first series of documents either understate or fail to place Protestant-Catholic attack and response in their social context. The succeeding papers and the final report mask the pivotal role played by religious conflict and violence in our history by identifying the relevant events with ethnic conflict only.

In *Violence in America: Historical and Comparative Perspectives, A Report Submitted to the National Commission on the Causes and Prevention of Violence,* edited by Hugh Graham and Ted Gurr (1969, p. xiv), Gurr commented: "Americans have always been given to a kind of historical amnesia that masks much of their turbulent past. All nations...sweeten memories...through collective repression, but Americans...magnified...selective recollection, owing to our historic vision of ourselves as a latter-day chosen people, a New Jerusalem." His conclusion: we have forgotten that violence is endemic to American history. Ironically, in spite of Gurr's own use of religious imagery the anthology ignores the religious conflicts that may have been fueled by that same imagery.

The only essay in this collection that discussed American religious conflict is by Richard M. Brown (1969a, pp. 45-84), "Historical Patterns of Violence in America." In it Brown distinguishes between "negative" and "positive" violence and finds religious violence subsumed under both categories. Included as cases of negative violence (i.e., in no direct way connected with any socially or historically constructive development), are the violence of racial, ethnic, and religious prejudice; urban violence; criminal, feud, and lynch mob violence; and free-lance mass murder. Not only is religious violence not separated from racial and ethnic violence, but it is separately listed under urban violence. It is even found under the category of "positive violence," when this form of violence was pursued by respectable members of the community taking law in their own hands to control the lawless (and later on, to attack groups such as Catholics, Jews, and labor organizers)!

There are innumerable problems with Brown's formulation: he does not consider the possibility that some forms of "negative" violence could be functional for maintaining the status quo. More generally, this formulation raises the complex question of how "historically constructive developments" are to be determined, as opposed to historically destructive developments. Further, the classificatory system consists of overlapping categories, and therefore, Catholic-Protestant violence could easily be scattered under different categories.

At one point, the author pursues a relatively extensive discussion of the Ku Klux Klan that concludes with the finding that Catholics and Jews, although the butt of verbal abuse, did not suffer violence during the Klan revival in the twenties, but WASPs who contravened the bounds of middle-class morality did. Brown (1969a, pp. 52-53) writes:

> Parallelling the Ku Klux Klan have been a host of other movements of racial, ethnic and religious malice. Before the Civil War the northeastern United States was lacerated by convent burnings and antiCatholic [sic] riots. This "Protestant Crusade" eventually bred the political Know Nothing movement. Anti-Chinese agitation that often burst into violence became a familiar feature of California and the West as the 19th century wore on. In 1891, 11 Italian immigrants were the victims of a murderous mob in New Orleans. The fear and loathing of Catholics (especially Irish and Italians) that often took a violent form was organized in the nonviolent but bigoted American Protective Association (APA) of 1887. Labor clashes of the late 19th century and early 20th century were often in reality ethnic clashes with native old-stock Americans ranged on one side as owners, foremen, and skilled workers against growing numbers of unskilled immigrants—chiefly Jews, Slavs, Italians, and others from Southern and Eastern Europe.

The confounding of ethnic and religious conflicts in this passage is difficult to account for, but typical of this chapter, and all commission reports.

Under "Urban Riots" we read: "Ulcerating slums along the lines of Five Points (in New York) and severe ethnic and religious strife stemming from the confrontation between burgeoning immigrant groups and the native American element made the 1830's, 1840's, and 1850's a period of sustained urban rioting, particularly in the great cities of the Northeast" (Brown, 1969a, pp. 53-54). After listing the numbers of riots in various cities, including those in the mid-west, Brown lists the various types of riots that accounted for this mayhem: labor riots, election riots, anti-Negro riots, antiabolitionist riots, anti-Catholic riots, "and the riots of various sorts involving the turbulent volunteer fireman's units." In no case is there any effort to discuss the relationship between ethnicity, religion, nativism, and violence.

The failure to put religious violence into focus is found in Brown's discussion of "vigilantism." This type of violence along with police, Revolutionary, Civil War, and Indian War violence is included under the category of "positive violence."

In discussing vigilante violence, a form of positive violence for him because it was indulged in by the elite to enforce proper behavior, Brown explains that vigilantism changed after the Civil War, and although members of the establishment continued to lead its ranks, it found other targets "connected with the tensions of the new America: Catholics, Jews, Negroes, immigrants, laboring men and labor leaders, political radicals, advocates of civil liberties, and non-conformists in general" (Brown, 1969a, p. 69).

These were all of the comments on religious violence in almost forty pages of text on "Historical Patterns of Violence in America." It is fair to say that Catholic-Protestant violence does not appear to be a salient category for Brown—one that could, if isolated and analyzed, throw light on the social implications of past as well as recent violence. His inattention to religious conflict is attested to throughout his work, but a telling example is the fact that when he mentions the San Francisco vigilance committee of 1856 in "Historical Patterns of Violence," he characterizes it as "led lock, stock and barrel by the leading merchants of the city who organized to stamp out alleged crime and political corruption" (Brown, 1969a, p. 68).

It is only in another essay by Brown (1969b, p. 197) in this volume, "The American Vigilante Tradition," that we learn, "The San Franciscan vigilantes were ethnically biased; their ire focused on one group: the Irish. The vigilantes were anti-Catholic; their hero and martyr was the anti-Romanist editor, James King of William, and most of their victims of 1856 were Catholics."

Brown's inattention to Protestant-Catholic conflict is difficult to explain given his familiarity with, and apparent approval of, Ray Billington's (1938) *The Protestant Crusade 1800-1860: A Study of the Origins of American Nativism.* That history reported Protestant-Catholic conflict much more extensively than Brown did. Brown's work can justifiably be characterized as "soft" social amnesia—but on the hard side of soft.

The coverage of Protestant-Catholic conflict moves to the level of "hard social amnesia" in the report's conclusion, authored by Graham and Gurr (1969, pp. 788-822). In seeking answers to the question, "What is happening to the political system in contemporary America?" against the background of the then current concern over violence, the authors assess the relevance of past episodes of violence for the contemporary situation. Religious violence is not mentioned as one of the historical types of violence whose relevance is to be assayed (although the irrelevent family feud draws the authors' sustained attention).

The anti-Catholic and anti-Semitic rhetoric of the KKK during the 1920s is mentioned as a backdrop to the empirical finding that KKK violence was directed not against Catholics and Jews but against WASPs who contravened traditional moral proscriptions.

There is only one allusion that brackets ethnic and religious violence, in a discussion that claims violence is not precipitated by a revolution of rising expectations, but on the contrary, is "protective resistance to undesirable change": "Most ethnic and religious violence in American history has been retaliatory violence by groups farther up the socioeconomic ladder who felt threatened by the prospect of the 'new immigrants' and the Negro getting both 'too big' and 'too close'" (Graham and Gurr, 1969, p. 805). Those are the only remarks in the conclusion about religious violence in American history. Notice, too, how the sentence reverts to racial and ethnic groups, negating the relevance of religious conflict which had just been offhandedly introduced. The lacuna is all the more dramatic against the authors' assertion that "historical amnesia or selective recollection... masks unpleasant traumas of the past" (Graham and Gurr, 1969, p. 792).

If religious violence was remembered haphazardly in the body of *The History of Violence in America* (1969) and forgotten in its conclusion, it is hardly surprising that the final National Commission report, *To Establish Justice, To Insure Domestic Tranquility* (1969, p. 8), failed to cure the earlier oversights. Indeed, the final report compounded the social amnesia in the conclusion of the early report by being positively misleading:

> Dominant Anglo-Americans rallied to 'nativist' movements that directed violence toward 'ethnic' scapegoats; in the 1790s with the Alien and Sedition Acts; in the 1850s with the sectional split; in the decade 1886-96 with the unrestricted immigration and labor and racial unrest; in World War I with the Red Scare; in World War II with the Nisei.

This statement completely expunges religious conflict and replaces it with ethnic conflict. The Commission (1969, p. 14) also repeats, for a third time, the discussion of the Klan in the 1920s which "despite its traditional rhetoric— focused its chastisement less upon Negroes, Catholics, and Jews than upon white Protestants...." This passage—the only mention of violence against religious groups in the Commission's final report—minimizes the interreligious violence by acknowledging only that Catholics and Jews were singled out for verbal attack by a redneck group during a short period of our history, but that they were less likely to be physically victimized than WASPs.

The Commission's soft-peddling of interreligious conflict, and its furtherance of social amnesia, cannot be explained merely as the consequence of poor scholarship. In another staff report to the Commission, (Kirkham, Levy, and Crotty, 1969) *Assassination and Political Violence*, Chapter Four, "Political Violence in the United States," does report part of the history of nativism that is completely ignored in the final report of the Commission. Drawn from yet another Commission paper written by Brown and from a paper submitted by the Anti-Defamation League, this chapter provides a historical overview which includes vigilantism, abolitionism and antiabolitionism, reimposing white supremacy in the South, agrarian reform, and labor violence, as well as one topic which includes "Defense of American Nativism and Moralism—Native

American Party-Know-Nothings-White Caps-Second Ku Klux Klan." Each of these topics—labor, agrarian reform, and the Native American Party and Know Nothings get about a page to themselves, and the authors report months of rioting in Philadelphia in which "Two Catholic Churches, two parochial schools, and at least a dozen homes owned by Catholics were burned to the ground" (Kirkham, Levy and Crotty, 1969, p. 174). Admittedly, only this one incident is reported, although Brown knew Billington's report of the famous burning of the Charlestown convent, and more to the point of political violence, his enumeration of the frequent pitched battles between Catholics and Protestants on election days.

The Commission, whose job it was to uncover the roots of violence in our history, ignored even the little information it was provided, obliterating any memory of the most significant intergroup violence we ever experienced other than Indian wars and lynch law: interreligious pitched battles. It may well be that the Commission was convinced by some historians of nativism who hold that religion played no part in it—but putting nativism aside, there is no doubt about the history of interreligious violence and the Commissions's failure to cure our social amnesia about it.

Curing Social Amnesia to Better Understand Interracial Conflict

How do the facts lost to social amnesia further our understanding of contemporary conflictual interracial and interethnic dynamics? I think that knowing the history of religious violence can help untangle the contradictory findings, analyses, and recommendations concerning the causes and prevention of collective violence in the various reports that were submitted to the Commission, as well as the paradoxes in America's history that baffled the Commission.

Graham and Gurr (1969, pp. 813-814) describe "one basic principle" supported by the historical evidence. Violence can be successful only if it has public support:

> Popular support tends to sanction violence in support of the status quo....[The evidence indicates that]. the prolonged use of force or violence to advance the interests of any segmental group may impede and quite possibly preclude reform....[This conclusion] represents a fundamental trait of American...character, one which is ignored by advocates of any political orientation at the risk of broken hopes, institutions and lives.

In other words, after reviewing the history of violence in America, but completely missing anti-Catholic violence and response, they advise blacks and antiwar protesters to "cool it." When that history is *not* ignored, it becomes clear that both interreligious and interethnic conflict and violence will certainly have political consequences, often strengthening the political party that supports the status quo, but the conflicts can be linked to significant social change nonetheless. The history they overlooked demonstrates how problematic it was to apply this "basic principle" to racial violence between 1940 and 1970, as it would be to apply the principle in the nineties, where the principle could only obscure the broader sociopolitical issues at hand.

Indeed, the principle suffers from the inevitable consequence of social amnesia. It rests on ignorance of the fact that groups using violence to support the status quo did not have carte blanch; to the extent that they encountered resistance, the larger society was brought into play, as were the various institutions and underlying values of that society. When the status quo can only be defended by power or the use of non-legitimate force, and it meets resistance, the larger society could no longer stand idly by.

It might be imagined that the social amnesia that underlies Graham and Gurr's conclusions accounts for the fact that others who prepared reports for the Commission came to very different conclusions and recommendations. For instance, in Jerome H. Skolnick's report to the Commission, *The Politics of Protest*, he takes a radically different view from that of Graham and Gurr.

Skolnick (1969, pp. 9-10) proposes an alternative to the myth of American peaceful progress: historically, various groups resorted to violence; they were neither "violence-prone" nor exceptional; their adoption of violence was "not merely capricious and temporary, but socially structured and predictable." He adds, "The proposition that domestic political violence has been unnecessary to achieve political goals...is historically fallacious...." and Skolnick (1969, p. 16) rejects the notion that the establishment is self-transforming, or allows "outsiders" to "move nonviolently up the politico-economic ladder." Skolnick recognizes that violence is neither always necessary nor always effective. Even so, the inertia built into the arrangements of economic and political power is likely to require the resort to violence or the threat of violence on the part of out-groups. Citing Native Americans, immigrant laborers, and African Americans, Skolnick points out that admitting them as groups into the socioeconomic power complex would have required transforming the existing system. He shrewdly comments that "American institutions seem designed to facilitate the advancement of talented individuals rather than of oppressed groups."

Skolnick's analysis may be persuasive, but ironically, the data he provides supports Graham and Gurr's position more than his own. He could have supported his case better with the data on interreligious conflict but yet again, social amnesia seems to have intervened. The solution hit upon eventually to integrate Roman Catholics into civil society was to recognize their individual rights to freedom of religion, and to reject any recognized status to the group, or in this case their church. It seems possible, therefore, that an examination of that forgotten history would not only provide data to support Skolnick's thesis more competently than his own, but that it could resolve the contradictory conclusions drawn by him and Graham and Gurr.

The Commission report (1969, p. 2) itself unnecessarily elevated this contradiction, intergroup conflict bringing about change (Skolnick) versus it impeding it (Graham and Gurr), to a paradox: "Americans have been, paradoxically, both [sic] a turbulent people but have enjoyed a relatively stable republic. Our liberal and pluralistic system has historically both generated and accommodated itself to a high level of unrest, and our turmoil has reflected far more demonstration and protest than conspiracy and revolution." Recognizing the economic, political, commercial, and professional power of the "original dominant immigrant group, the so-called Anglo-Saxons," the Commission concludes that later ethnic arrivals sought to wrest power from the dominant group and the latter used all their control over legitimate power (and one might add their use of illegitimate force as well) to retain their superior position.

Embedded in these words, even though they were stunted by social amnesia, is the truism that "so-called Anglo-Saxons" were virtually all Protestant. On the eastern seaboard and the mid-west, the ethnics were frequently Catholic. The Protestant ethnics, like the Irish Protestants and Scandinavians, did not raise sociopolitical problems. The division between the dominant group and others was not economic or ethnic alone, but religious as well. Deep religious conflict between Catholic and Protestant working folk produced the crosscutting loyalties that had such profound effects on the labor movement and thwarted workers' efforts to organize themselves against the Anglo-Protestant elites. Maybe ethnic differences could have done it alone, but they did not have to. As Klausner (1969, p. 1299) noted, Protestant-Catholic religious differences "absolutized" mundane competition for jobs or political office that would usually be dealt with in the market or in the polling booth, and turned them into the most bitter intergroup hostilities and even bloodletting.

It is impossible for the Commission to understand how our "stable republic," free of conspiracy and revolution, has evolved a liberal and pluralistic system that historically both generated and accommodated itself to a high level of unrest, without knowing the preeminent role of religious conflict in American history. Religious conflict deflected attention away from economic and social class antagonisms. Even as late as the 1940s Catholics were voting Democrat, and the more Catholic they were, the more Democrat they voted; working-class and middle-income Protestants voted Republican and supported party politics that often financially benefitted only the very rich or upper middle class. Knowing the history of religious conflict that accounts for these kinds of voting patterns (that survived well into the twentieth century) makes it a lot easier to see how contemporary racial conflict now fills the same role. African Americans are finally socially situated to press for their inclusion into social and economic life, hence replacing the Catholics who had been the internal enemy for so long; to the extent that they press, as Skolnick would have it, for inclusion as a group, rather than as individual successes, their demands will generate that much more resistance, becoming the cannon fodder of two-party politics.

The Inclining Political Significance of Race

African-American marginality to the two-party political system lasted until after 1950. Admittedly, the Democratic Party was aligned with the continuation of slavery, and the Republican Party came into existence in response to the threat of disunion over slavery, but after the Civil War, the role of Negroes in two-party politics was at best tangential. They were neither politically powerful nor were they a group whose interests large numbers of people had to specifically vote against, except possibly in the South, where blacks were so politically powerless that they were often excluded from the voting process itself. This very powerlessness that lingered into the twentieth century precluded recruiting Negroes as the preeminent internal enemy. Fifty years ago things began to change quite radically. Interracial violence and conflict that was no longer limited to lynch mobs, was the vehicle of that change.

Only the dynamics of interreligious conflict, and its political ramifications, will provide a meaningful context for interpreting the various types of violence that are usually lumped together under the title "Negro-riot," or "race riot," or even "commodity riot," because it is highly likely that what enabled blacks to step up into the role of internal enemy was the development, after World War II, of racial violence as a two-way street. They were finally situated to make demands, albeit modest ones, on the larger society. Hence, they took their place in the long-running drama of what the Commission described as the generation of, and accommodation to, high levels of unrest that go hand-in-hand with the absence of conspiracy and revolution.

To be granted the dubious distinction of being the preeminent internal enemy is to become central in the give-and-take of two-party politics, or more specifically, of wedge politics. The Democratic Party, at once the party in the north of the Irish Catholics, came to support the aspirations of the African-American community when President Kennedy supported Martin Luther King. And the Democratic Party has remained more sympathetic to the needs of the African American, supporting such efforts as affirmative action.

The modern Republican Party finds its spiritual predecessors among those parties that sought to benefit from religious wedge politics: the Federalists, the Know Nothings, the fledgling Republican Party of the 1860s, and the party as it survived through the 1940s. Contemporary Republican politics are merely an old chapter, wedge politics, in a new book, the possibility of race war. In the recent past there were the "wedge politics" first pursued by Richard Nixon under the euphemism "Southern Strategy"; it continued with the code words "welfare Cadillac queen" and "quotas" to describe affirmative action, that incited racial tension during the Reagan administration and probably accounted for at least some of President Reagan's great popularity. Wedge politics were more blatantly behind Mr. Bush's elevation of Willie Horton to public enemy number one; they backfired, however, when he lost the party platform to the antiabortionists, and turned over the 1992 Republican National Convention to his erstwhile rival, who offended the nation by his unvarnished attacks on feminists, and homosexuals, both of whom he sought to publicly designate as internal enemies.

Curing social amnesia allows us to see that wedge politics not only lasted throughout our history, but played a significant role in it. More importantly, wedge politics cease to appear unreasonable when one asks of them, cui bono? I contend that the answer to that question has always been that the small minority who possessed significant amounts of property, and whose interests were protected from the voting majority in a democracy, were those who benefitted from this form of politics.

REFERENCES

Billington, R.A. (1938) 1964. *The Protestant Crusade 1800-1860: A Study of the Origins of American Nativism.* Chicago: Quadrangle Books.

Brown, R.M. 1969a. "Historical Patterns of Violence in America." In *Violence in America: Historical and Comparative Perspectives,* edited by H.D. Graham and T.R. Gurr.

Brown, R.M. 1969b. "The American Vigilante Tradition." In *Violence in America: Historical and Comparative Perspectives,* edited by H.D. Graham and T.R. Gurr.

Cooke, T. 1969. "Religion and the Problem of Violence." Pp. 263-270 in *To Establish Justice, To Insure Domestic Tranquility, Final Report of the Commission on the Causes and Prevention of Violence,* edited by Government Printing Office. Washington, DC: Government Printing Office.

Douglas, M. 1986. "Institutionalized Public Memory." In *The Social Fabric: Dimensions and Issues,* edited by J.F. Short, Jr. Beverly Hills: Sage.

Elkins, S., and E. McKitrick. 1993. *The Age of Federalism: The Early American Republic, 1788-1800.*

Gouldner, A.W. 1970. *The Coming Crisis of Western Sociology.* New York: Basic Books.

Graham, H.D., and T.R. Gurr (eds.). 1969. *Violence in America: Historical and Comparative Perspectives. A Report Submitted to the National Commission on the Causes and Prevention of Violence.* Washington, DC: Government Printing Office.

Higham, J. (1955) 1969. *Strangers in the Land: Patterns of American Nativism 1860-1925.* New York: Atheneum.

Hunter, J.D. 1991. *Culture Wars: The Struggle to Define America.* New York: Basic Books.

Jahar, F.C. 1994. *A Scapegoat in the New Wilderness: The Origins and Rise of Anti-Semitism in America.* Cambridge: Harvard University Press.

Kirkham, J.F., S.G. Levy, and W.J. Crotty. 1969. "Assassination and Political Violence 8." A Report Submitted to the National Commission on the Causes and Prevention of Violence. Government Printing Office.

Klausner, S. 1969. "Invocation and Constraint of Religious Zealotry." Pp. 1291-1326 in *Crimes of Violence.* A Staff Report to the National Commission on the Causes and Prevention of Violence, Appendix 27, (volume 13), edited by D.J. Mulvihill and M.M. Tumin. Washington, DC: Government Printing Office.

Littell, F.H. 1962. *From State Church to Pluralism: A Protestant Interpretation of Religion in American History.* Chicago: Aldine.

National Commission on the Causes and Prevention of Violence. 1969. *To Establish Justice, To Insure Domestic Tranquility.* Washington, DC: Government Printing Office.

O'Dea, T.F. 1960. "American Catholics and International Life." *Social Order* X: 243-265.

Report of the National Advisory Commission on Civil Disorders. 1968. New York: Bantam Books.

Rossiter, C. (1953) 1956. *The First American Revolution: The American Colonies on the Eve of Independence.* New York: Harcourt Brace.

Schnachner, N. (1946) 1961. *Alexander Hamilton.* New York: A.S. Barnes.

Skolnick, J.H. 1959. *The Politics of Protest.* A Report Submitted to the National Commission on the Causes and Prevention of Violence. Washington, DC: Government Printing Office.

Smith, J.M. 1956. *Freedom's Fetter's: The Alien and Sedition Laws and American Civil Liberties.* Ithaca, New York:

A COGNITIVE-EDUCATIONAL APPROACH TO THE RESOLUTION OF RACIAL, ETHNIC, AND RELIGIOUS CONFLICT

Joseph B. Gittler

Relatively few societies in the contemporary nations of the world manifest a mono-ethnic population. Most countries contain prodigious numbers of ethnic groups[1] resulting in the development of a number of sociocultural philosophies and programs seeking to deal with this situation. Sociocultural assimilation dominated the positions in the early decades of the twentieth century. Since the late 1940s cultural pluralism (multiculturalism) became a competing and prominent policy, especially in democratic societies.

This paper is an interim statement of an ongoing investigation of the complementary and commutual coexistence of cultural congruities among the multi-ethnic (including racial and religious) groups.

Research in Human Social Conflict, Volume 1, pages 343-363.
Copyright © 1995 by JAI Press Inc.
All rights of reproduction in any form reserved.
ISBN: 1-55938-923-0

DEFINITION OF AN ETHNIC GROUP AND ETHNICITY

Ethnic group has been given many and diverse definitions.[2] The variety of definitions is numerous. They tend to reflect the difficulties in meaningfully comprehending a common social reality—the ethnic group.

Following the guidelines and rules in the logical criteria for formulating definitions (Gittler, 1977), I would like to suggest that an ethnic group constitutes an unorganized human-social group whose members interact and share in a distinctive set of commonly held symbols (culture): (a) on a plane of overt affiliation and behavior where common symbols are manifested and directly observable; (b) on a plane of covert identification, consisting of personal group identification, feelings of belongingness, and a "consciousness of kind," (that Giddings suggested many years ago); and (c) on a plane of societal designation where individuals are referred to and considered by others as belonging to a particular ethnic group.

That which is commonly shared by members of an ethnic group on these three levels consists of: (1) a historic ancestral and sometimes national origin; (2) language ("mother tongue" and body language); and (3) family surnames. These primary categories of an ethnic group give rise to a derivative and secondary set of categories.[3]

Accordingly, an ethnic group consists of those individuals acting in relation to, identifying with, and being referred to by others as related to one, or more aspects of an endemic symbolic set.

Ethnicity may be defined, as the *degree* to which a plurality of individuals share by behavior, practice, feeling, and denotation from "others" commonly held symbols and values. The dimensionality of ethnicity determines the degree of cohesiveness and singularity of ethnic groups. The techniques for determining the degree and extent of an individual's ethnicity is still to be formulated and tested.

HOSTILITY SPRINGING FROM ETHNIC DIVERSITY

Unfortunately, the ethnic diversity throughout the world, has led to a human history that is replete with the "dislike of the unlike," the discontent with the different. The xenophobias, the ethnocentrisms, and the ethnic stereotyping, prejudices, discrimination, scapegoating and too frequently, persecutions and even annihilations, have been noted by numerous social scientists.[4]

SOCIAL POLICY REACTIONS TO ETHNIC DIVERSITY

Two prominent and basic social philosophies and advocacies developed in relation to the ethnic diversities—sociocultural assimilation and sociocultural pluralism (multiculturalism).

Sociocultural assimilation refers to a process of reshaping the cultural characteristics of diverse ethnic groups to conform to the modes of the dominant and, sometimes majority, cultural group in a given society or nation. It advocates the adoption of the language and other cultural modus vivendi of the hegemonic social group. The doctrine was frequently expressed in the terms of creating a "melting pot." (The phrase was adopted from the title of a play written in 1909 by the English author, Israel Zangwill.)

The doctrine of assimilation found its advocates among leaders in industry, politics, and education. This position dominated the decades from the latter part of the nineteenth century until the 1940s, especially in the United States.[5]

Since the 1950s cultural pluralism (multiculturalism) came to the fore as a prominent canon, especially in democratic societies. This doctrine recognized that the diverse cultures and subcultures in a given society be permitted and encouraged to maintain their own unique identities.

Horace Kallen enunciated the ideas of cultural pluralism initially in a series of articles in 1915 and later in a number of volumes which extended the implications of cultural pluralism to many facets of American society (Kallen, 1915a, 1915b, 1924, 1956). Kallen developed his ideas in opposition to the extant policies of assimilation, prevalent at the time of his early writings. He considered cultural assimilation and the practical programs appended to this view as detrimental to the idea and creed of democracy. He criticized the assimilationists vigorously in his writings.[6]

Influenced by William James (Kallen was his student in philosophy at Harvard University), George Santayana, and John Dewey, Kallen's theory traced its roots to philosophical pluralism and radical empiricism which conceived of the world as a plurality of entities in constant flux and in constant change.[7]

In the decades following the 1930s in the United States, many social practitioners, research scholars, political leaders, jurists, and industrial leaders became eloquent spokespeople for the cogent richness and beneficial contributions of the immigrant cultures of American society.[8]

Ethnic surgence is not limited to the United States. Great Britain, France, Spain, countries of the former Soviet Union, Canada, Holland, Belgium, Sweden, and India are experiencing the impact of multiculturalism. The older doctrine of sociocultural assimilation was never fully realized.[9]

This is not to say that ethnic assimilation has disappeared as a social process. In the United States, Americanization, as assimilation, kept its substantial pace with pluralism. Second and third generation descendants of immigrant groups have adopted many lifestyles and traits of the dominant American culture. The English language has replaced the languages of the immigrant forebears. Their clothing has become more American. Food patterns included American eating habits (observe the universality of the hamburger). Entertainment and recreation became Americanized. The drive toward unity, identity, and fashion cannot be denied. Complete ethnicity (ethnicification) became unachievable however, and to many, undesirable. Assimilation therefore, remains a concomitant of ethnic pluralism, fluctuating with historical periods, waves of immigration, the degree and velocity of social change, the intensity of intergroup (interethnic) tension and conflict, and the socioeconomic status of America's ethnic populations. Nevertheless, concurrently with assimilation, ethnic identity and continuity have persisted.[10]

Shibutani and Kwan have observed that a simultaneity of assimilation and ethnic cultural differentiation is an ongoing evolutionary process.[11]

CHALLENGES SURROUNDING MULTICULTURALISM

Multiculturalism (and ethnic pluralism) arose in opposition to programmatic assimilationism as well as being an ameliorant and antidote to the antipathies encompasing ethnic differences. It held that knowing, understanding, and interacting with the different would result in interethnic concord, amicability, and collaboration.

The durability and persistence of ethnicity, in the minds of some individuals, was not a virtue. Multiculturalism and specifically, ethnic pluralism, have been criticized both as a social trend and as a social policy. The surgence of ethnicity during the decades of the sixties, seventies, and eighties alarmed even earlier advocates of ethnic pluralism. One of the most potent concerns is the fear that ethnic pluralism would give rise to the polarization of intra-ethnic feelings and interethnic hostility.[12]

Serious and real polemics have emerged, questioning the feasibility and plausibility of the doctrine and practicability of ethnic pluralism. A summary of the fears, concerns, criticisms, or outright rejections of ethnic pluralism includes the following propositions:

1. Ethnic pluralism "exhibits fluidity as well as diversity of value-standards. This fluidity makes it difficult for the pluralist system to achieve *consensus*" (Kornhauser, 1959, p. 104).
2. It is nigh impossible for ethnic pluralism to achieve equality in the larger society.
3. A community with dissonant value sets will make for a "disjunctive symbiosis" (Flower, 1956, p. 123).
4. Diversity is a basis of distrust (Greeley, 1971a, p. 13).
5. Without safeguards, pluralism is conducive to ethnic separatism.
6. Homogeneous grouping "considerably increases the potential for conflict" (Friedman, 1971, p. 239).
7. Ethnic groups tend to be special interest groups.
8. Special interest groups tend to be power groups.

9. Power groups are agents of intergroup conflict.
10. Enhancement and resurgence of ethnic identity and ethnic activity lead to the resurgence of ethnic prejudice and ethnocentrism.
11. Ethnic pluralism can result in divided loyalties during crises such as wars.
12. Ethnic pluralism is conducive to the polarization of ethnic feelings.
13. When strains arise, groups in pluralistic societies tend to become activist (Pinart, 1968, p. 689).
14. Militance and extreme behavior tend to result when a group is denied its objectives and goals (similar to "discrimination in reverse").
15. Complexity of group life increases the possibility of group tyranny over individuals (Kariel, 1968, p. 167).
16. Emotional irrationality of man results from a pluralistic, anomic society (Zijderveld, 1970, p. 25).
17. Educationists and agencies for pluralism are vague and unclear about their program goals and program operation.
18. Programmatic and goal vagueness has made for ambivalent attitudes among many Americans (Greeley, 1971b, p. 350).

A common thread runs through the concerns and criticisms of multiculturalism including ethnic pluralism. It involves the failure of the doctrine to delineate a modus operandi for the inclusion of important concomitant goals to ethnic pluralism: how to promote order within diversity; how to achieve the consensus groups necessary for a functioning society; how to integrate the parts of a culture with the whole of a culture.

It is difficult to deny that the responses to these charges have been vague and inefficacious. Kallen (1956, p. 58) suggested "an orchestration of diverse utterances of diversities." Similarly, one finds such expressions as the "balancing of group against group"; the need for an "ongoing diagogue" between groups; the need to bring the "ideal" of pluralism close to reality and practice; the need to establish an "effective mediating principle." A generic need for a unifying force while retaining the differences, appears to pervade these suggestions.

HUMANOCENTRISM

In the light of the alleged shortcomings, I wish to propose a *supplement— not a replacement—*to the doctrine of ethnic pluralism and multiculturalism: *Humanocentrism.*

By *humanocentrism* is meant the tendency for humans to know, feel, and act together around common values and symbols while simultaneously identifying themselves with and remaining part of sets of different symbols and values. *Humanocentrism* conceives of a common core of universal human-social-cultural elements in concentric relationship to the multiplicity of diverse sociocultural items in a community, in a nation, in the world. The pattern imitates the system of the planets in their ways around the sun by juxtaposing unblended cultural elements into a dynamic attractional and interactional system of relationships to a common cultural core. Instead of seeking harmony and unity "through an orchestration of the different," *humanocentrism* suggests that each culture and its subcultures circumvolve around a common cultural hub making for a system of social-cultural *species* in a conjuctive relationship to their human-social-cultural common *genera*. *Humanocentrism* is not hostile to cultural pluralism. Nor does pluralism deny the need of common factors in cultures. It is a matter of focus, emphasis, and supplementation.

Humanocentrism, though distinguishable, is not unrelated to the concept and philosophy of humanism. It is also related, but different from the concepts of synergism, syncretism, unilinear universalism, or social mass.[13]

Basically, *humanocentrism* emphasizes the oneness of the world (or near oneness) ontologically and epistemically along with the differences and varieties of its make-up, and recognizes that human society manifests pluriaspects as well as unifeatures. *Humanocentrism* blends cultural differences with cultural similitudes, pluralism with monism, diversity with uniformity, localism with universalism, heterogeneity with homogeneity, distinctivity with uniformity, antinomy with synonymity, and uniformism with heteromorphism.[14]

SELECTIVE ILLUSTRATIONS OF HUMANOCENTRISM

I shall not indicate the divergencies among the multitudinous ethnic groups. These are readily available. Our project has garnered and continues to collect the facts of commonalities among the multifold ethnic cultures.[15]

In this paper, I would like to illustrate the degree and types of commonalities present among the major religions of the world.

For centuries, religion has been a potent and crucial constituent of ethnic identity and frequently the basis of ethnic conflict. In some countries there is an outright fusion between religion and ethnicity. Ireland clearly illustrates the union between Catholicism and the general culture of the country (Potter, 1960). Those of Irish descent in countries other than Ireland, have continued to display integration between their Catholicism and Irish ethnicity.[16] The French-Canadians have also wedded their larger culture "to that of religion and asserts its separateness from English-speaking North America."[17] Several writers have observed similar intimate relations between the Polish Catholics and their church.[18]

Although the degree of association and linkage between religion and ethnicity varies from ethnic group to ethnic group, their contiguity is never totally absent. Although religion may not be a direct cause of interethnic conflict (causal nexus is very difficult to determine, especially in social phenomena,) it is nevertheless frequently related, sometimes in vigorous, active ways.[19] Several contemporary religious practices are also involved in changing the socio-politico-economic conditions in the Middle East, South Asia, Central Asia, and Eastern Europe.[20]

We referred to *humanocentrism* as the sharing of common and similar religious convictions. Are there common religious convictions? This appears difficult to answer, especially if we take into account that in the twentieth century there are at least twenty-seven large and comprehensive religious systems in the world and thousands of creeds and subsidiaries. Much research study and examination are needed.

I would like to illustrate some aspects of our research findings which would tend to contribute to reducing the antagonisms, by citing the commonalities found in the various religious scriptures.

On the virtues of the middle way, for example, Buddhist teachings constantly refer to the middle path. One of the treatises of Buddha's contemporary, Confucius, is entitled "The Doctrine of the Mean." A Sanskrit proverb says "Follow the middle course and avoid extremes;" Krishna of Hinduism expounds on the middle way: "He who avoids extremes in feed and fast, in sleep and waking, and work and play; he winneth Yoga, balance, peace and joy." Lao-tse, founder of ancient Taoism, says: "Continuing to fill a pail after it is full, the water will be wasted. Continuing to grind an ax after it is sharp will wear it away. Excess of light blinds the eye. Excess of sound deafens the ear. Excess of condiments deadens the taste. He who possesses moderation is lasting and enduring." From the Book of Proverbs in the Old Testament: "Give me neither poverty nor riches, feed me with food sufficient for my wants, lest I should be full and deny thee, or be poor and steal and profane the name of God." From the Talmud: "The horse fed too freely with oats, oft becomes unruly." From the New Testament: "Let your moderation be known to all men" (Phillipians, 4:5). "Meekness, temperance, against such there is no law" (Gal. 5:23). From the Second Epistle to Peter: "Make every effort to supplement your faith with goodness, goodness with knowledge, knowledge with self-control, self-control with steadfastness, steadfastness with piety, piety with a spirit of brotherhood." From the Koran of Mohammed: "All acts are good but in mid-degree." From the Shinto scriptures of Japan: "If man oversteps the limits of moderation, he pollutes his body and his mind."

On page 3 of the Episcopal "Book of Common Prayer" we find the identical prayers to those on page 343 of the Conservative Synogogue, Holiday Prayer Book. The Psalms of the Old Testament are listed in the Episcopal prayer book on page 68 as they are on page 10, of the Union Prayer Book, of the Reform Jewish Congregations.

Additional prayers in different religions appear almost like translations of one another. Most, if not all, religions prescribe expiation for man's sins. Most religions command charity to the deserving. Most call their scriptures by names that have the same significance, that is, the word of God. Most religions have pageants, processions, festivals, lamentations, and holy days. Each has a sabbath for rest and recuperation. All religions call their places of worship by names which have approximately the same meaning. All have subdivisions into sects. The sacred writings are replete with identities with faith, hope, worship, and transcendence. There are evidences of religious common ground.

Joachim Wach (1951, 1964), one of the world's major scholars of religious studies, published his findings on the universals in religious experience: (1) response to what is experienced as ultimate reality; (2) religious experience as the most intense experience; (3) as an imperative commitment which impels humans to act. Wach goes into great detail to present empirical evidence of these universalities.

Since the 1960s there have been a number of rapproachements between Catholicism and other religions, with a special focus on Judiasm. In 1965 the Second Vatican Council "officially removed negative mentions of Jews from the liturgy" (Charlesworth, 1991, p. 38, 123).

The Council issued a number of decrees.[21] Among the decrees was one on ecumenism.[22] It defines ecumenism as a movement for the restoration and fostering "of unity among all Christians." In recent years, a number of Christian theologians have sought to expand the concept of ecumenism to include, the non-Christian religions of the world. "The Jew and the Christian have an inextricably bound destiny," wrote a Calvinist theologian (Brown, 1967, p. 249).

An American rabbi wrote; "We are all involved in one another. Spiritual betrayal on the part of one of us, affects the fate of all of us.... Today, religious isolationism is a myth. For all the profound differences in perspective and substance, Judaism is sooner or later affected by the intellectual, moral, and spiritual events within the Christian society" (Heschel, 1966, p. 119).

Augustin Cardinal Bea, whom Pope John XXIII appointed as head of the Secretariat for Vatican Council II, wrote: "The modern world provides better means and resources than ever before to make mankind a family in the fullest sense, that is a family...in sharing...the physical, intellectual and spiritual resources of the world...and an awareness that there is a duty to make right use of the resources, so that the solidarity of the human family may not remain merely an ideal but may become effective and real" (Bea, 1964 pp. 2-3).

The Vatican Council's *Declaration on the Relationship of the Church to Non-Christian Religions* [*Nostra Aetate*] opens with the words: "In our times, when every day men are being drawn closer together and the ties between various peoples are being multiplied, the church is giving deeper study to her relationship with non-Christian religions. In her task for fostering unity and love among men [I wish that it would have used the word women also], and even among nations, she gives primary consideration here to what human beings have in common and to what causes them to live out their destiny together; [for] all people have a single community, and have a single origin, since God made the whole race of men dwell over the entire face of the earth."

Rabbi Herman Hailperin, in his book *The Three Great Religions: Their Theological and Cultural Affinities* (1978) points out: that the Eucharist, a basic Christian practice bears "a formal likeness to the ancient Aramaic interpretation of the unleavened bread" (p. 40); "the New Testament text itself contains in many places, Jewish exegetical treatments of words and ideas" (p. 11); "it is next to impossible to segregate the Jewish from the Christian elements in the formation of Islam" (p. 44).[23]

Professor Mittal (1986) University of Delhi, points out that Sikhism, Buddhism, Jainism, and Hinduism which had their origins in India (and which are in conflict frequently with one another) share many common beliefs.

In 1993, leaders representing more than 100 of the world's diverse faiths including, Christianity, Buddhism, Islam, Bahaism, Judaism, Confucianiam, Zoroastrianism...gathered to explore common ground, and concluded their discussions with a declaration *Towards a Global Ethic.*[24]

Father Allen Farrell, one time editor of the Catholic journal, *America*, once mentioned to me, that if I wanted to get an idea of Jesus and his disciples and what they were to each other, I should observe the Chasidim in Jerusalem.

It is of ceaseless interest to note, how contemporary Protestant theologians have used the concepts of the profound and devout Jew, Martin Buber.

Gotthold Lessing caught the essence of the common Christian-Judaic heritage in his drama *Nathan the Wise*. In Act 4, Scene 7, a conversation ensues between Nathan and the Friar. Touched by Nathan's devotion to God and his love of humankind, the Friar exclaims, "Nathan! Nathan! You are a Christian! By God, you are a Christian! No truer Christian ever was!" Nathan replies: "Happy for us, that what to you makes me a Christian, so makes you to me a Jew."

A COGNITIVE-EDUCATIONAL APPROACH TO IMPLEMENTING HUMANOCENTRISM

It is apparent that I have selected items of agreement among the religions. Crucial elements of disagreement and differences in belief among religious systems certainly exist and prevail: disagreements between Jew and Jew, disagreements between Christian and Christian, disagreements between Christians and non-Christians.

As we mentioned, *humanocentrism* seeks to present the cultural similarities with the differences and if the differences tend toward intercultural conflict, similarities can contribute to concord and compatibility. We suggest therefore, the practical implementation of the facts of *humanocentrism* by formally involving the school (including colleges), its curriculum, and the teacher.[25]

We are using cognition synonymously with factual knowledge, that is, clear understandings accomplished by statements that are verifiable and that include perceptions, thinking, and reasoning that are objective, logical, and empirical.[26]

We should state at this point that the cognitive-educational approach is but one procedure toward the reduction and possible resolution of intercultural conflict. Every human social problem involves a multiplicity of factors.[27] Therefore problems of multicultural conflict are multifaceted and involve a variety and combination of approaches toward the alleviation of intercultural conflict.

The cognitive-educational approach has its limitations, but it has its efficacies also. It has its limitations as far as the bigot is concerned. As the Supreme Court Justice Oliver Wendel Holmes once wrote: "The mind of the bigot is like the pupil of the eye; the more light you pour upon it, the more it contracts."

I would agree that bigots have to be treated more precipitously than through the cognitive-educational process.

I have sought to emphasize an approach that has been relatively ignored. In most countries, the school systems reach very large segments of their total populations. In the United States, for example, there are about 35 million pupils enrolled in the elementary schools, 14 million in high schools, and 13 million in colleges and universities.

Humanocentrism seeks consensus through cognition. While it has been shown that the attitudinal influences frequently shape the cognitive, the cognitive plays a significant role in shaping attitudes and behavior.[28]

I would like to include, as part of formal cognitive education, the study in the curricula of the criteria for straight thinking and types of distorted thinking. This can enable the student to recognize and evaluate the various statements and declarations that refer to and reflect on conflict. Many introductory texts on logic list, explain, and elaborate these types of distorted thinking, usually under the heading of "informal logical fallacies." (I remember reading that "those who believe in absurdities will commit atrocities.")

Part of the cognitive approach is, of course, the pursuit of scientific truth. Bertrand Russell (1945) states in the last paragraph of his volume, *A History of Western Philosophy*: "In the welter of conflicting fanaticisms, one of the few unifying forces is scientific truthfulness, by which I mean the habit of basing our beliefs upon observations and inferences as impersonal, and as much divested of local and temperamental bias, as is possible for human beings.... The habit of careful veracity can be extended to the whole sphere of human activity, producing wherever it exists, a lessening of fanaticism with an increasing capacity of sympathy and mutual understanding" (p. 836).

There is a beautiful poem by William Blake that enunciates the *humanocentric* idea lyrically:[29]

> To reason, truth, coherence, and love
> All should pray in their distress;
> And to these virtues of delight
> Return their thankfulness.

* * *

> For reason, truth, coherence and love
> Are symbols of God-thought. Found so rare,
> Reason, truth, coherence and love
> Are God's true children and his care.

* * *

> For reason can have the human mind,
> Truth the human heart;
> Love, the human form divine,
> Coherence, the human dress.

* * *

NOTES

1.   Over 100 new countries have come into existence since 1943. This separatism is based on ethnic differences in addition to political factors. "Through the 1950's and 1960's, the number of new Afro-Asian states steadily increased....Seventeen new states were formed in the single year of 1961" (Worsley, 1990, p. 83). See also Smith, 1986. For a view of ethnic populations in other countries see: Aaronson, 1990; Barth, 1969; Ben-Rafael and Sharot, 1991; Fishman, 1985; Holloman and Serghei, 1978; Hunt and Walker, 1974; Kaplan, 1993; Krag and Yukhneva, 1991; Lind, 1955; Milojkovic-Durič, 1994; Nash, 1989; Sigler, 1987; Times of India, 8/18/86, p. 5; Schwartz, 1975, pp. 106-132; Milosz, 1975, pp. 339-352; Messina, Fraga, and Rhodebeck, 1992; Schechterman and Slann, 1993.

Brass (1985) delineates ethnic compositions in Hungary, Spain, Belgium, and Yugoslavia; Cohen (1993) deals with the ethnic composition and their conflicts in Yugoslavia; Boucher and colleagues (1987) analyze ethnicity in Sri Lanka, Hong Kong, China, Malay Peninsula, Philippines, Soloman Islands, and Hawaii.

The United States has been and is one of the large multi-ethnic societies. Eighteen different languages were spoken in early Dutch Manhattan (Quinn, 1994). Oscar Handlin, one of the major American historians and Pulitzer Prize winner, wrote: "Once I thought to write a history of immigrants in America. Then I discovered that the immigrants were America" (Handlin, 1951, p. 3). In one New York City block, in 1865, there were 382 families consisting of "812 individual Irish, 218 Germans, 186 Italians, 189 Polanders, 39 Negroes...." (Howberger, 1994). For a contemporary view of the ethnic population in the United States see Glazer and Moynihan, 1970, 1975; Handlin, 1957; Alba, 1990; Nelli, 1983; Schaefer, 1993; Thernstrom, 1980; Van den Berghe, 1981.

2.   "In a general definition, an ethnic group is a segment of a larger society whose members are thought, by themselves or others, to have a common origin and to share important segments of a common culture, and who in addition, participate in shared activities in which the common origin and culture are significant ingredients" (Yinger, 1994, p. 3). "Ethnic groups...are groups set apart from others because of their national origin or distinctive cultural patterns" (Schaefer, 1990, p. 10). "An 'ethnic group' is a reference group invoked by people who share a common historical style (which may be only assumed), based on overt features and values, and who, through the process of interaction with others identify themselves as sharing that style" (Royce, 1982, p. 17). "A large collectivity, based on presumed common origin, which is, at least on occasion, part of a self-definition of a person, and which also acts as a bearer of cultural traits" (Greeley and McCready, 1975, p. 210). A group "distinguished by culture, language, or nationality" (Rose and Rose, 1948, p. 5). "A human group bound together by ties of cultural homogeneity" (Barron, 1957, p. 32). "A group with a foreign culture" (Warner and Srole, 1945, p. 28). "Any group which is defined or set off by race, religion, or national origin, or some combination of these categories.... All of them serve to create, through historical circumstances, a sense of peoplehood" (Hunt and Walker, 1974, p. 23). "A group with historical memory, real or imaginary" (Novak, 1973, p. 47). See also Williams, 1947, p. 42; Shibutani and Kwan, 1965, p. 47; Greeley, 1974, p. 172; Parsons, 1951, p. 172; Gordon, 1964, p. 24; Morris, 1967, p. 167; Leslie, Larson, and Gorman, 1973, p. 446.

3.   The derivative categories find their institutionalized expressions in marriage, famileal relations, kinship relations; religion and philosophy; politics; education; economic life; dress; cuisine; fine and performing arts; crafts; voluntary associations; play and games (recreation).

4.   Paul Radin (1934) traced the history of ethnocentrism from ancient times. "Whatever is different in social custom always arouses attention and tends to set up antagonisms" (Young, 1935, p. 489). "It would seem a safe estimate that at least four-fifths of the American population lead mental lives in which feelings of group hostility play an appreciable role (Allport and Kramer, 1946, p. 9). David Allen (1991) accounts for ethnic conflict in multi-ethnic societies as a universal phenomenon among all human life forms arising even in the early months after birth. Zia Sardar (1993) has researched a history of racism and xenophobia (she also uses the term "otherness") from ancient Greece to contemporary times. Rupesinghe and Kusoda (1992) reviewed the proliferation of ethnic conflict in many areas of the contemporary world—Europe, India, Middle East, Africa. See also Barkun, 1994; Fein, 1993; Jordan, 1968; Lambropoulos, 1993; Pieterse, 1992; Roback, 1944; Hacker, 1992; Esman, 1988; De Silva, 1986; Evans, 1973, 1993; Horowitz, 1985; Puddington, 1994; Stavenhagen, 1990. Moynihan (1993) states: "...ethnicity will become the dominant issue of world affairs."

Bertrand Russell (1938), a Nobel Laureate and a major philosopher of the twentieth century, cites an interesting and relevant tale: "In passing by the side of Mount Thai, Confucius came on a woman who was weeping bitterly by a grave. The Master pressed forward and drove to her...'You are wailing,' said he; 'is that of one who has suffered sorrow on sorrow?' She replied, 'That is so. Once my husband's father was killed here by a tiger. My husband was also killed, and now my son has died in the same way.' The Master said, 'Why do you not leave this place?' The answer was, 'There is no oppressive [leadership, tyranny and prejudice] here. 'Remember this my children, oppressive environment is more terrible than tigers.'"

Ethnocentrism, a term coined by Sumner, appeared to him to be a universal characteristic of human social group life. In Sumner's classic study, *Folkways*, he states that ethnocentrism is the "view of things in which one's own group is the center of everything and all others are scaled and rated with reference to it.... Each group nourishes its own pride and vanity, boasts itself superior, exalts its own divinities and looks with contempt on outsiders" (Sumner, 1906).

5. The policy was advocated by President Theodore Roosevelt, August Hecksher (a prominent philanthropist) in the early decades of the twentieth century), Ellsworth Faris, E. A. Ross, and A. P. Fairchild (prominent social scientists also of the early decades of the twentieth century).

The New York City superintendent of schools, in 1918, when eighty percent of the school children in the city were immigrants or children of immigrant parents, defined Americanization "not only as an appreciation of the institutions of this country, which would be unexceptionable, but also as absolute forgetfulness of all obligations or connections with other countries because of descent or birth...." (Schappes, 1970).

Seventy percent of Henry Ford's work force were foreign born, in the early decades of his automobile factory. "On a stage of Ford's English language school, in front of the painted backdrop of an immigrant ship stands a cauldron as big as a house—the melting pot. Down a gang plank come the members of the class dressed in their national garb and carrying their luggage. They appear to enter the cauldron, the contents of which are being stirred with long ladles by the teachers. As the pot boils, the graduates emerge on the other side dressed in their best American clothes and holding American flags" (New York Times Book Review, July 13, 1986, p. 36). "He tried to make over his workers in terms of 'Americanization and Fordliness'" (New York Times Book Review, July 13, 1986, p. 36).

6. "...what troubles Mr. Ross [E. A. Ross, a sociologist who advocated assimilationism] and so many other American citizens of British stock is not really equality; what troubles them is *difference*. Only things that are alike in fact and not abstractly, and only men that are *alike* in origin and in feeling and not abstractly, can possess the equality which maintains that inward unanimity of sentiment and outlook which make a homogeneous culture...." (Kallen, 1924, pp. 115-116). "The unison [in American society] to be achieved cannot be a unison of ethnic types" (Kallen, 1924, p. 120).

7. Kallen's metaphysics saw the world as a "seething plurality of entities, each *there*, each trying to stay *with* if not *on*, and by means of its fellows. The 'total' always exceeding itself from moment to moment, is not a whole, but an aggregate of *eaches*, each with a vote that it casts for itself, each involving novelties, chances, mutations, and discreteness as well as necessities and continuities and uniformities" (Kallen, 1924, pp. 27-28).

The world according to Kallen, is further conceived as a continuous evolutionary process of "differentiation of the One into the Many. When mankind began, the world was already an endlessly diversified manifold, and there has been no cessation of increase in the variety and number of the natures whose aggregation it is" (Kallen, 1956, p. 270).

Philosophical pluralism which also influenced Kallen dates back to Empedocles (490-430 B.C.), Anaxagoras (500-425 B.C.), Democrities (460-370 B.C.), and the later Pythagareans. These philosophers broke with the metaphysical monists of Thales, Anaximander, Parmenides, and Zeno.

8. Jane Addams, director of Hull House, one of the earliest community centers (then called settlement houses) in Chicago, Lillian Wald of the Henry Street Settlement in New York City, Robert Wood of the South End House in Boston, and the director of the Education Alliance in New York City; Glazer and Moynihan (1963); Greeley (1974b); Novak (1973). Louis D. Brandeis, associate justice of the United States Supreme Court in the 1920s and 1930s wrote: "America has believed that each race had something of peculiar value which it can contribute to the attainment of those high ideals for which it is striving....America has believed that in differentiation, not in uniformity, lies the path of progress" (Peare, 1970, p. 188). Morris R. Cohen, one of America's major philosophers and professor of philosophy in the 1920s and 1930s at City College of New York, declared in a number of lectures that "heterogeneity in a community breaks down fixed beliefs and enables progress." Professor Cohen frequently quoted Goethe's statement: "He who knows his own language only, does not know his own language." Langston Hughes, the highly recognized African-American poet, wrote in a poem entitled "Color": "Wear it/Like a banner/

For the proud—/Not like a shroud. Wear it/Like a song soaring high—Not moan or cry." In very recent years a number of scholarly analyses and rationales for multiculturalism has been published. See Foster and Herzog, 1994; Markham, 1994; McAdoo, 1993; Pankratz 1993.

The National Association of Intergroup Relations Officials estimated that in the 1980s, ethnic organizations in the United States numbered 345. Ethnic studies had spread to about 500 colleges and universities.

9. A number of factors may account for the durability of ethnicity. I have listed sixteen of these in a prior publication (Gittler, 1974, pp. 330-332).

10. Gordon (1954, p. 15) distinguishes between behavioral assimilation and structural assimilation. Descendants of immigrants, "as a result of their exposure to the larger environment...have been socialized into it so that its behavior patterns are as indigenous to them as to the children of Anglo-white Protestants. On the other hand, structural assimilation, which includes religious practices, ancestral literature, folk music and dance has not taken place to the same degree as the behavioral kind."

11. "Actually the disappearace of some ethnic minority as it is integrated into a larger population only means that a new ethnic group has come into existence, something that has happened hundreds of times in the history of mankind. The integration does not herald in the millenium. When the new group meets another ethnic group—which in turn had been formed elsewhere through the same processes—the whole cycle begins all over again" (Shibutani and Kwan (1965, pp. 567-568).

12. The late David Danzig, originator of the Institute of Cultural Pluralism in New York City, when citing the reality and persistence of group differences and group conflict in American society, posed the question: "Has America substituted for its goal of a unitary integrated community of individuals a compartmentalized society of groups?" (From personal notes of Joseph B. Gittler).

Louis Adamic, author of *From Many Lands* and the editor of *Common Ground*, stated in one of his editorials, "Never has it been more important that we become intelligently aware of the ground that Americans of various strains have in common" (From Gittler's personal notes).

Irving Howe, author of *The World of Our Fathers* who has done much to foster Jewish ethnicity, warned that the return to ethnicity is dangerously sentimental.

Opponents of multiculturalism appear to multiply and increase in acrimony (Bernstein, 1994; Connolly, 1973; Friderers, 1983; Geertz, 1986; Goulbourne, 1991; Hughes, 1993; Lasch, 1994; Rauch, 1993).

Higher education has often been the focus of debate relative to multicultural education (Bullivant, 1981; D'Souza, 1991).

The Chronicle of Higher Education has frequently reported the extant controversies between multicultural versus traditional curricula approaches. See Chronicle of Higher Education 1/15/92, p. A-9; 1/29/92, p. A-8; 12/8/93, p. B-5; 12/15/93, p. A-22; 1/12/94, p. B-3; 3/23/94, p. A-64; 11/16/94, p. B-3).

13. Humanism stresses the values and significances of the human being per se rather than that which focuses on naturalism of the physical world or theism of conventional religion. Humanism locates in humans the source of goodness, value, and creativity. It also stands in opposition to absolutism and emphasizes pluralism and human freedom.

Synergy (or synergism) from the Greek *synergein* means "to work together, or work with." The term has been used in medicine to refer to the greater effect of a combination of drugs than that produced by one drug. Buckminster Fuller used the terms "energetic synergetic geometry" as a principle in his structural design, by which he meant the combination "of structural units to make greater structural strength than separate units." In theology synergism consists of the position that there is more than one principle actively working toward human salvation. The doctrine of Melanchthon states that "the Holy Spirit, the word, and the human will work together in man's regeneration" (Reese, 1980, p. 565).

Syncretism from the Greek *synkretizein* means "to combine." The term, introduced by Plutarch, refers to the "blending of philosophical doctrines from opposing schools, or religious doctrines from different faiths."

Humanocentrism is different from unilinear universalism in that the latter refers to the inclusion of every group into a common category of social and cultural attributes.

By social mass is meant an undifferentiated aggregate of persons and groups similarly exposed and reactive to social stimuli. A social mass is contradictory to the concept of pluralist society. Mass uniformity is antinomous to group heterogeneity and our definition of humanocentrism.

14. Frequently, artists and poets, in their picturesque and dramatic expressions, reflect the urgencies of humanocentrism. From my personal notes and memory:

    a. Shelly's lines come to mind:
       "Nothing in the world is single,
       All things by a law divine
       In one spirit meet and mingle;
    b. John Donne: "No man is an island;"
    c. Pablo Cassals: "We ought to think that we are one of the leaves of a tree, and the tree is all humanity. We cannot live without the others, without the tree;"
    d. When anyone asked Diogenes Laertius where he came from, he said: "I am a citizen of the world;"
    e. Alexander Pope in his *Essay on Man*: "God loves from whole to Parts; but human soul
       Must rise from Individual to the whole.
       Self-Love but serves the virtuous mind to wake,
       As the small pebble stirs the peaceful lake;
       The Centre mov'd, a circle strait succeeds,
       Another still, and still another spreads,
       Friend, parent, neighbour, first it will embrace,
       His country next, and next all human race."

15. Our research catalogs the commonalities among the major religions, technical philosophies, fine and performing arts, laws and politics, family functions and structures, ecological problems, scientific and technological trends, social stratifications, ethical beliefs and values, problems of aging, gender relations, psychological needs and behaviors, intergenerational problems, problems of crime and substance abuse, problems of increasing urbanization trends, recreational activities, health problems, wars, and youth culture problems.

16. "Perhaps the greatest difficulty which confronts the historian of the Irish is that of differentiating between the specifically Irish and specifically Catholic aspects of their lives. They had emerged into the modern world from a past in which Catholicism had played a stronger role than among any other people of western Europe" (Brown, 1966, pp. 34-35).

17. Wade (1960, p. 22) "The French-Canadian ideology has always rested on three characteristics of the French-Canadian culture—the fact that it is a minority culture, that it is Catholic, and that it is French" (Dumont, 1965, p. 392; Abramson, 1973, p. 13). "The history of French Canada is the history of the [Catholic] church in Canada and vice versa" (Falardeau, 1965, p. 342).

18. Baron, 1960, pp. 96-108; Nahirney and Fishman, 1966. Florian Zaniecki differs from Baron and Nahirney and Fishman regarding the degree of identification between the Poles and their church (Abramson, 1973, p. 142). Welaratna (1993) has observed the interfusion between religion with ethnic culture among the Cambodians and Jews.

19. "The role of religion is paradoxical. It makes prejudice and it unmakes prejudice. While the creeds of the great religions are universalistic, all stressing brotherhood, the practice of these

creeds is frequently divisive and brutal; the sublimity of religious ideals is offset by the horrors of persecution in the name of these same ideals. Some people say the only cure for prejudice is more religion; some say the only cure is to abolish religion" (Allport, 1954, p. 444).

20.   Religio-ethnic conflict has expressed itself vigorously throughout history between Christian and Judaic relations (Juergensmeyer, 1993; Nash, 1989; De Silva, Duke, Goldberg, and Katz, 1988).

21.   The Second Vatican Council was opened by Pope John XXIII on October 11, 1962, after several years of preparation and planning. Pope John died during the early years of the Council. Pope Paul VI, who succeeded Pope John, closed the Council on December 8, 1965.

Sixteen documents were issued by the Council; four constitutions, three declarations, and nine decrees. Among the nine decrees was the one on ecumenism.

22.   Neither the term ecumenism nor the religious movement it signifies originated with the Second Vatican Council. Protestant ecumenism goes back four and one-half centuries, to the Colloquy of Marburg of 1529. Catholic ecumenism also dates back many years with the earliest instances dating as far back as the year 325.

23.   See also Wolfson, 1964, p. 97, 1968, p. 178; Robertson and Garrett, 1991; Adler, 1990; Armstrong, 1993; Beyer, 1994; Chatterjee, 1984; Charlesworth, 1991.

24.   U.S.A. Weekend, December 17-19, 1993, p. 11.

25.   Our project is now engaged in implementing the facts of humancentrism on various levels of formal education from preschool to university. See also Verma and Zec, 1994; Devine, 1994; Meyer, Kamens, and Benavol, 1992; Savitt, 1993.

26.   We recognize that the cognitive process also involves factors of motivation, skills, memory, intelligence, style of teaching, motivation, and attitude. All of these factors get linked to the variety of learning theories which include B.F. Skinner's operant conditioning, Robert Gagne's conditions of learning, information processing theory, Jean Piaget's cognitive development theory, Albert Weiner's attribution theory (Bell, 1986).

27.   Every social problem including intercultural conflict is multifacted and involves multidisciplines to understand and resolve the conflicts. (Alfred North Whitehead's famous observation applies here: "Seek simplicity and distrust it.")

Intercultural and intergroup discord involve different kinds of discord—prejudice, predilection, discrimination, scapegoating, persecution, annihilation. These different types of discord call for different approaches to their resolutions.

Each of these types of conflict vary in the degree of prejudice, discrimination, and so forth by place and time.

These different types of discord and opposition are not necessarily separate from one another. They weave in and out of each other at different times and places.

Just as a variety of factors contribute to intercultural conflict, a variety of approaches contribute to reducing conflict. They include: controlling and changing personality ingredients, educational approaches, intercultural contacts, informal and formal negotiation procedures, institutional leadership, law and government, protest movements, mass media approaches, short- and long-term procedures.

28.   Morton Deutsch (1973) states that "each participant in a social interaction responds to the other in terms of his perceptions and cognitions of the other...."

Robin M. Williams (1947) summarized nine studies in which the cognitive approach was the basic orientation. Three studies focussed on African-Americans, one on Oriental-Americans; the rest on a variety of racial and ethnic groups. 1906 highschool and college students were involved. They were given before and after tests. Six of the studies showed slightly favorable to significantly favorable attitude changes. Three showed no changes. None showed unfavorable changes.

Gordon W. Allport (1954) concludes his survey of studies of the relation between education and attitudes: "...general education does to an appreciable degree help raise the level of tolerance, and that the gain apparently is passed along to the next generation" (p. 434). He does point out that the whole problem of prejudice "is not solely a matter of education."

Weil (1985) in his analysis of the role of education concludes: "Many studies of thousands of adults aged 25 to 72 drawn from 38 national sample surveys conducted from 1949 to 1975...establish that education produces large and lasting good [by which is meant liberal] effects in the realm of values (p. 458).

See also Denti, 1992; Chetkow-Yanoov, 1992.

On the other hand, others have argued that education does not directly reduce prejudice and conflict. See Bailey,1992; Combs and Avrunim, 1988; O'Keefe, 1990.

29.   From personal notes.

REFERENCES

Abramson, H.J. 1973. *Ethnic Diversity in Catholic America.* New York: John Wiley.

Adler, M.J. 1990. *Truth in Religion: The Plurality of Religions and the Unity of Truth.* New York: Macmillian.

Allen, D. 1991. *Fear of Strangers and Its Consequences.* Garnersville, NY: Bennington Books.

Alba, R.D. 1990. *Ethnic Identity: The Transformation of White Americans.* New Haven: Yale University.

Allport, G.W., and B.M. Kramer. 1946. "Some Roots of Prejudice." *Journal of Psychology* 22: 9-39.

Allport, G.W. 1954. *The Nature of Prejudice.* Cambridge, MA: Addison-Wesley.

Armstrong, K. 1993. *The History of God: The 4000-Year Quest of Judaism, Christianity and Islam.* New York: Knopf.

Aaronson, G. 1990. *Israel, Palestinians and the Intefada.* London: Kegan Paul.

Bailey, J.E. 1992. *Aspects of Relativism: Moral, Cognitive, and Literary.* Lanham, MD: University Press of America.

Barkun, M. 1994. *Religion and the Racist Right: The Origins of the Christian Identity Movement.* Chapel Hill: University of North Carolina.

Baron, S.W. 1960. *Modern Nationalism and Religion.* New York: Meridian Books.

Barron, M.L. 1957. *American Minorities.* New York: Alfred A. Knopf.

Barth, F. 1969. *Ethnic Groups and Boundaries.* Boston: Little Brown.

Bea, A.C. 1964. *Unity in Freedom.* New York: Harper and Row.

Bell, M.E. 1986. *Learning and Instruction: Theory into Practice.* New York: Macmillan.

Ben-Rafael, E., and S. Sharot 1991. *Ethnicity, Religion and Class in Israeli Society.* Cambridge, UK: Cambridge University Press.

Bernstein, R. 1994. *Dictatorship of Virtue: Multiculturalism and the Battle for America's Future.* New York: Alfred A. Knopf.

Beyer, P.F. 1994. *Religion and Globalization.* Newbury Park, CA: Sage Publications.

Boucher, J. 1987. *Race Relations.* Newbury Park, CA: Sage Publications.

Brass, P. (ed.). 1985. *Ethnic Groups and the State.* Totowa, NJ: Barnes and Noble.

Brown, R.M. 1967. *The Ecumenical Revolution.* Garden City, NY: Doubleday.

Brown, T.N. 1966. *Irish-American Nationalism, 1870-1890.* Philadelphia: J.B. Lippincott.

Bullivant, B.M. 1981. *The Pluralist Dilemma in Education.* Sydney: Allen and Unwin.

Charlesworth, J.H. 1991. *Jesus' Jewishness: Exploring the Place of Jesus in Early Judaism.* Crossroad, NY: American Interfaith Institute.

Chatterjee, M. 1984. *The Religious Spectrum.* New York: Allied Publishers.

Chetkow-Yanoov, B. 1992. "Preparing for Survival in the 21st Century: Some approaches to Teaching Conflict Resolution in Our Schools and Universities." *International Journal of Group Tensions* 22: 277-290.

Cohen, L.J. 1993. *Broken Bonds: The Disintegration of Jugoslavia.* Boulder: Westview Press.
Combs, C.H., and G.S. Avrunim. 1988. *The Structure of Conflict.* Hillsdale, NJ: Lawrence Erlbaum Associates.
Connolly, W.E. (ed.). 1973. *The Bias of Pluralism.* New York: Atherton Press.
Denti, L.G. 1992. "Reconciling Differences: A Commentary on Special and Regular Education." *International Journal of Group Tensions* 22 (4): 265-276.
De Silva, K.M. 1986. *Managing Ethnic Tensions in Multi-Ethnic Societies: Sri Lanka 1880-1985.* Lanham, MD: University Press.
De Silva, K.M., P. Duke, E.S. Goldberg, and N. Katz. 1988. *Ethnic Conflict in Buddhist Societies: Sri Lanka, Thailand, and Burma.* Condon: Printer Publishers.
Deutsch, M. 1973. *The Reduction of Conflict: Constructive and Destructive Processes.* New Haven: Yale University Press.
Devine, P.J. 1994. *Social Cognition. Input on Social Psychology.* San Diego: Academic Press.
D'Souza, D. 1991. *Illiberal Education: The Politics of Race and Sex on Campus.* New York: Free Press.
Dumont, F. 1965. "The Systematic Study of the French-Canadian Total Society." Pp. 386-405 in *French-Canadian Society* (volume 1), edited by M. Rioux and Y. Martin. Toronto: Mc Clelland and Stewart.
Esman, M.J. 1988. *Ethnicity, Pluralism and the State in the Middle East.* Ithaca: Cornell University Press.
Evans, E.N. 1973. *The Provincials: A Personal History of the Jews in the South.* New York: Atheneum.
Evans, E.N. 1993. *The Lonely Days Were Sundays: Reflections of a Jewish Southerner.* University, MS: University of Mississippi Press.
Farlardeau, J-C. 1965. "The Role and Importance of the Church in French Canada." In *French-Canadian Society* (volume 1), edited by M. Rioux and Y. Martin. Toronto: Mc Clelland and Stewart.
Fein, H. 1993. *Genocide.* Newberry Park, CA: Sage Publications.
Fishman, J.A. 1985. *The Rise and Fall of the Ethnic Revival.* Berlin: Mouton.
Flower, E.F. 1956. "Commitment, Bias, and Tolerance." In *Cultural Pluralism and the American Idea,* edited by H.M. Kallen. Philadelphia: University of Pennsylvania Press.
Foster, L., and P. Herzog (eds.). 1994. *Defending Diversity: Contemporary Philosophical Perspectives on Pluralism and Multi-culturalism.* Boston: University of Massachussetts.
Frideres, J.S. 1983. *Native People in Canada: Contemporary Conflicts.* Scarborough: Prentice-Hall of Canada.
Friedman, M. (ed.). 1971. *Overcoming Middle Class Rage.* Philadelphia: Westminster Press.
Geertz, C. 1986. "The Uses of Diversity." *Michigan Quarterly* 25 (1): 114-115.
Gittler, J.B. 1974. "Cultural Pluralism in Contemporary American Society." *International Journal of Group Tensions* 4 (3): 322-345.
Gittler, J.B. 1977. "Toward Defining an Ethnic Minority." *International Journal of Group Tensions* 7: 4-19.
Glazer, N., and D.P. Moynihan. 1963. *Beyond the Melting Pot: The Negroes, Puerto Ricans, Jews, Italians and Irish of New York City.* Cambridge, MA: M.I.T. Press.
Glazer, N., and D.P. Moynihan. 1970. *Beyond the Melting Pot: The Negroes, Puerto Ricans, Jews, Italians and Irish of New York City* (2nd ed.). Cambridge, MA: M.I.T. Press.
Glazer, N., and D.P. Moynihan. 1975. *Ethnicity: Theory and Experience.* Cambridge: Harvard University Press.
Gordon, M.M. 1954. "Social Structure and Goals in Group Relations." In *Freedom and Control in Modern Society,* edited by M. Berger. New York: D. Van Nostrand.
Gordon, M.M. 1964. *Assimilation in American Life: The Role of Race, Religion and National Origins.* New York: Oxford University Press.

Goulbourne, H. 1991. *Ethnicity and Nationalism in Post-Imperial Britain.* New York: Cambridge University Press.

Greeley, A.M. 1971a. *Why Can't They Be Like Us? America's White Ethnic Groups.* New York: E.P. Dutton.

Greeley, A.M. 1971b. "The Rediscovery of Diversity." *Antioch Review* 31 (Fall): 343-366.

Greeley, A.M. 1974a. "Political Participation Among Ethnic Groups in the United States: A Preliminary Reconnaisance." *American Journal of Sociology* 80: 170-204.

Greeley, A.M. 1974b. *Ethnicity in the United States: A Preliminary Reconnaisance.* New York: John Wiley and Sons.

Greeley, A.M., and W.C. McCready. 1975. "The Transmission of Cultural Heritages". In *Ethnicity:Theory and Experience*, edited by N. Glazer and D.P. Moynihan. Cambridge, MA: Harvard University Press.

Hacker, A. 1992. *Two Nations: Black and White, Separate, Hostile Unequal.* New York: Charles Scribners.

Hailperin, H. 1978. *The Three Great Religions: Their Theological and Cultural Affinities.* Pittsburg: Duquesne University Press.

Handlin, O. 1951. *The Uprooted: The Epic Story of the Great Migrations That Made the American People.* New York: Grossett and Dunlap.

Handlin, O. 1957. *Race and Nationality in American Life.* Boston: Little Brown.

Heschel, A. 1966. "No Religion is an Island." *Union Seminary Quarterly* 21 (January).

Holloman, R.E., and A.A. Serghei. 1978. *Perspectives on Ethnicity.* Hague: Mouton.

Homberger, E. 1994. *Scenes from the Life of a City: Corruption and Conscience in Old New York.* New Haven: Yale University Press.

Horowitz, D. 1985. *Ethnic Groups in Conflict.* Berkeley: University of California Press.

Hughes, R. 1993. *Culture of Complaint: The Fraying of America.* New York: Oxford University Press.

Hunt, C.L., and L. Walker. 1979. *Ethnic Dynamics: Patterns of Intergroup Relations in Various Societies.* Homewood, IL: The Dorsey Press.

Jordan, W.D. 1968. *White Over Black: American Attitudes Toward the Negro, 1550-1812.* Chapel Hill: University of North Carolina.

Juergensmeyer, M. 1993. *The New Cold War? Religious Narionalism Confronts the Secular State.* Berkeley: University of California Press.

Kallen, H. 1915a. "Democracy versus the Melting Pot." *The Nation* 100, February 18: 190-194.

Kallen, H. 1915b. "Democracy versus the Melting Pot." *The Nation* 100, February 25: 217-221.

Kallen, H. 1924. *Culture and Democracy.* New York: Arno Press.

Kallen, H. 1956. *Cultural Pluralism and the American Idea.* Philadelphia: University of Pennsylvania Press.

Kaplan, R.D. 1993. *Balkan Ghosts: A Journey Through History.* New York: St. Martin's Press.

Kariel, H.S. 1968. "Pluralism." *International Encyclopedia of the Social Sciences* 8: 164-168.

Kornhauser, W. 1959. *The Politics of Mass Society.* New York: Free Press.

Krag, H., and N. Yukneva (eds.). 1991. "The Leningrad Minority Rights Conference." Leningrad Association of Scientists, June 2-4, Leningrad.

Lambropoulos, A. 1993. *The Rise of Eurocentrism.* Princeton: Princeton University Press.

Lasch, C. 1994. *The Revolt of the Elites and the Betrayal of Democracy.* New York: W.W. Norton.

Leslie, G., R.F. Larson, and B.L. Gorman. 1973. *Order and Change.* New York: Oxford University Press.

Lind, A.W. (ed.). 1955. *Race Relations in World Perspective.* Honolulu: University of Hawaii Press.

Markham, J.S. 1994. *Plurality and Christian Ethics.* New York: Cambridge University.

McAdoo, H.P. 1993. *Family Ethnicity: Strength in Diversity.* Newbury Park, CA: Sage.

Messina, A.M., L.R. Fraga, and L.A. Rhodebeck. 1992. *Ethnic and Racial Minorities in Advanced Industrial Democracies.* New York: Greenwood Press.

Meyer, J.W., D. Kamens, and A. Benavol. 1992. *School Knowledge for the Masses: World Models and National Primary Curricular Categories in the Twentieth Century.* Bristol, PA: Falmer Press.

Milojkovic-Duric, J. 1994. *Panslavism and National Identity in Russia and the Balkans, 1830-1880: Images of Self and Others.* New York: Columbia University Professor Press.

Milosz, C. 1975. "Vilnius, Lithuania: An Ethnic Conglomerate." In *Ethnic Identity: Cultural Continuities and Change,* edited by G. DeVos and L. Romanucci-Ross. Palo Alto, CA: Mayfield Publishing.

Mittal, K.K. 1986. "Philosophy of Inter-Faith Relationship." Pp. 74-94 in *Religious Pluralism and Co-existence,* edited by W. Singh. Patiola: Punjabi University.

Morris, H.S. 1967. "Ethnic Groups." *International Encyclopedia of the Social Sciences* 5.

Moynihan, D.P. 1993. *Ethnicity in International Politics.* New York: Oxford University Press.

Nahirny, V.C., and J.A. Fishman 1966. Pp. 318-357 in *Language Loyalty in the United States,* edited by J.A. Fishman et al. The Hague: Mouton.

Nash, M. 1989. *The Cauldron of Ethnicity in the Modern World.* Chicago: University of Chicago Press.

Nelli, H.S. 1983. *From Immigrants to Ethnics.* New York: Oxford University Press.

New York Times Book Review. July 13, 1986, p. 36.

Novak, M. 1973. *The Rise of the Unmeltable Ethnics: Politics and Culture in the Seventies.* New York: Collier.

O'Keefe, D.J. 1990. *Persuasion: Theory and Research.* Newbury Park, CA: Sage.

Pankratz, D.B. 1993. *Multiculturalism and Public Arts Policy.* New York: Bergin and Garvey.

Parsons, T. 1951. *The Social System.* Glencoe, IL: The Free Press.

Peare, C.O. 1970. *The Louis D. Brandeis Story.* New York: Thomas Y. Crowell.

Pieterse, J.N. 1992. *White On Black: Images of Africa and Blacks in Western Popular Culture.* New Haven: Yale University Press.

Pinard, M. 1968. "Mass Society and Political Movements: A New Formulation." *American Journal of Sociology* 73: 682-690.

Potter, G.W. 1960. *To The Golden Door.* Boston: Little, Brown.

Puddington, A. 1994. "Black Anti-Semitism and How It Grows." *Commentary* 97 (April): 19-24.

Quinn, A. 1994. *A New World: An Epic of Colonial America From the Foundation of Jamestown to the Fall of Quebec.* Boston: Faber and Faber.

Radin, P. 1934. *The Racial Myth.* New York: McGraw-Hill.

Rauch, J. 1993. *Kindly Inquisitors.* Chicago: University of Chicago Press.

Reese, W.C. 1980. *Dictionary of Philosophy and Religion: Eastern and Western Thought.* Atlantic Highlands, NJ: Humanities Press.

Roback, A.A. 1944. *A Dictionary of International Slurs.* Cambridge, MA: Sci-Art Publishers.

Robertson, R., and W.R. Garrett. 1991. *Religion and Global Order.* New York: Paragon House.

Rose, A., and C. Rose. 1948. *America Divided: Minority Group Relations in the United States.* New York: Alfred A. Knopf.

Royce, A.P. 1982. *Ethnic Identity: Stratigies of Diversity.* Bloomington: Indiana University Press.

Rupersinghe, K., and M. Kusoda 1992. *Early Warning and Conflict Resolution.* New York: St. Martin's Press.

Russell, B. 1938. *Power: A Social Analysis.* New York: W.W. Norton.

Russell, B. 1945. *A History of Western Philosophy: And Its Connection With Political and Social Circumstances from the Earliest Times to the Present Day.* New York: Simon and Schuster.

Sardar, Z. 1993. *Barbaric Others: The Origins of Western Racism.* Boulder, CO: Westerview Press.

Savitt, W. (ed.). 1993. *Teaching Global Development: A Curriculum Guide.* South Bend: University of Notre Dame Press.

Schaefer, R.T. 1990. *Racian and Ethnic Groups.* Glenview, IL: Scott, Foresman.

Schaefer, R.T. 1993. *Racial and Ethnic Groups.* New York: Harper Collins.

Schappes, M.U. 1970. "The Jewish Question and the Left—Old and New." *Jewish Currents*, reprint #7.

Schechterman, B., and M. Slann (eds.). 1993. *International Relations.* Westport, CT: Praeger.

Schwartz, T. 1975. "Cultural Totemism: Ethnic Identity." In *Ethnic Identity: Cultural Continuities and Change*, edited by G. DeVos and L. Romanucci-Ross. Palo Alto: Mayfield Publishing.

Shibutani, T., and K.M. Kwan. 1965. *Ethnic Stratification: A Comperative Approach.* New York: Macmillan.

Sigler, J.A. (ed.). 1987. *International Handbook of Race and Race Relations.* New York: Greenwood.

Smith, M.G. 1986. "Pluralism, Race and Ethnicity in Selected African Countries." Pp. 178-225 in *Theories of Race and Ethnic Relations*, edited by J. Rex and D. Mason. New York: Cambridge University Press.

Stavenhagen, R. 1990. *The Ethnic Question: Conflicts, Development and Human Rights.* Tokyo: United Nations University Press.

Sumner, W.G. 1906. *Folkways.* New York: Ginn.

Thernstrom, S. (ed.). 1980. *Harvard Encyclopedia of American Ethnic Groups.* Cambridge: Harvard University Press.

Times of India. August 18, 1986. New Delhi, India.

Van den Berghe, P. 1981. *The Ethnic Phenomenon.* New York: Elsevier.

Verma, G.,, and P. Zee. 1994. *The Ethnic Crucible.* Bristol, PA: Falmer Press.

Wach, J. 1951. *Types of Religious Experience: Christian and Non-Christian.* Chicago: University of Chicago Press.

Wach, J. 1964. "Universals in Religion." Pp. 38-52 in *Religion, Culture and Society*, edited by L. Schneider. New York: John Wiley and Sons.

Wade, M. (ed.). 1960. *The French-Canadian Outlook.* New York: Viking.

Warner, W.L., and L. Srole. 1945. *The Social Systems of American Ethnic Groups.* New Haven: Yale University Press.

Weil, F. 1985. "The Variable Effects of Education on Liberal Attitudes: A Comparative-Historical Analysis of Anti-Semitism Using Public Opinion Survey Data." *American Sociological Review* 50: 458-474.

Welaratna, U. 1993. *Beyond the Killing Fields.* Stanford: Stanford University Press.

Williams, R.M., Jr. 1947. *The Reduction of Intergroup Tensions.* New York: Social Science Research Council.

Wolfson, H.A. 1964. *The Philosophy of the Church Fathers.* Cambridge, MA: Harvard University Press.

Wolfson, H.A. 1968. *Philo: Foundations of Religious Philosophy in Judaism, Christianity, and Islam.* Cambridge, MA: Harvard University Press.

Worsley, P. 1990. "Models of the Modern World-System." *Theory, Culture and Society* 7: 83.

Yinger, J.M. 1994. *Ethnicity: Source of Strength? Source of Conflict?* Albany: State University of New York Press.

Young, K. 1935. *Social Psychology.* New York: F.S. Crofts.

Zijderveld, A.C. 1970. "Rationality and Irrationality in Pluralistic Society." *Social Research* 37 (March): 23-47.

RACIAL AND ETHNIC CONFLICT STUDIES:

METHODOLOGICAL DILEMMAS

John H. Stanfield, II

In order to discuss methodological problems and prospects in studies of racial/ethnic conflict, it is necessary to come to terms with the word "methodology." Usually in the traditions of Western social sciences, discourses on methodology have been reduced down to discussions on technical strategies targeting the collection and analysis of empirical data. As central as technical aspects are to understanding methodologies, we should not forget that methods are human constructs and are embedded in at least implicit conceptual infrastructures. That is to say, methods are human inventions and thus can and should be studied as (1) extensions of the life histories of their inventors and users; (2) as ethical and moral issues; and (3) as phenomena influenced by external events such as historical location, politics, economics, and technology. Methodologies, in a word, have epistemological grounding and social orientations and should be studied as such.

Research in Human Social Conflict, Volume 1, pages 365-381.
Copyright © 1995 by JAI Press Inc.
All rights of reproduction in any form reserved.
ISBN: 1-55938-923-0

To say that methodologies are rooted in conceptual infrastructures is to admit to the fact that we can speak of theories of methods and the intellectual history of methods (Stanfield and Dennis, 1993). In the next section, I discuss some epistemological and theoretical issues regarding the epistemologies and intellectual histories of research methods in racial/ethnic conflict studies. This discussion is imperative for grounding the more technical discussion on research methods in racial and ethnic conflict studies at the conclusion of this paper.

EPISTEMOLOGICAL GROUNDINGS
AND INTELLECTUAL HISTORIES

From the standpoint of the 1990s, it is no radical gesture to claim that methodologies have epistemological groundings and intellectual histories. By epistemologies we mean the unintentional and intentional consequences of methodologies being human experiences and thus embedded in autobiographies, moral standards, ethics, politics, and in the nature of society and community in particular historical moments. By intellectual histories we mean that as human inventions, methodologies are embedded in conceptual frameworks and frames of references which can be analyzed and assessed in historical terms. Intellectual histories in this context also refers to the important intrinsic ways in which methodology is, or at least should be, linked to theory-building attempting to explain something in an empirical reality.

To speak of epistemological groundings in methodological traditions in racial/ethnic conflict research and policy-making is to bring to the surface the obvious autobiographical, social, cultural, and political biases which, more often than not, contaminate validity and reliability of inquiries into this most important issue. Obviously, the numerous facets of bias flow from the profound degrees of emotionalism and crisis management needs and demands which shape most of what we know about racial/ethnic conflict. As in other areas of social problems research and policy-making, the study of racial conflict/ethnic conflict in many, if not in most cases, is from the perspective of the dominant. This is more than apparent in the ways in which racial/ethnic conflict problems are often articulated in terms which victimize subordinates, often pointing out their individual and psychological deficiencies (Crowell, 1992; Flamming, 1968; Fred and Wilkins, 1988; McKernan, 1982; Moniat and Raine, 1970; Murphy and Watson, 1967; Sawyer and Senn, 1973; Sears and McConahay, 1970; Singer, Osborn, and Geschwender, 1970; Spiegal, 1967a, 1967b; Tomilson, 1967; Wall, 1992; Warren, 1973) .

Seldom are those who rebel against standing sociopolitical orders asked about their perspectives using their indigenous experiences and interpretations. There is little sense in the racial/ethnic conflict literature that conflict in multiethnic/racial institutions, communities, societies, and regions takes place in plural social organizations. Plural social organizations have members with diverse cultural backgrounds and thus moral standards. To attempt to gauge the attitudes of or interpret the behavior of culturally different people involved in conflictual circumstances solely in terms of the dominant has little use value. The only thing it does offer is insights into how the dominant feel subordinates should be thinking or dominant impressions of how subordinates behaved. This is why even though there has been an increasingly sophisticated methodological literature on racial/ethnic conflict emerging, it speaks more to the norms of academic and policy-making communities than to actual empirical realities.

There are also ethical and political issues in methodological studies of racial/ethnic conflict stemming from the sensitivity of asking and responding to questions and the growing reluctance of culturally different people to allow dominant group researchers to probe deeply into their institutions and communities. There is also the problem of the crisis management mentality that obsesses most government and academic policy research. This political imperative of much racial/ethnic conflict research results in certain questions not being asked and others being asked with little or no in-depth reflection. For instance, in school desegregation research (Buell, 1982; Kirp, 1979; Rist, 1978) and in other conflictual institutional spheres such as prisons (American Correctional Association, 1981, 1990; Braswell, Dillingham, and Montgomery, 1985; Collective Violence Research Project, 1973; Colvin, 1992; Cummins, 1994; Fox, 1973; Muller, 1986), the focus is solely on racial attitudes and interracial behavior with little or no examination of contextual issues such as family and community of origins, and the ways in which institutions fit into political, economic, and even technological climates. It is as if some how or another racial/ethnic conflict is suspended in mid-air isolated from the social organizations shaping its processes and products (Carithers, 1970; Conforti, 1974; Gould, 1973; Lauruffa, 1992; Miracle, 1981; Ottaway, 1976).

Also, the intense interpersonal emotions that embed processes and products of racial/ethnic conflict—anger, fear, hostility—makes truth-telling profoundly problematic (Alan, 1994; Gitter, Black, and Motofsky, 1972; Knopf, 1975; Mohajer and Steinfatt, 1982). Such emotions, running high sometimes across generations and centuries, makes it difficult for researchers and policymakers to distinguish between gross exaggerations of facts due to the duress of affliction and the actual empirical realties of incidents and circumstances (Boucher, Landis, and Clark, 1987). The probability of distortion and information withholding increases when research subjects perceive they have much to lose by telling the truth about their participation in racial and ethnic conflicts. Possibilities such as arrest, harassment, unemployment, and death are some of the more important reasons why, say for instance, race rioters refuse to talk to researchers or tell them the truth. This observation, incidently, makes many interview studies on why Afro-

Americans and white urban dwellers rioted during the course of the past two centuries suspect (Belknap, 1991; Boskin, 1967; Bullock, 1969; Capeci, 1970; Chikota, 1970; Cohen, 1972; Cohen, 1966; Crump, 1966; Culver, 1994; Fogelson, 1969; Kinnear, 1911; Lane, 1971; Lee, 1943; May, 1974; Nerner, 1986; Porter, 1984; Rist, 1972; Rossi, 1970; Schlemmer, 1968; Senechal, 1990; Slaughter, 1991; Spilerman, 1974; United States Kerner Commission, 1968; Weskow, 1966; Williams, 1927, 1991). The same goes for the interview data gathered by government commissions investigating racial and ethnic riots in nineteenth- and twentieth-century societies such as the United States, India, Great Britain, and South Africa (Akbar, 1988; Akron, Ohio, 1969; Belknap, 1991; Burma, 1939; Button, 1993; California Governor's Commission on the Los Angeles Riots, 1966; Chakavarti, 1987; Cohen, 1967; Cowell, Jones, and Young, 1982; Fogelson, 1967; Finkleman, 1992; Jacobson, 1985; Johannesburg, 1958; Joshua, 1983; Miami Study Team on Civil Disturbances in Miami, Florida, 1969; Samuel, 1930; Sears, 1967; South Africa, 1941, 1949, 1980; Spiegal, 1967; Webb and Kirkwood, 1949).

This observation raises the interesting question: how can researchers and policymakers faced with this problematic of truth-telling under duress (even when it is a historical tradition and not a contemporary occurrence) develop methodologies to assure maximum data reliability and validated? It is a question certainly not easy to resolve.

The last and perhaps the most important epistemological problem is the unpackaging of the terms race, ethnicity, and conflict. In race/ethnic conflict analyses, those three terms tend to be naturalized or utilized in mundane fashions and therefore not explicitly defined. What are race and ethnicity as human experiences and how are they linked to conflict as processes and consequences in social life? This intricate question becomes even more complex when we consider the variation of historically located cultures within and among societies and global regions which give race and ethnicity so many contrasting meanings and manifestations.

No matter the society, region, or historical context, it is important to understand epistemologically that race and ethnicity are very much social constructions of reality with political and economic functions. Race is a cluster of myths regarding the correlates of real or imagined phenotypical attributes with human qualities such as intellectual abilities, personality, and moral fiber. Ethnicity is the combination of socially defined ancsetery and cultural attributes such as language, religion, life cycle phases, and values. Both races and ethnicities are created, maintained, and transformed through power and privilege-oriented categorization processes that homogenize the individual characteristics of people into collective images and stereotypes of populations in official definitions of institutions, communities, societies, and global regions (Stanfield, 1994).

The categorization processes that create races and ethnicities function as a major source for legitimating patterns of unequal access to power, privilege, and prestige in thought, human development, stratification, and social organization. Racial and ethnic categorization is a political practice within historically specific social and cultural contexts which becomes most eruptive when the two homogenization practices become intertwined in such a way that ethnicity becomes racialized (Stanfield, 1994; Van den Berghe, 1967). This point is important since after all, while ethnicity as a mode of categorization can occur without racialization, race cannot stand without ethnicity.

When ethnicity becomes racialized, it magnifies ideologies and sociopolitical practices of unequal access to human and natural resources. This is because cultural differences between dominant and subordinate populations are exacerbated by manufactured racial differences. Concretely the more cultural attributes such as language, religion, and behavioral patterns differ between populations defined socially as different races, the more intense and rigid is the mode of inequality.

CONFLICT

When we think of the term "conflict" in social relations, usually overt episodes of intergroup antagonism come to mind (Allen, 1970; Lee, 1945; Walters, 1982; Wilson, 1961). Indeed, it is the episodic meaning of conflict and its resolution that undergirds conflict analysis as an area of research and policy. The epistemological impetus behind this meaning of conflict are functional and organic notions of institutions, communities, and societies. In functional and organic interpretations of such social organizations, it is assumed that intergroup conflict is an exceptional if not dysfunctional and pathological episodic experience. Conflict is a relational process that must be resolved through natural evolution or through intervention if a mode of social organization is to regain its homostatic balance.

It is no great surprise to find that conflict analysis is rooted in such epistemological reasoning since most of this research and policy-making field was established during the heyday of functional and organic interpretations of social organizations. The problem with this functional and organic approach to conflict analysis is that it ignores the normal aspects of conflict in everyday life as well as the power and privilege relations characteristic of social organizations of all levels. No matter the institution, community, or society, people differ in perceptions, values, and material resources, and therefore, conflict is an integral part of daily life in all social organizations. To assume that it is possible for a social organization to exist without some degree or kind of conflict is to resort to utopian thinking.

These points have special credence in regards to the racial/ethnic conflict literature. As in the more general approach, researchers and policymakers tend to define racial/ethnic conflict issues in overt episodic terms in at least two ways. Both approaches have shaped two dominant schools of thought utilizing episodic perspectives in racial and ethnic conflict studies. The first perspective as exemplified by the classical Chicago School of Race Relations, argues that interracial and interethnic conflict are inevitable intergroup interactions leading to eventual intergroup assimilation into functional or organic social organizations. William I. Thomas' organization-disorganization-reorganization model and Robert E. Park's race cycle model, for instance, assumed that white immigrants and Afro-Americans, respectfully, may enter into temporary conflict with the dominant society as they enter in but gradually internalize mainstream values and behavior codes as they enter accommodation and assimilation phases. Park's student, Charles S. Johnson, did more than any other member of his generation to explore the conflict phase of the Parkian race cycle (Park, 1950; Johnson, 1987; Thomas and Znaniecki, 1958).

The second perspective promotes case studies of interracial and ethnic collective violence. From a broad array of theoretical and methodological approaches, most of this literature concentrates on analyzing interracial and ethnic riots, pogroms, and massive genocide. By far, the case study approach is the most popular way in which racial/ethnic conflict has been studied.

During the 1960s, under the influence of Parsonian functionalism, social scientists attempted to explain the race riots that rocked American cities in episodic terms (Armstrong, 1975; Coser, 1956; Enloe, 1972; Himes, 1974, 1980; Montagu, 1942; Stanfield, 1992). Particularly, the work of Joseph Himes attempted to apply functional principles to the study of racial conflict. As much as these studies helped to shed needed light on the power and privilege aspects of interracial conflict (a departure from conventional Parsonian functionalism), nevertheless, they have contributed to the notion that racial/ethnic conflict is episodic.

It has only been during the past twenty-five years that scholars have begun to suggest, as mainstream ideas, that racial/ethnic conflict is a routine characteristic of human life (Essed, 1991; Van Dijik, 1987, 1993). It is true we should not ignore the episodes of racial and ethnic conflict. But more importantly, we should not overlook the routinization of such intergroup antagonism in the daily affairs of people in multi-ethnic/racial social organizations. The routinization of conflict in multi-ethnic/racial social organizations is the direct result of the sociocultural correlations applied to real or imagined phenotypical characteristics and subsequent collective differences in values, beliefs, identities, codes of behavior, and material and symbolic resources. Occasionally the discrepancies in the organized lives and material and symbolic interests of the racially and/or ethnically dominant and subordinate spark sociopolitical explosions such as riots. But for the most part, intergroup antagonism is quite routinized to such a point that the conflict proness of multi-ethnic/racial social organizations seems to be natural. Just a casual look at the front page of elite newspapers such as *The New York Times* or *The London Times* reveals how much racial conflict is a well-routinized public cultural obsession often hidden underneath obscure discourse styles. Indeed, racial conflict is so routinized in dominant public culture that it takes on the form of public rituals that affirm personal and collective identity and reaffirms the perceived identity of racialized outsiders (Van Dijk, 1993).

The reason why routinized racial and racialized ethnic conflict is so difficult to resolve is that it is an integral part of precisely what makes a multi-ethnic/ racial institution, community, society, or region. Racial and racialized conflict ceases when race ceases being so essential for defining and organizing daily life in social organizations. What this means from a policy perspective is that the resolution of racial and racialized ethnic conflict lies in the success in resocializing populations and/or giving them incentives to think, act, and live in nonracial ways.

LOGIC OF INQUIRY PROBLEMS AND PROSPECTS

There are daunting logic of inquiry problems in studying racial and ethnic conflict. I have already mentioned how intense emotions and crisis management agendas enveloping racial and ethnic conflict issues have impeded the development of adequate research designs. The psychological reductionism that dominates researcher approaches to the study of race riots and their participants has distracted attention from more macro explanations as to why such sociopolitical explosions occur. Last, and certainly not least, the preoccupation with episodes of interethnic/racial violence has left us methodologically silent when it comes to the study of routinized ethnic/racial conflict in conventional social and policy sciences.

There are three bodies of literature we must consult to grasp the nature of rountinized ethnic/racial conflict. First there is the resistance literature in African descent slavery and genocide (state violence) studies that documents the mundane efforts of the racialized oppressed to mundanely circumvent and otherwise undermine the authority of the racialized dominant. This resistance literature has been greatly expanding during the past two decades as scholars have begun to realize that the oppressed are more than passive pawns or victims even in the most dire forms of inequality (Blassingame, 1972; Chaliand, 1983; Chalk and Jonassohn, 1990; Horowitz, 1980; Mazian, 1990; Melson, 1992; Van Den Berghe, 1990).

Methodologically, the study of resistance involves using records created by the oppressed as well as those of oppressors. It is also a matter of searching for instances of rebellion in official records which have tended to be overlooked by scholars in the past who embraced passive perspectives regarding the plight of Africans in slavery and Jews in extermination camps or in resistance movements. It is important to analyze such records not only to document an episode but to also to raise questions regarding the processes of on-going mundane resistance to dominant racialized authority. The most obvious problem with the resistance literature is that it is quite anti-institutional and (ironically) ahistorical. Slavery and the holocaust occurred within different kinds of institutional frameworks and historically grounded political economies and external eco-systems. Also, resistance has become a catchall term with little attempt to discuss the different ways in which the oppressed have attempted to circumvent the authority of the dominant.

Secondly, phenomenological and neo-Marxist perspectives and their synthetic products such as critical and postmodern theories, have recently begun to be fashionable ways to explain racial and ethnic conflict issues in the construction of everyday realities. Particularly postmodernists have been interested in exploring the problematics of creating and maintaining identity in multi-ethnic/racial societies such as the United States and other Western nation-states (Collins, 1990; Gates, 1987, 1992; Gilroy, 1987, 1993; Henry, 1986; Winant and Omi, 1986). Unfortunately, the major weakness of postmodernism is an over dependency on literary and textual analysis with little real context. Therefore, even though postmodern studies have proliferated the study of racial and ethnic conflict, it's literary/textual methodological approach makes it inadequate for understanding empirical realities.

Nevertheless, the postmodern perspective social theory construction offers a needed reminder that societies such as the United States are intricate plural entities in constant flux rather than static organic and functional wholes. It is a matter of designing methodologies to test and modify theories that finally are articulating the normality of racial and ethnic conflict in the daily lives of Americans and in other multiethnic/racial societies and regions.

There are three possible logic of inquiry approaches in the study of racial and ethnic conflict and four different levels of analysis. There are also three different methodological strategies which can be constructed and put to good use. The three possible approaches are the examination of: (a) routinized racial/ethnic conflict; (b) episodic racial/ethnic conflict, and (c) the inter-linkages of routinized and episodic racial/ethnic conflict. The examination of routinized racial/ethnic conflict acknowledges the normality of intergroup antagonisms in historic multiethnic/racial social organizations and the ways in which relatively ethnically/racially homogeneous social organizations (e.g., Western or Northern Europe) become normatively conflictual along racial lines as culturally different populations migrate voluntarily or involuntarily (e.g., slaves or refugees) into the same geographical spaces such as institutions, communities, nation-states, or regions. The later process, when homogenous social organizations between culturally pluralistic, the routinization of intergroup conflict and subsequent mundane socialization processes become acutely problematic and violent prone when "migrants" are phenotypically as well as culturally distinct from the dominant "natives." On a community level, this is precisely what sparked race riots in Chicago after World War I, as the predominantly white ethnic city, virtually overnight, gained a tremendous influx of southern migrant African Americans (Bernstein, 1967; Illinois, 1922; Sandburg, 1969) and on the national and regional/international levels, this is the story behind the rash of racial problems Europeans are experiencing as third world immigrants are transforming their countries and continent into multiracial social organizations.

Episodic ethnic/racial conflict, which has most of the attention of scholars, policymakers, and the media includes examples of the sociopolitical volcanic eruptions which occur from time to time in multiethnic/racial social organizations. Episodic ethnic/racial conflict cases are windows through which we can observe the inner-workings of multiethnic/racial social organizations in sociopolitical processes of change. In this vein is not only useful to examine intergroup antagonisms as an episodic event but also the responses of the status quo to the event. Does the government, for instance, respond to a race riot by ignoring it or through engaging in real or cosmetic change-oriented activity?

Linking routinized and episodic ethnic/racial conflict processes and events is to recognize the normal ways in which multiethnic/racial social organizations originate, are maintained, and change. Making links between routinization and episodes of ethnic/racial conflict avoids the reification problems of the first two logic of inquiry perspectives which inadequate either or discussions. People, such as most Americans and other members of race-centered societies, are surprised when they have no, or little, understanding of the routinization of race in everyday life and then a race riot occurs or an interracial fight breaks out in a desegregating middle school, both "out of no where." They are baffled as to how is it interracial conflict can occur in a society they presume is color-blind or in other ways, is not racially prejudiced. This is also the reason why local and national race riot commission reports in multiethnic/racial societies are highly political documents which usually fail to get to the bottom of why the riot occurred. Namely, the reluctance to acknowledge or the inability to realize the integral place of race in the daily lives of all societal residents encourages a reified approach which targets the troubled community out of context of a racially troubled society. Even when commissioned reports such as the Carnegie Corporation's *American Dilemma* complied by Gunnar Myrdal or the U.S. Government's Kerner Commission Report on the 1960s urban riots publicly condemns racism as a national problem, the public norm has been to ignore, criticize, or explain away the normality of race in the ways in which race-centered societal members define themselves, others, and mundanely organize their daily lives.

Whether a researcher chooses the rountinized or episodic or synthesis approach to the study of racial/ethnic conflict, there are four basic levels of analysis with a number of possible syntheses across levels. The four basic levels of analysis are: local (institutions and communities), ecosystem (metropolitan areas, rural sectors, and regions within societies), societies (nation-states, colonies, empires, kingdoms), and regional/international (cross-societal geographical regions, continents, intercontinental spheres). Up until very recently, most ethnic/racial conflict studies tend to focus on local and societal levels. The post-Cold War breakdown of highly eruptive regional/international areas in Eastern Europe, sub-Saharah Africa, Latin America, and Southeast Asia is generating more scholarly and policy-related interest in more broadly macro-analyses of ethnic/racila conflicts and their resolutions. With this growing interest and concern is the increasing awareness of the fallacies of research paradigms which encourage inquires which remain within the boundaries of nations with no appreciation of the greater relevance and saliency of ethnic and racialized ethnic ties which cut across subcontinents, continents, and among continents (one can argue with some persuasion that the current ethnic and racialized ethnic flareups around the post-1970s globe will stimulate significant changes in the ways in which "area studies oriented" scholars such as historians and political scientists define their intellectual crafts).

No matter which theoretical perspective or unit of analysis a researcher selects, there are three possible technical methods in ethnic/racial conflict studies to choose from: quantitative or qualitative or a synthesis of quantitative and qualitative strategies. Quantitative approaches have ranged from formal cost/benefit analyses of the consequences of racial/ethnic conflicts to the use of survey and psychological testing instruments on samples of involved populations (California Bureau of Criminal Statistics, 1966; Lemburg Center for the Study of Violence, 1967; Levine, 1977; McConahay and Hardee, 1981; Montero, 1977; Morrison, 1993; Ridenour, Leslie, and Oliver, 1965; Sampson and Kardish, 1965; Timol, 1977). In the logical positivistic framework, quantitative approaches have the advantage of offering impartial data collection and analyses and opportunities to predict future trends and outcomes. But, the problem with quantitative approaches is that the human decision making which go into the construction of questions and the selection of secondary data sources are culturally-based; usually within the context of the dominant group. The reams of self-esteem studies conducted on residents of urban riot torn areas during the 1960s and post-1970s are rooted in conceptions of self derived from Euro-American experiences and therefore their reliability and validity must be questioned seriously. Attempts to measure and quantify attitudes and behavior of people reared in race-centered social organizations about their views about racial conflict are actually quite problematic as seen in research which indicates that more often than not there is a discrepancy between what people think and do when it comes to racial issues (also consider the public opinion poll data which indicates that on the part of Euro-Americans, racial liberalism tends to be situational—rooted in growing tolerance for "race mixing" in public places while Euro-American attitudes toward integrating their families, peer groups, and other private spheres has remained quite negative over the decades). This problem increases when there is an episode of collective interracial violence since the intensity of emotions diminishes the probability of the involved persons sharing their true attitudes and beliefs and revealing what they really did or wanted to do.

When it comes to quantitatively exploring rountinized forms of racial/ethnic conflict, there are conceptual and measurement dilemmas stemming from the misinformation researchers and subjects have about the ways in which race and ethnicity shapes their lives. Afterall, multiethnic/racial social organizations are maintained and reproduced through involved populations being systematically miseducated and otherwise being misinformed regarding the intricacies of race and ethnicity as modes of socialization processes as well as attitudes, beliefs, and behavior. It is no wonder then that racial and ethnic matters tend to be defined so vaguely and superficially in dominant public culture—when the issues are explicitly defined at all. It is for this reason, so much race and ethnic conflict research is impeded by implicit folkwisdoms regarding race and ethnicity as well as convoluted or overly simplistic concepts and subsequent poorly contrived measurements. As well, more often than not, whether or not we are referring to routinized or episodic racial/ethnic conflict, survey respondents are more than likely quite varied in their subjective impressions of what racism and ethnocentrism are (if they even have a vague clue) even though their responses are coded and put into neat little analytical boxes. This certainly is not helped by researchers who may be the best of all scholars but as products of a society and world in which race and ethnicity are so mundanely central, more often than not fail to move beyond folkwisdoms which constructing and coding survey questionnaires and collecting and analyzing data drawn from secondary quantitatively oriented sources such as census reports.

Some of the observations just made about logic of inquiry problems in conducting quantitatively oriented research on racial/ethnic conflict can be applied to qualitative approaches (Stanfield and Dennis, 1993; Stanfield, 1994). The strength of qualitative methods in racial/ethnic conflict research is that it emphasizes the subject views of the subject and increasingly of the researcher and those who engage in policy-related work. The subjective orientation of qualitative research allows us to include critical role of emotions in racial/ethnic research. In the haste to develop rational models of racial/ethnic conflict, it is easy to forget the critical role of routinized or episodic intense emotions in intergroup antagonisms. In most cases, no matter the degree or kind of racial/ ethnic conflict, the antagonistic experiences are rooted in intense emotionalism rather than in "rational choice" or "rational action." What appears to be a rational choice or action in a mathematically formulated model of racial/ethnic conflict is grounded in intense emotionalism which must be accounted for if we are to grasp the meaning of the intergroup antagonism. Thus qualitative approaches such as oral histories, long interviews, participant-observation, archival research, and visual arts, which help us understand emotions as well has human motivations are valuable methodological strategies (Davis, Burleigh, and Gardner, 1941; Dollard, 1937; Essed, 1991; Van Dijk, 1987, 1993).

But, as in the case of quantitative approaches, conceptual convolution and superficiality as well as measurement regarding the character of race and ethnicity have been, to say the least, severe problems. The major difficulty with qualitative approaches is that as much as there is concerned for the subjective experiences of the research respondent, such experiences are defined within the subjective experiences of the researcher. Thus, a vicious cycle is constructed in which the researcher sympathetic with the subjective experiences of the respondent taints the process of data definition, collection, and analysis through defining such experiences in his or her own terms. In a most profound and, I should add, problematic sense, the dilemma qualitative researchers face of having their values, beliefs, and biography intrude in research processes cannot be helped if the researcher is going to be able to communicate "findings" to professional colleagues and publishers who more than likely have a different set of discourse styles and norms from the research respondents. Thus otherwise excellent qualitative studies of routinized and episodic racial/ethnic conflict must be read with caution since their analytical frameworks are usually rooted in the experiences of the researchers. Even when a qualitative analytical framework is grounded in the experiences of the researched, the actual production of the study as an academic or policy-making commodity makes it very likely that it is at most a modified version of who the researched are as human beings.

Synthesizing quantitative and qualitative approaches certainly have distinct advantages over "either or approaches." This is because as important as it is to descriptively or inferentially quantify human experiences, we cannot forget that people are more than numbers. Conversely, it is critical to realize that human experiences are not merely subjective events with no generalizability. Some human experiences can be categorized and otherwise placed in measurable analytical constructs to explore trends and to make predictions. It is no accident that the best racial/ethnic conflict academic and policy-making studies are those which utilize a combination of quantitative and qualitative methods such as census and survey data, archival materials, long interviews, and videotaping. Nevertheless, what commonly haunts quantitative and qualitative studies of racial/ethnic conflict also disturbs the validity and reliability of studies which attempt to combine both approaches.

The purpose of these critical observations of the racial/ethnic conflict literature as methodological dilemmas is not to say such analyses cannot be done well. The point is threefold. First, researchers interested in the study of racial/ethnic conflict should familiarize themselves with the intricacies of race and ethnicity as human events on a more sophisticated level. The misinformation and uncomfortable silences that characterizes the ways in which race and ethnicity are learned in multiethnic/racial societies fosters much inadequacy in how racial/ethnic research is conducted. Second, even in the midst of a crisis, researchers should be mindful of the validity and reliability problems of studies which victimize populations and reify conflictual processes. It does little good to study conflict without context and with no or little understanding of power and privilege as relational processes and structures.

Third, the crisis-management bias in racial/ethnic conflict studies has discouraged the development of a most fascinating and still grossly under-studied area of research. The 1992 Los Angeles riot and other urban race riots in the post-1970s United States, as well as in other parts of the world, are sore reminders of how inadequate our theoretical and methodological knowledge continues to be regarding why riots occur. More generally, we still are without comprenhensive studies on why episodic and routine racial/ethnic conflict occurs; particularly across national boundaries. This is why with the growing interest in racial/ethnic conflict issues, there is the increasing need for us to begin serious thinking regarding the logic of inquiry problems which should at least be considered in asking and revising conventional questions about such intergroup antagonisms as well as asking new ones.

REFERENCES

Akbar, M.J. 1988. *Riot after Riot: Reports on Cast and Communal Violence in India.* New York: Penguin Books.

Akron, Ohio. 1969. *The Report of the Akron Commission on Civil Disorders.* Akron: The Commission.

Alan, G.W. 1994. *A Gathering of Heroes: Reflections on Rage and Responsibility: A Memoir of the Los Angeles Riots.* Chicago: Academy Chicago Publishers.

Allen, V.L. 1970. "Towards Understanding Riots: Some Perspectives." *Journal of Social Issues* 26: 1-18.

American Correctional Association. 1981. *Riots and Disturbances in Correctional Institutions; A Discussion of Causes, Preventive Measures and Methods of Control.* College Park, MD: ACA.

American Correctional Association. 1990. *Causes, Preventive Measures, and Methods of Controlling Riots and Disturbances in Correctional Institutions.* Laurel MD.: Ameican Correctional Association.

Armstrong, E.G. 1975. "The System Paradigm and the Sociological Study of Racial Conflict." *Phylon* 36: 8-13.

Belknap, M.R. 1991. *Urban Race Riots.* New York: Garland Pub.

Bernstein, S. 1967. *Alternatives to Violence; Alienated Youth, Riots, Race, and Poverty.* New York: Association Press.

Blassingame, J.W. 1972. *The Slave Community.* New York: Garland Publishers.

Boskin, J. 1967. *Urban Racial Violence in the Twientieth Century* (2nd ed.). Beverly Hills: Glencoe Press.

Boucher, J. D. Landis, and K.A. Clark. 1987. *Ethnic Conflict: International Perspectives.* Newbury Park, CA: Sage Publications.

Braswell, M., S. Dillingham, and R. Montgomery, Jr. 1985. *Prison Violence in America.* Cincinnati, OH: Anderson Pub. Co.

Buell, E.H. 1982. *School Desegregation and Defended Neighborhoods.* Lexington, MA: Lexington Books.

Bullock, P. 1969. *Watts: The Aftermath.* New York: Grove Press.

Burma. 1939. Riot Inquiry Committee. Rangoon, Supdt., Govt. printing and Stationary.

Button, J. 1993. "Racial Cleavage in the Local Voting: the Case of School and Tax Issue Referndums." *Journal of Black Studies* 24: 29-41.

California, Bureau of Criminal Statistics. 1966. Watts riots Arrest, Los Angeles, August 1965, Final disposition.

Capeci, D.J. 1970. *The Harlem Riot of 1963.* Riverside: University of California, Thesis Collection.

Carithers, M.W. 1970. "School Desegregation and Racial Cleavage, 1954-1970: A Review of the Literature." *Journal of Social Issues* 26: 25-48.

Chailand, G. 1983. *The Armenians: From Genocide to Resistance.* London: Zed Press.

Chakavarti, U. 1987. *The Delhi Riots: Three Days in the Life of a Nation.* New Delhi: Lancer International.

Chikota, R.A. 1970. *Riot in the Cities.* Rutherford: Fairleigh Dickinson University Press.

Cohen, N.S. 1972. *Civil Strife in America.* Hinsdale: Dryden Press.

Cohen, N.E. 1967. *Los Angeles Riot Study: Summary and Implications for Policy.* Los Angeles: Insitute of Government and Public affairs, University of California.

Cohen, J. 1966. *Burn, Baby, Burn! The Los Angeles Race Riot, August, 1965.* New York: Dutton.

Collective Violence Research Project. 1973. *Collective Violence in Correctional Institutions: A Search for Causes.* Columbia, SC: Dept. of Corrections.

Collins, P.H. 1990. Black Feminist Thought: Knowledge, Consciousness, and the Politics of Empowerment. Boston: Unwin Hyman.

Colvin, M. 1992. *The Penetentiary in Crisis: From Accomodation to Riot in New Mexico.* Albany: State University of New York Press.

Conforti, J.M. 1974. "Racila Conflict in Central cities: The Newark Teachers Strikes." *Trans-Action* 12: 22-33.

Coser, L.A. 1956. *The Functins of Social Conflict.* Glencoe, IL: Free Press.

Cowell, D., J. Trevor, and Y. Jock. 1982. *Policing the Riots.* London: Junction Books.

Crowell, A. 1992. "Helping People Cope with the Riots: Los Angeles Department of Health." California County. Sept.-Oct. 1992.

Crump, S. 1966. *Black Riot in Los Angeles* (1st ed.). Los Angeles: Trans-Anglo Books.

Culver, J.H. 1994. "Los Angeles a Year after the Riot." *Comparative State Politics* 15 (1).

Cummins, E. 1994. *The Rise and Fall of California's Radical Prison Movement.* Stanford: Stanford University Press.

Davis, A., B. Burleigh, and M.R. Gardner. 1941. *Deep South.* Chicago: University of Chicago Press.

Dollard, J. 1937. *Caste and Class in a Southern Town.* New Haven: Yale University Press.

Enloe, C. 1972. *Ehnic Conflict and Political Development.* Boston: Little Brown.

Essed, P. 1991. *Understanding Everyday Racism.* Newbury Park, CA: Sage Publications.

Finkelman, P. 1992. "Lynching, Racial Violence and Law." *Race, Law, and American History, 1700-1990* 9.

Flamming, K.H. 1968. *Who "Riots" and Why? Black and White Perspectives in Milwaukee.* Milwaukee Urban League.

Fogelson, R.M. 1967. *White on Black: A Critique of the McCone Commission Report on the Los Angeles Riots.* Los Angeles: University of California, Special Collection

Fogelson, R.M. 1969. *The Los Angeles Riots.* New York: Arno Press.

Fox, V.B. 1973 (1956). *Violence Behind Bars.* Westport, CT: Greenwood Press.

Fred, H.R., and R.W. Wilkins. 1988. *Quiet Riots: Race and Poverty in the United States.* New York: Pantheon Books.

Gates H.L. 1987. Figures inBlack: Words, Signs, and the "Racial" Self. New York: Oxford University Press.

Gates, H.L. 1992. *Loose Canons: Notes on Culture Wars.* New York: Oxford University Press.

Gilroy, P. 1987. *There Ain't No Black in the Union Jack: The Cultural Politics of Race and Nation.* London: Hutchinson.

Gitter, G.A., H. Black, and D. Mostofsky. 1972. "Race and Sex in the Perception of Emotion." *Journal of Social Issues* 28: 63-78.

Gould, W.S. 1973. "Racial Conflict in the U.S. Army." *Race* 15: 1-24.

Himes, J. 1974. *Racial and Ethnic Conflict.* Dubuque, IO: W.C. Brown Co.

Himes, J. 1980. *Conflict and Conflict Management.* Athens: University of Georgia Press.

Horowitz, I. 1980. *Taking Lives: Genocide and State Power.* New Brunswick, NJ: Transaction Books.

Illinois. 1922. *Chicago Commission on Race Relations.* Chicago: The University of Chicago Press.

Jacobson, C.K. 1985. "Resistance to Affirmative Action: Self-Intrestor Racism." *The Journal of Conflict Resolution* 29: 306-329.

Johannesburg (South Africa). 1958. *Report of The Riots Commission.* Johannesburg: The Commission.

Johnson, C.S. 1987. Bitter Canaan. New Brunswick, NJ: Transaction Books.

Joshua, H. 1983. *To Ride the Storm: The 1980 Bristol 'Riot' and the State.* London: Heineman.

Kinnear, G. 1911. *Anti-Chinese Riots at Seattle.* Seattle: .

Kirp, D. 1979. *Doing Good by Doing Little.* Berkeley: University of California Press.

Knopf, T. 1975. *Rumors, Race, and Riots.* New Brunswick, NJ: Transaction Books.

Lane, A.J. 1971. *The Brownsville Affair.* Port Washington, NY: Kennikat Press.

Lauruffa, A.L. 1992. "Howard Beach and Belmont: Studies in Ethnic-Racial Conflict." *Studies In Third World-Societies* 48: 99-105.

Lee, A.M., and N.D. Humphrey. 1943. *Race Riot.* New York: Dryden.

Lee, A.M. 1945. *Race Riots aren't Neccessary.* New York: Public Affairs Committee,Inc.

Lemburg Center for the Study of Violence. 1967. *Six-city Study, A Survey of Racial Attitudes in Six Northern Cities: Preliminary Findings.* Waltham, MA: Lemburg Center for the Study of Violence, Civil Disorder Data Clearinghouse, Brandeis University .

Levine, G.W. 1977. "Some Concluding Remarks: Research Among Racial and Cultural Minorities." *Journal of Social Issues* 33: 175-178.

May, R. 1974. *The Interaction Between Race and Colonialism: A Case Study of the Liverpool Race Riot of 1919.* Birmingham: University of Birmingham, Faculty and Commerce and Socail Science.

Mazian, F. 1990. Why Genocide: The Armenian and Jewish Experiences in Perspective. Arms: Iowa State University Press.

McConahay, J.B., and B.B. Hardee. 1981. "Has Racism Declined in America? It Depends on Who's Asking and What is Asked." *The Journal of Conflict Resolution* 25: 563-580.

McKernan, J. 1982. "Value Sytems and Race Relations in Northern Ireland and America." *Ethnic and Racial Studies* 5: 156-174.

Melson, R. 1992. *Revolution and Genocide: On the Origins of the Armenian Genodice and the Holocaust.* Chicago: Chicago University Press.

Miami Study Team on Civil Disturbances in Miami, Florida. 1969. *Miami Report: The Report on the Miami Study Team on Civil Disturbances in Miami, Florida During the Week of August 5, 1968.* Washington, DC: U.S. Government Printing Office.

Miracle, A.W. Jr. 1981. "Factors Affecting Interracial Cooperation: A Case Study of a High School Football Team." *Human-Organization* 40: 150-154.

Mohajer, F., and T.M. Steinfatt. 1982. "Communication and Interracial Conflict; The Role of Disagreement, Prejudice, and Physical Attraction of the Choice of Mixed Race, Mixed Sex Partners." Annual Meeting of Western Speech Communication Association, Denver, CO, February 19-23.

Moinat, S.M., and W.J. Raine. 1970. "Black Ghetto Residents as Rioters." *Journal of Social Issues* 26: 45-62.

Montagu, A. 1942. *Man's Most Dangerous Myth.*

Montero, D. 1977. "Research Among Racial and Cultural Minorities: An Overview." *Journal of Social Issues* 33: 1-10.

Morrison, P.A. 1993. *A Riot of Color: The Demographic Setting of Civil Disturbance in Los Angeles.* Santa Monica, CA: Rand.

Muller, E.N. 1986. "Rational Chioce and Rebellious Collective Action." *The American Political Science Review* 80 (2).

Murphy, R.J., and J.M. Watson. 1967. *The Structure of Discontent: the Relationship Between Social Structure, Grievance, and Support for the Los Angeles Riot.* Los Angeles: Institute of Government and Public Affairs.

Nerner, J.M. 1986. *Reaping the Bloody Harvest: Race riots in the United Staes during the age of Jackson, 1824-1849.* New York: John M. Werner.

Ottaway, R.N. 1976. "Developing the White, Moderate Leadership of a community in Racial Conflict." *Centro-Sociale* 23: 119-136.

Parrenas, C.S., and F.Y. Parrenas. 1993. "Cooperative Learning, Multicultural Functioning, and Student Achievment." *National Association for Bilingual Conferences* 93: 181-189.

Porter, B. 1984. *The Miami Riot of 1980.* Lexington MA: Lexington Books.

Ridenour, R., A. Leslie, and V. Oliver. 1965. *The Fire This Time: The W.E.B. DuBois Clubs View of the Explosion in South Los Angeles.* Los Angeles, CA: W.E.B. DuBois Clubs.

Rist, R.C. 1972. "The Quest for Autonomy: A Socio-Historical Study of Black Revolt in Detroit." University of California Los Angeles, African American Studies Center Monograph Sereis no.4.

Rist, R.C. 1978. *The Invisible Children.* Cambridge, MA: Harvard University Press.

Rossi, P.H. 1970. *Ghetto Revolts.* Chicago: Aldine Publisher Co.

Rule, J.B. 1988. *Theories of Civil Violence.* Berkeley: University of California Press.

Sampson, E.E., and M. Kardish. 1965. "Age, Sex, Class, and Race Differences in Response to a Two-Person non-zero Sum Game." *Journal of Conflict Resolution* 9: 212-220.

Samuel, H.B. 1930. *Beneath the Whitelash: A Critical Analysis of the Report of the Commission on the Palestine Disturbances of August, 1929.* London: Hogarth Press.

Sandburg, C. 1969. *The Chicago Race Riots, July 1919.* New York: Harcourt.

Sawyer, J., and D.J. Senn. 1973. "Institutional Racism and the Ameican Psychological." *Journal of Social Issues* 29: 67-80.

Schlemmer, L. 1968. "The Negro Ghetto Riots and South African Cities." *South African Insitute of Race Relations* 15.

Sears, D.O. 1967. *Los Angeles Riot Study.* Los Angeles: Insitute of Government and Public Affairs.

Sears, D.O., and J.B. McConahay. 1970. "Racial Socialization, Comparison Levels, and the Watts Riot." *Journal of Social Issues* 26: 121-140.

Senechal, R. 1990. *The Sociogenesis of a Race Riot: Springfield, Illinois, in 1908.* Urbana: University of Illinois Press.

Singer, B.D., R.W. Osborn, and J.A. Geschwender. 1970. *Black Rioters.* Lexington, MA: Heath Lexington Books.

Slaughter, T.P. 1991. *Bloody Dawn: The Christiana Riot and Racial Violence in the Anti-Bellum North.* New York: Oxford University Press.

South Africa. 1941. Commission to Inquire into Riots in Johanssesburg on 31 January and 1st February, 1941. Cape Town: Cape Times ltd.

South Africa. 1949. Commission of Inquiry into Riots in Durban. Cape Town: Cape Times.

South Africa. 1980. Commission of Inquiry into the Riots at Soweto and Elsewhere. Pretoria: Government Printer.

Spiegal, J.P. 1967a. *The Social and Psychological Dynamics of Militant Negro Activism.* Waltham, MA: Brandeis University.

Spiegal, John Paul. 1967b. *Race Relations and Violence: A Social Psychiatric Perspective.* Waltham MA: Lemburg Center for the Study of Violence, Brandeis University.

Spilerman, S. 1974. *Structural Characteristics of Cities and the Severity of Racial Disorders.* Institute for Research on Poverty, University of Wisconsin.

Stanfield, J.H., and R. Dennis. 1993. Race and Ethnicity in Research Methods. Newbury Park, CA: Sage Publications.

Stanfield, J.H. 1992. "America and Other Race Centered Societies." *International Journal of Cooperative Sociology.*

Stanfield, J.H. 1994. "Ethnicity in Qualitative Methods." In *Handbook on Qualitative Methods,* edited by Y. Lincoln and N. Denzine. Newbury Park, CA: Sage Publications.

Timol, R. 1977. *Soweto: A People's Response: Sample Survey of the Attitudes of People in Durban to the Soweto Violence of June 1976.* Durban, South Africa: Institue of Black Research.

Tomilson, T.M. 1967. *Los Angeles Riot Study Method: Negro Reaction Study Method.* Los Angeles: Insitute of Government and Public Affairs, University of California.

United States Kerner Commission. 1968. *Report to the National Advisory Commission on Civil Disorders.* New York: Dutton.

Useem, B., and P. Kimball. 1989. *States of Seige: US Prison Riots, 1971-1986.* New York: Oxford University Press.

Van den Berghe, P. 1967. *Race and Racism.* New York: Wiley.

Van den Berghe, P. 1990. *State Violence and Ethnicty.* Niwot, CO: University Press of Colorado.

Van Dijk, T. 1987. *Communicating Racism.* Newbury Park, CA: Sage Publications.

Van Dijk, T. 1993. *Elite Discourse and Racism.* Newbury Park, CA: Sage Publications.

Wall, B. 1992. *The Rodney King Rebellion: A Psychopolitical Analsis of Racial Despair and Hope.* Chicago: African American Images.

Walters, R.W. 1982. "Race, Resource, Conflict." *Urban League Review* 7: 53-64.

Warren, D.I. 1973. "Some Observation from Post-Riot Detriot: The Role of the Social Researcher in Contemporary Racial Conflict." *Phylon* 34: 171-186.

Webb, M., and K. Kirkwood. 1949. *The Durban Riots and After.* Johannesburg: S.A. Institute of Race Relations.

Weskow, A.I. 1966. *From Race Riot to Sit-in, 1919 and the 1960's.* Garden City, NY: Anchor Books.

Williams, L.E. 1927. *Anatomy of Four Race Riots.* Hattiesburg MS: College Press of Mississippi.

Williams, L.E. 1991. *Post-War Riots in America, 1919 and 1946: How the Pressure of War Exacerbated American Urban Tensions to the Breaking Point.* Lewiston, NY: E. Mellen Press.

Wilson, J.Q. 1961. "The Strategy of Protest: Problems of Negro Civic Action." *The Journal of Conflict Resolution* 5: 291-303.

Winant, H., and M. Omi. 1986. *Racial Formation in the U.S.: From the 1960s to the 1980s.* New York: Routledge and Kegan Paul.

J
A
I

P
R
E
S
S

Research in
Inequality and Social Conflict

Edited by **Isidor Wallimann,** *School of Social Work,
Basel* and **Michael Dobkowski,** *Hobart & Wm. Smith
College*

Volume 2, 1992, 279 pp. $73.25
ISBN I-55938-093-4

CONTENTS: Introduction. Sovereignty, Inequality, and Con-
flict: The Conflict Over Palestine as a Case Study of the Dys-
functionalism of the Existing International System and the
Utility of a World Order Perspective for Comprehending the
Conflict, *Cheryl A. Rubenberg.* Rural Crisis and Migration: A
Variable of Revolution in Iran, *Abol Hassan Denesh.* The De-
clining Middle Class in an Age of Deindustrialization, *Tim
Knapp.* The Retreat of the Welfare State, *Peter Taylor-Gooby.*
Inequality and Political Activism in Australia, *Brian Graetz.*
From Class Bearers to Civil Subjects: Reconceptualizing the
Relation Between Structure, Identity and Collective Action,
Michael Emmison, Paul Boreham, and Stewart Clegg. Minor-
ity Group Threat and Social Control Twenty Years of Investi-
gation, *Pamela Irving Jackson.* Ethnic Density and the
Classroom Climate: The Effect on Attitudes Toward Others in
the Multicultural Classroom, *Karen L. Parsonson, Raymond
P. Perry, and Rodney A. Clifton.*

Also Available:
Volume 1 (1989) $73.25

JAI PRESS INC.
55 Old Post Road # 2 - P.O. Box 1678
Greenwich, Connecticut 06836-1678
Tel: (203) 661- 7602   Fax: (203) 661-0792

Research in Social Movements, Conflicts and Change

Edited by **Louis Kriesberg,** *Department of Sociology, Syracuse University,* **Michael Dobkowski,** *Hobart and William Smith College* and **Isidor Wallimann,** *School of Social Work, Basel*

REVIEWS: "... recommended for graduate libraries."

— *Choice*

"... The papers are generally of excellent quality ... a useful series of annual volumes ...."

— *Social Forces*

"... an excellent series of original articles ... the papers are broad in scope and methodologically diverse ... a welcome departure from the traditional social roots approach and offers new insights into feedback effects of social movements ... useful anthologies that are theoretically informed and timely."

— *Political Sociology*

Volume 17, 1994, 316 pp. $73.25
ISBN 1-55938-890-0

CONTENTS: Protest Demonstrations and the End of Communist Regimes in 1989, *Anthony Oberschall.* Post Generational Theory and Post-Communist Youth in East-Central Europe, *John D. Nagle.* A Dynamic View of Resources: Evidence From the Iranian Revolution, *Charles Kurzman.* Strategy and Identity in 1960s Black Forest, *Francesca Polietta.* Action and Consensus Mobilization in the Deaf President Now Protest and Its Aftermath, *Sharon N. Barnartt.* The Institutional Structuring of Organized Social Action, 1955-1985, *Debra C. Minkoff.* On Studing the Cycles in Social Movement, *Andre Gunder Frank and Marta Fuentes.* Resistance to Resettlement: The Formation and Evolution of Movements, *Anthony Oliver-Smith.* Expansion of the Informal State and Disempowerment of Grass-Roots Activism: A Case Study, *Neghin Modavi.* Social Movements and Social Problems: Toward A Conceptual Rapprochement, *Harry H. Bash.*

Also Available:
Volumes 1-16 (1978-1993)
   + Supplements 1, 2 (1987-1992) $73.25 each

Advances in Group Processes

Edited by **Edward J. Lawler**, *Department of Organizational Behavior, Cornell University*

This series publishes theoretical, review, and empirically based papers on group phenomena. The series adopts a broad conception of "group processes" consistent with prevailing ones in the social psychological literature. In addition to topics such as status processes, group structure, and decision making, the series considers work on interpersonal behavior in dyads (i.e., the smallest group), individual group relations. Contributors to the series include not only sociologists but also scholars from other disciplines, such as psychology and organizational behavior.

REVIEWS: "A major impression one gets from this volume is that far from being dormant, the social psychology of groups and interpersonal relations is quite vibrant, and very much involved with compelling problems.

"Concerns about the imminent demise of group processes as an area of study in social psychology are clearly exaggerated. But should doubts remain, they ought to be allayed by the range and quality of the offerings in this volume."

" . . . should be of interest both to specialists in group processes and to sociologists who are interested in theory, particularly in theoretical linkages between micro and macro analysis. Because many of the papers offer thorough reviews and analyses of existing theoretical work, as well as new theoretical ideas, they are also useful readings for graduate students.

— *Contemporary Sociology*

Volume 11, 1994, 239 pp. $73.25
ISBN 1-55938-857-9

Edited by **Barry Markovsky, Karen Heimer,** and **Jodi O'Brien,** *Department of Sociology, University of Iowa.*

CONTENTS: Preface, *Barry Markovsky, Karen Heimer, and Jodi O'Brien.* Persons, Identities, and Social Interaction, *Lee Freese and Peter J. Burke.* Discrete Event Simulation and Theoretical Models in Sociology, *Thomas J. Fararo and Norman P. Hummon.* Action, Social Resources and the Emergence of Social Structures: A Rational Choice Theory, *Nan Lin.* Relating Power to Status, *Michael J. Lovaglia.* A New Theory of Group Solidarity, *Barry Markovsky and Edward J. Lawler.* Conflict and Aggression: An Individual-Group Continuum, *Jacob M. Rabbie and Hein F. M. Kidewujkx.* Coherent Structure Theory and Decision-Making in Social Networks: A Case Study in Systems Isomorphy, *D.H. Judson and L.N. Gray.* Structure, Culture and Interaction: Comparing Two Generative Theories, *Cecilia Ridgeway and Lynn Smith-Lovin.*

Also Available:
Volumes 1-10 (1984-1993) $73.25 each

J A I   P R E S S

Advances in
Social Science Methodology

Edited by **Bruce Thompson**, *Department of Educational Psychology, Texas A & M University*

Volume 3, 1994, 289 pp. $73.25
ISBN 1-55938-379-8

CONTENTS: Foreword, *Bruce Thompson.* Section 1: The Use of Multiple Contrasts. Planned Versus Unplanned and Orthogonal Versus Nonorthogonal Contrasts: The Neo-Classical Perspective, *Bruce Thompson.* Analysis of Variance and the General Linear Model, *Allen L. Edwards and Lynne K. Edwards.* Choosing a Multiple Comparison Procedure, *Roger E. Kirk.* Group Contrasts in the Multivariate Case, *Carl J. Huberty, Tungshan F. Chou, and Elisa B. Benitez.* Section 2: Other Amalytic Issues. Quantitative Research: What It Is, What It Isn't, and How It's Done, *Margaret D. LeCompte and Judith Preissle.* Judging Variable Importance in Multidimensional Scaling, *J. Douglas Carroll and Sharon L. Weinberg.* Logistic Regression: An Introduction, *Janet C. Rice.* The Critique of Pure Statistics: Artifact and Objectivity in Multivariate Statistics, *Stanley A. Mulaik.*

Also Available:
Volumes 1-2 (1989-1992) $73.25 each

JAI PRESS INC.
55 Old Post Road # 2 - P.O. Box 1678
Greenwich, Connecticut 06836-1678
Tel: (203) 661- 7602   Fax: (203) 661-0792

Symbolic Interaction
Official Journal of the Society for the Study of Symbolic Interaction

Editor:
Andrea Fontana
Department of Sociology
University of Nevada, Las Vegas

Associate Editors:
Ruth Horowitz, *University of Delaware*
E.Doyle McCarthy, *Fordham University*
Dmitri Shalin, *University of Nevada, Las Vegas*

Symbolic Interaction is a scholarly journal devoted to the empirical study of human behavior and social life. It examines the nature, forms, conditions, and consequences of communicative interaction within, between, and among such social actors as individuals, groups, organizations, institutions, communities and nations.

Contributions are not only from sociologists and social psychologists, but also anthropologists, philosophers and specialists in speech and communication. Topics covered include: the social construction of reality; the negotiation social orders; the link between power and meaning; socially motivated interpersonal control; the dynamics of situated interaction; the acquisition and transformation of social identities; and socialization through the life cycle. The journal also carries special features such as: interviews, reviews, feature articles, commentaries, and updates by foriegn-based corresponding editors.

Abstracts of articles published in *Symbolic Interaction* may be found in Sociological Abstracts, The Social Sciences Citation Index, and Current Contents: Behavioral and Social Sciences.

Subscription Rates:
(all subscriptions are for the calendar year only)

Volume 19 (1996)	**Published Quarterly**
Institutions:	$170.00
Personal:	$70.00

ISSN 0195-6086

Volumes 16-18 (1993-1995) $170.00 per volume
Outside the U.S. add $20.00 for surface mail or $40.00 for airmail.